MW00988439

CREATORS, CONQUERORS, AND CITIZENS

OTHER BOOKS BY ROBIN WATERFIELD
PUBLISHED BY OXFORD UNIVERSITY PRESS

Dividing the Spoils: The War for Alexander the Great's Empire (2011)
Taken at the Flood: The Roman Conquest of Greece (2014)

Translations
Plato: Republic (1993)
Plato: Symposium (1994)
Plato: Gorgias (1994)
Aristotle: Physics (1996)
Herodotus: The Histories (1998)
Plutarch: Greek Lives (1998)
Plutarch: Roman Lives (1999)
The First Philosophers: The Presocratics and the Sophists (2000)
Euripides: Orestes and Other Plays (2001)
Plato: Phaedrus (2002)
Euripides: Heracles and Other Plays (2003)
Plato: Meno and Other Dialogues (2005)
Xenophon: The Expedition of Cyrus (2005)
Plato: Timaeus and Critias (2008)
Polybius: The Histories (2010)
Demosthenes: Selected Speeches (2014)
*Lives of the Attic Orators: Texts from Pseudo-Plutarch, Photius, and the
Suda* (2015)
Plutarch: Hellenistic Lives (2016)
Aristotle: The Art of Rhetoric (2018)

CREATORS, CONQUERORS, AND CITIZENS

A HISTORY OF ANCIENT GREECE

ROBIN WATERFIELD

OXFORD

UNIVERSITY PRESS

OXFORD
UNIVERSITY PRESS

Oxford University Press is a department of the University of Oxford. It furthers the University's objective of excellence in research, scholarship, and education by publishing worldwide. Oxford is a registered trade mark of Oxford University Press in the UK and certain other countries.

Published in the United States of America by Oxford University Press
198 Madison Avenue, New York, NY 10016, United States of America.

Library of Congress Cataloging-in-Publication Data
Names: Waterfield, Robin, 1952– author.
Title: Creators, conquerors, and citizens : a history of ancient Greece / by Robin Waterfield.
Description: New York, NY : Oxford University Press, 2018. | Includes bibliographical references and index.
Identifiers: LCCN 2017049709 (print) | LCCN 2017050452 (ebook) | ISBN 9780190234317 (updf) | ISBN 9780190234324 (epub) | ISBN 9780190234300 (hardback)
Subjects: LCSH: Greece—History. | Greece—Civilization. | Civilization, Ancient. | BISAC: HISTORY / Ancient / Greece.
Classification: LCC DF214 (ebook) | LCC DF214 .W38 2018 (print) | DDC 938—dc23
LC record available at https://lccn.loc.gov/2017049709

1 3 5 7 9 8 6 4 2

Printed by Edwards Brothers Malloy, United States of America

For Kathryn, with love
impossible without you

Contents

ACT I: THE ARCHAIC PERIOD (750–480): THE FORMATION OF STATES

ACT II: THE CLASSICAL PERIOD (479–323): A TALE, MAINLY, OF TWO CITIES

ACT III: THE HELLENISTIC PERIOD (323–30): GREEKS, MACEDONIANS, AND ROMANS

Preface and Acknowledgments

Aristophanes, who lived and worked at the end of the fifth and beginning of the fourth century BCE, was the greatest writer of humorous plays in Athens. Alongside amusing the audience, it was his job, and that of his fellow writers of Old Comedy (as this style is known), to comment on current affairs, often with a sarcastic tongue. At one point in his hilarious *Lysistrata*, produced in 411, he has the protagonist, Lysistrata herself, say this to the warring Athenians and Spartans:[1]

> Now that I've got you here I'm going to tick you off
> For all to hear, and with good reason, because although
> At places like Olympia, Thermopylae, and Delphi
> (And so on and so forth: I'll keep it short)
> You purify altars with the same holy water
> As though you were kin, and although the enemy
> Is looming with his barbarian horde, it is
> Fellow Greeks and their cities that you destroy.

Aristophanes had a good point. Other writers and other events could be adduced to the same effect: the Greeks recognized their kinship and their common culture, but failed to make these shared features a foundation for a common political life. They were culturally one, but politically many.

The primary purpose of this book is to provide an engaging, accessible, and up-to-date history of the ancient Greeks, but exploration of the Greek world very quickly brings one up against this one–many issue. If I were writing the history of ancient Rome or medieval Spain, I would be writing about a single place, but in the ancient world there was no single place called "Greece" ("Hellas" to the Greeks, then as now). The land that currently makes up the modern country of Greece was occupied by a large number of peoples, living typically in city-states (that is, towns with their surrounding farmland), and other city-states, equally populated by peoples who called themselves "Greeks," were dotted all the way around the

---

1 Aristophanes, Lysistrata 1128-1134.

coastlines of the Mediterranean and the Black Sea. In the Classical period, there were well over a thousand of these statelets.

When the ancient Greeks spoke of "Greece," they meant the abstract sum of all these communities, but in reality there was no shared homeland, and the citizens of each city-state gave their loyalty primarily to the place where they lived: they were Athenians, rather than Syracusans or Spartans. They were divided enough even to go to war with one another, and yet they knew themselves to be, in some sense, a single people. The political cultures of the Greek states play an important part in the book, then, because it was these that motivated them and governed their behavior. The one–many issue is the thread that binds the book together and leads to its concluding chapter.

But my principal aim, as I have said, is to provide a general history of the ancient Greeks. It is time for a new one. Every generation of historians is obliged to revisit old territories and re-examine them in the light of current conceptions, approaches, and information. And the past few decades have seen great progress—sometimes of a revolutionary nature—attend almost every field of Classical and ancient historical studies. New ways of reading social history from archaeological data have made the so-called Dark Ages less dark, for instance. Survey archaeology, in which walkers systematically transect a given area of land, is revealing more and more about the uses of the countryside. New sites are still being discovered and explored. Environmental history has progressed by leaps and bounds. The use of models, drawn especially from the social sciences, and of comparative data from other societies, has cast new light on what we thought we knew. Increased skepticism about what our ancient sources were writing, and why they were doing so, has brought great changes in its train. The way we see Spartan society, for instance, has changed radically; Alexander the Great's character and achievements have been up for reassessment.

Then again, it used to be acceptable for a history of the Greeks to stop toward the end of the fourth century, as though nothing of political significance happened after they became subject to the Macedonians. In this book, however, roughly equal weight is given to all three of the major periods of ancient Greek history, under their traditional names: Archaic, Classical, and Hellenistic. Actually, I have written just a little less about the Hellenistic period than the other two. The reason for this is that, by then, Greeks were scattered all over Egypt and Asia, as well as the Mediterranean. If I had given these eastern Greeks equal space, the book would have been considerably longer, and we would have lost sight of the mainland Greeks whose history I had largely been telling up to that point. So, even in the Hellenistic period, I have focused on the mainland Greeks a bit more than I have on their eastern or Egyptian peers. The "Recommended Reading" chapter makes up for this deficiency, as for others.

There is also another kind of imbalance between the three periods of the book. The sources for them are uneven, and necessitate different approaches. For the Archaic period, for which sources are scanty and difficult to interpret, we can talk mainly about general trends rather than specific events, and I have therefore taken the opportunity to illuminate not just the history of the period, but also some of the commonalities of the Greek world, which were laid down in the Archaic period: religion and warfare, for instance, are covered in this section, and return only intermittently thereafter. For the rest, we have sufficient sources (far better for the Classical period than the Hellenistic) to put together a narrative, but in the Hellenistic period the Greek world was so extensive that again it is better from time to time to raise general issues and explore the big picture, as well as telling the stories.

The conventional boundaries of the three traditional periods are significant moments in the history of events (rather than, say, the history of sculpture, which followed its own timeline): 776 was the alleged foundation of the Olympic Games, and therefore the start of datable history, since the primary dating system employed by the Greeks was the four-year Olympiad (they pinpointed events as having taken place, for instance, "in the second year of the twelfth Olympiad"); 479, the start of the Classical period, was when the Persians were driven out of Greece and Athens began its rise to true greatness; 323, the end of the Classical period, saw the subjection of the Greeks to Macedonians and the vast expansion of the Greek world in the wake of Alexander the Great's eastern conquests; 30, the end of the Hellenistic period, was when the last of the Greco-Macedonian kingdoms was taken over by Rome, and Greek political history became a facet of Roman history.

The terms "Archaic," "Classical," and "Hellenistic" are conventional, and there is no point in trying to invent new ones, but they are not unproblematic, especially since they privilege the Classical period. To call something "classical" implies that it is excellent and the standard against which other things should be measured: "That football game was a classic!" The implication, then, is that the other two periods of Greek history are somehow less satisfying as history or less perfect culturally. This was a view that was held by generations of scholars, for whom the Archaic age was merely a forerunner of Classical perfection and the Hellenistic era a disappointment after Classical glories, but it is a view that is firmly rejected in this book. All three periods are given equal weight, because they are equally important and exciting stretches of Greek history.

Writing a book like this is daunting as well as difficult. I received early encouragement from Paul Cartledge, Michael Flower, and Greg Woolf. For conversations and responses to queries, I thank Paul Cartledge (especially as one of the readers of the final draft of the book), Paul Christesen, Klaus Freitag, Brian McGing, Jeremy McInerney, Ian Morris, Jacob Morton, William Murray, John Porter, David Pritchard, Lawrence Tritle (the other reader of the "finished" book), Christopher Tuplin, Robert Wallace, and Nigel Wilson. For assistance with mathematics and economics, I consulted two old friends, Ian Maclean and Andrew Lane, respectively. As usual, I wrote to scholars around the world asking for offprints of articles, and as usual met with nothing but kindness. For help during extended visits to the libraries of the British and American Schools in Athens, once again I thank the staff of both institutions. I am grateful to John Hale for thinking up the title, and to Olga Palagia for letting me use her photograph of the Nabis coin. At the Press, Stefan Vranka, as always, was the perfect editor—knowledgeable and wise—and John Veranes did sterling work, especially over the illustrations. Stephen Dodson's copy-editing improved the book in a number of ways. The book is dedicated to Kathryn, not just for the usual wifely virtues (which, in her case, include being pestered with historical questions and being the first reader of the book), but because its writing brought out, even more than usual, the self-absorbed and obsessive author in me, and she never flinched.

Conventions and Abbreviations

All dates are BCE unless otherwise indicated.

Many works of Greek literature survive only in fragments. Different collections of fragments might have different numbering. I have always indicated which collection I have used. Thus "Hesiod, F 35 Merkelbach/West" refers to Merkelbach and West's edition of Hesiod's fragments.

"Pseudo-" before an author's name (pseudo-Aristotle, pseudo-Hesiod, etc.) means that a work that has been transmitted to us as a genuine work of Aristotle or Hesiod or whomever was probably written by someone else. It does not mean that the writer was trying to pass himself off as Aristotle, Hesiod, or whomever.

Abbreviations of collections of inscriptions and other sources:

Arnaoutoglou	I. Arnaoutoglou, *Ancient Greek Laws: A Sourcebook* (Routledge, 1998).
Austin	M. Austin, *The Hellenistic World from Alexander to the Roman Conquest: A Selection of Ancient Sources in Translation* (2nd ed., Cambridge University Press, 2006).
Bagnall/Derow	R. Bagnall and P. Derow, *The Hellenistic Period: Historical Sources in Translation* (2nd ed., Blackwell, 2004) (1st ed. title: *Greek Historical Documents: The Hellenistic Period*).
Burstein	S. Burstein, *The Hellenistic Age from the Battle of Ipsos to the Death of Kleopatra VII* (Cambridge University Press, 1985). Translated Documents of Greece and Rome 3.
Crawford/Whitehead	M. Crawford and D. Whitehead, *Archaic and Classical Greece: A Selection of Ancient Sources in Translation* (Cambridge University Press, 1983).
F	fragment.
FGrH	F. Jacoby, *Die Fragmente der griechischen Historiker* (Berlin/Leiden: Weidmann/Brill, 1923–).

Fornara	C. Fornara, *Archaic Times to the End of the Peloponnesian War* (2nd ed., Cambridge University Press, 1983). Translated Documents of Greece and Rome 1.
Harding	P. Harding, *From the End of the Peloponnesian War to the Battle of Ipsus* (Cambridge University Press, 1985). Translated Documents of Greece and Rome 2.
IC	M. Guarducci, *Inscriptiones Creticae*, 4 vols (Libreria dello Stato, 1935–1950).
IG³	D. Lewis, *Inscriptiones Graecae* (3rd ed., de Gruyter, 1981).
Meiggs/Lewis	R. Meiggs and D. Lewis (eds.), *A Selection of Greek Historical Inscriptions to the End of the Fifth Century BC* (2nd ed., Oxford University Press, 1988).
P.	Papyrus, or collection of papyri.
Phillips	D. Phillips, *The Law of Ancient Athens* (University of Michigan Press, 2013).
Rhodes	P. Rhodes, *The Greek City States: A Source Book* (2nd ed., Cambridge University Press, 2007).
Rhodes/Osborne	P. Rhodes and R. Osborne, *Greek Historical Inscriptions 404–323 BC* (Oxford University Press, 2003).
Rigsby	K. Rigsby, *Asylia: Territorial Inviolability in the Hellenistic World* (University of California Press, 1996).
SEG	*Supplementum Epigraphicum Graecum* (Gieben, 1923–).
Sherk	R. Sherk, *Rome and the Greek East to the Death of Augustus* (Cambridge University Press, 1984). Translated Documents of Greece and Rome 4.
Syll.³	W. Dittenberger et al. (eds.), *Sylloge Inscriptionum Graecarum*, 4 vols. (3rd ed., Hirzel, 1915–1924).
Welles	C. Welles, *Royal Correspondence in the Hellenistic Period: A Study in Greek Epigraphy* (Yale University Press, 1934; repr. Ares, 1974).

Chronology and King Lists

All dates BCE

Timeline of Cardinal Moments

c. 1200	Trojan War
c. 1200–1125	destruction of Mycenaean centers
c. 1200–750	hellenization of Anatolian coastline
c. 900–700	Geometric pottery and artwork
c. 800–700	invention and diffusion of the Greek alphabet
c. 790	first Heraion on Samos
776	traditional date of the first Olympics
c. 775	foundation of port-of-trade on Pithecusae
c. 750–610	Spartan takeover of Messenia
734	foundation of Syracuse in Sicily by Corinthians
c. 700	Homer and Hesiod composing their epic poems; first stone temple of Apollo at Corinth
669	Argive defeat of Sparta at Hysiae
c. 650–510	period of Archaic tyrannies in Greece
c. 650–500	diffusion of hoplite weaponry in Greece; rise of a middle-income group
c. 650–470	flourishing of Archaic lyric poetry
c. 650	Pythia festival established in Delphi
630–480	*kouroi* and *korai* statues in fashion
625–550	Corinthian pottery workshops flourish
625–475	Athenian black-figure vase-painting flourishes
621	Dracon appointed legislator in Athens
by 600	Doric architectural order perfected
c. 595–590	First Sacred War
594	Solon's emergency appointment in Athens
c. 590	Great Rhetra of Sparta
by 560	Ionic architectural order perfected; circuit of crown games established (at Olympia, Delphi, Corinth, Nemea)
559–330	Achaemenid dynasty rules Persian Empire

c. 550	Anaximander of Miletus (science); first Greek coins; foundation of Spartan alliance (later the Peloponnesian League)
547	Cyrus the Great annexes Lydia and the Greek dependencies of Lydia
546	Peisistratus establishes his tyranny in Athens
c. 530–320	Athenian red-figure vase-painting
c. 525	birth of Aeschylus (drama)
520–490	Cleomenes I, Agiad king of Sparta
518	birth of Pindar (poetry)
510	end of Peisistratid tyranny in Athens
c. 510	drama performances begin at reformed City Dionysia in Athens
508	Cleisthenes initiates democratic reforms in Athens
499–494	Ionian Rebellion
494	severe defeat of Argos by Sparta at Sepeia
490	first Persian invasion; battle of Marathon
488	first ostracism in Athens
487	sortition introduced for selection of Archons in Athens
485	Gelon becomes tyrant of Syracuse
480	Xerxes' invasion of Greece; Carthaginian invasion of Sicily; battles of Artemisium, Thermopylae, and Salamis in Greece; battle of Himera in Sicily
479	battles of Plataea and Mycale
477	Athenians form Delian League
472	Aeschylus' *The Persians*, first extant tragedy
c. 466	battle of the Eurymedon
465	earthquake flattens Sparta; helot revolt
462	reforms of Ephialtes in Athens
461–446	First Peloponnesian War
457	start of ten-year control of central Greece by Athenians
455	Pericles' first Generalship in Athens
449	?Peace of Callias ends hostilities between Greeks and Persians
447	construction of Parthenon begins in Athens
446	Thirty Years' Peace between Sparta and Athens
437	Athenians found Amphipolis
431–404	(Second) Peloponnesian War
430–427	typhoid fever ravages Athens
420s	Herodotus writing his *Histories*
429	death of Pericles
427–424	Athenian forces in Sicily
425	Aristophanes' *The Acharnians*, first extant comedy
c. 425	first Corinthian capital (temple of Apollo at Bassae)
421	Peace of Nicias
415–413	Athenian expedition to Sicily

413	Peloponnesian War resumes; Spartan fortification of Decelea
411	regime of the Four Hundred in Athens
c. 410	Zeuxis of Heraclea's floruit (painter)
406	deaths of Sophocles and Euripides (drama)
405	Dionysius I becomes tyrant of Syracuse
404	siege and surrender of Athens
404–403	regime of the Thirty in Athens
404–371	Spartan ascendancy in the Greek world
404–343	Egyptian rebellion against Persian Empire
c. 400	death of Thucydides, historian
400–360	reign of Agesilaus II in Sparta
399	trial and death of Socrates in Athens
395–386	Corinthian War
c. 390	Isocrates opens his school in Athens
387	Plato opens his Academy in Athens
386	the King's Peace (Peace of Antalcidas)
384	birth of Demosthenes (oratory/politics) and Aristotle (philosophy)
378	foundation of Second Athenian League
378–371	Boeotian War
371	Spartan power broken at battle of Leuctra
371–362	Theban ascendancy on mainland Greece
369	liberation of Messenian helots; foundation of Messene
368	foundation of Megalopolis
359	Philip II ascends to Macedonian throne
357–355	Social War (Athens vs. allies)
356	birth of Alexander the Great
355–346	Third Sacred War
from c. 350	aristocratization of Greek cities
346	Peace of Philocrates between Philip and Athens
344–337	Timoleon saves Greek Sicily
338	battle of Chaeronea; subjection of Greeks to Macedon
337	League of Corinth founded and declares war on Persia
336	assassination of Philip II; accession of Alexander III
335	destruction of Thebes
334	Alexander's eastern expedition begins
c. 330–30	Megarian bowls (relief ware) popular
323	death of Alexander in Babylon
323–322	Lamian War
323–281	Alexander's Successors carve up the empire
321	first victory of Menander of Athens (comedy)
317–307	regime of Demetrius of Phalerum in Athens
315	death of Lysippus of Sicyon (sculpture)
311–306	Agathocles of Syracuse vs. Carthage

308	Cassander kills the last Argeads
306	Epicurus founds his commune/school in Athens
306–304	the Successors (and others) assume royal titles
301	battle of Ipsus
c. 300	Zeno of Citium founds Stoic school of philosophy
c. 285	birth of Archimedes of Syracuse (mathematics); foundation of Museum of Alexandria
281	deaths of the last Successors; broad divisions of Alexander's empire become clear
c. 280	Aristarchus of Samos develops heliocentric theory; Theocritus of Syracuse active in Alexandria (poetry)
280–279	Celtic invasion of Greece
c. 275	Antigonus Gonatas secure in Macedon
274–168	series of six Syrian Wars between Seleucids and Ptolemies
c. 270	birth of Euclid (mathematics)
c. 260	floruits of Callimachus of Cyrene and Posidippus of Pella (poets)
260–215	rise of Pergamum
250s–230s	growth of Achaean and Aetolian confederacies
241–239	War of the Brothers: Seleucus II vs. Antiochus Hierax
c. 240	Bactria becomes independent Greek kingdom
235–222	Cleomenes III king in Sparta
232	overthrow of Aeacid monarchy in Epirus
229–222	Cleomenean War
229	First Illyrian War brings Romans to Greek lands
227	Cleomenes' reformation of Sparta
224	Antigonus Doson founds Common Alliance of Greek confederacies
221	Philip V comes to the Macedonian throne
220–217	Social War (Macedonian Common Alliance vs. Aetolians)
218–202	Second Punic War (Rome vs. Carthage)
215	alliance of Philip V with Hannibal of Carthage
214–212	Roman siege of Syracuse
214–205	First Macedonian War
213	death of Aratus of Sicyon
212–205	Antiochus III's eastern expedition
207–192	Nabis king in Sparta
206–185	disturbances in the Thebaid in Egypt
200–196	Second Macedonian War
198	Achaean Confederacy leaves Common Alliance
196	Isthmian Declaration of T. Quinctius Flamininus
192–188	Roman war against the Aetolians and Antiochus III
182	death of Philopoemen

171–168	Third Macedonian War
168	Antiochus IV expelled from Egypt by Rome
167	end of Macedonian monarchy; partitioning of Macedon and Illyris
166	Delos declared a free port
150s	Polybius writing his *Histories*
147	Roman military governorship of Macedon begins
146	Achaean War; sack of Corinth; sack of Carthage
133	Attalus III of Pergamum bequeaths kingdom to Rome
132–102	severe dynastic conflict in Egypt
131–129	Antiochus VII's eastern campaigns
128–111	severe dynastic conflict in Syria; diminution of the empire
96	Cyrenaica bequeathed to Rome
89–63	Roman wars against Mithridates VI of Pontus
87	Egypt bequeathed to Rome
87–86	Sulla's blockade and destruction of Athens and Piraeus
83–69	Tigranes of Armenia expands and takes over Syria
74	Rome accepts bequest of Cyrenaica; Bithynia bequeathed to Rome
64	Pompey annexes Syria for Rome
58	Romans take over Cyprus
44	assassination of Julius Caesar
31	battle of Actium; Cleopatra and Antony retreat to Alexandria
30	Octavian annexes Egypt for Rome
27	Greece becomes Roman province of Achaea

King Lists

Rulers of Egypt (Ptolemies)

Ptolemy I Soter (305–283)
Ptolemy II Philadelphus (283–246)
Ptolemy III Euergetes (246–221)
Ptolemy IV Philopator (221–204)
Ptolemy V Epiphanes (204–180)
Ptolemy VI Philometor (180–145)
Ptolemy VIII Euergetes II (145–116)
Cleopatra III & Ptolemy IX Soter II (116–107)
Cleopatra III & Ptolemy X Alexander (107–101)

Ptolemy X Alexander & Cleopatra Berenice (101–88)
Ptolemy IX Soter II (restored) (88–81)
Cleopatra Berenice & Ptolemy XI Alexander II (80)
Ptolemy XII Neos Dionysus (80–58)
Berenice IV (58–56)
Berenice IV & Archelaus (56–55)
Ptolemy XII Neos Dionysus (restored) (55–51)
Cleopatra VII Philopator (51–30)

Rulers of Macedon (from the fourth century)

Archelaus (413–399)

Orestes (399–398)

Aeropus II (398–395)

Amyntas II (395–394)

Pausanias (394–393)

Amyntas III (393–370)

Alexander II (370–367)

Ptolemy (367–365)

Perdiccas III (365–360)

Philip II (360–336)

Alexander III the Great (336–323)

Philip III Arrhidaeus (323–317)

Olympias (for Alexander IV) (317–316)

Cassander (316–297)

Philip IV (297)

Antipater (297–294)

Alexander V (297–294)

Demetrius I Poliorcetes (294–287)

Pyrrhus (287–284)

Lysimachus (287–281)

Ptolemy Ceraunus (281–279)

Antigonus Gonatas (276–239)

Demetrius II (239–229)

Antigonus III Doson (229–221)

Philip V (221–179)

Perseus (179–168)

Rulers of Pergamum (Attalids)

Philetaerus (283–263)

Eumenes I (263–241)

Attalus I (241–197, the first king)

Eumenes II (197–159)

Attalus II (159–138)

Attalus III (138–133)

Rulers of Persia

Cyrus the Great (559–530)

Cambyses (530–522)

Darius I (521–486)

Xerxes (486–464)

Artaxerxes I (464–424)

Darius II (424–405)

Artaxerxes II (405–358)

Artaxerxes III (358–338)

Artaxerxes IV (338–336)

Darius III (336–330)

Artaxerxes V (330–329)

Rulers of Syracuse

Gelon (485–478)

Hieron I (478–466)

Thrasybulus (466–465)

Dionysius I (405–367)

Dionysius II (367–357)

Dion (357–355)

Callippus (355–353)

Hipparinus (353–351)

Nisaeus (351–346)

Dionysius II (restored) (346–344)

Timoleon (344–337)

Agathocles (317–289)

Hicetas (289–280)

Pyrrhus (278–276)

Hieron II (275–215)

Hieronymus (215–214)

Rulers of Syria (Seleucids)

Seleucus I Nicator (305–281)
Antiochus I Soter (281–261)
Antiochus II Theos (261–246)
Seleucus II Callinicus (246–225)
Seleucus III Soter (225–223)
Antiochus III Megas (223–187)
Seleucus IV Philopator (187–175)
Antiochus IV Epiphanes (175–164)
Antiochus V Eupator (164–162)
Demetrius I Soter (162–150)
Alexander Balas (150–145)
Demetrius II Nicator (145–140)
Antiochus VI Epiphanes (145–138)
Antiochus VII Sidetes (138–129)
Demetrius II Nicator (restored)
  (129–126)

Cleopatra Thea (126–123)
Antiochus VIII Grypus (126–96)
Seleucus V (126)
Antiochus IX Philopator (114–95)
Seleucus VI (95)
Antiochus X Eusebes Philopator (95)
Demetrius III Philopator Soter
  (95–88)
Antiochus XI Epiphanes
  Philadelphus (95)
Philip I (95–84)
Antiochus XII Dionysus (87)
Philip II (87–83)
Antiochus XIII Philadelphus (83)

Maps

A. THE PELOPONNESE AND CENTRAL GREECE

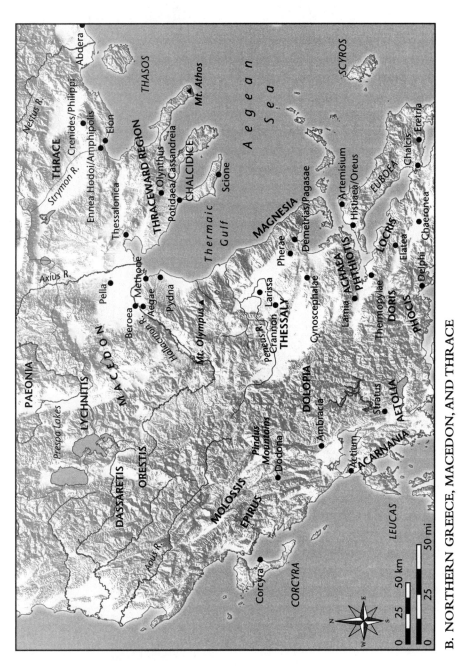

B. NORTHERN GREECE, MACEDON, AND THRACE

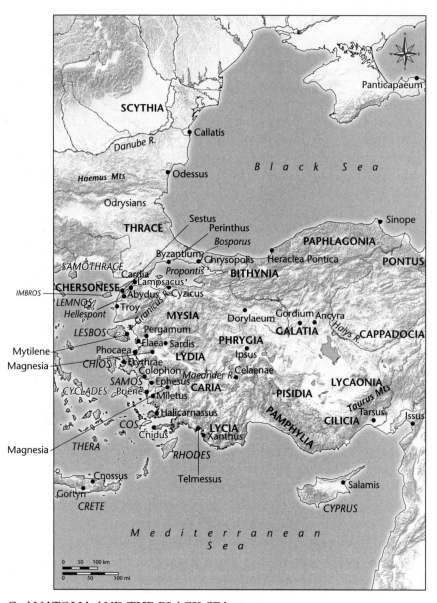

SCYTHIA

Danube R.

Haemus Mts

Callatis

Odessus

Odrysians

B l a c k   S e a

Panticapaeum

Sinope

PAPHLAGONIA

THRACE

Sestus

Perinthus

Bosporus

Byzantium

Chrysopolis

Heraclea Pontica

PONTUS

SAMOTHRACE

Cardia

Propontis

BITHYNIA

IMBROS —

CHERSONESE

Lampsacus

Abydus

Cyzicus

LEMNOS

Troy

Hellespont

Granicus

MYSIA

Dorylaeum

Gordium

Ancyra

GALATIA

Halys R.

CAPPADOCIA

LESBOS

Pergamum

Elaea

Sardis

PHRYGIA

Mytilene —

Phocaea

Magnesia —

CHIOS

Erythrae

Colophon

LYDIA

Ipsus

Celaenae

Maeander R.

LYCAONIA

SAMOS

Ephesus

CYCLADES

Priene

Miletus

CARIA

PISIDIA

Taurus Mts

Halicarnassus

Tarsus

Issus

COS

Cnidus

LYCIA

Xanthus

PAMPHYLIA

CILICIA

Magnesia —

THERA

RHODES

Telmessus

Cnossus

Salamis

Gortyn

CRETE

CYPRUS

M e d i t e r r a n e a n
S e a

0   50   100 km

0   50   100 mi

C. ANATOLIA AND THE BLACK SEA

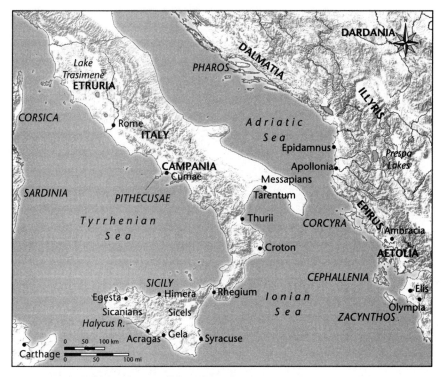

D. THE CENTRAL MEDITERRANEAN

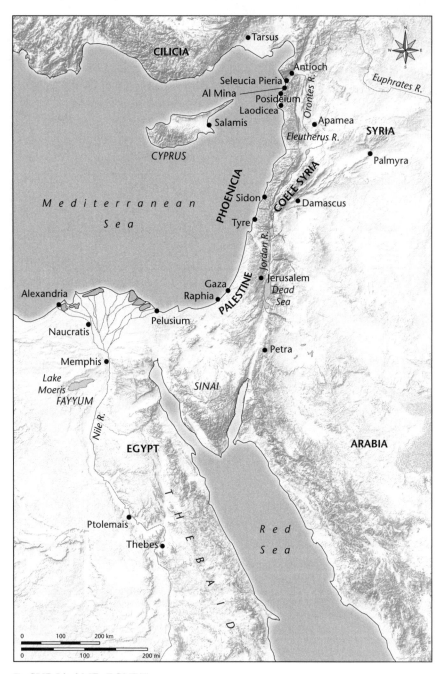

Tarsus

CILICIA

Antioch

Seleucia Pieria

Al Mina

Posideium

Laodicea

Orontes R.

Euphrates R.

Apamea

SYRIA

Eleutherus R.

Salamis

CYPRUS

Palmyra

Mediterranean
Sea

PHOENICIA

COELE-SYRIA

Sidon

Damascus

Tyre

Jordan R.

Gaza

Jerusalem

Raphia

Dead
Sea

PALESTINE

Alexandria

Pelusium

Naucratis

Petra

Memphis

Lake
Moeris

FAYYUM

SINAI

Nile R.

EGYPT

ARABIA

Ptolemais

THEBAID

Red
Sea

Thebes

0   100   200 km

0   100   200 mi

E. SYRIA AND EGYPT

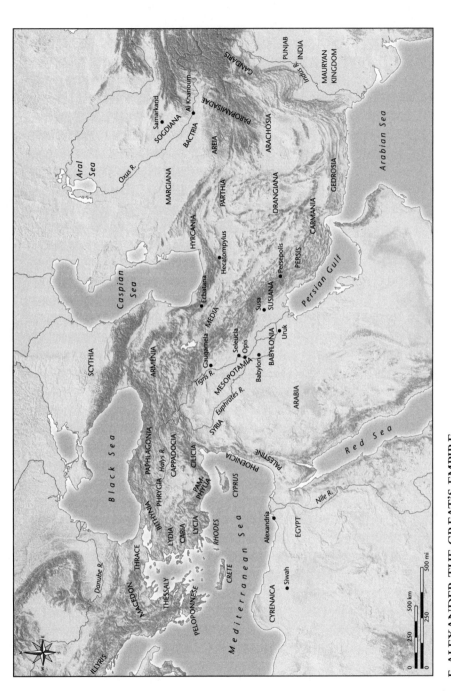

F. ALEXANDER THE GREAT'S EMPIRE

Introduction I
Environmental Background

The Greek peninsula, the heartland of the Greek world, sits right on top of the most active tectonic plate in the Mediterranean, and as a result approximately 75 percent of the Greek mainland consists of hills and mountains, usually of limestone, which make good farmland scarce and communication by land difficult. There were inland valleys and highland plains that were fertile enough to permit habitation, but most towns were founded on the often narrow strip of land that divides the coastline from high ground inland. The country consists of a large number of small habitable areas with formidable natural boundaries—a description that applies also to the hundreds of Greek islands with their watery boundaries. In many cases, it was easier and more usual to travel by boat rather than oxcart or mule or foot.

The Dalmatian mountains that run south-southeast from the European Alps spread eastwards into Macedon and Thrace and southwards into northern Greece, where they are known as the Pindus Mountains. The Pindus range reaches all the way down to the Gulf of Corinth and effectively divides northern Greece into eastern and western parts. The same north–south pattern of mountains characterizes the Peloponnese as well, the great southern peninsula of Greece. The western side of Greece is much better watered than the eastern half, and has a number of good, fertile plains, but, as everywhere in Greece, the mountains often come down close to the sea.

The eastern part of northern and central Greece is divided by lesser mountain ranges running roughly west to east, with the great, well-watered plains of Thessaly divided in this way from Macedon to the north by the Mount Olympus massif, and from central Greece to the south. Then Boeotia in its turn is similarly separated by the Parnes range from Attica to the south. The range that extends south from Mount Olympus down the Magnesia

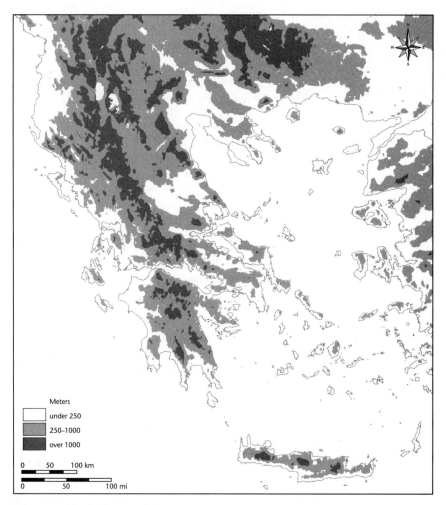

Map 0.1. Physical map of Greece.

peninsula continues along the long island of Euboea that lies off the east-ern Boeotian and Attic coastlines. The islands that swirl like pendent jewels from the south of Euboea are the peaks of this continuing mountain range, jutting out of the water. And then there are the many other islands of the Aegean Sea: "As the sky is decorated with stars, the Aegean is decorated with islands."[1]

1 Aelius Aristides, *Speeches* 44.14 (2nd century CE).

Two arms of the sea, the Corinthian and Saronic gulfs, almost meet and make the Peloponnese an island. Strictly, it is an island now, since the completion of a canal linking the two gulfs in 1893, the fulfillment of a plan first imagined in the seventh century BCE but foiled by lack of technology (the current canal is the deepest in the world, cut through solid rock). Instead, late in the seventh century, the Corinthians built a paved trackway called a *diolkos* across the isthmus, along which light ships could be rolled while their cargoes were transported by oxcart and mule. The north–south mountain ranges of the Peloponnese extend with decreasing height down its four promontories: from west to east, fertile Messenia, the arid Mani peninsula, the Cape Malea peninsula, and Argolis. Each of the four quarters of the Peloponnese has good agricultural land, but Achaea and Arcadia are mountainous regions, notoriously poor for much of antiquity.

Climate

Far more Greek literature has been lost than survives. Luckily, two of the books that survive from the hand of Theophrastus of Eresus (c. 370–287), who succeeded Aristotle as head of his school at Athens, contain his botanical researches. One important deduction they allow us to make—which has been supported in recent years by the evidence of pollen analysis and dendrochronology—is that the climate of the Mediterranean in antiquity was broadly similar to that of today. The flora Theophrastus describes and discusses still grow there. Obviously, many new species have been introduced to the region over the centuries, and some old ones have become extinct, but the basic set of plants is more or less the same in kind and in distribution. In antiquity, natural disasters had a far more devastating impact on the environment than mankind. Soil erosion as a result of human intervention has only ever had local effects, and the infamous deforestation of Greece seems to have been a phenomenon more of the modern period than classical antiquity.

The chief features of the Mediterranean climate are mild, wet winters and hot, dry summers. In many places, the summers are dry enough to arrest natural plant growth, but, on the other hand, the growing season is long. In southern Greece, most of the total annual precipitation occurs in the months of October to May, with prolonged frost being very rare in the lowlands of the south. But the Mediterranean climate does not extend to northern Greece, where mountainous regions suffer bitter winters, and in the summer the snowmelt provides plenty of water for irrigation. In fact, Greece includes four main hydrographic regions, with rainfall varying from less than four hundred millimeters (sixteen inches) a year in a zone that covers Attica (the territory of Athens), the Aegean islands, and the southern tip of the Peloponnese, to more than two thousand millimeters a year in the high mountains of the Peloponnese and northern Greece. This simple fact had profound consequences: the drier areas could not grow wheat, for instance, and had to import wheat or rely on barley, which is less nutritious and harder to process. Along with the rest of the Mediterranean, Greece consists of many microregions with their idiosyncratic microclimates. A town that nestles under a mountain receives noticeably more rainfall than its immediate neighbors on the plain.

The Greek climate was and is extremely capricious. It is no exaggeration to say that anywhere in ancient Greece might have experienced a difference of up to 60 percent in its annual rainfall, with the variations occurring especially in autumn and spring, the most critical times for crop growth in a dry-farming regime. In regions where the rainfall was barely sufficient, a year or two of relative drought could be disastrous, and it is likely that catastrophic crop failure occurred several times a century. "It is beyond human ability," Xenophon of Athens remarked around 350 BCE, "to foresee the majority of factors relevant to agriculture. Hailstorms and occasional frosts, droughts, unexpected rainstorms, crop diseases—all these and other factors often undo even well-planned and well-executed work."[2] Living also with frequent warfare, Greek peasants were threatened by fear, grief, hunger, injury, and early death. It is little wonder that Greek gods were fickle and unpredictable.

Farming

Once upon a time, it is said,[3] the sixth-century Athenian tyrant Peisistratus was inspecting the countryside outside the city when he came across a field that was nothing but boulders and stones. Now, Peisistratus had recently

2 Xenophon, *On Estate Management* 5.18.
3 Pseudo-Aristotle, *The Athenian Constitution* 16.6 (written c. 330); Crawford/Whitehead no. 70.

tried to regularize the city's public finances by imposing a 10 percent tax on agricultural produce, and he asked the man working the field how much his land produced. "Nothing but aches and pains," the farmer replied. "Peisistratus should have 10 percent of those too." The story captures two things. First, that agriculture was the basis of society; it was the primary and essential livelihood for many families, and taxing it was a primary source of revenue for a Greek state. And, second, that for the majority of farmers, life was tough. As a rule of thumb, the annual grain yield of one hectare (about 2.5 acres) could maintain one member of a household, but many farms were so small and poor that the owners must have struggled to make ends meet and put food on the table. Farming was essentially dry farming, with little or no reliance on irrigation other than that provided by the weather.

The hazards and variability of conditions in Greece were such that farming there in antiquity was in no sense uniform year by year or region by region. Not only did different parts of Greece tackle the hazards differently, but individual farmers had to be flexible. They experimented with different crops and knew what grew under what circumstances. They channeled streams for irrigation, where they could, and built terraces to increase area and impede erosion. Bare fallowing was widely practiced—the method of avoiding soil exhaustion by taking a field out of production for a year, letting animals roam on it, and then plowing in the weeds and manure (and well-rotted human waste). A few pigs, sheep and goats, and a couple of donkeys or mules would supply the basic needs of a subsistence farmer (along with poultry and bees), without taking too much of his land away from producing food for the household. Only those with a farm of at least five hectares (twelve acres) would even consider keeping a team of two oxen. Animals were kept for their manure, as a food resource in years of poor harvests, to provide energy for traction and transportation, and for their wool, hair, and hides.

Many people owned several different plots of land (as a result of inheritance or purchase), which might be near or at some remove from their residences. A farmer might use one plot for olives, another for vines, another for grain, and so on, to spread the risk. More likely, he would give each plot of any size over to a mixture of crops. If hail or warfare or a wild boar destroyed one field, he would still be able to count on the others. Much of the countryside was an intricate patchwork of small plots.

In short, Greek subsistence farmers were forced to diversify in order to manage the risks they faced; the "Mediterranean triad" of grain, olives, and grapes was supplemented by legumes (in wetter areas, where they grow well) and a little animal husbandry. A certain amount of food was also foraged, trapped, hunted, and fished from countryside, forest, wetlands, rivers, and sea. It was crucial not just to survive, but also to make enough of a surplus to trade for items such as salt, tools, storage jars, and footwear. Many other farmers, however, were prosperous enough to focus less on risk-management and more on profit-making, by specializing and producing enough of their crops to sell in local or international markets. As urbanization increased, with more people choosing to live in towns (necessarily, because all premodern cities were unhealthy places, where deaths outnumbered births, and immigration was therefore essential), more food was grown just for markets, or imported from elsewhere.

Most cereal crops were sown just before the winter rains and harvested in the early summer. Storage was therefore another fundamental strategy: cereals are relatively easy to store, dried legumes keep well, and good olive oil keeps for two or three years under the right conditions. It is a nice symbol of the importance of storage that some of the eighty-one gifts placed in a grave known as the Athenian Rich Lady's grave of around 850 BCE were models of grain bins. And then the third aspect of risk-management for the individual farmer was exchange: he could remedy a shortfall by exchanging his surplus products. The microregional makeup of the Mediterranean made it likely that, even if a farmer was short of grapes one year, he would not have had to travel far to find someone else whose vines had flourished.

By the historical period, animal husbandry was less important—at any rate, in the less hilly regions of Greece—than it had been in the past, but it still made up a good portion of the agricultural economy, and in some regions ownership of livestock remained a measure of wealth. Vertical transhumance, the regular movement of flocks of sheep and goats from low winter pastures to high summer pastures and back again, was practiced (though over no great distances) in regions short of lowland pasturage if flocks were large enough to require it. In other places, there were enough lowland pastures or wetlands (around Lake Copais in Boeotia, for instance) to satisfy summer needs even for larger flocks and herds. Small, deserted islands were used for temporary pasturage as well.

Large quantities of animals were required every year for state and private religious sacrifices: where we have figures, we know that in the 330s the Athenian state was sacrificing over six thousand oxen and more than fifteen thousand sheep and goats a year. This was the regular turnover, but there were also unexpected celebratory or other sacrifices. Fourth- and third-century monarchs were given to marking special occasions with even more ostentatious sacrifices: Jason, ruler of Thessalian Pherae, once levied a thousand oxen and over ten thousand sheep, goats, and pigs for a single festival. Many states or temples kept their own sacred herds and flocks, but this was still a lucrative market for animal farmers, who, with their teams of oxen, were also prominent in the transport business.

A horse's demand for rich pasturage largely limited commercial horse-rearing to regions with sufficient and well-watered flatland, such as Macedon and Thessaly. In central and southern Greece, it was a rich man's hobby: no one else could afford to give up so much productive land. One horse eats as much barley as a household of five or six people. Ownership of a horse, in a dry region such as Attica, was therefore a showy sign of social distinction, like owning a Ferrari today. Horses were not used for farm work, but mainly for warfare and racing. Animals other than horses and cattle in large quantities could be maintained largely from woodland

Figure 0.1. Plowing and sowing. From an Athenian black-figure Siana cup of the first half of the sixth century. Seed was sown in the autumn, but further plowings took place after the spring harvest, to bury weeds as green fertilizer and keep the soil friable. BM 1906,12–15.1 side A. Photo © Trustees of the British Museum.

and scrubland, just as in some parts of Greece nowadays cattle graze freely in the hills.

The Silent Majority

Something like this, then, is how we should imagine the lives of the majority of the population of Greece—perhaps 90 percent at the start of the book, and about 60 percent at the end. Their lives were defined by good or bad harvests. But despite the predominance of agriculture in the lives of the Greeks, ancient agricultural practices have left little trace in the archaeological record, and although farming manuals were written, none has survived. We remain ignorant about some very basic facts, but we should imagine the majority of this majority working small farms of between 3.5 and 6 hectares (9 to 15 acres), though there were regions, such as Thessaly, where there were large estates.

Imagination is the best tool we have, because it is otherwise very hard to detect their voices. From the third century BCE onward, tens of thousands of papyri from the sands of Egypt enable some microhistory, but it is still largely the history of a literate elite, not of the underclasses. Surface surveys go some way toward revealing the lives of farmers, but the situation is even worse for those farther down the economic scale—those who owned no land, or too little to make a difference, and who were dependent mainly on selling their labor, often moving from place to place. Their lot was so miserable that they became a byword for wretchedness, so that, when questioned by Odysseus in the underworld, heroic Achilles claimed that he would rather be one of these men, "a laborer for hire to a landless man," than a king of the dead.[4] Unless or until miraculous new methods of analysis are developed, individual details of the lives of most Greeks will remain largely inaccessible.

Almost all the literature of ancient Greece was written by male members of the urban elite, and their concerns were different. They wrote about politics, philosophy, and war, about love and loathing, but what occupied the minds of the majority was putting food on the table; a popular fantasy was that the Age of Cronus, the deity who preceded Zeus as king of the gods, had been a time when food grew from the ground with no need of human labor. We stand in awe of the creations of countless ancient artisans—the Parthenon, beautifully

---

4 Homer, *Odyssey* 11.487–491.

painted vases, sculptures in bronze and marble, magnificent cities—but we know almost nothing about the lives of those who made them. As Bertold Brecht ironically asked, in his 1935 poem "A Worker Reads History":

> Who built the seven gates of Thebes?
> The books are filled with names of kings.
> Did kings haul the rough blocks of stone?

Diet, Life Expectancy, Population

A typical Greek meal consisted of bread, *opson* (small quantities of savories such as olives, small fish, shellfish, cheese, eggs, onions, garlic, vegetables, pickles), and wine, which was generally diluted to about half strength with water, and was often flavored with herbs or spices—or even with grated cheese and barley, in one famous episode in Homer's *Iliad*.[5] Legumes (mainly broad beans, chickpeas, lentils, and peas) might also be served, especially in the form of soups; they were a very important source of protein for a diet that was otherwise borderline in this respect. Olive oil and salt were the usual condiments. Big fish were an expensive luxury (as they still are). A meal might be rounded off with some fruit or honeyed pastries. Food was eaten with the fingers and a piece of bread, not with cutlery.

In the historical period, meat reached the dining table usually only after a blood sacrifice. Meat was a more common element of the diet in areas where animal husbandry remained important; soldiers out on campaign might find it more readily available than other foodstuffs, athletes in training bulked up on it, and peasants might reluctantly slaughter livestock to see them through a bad summer, but essentially animal meat was a treat. There was simply not enough good land for livestock to graze; plants produce more food per unit of land than animals do.

A big animal sacrifice sponsored by the state was therefore a festive occasion for the whole citizen community, with a procession before the sacrifice and a banquet afterwards for as many as could be fed. In prosperous Classical Athens, a man could expect to take part in a sacrifice about once a week. Private individuals might perform a sacrifice in celebration of some event or a successful hunt and invite their friends to a meal at which the meat was eaten, or a rich man might feast the members of his village as a benefaction.

---

5 Homer, *Iliad* 11.638–641.

The gods usually received, as smoke and smell, the bones and other inedible bits, but the rest was consumed by humans, with a special cut set aside for the presiding priest.

Rich and poor ate much the same food, although the rich had more; they also had greater access to spices and other imports. Cereal products dominated the diet. Wheat was usually eaten in the form of bread (leavened or unleavened), and barley as porridge. Cereals are a good source of calories and protein, and they have a couple of important vitamins (B and E), but other elements of the diet had to supply the other vitamins. Generally speaking, the Greek diet was nutritious enough, provided one had an adequate supply of it.

As my survey of the Greek climate has shown, many regions or microregions of Greece might in any year suffer from a poor harvest. Famines were rare, and more likely to be caused by humans rather than nature (for instance, during the siege of a city), but shortages were not uncommon. A certain degree of malnutrition was widespread in Greece, and helps to explain the high incidence of child mortality and the fairly short stature of ancient Greeks: even in the relatively prosperous Classical period, men averaged about 170 centimeters (67 inches), women about 156 centimeters (61.5 inches). A tall woman was judged beautiful by that standard alone.

By the Classical period, the average age at death for a man was the mid-forties, and for a woman the mid-thirties. Warfare, complications in pregnancy and childbirth, diseases—all took their toll. The rich were better protected against these hazards than the poor. Most men who made it to adulthood faced a hard life of agricultural toil and soldiering, supported by a barely adequate diet. Standards of living rose over the centuries, but still the disease-ridden and impoverished peasants of Greece bore little resemblance to the heroic, unsullied figures of Classical statuary and biography. A high rate of morbidity has to be offset by high fertility: women gave birth, on average, to 4.3 children in the Classical period and 3.6 in the Hellenistic period, while the infant survival rate was 2.7 in the Classical period and 1.6 in the Hellenistic period. According to Aristotle, "most infant deaths occur before the seventh day."[6] It was considered a rare but real blessing to have more than two or three children, just as it was considered exceptional for a mature child to have both parents alive.

6 Aristotle, *Researches into Animal Life* (*Historia Animalium*) 588a9.

Population growth was constrained by late marriage for men (they were in their late twenties or even early thirties, typically, while their brides were fourteen or fifteen), by birth control (either by spacing out pregnancies, by practicing anal sex, or by contraception, for which a wide range of more or less effective herbs was available), by abortion (again, certain herbs were known to be effective), or by abandoning unwanted infants. Some of these were found and reared as slaves in other homes, but not all. Seriously deformed children were more likely to be exposed; a second son was at risk because, if two sons lived, the estate would be divided between them, with the possibility of making it too small to be viable, or of dropping a rung on the status ladder; a second daughter was at risk, or even a first, because of the need to give her a dowry in due course of time and her negligible economic value.

In the times covered by this book, populations fluctuated locally as a result of war, natural disaster, disease, and emigration (Athens, for instance, lost about half its population to warfare and disease in the last third of the fifth century), but maintained an overall long-term growth. If the population of the Greek mainland in 700 BCE was 1.5 million, it may have reached about eight million by the end of the fourth century, when it peaked. But, lacking statistics, this is no more than an informed guess. And then in addition to the Balkan peninsula itself, there was an increasing number of Greek settlements abroad—a substantial trickle in the Archaic and Classical periods, and a flood in the Hellenistic period. These settlements contained several million more Greeks or Greek-speakers, but the really significant figure is that, in the Hellenistic period, Greek-speakers came to control kingdoms and empires with a total population of perhaps forty million. What counted as "the Greek world" exploded in extent.

Introduction II

Historical Background

By the time this book opens around 750 BCE, a great deal has already happened in the Greek world. The Aegean basin, which formed the heart of that world, always bustled with human activity. A fossilized skull, discovered in the Petralona Cave in Chalcidice (the three-fingered peninsula of northern Greece), of a crossbreed man, half Neanderthal and half *Homo erectus*, may be two hundred thousand years old. A chert quarry flourished on the island of Naxos for thousands of years up to the eighth millennium, and obsidian (a kind of volcanic glass) was quarried on Melos and other Aegean islands from about 13,000 onward. Meanwhile, the Franchthi Cave in Argolis was home to a village that flourished both inside and outside it for perhaps thirty thousand years until about 3000, far longer than any modern city or settlement. There are dozens of other Stone Age sites all over Greece, with the more recent ones, such as Sesklo (near modern Volos/ancient Pagasae), showing considerable sophistication in terms of social structures, fortifications, and economic life.

Crete and Cyprus were also settled during Neolithic times, as well as some of the Cycladic islands. By 3000 BCE, the mineral-rich Cyclades were key elements in eastern Mediterranean trade involving Crete, Egypt, Phoenicia, and mainland Greece. For the next several hundred years, spanning the end of the Stone Age and the beginning of the Bronze Age, the Aegean islands supported a culture, called "Cycladic," which is most familiar to visitors to today's museums from its iconic product—flat marble idols with triangular noses and crossed arms, strikingly modern in appearance. Subsequently, the islands fell under the influence first of Crete and then of mainland Greece. Meanwhile, on Crete the Minoan civilization (named in modern times after legendary King Minos) was emerging in its full glory, as the ruins of Cnossus testify, or the delicately wrought jewelry of the British Museum's Aegina Treasure.

The familiar story that until Theseus' intervention the Athenians used to send seven young men and seven young women to Crete to be sacrificed to the terrible Minotaur perhaps reflects a time when some parts of the Greek mainland were subject to Crete. Certainly Minoan culture spread northward from Crete to the Aegean basin, until decline set in from about 1450 BCE. The reasons for the decline are unknown; despite popular lore, it had little or nothing to do with the massive eruption of the Thera volcano (the modern island of Santorini), about 140 kilometers (ninety miles) north of Crete. This event, the fallout from which certainly affected Crete, should more properly be dated to around 1600 BCE, many years before the decline of the Minoan civilization.

The Mycenaeans

The first great civilization of the mainland Greeks is called "Mycenaean," after one of the largest and best-known sites, Mycenae in the northeast Peloponnese. In this sentence, the word "Greeks" now gains extra significance. The Mycenaean script, known as Linear B, was syllabic, which is to say that each of its ninety or so signs represented a syllable, not a single letter as in an alphabetic script such as ours. More than six thousand clay tablets with Linear B characters impressed on them have survived. For several decades after the discovery of the first of these tablets they remained undeciphered, and Linear B was lumped in with one of the two undeciphered languages of Minoan Crete, Linear A, with which it shares a number of features. This Cretan language still remains largely a mystery, but the breakthrough with Linear B came in the 1950s, when it was found to be Greek. So the Balkan peninsula was now occupied by Greeks. They probably arrived, perhaps from a northerly direction, not long before 2000 BCE, bringing the horse with them.

Mycenaean sites began to be developed around 1650, but the time of their main flourishing was the three hundred years from 1500 to 1200, when Minoan influence diminished and a distinct culture evolved. Each main site consisted of a defensible palace-dominated town, with outlying farmland and hamlets. The palace was occupied by a king, who, with the help of a cohort of high-ranking assistants, was simultaneously the military, political,

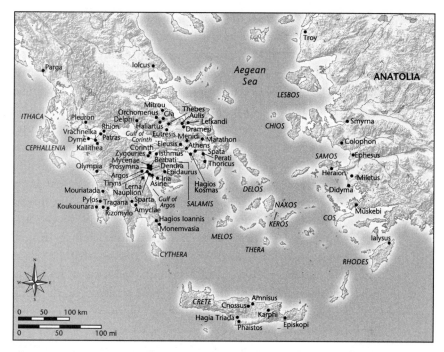

Map 0.2. The main Mycenaean sites.

and religious leader of his people and the CEO of a commercial enterprise based largely on agricultural produce. Scribes used Linear B to record the king's possessions and his commercial and religious transactions. As a way of legitimizing their authority, the king and his courtiers were given to ostentatious display, especially in acquiring luxuries from the Near East and burying valuables along with their dead.

Trade was supported by extensive division of labor: the Linear B tablets include the names of some twenty kinds of artisan, from goldsmith to headband-maker. So powerful did some Mycenaean states become that they were able to extend their influence to Crete and dominate the declining Minoan culture there. And the legends preserved for us most notably by Homer (under whose name the first European books, the epic poems *Iliad* and *Odyssey*, have come down to us) tell of a Greek assault on the city of Troy in northwestern Anatolia. The Mycenaeans were a dynamic and warlike people, and proud of it; weapons are common in their graves.

All the Mycenaean sites around the Aegean display a surprising uniformity of culture. The same thing was happening elsewhere in Europe: the local differences that had characterized the Neolithic era gave way in the Bronze Age to broader cultural groupings, such as the Atlantic tradition, which was followed in Britain, northern France, and northern Spain. So in Greece, within the Aegean–Balkan tradition, local differences consisted not so much of new styles or burial practices as variations on the same themes. They spoke the same or a similar language; they worshipped the same or similar gods.

As we shall see, this is normal for Greece. A fairly high degree of cultural homogeneity, in combination with political diversity, is the recurrent pattern of Greek life and history, and a recurrent theme of this book. Despite the cultural uniformity, it is quite likely that some Mycenaean towns were trading rivals rather than allies, and it is not unlikely that it was inter-Mycenaean warfare that brought about or hastened the eventual demise of the civilization in at least some areas of Greece in the twelfth century. Perhaps, if they had survived, greater units would have been formed. It seems that the palace at Pylos controlled much of Mycenaean Messenia, and Athens held sway over much of Attica. Probably more areas would have coalesced in the same way, but the Mycenaeans never had the chance to find out.

Ancient Greek Historical Periods

Name	Dates (BCE)
Bronze Age	c. 3000–1200
Bronze Age on Crete/Minoan Period	c. 2600–1400
Late Bronze Age/Mycenaean Period	c. 1600–1200
Early Iron Age/"Dark Age"	c. 1200–750
Formative	c. 900–750
Archaic	c. 750–479
Classical	479–323
Hellenistic	323–30
Roman Imperial	146 BCE–1453 CE

A Dark Age?

By 1100 it was all over. Frustratingly, we do not know why. Probably different factors caused the collapse of the palace culture in different places. There is evidence of serious earthquake damage at Boeotian sites, and of destruction by enemy action elsewhere. There seems to have been a prolonged period of drought from the thirteenth century for two or three hundred

years, which might have led to grain shortages, migration, and general turmoil. It is possible that the whole economic structure collapsed, as a result
of this drought and of disruption among the Mycenaeans' Near Eastern
trading partners, due to warfare between the Hittite and Assyrian empires,
based respectively in Anatolia and Mesopotamia (modern Iraq). There were
disturbances all over the eastern Mediterranean, even as far west as Sicily.
For much of the thirteenth century, and into the twelfth, the coastlines of
the eastern Mediterranean were liable to raids by the Sea Peoples, as they
are popularly known, who seem to have been organized pirates, or perhaps
waves of migrants looking for new homes.

On the Greek mainland, the story of the centuries following the downfall of the Mycenaean civilization is one of gradual recovery and the re-
formation of states. The immediate result of the downfall was the dispersal
of the surviving population into a large number of smaller settlements,
on the mainland and elsewhere. This was when the Greeks first settled on
Cyprus, for instance, sharing the island with Phoenicians. Distinct regional
styles of pottery suggest that these places were relatively isolated from one
another; the cultural unity of the Mycenaean world had become fragmented. Housing was small and poor, civic amenities were almost non-
existent, and sophisticated craft techniques had been forgotten. There was
no need for writing, because writing had been exclusively wedded to the
palace bureaucracy, and that was a thing of the past.

But the end of the Mycenaean palaces was not the utter break that scholars used to suppose, nor was what followed universally a "Dark Age," as
it is still sometimes called. In fact, to call it a Dark Age is in many ways a
confession of failure. Recent finds, new ways of reading cultural history
from archaeological evidence, and the evidence of the Homeric poems shed
enough light to make it better to refer to the period neutrally as the Early
Iron Age. True, there was a sharp decline in population and culture, but the
effects were not everywhere catastrophic. Graves at Lefkandi in Euboea,
and elsewhere, display substantial wealth and refined tastes, and prove that
Greeks were still trading with the Near East. One of the Lefkandi tombs,
dating from the second quarter of the ninth century, was clearly that of
a wealthy trader: it contained (among many valuable objects) sets of balance weights for the three dominant standards used in Phoenician ports
(the Babylonian, the Syrian, and the Palestinian). Even if many places were
family-based hamlets, others had ranked societies, with kings or a wealth-
and-warrior elite dominant over a population of peasants and artisans.

Important developments were taking place, especially learning to work with iron. It is not impossible that the collapse of the Mycenaean palaces so badly disrupted the trade in copper and tin (the ingredients of bronze) that the Greeks were forced to take up ironworking. The necessary techniques seem to have been acquired first on Cyprus, and had spread all over Greece by the eighth century. The main advantages of iron were that it was more readily available and made lighter and sharper tools and weapons. The invention of a faster potter's wheel made it possible to make pots on a larger and more impressive scale and supported the emergence of Geometric pottery, one of the supreme accomplishments of Greek art. The Athenians invented it, around 900, and Athenian work always held pride of place, but Argos and Corinth were also major centers of production. This style flourished for the best part of two hundred years, and though there were regional differences, and the northern Aegean seems to have largely resisted the fashion, for a

Figure 0.2. Geometric vase. This large belly-handled amphora, 0.7 meters in height (over 2 feet), comes from an Athenian tomb of c. 850. It is an astonishing piece of work for what is still commonly thought of as the "Dark Age." Agora Excavations P27629.

while the taste for geometrical designs united the elites of many Greek communities, on the mainland and in the Aegean.

Homer

Some flesh can be added to the rather sparse picture of the Early Iron Age that is given us by archaeology. We have an alternative source of evidence as well: Homer's epic poems. Two have survived under his name: the *Iliad* focuses on the conflict between two Greek leaders, Agamemnon and Achilles, in the last year of the legendary siege of Troy, and the *Odyssey* tells of the adventures of one Greek hero, Odysseus, as he struggled to return home after the war. Homer probably practiced as an oral bard, but his chief importance is that he wrote down or dictated these two poems, or some of them, drawing on a pool of stories that had been transmitted down to his time as a result of centuries-old traditions. This is why these poems, the very first works of European literature, are already mature and skillful works. Whenever it was that the poems began to be written down—estimates range from before 750 to around 650—at many points they take for granted certain features of society. The question is whether they describe a single coherent society (and if so whether it was the society that was contemporaneous with the final form of the poems or an idealized view of a past society) or reflect features from a number of different stages of the evolution of Greek society in the Early Iron Age.

Since Homer came at the end of a long line of bards, each of whom had added to and altered the stories they received, it is possible that, rather than reflecting a single society, his poems contain layers of material from different eras and the final construct is little more than a poetic fantasy. Nevertheless, since Homer was an entertainer, the society he assumed must have been broadly recognizable to his audiences. Of course, there are fantastic elements in the stories—men are larger than life, the gods walk the earth along with witches and monsters—and there are also artifacts and features of society that belong to earlier phases of the poems' historical development. But Homer's audiences would have taken these features in their stride, as enhancing the fantastic and heroic dimension of the stories.

So Homer can be mined for information about Early Iron Age society, provided that archaeology is our primary guide. The central theme of the *Iliad*—how leaders should behave in order to do the best for their

communities—is timeless, but there are other aspects that are more specific. Homeric society is clearly hierarchical, divided between the haves and
the have-nots. The dominant elite owe their wealth and their standing in
society to agriculture (especially livestock) and the profits of long-distance
trading, piracy, and cattle-rustling. Wealth, however gained, is regarded as
proof of a man's caliber, and so he puts it on display, especially by gift-giving
and feasting others in competition with his peers. A man is what he seems
to others to be; hence both his insecurity and sense of shame (rather than
guilt, shame's internalized equivalent), and his urge to win distinction. Each
Homeric hero is the head of a household, which consists of his immediate family and attendants (free or slave) and his valuables. His position is
entrenched, but not absolutely certain, since it depends not just on inheritance but to a certain extent on charisma and leadership (or, more cynically,
on bribery and rhetorical persuasion). Leaders are chieftains, whose power
depends on the resources of their households, their martial prowess, and
their ability to attract followers.

There is little in the way of social justice; the process of seeking redress
was initiated by the injured party and ended in a solution that satisfied both
parties, rather than one which followed an objective code. And for members
of the elite, considerations of personal and familial honor outweigh equity.
It would have been morally right (by our lights) for Achilles to stop sulking
and return to the fray to save Greek lives and prevent their imminent defeat,
but he felt he could not do so, because his honor had been besmirched. And
when he does return to battle, it is because his friend Patroclus has been
killed, not because the Greeks need him. Trojan Hector's motivations are
the same: in a famous passage of the *Iliad*, as he takes leave of his wife he
lists his reasons for going into battle as personal honor and concern for his
family; loyalty to the wider community plays little part.[1]

There is just enough sense of community for a typical question, on meeting a man for the first time, to be whether he has come on private or public
business. Homeric heroes meet in council to discuss matters that affect all
households in common, but otherwise they are their own bosses, lords of
their households and estates. They call assemblies of the common people for
decisions affecting the whole community, but the people's role is no more
than to acclaim the heroes' decisions. The people had no right of free speech
and no right to vote, nor to assemble of their own accord; nevertheless, the

---

1 Homer, *Iliad* 6.440–465.

right of assembly was an old and respected tradition, and, even if they lacked institutional power, the assembled people had a degree of moral authority, so that aristocrats usually wanted their backing and won honor for their success in gaining the people's acclaim as they did for their success in war.

This, in outline, is how we should conceive of Early Iron Age society in the Greek world. Given that this is the start of the Iron Age, it is surely no coincidence that in later years, despite the superiority of iron to bronze, "the race of iron" came to signify people living in a grim society. "Would that I had died before or been born later!" laments Hesiod of Ascra in Boeotia, the poet of the early seventh century who preserves the myth for us. "For now truly is a race of iron: there is no end to toil and misery by day, nor to perishing by night."[2] Some communities were so small that their inhabitants must have been little more than an extended family. Even Lefkandi in Euboea, the largest and wealthiest settlement so far excavated from this period, probably had a population of no more than a few hundred at its height (it was abandoned around 700). Some places, such as Tiryns, which survived the immediate collapse of the palaces fairly well, went into further decline later. The Myth of Metals—that the Age of Gold and of heroes is in the past and things are much worse now—was a charter myth for the new era.

The Settlement of Anatolia

Later Greeks had a particular tale to tell about the diaspora that followed the collapse of the Mycenaean palaces. By the historical period, there were three language groups on the west coast of Anatolia (modern Turkey): Aeolian Greek was spoken in the cities of the north, Ionian in the center, and Dorian in the south. And it was said that these areas had been settled by Greeks at the time of the Mycenaean diaspora—that Ionian-speaking Mycenaean refugees who settled in Attica (the territory of Athens) slowly spread across the Aegean until they occupied the central coastline of western Turkey, that Aeolian-speaking emigrants mainly from Thessaly and Boeotia did the same in the north, and that Dorian-speaking Peloponnesian emigrants took the south.

The trouble is that archaeology does not support this story. There is no evidence for Aeolian Greek in northwest Anatolia, for instance, until the

---

2 Hesiod, *Works and Days* 175–178; the full myth occupies 109–201.

eighth century. It now seems more likely that the Eastern Greek cities were originally indigenous, with small Greek populations (in the three dialect bands), but that Greek language and culture gradually became dominant until, by the historical period, the places spoke Greek and were effectively Greek cities. Legends of early migrations arose, as legends often do, for contemporary political purposes; for instance, it was very useful for Athens in the fifth century to claim to be the mother city of the Ionian Greek cities, which it was trying to amalgamate into a grand alliance. The old, familiar story has to be discarded. The Greeks scattered, to be sure, but not in sufficient numbers for this to count as a time of mass emigration.

ACT I

The Archaic Period
(750–480)

The Formation of States

I

The Emergence of the Greeks

The two and a half centuries that make up the Archaic period, roughly 750 to 480 BCE, saw the lives of the Greeks change fundamentally. Above all, there was the gradual development of statehood and civilized life, from primitive and hierarchical beginnings to far greater collectivism, equality under the law, and general participation in public life. From a broad perspective, this was an astonishing development. For hundreds, if not thousands of years, the chief form of political and social organization in the Near East and Mediterranean had been the hierarchically organized kingdom. Yet the Greeks evolved a different form, which became dominant in the Mediterranean world for several centuries. Politically, it was more egalitarian; economically, property belonged to private individuals, not just the king or a temple.

Within the Archaic period also, the art of writing, lost since the collapse of the Mycenaean palaces, was reintroduced. Creative geniuses such as Homer, Hesiod, the lyric poets, and the Presocratic natural scientists showed what could be done with words and ideas. Brilliant experimentation governed the changing styles of vase-painting; Greek art was valued all over the Mediterranean. Temple architecture evolved from modest to monumental, and sanctuaries were filled with often strikingly impressive buildings and beautiful artifacts. Coined money spread rapidly. New forms of warfare were developed. The Greeks founded cities and trading posts all over the Mediterranean, impelled by the quest for wealth, or at least for relief from poverty, and supported by the god Apollo's oracle at Delphi, which became the hub for many networks in the Mediterranean. The institutions, artifacts, and practices that define the better-known Classical period have their roots in the Archaic period.

The Great Land Grab

A tipping point was reached in Greece in the eighth century. Perhaps as a result of better nutrition and of changes in marriage practices, so that women married younger than they had before, the population increased dramatically over the course of the century, particularly in the second half, on both the mainland and the islands. The results of this population increase make the eighth century one of the most dynamic periods of Greek history.

A growing population needs new land, and everywhere we find signs of expansion, at home and overseas. At home, large villages (as they were at the time) such as Athens and Corinth generated further villages, occupying more of the land that would in due course of time become Attica and Corinthia. The most extreme case of this kind of internal expansion was pursued by the Spartans. Sparta had already taken over and developed its home territory of Laconia in the ninth century, and by the end of the eighth it had also annexed the most fertile part of neighboring Messenia, awarding itself an enormous territory, compared to others.

Abroad, the emigrants first looked westward, where they had long had trade links. Corinth, for instance, established what would become the great Sicilian city of Syracuse and occupied much of the northwestern coastline of Greece, from Epirus to Illyris, including foundations on the Ionian Islands, so that it came to dominate the western trade routes. Soon a fair sprinkling of new Greek towns dotted the coastlines of Sicily and southern Italy. Euboeans joined Phoenicians in founding a highly successful emporium (port-of-trade) on the island of Pithecusae (modern Ischia), off the west coast of southern Italy. In the last third of the eighth century, a Greek overseas settlement was being founded roughly every two years. Generally speaking, the emigrant party consisted entirely of men, numbering in the dozens; women would be found where they settled, and further settlers would arrive once the place seemed viable.

Pithecusae was not favored with fertility. The chief purpose of the venture was to gain access to minerals from mainland Italy. Clearly, land-hunger caused by a growing population was not the only spur to emigration. Personal profit was also a relevant factor. There were fortunes to be made in the eighth century, and international trade increased rapidly, as shipbuilding

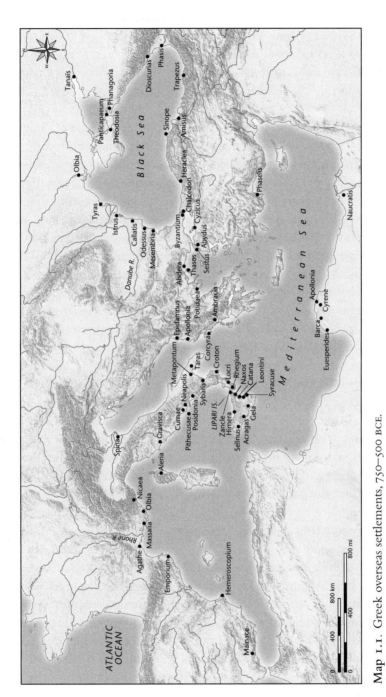

Map 1.1. Greek overseas settlements, 750–500 BCE.

techniques improved and prosperity recovered. At the mouth of the Orontes River in Syria, a trading post was set up around 820 by Phoenicians (its ancient name is unknown, and today it is called simply Al Mina, "the emporium"), to bring goods from farther east—textiles, slaves, spices, perfumes, jewelry—into the Mediterranean in return for Greek agricultural products and minerals. There was another such trading post about forty-five kilometers (twenty-seven miles) farther south down the Levantine coast, which later came to be known as Posideium to the Greeks (Ras al-Bassit today). Greek penetration, if not actual residence, at Al Mina, Posideium, and elsewhere on the Phoenician and Cilician coasts has been confirmed by pottery finds.

A little later, starting at the beginning of the seventh century, the northern Aegean, the Hellespont, the Propontis (the Sea of Marmara), and the Black Sea were also opened up by Greek settlers, so that they could exploit the commercial potential of the Black Sea coastline and inland Thrace. Euboea and Megara were as important in this movement as they had been westward, but so were states closer to the region, especially Samos and Miletus, which was an exceptionally prolific colonizer, sometimes in partnership with Megara. Toward the end of the seventh century, Eastern Greeks from these two places and elsewhere jointly founded the most successful Greek overseas emporium, Naucratis, on the western Nile Delta in Egypt. It was located close to the largest natron bed in Egypt, and natron, the ancient Mediterranean's basic cleaning product, was always one of Egypt's largest exports, along with wheat (and, later, papyrus). All Greek trade with Egypt was obliged by law to pass through Naucratis, so the place flourished. The foundation of Massalia (Marseilles) in southern France by Phocaeans, around 600, extended the reach of Greek traders to the mineral wealth of Spain and inland Europe. This was the route that brought British tin to the Mediterranean.

The overall result of the new foundations established in the eighth and seventh centuries was a huge extension of Greek horizons, until they encompassed almost the whole of the Mediterranean Sea, and much of the Black Sea as well. But in addition to extension, there was also an increased intension or concentration, since the Greeks no longer lived in individual communities, but were interlinked with other states in networks all over the Mediterranean. These networks were laid down in the Archaic period, and so Greek history became not, or not just, a matter of one state interacting with another, but of networks and alliances. Through these networks, ideas spread, and as a result the common features of Greek culture could be found everywhere—architectural styles, artistic motifs, clothing fashions, scripts and dialects, forms of worship.

Perhaps forty thousand adult male Greeks emigrated from Greek communities between 750 and 600. Some places, such as Achaea, sent a fair proportion of their population, with the primary purpose of relieving poverty at home, and the Megarians similarly established overseas settlements for those of their citizens who had been dispossessed by Corinthian encroachment, but overall the emigrants constituted only a small percentage of the total population of mainland Greece at the time, and trade was often the primary purpose. It is very likely that many of these expeditions, especially the early ones, were funded by private citizens rather than being "colonies" sent out officially by the state, though all the new overseas settlements seem to have retained ties of some kind and degree with their mother cities.

Long-distance trade was in the hands of the elite of Greece, either directly or through agents; they were the only ones with the capital, and they had, or they soon established, networks of wealthy friends in Greece and abroad to seize opportunities and ease passage. Plenty of local trade also went on in everyday goods such as wine, grains, and textiles—the volumes involved were far greater than those of international trade—but long-distance trade continued to be in and of itself an activity that brought prestige to the elite participants. They opened up the routes, gained acquaintance with the land, manned a ship with fifty oarsmen (who doubled as settlers), and set out in search of the good life.

Greekness

One of the most important phenomena of these early migrations was a growing sense of Greekness. In recent scholarship on Greek ethnicity, a great deal has been made of the Persian Wars of the early fifth century as a watershed in how the Greeks perceived themselves. Before this watershed, it is said, the Greeks began to notice certain similarities—of language, worship, clothing, foodways, heritage, laws, stories, political institutions, and so on—and by aggregating these qualities they arrived at a sense of what it was to be Greek and postulated a common kinship. And then, after violent and victorious contact with the Persians, they defined themselves as possessing the opposite set of qualities to those possessed by Persians and other "barbarians."

This is an important insight, but the contrast between aggregation and opposition is too stark. The two processes go hand in hand: a growing sense of what it is to be Greek entails a growing sense of what it is that makes Greeks different from others. And this dual process was inevitably accelerated by contact with the peoples who, sometimes reluctantly, became neighbors of the new Greek immigrants. Indeed, one could argue that the Greeks already brought a fairly strong sense of Greekness with them—that it was their traditions and religious practices that gave them the courage to hazard the dangerous venture of emigration, never to return home. Many of the new settlements were populated by men not from a single Greek community but from several, who naturally came to recognize what they had in common. Archilochus of Paros, one of the settlers of the northern Aegean island of Thasos in the mid-seventh century, described his fellow settlers as *panhellēnes*, "the Greeks collectively."[1]

Even though they spoke different dialects of Greek, Greeks could understand one another, if occasionally with a little difficulty, but they could not understand the non-Greeks with whom they came into contact. An early Greek word for "foreigner" was just "other-language-speaker." By the middle of the sixth century, the nine Greek communities that had founded the emporium at Naucratis, surrounded by Egyptians, were acknowledging their similarity by worshipping at a sanctuary called the *Hellēnion*, dedicated to "the gods of the Greeks." Something similar was happening in southern France: in Massalia there was a temple to Apollo Delphinios that was intended to be shared by "all Ionians," which means "all Greeks." By the early fifth century, there was a temple to "Zeus of the Greeks" on the island of Aegina.[2]

A sense of solidarity was evolving. By making Greeks aware of themselves, the new overseas foundations did not reproduce the culture of mainland Greece so much as consolidate it. Here is a nice example: emigrants from the three main towns on Rhodes founded settlements on Sicily, where their particular town-identities were less relevant than the fact that they were all Rhodians, and before long we find that, back home, the islanders too began to identify themselves for the first time as Rhodians; and then, in due course (late in the fifth century), the three towns joined together to found Rhodes town. Local identities became subsumed under a broader tier

---

1 Archilochus F 102 West.
2 Herodotus, *Histories* 2.178; Strabo, *Geography* 4.1.4; Isocrates 9.15 (*Evagoras*).

of pan-Rhodian ethnicity. Paradoxically, it was the Greek dispersal that first confirmed Greek identity.

Already in Homer's poems (around 700) there are common words for the Greeks, even if none of them is the term "Hellenes," which would later come to designate all Greeks everywhere. (Our word "Greek" is derived from *Graecus*, the word the Romans used.) Homer has several terms available when he wants to generalize about the Greeks at Troy: they are called, interchangeably, "Danaans" or "Achaeans" or "Argives," and they act in concert to avenge the kidnapping of Helen by a non-Greek prince. By an audacious act of imagination (since in his day Greek separatism was at its height), the poet insisted that the Greeks were unified by kinship, seeding a fruitful idea. In later years, a common way to lay claim to Greekness was to point to a passage in Homer where one's city or alleged ancestor was named as having taken part in the expedition.

At much the same time, we find the Greeks of Anatolia and the Aegean islands consistently and collectively described as "Ionians" in Near Eastern documents, and this seems to have been the label they accepted in that part of the world. It is very likely, then, that in contact with non-Greeks the newcomers would have called themselves "Greeks," even if the term they used for that differed in different parts of the world. In short, Greek ethnicity became tiered: I am a Chalcidian, from the Ionian island of Euboea, and Greek. The different tiers had different inherent strengths for different individuals, and they identified with whichever tier was appropriate to the circumstances. The flexibility of ethnicity is precisely what makes it a powerful political tool, used to distinguish "us" from "them."

Ethnicity is not a given. Ethnicity is a construct, self-ascribed or ascribed by others on the basis of perceived cultural differences and perceived common descent. I say "perceived" descent because, although nowadays DNA analysis can show the realities of descent, this science was of course unavailable to the Greeks. It is an important part of the construct that it soon becomes associated with notional (or real) ties of blood and common descent; this is the glue that joins all the disparate elements that contribute in an aggregative fashion to ethnicity, and the source of strong emotional attachment. And so a myth-history is invented, which gives residents pride and also a first calendar of festivals, to celebrate events in the myths.

A myth-history for the Greeks was invented with particular crudity. At some point—certainly by the early sixth century, when the anonymous poem *The Catalog of Women* first records it—a man called Hellen was inserted at the head of the main Greek genealogy, so that the majority of Greeks became descendants of Hellen, or *Hellēnes*.[3] The artificiality of this addition seems to have troubled no one, because they were trying to explain their actual experience of kinship rather than making something up out of the blue, and it was a tactic that was used more than once: in the fourth century, for instance, when the Triphylians of the western Peloponnese wanted to be thought of as Arcadians, the Arcadians agreed to create a new son called Triphylus for their own eponymous hero, Arcas.

Hellen was made the son of Deucalion (the Greek Noah figure, who with his wife survived the deluge and restarted the human race), with Aeolus and Dorus, the putative ancestors of the Aeolians and Dorians, his immediate children, and Ion and Achaeus, the ancestors of the Ionians and Achaeans (a small, but distinct dialect group), as grandchildren. These were not figures who had previously existed in the mythological canon. No rich stories had accumulated around them, nor were they the recipients of cult; they were invented just to serve the purposes of ethnicity-construction. In this way, all the major subdivisions of the Greeks were incorporated. The Greeks were one and many—one at the level of Greekness, many as Ionians (as distinct from Aeolians and Dorians) or as Chalcidians (as distinct from citizens of all other communities).

Signs of State Formation

If the eighth century saw an increase in Greek mobility over the Mediterranean, there was also a lot of significant activity back on the Greek mainland. I have suggested that the majority of the new overseas settlements were funded and founded by members of the Greek wealth elite, acting as individuals, so that they were not exactly "colonies" of already existing states back in Greece. Still, it is likely that some of these ventures were sponsored and assisted in some sense by the state, especially in those cases where the point was to relieve poverty or get rid of unwanted citizens, and so we can count them as indicating a greater degree of centralization of authority in at least some parts of Greece. Fire from the sacred hearth of the mother city was often carried to the new settlement, maintaining a religious link forever between the two communities. This degree of centralization is just

---

3 Pseudo-Hesiod, *The Catalog of Women*, F 9 Merkelbach/West.

one sign that in eighth-century Greece communities were evolving toward statehood.

To explain the initial coalescence of separate villages into what would become states, we might imagine that warfare demonstrated the benefits of cooperation, or that overlapping village territories and a rising population led to disputes over matters such as land, water, mineral resources, waste, strong points, and burial plots, and it was in everyone's interest to combine and generate an apparatus to arbitrate such conflicts and, in general, to regulate social behavior, manage resources, and delimit and protect private property. In some cases, perhaps, the process was not so peaceful, if the headman of one village was aggressive enough to defeat a neighboring chieftain and add his retainers to his own. Or we might imagine that a particular man proved good at giving fair judgments, until his village began to be recognized as the center for such decisions.

By the end of the eighth century, especially in the more prosperous parts of central Greece, plots of land were being set aside outside settlements, away from habitation areas, for civic cemeteries. Here, for the first time, people of all ages and both genders were buried, and burial goods came not just from the privileged class but from those lower down the social scale as well. Relatedly, whereas earlier forms of religious worship have left little trace in the archaeological record, now we find land, both within centers and out in the countryside (especially on hilltops), given over to the construction of sanctuaries. Clearly, the will was there to invest in the community, and to see it as an enduring entity.

A crude sanctuary of the early eighth century might consist of no more than an altar stone and a low surrounding wall, dividing the sacred ground from outside; at the most, it might contain a small building to house votive offerings or a temple that was architecturally little different from a private house. The altar, the focus of sacrificial rituals, was the essential thing. But in the middle of the century, distinctive temples were being built, in larger numbers and on a grander scale than before, as permanent cult centers. The first Heraion (temple of Hera) on the island of Samos, for instance, which was built not long after 800, was about six meters wide and over thirty meters long (about twenty by a hundred feet), and that became the preferred length elsewhere as well for monumental temples sacred to a community's main deity. No building had been attempted on this scale for hundreds of years. There were two main motives for such monumental constructions: to display extravagant piety and to create a place where valuable dedications could safely be housed. A seventh-century decline in burying valuables along with the dead was accompanied by an increase in the practice of dedicating valuables at sanctuaries.

Fully stone temples (with wooden roofs covered with terracotta or stone tiles) did not appear until the manufacture of iron tools had sufficiently developed to make the necessary stonework feasible. By the middle of the seventh century, there was a fair scatter of monumental stone temples in the Greek world, and, in emulation of their neighbors, pretty much every village had its own small temple made of more perishable materials. The construction process was hugely helped by the invention of the pulley hoist (a kind of crane) at the end of the sixth century; previously, the only way to elevate large stones had been with ramps and levers, and with considerably more danger and sweat.

Coalescing Communities

All this activity shows that, in the more prosperous parts of Greece, there was a strong impetus toward the formation of states. The shared effort alone bound people together and gave them a sense of belonging and community, as did the building of city walls when that became a priority (in the end, about 40 percent of Archaic settlements had fortification walls), or the regularization of the layout of streets. There must have been enough of a central authority for a considerable workforce to be mobilized for such large-scale building projects, and probably communal funds too. A few of the temples that were built at this time were placed in the countryside in such a way that they seem to mark out territory—a clear sign of state formation. Processing out to these temples for religious festivals, or trundling to putative "borders" for fairs, gave people a sense that all the space they traversed belonged to them. And many of these temples remained in use for the rest of antiquity; the sacred landscape of Greece was laid down in the Archaic period.

Within settlements, in the course of the eighth century we start to find open spaces designed for public meetings and events, and soon the first public buildings are being built in these spaces, and water sources are being structured and embellished with fine architecture. Public land is distinguished from private land. The concept of citizenship evolves as long-term residents meet in these public spaces and play peaceful parts in sustaining the fledgling entity, as well as defending it on the battlefield if necessary. An early institution, once a village gets to be of any size, is the division of the population into artificial tribes or some such units to facilitate civic and military management and the absorption of new immigrants.

A state by definition uses ideological, economic, and coercive power to rule over a certain territory. It is also its duty to keep the gods smiling on the community, to defend it, to expand it, to increase its prosperity, and to keep the peace internally. In order to achieve and maintain this rulership, a state has to have central administrative facilities, a judiciary, a militia, and revenues to pay for all this. In these early days, it is not clear what sources of revenues communities had. A share of plunder, donated by the man who had gained it, probably featured as prominently as taxes, harbor fees, fines, and so on.

There were many little border wars as the new states flexed their muscles and tried to fix their frontiers, but plunder came also from farther afield. The Greeks of the Archaic period were known all over the Mediterranean as traders, mercenary soldiers, and pirates, and the occupations overlapped to a considerable degree. As the Athenian historian Thucydides said, many years later: "In those days piracy was not yet a source of shame, but was even considered quite honorable."[4] An elite name on Archaic Samos was Syloson, "Plunderer." In Homer's *Odyssey*, a typical question on meeting a high-born stranger is "Are you here on business, or are you traversing the seas as reckless raiders?" The Archaic Greeks were the Vikings of the Mediterranean.

A wealthy man recruited enough of his retainers to man a ship (usually thirty or fifty men, doubling as rowers and fighters), loaded some goods, and set sail in search of profit. If barter failed, goods might be seized by force. Or he might hire himself and his men out as warriors: the brother of the poet Alcaeus of Lesbos (born around 620) was a mercenary captain in the hire of Nebuchadnezzar II of Babylon, and another high-ranking mercenary (because he was elite enough to be able to write) was the wag who, along with other Greeks, vandalized a colossal statue of Rameses II at Abu Simbel in Egypt, also early in the sixth century. Using an axe to carve his name, he wrote: "Archon son of Amoebichus and Axe son of Nobody wrote these words."[5]

---

4 Thucydides, *History* 1.5.1 (late fifth century); Crawford/Whitehead no. 82.
5 Meiggs/Lewis no. 7 = (translated) Fornara no. 24A.

Eventually, with the economic, political, and military sources of social power in place, a giant step toward the formation of the community, and its citizens' loyalty, is taken by the invention or adoption of a myth-history, an ideological basis to justify rulership of their territory and probably also their expansion into others' territory. The state now has a past as a distinct ethnic entity, to be remembered collectively by its inhabitants and enhanced by further acts of commemoration in religious rituals. Another layer of history is supplied by canonizing a particular person as the founder of the state and instituting his worship as a semi-divine hero: Theseus in the case of Athens, Phoenician Cadmus for Thebes, and so on. This heroization was easier in the case of the new overseas settlements, which often had or claimed to have a single, identifiable leader.

Seeing that each town was a state in its own right, urbanization, the concentration of the population in towns (and the consequent development of a limited market economy), marched in tandem with state formation. Many landowners lived in town and commuted from there to their farms. Craftsmen and others who were prepared to pursue urban living arrived and swelled the population. By the middle of the eighth century, artisans in Athens, Corinth, and Argos, at least, already had their own quarters.

Craft specialization in turn allows a town to develop its own local styles and to offer particular products on the international markets, helping to fix its identity. Rhodes began to specialize in gold jewelry, Naxos and Paros in marble sculpture, Samos in metalwork and marble sculpture, Sparta in carved ivories and lead figurines, Corinth and Athens in fine pottery, Corinth in perfume and roof tiles. Other places were famous for specializing in various agricultural products: wine from Thasos, wool from Miletus, grain from Cyrene and Sicily, vegetables from Phleious.

But urbanization does not happen overnight. It may have taken decades before one could have said that Corinth or Athens was a proper town, rather than a cluster of prosperous villages, and, of course, some regions were more backward in this respect than others. By the fourth century, probably 30 percent of all Greeks lived in towns with populations of five thousand or over, and there were dozens of such towns around the Mediterranean. They had the same feel to them; they were distinctively Greek. By the imitative process called "peer polity interaction," Greek states influenced one another and developments were channeled in similar directions.

The Polis

By far the most famous form of state in ancient Greece is the polis, the city-state. There were, at any moment in the Classical period, more than a thousand Greek city-states (poleis) on the Greek mainland and around the Mediterranean and Black Sea coastlines, and many more were established in Asia in the Hellenistic period. No other Mediterranean people did this, or not on this scale; Phoenicians came second, but a long way behind.

A polis was a small, self-governing (though not necessarily fully independent) community of male citizens, living with their wives and children in an urban center and its hinterland (Attica for Athens, Argolis for Argos, and so on), and sharing common political, social, and religious institutions. Typically, a polis would be centered in physical terms on an acropolis, a hill where people could take refuge, and in religious terms on the cult of a patron deity (Athena for Athens, Hera for Argos, and so on).

Citizens were so closely involved with the running of a polis that in both literature and official documents the state is called, for instance, "the Athenians" rather than "Athens." Even if Athenians were ethnically more or less indistinguishable from their immediate neighbors, they felt loyalty first and foremost to Athens, and differentiated themselves from the citizens of other states on this basis. Some poleis were sometimes parts of larger political units and so lacked full autonomy, but much Greek history is comprehensible only if we suppose that citizens were motivated by the desire to gain, preserve, or regain their city's right to self-government. Small states even risked the wrath of large states over the issue. This loyalty is the primary reason why the Greeks were simultaneously one and many. This was the tier of ethnicity with which Greeks most commonly identified, because this was where they lived. The Greeks had no fatherland or motherland, but the Athenians did. Citizenship gave a man his primary tier of identity.

The loyalty the state engendered in its citizens meant that citizenship was invariably a closely guarded privilege, at any rate until the circumstances of the Hellenistic period made such parochialism redundant; by the Classical period, it also gave the inhabitants of a polis a tendency to regard one another as equal qua citizens, no matter how rich or poor they were, and

to marry exclusively among themselves. However, even though the fundamental ideology of the Classical polis was equality among citizens, poleis
differed from one another in what proportion of the citizen body enjoyed
full legal and political rights. Citizenship might be limited by birth (as in
Sparta, and in Athens from the middle of the fifth century), by landownership (as in Macedon), or by wealth (commonly). Everywhere, it was limited
by gender.

Greek city-states differed hugely in extent: by the time Sparta had taken
over all of Laconia and Messenia, its territory was over 8,500 square kilometers (3,300 square miles); for a brief period in the fourth century, Syracuse
in Sicily controlled over ten thousand square kilometers; Cyrene in North
Africa stood at over four thousand, Panticapaeum in the Crimea at more
than three thousand, and Athens at 2,400 square kilometers (about the size
of modern Luxembourg). Crete in the Hellenistic period consisted of a
small number of large blocs, each ruled by a single city. At the other end of
the scale, there were tiny poleis, with only a few hundred residents (whereas
the population of Athens at its height, around 430, was about 340,000).

The smallest city-states consisted of the urban center and outlying farmsteads in a single valley or coastal plain, with the great majority of the population living in the town rather than hamlets; the largest included a number
of large villages and even towns within their territories, as well as a scatter
of farmsteads. The great difference in size between poleis inevitably equates,
in historical terms, to a great difference in visibility. That is one reason why a
lot of Greek history is about Athens, Sparta, and Syracuse, while the history
of many smaller states is virtually irrecoverable.

Federalism

The polis, however, was not the only form of political organization in
Greece. Some Greeks, such as the peoples of Macedon, Epirus, Cyrenaica,
Sicily, and several semi-Greek Cypriot towns, lived for much of their history under monarchies; for centuries, the Spartans had two simultaneous
kings. Syracuse veered from monarchy to republicanism and back again.

The highest level of administration (that is, not concerned with day-to-
day matters) of some sanctuaries was provided by a committee made up of
delegates of *amphiktuones*, "neighboring communities." We know of a few
of these amphictyonies, and infer the existence of more—I mean, more
international amphictyonies; there were also local ones, groups of villages

or towns within a single state that shared worship at and the administration of a single sanctuary. Typical international amphictyonies were the one that administered the island of Delos, sacred to the twins Apollo and Artemis, which included Athens as well as the larger Cycladic islands, and the one that was responsible for the sanctuary of Poseidon on the island of Calauria (modern Poros), which also included Athens besides other mainland states surrounding the island.

The most famous international amphictyony was originally responsible for the sanctuary of Demeter near Thermopylae, but in the first decade of the sixth century its reach extended southward as it also took over the administration of Delphi from the people of Phocian Crisa in the First Sacred War. By the end of the war, Crisa's farmland had been turned into a sacred plain stocked with animals to be bought and sacrificed by pilgrims to Delphi, and Delphi was under the control of an expanded amphictyony (eventually, about twenty-four members, but originally twelve). The sacred-ness and prestige of Delphi made its Amphictyonic Council an authoritative entity, even in international affairs. Not all their power was spiritual; consen-sus was required for their decisions, and that degree of cooperation between twelve (or more) Greek states was rare enough to command attention.

But there were also different forms of republics. A people, such as the Athenians, might choose to organize themselves politically as a polis, and all of the newly established overseas settlements were poleis, but on the Greek mainland the polis system emerged at first only in the south and east of the Peloponnese and in eastern central Greece—precisely those areas where state structures had been most securely established in the Late Bronze Age, the Mycenaean period. Elsewhere, or where there was a multiplicity of poleis or villages, with none dominant over the others, the *ethnos* was the preferred structure.

In origin, an *ethnos* was a collection of communities within a single region where the inhabitants identified themselves as kin, met together at fairs and religious festivals, and gave themselves a shared history; but when (chiefly in the Hellenistic period) the inhabitants began to cement their chosen ethnic identity with a layer of political unification, the term *ethnos* gained politi-cal weight, as a "tribal state." Since a tribal state is a form of federation, the word may be translated "league" or "confederacy," but strictly *ethnos* applies only to people who have identified themselves as kin, and the political system, the "federal state," is a *koinon* ("shared venture," plural *koina*). But "We belong to a single *ethnos*" was always more emotive than "We belong to a single *koinon*," because of the implication of shared blood. The rights of member communities to intermarry with and own land in other member communities were always important aspects of *koina*.

Koina, however, could and did overstep their ethnic boundaries, usually by extending grants of citizenship to foreign communities. Some *koina* even lacked ethnic origins altogether and were purely political entities, such as the Confederacy of Islanders that united many of the Aegean islands at the end of the fourth century; they came together for reasons of economics and security rather than because they felt themselves to be kin. Sometimes more than one *ethnos* might unite under a broader ethnic identity, as the Molossians, Chaonians, and Thesprotians of Epirus formed themselves into the Epirote Confederacy. However formed, and whether large or small, *koina* came together by agreement, and that is enshrined in the term "federalism," the Latin root of which is *foedus*, a compact. At times of stress, relations between the center and the periphery could well be up for renegotiation.

A citizen of a federal state had a kind of dual citizenship: he was, for instance, "an Acarnanian, from Stratus," to indicate the two tiers with which he was identified, the *ethnos* and the member community. The difference between polis and *ethnos* lay in the degree of centralization involved. In the polis system, the largest urban center was also the dominant political center; in a confederacy, each of the member communities usually remained responsible for its own finances, citizenship rolls, sanctuaries, offices, laws, festivals, and nonmilitary forms of interaction with others.

Confederacies differed in their constitutions, but each of them elected officials to take care of common diplomatic and military matters; had a common meeting-place for political assemblies; shared military duties; had common judicial, deliberative, legislative, and executive systems; exacted financial contributions from its members; minted a common coinage; and acknowledged its presiding deity with a common sanctuary (so that a *koinon* resembled an amphictyony), which was often also where council and assembly meetings took place. Otherwise it was supposed to interfere little in the day-to-day running of its member communities. Some confederacies, however, found it hard to maintain the notional equality of all member communities: Thebes frequently had control of the Boeotian Confederacy, for instance, and Olynthus always dominated the Chalcidian Confederacy.

Koina were sensible ways for weaker communities to band together so that they could resist their stronger neighbors. The Acarnanian Confederacy, for instance, was formed to stand up to the powerful Corinthian colonies on the west coast. Many Greeks, however, did not see the *koinon* just as an alternative form of political system to that of the polis. So enamored were they of the republican polis as an ideal political set-up, as the only (literally) "civilized" way to live, that they tended to look down on other forms of political organization—monarchy, confederacy—as primitive. And it was true that confederacies were often formed by more dispersed and rural communities, the kind that the snobbish polis Greeks could sneer at as boorish farmers. It was also true that the confederacies tended not to produce writers and artists of caliber—the poet Pindar (a Boeotian) being a notable exception. And, finally, it was also true that some confederacies were made up of poleis, and over the centuries more confederacy members evolved into poleis themselves, giving the Greeks the impression that this was somehow a predetermined evolution—that the polis was the natural end of political life.

But in fact federation was a genuine alternative. The processes that led to the formation of *koina* were little different from those that led to polis-formation: they marked out their territories and developed administrative apparatus to take care of them; they had similar expenses and sources of revenue; their actions and self-presentation were often indistinguishable from those of a polis. Constitutionally, too, confederacies were no different from city-states, since they could occupy any point on the spectrum running from oligarchy to democracy, though they tended more often toward oligarchy, dominance by wealthy landowners in rural regions. And in the course of time, more Greeks on the mainland and the Anatolian coastline became members of confederacies than of stand-alone city-states. The fame of the polis has created a distorted picture of ancient Greek political life.

2

Aristocracy and
the Archaic State

The first to benefit from the increased commercial and political opportunities that statehood provided became the new aristocracy of Archaic
Greece. They were also often the old aristocracy, those who had emerged
since the Mycenaean collapse with the largest and best landholdings, and
with the best trade contacts abroad. But wealth rather than birth was always
the chief determinant of membership in the Greek aristocracy, and I use the
term "aristocracy" as synonymous with "wealth-and-warrior elite" or "leisure class"—the class, in Marxist terms, of those whose income is derived
from the labor of others. These "aristocrats" did not form a closed set: some
families were bound to fail economically, or to fail to produce a living son
to perpetuate their standing; they did not have a monopoly on landownership or trade, and new fortunes were made that elevated outsiders into
their ranks. Status was never entirely a given, but was always subject to
negotiation and merit. Elite authority came not just from the economic and
military power that they wielded, but also from their leadership of local religious cults and from symbolic strategies such as conspicuous benefactions
to the community, designed to legitimate their leadership.

In the eighth century, it is unlikely that the average poor farmer even
dreamed of wielding political power, and it was members of this elite who,
with the departure of kings and chieftains, became responsible as an oligarchy for the incipient state, with collegial groups of elite families first inventing political offices and then controlling them and rotating them among
themselves. In the middle of the eighth century, the hereditary kingship at
Corinth was replaced by the hereditary oligarchy of an elite group, numbering about two hundred, who called themselves the Bacchiads (alleged
descendants of an early king, Bacchis) and married exclusively among

themselves so as not to disperse wealth and power; not much later, the same happened on Samos, where the rulers were called the Geomoroi, the landholders. The wealth-and-warrior elite held sway in so many places we know of that it is safe to infer that they did so in general. "In the hands of the good lies the noble piloting of cities, handed from father to son," as the praise-poet Pindar put it, early in the fifth century, in an ode written for a Thessalian client. In Athens "offices were filled according to the qualifications of noble birth and wealth," by men who called themselves the Eupatridae, "the descendants of good fathers."[1]

Class Turmoil?

Homer, in the *Iliad*, had reminded his elite audiences of their obligation to rule well, and a few decades later, early in the seventh century, the poet Hesiod did much the same, contrasting "gift-devouring barons" with those who pass "straight judgments."[2] As entertainers, both Homer and Hesiod were dependent on the elite for their living, so they were careful not to protest against injustice too loudly, but they took seriously the traditional role of poets as educators and advisers.

This role was also taken on by the lyric poets. Further epic poems, now almost entirely lost, were being written in the Homeric style, but the most prolific form of literature in the Archaic period consisted of lyric verse, shorter poems in various non-epic meters. There was already a long tradition of lyric poetry, but now at last we have fragmentary remains, amounting to about three thousand lines in all, almost half of them ascribed to Theognis of Megara (mid-sixth century), and complete poems from later authors. Such was their genius that several of the poets, such as Sappho of Lesbos (late seventh century) or Pindar of Boeotian Cynoscephalae (early fifth century), are well known even today, a lingering effect of their immense popularity in the ancient world. They were great innovators, experimenting with the effects of different meters, creating real poetry.

Depending on their meters, the poems were sung to the accompaniment of the lyre or of the *aulos* (a double reed-pipe with a sound like an oboe). Largely eschewing weighty themes, the poems are personal; they focus on real-life

---

1 Pindar, *Pythian Odes* 10.71–72; pseudo-Aristotle, *The Athenian Constitution* 3.1.
2 Hesiod, *Works and Days* 38–39, 225–236; *Theogony* 84–92.

experiences, they express emotions such as love and hatred, and are sometimes charged with eroticism; they could be used for satire or invective; they are often not entirely serious; they occupy a range of registers from high to low.

Some of the poems were sung by choirs during festivals, for celebration or competition, but many of them were solo songs, and they were sung chiefly at elite all-male drinking clubs—at symposia, or the common messes of Sparta. We will look in more depth at symposia shortly, but for now all we need to know is that a symposium was a very exclusive affair, at which elite men could say (or sing) what they wanted and get away with it. The attitudes expressed there could therefore be quite extreme: some lines of Theognis, for instance, urged men to "Trample underfoot the empty-headed people, prick them with the sharp goad, and burden them with the yoke." And he goes on: "For you shall not now find a people so ready to accept servility among the whole race of mankind."[3] But lines like these do not mean that the elite were putting such ideas into practice in the real world, that the Archaic cities were riven with class turmoil. They expressed ideas with which the singers were in sympathy—here, the superiority of the elite to the commons—but they tell us little about actual historical events.

Nevertheless, the lyric poets can afford us historical insights. It is not just that the verses of Alcaeus of Lesbos comment directly on the infighting, in which he participated, among the elite of Mytilene, as those of Solon of Athens comment on the social and political difficulties of early-sixth-century Athens, but, more generally, that not all their work was tongue-in-cheek. These poets can occasionally reveal something of the events and issues that were salient at the time, and the impression they give us is that the ranks of the elite had become permeable as new men made money and gained entry. Good birth was no longer sufficient on its own, and superior moral qualities were stressed instead. There were now enough members of the elite for them to have to compete for resources. This competition could threaten violence, and in order to gain an edge over their rivals some of them had even begun, in economic terms, to oppress the lower classes; hence they are warned against greed and the exploitative or illegitimate pursuit of wealth.

No one literally trampled anyone else underfoot, nor do later historians recall a period of class warfare in their Archaic past, as they surely would have

3 Theognis, *Elegies* 847–850.

had there been one. Megara may be the exception that tests this rule, since
we hear of a period of "disorder and anarchy" in the sixth-century transition from a narrower to a broader oligarchy,[4] but otherwise there is little
that would lead us to such a conclusion. Aristotle tells us in his *Politics* (that
is, "matters pertaining to the polis") that the upper classes of Lesbos used
to club their opponents into submission—their opponents, not the lower
classes.[5] When Theognis talks (as he frequently does) of the bad becoming good, the conclusion he draws is not that the bad should therefore be
crushed, but that the good should endeavor to become even better, proving
their right to rule. This is not a scenario of class warfare but of intra-elite
competition. Elite rule of Archaic Greece was secure.

   The elite appear to have retained their privileged position in Athens longer than elsewhere. In Athens, as elsewhere, from around the middle of the
eighth century we find civic cemeteries allowing for the first time the burial
of poorer members of the community alongside members of the elite. But
only fifty years later, the archaeological picture reverts to a situation where
formal burial—of the noncasual kind that leaves traces in the archaeological
record—is reserved for the rich. This situation continued until well into the
sixth century. The rich retained their exclusive control of Athens for longer
than they did in other central Greek communities—and as a result, as we
shall see, the reaction, when it came, was especially dramatic.

Archaic Elite Culture

The wealth-and-warrior elite of central Greece and the prosperous cities
of Anatolia, Sicily, and southern Italy matched their privileged position
with an extraordinary lifestyle that emphasized their superiority to other
men, even their proximity to the gods, and therefore reinforced their
fitness to rule. There was a risk inherent in this strategy: if aristocrats raised
themselves too far above the common herd, they would undermine their
attempts at legitimation by seeming too arrogant and remote. So they
tempered exclusivity by showing themselves also to share the values of the
community, and to be special only because they were better placed than
others to perpetuate those values—by, say, protecting the community from

---

4 Aristotle, *Politics* 1302b31–32.
5 Aristotle, *Politics* 1311b26–28.

enemies with their courage and administering it with their literacy. And if they tended toward ostentatious displays of wealth, that was not intended to alienate people, but only to make them envious and emulous, because everyone wanted to be rich.

Above all, they needed long, noble lineages, because, in reality, their roots were unlikely to go back more than a few score years. And so for many decades, from the second half of the eighth century, we meet signs of attempts to reinforce the antiquity and superiority of their lineages, above all by worshipping at old tombs, which were now alleged to contain their ancestors, on the understanding that earlier inhabitants of the land must be kin. The impressive Mycenaean-period tholos (rotunda) tombs were naturally the prime sites for these cults. The phenomenon is familiar from other cultures: the Irish megalithic complex at Newgrange, for instance, was receiving rich votive offerings in the third century CE, three thousand years after its establishment.

In addition to stressing their lineages in this way, the privileged class developed other lifestyle strategies. Outsiders were excluded largely because they lacked the resources to participate, or the leisure time, or the desire to behave with such ostentation. Members of the elite continued to bear arms in the streets, for instance, throughout the Archaic period. By the end, this had become purely a matter of ostentation, since legitimate forms of violence had become the responsibility of the state, not of individuals, but at the beginning it was a reminder that the defense of the state was in their hands, and that they had the right to resolve personal issues by violence. They distinguished themselves also by hunting, sport, and feasting, and by traveling abroad—all pursuits that require leisure or at least money. But the most important of the elite lifestyle choices was the adoption of effete, eastern affectations.

They took to wearing long, flowing garments of expensive material in the eastern fashion—clothing that was imported and bought rather than being made by the household's womenfolk, as was usual. Their hair was worn long and elaborately coiffured; they wore gold jewelry and perfume, and spent as much of their leisure time as they could over wine and song, as if to emphasize that they did not have to labor. Rather than the purely Greek idiom of Geometric pottery, they preferred eastern styles (though the pots were made in Athens and Corinth), with linear orderliness replaced by a profusion of images of animals, plants, and exotic creatures such as sphinxes and griffins.

Eastern influence is evident in other artistic fields as well—in, for instance, the introduction of filigree in jewelry. In sculpture, the monumental *kouros* statues of naked young men that began to be carved in marble from the end of the seventh century derived their striding stance, proportions, hairstyle, and overall appearance from Egypt, though their full nudity was a Greek innovation. (See the picture on p. 195.) Their female equivalents, *korai* (singular *korē*), were clothed; men could be heroically nude, but women had to be modest. A typical *korē* grasps her skirt with one hand, while her other hand holds an offering to a deity. *Kouroi* gave sculptors the chance to focus on musculature, *korai* on drapery. *Kouroi* and *korai* were made to be dedicated in sanctuaries by those who could afford the enormous expense. Some sanctuaries had over a hundred of these pieces. Some were so colossal that they would have overtopped the temples where they were dedicated. Thousands of these statues were made in the Archaic period. They became a truly pan-Hellenic idiom of elite taste.

Even the literature written for elite consumption was heavily influenced by eastern ideas—or perhaps one should say that, at this period of Greek history, it is artificial to divide Greek literature, painting, fashion, and so on from their eastern equivalents; they were all part of the same network, drawing on the same set of idioms. The Greeks developed some of their own styles, such as Geometric pottery, but generally speaking, for much of the Archaic period, Greek culture was essentially eastern culture. It would distress nineteenth-century believers in Greek uniqueness to know that fundamental ways of viewing the world came from the East. Not a few of what we think of as "the Greek myths" are Anatolian or Near Eastern in origin.

Symposia

One of the main symptoms of elite exclusivity was the symposium. The word literally means "drinks party," but that has misleading connotations for the modern reader—the Greeks did not sip sherry and nibble salted nuts. The consumption of alcohol was indeed the main purpose of the party, but the evening meal was eaten first. There was a distinct break after the meal while the room was cleared and rituals performed, and then the drinking started. Symposia were both common and notorious, so that we have plenty of evidence from scattered references in all genres and periods of Greek literature, but especially from the fourth century, when Plato and Xenophon each wrote a *Symposium* as a setting for their mentor, Socrates, and both works have survived.

For as far back as we can trace it, upper-class Greek men had always, as warriors or as devotees of a deity, practiced communal dining accompanied by music, but the desire for exclusivity introduced some changes. Symposia moved out of sanctuaries and public halls and into private homes, and they no longer needed a sacrifice as an occasion for meeting. The guests came to imitate the languid eastern practice of reclining on couches to eat and drink, rather than sitting upright on chairs; and whereas women had been a presence, if only a marginal one, in upper-class banquets, they were sternly excluded from late-Archaic and Classical symposia, unless they were entertainers or prostitutes. The exclusivity of the occasion was also fed by the fashion for competitive singing and games, because it took time and commitment to acquire the relevant skills.

In a private house, symposia were held in a room known as the *andrōn*, the men's room, which was largely reserved for entertaining. There was space, typically, for seven or eleven couches, on each of which one or two guests reclined. The couches were placed around the walls of the room, so that symposiasts looked inward at one another. A "king" was appointed to regulate the symposium, choose the proportions of wine and water to be mixed in the great jar by slaves, and decide how many of these jars to get through during the night, given that each one held between seven and fourteen liters (1.5 to three gallons). It was his job to try to keep each of the symposiasts on the creative edge of intoxication. Drinking-cups were shallow, better for sipping than gulping, to curb drunkenness and encourage conversation—or at least they started shallow, but as the night wore on, deeper cups might be brought into use. Since the wine was heavily diluted (though ancient wines were a little stronger than most modern ones), at many symposia guests would become no more than tipsy.

Following a hymn to the gods, the guests settled down to make witty and elegant conversation, sing songs (perhaps on a theme set by the "king," such as "What is best?"), ask riddles, tell jokes, play games (such as *kottabos*, the flicking of drops from the bottom of one's cup at a target), and be entertained by one another. The point of such games was to test inebriation levels, since the more alcohol was consumed, the harder they became. This was an initiatory procedure, a way of seeing if a man had the moral character to be a member of the elite and take his place as one of the leaders of the community; the truism that a man who cannot rule himself cannot hope

to rule others was later a recurrent theme in the books of the blue-blooded
Xenophon of Athens. If there was hired entertainment, it might consist of a
show put on by dancing-girls, acrobats, or mimes.

Symposia were orchestrated to include nothing from the humdrum
world: guests ate and drank from utensils of precious metal or painted clay
decorated with versions of themselves; they sang special songs, played special
games, and focused entirely on pleasure. The symposium occupied its own
universe, created by the inward-looking circle of couches. It was separated
from the normal rules of society, and opening and closing rituals marked the
event as special. They met after dark and drank through the night, turning
normality on its head in this regard too. It was all a far cry from the humble
and sordid taverns frequented by the poor, with sawdust on the floors and
simple, unadorned cups.

Readers familiar with museums housing ancient Greek pots will have
noticed that sexual acts are sometimes depicted. A large number of surviving vases, especially from the Athenian black- and red-figure periods, were
designed for use in symposia. These pots tended to display scenes typical of
symposia—drinking (symbolized by Dionysus, the god of wine, or by satyrs,
his servants), sex, or the kind of mythological or historical story that would
have formed the theme of symposiast songs.

It is possible that the vases display possibilities rather than certainties. Just
as a vomiting drunk on a vase represented one possible outcome, so sex
on vases might represent another. But it does seem to be the case that sex
was available at symposia. The entertainers and servers may even have been
required to be naked; at any rate, that is how they commonly appear on pots.
Sex was available either with a fellow guest, or, more likely, with a pipe-girl
or imported prostitute. From the early sixth century onward, younger, teenaged male guests might be invited to the affair, whether as some member's
son who was due to be initiated into their circle or as the sexual partner of
one of the older men. The boys might be asked to serve the wine, as young
Ganymede served wine at the table of the gods on Olympus, but their main
job was to watch, listen, and learn. Even though the rooms were not well
lit, having sex in the company of others is bound to be a strong bonding
mechanism.

Symposia were not supposed to get out of hand, but they did, of course,
and then the guests might spill out on the street in a *kōmos*, a revel or riotous
party. The boisterous group would dance and careen through the streets, still
dressed as symposiasts and still singing to the women's pipes, carrying their

Figure 2.1. Symposiast sex. A red-figure kylix, attributed to the Triptolemus painter, from the early fifth century. The couch and table suggest a symposium, and sex was commonly available at symposia, with a prostitute or other slave-girl or with fellow symposiasts. Museo Nazionale Archeologico, Tarquinia RC2983. Photo © Immagini della Soprintendenza per I Beni Archeologici dell'Etruria Meridionale.

cups and instruments and torches and even the great jar of wine (or having their slaves do so), perhaps also carrying a large model phallus in honor of Dionysus, abusing innocent passersby with coarse humor, and gate-crashing other symposia. Pots show komasts fighting or engaging in rough sex. The *kōmos* was a ritualized display of elite arrogance: they could make nuisances of themselves and get away with it.

The symposium was an essential part of elite culture in the Archaic period and remained an important refuge for members of the wealth elite in the Classical period as well. But as elite dominance faded, so the symposium became more arcane, a place of nostalgia for the "good old days" when their power was uncontested. Archaeological evidence suggests also that by the middle of the fifth century symposia were being held in the homes of those lower down the social scale than the super-rich, so that the event had lost its exclusivity. Then in the fourth century, the practice began of inviting professional musicians to entertain a symposium. *Andrōnes* accordingly grew larger, sacrificing intimacy for ostentation. Since the spotlight was now on the entertainers rather than the guests, this spelled the end of the institution.

International Friendships and Games

The common elite culture of Archaic Greece was fostered by the deliberate cultivation by aristocrats of relationships with their peers abroad, in other Greek or non-Greek communities. On the one hand, such friendships could help a man in trade, for instance, since he had sources of information and a guaranteed welcome in ports on his chosen route. On the other hand, these elite friendships were sometimes pretty much all there was in the way of interstate relations, and so they served the interests of the community as well. Moreover, the more friends a man had abroad, the less likely his community was to suffer plundering raids, for the network of international friendships also highlighted who were one's enemies, or at least who were potential targets for brigandage and piracy. There were gray areas, however, and a man with these foreign friendships could be suspected of disloyalty to his community, with the gifts he received regarded as bribes in exchange for political favors.

This form of elite friendship was called *xenia*, which literally means just "the condition of being a host or a guest" and is usually translated "guest-friendship." It was a sacralized and ritualized relationship. Once it had been initiated by ritual means and the exchange of gifts of equal value, it was perpetuated by means of hospitality and the free and generous donation of goods or services. *Xenia*, which imitated kinship, was expected to be passed down through the generations. No doubt *xenoi* were generally fond of one another—that is, were friends as well as guest-friends—though that was not essential to the relationship, which was formed by a ritual act rather than by familiarity and acquaintance, and could even lie in abeyance for a generation or two.

International festivals were good places to form or renew guest-friendships. But primarily they were celebrations of aristocratic class solidarity and venues for elite display (hence the athletic contests) and legitimation. Who else might have been interested in taking part in such ritualized conflict?

Besides, they were the only ones who could afford to pay for the kind of physical training that would turn their sons into competitive athletes, they were the only ones who could afford to breed horses, and they were the only ones who could afford to take time off to train for and participate in athletic events.

The earliest and most important of the international festivals were those at Olympia (sacred to Zeus) and Delphi (sacred to Apollo), with Apollo's island of Delos coming a close third. All these places were neutral, remote enough from centers of political power to be able to act as arenas where members of the wealth elite could meet as equals. In fact, Delphi claimed to be the center of the world, equidistant from everywhere. It was certainly of central importance to the Greek world, and when the temple was destroyed by an earthquake in the late 370s, cities and individuals from all over the Mediterranean contributed to its restoration.

Late in the fifth century, Hippias of Elis calculated the date of the first Olympic games as the year 776 (by our reckoning), but archaeological evidence suggests a date closer to 700, and that the place was still of minor importance then, attracting only local participation. Hippias' date, however, remains the start of the Olympiad dating system. Gradually, over the course of the seventh century, the festival grew and attracted participants first from the rest of the Peloponnese and then farther afield, until eventually (the games continued in some form until the late fourth century CE) competitors came from all over the Mediterranean. Cult buildings and monuments began to be erected late in the seventh century, along with the first stadium and gymnasium (literally, "place for exercising naked"); by the early sixth century, victory statues were beginning to be erected and poems composed to order for victorious competitors. By the end of the sixth century, however, rather than individual dedications, the first treasuries were being built by states to house dedications, indicating that the glory of victory was now being appropriated by states rather than just individuals.

Delphi opened for oracular business in the eighth century, but the festival known as the Pythia was probably instituted around 650. Since Delphi was sacred to Apollo, the festival originally emphasized musical competition, but it underwent a major overhaul early in the sixth century when the amphictyony took over responsibility for the sanctuary (p. 39), and became largely a regular athletic meeting along Olympic lines. Cult buildings and monuments began to be erected in the sixth century, and over the subsequent decades and centuries of its existence the place became crowded with magnificent dedications and monuments—more crowded even than Olympia. The Pythia festival too gradually expanded until participants came from all over the Greek world.

Olympia and Delphi founded the earliest international athletic competitions, but there came to be others. In the first third of the sixth century, the Nemean games were established at Nemea (sacred to Zeus), the Isthmian games near Corinth (for Poseidon), and the Greater Panathenaea at Athens (for Athena). Every town of any size now supported at least one gymnasium, with a wrestling-ground attached, for elite men and boys to practice and stay fit.

The big four festivals (excluding the Panathenaea, because it was too closely connected with a major polis rather than being on neutral ground) were coordinated with one another as a circuit: in any four-year period (an Olympiad), games were held at Olympia in August/September of the first year, at Delphi in August/September of the third year, at Nemea in July of the second and fourth years, and at Corinth in April of the second and fourth years. The Pythia was considered the second most prestigious after the Olympics, but in time the Isthmia grew to be the best attended, until by the Hellenistic period it was "the meeting place of Asia and Greece."[6]

The elite participants at these festivals demonstrated their superiority to money by making crowns rather than cash the prizes. At Olympia the crown was of olive, at Delphi of bay, at Nemea of wild celery, and at Corinth of pine or celery (at different times). In the Hellenistic period, one way in which cities (especially in Anatolia) gained international prestige was by having one of their festivals declared equivalent in status to one of the four original crown festivals of the Greek mainland.

The fact that Archaic Greece could support a circuit of four magnificent athletic festivals (in addition to many locally organized athletic and musical contests) is a measure of the competitiveness of the Greek elite of the time. For the contestants, there was a lot at stake. It was not just that they stood to win or lose pride and prestige, which was a serious enough business in itself. A victor in one of the crown games was also likely, especially in the Classical period, to be rewarded in his hometown. He might be dined for life at state expense, or become exempt from certain taxes; he might even translate his success into senior political posts and military commands. At the Panathenaea, winners—and even, unusually, those placed second and

6 Livy, *History of Rome* 33.32.2.

third—received valuable prizes, usually in the form of large quantities of high-quality olive oil in fancy jars.

Commemorative statues and praise poets such as Pindar and Bacchylides (from the island of Ceos) translated temporal victory into eternal fame. For some particularly famous and successful athletes, the glory continued even after their deaths, and they were worshipped as heroes, more than human but less than gods. An inscription has survived on the island of Thasos,[7] showing that its most famous athlete, Theogenes (said to have won 1,300 victories overall), received such worship. Each person sacrificing to him was to pay at least one obol, and when the total had reached a thousand drachmas (six thousand sacrifices, if everyone paid the minimum rate) a decision was made as to how to spend it on a suitable offering to Theogenes—a statue, an inscribed epigram. If a man was victorious in an athletic event, the implication was that he had found favor with the presiding deity, or even that he had been possessed by the god in order to win. You wanted such a man on your side, so you gave him honor. In Sparta, Olympic victors were rewarded not in material terms but with the privilege of fighting alongside the kings in battle.

But glory is always in short supply. These festivals came to be attended by people from all over the Greek world, and one might have thought that they therefore fostered a unified sense of Greekness. This was not really so. In the first place, that tier of ethnicity was not an issue for several centuries: it was only after Olympia and Delphi had come to attract contestants from much farther afield that questions were asked, perhaps first in the fifth century, and officials were appointed to verify the Greekness of contestants. Then Greekness was a prerequisite for several centuries, until the rule was bent for eminent Romans.

In the second place, both Olympia and Delphi were often under the control of some state; in the case of Olympia, it was usually Elis, but other Peloponnesian states also had their turns, and at different times in the history of Delphi different states—Thessaly, Corinth, Sparta, Athens, Macedon, Aetolia—exerted the most influence on policy, bringing their friendships and enmities with them. Enemies might be banned from taking part in the games, as the Spartans were prevented by the Eleans from taking part in the 420 Olympics. Moreover, the official state dedications that crammed both sites were often positioned aggressively in relation to monuments erected

7 *Syll.*³ 64a.

by other states, and in so far as they boasted about victory over other Greeks in war or some other field of glory, they hardly fostered a warm feeling of pan-Hellenic identity.

International sites such as Olympia and Delphi functioned as places of memory, but the memories were not always happy ones. Local identities were just as likely to be reinforced as any sense of shared Greekness. It was only after the Persian Wars that a wider sense of Greek unity emerged, and at both the Olympic and Isthmian festivals dedications of battlefield trophies commemorating victories over fellow Greeks died down, perhaps by official edict (though the practice was revived with vigor in the third century). In the Archaic period, the Greeks remained, as ever, simultaneously one and many.

3

The Archaic Greek World

We have so far barely touched on one of the major developments of the early Archaic period—the rediscovery of literacy, which had been lost with the downfall of the Mycenaean palaces. The topic is relevant to state formation because states of any complexity need literacy and numeracy to function. The Greek alphabet was invented around 800, and over the course of the next few centuries the Greeks attained a higher degree of literacy than any earlier society. This was due to the excellence of their alphabet; the one they learned from the Phoenicians had no vowels, and by adding vowels or adapting some of the Phoenician signs as vowels, the Greeks produced a far more useful tool, with which spoken language could be accurately reproduced.

The likely context for the invention of the Greek alphabet was the polyglot interaction between Phoenicians and Greeks at places such as Al Mina and Pithecusae. The similarities between local Greek scripts show that there was an original "mother script" from which they evolved, and it was probably one or the other of these two places where it came into being. It spread quickly: there are eighth- and seventh-century examples of writing from Rhodes and Samos in the east, Methone in the north, Pithecusae in the west, and many places in between. But writing was rare until the sixth century, and the earliest examples are mainly graffiti scratched on shards of pottery, the ancient equivalent of scraps of paper.

Since Al Mina and Pithecusae were places of commerce, the alphabet was probably adopted to aid commercial transactions; this was the main use to which the Phoenicians were putting theirs. Quite a few early inscriptions are claims to ownership, and this must have been the first and basic function of writing in commercial contexts: the maker's or owner's mark. Even some incomprehensible graffiti may be coded trademarks. In an extension of this usage, potters were soon signing some of their pots: "So-and-so made me."

Figure 3.1. Early writing. This small Subgeometric cup was made in Rhodes c. 700. The graffito, which reads from right to left, says: "I am Qoraqos' cup." Copenhagen National Museum no. 10151.

Trade not only enabled the geographical expansion of the Greek world, but also its cultural growth, by making that world literate.

But what is fascinating about early Greek writing is that it very quickly exploded beyond commerce into many other realms. Writing was not to be the province of a few scribes, as it had been in the past and still was in the Near East. On the shoulder of a wine jug from Athens, dating from around 740, is a graffito the first part of which is a perfect hexameter in Homeric language—"Whoever, of all the dancers, now disports most daintily, to him this . . ."—before descending into unmetrical nonsense by a second hand. Seventh-century shards found on Mount Hymettus in Attica seem to have been offered to Zeus just as they were, as if the act of writing alone, at this early stage, made even a piece of broken pottery a worthy dedication to a deity. A number of graffiti, especially those scratched on rocks on the island of Thera, are homosexual, commending the good looks or the dancing of favorites, or recording sex acts. By early in the seventh century, the names of the deceased were beginning to be inscribed on tombstones; by the end of the sixth, curses were being fixed by being written down and buried. By the middle of the sixth century, writing was even being used for private communication, as is proved by a shard recovered from the Athenian Agora: "Thamneus, please put the saw under the threshold of the garden gate."[1]

The uses of writing more or less immediately ranged from the serious to the frivolous, from the permanent to the transient, and from the public to the private, as they still do today. It did not impinge much on the lives of the poor, who could perhaps do little more than recognize and write their own names, but it was useful in elite contexts such as office-holding, trade, commemoration, warfare, and symposia. The acquisition of such a recondite skill further enhanced their social status.

Written Law and Archaic State Institutions

One early use of writing deserves to be singled out for what it tells us about Archaic Greek communities. This is the inscribing of laws on bronze or stone—and on other materials, of course, no doubt in larger quantities, but they have all perished. The Greeks later attributed comprehensive law codes to great lawgivers of the Archaic period—men such as Zaleucus of Locri in southern Italy, Lycurgus of Sparta, and Dracon of Athens—but surviving laws are not like that. Only Gortyn in Crete seems to have made any attempt, this early, to relate new laws to old ones in a systematic fashion. Elsewhere they are piecemeal attempts to solve outstanding problems in a number of spheres: commercial transactions, inheritance and property rights, land division, conspicuous exploitation of wealth, and injury. These early laws already demonstrate a marked feature of Greek law in general: they are very commonly procedural rather than substantive. That is, rather than defining a given crime, they state what is to be done if someone is convicted of that crime and what the penalty is to be. The definition of the crime, and deciding whether someone is guilty of it, were in this way left to the judges to decide on the day.

Quite a few of these early written laws stipulate regulations about political officeholding—that such-and-such an office is to be held only for one

---

1 American School of Classical Studies at Athens, Agora Excavations, P 12784.

year in every ten, for instance. This affords us a very important window onto the Archaic Greek state. The assumption, from this early in the formation of the state, was that those who were equipped to rule would share power—that there would be *isonomia* among them, "fair shares," equality of opportunity and equality under the law. The sharing of power, rather than monarchy, lay at the very foundation of the Greek state. For the next several centuries, one of the critical issues that divided Greek states both externally and internally was precisely whether power should be shared among all, or only a few.

The inscribing of laws clearly represents an attempt to overcome arbitrariness in the making of legal decisions. At least some legal decisions would no longer depend on the memories of the aristocratic council or an all-too-human judge. But many problems and procedures were still covered by oral tradition, and a number of communities had an officer called a "remembrancer," one of whose jobs was to preserve relevant oral traditions alongside the newly inscribed laws. He often doubled up as the scribe as well.

Since oral tradition still covered most crimes and penalties, only laws that were felt to be too complex to be remembered, or interestingly new, were inscribed. The visual impressiveness of the inscription was as much a factor as what it actually said. The inscription was an icon: the new art of writing displayed the grandeur of the law and of elite administration to a largely illiterate population, for whom such inscriptions would have to be read out. Written law was also a way of creating the history of a community, by recording its decisions for posterity.

All this is, of course, a further sign of statehood. Indeed, many of these early laws explicitly say: "The polis decided the following"—the first instances of the use of the word to refer to the political community made up of citizens, rather than the physical entity, the town or city.[2] And so inscribed laws of the Archaic period also occasionally reveal quite a lot about administrative structures. A mid-sixth-century inscription from Chios, for example, reads in part as follows: "Let him appeal to the Council of the People. On the third day after the Hebdomaia let the Council assemble, the People's fine-imposing Council, consisting of fifty men from a tribe."[3] So the citizens of

---

2 E.g. Meiggs/Lewis no. 2 = (translated) Fornara no. 11; Rhodes no. 44; Crawford/Whitehead no. 37.
3 Meiggs/Lewis no. 8C = (translated) Fornara no. 19; Rhodes no. 346; Crawford/Whitehead no. 38.

Chios, at any rate, were divided into tribes for administrative purposes, and there existed a People's Council with the right to exact fines from wrong-doers, which met at regular intervals (the Hebdomaia was the seventh day of each month, sacred to Apollo). Regularly scheduled meetings afforded protection against the system where meetings were convened only at the whim of an aristocrat.

But the existence of a structure does not guarantee its efficacy; authority and the right to carry out political acts were certainly not restricted to office-holders in the Archaic period. In mid-seventh-century Athens, for instance, the influence of the Alcmaeonid family far outstripped the official positions any members of the family might have held. When Peisistratus came to power in Athens a century later, the appointed officeholders apparently played no part in either supporting or resisting the coup, and Cleisthenes was not in office when he triggered democracy in Athens. When the Argive authorities refused help to the people of Aegina in the 490s, Argive aristocrats raised a force and went to the island of their own accord. The duties of the few offices that existed at the time were probably still being shaped by individual officeholders themselves. The wealth-and-warrior elite eventually learned to accept confinement within the laws of their societies, rather than choosing their own goals, but it took time.

Archaic Hoplites

It goes without saying that defense was a crucial state function. Looking ahead, by the middle of the fifth century there was a high degree of similarity among the land armies of the advanced cities, in that they relied above all on heavy-armed infantrymen known as hoplites, fighting in a massed formation called a phalanx. We shall examine the hoplite phalanx as a form of fighting in more detail later, in order to focus now on its possible socio-political implications in the seventh century. The main one is commonly said to be that hoplites, who came from farther down the social scale than the aristocracy, could see that they, not just the elite, were responsible for the safety of the community, and so demanded a greater share in its administration. It was hoplites, then, who were chiefly responsible for the eventual restriction of elite power.

The argument is less plausible than it might seem. By the time there were enough hoplites to make a difference, they came from a broad economic spectrum, excluding only the poorest members of society, and there is no reason to think they shared political ambitions. The argument is also mis-timed, because there is no reliable evidence for the introduction of hoplite tactics until the end of the sixth century. The details of every early portrayal of hoplites on vases make it more or less certain that the intention was not to try to depict a phalanx, since the soldiers' weaponry and behavior are inappropriate. Literary evidence, such as the poems of Tyrtaeus of Sparta (mid- to late seventh century), fares no better: Tyrtaeus sang about a Homeric kind of warfare, in which "forward fighters" dash forth from the mass of the army to duel an opponent before withdrawing back to the lines again, or at the most a few warriors fight side by side in a line that could be chest to chest with the enemy.[4]

There is no doubt that the hoplite panoply was evolving in the seventh century, probably as a result of Greek mercenary experience abroad. What we have no evidence for is that they fought in massed phalanxes. No state at the time had enough men to field the requisite thousands. The point of adding an extra hand grip on the large, round shield that came to be favored early in the seventh century was to enable soldiers to hold such a large piece of equipment steady, so that they could benefit from its added protection; the shield was more than half a man's height. It was an extra benefit that it also came in useful when men were standing side by side, and later in tightly packed phalanxes, where a man's right side, when he was standing chest forward, was protected more by his neighbor's shield than his own. Even so, it was not one of universal application, because hoplites were not always equipped with this kind of shield (as in the picture on p. 158), and when a man turned sideways on to the enemy, to give his spear thrust force, his shield protected his body, but not that of his neighbor.

There was no hoplite revolution in the seventh century, no sign of a numerous middle-income group fighting in an egalitarian phalanx or form-ing common political goals. There was certainly a military reform (led by Argos, Corinth, and Sparta), but it seems to have been spread out over many decades—evolution rather than revolution—and so far from being over by the middle of the seventh century, it had hardly begun. Warfare remained very much an elite affair until the Persian Wars of the early fifth century; they were the only ones who could afford the equipment. Like Homer's

4 Tyrtaeus, F 10, 11, and 19 West.

Figure 3.2. Corinthian helmet. There was no hoplite uniform as such, but by 700 many soldiers were choosing this kind of helmet, which afforded maximum protection, at the cost of some restriction to vision and hearing. The owner of this one presumably died from the blow to his head. BM 1977,0101.8. © Trustees of the British Museum.

heroes, the seventh-century elite fought beside or in front of poorer farmers and serfs who wielded sticks, stones, and agricultural tools rather than expensive weapons.

The sixth century is when conditions changed. Under the benign tax regimes of the Greek poleis, it was not difficult for individuals to create surpluses. Many states and individuals grew richer over the course of the sixth century by trading their surpluses, and the potential for profit was a constant incentive to produce more and better goods. Wealth began to trickle down the social scale, and a class of middling farmers, craftsmen, and traders emerged. The cost of the hoplite panoply came within the reach of more people, eventually perhaps 40 percent of the adult male population, and at some point there were enough in the larger cities to form a proper phalanx.

But, throughout the Archaic period, the elite could argue that they deserved their privileged position because they were responsible for the safety of all.

Tyranny

Those scholars who believe in a hoplite revolution in the Archaic Greek poleis often connect it with another phenomenon—the rise to power in a fair number of poleis by sole rulers known as *turannoi*, "tyrants." It is said that these tyrants gained power by exploiting the political ambitions of the middling farmers, the hoplite class. But, since we have just seen reason to doubt that there was much of a middle-income group until toward the end of the Archaic period or that they developed any class loyalty or common political ambitions, this scenario seems unlikely.

Apart from Sparta, in the seventh and sixth centuries few of the advanced cities in mainland Greece and Anatolia avoided tyranny. The period of Archaic tyranny lasted from around 650, when Cypselus came to power in Corinth, until 510, when Hippias was expelled from Athens. On Sicily, the phenomenon started later and lasted longer: men called "tyrants" arose there at the end of the sixth century and remained in power, with interruptions, until close to the end of the third century. Tyrants reappeared in mainland Greece and Anatolia in the late fourth and third centuries, usually imposed by some external and imperial power.

The fact that tyranny was such a common phenomenon in the Archaic period gives us our first clue as to its nature in the Greek world: while tyranny to us is an exceptional position, Archaic Greek tyrants were not exceptional. Tyranny could not have been so widespread unless in some sense it was an organic outgrowth from its predecessor, which was, as we have seen, aristocracy.

In the Archaic state, aristocrats could either agree to work together as equals, sharing power among themselves, or they could allow their competitiveness free rein. In the latter case, sometimes one man proved more powerful than his rivals, and seized sole power for himself and his family. That was all an Archaic Greek tyrant was. Later Greeks associated tyranny with despotism, just as we do, but all the very earliest occurrences of the word, contemporary with the phenomenon itself, acknowledge that the unregulated power of tyranny is something most men would regard as enviable:[5]

---

5 Archilochus F 23 West (last two lines).

> Rule this place and hold the tyranny,
> And many men will envy you for sure.

Greeks also later came to vilify tyrants as the possessors of unconstitutional power, but since, as we have seen, states did not really have constitutions at the time, this too is a later gloss. It was mainly in democratic Athens in the fifth century that the negative image of tyranny arose, because for Athenian democrats tyranny was the polar opposite of democracy.

As soon as we begin to see tyrants as practitioners of Archaic elite politics, distinguished only by their success, everything falls into place. They practiced *xenia*, especially with other tyrant families, and intermarried among themselves. They ruled with the help of their friends. They legitimated their positions by charismatic means, especially their heroic prowess at athletics and warfare, and by lordly munificence. Cylon attempted a coup in Athens on the strength of Olympic victory; Cleisthenes of Sicyon dedicated his victorious chariot at Delphi in a specially constructed treasury. They patronized poets and artists. In many cases, they developed the public spaces of their cities with magnificent buildings and structures. Polycrates of Samos, especially, used his piratical wealth to make his city the showpiece of the Greek world.

The good they did meant that they were not unpopular. Many tyrants came to power on the strength of their success as military leaders, and held on to power without much difficulty for the same reason and because they increased their citizens' prosperity. Many of them were honored in their lifetimes or after their deaths by their communities. The only rebellions we hear about were strictly inter-elite affairs, as when one of the Athenian noble families, the Alcmaeonidae, withdrew to a fortress in the countryside and tried, but failed, to depose Hippias by force. We never hear of tyrants being deposed by popular uprisings. The dissatisfaction that built up and eventually caused their downfall came, unsurprisingly, from their elite rivals.

Tyrants, already rich and powerful, aimed to make themselves and their families supremely rich and powerful. Paradoxically, however, they did often pave the way for political power to devolve farther down the social scale. First, they strengthened and fixed the powers of the various political offices of a community, because they limited their rivals—those they did not kill or banish or send to found settlements overseas—to these offices. Second, quite a few of the tyrants regularized tax-collection in their states, accustoming citizens to accept the existence of state institutions. Third, in so far as sole power is precarious, they had to take the interests and concerns of ordinary people into consideration.

Economic factors were creating a middle-income group anyway, as we have seen, so by the end of the period of tyranny there was not only a more determinate state structure, but there were many more people who were willing and able to play their parts within that structure. In reaction to the tyrants, it now seemed more attractive to give one's loyalty to the state than to individual barons. This is not to say that elite feuding did not break out again here and there—it did in Athens, as we shall see—but it was not allowed to last long, and was capable of being channeled in other directions. In the backlash from tyranny, the state was reimagined as a collective institution, and its formation was more or less complete: monarchy had given way to aristocracy, and aristocrats in their turn were learning that they had to make constitutional concessions to the poorer majority.

Coinage and Statehood

Coined money appeared first in Lydia and certain Eastern Greek cities that were neighbors or dependencies of Lydia a decade or two before 600 BCE, but soon spread to mainland Greece, as well as all over the Mediterranean and deeper into the Near East. The probable reason for its introduction was that it made it easier for a state to collect revenue and disburse it. At the same time, it was a brilliant new way for the aristocrats who constituted the state at the time and were minting the coins to raise their own status and advertise the prestige of their city. Besides, states profited from minting coins, or at least covered their costs, because they shaved a tiny bit off each coin.

So, having decided to regularize and simplify their finances by ordaining that taxes and fines are to be paid in coined money, the state first pays for goods and services in coined money, to get it circulating around the community. The convenience of coined money is recognized, it boosts the economy by reducing transaction costs, and the community enthusiastically moves toward monetization. No Greek state achieved more than partial monetization, however, since barter was still used for many small exchanges, and weighed lumps of bullion for exchanges both large and small. The least degree of monetization was achieved by the Spartans, who deliberately impeded it. The greatest degree of monetization was achieved by Athens, with the assistance of its very own slave-worked, silver-bearing lead mines—up until the first century BCE, when they were exhausted. By the second half of the fifth century, coined money was used in Athens for almost all private and public financial transactions. By the Hellenistic period, coins were ubiquitous throughout the Greek world.

Given how useful coined money is to both state and individual, it is no surprise to see how quickly it took hold. The first states (Aegina, Corinth, Samos, and Athens led the way) began to coin money around the middle of the sixth century, and less than a hundred years later, over a hundred states had their own mints. Over time, the number of standards in the Greek world fell, but there was never the political will to attempt to create a single monetary zone. There were moneychangers in every port. Many centuries later, the Romans came close to unification throughout their empire, but the Greeks remained, as always, both one and many. They supported trade, but in the last resort political considerations such as alliances and enmities outweighed the desire to make life easier for businessmen.

Silver very quickly established itself as the metal of choice for Greek coins; the decision to assign value to silver had been taken way back in the mists of time, and silver bullion had long been in use as money. Gold was rarely coined in Greece until the Macedonian conquest, though they accepted foreign gold coins; the gold–silver ratio was about 15:1 in the

Figure 3.3. Aeginetan coin. A typical early (sixth-century) coin, made of a weighed piece of silver with a hammered image. This is a stater, worth/weighing two drachmas. The turtle was the standard emblem of the prosperous trading island of Aegina. BM 1926,0116.693. © Trustees of the British Museum.

Classical period and 10:1 in the Hellenistic period, after Alexander the Great had driven the value down by releasing huge quantities of precious metals onto the market. In addition to small silver fractions, states also issued low-denomination coins in non-precious metals, so that Greek society at all levels became relatively monetized quite quickly.

But monetization was rarely accompanied by the minting of enough coins. This meant not just that other means of exchange continued, but also that a thriving culture of credit emerged. There were even "friendship groups" (*eranoi*) that would provide small loans interest-free. Lending and borrowing took place especially among friends, but loans were also provided by temples (whose liquidity came from rents and the fees they charged for their services; their valuable dedications were only to be touched in the direst emergencies), and other institutions with their own revenues. Banks (or rather, bankers, because there was no concept of businesses as separate legal entities) emerged in fourth-century Athens and elsewhere, but they were few and for the rich alone.

The basic unit of weight in Greece was the mina, which was subdivided in different monetary zones into different numbers of drachmas (although 100 soon became standard), each of which was the equivalent of six obols. These names reveal their marketplace origins: "obol" means "spit" or "nail," and "drachma" means "handful," so that six nails constituted a handful. Then, to express great wealth, a talent was equivalent to 60 minas. Since a mina weighed about 430 grams (15 ounces) and a talent over 25 kilograms (about 55 pounds), neither of them were coined weights; they were found as bullion, or as a virtual expression of worth. So the basic units of Greek money were: 1 silver talent = 60 minas = 6,000 drachmas = 36,000 obols. Another denomination in common use was the stater, equal to two drachmas. At the end of the fifth century in Athens, a laborer in the public sector could expect, at best, 1.5 drachmas for a day's work; at the other end of the scale, possession of an estate worth 4 or 5 talents made you very well off.

The long-term effects of the introduction of coined money have been profound. Greek money is the ancestor of modern money in all its forms, virtual or actual; the Greeks were the first to use money as a way to evaluate everything, all goods and services. But in historical terms, the chief short-term points of interest are two: that it reveals traces of international networks among Greek communities that chose to adopt the same standards, and that it absolutely confirms the widespread existence of the state in Greece by the middle of the sixth century. It is not just that minting coins and stamping them with insignia are assertions of proud independence by the issuing state, but also that, with the advent of coined money, we can more readily talk of "taxation" and "revenue collection," and of the economy of the state as an entity in its own right, where previously we have struggled to guess what revenues Archaic states might have had.

The "Greek Miracle"

When the Scottish philosopher John Burnet appropriated (from the French thinker Ernest Renan) the phrase "the Greek miracle" at the end of the nineteenth century, he meant to capture two things: that something wonderful happened in sixth-century Greece, and that it was inexplicable. The wonderful thing that happened was nothing less, according to Burnet and the many who agreed with him, than the birth of rational thinking, science, and philosophy, all at once, in sixth-century Miletus. It was inexplicable because there was no telling what triggered it at that time and place. It was therefore best regarded as a product of individual genius, and we know of three sixth-century Milesians who gain the credit for it: Thales, Anaximander, and Anaximenes. These were the first of the thinkers whom scholars call the Presocratics, because their work predated the philosopher Socrates, after whom philosophy could never be the same again: Socrates made philosophy self-reflective, rather than focused on the outside world.

There were two revolutionary aspects of the Presocratics' work. First, they attempted to explain the origin and nature of the world by means of a single substance; Anaximenes, for instance, said that air was the primary substance, and that everything else was air transformed by thickening or thinning. This is reductionism, the essential principle of rational thought that things are to be explained by as few causes as possible. Second, the means chosen for explaining the world was itself a natural substance, not something like a god. The idea that the world is orderly and comprehensible by the human mind was the greatest gift of these early thinkers to future generations.

These are remarkable and profound developments, but the first scientists had many limitations. They lacked telescopes and microscopes, let alone hadron colliders, with which to study the universe and its origins, and so they were necessarily visionaries as much as scientists. The kinds of argumentation they used were fairly primitive, relying above all on polarity or analogy. Arguments based on the polarity of opposites such as light and dark abound, and analogy afforded them numerous insights. Anaximenes, for instance, inferred some of the cosmic properties of air on the basis of its effect on human beings, supposing that the universe at large, the macro-cosm, worked on the same principles that could be observed in the micro-cosm. One could say that the Presocratics had scientific attitudes, but little in the way of scientific reasoning or methodology.

We have a tiny fragment of Anaximander's own writing—the first frag-ment of literary prose from Greece:[6]

> Anaximander says that the original sources of existing things are also
> what existing things die back into according to necessity; "for they give
> justice and reparation to one another for their injustice in accordance with
> the ordinance of Time," as he puts it in these somewhat poetic terms.

Why did Anaximander choose to write in prose, when poetry was the usual medium for the transmission of wisdom? I think the difference he was trying to mark was that, whereas wisdom had previously been expressed in a dogmatic form, by divinely inspired poets, his words were part of an argument. The new idea, that claims should be backed up by argument and evidence, required a new medium. Wise men subsequent to Anaximander continued to publish in verse, but prose became the most accepted medium for philosophy, science, history, biography, and rhetoric—all of which use argument and evidence to close in on truth. Later, of course, prose was used for other purposes, such as fiction, but these were its original functions.

So Anaximander's idea was that the world consists of the orderly inter-play of opposites—orderly in the sense that none is capable of encroaching too far on its opposite. Instead of being the playground of the gods, the world was reinvented as a *kosmos*, a beautiful and orderly entity. The hot, dry season cannot go on forever, but is replaced by the cold, wet season; night gives way to day. This is a matter of necessity, and has nothing to do with the whims of fickle gods who need appeasing by ritual. The universe is ordered by cosmic justice.

Should we agree with Burnet that this was a miracle? I do think these three Milesians played a large part in teaching future generations how to make sense of the world. But we should also acknowledge that a great deal of scientific and mathematical work had long been carried out in Egypt and

---

6 Anaximander, F 1 Diels/Kranz, embedded in Simplicius, *Commentary on Aristotle's* Physics, 24.14–25 Diels (sixth century CE).

Babylonia. We cannot track in detail what ideas the Greeks might owe to these neighbors, but ideas travel along trade routes, and Miletus was one of the major trading centers of the time.

There may have been other, less concrete preconditions. Perhaps the idea that the cosmos was orderly was a projection of the increasing orderliness of the Archaic Greek state; after all, Anaximander used civic justice as a metaphor for cosmic justice. Increasing contact with and knowledge of other societies also encourages critical thinking, seeing that not everyone thinks and behaves in the same way. Perhaps even the invention of coinage played a part, by instilling the idea of infinite substitutability—that one thing could become many things, as the same coins could purchase many items and Anaximenes' air could become wood and stone. At any rate, Heraclitus of Ephesus, a somewhat later thinker (c. 500), liked the metaphor: "Everything is a compensation for fire, and fire is a compensation for everything, as goods are for money and money for goods."[7]

But in all likelihood the most powerful precondition—because more peculiarly Greek, and more particularly contemporaneous with these three Milesians—came from the nature of the city-state. By the sixth century, in many states political debate took place in an aristocratic council or even before a people's assembly. People were expected to weigh up the pros and cons of alternative proposals, and in their turn they expected speakers to justify what they were saying. The city-state was fostering the habits of rational argument and critical thinking, in which the authority of the speaker counted for less than what he said and was even dependent on the validity of what he said. Rational argument was becoming the norm, and the Presocratics simply extended it to the study of the world.

Ceramics

The sum total of surviving Archaic literature is pitifully small: a few of many epic poems, a few thousand lines of lyric poetry, some of the fables attributed to Aesop (if we can distinguish those that are early from later additions to the corpus, which was compiled in the Roman era), and some fragments of the early philosopher–scientists. Fortunately, the same cannot be said of

---

7 Heraclitus, F 90 Diels/Kranz.

another extraordinary achievement of the Archaic period: the glorious and continuously evolving artwork on vases of fired clay.

Human and other figures were first painted on Geometric pots in Athens in the middle of the eighth century. They were painted in black, with features defined by incision (a technique invented in Corinth), so that the pale clay showed through the incised black glaze. The possibilities afforded artists by this technique confirmed the Greeks in their love of depicting the human figure in as realistic—and occasionally grotesque—a way as possible, and by about 625 potters working in Athens were specializing in the human figure, while Corinthian potters continued to do fine work on small pots, still drawing on eastern motifs and techniques. But the human figure dominated Greek and Greek-influenced vase-painting until the Hellenistic period, when it was overtaken by relief ware—pieces with raised figures and patterns on them, imitations in clay of metal originals.

In the sixth century, Athenian potters discovered how to make a particularly high-quality black glaze, and developed their famous black-figure style. This soon enabled Athens once again to surpass Corinth as the producer of the most widely exported pottery, and it retained this position for centuries, eclipsing regional styles. On the next page is shown one of the masterpieces of the painter Exekias, painted around 540.

Achilles and Ajax, whose names are written over their heads, are playing dice and calling out their rolls: *tesara* (four) emerges from Achilles' mouth, and *tria* (three) from Ajax. The scene is symmetrical, with triangles dominant—the revelation at a second glance of underlying symmetries and structures is very typical of Classical Greek art in all its forms, with its emphasis on harmony, rhythm, and proportion. Particular care has been taken over incising the details of their gorgeous cloaks, their hair, headgear, and resting shields. The pair of heroes stand out from the background as though backlit. The scene is tranquil, and its dignity is typical of the best Athenian black-figure pieces, but there are disturbing narrative undertones. Both men are fully armed and seem ready to disturb the tranquility by leaping to their feet and returning to the bloody fray of the Trojan War. Furthermore, the viewer of the scene would have known that neither man would survive the war—Achilles famously struck in his vulnerable heel by Paris' arrow, and Ajax a maddened suicide (an event also painted by Exekias on a surviving pot).

Black-figure vases continued to be made in quantity up until the end of the sixth century, and occasionally thereafter, and there were other

Figure 3.4. Exekias' "Dice-players." Exekias was one of the greatest masters of the Athenian black-figure technique. He worked in the third quarter of the sixth century, during the Peisistratid period. This amphora is signed, so that we know that he was both the potter and the painter of the piece. Vatican Museums, Gregorian Etruscan Museum 16757. Photo © Scala / Art Resource, NY.

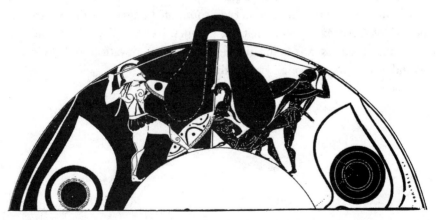

Figure 3.5. "Bilingual" eye cup. This is a detail from a cup by the "Andocides Painter," made c. 525 in Athens. The painter was one of the pioneers of red-figure, and used this cup to advertise his preference for the new technique. Palermo Museo Archeologico Regionale 200014.

techniques, such as white-ground, in which the clay of the vase was covered with a white slip before being painted. But around 530 a new technique was discovered in Athens, which swept black-figure aside and retained its popularity for about two hundred years, not just in Greece but over much of the Mediterranean. This was red-figure painting. Other places, especially southern Italy and Etruria, began to produce their own imitations, but Athens remained the place where you went for quality, at least up until the late fourth century, when production declined as Athenian trade tailed off. Many thousands of Athenian red-figure vases have survived, and the quality of the best of them—the glaze as well as the artistry—is the envy of potters and painters even today. But, like their black-figure counterparts, few are of exceptional quality (though many are good), and this reminds us that most of these pots were cheap, affordable by almost anyone.

The new red-figure technique—figures are red, the color of the original Attic clay, against a black glaze background rather than the other way around—allowed painters to paint details directly on to figures with a brush, rather than incising them as before, so that they achieved even greater naturalism. On the cup shown on the previous page, the "Andocides Painter" (that is, the man of unknown name who painted pots produced in Andocides' workshop) combines both red-figure and black-figure techniques, and (a telling detail) has the red-figure warrior outclassing two black-figure fighters. He also expresses the superiority of the new technique by having the shield of one of the black-figure fighters cross the boundary into the red-figure space. The cup summarizes some of the qualities of the Archaic period of Greece: experimentation, competitiveness, playfulness, and the sense that progress was being made—that each innovation and discovery would lead in the future to greater things.

4

Early Athens

Early in the fifth century, Greeks reflected on the political systems that their communities had ended up with, or could end up with, and developed a simple framework that divided constitutions into three: monarchy, oligarchy, and democracy. The division was clearly based in the first instance on what proportion of the citizen body held power: one man, a few men (that is, the rich), or all full citizens. But as well as being a linear division in this way, it could also be seen as two extremes—monarchy and democracy—with some kind of compromise or balance in the middle. And so oligarchy was often touted as an ideal "mixed" or "balanced" constitution. In fact, this is the form in which the threefold division is first found, in one of Pindar's odes from the late 470s: "Under every kind of administration," the poet says, "a man of straight speech stands out for his excellence, whether he is in the court of a tyrant, or whether political power is in the hands of the impetuous rank and file or of the wise." The wise, Pindar implies, strike a balance between tyranny and the reckless mob.[1]

We have already looked at monarchy in the Greek states, in its manifestation as tyranny, and monarchy will return to Greece in a big way in the Hellenistic period. Athenian democracy and Spartan oligarchy will occupy the next chapters. Although there were many other democracies and oligarchies in Greece, our evidence is far better for these two places than for others. In any case, the Athenians were probably the inventors of democracy. Some other places are occasionally described as democracies in the sixth century (Ambracia, Chalcis, Naxos, Cyrene, Megara, and some of the new Sicilian settlements), but always by historians writing many decades later. And we can never be sure quite what they meant by "democracy," which

---

1 Pindar, *Pythian Odes* 2.86–88. Then see the famous constitutional debate (among Persian nobles!) at Herodotus, *Histories* 3.80–83.

was a flexible term and was commonly used to describe what we would call moderate oligarchies, where several thousand citizens, rather than just a few dozen, held power.

In any case, Athenian democracy was exceptional in its longevity and stability. If we date its start to 500, when we hear that the new Council first took oath,[2] it lasted until the Macedonian conquest of Athens in 322, with only two brief oligarchic interruptions toward the end of the fifth century. In the Classical period, there were few other places—perhaps only Argos, Thebes, Elis, Syracuse, Tarentum, and Methymna on Lesbos—where democracy lasted more than a couple of decades without being replaced or tempered.

Oligarchy in Archaic Athens

We know very little about Archaic Athens. There were no contemporary historians, later material is often contaminated by current affairs, and there are few inscriptions, the other main form of contemporary evidence. The city seems to have lurched from crisis to crisis. An attempt at tyranny by Cylon in 636 was followed by two emergency appointments (Dracon in 621 and Solon in 594), and then three further attempts at tyranny (Damasias in 581 and Peisistratus in both 560 and 556), before Peisistratus was finally successful on his third attempt in 546. Evidence has turned up recently of the violence of at least one of these lurches: in 2015 archaeologists discovered, in a mass grave in a suburb of Athens, the remains of eighty young men, dating from the second half of the seventh century; they were tied together at their wrists, and all eighty of them had been executed by heavy blows to the head. Perhaps they were supporters of Cylon.

By the middle of the seventh century, the oligarchic system was in place that would last, with modifications, for about 150 years, until being replaced by democracy. A board of nine Archons ("leaders") was elected every year, who were responsible between them for carrying out all legislation. One—the "Eponymous" Archon, because his name was used to pinpoint the year for dating purposes—was the head of state for the year, with responsibility for all civic matters. Since the Athenian year started in late June or early July, at the first new moon after the summer solstice, an Athenian year, when

---

2 Pseudo-Aristotle, *The Athenian Constitution* 22.2; Crawford/Whitehead no. 119.

referred to as a whole, should strictly be written, for example, 645/4 in our terms—that is, from July 645 until July 644; to the Athenians, however, it was "the Archonship of Dropides."

The other Archons were a "king," with largely religious responsibilities; a Polemarch ("war leader"), who was assisted by a board of four Generals, one from each of the four Athenian hereditary tribes into which citizens were divided for administrative purposes; and six *thesmothetai* ("regulators"), whose role at this time is obscure. Each of the Archons also had various judicial responsibilities, but homicide cases were heard by a court of fifty-one men who met on the Areopagus hill west of the Acropolis.

The way the system worked was that the aristocratic Council, after consultation with the Archons, presented the results of its deliberations to the popular Assembly for acclamation, and then the Council instructed the relevant officer or officers to execute the decision. The Assembly must have been thinly populated, because only those who bore arms counted as citizens, and we are assured that the poor played little or no part in the political life of the city.[3] All it was required to do, apparently, was rubber-stamp the Council's decisions.

Not long after Cylon's attempted coup, a man called Dracon was swept to power during some emergency. We know little of his legislation, because within thirty years all of it, except his homicide laws, had been superseded. It seems that his work was rather primitive, with fines expressed in numbers of oxen and with death the likely consequence of a wide range of crimes. A fourth-century Athenian orator famously quipped that Dracon ("Snake") had written his laws not in ink, but in blood;[4] we still use "draconian" as a synonym for "harsh." But the importance of his legislation was that it made uniform the various systems that had arisen over time in various parts of Attica. Now all those parts of Attica that owed allegiance to Athens would follow the same procedures. It goes hand in hand with this that Dracon distinguished citizens from noncitizens, in the sense that murdering a non-Athenian incurred a lesser penalty.

Dracon only partially replaced the existing self-help system, the aristocratic code of honor that demanded swift and personally executed retaliation for wrongs. That is, he seems not to have given the courts the right to exact penalties, but only to pronounce verdicts. If the defendant was found

---

3 Pseudo-Aristotle, *The Athenian Constitution* 2.3, 4.2; Crawford/Whitehead nos. 66, 65B.
4 Demades, F 23 de Falco.

guilty, the court pronounced him without rights, and he was then handed over to the injured party or the injured party's closest relatives (descendants of a common great-grandfather), who could deal with him as they wished, up to and including killing him. The courts were there to slow things down as much as anything—to give the injured party time to calm down and the criminal time to flee into exile, if he wanted. Archaic society, in Athens as elsewhere, remained one in which violence was often a distinct possibility.

Solon and the Debtors

The next crisis we hear about occurred early in the sixth century. The main symptom was that many of the poor had got themselves into a vicious cycle of escalating debt to the rich, which was exacerbated by the fact that security for debt was taken out on the debtor's own person. This was not an uncommon procedure in the ancient world—the Babylonians were already doing it early in the second millennium BCE, for instance—but it meant that if the debtor defaulted, the creditor sold him and his family abroad into slavery to recover what he was owed, or turned them into debt-bondsmen to work for him for free.

The dependence of the poor on the rich is what we would expect at this period of history, but clearly Athens was about to explode and Solon was appointed to dissolve the tension. We have about three hundred lines of his verse, and plenty of discussion in later authors, but much is uncertain about his aims and achievements. He became so famous later that the whole Athenian law code was held to have originated with him, so that the historical record is confused by the attribution of much later legislation to him. Solon became Archon for the year 594/3 and was granted plenipotentiary powers, but his legislation must have taken longer than a year to enact (he covered a great deal, from fixing the festival calendar to legislating for the placement of beehives), and so he probably also held an unconstitutional sole Archonship for a while, little different from tyranny except that he was working for the good of all, not for the enhancement of his family, and did not have to resort to force to establish or maintain his authority.

It is not clear how the miserable debtors had got into debt. Perhaps the rising population of Attica had made labor so cheap that the poor could be badly exploited and reduced to dependency. Probably the rich, who already owned all the good land, had by now enclosed common land as well and gained control over access to water; at any rate, Solon accused them of "stealing public and sacred land."[5] Any poor man who wanted to start his own farm had to both borrow the startup costs and materials from a rich neighbor, in return for a share of the produce at harvest-time, and give over more of his produce as rent. Even though the rents do not seem to have been extortionate (we hear of one-sixth),[6] they were high enough, in combination with other debts, and in any case it is likely that the rich were releasing only marginal land, keeping all the good land for themselves. Or, possibly, one-sixth was the rate of interest per month rather than per year, which would soon add up to a crippling burden.

Solon called his solution to this nest of problems a *seisakhtheia*, a "disburdening." First, he forced the big landowners to disenclose common land and return it to public use, and he set limits on the amount of land that one man could own in Attica.[7] These measures must have hurt, but the landowners had agreed to Solon's appointment, and so they agreed also to his reforms, for the sake of stability. In the short term, this made more land available for public grazing. In the longer term, it also opened up this land for purchase, and indeed the evidence of archaeology shows that by the end of the sixth century the countryside of Attica was filling up. It took several decades for this measure of Solon's to take effect, but it meant that many former tenants and sharecroppers became landowners. Solon also helped them by allowing only olive oil to be sold abroad; olives can be grown on the poorer land that his new farmers were developing, so he was helping them to find the best price, at home or abroad.

He also canceled all current debts and made it illegal in the future to enslave a man for debt. He did not make debt-bondage illegal—a man may still have had to repay a debt by providing the creditor with labor or services—but he extracted the deadly sting of potential enslavement. But in guaranteeing for the Athenian peasant relative freedom from exploitation, Solon created a gap that those in search of cheap labor needed to fill, and so the trade in foreign slaves rocketed. Athenians may have been barred from enslaving other Athenians, but the same consideration was not offered

5 Solon, F 4.12–13 West.
6 Pseudo-Aristotle, *The Athenian Constitution* 2.1–3; Crawford/Whitehead no. 66.
7 *Seisakhtheia*: pseudo-Aristotle, *The Athenian Constitution* 6.1 (Crawford/Whitehead no. 67). Disenclosure: Solon, F 36.4–7 West. Limit on land: Aristotle, *Politics* 1266b17–19.

to others. We will see later how embedded slavery was in the Athenian economy.

Solon and the Constitution

Having resolved the immediate issue, Solon turned to further reforms, designed to come up with a workable form of aristocratic oligarchy. He divided all Athenians into four property classes, according to how many measures of barley their estates could potentially provide—barley being the "monetary" standard of the time. Some way of reckoning equivalents must have been involved, since people always had other sources of income than barley. But the system was unlikely to have been policed by officials tasked with assessing a landowner's means; it is more likely that a man self-identified as a member of a particular class, and remained in it as long as he kept up the obligations of that class and behaved in an appropriate fashion.

The four classes were: the *Pentakosiomedimnoi*, those whose estates produced a minimum of 500 *medimnoi* of barley a year, where the *medimnos* was a dry measure equivalent to about 50 liters (11 gallons) and weighing about 30 kilograms (70 pounds) of barley or 40 kilograms (90 pounds) of wheat; the *Hippeis*, "Horsemen" or "Knights," whose estates were valued at 300 *medimnoi*; the *Zeugitai* (200 *medimnoi*)—"Teamsters," perhaps, since they seem to have been named for their oxen; and, finally, the Thetes (a word whose original meaning was "wage laborers"), a broad class encompassing about 80 percent of the population at this time, and ranging from reasonably prosperous farmers and craftsmen to, for instance, casual laborers. This 80 percent constituted what the Greeks called "the poor," because they were not gentlemen of leisure but had to work for others in order to make a living. The top three classes ranged from the rich to the super-rich.

In Solon's legislation, only members of the top two classes were eligible for the highest political offices; members of the top three classes could be members of the new Council of Four Hundred he created, a hundred from each tribe, to prepare business for the Assembly; and Thetes were for the first time allowed to participate in the Assembly and as jurymen in the popular courts. Never before in history had political participation of any kind been permitted for the peasant class.

Only members of the first three classes were obliged to serve in the army as hoplites, though richer Thetes could afford hoplite armor as well. As a check on officers of the state, Solon gave the Areopagus Council, previously a purely judicial body, a broad brief to "safeguard the laws." This council was from now on made up of former Archons after their year of office, so it had considerable prestige as a council of experienced men. "Safeguarding the laws" seems to have involved the right to receive reports about the conduct of officers during their term of office, on moral as well as political grounds, and to punish them if necessary.

The importance of the establishment of the census classes was that it redefined what it was to be a member of the elite, which now depended on wealth, not birth. By Solon's time, the birth elite did not necessarily coincide with the wealth elite; there were plenty of nouveaux riches, and plenty of impoverished aristocrats. By opening up membership of the military and political elite to the new rich, Solon appeased their greatest complaint. Moreover, from now on anyone who could make himself rich enough, even a farmer or a craftsman, could stand for election as an Archon, however noble or ignoble his lineage. That this was not impossible is proved by a fifth-century inscription, once attached to a now-lost statue group: "Anthemion, son of Diphilus, made this dedication to the gods on exchanging the rank of Thete for that of Knight."[8] The regime of the Eupatridae, the birth elite, was over.

We do not know how members of the new Solonic Council were selected, or whether their tenure was lifelong or limited (in fact, some scholars even doubt that this council existed). The Archons were perhaps chosen by the Council from a short list prepared by the four tribes and approved by the Assembly. The Assembly began to meet more regularly, when convened by the Council, though it could still only vote on issues, not debate them, and voting was still probably by acclamation rather than a show of hands.

Solon also guaranteed the people's juridical independence from the landowning class by giving them the right to sit as a court of appeal (known as the Heliaea) against verdicts handed down by the higher courts in certain categories of case, and he made it possible for any Athenian citizen to initiate a court case in the public interest. Cases were now divided into *dikai* and *graphai*. For a *dikē*, a "suit" (in effect, a private suit), the prosecutor had to be the injured party himself or, if he was dead, his close kin. For a *graphē*, a "writ" (in effect, a public suit), the prosecutor could be anyone at all—any disinterestedly concerned citizen, acting on behalf of the community.

Solon was trying to make justice the concern of the community as a whole, rather than just the elite, but in actual fact prosecutors in *graphai* were

8 Pseudo-Aristotle, *The Athenian Constitution* 7.4.

rarely disinterested, and such cases could be and often were hijacked for political purposes, especially when the "writ for introducing an illegal measure" came into force in the last quarter of the fifth century. But for the first time, in the Heliaea, verdicts were reached by counting votes rather than by shouting "Yea" or "Nay." This, of course, is a critical democratic innovation, with its implication that every citizen is as good as every other citizen.

Despite frequent claims by fourth-century Athenian writers, however, who saw Solon as the founder of their democracy, he was no democratic idealist; he had a crisis to resolve, and he did so by giving the poor just enough so that they would not escalate their challenge to elite rulership. He himself said that he gave the poor no more than was fitting.[9] After his reforms, rich landowners were still dominant both economically and politically. But the Athenian system needed citizens who were not dependent on others, and who could therefore afford to serve the state in the administration and the army, and it was Solon who made this future possible. And by limiting the amount of land men could own, he created one of the remarkable features of Classical Athens: that although there were of course some who were filthy rich and others who were wretchedly poor, overall there was no great inequality of income. He changed the status of the poor from subjects to citizens.

Peisistratus and His Sons

Athens remained destabilized by elite rivalries over the years following Solon's reforms, and the city lurched toward its first sustained tyranny. Peisistratus, from the Neleid family, had come to prominence by successfully realizing a long-held Athenian dream, wresting the nearby island of Salamis from Megara. On the strength of this, he entered the lists with the Alcmaeonidae and Boutadae, the two most powerful families of Athens, led respectively by Megacles and Lycurgus. These were powerful adversaries: Lycurgus was the priest of Athena Polias, the presiding deity of the city, and Megacles was the son-in-law of the tyrant of Sicyon.

Peisistratus made good use of his years of exile after his second failed coup. He took out leases on gold and silver mines around Mount Pangaeum in Thrace (next to Ennea Hodoi), and with the help of his new wealth gained support and mercenaries from friends in southern Greece. He landed at

9 Solon, F 5 West.

Marathon, perhaps in 546, marched on Athens with an army numbering in the low thousands, and established a tyranny that lasted for thirty-six years, until his death of natural causes in 528/7. Then his son Hippias took over, with the assistance of his brother Hipparchus.

We have already looked at tyranny in general, and Peisistratus and his sons conformed to the type. They worked with the other noble families as much as they could; the chance survival of a fragmentary list of Archons lets us know that Cleisthenes, son of Megacles and head of the Alcmaeonidae, was Eponymous Archon for 525/4 (even though the Alcmaeonidae later claimed that they had been in exile throughout the tyranny), and that Miltiades, of the Philaidae, was Archon for 524/3, even though his father had been assassinated, probably by the tyrants, a few years earlier.[10]

The Athenian tyrants embellished and improved the city's public facilities, especially the delivery of water to the city, and cleared a large space to the northwest of the Acropolis as a public park, complete with athletic race track and military parade ground. They extended Solon's drive to weaken the dependency of the poor on the rich by making it possible for poor farmers to borrow money from the state rather than from landowners. They supported the continuing development of Athens as a center of culture by encouraging poetry, sculpture, architecture, and vase-painting. They oversaw the continuing expansion of Athenian trade networks abroad and its trend toward becoming an international commercial hub.

The first Athenian coins were minted under the Peisistratids; an early series of "blazon money" (dump silver two-drachma pieces marked with various blazons) under Peisistratus was replaced under his sons by the first series of Athens' famous "owls." These were four-drachma pieces of about seventeen grams (a bit more than half an ounce), made out of high-grade Attic silver from the Laurium mines in the southeast of the peninsula. The mines were probably now taken into state ownership (though working them was leased out to individuals), because a new vein of exceptional richness had just been discovered. Athens rapidly became the most important minting center in the Aegean; everyone trusted the quality of the silver, whether they were using owls as coin or as bullion.

Hippias and Hipparchus planned and began work to replace an existing temple of Olympian Zeus, southeast of the Acropolis, with an enormous

---

10 Meiggs/Lewis no. 6 = (translated) Fornara no. 23; Rhodes no. 60; Crawford/Whitehead no. 71.

Figure 4.1. Athenian "owl." A typical earlyish Athenian "owl," worth four drachmas. The Athenians were the first to mint coins with the place name. Athenian owls were the most highly regarded currency of the eastern Mediterranean for many decades, and were one of the sources of Athenian wealth. BM 1948,0506.9. © Trustees of the British Museum.

structure that was clearly meant to outdo all other tyrant temples, such as Polycrates' Heraion on Samos. The project was very grandiose, and was abandoned when the tyranny fell in 510; it was not finally completed until six hundred years later, by the Roman emperor Hadrian. Hippias' son (another Peisistratus, Archon in 522/1) built, among other things, the Altar of the Twelve Gods in the Peisistratid park. Apart from its religious function, the altar represented the center of Athens, in the sense that distances were henceforth measured to and from that spot, and at the same time the roads of Attica were improved and milestones (with inscribed moral maxims by Hipparchus) indicated when one was halfway between Athens and outlying villages. Peisistratid Athens was evidently evolving as the central place of Attica, and by the end of the century all the important rural sanctuaries of Attica had branches in Athens, but nowhere else.

But elite resentment of the tyranny was building up, and in 514 Hipparchus was murdered. He had made sexual advances to a young man called Harmodius, and Harmodius and his older lover, Aristogeiton, members of the Gephyraioi family, decided to kill him—which meant killing his brother first. They planned to take advantage of the happy chaos of the Panathenaea festival, when the streets would be filled with celebrants and

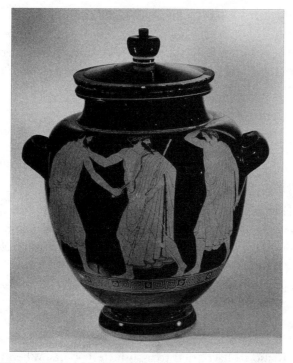

Figure 4.2. Harmodius and Aristogeiton. This Athenian red-figure stamnos of c. 470 shows the two tyrannicides striking down Hipparchus. Aristogeiton, the older man (and therefore bearded), is the one on the left. Museum der Universität Würzburg, Antikenabteilung L.515. Photo: Wikimedia.

spectators. But something went wrong and only Hipparchus was murdered. Harmodius was killed on the spot, and Aristogeiton was arrested and tortured to death (leading, after the fall of the tyranny, to a law that Athenian citizens were not to be tortured). Hippias regained control of the situation and, faced with more active resistance from the rival families (inspired, presumably, by the lovers' attempt), instituted a much more oppressive regime.

The Noble Liberators

In later years, in democratic Athens, the main version of these events hailed Harmodius and Aristogeiton as "the tyrant-slayers" and the institutors of democracy. They were the subjects of an impressive sculpture group, which was erected in the Agora, the first time men rather than gods had been so honored. Their cult as heroes was a prominent part of the Panathenaea, the central Athenian festival, and their descendants were awarded certain privileges in perpetuity. They were celebrated in popular songs:[11]

> I shall carry my sword in a myrtle bough
> As did Harmodius and Aristogeiton
> When they killed the tyrant
> And gave the Athenians equality.

This was the version of events that entered Athenian social memory, but it was plainly false, as the Athenian historian Thucydides was the first—or the first we know of—to point out.[12] So far from ending the tyranny, the pair of lovers made it worse. A sordid tale of lovers' jealousy was transformed into high-minded politics. Why?

Elite competition was probably at the bottom of it, with some families championing Harmodius and Aristogeiton over an alternative version that was broadcast by the Alcmaeonidae. After the murder of Hipparchus, the Alcmaeonidae attempted to raise an armed rebellion; one of their number, Cedon, seems also to have tried to assassinate Hippias. When these efforts failed, they resorted to more subtle methods—or so they said subsequently. Their influence in Delphi was great, as a result of their generous rebuilding of the temple after a fire, and they got the Delphians to persuade the Spartans to get rid of the Athenian tyranny. The story in Herodotus is that every time a Spartan came to Delphi to consult the oracle, the priests urged him to liberate Athens.[13]

The powerful and far-sighted Spartan king, Cleomenes I (reigned c. 520–490), was easily persuaded. Sparta never had a tyrant, and had gained the reputation of being opposed on principle to tyranny, but it was not as straightforward as Cleomenes had expected. On his second attempt, however, in 510, he invaded Attica in force and succeeded in driving Hippias out of Athens with his family to seek Persian protection. We will shortly see how Athens managed to avoid Spartan domination, but the point is that Athens owed its freedom from tyranny to a foreign power—an awkward

---

11   Preserved by Athenaeus of Naucratis, *Wise Men at Dinner* 695a–b (second/third century CE); Fornara no. 39A; Crawford/Whitehead no. 73.

12   Thucydides, *History* 6.54–59.

13   Herodotus, *Histories* 5.63; Crawford/Whitehead no. 74.

fact that many Athenians chose to forget by promoting Harmodius and Aristogeiton over the Alcmaeonid version of events. The cult of the tyrannicides suited the image of itself that Athens was trying to develop in the early fifth century, and so that was the version of events that came to take pride of place in the Athenian imagination.

5

The Democratic Revolution

Following the expulsion of Hippias by Cleomenes, Athens was effectively a client state of Sparta, and, with Spartan encouragement, in 509/8 an Athenian aristocrat called Isagoras, who was Archon for the year, attempted to reinstate old-style aristocracy. Isagoras' main opponent was Cleisthenes. Isagoras had the support of the majority of the noble families, so Cleisthenes turned to the people—perhaps the Assembly, or the Council—and proposed radical constitutional reform. We cannot know how much detail he went into at this stage; perhaps he did no more than speak vaguely but effectively about *isonomia*, "fair shares"—about transferring to the whole population the equality and power-sharing that aristocrats had created among themselves. At the time, only the wealth elite ruled and were ruled in turns; Cleisthenes suggested that the entire population submit itself to the same dynamic. Now under threat, with Spartan help Isagoras threw the Alcmaeonidae and their allies out of Athens.

Cleisthenes had sown seeds of unrest, however, and Cleomenes garrisoned the city to ensure the safe establishment of Isagoras' oligarchy. But the Council—Herodotus' word[1] refers to the Areopagus Council for those scholars who deny the existence of the Solonic Council—refused to accept subordination to Sparta, and it was probably with the councilors' encouragement and leadership that the Athenian people (members of the hoplite class, probably) pinned the Spartan garrison on the Acropolis without much in the way of supplies, and after a few days let them leave the city peacefully. Isagoras fled, and some of his supporters were killed. The hoplite class that had been growing in numbers and strength over the course of the sixth century had found its voice. Athenian society had been more thoroughly

---

1 Herodotus, *Histories* 5.72.2; Crawford/Whitehead no. 75.

elitist than any other contemporary state, and the reaction when it came was extreme.

The critical moment here was the Council's resistance, which triggered the uprising. Inspired by Cleisthenes' promises—in fact, probably more inspired than Cleisthenes himself had meant them to be—the people rioted. It is hard to tell whether Cleisthenes was a democratic idealist or was aiming for personal power. But events overtook him, and once he and his allies had returned from exile, they kept their promises and passed the series of reforms that turned Athens into a democracy—a *dēmokratia*, "government by the people for the people" (though the word seems not to have been coined until the 460s). The great Athenian families seem to have capitulated, and to have faced the fact that from now on they would have to find other ways to retain their dignity and prominence. Cleisthenes certainly reassured them that their families and his would still occupy all the top positions in the new system. A true revolution had taken place, with minimal bloodshed.

The Spartans persisted over the next few years in trying to bring the Athenians to heel, but failed—most dramatically in 506, when in a single day the Athenians beat off simultaneous attacks from Spartan allies to the east (Chalcis) and north (Boeotia). There was then a third, more serious attempt from the west, by the Spartans and their Peloponnesian allies, but the Corinthians thought the attack unjustified by the terms of their treaty with Sparta and caused a split in the leadership. One of the kings, Damaratus, turned back with the discontented allies, leaving Cleomenes frustrated in the field. (Subsequently, the Spartans passed a law forbidding joint command by two kings of the same expedition.) The victories made the new democracy proud; inadvertently, Cleomenes helped the new political system find favor in Athens. His repeated attempts to crush the new democracy also created a dynamic of hostility between Sparta and Athens that would endure, with peaks and troughs, for 150 years.

A New Dispensation for Athens

Curiously, given his importance, Cleisthenes is not prominent in our sources. It is hard to get a sense of him as a person. In fact, he is never mentioned outside the context of his reforms. Perhaps he died shortly after instigating

THE DEMOCRATIC REVOLUTION

the reforms; he was probably born in the early 560s. In what follows, I will talk of Cleisthenes as though he were at least the prime mover, but other scenarios are possible.

Having obtained the blessing of Delphi, Cleisthenes divided the whole of Attica into three geographical areas: the various coastal regions, the inland, and the city (including the farmland and coastline near the city—more or less the area covered by the modern city of Athens). Within these three regions, he found or created 139 "demes" (parishes), with those outside the city centered on a town or village.

He replaced the four tribes with ten. Each of the new tribes was made up of three *trittyes* ("thirds" or "ridings"), one from the coast, one from the inland, and one from the city. Each riding contained one or more demes, depending on population. In the end, then, every tribe had a roughly equal population and contained a cross section of the citizenry, since all three regions were represented in it. Just as importantly, each tribe included city demes, where the most politically experienced men resided, so that the tribes would start equal in this respect too. In a sense, Cleisthenes mapped Attica, relating its elements to one another and confirming its extent in all directions.

It was probably now that more remote Attic towns and villages, up to two days' journey away from Athens by foot, finally became fully incorporated into the state. The thousands of new citizens created by the incorporation of outlying villages and towns were the chief reason for increasing the number of tribes from four to ten; new citizens in the future would easily be accommodated as well. Those towns that were the homes of significant cults were given money for building work, forcing them to acknowledge their dependency on Athens. However they had been administered previously, all the demes now had the same political structure, which mirrored that of Athens itself.

The new system was an attempt to sweep away old land- and kin-based loyalties and replace them with loyalty to artificial constructs—deme, tribe, and the state as a whole. This promise would naturally take some years to be realized, as old loyalties died hard, but a generation would soon exist that had known no other system. Now fellow tribesmen from different ridings might live miles apart from one another and have no genuine kinship ties or shared local interests. Instead, they were united by the shared religious practices that came with membership of the new tribes, by the fact that they were often called upon to represent their tribe in competition against the others, and by the fact that tribesmen fought shoulder to shoulder in the army. Any authority an aristocrat might be able to exert at the deme level could be counteracted by the tribe. This was the moment when the aristocratic households ceased to be at the center of Athenian political and religious life and were replaced by the state. Aristocracy remained a social distinction, but it lost its political force. In theory, men were political equals now.

One of the first moves of the new state was to expand aggressively beyond its borders: after the defeat of Chalcis in 506, the first Athenian "cleruchy" was established—an overseas settlement on occupied territory where the emigrant cleruchs ("allotment-owners") lost neither the privileges nor the obligations of Athenian citizenship. Poorer cleruchs, on receipt of their allotment, became middling farmers and capable of serving Athens as hoplites; perhaps that is how Anthemion got his start (p. 81). Cleruchs, who numbered between two hundred and two thousand, could serve as garrisons, to secure strategic or fertile islands or cities for Athens. Wealthier cleruchs were often absentee landlords, however, preferring to live in Athens and rent their other property, and enough men chose this route for cleruchies rarely to have formed actual communities or villages. They were always extras, grafted on to existing communities of unwilling residents, so it is no surprise that "an Attic neighbor" came to be proverbial for someone you did not want nearby. The Euboean cleruchy did not last long: it was brought to an end a dozen or so years later under unknown circumstances. But Salamis seems to have received one too (some of the regulations survive on an inscription, the earliest surviving official Athenian inscription), and henceforth Salamis was always regarded as Athenian territory, though it was never divided into demes.[2]

The Board of Generals

All political appointments and the provision of regiments for the army were based on the new tribal system; for the first time, there was to be a proper citizen army, with each tribe supplying a small number of cavalrymen and a

2 Meiggs/Lewis no. 14 = (translated) Fornara no. 44B.

much larger number of foot soldiers from those of its members who could afford the panoply. The army was mustered by tribes and formed up for battle in tribal units, rather than as retainers of this landowner or that. This system remained in place until the 340s, when troops began to be recruited by age group alone, rather than by tribe and age group.

A board of ten democratically elected Generals was created to advise the Polemarch, who owed his position merely to his membership in one of the highest Solonian property classes. Within two decades, however, as we shall see, when all the Archons were downgraded in the interests of democracy, the Polemarch fell too, leaving military matters to the board of Generals. At first, each tribe elected one General for a year, but within a few decades the system had become more flexible, and the same tribe could supply more than one General. Generalship was subject to election, not sortition (that is, a lottery), and a man could be General any number of times, even in consecutive years, because it required not just loyalty to the democracy but expertise; that is also why certain positions requiring financial expertise were also subject to election.

Appointed by the state, Generals were answerable to the state. Of course, they were allowed some discretion in the field, but they often received express orders from the Assembly before and during a campaign, and always had to be aware of what might please the people. We quite often hear of Generals being prosecuted in Athens for unsuccessful missions; on one notorious occasion in 406, six were condemned to death at once. In democratic Athens, it was possible to regard an important failure as equivalent to treason. The carrot of honor and the stick of prosecution were the means by which the Athenian people controlled their officers.

Generals were responsible for both army and navy, and had no specializations until sometime in the fourth century, when one took command of the hoplites if they were campaigning abroad, two became responsible for the security of Piraeus, one was responsible for homeland security, one for seeing that the navy was seaworthy, and the remaining five were without specific portfolios. Later still, further divisions of responsibility occurred, depending on pragmatic considerations, and there seem to have been as many as fourteen Generals, in a kind of loose hierarchy, with the Hoplite Generalship the most prestigious. Later still, this post came to be the second most important in Roman Athens, after the

Eponymous Archon, whose position was by then subject to election rather than sortition.

The Democratic Council

Cleisthenes raised the number of members of the Council (*Boulē*) to five hundred, with each tribe supplying fifty. Councilors, who had to be aged thirty or over, were elected annually, and at first could be chosen only once in a lifetime, though that was later increased to twice, but not in consecutive years. If a man wanted to become a councilor, it seems that he was able to do so. He proposed his name to his deme, and the deme assembly checked his credentials and accepted his candidacy. All the demes put forward a pool of candidates, from which their quota of councilors was drawn by election (or, from 486, by sortition) at a meeting of the tribal assembly. The fact that demes chose their councilors makes Cleisthenes' Council the first council of representatives in world history; through his deme and tribe, the voice of even the most distant inhabitant of Attica could, in theory, be heard in Athens.

It was clearly not in keeping with the spirit of the new democracy that Thetes, the majority of the population, should be excluded from the Council, nor was it practical to shrink the pool of available councilors in this way, since no one was allowed to stand more than twice in a lifetime. So before long Thetes were allowed into the Council as well as the Assembly—but this made a difference only to town-dwelling Thetes, since there was no pay (yet) for public service, and their country cousins could not afford to take time off. It is a full day's walk from Marathon, for instance, to Athens, and Assembly meetings might be called at short notice. The frequency of Council meetings (every day except for holidays and days of ill omen) made it difficult for the poor to serve in this capacity too, even after councilors began to receive a daily allowance. Throughout democratic Athens' history, the Council tended to be peopled by those who were better off, and politics in general was played more by those who lived in or near the city than by those whose homes were farther away, who, if they cared, focused more on local deme politics.

The first job of the new Council was to prepare the agenda for the people's Assembly, the *Ekklēsia*. In order for the people to function efficiently as the decision-making body, they had to be fed predigested proposals. So the Council received petitions from citizens and officers, or generated them by itself, and no proposal could come before the Assembly that had not been previously debated by the Council. Four days in advance of the date chosen for an Assembly meeting the Council posted the agenda in the Agora, either as formulated proposals to be voted on or as topics to be debated before voting; it attached its recommendations to some items on the agenda, and had the right to call extra meetings of the Assembly.

Its second job was to see that the Assembly's decisions were carried out. It gave the state's officers their orders and supervised their work; it generated subcommittees out of its members to see that things got done, and supervised their work too. It was responsible, then, for all daily business, and this meant that it controlled state finances. It ensured that the navy was seaworthy, negotiated with foreign states, and received their representatives, although the declaration of war or peace was up to the Assembly. It acted as a law court for matters relating to administration, especially in the financial sphere, but passed serious cases, involving large fines, on to the regular law courts.

Since it was impractical to have five hundred councilors in permanent session, at some point each year was divided into ten stretches of thirty-five or thirty-six days (each one a *prytanis*), with the fifty councilors of each tribe acting as a sitting board, the *prytaneis* (presidents, presidium), for one of those ten periods—with fifteen or so of their number sleeping over as well, to be a permanent presence. Their jobs were to receive business and prepare the agenda for the full Council when it met, and one of their number was selected to chair Assembly meetings (which had previously been the Archons' job); later, in the 350s, as a hedge against corruption, the *prytaneis* daily chose a man from one of the *other* nine tribes to preside over Council and Assembly meetings, so that no one could know in advance who it was likely to be.

The division of the political year into prytanies acted as a kind of calendar—a political calendar to go along with the largely agricultural calendar of religious festivals. Coordination of the two calendars was often a nightmare, which explains why Assembly meetings could not take place on fixed days, say the third of every month, because in any month the third day might coincide with a festival day from the religious calendar, when secular meetings were prohibited. Moreover, the Assembly could not meet on the same day as the Heliaea, because the personnel were the same.

The regulation that no one could be a member of the Council more than twice in a lifetime appears to have been relaxed by early in the third century, when a declining population and a Council of six hundred made it hard to fill all the seats if men were allowed to stand only twice. But, while it lasted, the rule prevented individuals from becoming prominent

and ensured that as many people as possible would gain political experience.
At any given moment, up to 25 percent of Athenian males over the age of
thirty would have served as councilors. This in turn guaranteed a politicized
and informed Assembly, because there would always be a good number of
ex-councilors in the Assembly.

The exact timetable is impossible for us to establish, but the developments
I have been describing emerged over the decades following Cleisthenes' initial reforms. Athenian democracy was always a work in progress. In 487/6
the Archonship was finally sidelined as a route to power by being made subject to sortition (from a pool of perhaps a hundred candidates put forward
by the demes) rather than election. Men still wanted to be Archons for the
prestige, but they also began to covet Generalship, since this was now the
most important position still open to voluntary election and to which one
could be repeatedly re-elected, even year by year, so that it could act as a
platform for personal power. Not long after this date, the Polemarch appears
with only civilian functions.

The possibility of repeated election year after year meant that politics
could now become a profession. But only the wealthy could afford to make
politics their profession, and so Athens became a democracy in which legislative power was in the hands of the people, while advisory power remained
in the hands of the rich. Following Cleisthenes' example, the rich had
learned that, from now on, it was only by gaining the support of the poor
that they would be successful. The stability of the Athenian democracy was
due in large part to the degree of communication and cooperation between
rich and poor.

People Power

Before Cleisthenes, as we have seen, the Assembly seems to have had little to
do apart from rubber-stamp the aristocratic Council's decisions. Many popular assemblies in the Greek world continued like that, but Cleisthenes gave
real power to the Athenian people—or to adult male Athenians anyway. At
first, probably, there were ten statutory meetings of the Assembly each year.
By the mid-fourth century, the number had crept up to forty—four each
prytany, with one being a principal meeting, at which the most important
issues (defense, religious matters, the grain supply) were prioritized. Even

though urban residents were bound to be more strongly represented than country folk, Assembly meetings seem to have included a fair cross section of the population—that is, with the poor in the majority, and the elderly poor in wartime. Instead of merely listening to predebated topics, many issues were now debated within the Assembly and voted on immediately. Rhetorical skills—the ability to persuade mass audiences—became of critical importance to the practice of Athenian politics.

As a symbol of its independence, by about 500 the Assembly had gained its own permanent meeting-place on the Pnyx hill, a natural auditorium just west of the Acropolis and the Areopagus hill; since right from the start the Pnyx was adapted to accommodate several thousand people, clearly mass involvement in politics was assumed. Decisions in the Assembly were now taken by a show of hands, with a simple majority carrying the day, rather than by acclamation. This is a more accurate and democratic procedure, though not as accurate as counting pebbles, which was used in the courts and when the Assembly was acting as a court (it heard cases affecting the stability of the community). But counting pebbles takes too much time for a body of thousands that could be required to make dozens of decisions in a day.

People power (a literal translation of the Greek *dēmokratia*) was also hugely increased by the process of ostracism, another measure put in place to curb the elite; it might have been Cleisthenes' doing, but it remained unused until the early 480s. Each year the Assembly could decide to cast a secret ballot that would result in a ten-year exile for one man, whoever gained the majority of the votes, provided that a minimum of six thousand votes were cast. This was a large vote, designed to make sure that such a powerful instrument was used only when it was really necessary. The "winner" was punished not because of any crime he had committed, but just because he was felt to be a threat to the democracy, and his exile involved no confiscation of property or loss of rights when he returned or was recalled. It was an institutionalization of the long-standing aristocratic practice of sending one's opponents into exile, either by the threat of killing them in retaliation for their crime or by official means.

For ostracism under the democracy, each attending citizen wrote or had written on a pottery shard (an *ostrakon* in Greek) the name of the man he wanted to see removed, probably from a published list of candidates. The practice was curiously similar to that of "fixing" curses by inscribing the name of one's enemy. Surviving *ostraka* (we have well over ten thousand) display a bizarre range of allegations, on those rare occasions when they give a reason at all for wanting to send a man into exile, from treason to buggery.

But the Athenians handled this power responsibly. Ostracisms were rare: the first was in 488/7, and there were only fifteen in total over the next seventy years. But whether or not one happened in any given year, by debating the issue the people publicly reaffirmed their power over the lives of powerful individuals. By the last quarter of the fifth century, however, it had become less a matter of getting rid of powerful individuals than of forcing a choice between the political platforms of rival politicians—much as politicians nowadays call snap elections or referendums in an attempt to show their critics that they have popular support for their

Figure 5.1. Ostraka. These ostraka, found in the Athenian Agora, bear the names and patronymics of four of the fifth century's most famous Athenian statesmen: (clockwise from top left) Aristeides, Themistocles, Pericles, and Cimon. Agora Excavations P16755, P 18555, P 9973, P 9950.

policies. Since this was not the original intention, the process fell into disuse.

Citizens and Metics

What it was to be an Athenian citizen became much clearer as a result of Cleisthenes' reforms. Formally, a man (only men were full citizens) was enrolled at the age of eighteen into his hereditary deme—that is, where his ancestor had been enrolled at the time of the reforms, whether or not he himself still lived there. From the moment of registration onward, provided he was also acknowledged by his phratry (a kinship group) as the legitimate son of his parents, he was a citizen of Athens. Over the decades following the institution of this practice, it became quite common to identify a person by his deme, not just his father—as, for instance, *Sōkratēs Sōphroniskou Alōpekēthen*, Socrates, the son of Sophroniscus, from the deme Alopece.

Before long, the distinction between full citizen inhabitants of Attica and resident foreigners, or metics (*metoikoi*, "immigrants"), became more fully developed. Metics had fewer rights and occupied a kind of intermediate position between slaves and citizens (so that, in Athens at any rate, freed slaves gained metic status, and a lot of metics were in fact freed slaves rather than immigrants). If they stayed in Athens longer than a month, they had to register as resident foreigners. Their residence had to be sponsored by a citizen "protector" or "patron," who might also have had to represent them in court, if the occasion arose. Metics were not allowed to own land (unless granted this as a special privilege), play an active political role, or sit on a jury; unless exempted, they had to pay a special poll tax (twelve drachmas a year for a man, six for a woman); and they were obliged to serve in the military and, if rich, support the state financially.

What was most important to them, however, was that they obtained legal protection:[3]

> As immigrants to this land, we shall be free and inviolate,
> Protected against men's reprisals. No one, whether citizen

3 Aeschylus, *Suppliant Women* 609–614.

> Or foreigner, shall be allowed to seize us. If force is used against us,
> Any of the landowners who fails to help us shall be punished
> With loss of rights, and be driven into exile by the people.

Metics, women, slaves—each was a class apart from full citizens, and while the Athenians, like all ancient Greeks, were intensely aware of social status, the dynamic of every city was the outcome of the daily interaction of citizens and noncitizens, not just of citizens alone.

The obligations of citizenship were important. An Athenian citizen was expected to obey the laws and be useful to the community; in fact, all Greek states, but especially democracies, absolutely depended on the involvement of their citizens in political life. In Athens, after the age of eighteen, a citizen would participate in the civic religious rites that kept the gods smiling on the city, and after the age of twenty could attend and address meetings of the Assembly. At thirty he could serve as a juror in the law courts and on the Council, and could stand for any of the public offices. He could own property in Attica (though citizenship in Athens did not depend on it), and if there were any handouts he could receive them. He was expected (until the 460s) to serve unpaid in the army or navy, and, if rich, to use his wealth for the common good.

The new Athens needed a new heart, and the space cleared and partially developed by the Peisistratids northwest of the Acropolis became the new Agora, replacing an old one to the east of the Acropolis. It was rapidly developed as an administrative area and marketplace. The erection of Antenor's "Harmodius and Aristogeiton" there in the 490s confirmed its status as the heart of the democracy.

The Acropolis was also further developed. Most importantly, the seventh-century temple of Athena Polias was demolished and replaced by what is known as the Old Athena Temple; it and the mid-sixth-century "Bluebeard" temple (named after a surviving character from the temple's pedimental sculptures, now in the Acropolis Museum), each about forty meters long (130 feet), were the most impressive structures up there. Both would soon be destroyed by the Persians, who would also carry off Antenor's statue group.

Democracy came to Athens on the wings of a genuine revolution: if the Athenian people had not made Cleomenes' position in Attica untenable and had not then beaten off his next invasions, Athens might have become a puppet of Sparta. The act of rioting, even if limited to the hoplite class,

was itself an affirmation of the people's right to determine their political future; nothing could more quickly have strengthened and quickened
the incipient democracy. But the fact that democracy took root so quickly
reminds us that Cleisthenes, like all innovators, owed a great deal to past and
current trends. The most important current trend was a greater degree of
egalitarianism throughout the foremost Greek cities. The most important
longer-standing trend was the gradual empowerment and enrichment of
the poorer citizens of Athens since Solon's time. If the Athenian people had
not had a taste of relative freedom, they would not have been inspired to
seize more.

6

Sparta

There are two rather curious impediments to writing an account of early Spartan history—in addition, that is, to the paucity and unreliability of our sources for Archaic history in general. The first arises from the fact that Sparta was, by the Classical period, a somewhat xenophobic society, not an attractive place for foreigners to stay. In fact, from time to time the Spartans expelled foreigners from their territory. As usual, rumor filled the void created by lack of solid information, leaving us with as many exaggerations as hard facts, and rarely any way of telling which is exaggeration and which is fact. For instance, the Spartans were said to weed out unfit and deformed infants and put them to death.[1] But we know that one of the Spartan kings, Agesilaus II, was lame from birth, and he was not put to death as an infant. So probably the Spartans did not practice infanticide—or at least no more than other Greek states—and this was just a rumor.

The second impediment is that the Spartans themselves constantly reinvented aspects of their early history. Most of the literary evidence is tainted by the ideas that, instead of the piecemeal legislation that we have found typical of early Greek states, the Spartan constitution was drafted in its entirety by a single individual, a man called Lycurgus, way back in the mists of time, and had remained in force, unchanging, ever since.

This entire picture, including the person of Lycurgus, might be an invention; at least some of it is demonstrably false. For instance, Lycurgus was said to have banned coined money,[2] but there was no coined money anywhere in the world at the time he is supposed to have lived.

---

1 E.g., Plutarch, *Lycurgus* 16 (written c. 100 CE).
2 Plutarch, *Lycurgus* 9; Crawford/Whitehead no. 53.

Furthermore, even though the Spartans did not mint their own money until early in the third century, other forms of currency were recognized (especially weighed ingots of iron), and of course they must have made use of coined money for international trade and so on. An inscription exists, for instance, from the end of the fifth century, detailing the receipt of money from Sparta's allies.[3] Full Spartan citizens did not sully their hands with moneymaking activities, but that did not mean there was no money circulating in the state.

The idea that the traditional Spartan way included a ban on coined money was most likely invented early in the fourth century, when the state was having to cope for the first time with great wealth, and avarice had become a real social problem. A great debate raged about the issue, and some conservative group in Sparta must have tried to invoke Lycurgus (who was worshipped as a god) for the idea that Sparta should remain austere. It worked: the private possession of coined money (but not its public use) was officially banned for a few decades in the early 300s. But other aspects of the "Lycurgan system" were probably invented even later, during the revolutionary reigns of Agis IV and Cleomenes III in the third century; they too, as we shall see, attributed their reforms to Lycurgus as a way of validating them.

All other evidence suggests that early Sparta was, apart from its exceptional size, a normal Greek polis. It was a center for the manufacture of luxury goods for the internal elite market and for export; it was particularly famous for its ivory carving (the ivory was imported), lead figurines, fine black-figure pottery, and bronzes. More poetry was being crafted in seventh-century Sparta, by both native-born and foreign poets, than anywhere else in Greece at the time. The competitive Spartan elite were importing luxuries from the Near East, making conspicuously valuable dedications in their sanctuaries, forging links with their peers abroad, and entering all the equestrian events at Olympia. But, early in the sixth century, their priorities changed. There was a sharp decline in artistic production, and no literary production at all. The Spartans had set their collective face against such things. Even laws were rarely written up and archived; justice was administered on principle, and the chief guiding principle was the preservation of Spartan society.

---

3 Meiggs/Lewis no. 67 = (translated) Fornara no. 132; Crawford/Whitehead no. 188.

Figure 6.1. Spartan ivory. This striking image of a goddess, perhaps Artemis Orthia, perhaps the Mistress of Animals, was made c. 660 in Sparta. The plaque was originally the catch-plate of a brooch. National Archaeological Museum, Athens, 15511. Photo: Wikimedia.

The Conquest of Messenia

In the middle of the eighth century, a cluster of four villages in the Eurotas River valley of the district of Laconia annexed the territory of a fifth, a short way south. The newly formed statelet of Sparta then followed the pattern typical of prosperous early Greek states by expanding into its hinterland, Laconia, and establishing borders. But Laconia was apparently not enough for them. The First Messenian War (probably more like a series of raids) was over by about 690, though the dates are uncertain, and gained the Spartans southeastern Messenia, the exceptionally rich Pamisus River valley—and even more subjects. Next they tried to challenge Argos for Cynouria, the southeastern coastline of the Peloponnese, especially for the fertile plain at its northern end called Thyreatis. The attempt was sustained for several decades, but Sparta was finally and decisively defeated at the battle of Hysiae in 669, not far southwest of Argos, creating a permanent enmity between them and the Argives. But the Spartans had completed the annexation of Messenia by about 610, as a result of the lengthy Second Messenian War. In territorial terms, Sparta had become by far the largest state in Greece.

With the conquest of Messenia, the Spartans were hugely outnumbered by subjects who had reason to hate them. At the same time, they seemed incapable of getting the better of Argos. Their response presumably took some years to implement, but by the end they had turned themselves into a landowning elite of full-time servants of the community, who underwent a special form of training and adopted a particular lifestyle designed to make them supreme battlefield warriors, capable of keeping their subjects quiescent and enemies at bay. That is why the leisurely habits of earlier times had to be abandoned.

Perioeci and Helots

Spartan subjects fell into two categories. Closest to independence were the inhabitants of the eighty or so outlying towns and villages of Laconia and Messenia, known as the *perioikoi*, "those who live around us." They retained self-government and were personally free, but had no say in policy-making, even though they were required to serve in the army. A Perioecic community was little different from any other Greek town, with the same ranges of wealth and occupations, from hoplites to slaves. Full Spartan citizens, known as Spartiates, did not engage in farming, crafts, or trade. They had serfs for agriculture, but most of the rest of Spartan economic activity was in Perioecic hands.

The rest of the population of Laconia and Messenia was reduced to serfdom. It is not clear why Perioeci remained free while others did not. Perhaps they occupied a higher social rung at the time of the Spartan conquest and were allowed to remain free while their tenants and dependents were not. These serfs were called "helots," which means "captives" or "the conquered," so it seems that they were reduced en masse as a result of conquest.

Gangs of helots worked the farms of their Spartiate masters and were obliged, on pain of death, to hand over 50 percent of the produce to sustain their masters and their families, who lived in Sparta itself, and to allow them to dedicate themselves full time to service to the state. Helots were publicly owned, because only the state could emancipate them, but otherwise were entirely subject to their particular masters. This was not slavery, because they were not bought and sold, and they lived apart from their masters and were allowed a family life and their own culture. There were slaves in Laconia, owned by both Spartiates and Perioeci, but otherwise the Spartans were little involved in the international slave trade, since the helot population was self-perpetuating. Sparta was always closer to self-sufficiency than other states, thanks to its huge territory.

Although Laconian helots generally lived on their masters' estates, their counterparts in Messenia were more likely to be found in nucleated villages. In terms of security, both systems had advantages: dispersed helots would find it hard to organize; nucleated helots were easier to watch. But compliance was won chiefly because, besides having family lives, helots could even make money, since they were obliged to hand only half of their produce over to their masters. In the third century, when there were far fewer masters, and therefore far more well-off helots, Cleomenes III of Sparta raised five hundred talents by offering freedom at five minas a head—so six thousand helots, at least, had considerable wealth to spare. But the same factors that made for compliance also made for rebellion, because they meant that, over time, helots could develop a sense of identity, the prerequisite for rebellion. Nevertheless, helots were not infrequently armed and incorporated into the army, with the state providing their weaponry.

The arming of helots implies that the Spartans thought they had the situation under control, and even that they could expect loyalty. There may have been an implicit threat: their families at home could have been considered hostages for the helots' good behavior while out on campaign. Anyway, it is remarkable that the majority of the helots, those in Messenia, lived on the other side of the Taygetus mountain range from Sparta, where all Spartiates lived; since the Taygetus is one of the more formidable barriers in Greece, the helots were unsupervised except by Perioeci or trustees from their own number. Helots fought alongside their masters because they too were defending their homes, ancestral shrines, and families.

The two major helot rebellions of which we know (one in the mid-460s and the other, the decisive one, in 369) were both prompted by extraordinary circumstances. There probably were more uprisings, but they were small enough to be successfully quelled and successfully kept from the knowledge of outsiders. But the precariousness of Spartan society was underlined by the attempted coup in 399 of a former Spartiate called Cinadon, now demoted to Inferior status, who claimed (before being flogged to death by the authorities) that all non-Spartiates would happily eat the Spartiates, even uncooked.[4]

Helots were kept in fear of their masters. As part of their training, a few twenty-year-old Spartiates (perhaps ten or fifteen in any year), selected from their year-group, were sent out into the Messenian wilderness for a week or two. They were lightly clad and armed only with daggers. They were under orders to stay hidden in the daytime, and after dark to come down from the hills where they were hiding to hunt down helots. The selected young men had been earmarked for greater things, and were to prove their manhood and their absolute loyalty to the state by means of this challenging and brutal ritual. It was a form of initiation; the number of helots killed in this way was not enough to keep the population down— but it was enough to keep them terrified. At the start of every year, war was formally declared by the Spartiates on their helots, so that the killing of a helot would be legitimate and would not pollute the state with wrongly spilled blood.

The *Agōgē*

Absolutely central to Spartan society was its educational system, the *agōgē* or "raising." Uniquely for the Greek world, this was compulsory education: the sons of rich and poor alike were educated—as long as they were Spartiates. The evolution of the *agōgē* is impossible to recover. It is never

---

4   Xenophon, *Hellenica* 3.3.6; Crawford/Whitehead no. 264.

certainly mentioned in our sources until the third quarter of the fifth century, but it or some elements of it must have been in place earlier, since it fits so well with other Spartan practices.

Up until the age of seven, a Spartiate boy lived at home. Then there were two phases of school education, from seven to twelve and from thirteen to eighteen. There were similarities between the two stages—bonding activities such as dancing, singing, and sports continued throughout, and evening meals were eaten in year-groups—but the second phase was far tougher than the first. Softer aspects such as reading and writing were de-emphasized in favor of more exercise, now including weapons training, tactical exercises, drilling, hunting, and mock battles in which real violence was encouraged and failure was punished. The emphasis now was not just on lessons but on austerity: cold baths, food that was plain at best and came in small portions, reed beds, thin clothing.

The boys lived away from home. Their rations were occasionally made so short that they were encouraged to steal food (but nothing else); they were punished only if they were caught. They were being trained to act as foxes. Their success at this was constantly monitored by their elders, and talented boys, those who conformed exceptionally well to Sparta's values, would find themselves on graduation rewarded with privileges. Rivalry was encouraged, competitiveness was the dominant dynamic, and honor the constant goal. The point of the *agōgē* was not just military training; it also allowed elders to judge who was likely to serve the state well in any capacity.

In order to graduate, fledgling Spartiates had to undergo, or survive, certain rites of passage, which could be extreme. The most famous was a development of the Spartan virtue of stealing: in the sanctuary of Artemis Orthia, the boys had to try to steal as many cheeses as possible from the altar while avoiding whip-wielding adults. Marcus Tullius Cicero, writing in the first century BCE, and Plutarch, 150 or so years later, assure us that in their day boys died during this ritual;[5] but Sparta had by then become a tourist destination, a museum of customs attributed to Lycurgus, and the rite had become a spectator sport, with banked seats from which the audience could watch blood fly. Endurance of the flogging had become the perverted point, and we hear nothing about cheeses.

5 Cicero, *Tusculan Disputations* 2.14; Plutarch, *Lycurgus* 18.

Another institutionalized practice was pederasty: at age thirteen, a Spartiate boy received an older man, aged twenty or so, as a lover. This man was his "inspirer" (the word also connotes "inseminator," the idea being that the older man injected valor into his lover along with his semen), and his job was to teach the boy Spartan virtues. Socially regulated, compulsory pederasty is known from other societies, such as Crete, as an initiatory procedure: the boys are thought to be tamed by their older lover and initiated into adulthood. The boy and his inspirer remained a couple throughout the final phase of the boy's education, and the older man retained some responsibility for his younger charge for the rest of their lives, but it is not clear whether he remained a lover past the boy's graduation. If comparative anthropological data are anything to go by, he did not.

In short, the *agōgē* discouraged affection for anyone or anything except the state itself and a man's fellow Spartiates, with whom he messed, participated in religious rituals, competed, danced, played sports, and suffered. This was where his loyalty lay. A Spartan man got married in his twenties, but did not spend time with his wife until he was discharged from sleeping over at the mess (but not from military call-up) at the age of thirty; even then, the center of his life remained the mess. In any case, being in his twenties, he was involved at the time in a homosexual relationship as an "inspirer" of a teenager. From the middle of the fifth century, faced with declining Spartiate numbers, the Spartans introduced a form of eugenics: an elderly husband could get a younger man to sleep with his wife if he felt that a good soldier would be the result, and brothers might share wives. In the developed system of Classical Sparta, loyalty might not be given in the first instance even to the family.

Having fully absorbed his social conditioning and undergone the same education as his peers, a Spartiate was now one of the *homoioi*, the "Similars." This was reflected in a certain uniformity of appearance and lifestyle, which was reinforced by state-instituted restrictions on the use of wealth. In reality, things were not quite so uniform: men who were considered exceptional were rewarded with higher ranks in the army, as I have already mentioned, and with occasional posts such as ambassadorships. Some messes were more prestigious than others. Three hundred soldiers who had proved their valor formed the kings' lifeguard on the battlefield and policed the city at home; their name, the Knights, reveals their origin as mounted warriors, but by the time we hear about them they were hoplite foot soldiers. There were plenty of inequalities among the *homoioi*, but everyone equally served the state to the best of his abilities.

Messes

From the age of twenty onward, a Spartiate took his evening meal with his messmates. Each mess consisted of only about fifteen men (symposium-size), so there were a lot of them, but the small numbers made for tight bonding, critical for Spartan military success. Graduation from the *agōgē* was the precondition for membership in a mess, which in turn was the criterion of citizenship. In order to retain his membership, a man had to supply his own daily rations from his farm, plus some extra (for the mess servants; for those, like the kings, who were maintained by the state; for guests), and a modest, but not negligible state tax.

At the age of thirty, he was allowed to leave the barracks and spend time at home with his wife, but until he stopped soldiering at the age of sixty he continued to take his evening meals in his mess, and to exercise and dance with his mates. A Spartiate was eligible to attend the assembly at the age of twenty; ten years later, as at Athens, he also became eligible for political office. He was expected to keep fit in case of military need and to play a part in the chastisement of the young that he came across: every senior Spartiate was a surrogate father in this way, tasked with the constant scrutiny to which juniors were subjected.

If a man failed to keep up his contribution to his mess, he was expelled from it and lost his citizenship, to his everlasting shame. He was classified as an "Inferior," along with those who failed to graduate from the *agōgē*, and treated with disdain. A fundamental dynamic of Spartiate society was the struggle to avoid becoming an Inferior. Citizens would always be Similars, because anyone dissimilar was denied citizenship. But it was possible for the son of an Inferior to regain his lost status if a wealthy family agreed to sponsor him through the *agōgē* as their own son's *suntrophos* ("brother by upbringing").

It is curious that, without the cooperation of his helots, a man would not be able to retain membership of a mess and would be demoted. This dependency had to be denied, and Spartiate boys were taught to identify themselves as the very opposites of helots. To this end, helots were sometimes brought into the messes and ritually abused or humiliated. They might be forced to get drunk, for instance, to remind the Spartiates present of the importance of self-discipline, the fundamental Spartan virtue; or they might be made to perform degrading dances, to contrast with the sober dances of the *agōgē*. This too the helots tolerated—until they reached breaking point.

The Great Rhetra

Plutarch of Chaeronea was an essayist and a biographer—very good in both fields—who died around 120 CE. Despite the distance in time and the possibly dilettantish nature of both genres in which he worked, he was a good researcher and often preserves precious information. Thanks to him, we have the authentic wording of a fundamental Spartan constitutional document, which was known as the Great Rhetra ("covenant"). The Spartans themselves, of course, attributed this Rhetra to Lycurgus, and it has commonly been dated to the early seventh century in the belief that their national poet, Tyrtaeus, displayed knowledge of it. But Tyrtaeus' words are not that precise, and the document was probably formulated a few decades later, when the state was beginning to cohere in its enduring form.

The Great Rhetra reads as follows:[6]

> Having founded a sanctuary for Zeus Syllanios and Athena Syllania, having divided the people into tribes and obes, and having established a Council of thirty Elders including the Leaders, perform Apellai season in and season out between Babyka and Knakion and in this way introduce and set aside proposals. To the people belongs the right to give decisive verdicts, but if the people make a crooked decision, the Elders and the Leaders are to be dismissers.

There is much that is obscure about this—perhaps deliberately so, to give it an aura of ancient authority, as though the divine Lycurgus were making a covenant with his people. But basically, in the manner of early legislation from other states, the Rhetra establishes procedure: assemblies are to be held at regular intervals (every Apella, the seventh day in the month, sacred to Apollo) and at a determined place. Proposals are introduced to the assembly by the Council, made up of twenty-eight Elders and the two kings (called here "Leaders").

The assembled Spartiates had the authority to approve decisions, but the Elders could ignore or veto their preferences if they felt they were "crooked." Clearly, the assembly's decision-making power was more or less

---

6 Plutarch, *Lycurgus* 6; Crawford/Whitehead no. 49.

a formality, and this is corroborated by the fact that voting was by shouting, which is a crude and fallible method. They were more like troops being addressed by their officers than political participants. The assembly existed to confer legitimacy on decisions taken elsewhere, by the leading men, and many decisions were taken without its slightest involvement. There were no written laws; as already mentioned, the memory and judgment of the ruling class were considered sufficient.

The Officers of the State

Despite the deliberate archaizing, the Rhetra does not reflect a primitive stage of Spartan politics. Judging by their title, the kings must have wielded greater power in the past, but in the Rhetra they are simply two special members of the Council of Elders (*Gerousia*). The two kings were members of aristocratic families that claimed descent from Heracles via a different twin son, the Agiads from Agis and the Eurypontids from Eurypon. In theory, the latter was the junior branch, but in practice the king who had ruled longest often wielded more authority than the other, whichever house he was from.

As the titular heads of state, the kings were sacred. No one was allowed to touch their persons, and on dying they received ten days of extravagant mourning. All ancient kings based their legitimacy ultimately on their alleged relationship with the gods, and the Spartan kings constantly reinforced their aura of sacredness by their conspicuous role in public ceremonies and sacrifices. Their families were among the wealthiest in Sparta, with landholdings all over Laconia, but their mess was maintained at public expense. They were excused the *agōgē*: in so far as that was a way to test the fitness of a man to be a Spartiate, it was assumed that the kings already had what it took. They were a cut above all the Similars. As figureheads, they tended to become the focus of political factions in Sparta, so that, not uncommonly, the Agiad king and the Eurypontid king might have different political agendas.

By the time we first meet them, the kings were embedded within the collegiate leadership of Sparta. By the Classical period, they were further humbled by having to declare on oath, once a month, that they would obey the laws or risk impeachment and deposition, and their judicial powers had been greatly restricted: they judged only cases concerning heiresses, adoptions, and public roads. Kings came closest to being absolute monarchs at times of war, and they also had the important right to address the assembly first on any issue. With the help of these ceremonial and military powers, along with his wealth, a determined king could accumulate sufficient personal capital and followers to gain authority. Besides, kings were lifelong members of the Council of Elders, and a young king could spend years, even decades, learning how to bend it to his will, while Elders came and went. Some kings—we have already met Cleomenes I, and Agesilaus II will prove to be another—gained and retained sufficient dominance to develop long-term policies.

The Council of Elders consisted of twenty-eight senior men aged over sixty (that is, past military age) and the two kings. Members other than the kings were elected by assembly acclamation when a place fell vacant; membership was for life, and a councilor never had to submit to an audit of his time in office. Only the most powerful and rich seem to have been represented on the council, so membership might have been restricted by some criterion to a select few families. The Council of Elders was an enormously prestigious institution, with real power, based on its preparation of business for the assembly. As the Rhetra shows, it even had the right to override the assembly. It also sat as a court for all the most important cases, including political trials and homicide suits, since it was the only body that had the right to impose severe penalties, such as exile, execution, and demotion to Inferior status.

The Rhetra makes no mention of another office that came to wield great power in Sparta, that of the Ephorate. The failure of the Rhetra to mention the Ephorate was, curiously, the occasion for the original publication of the document early in the fourth century: the exiled Spartan king Pausanias included the Rhetra in a pamphlet in order to prove that the Ephorate postdated the Lycurgan reforms and was therefore un-Spartan— and that therefore he should not have been exiled by a court that included them among the judges. The Spartans responded by claiming that the office began in the eighth century, but that was a fiction.[7] Be that as it may, by the time we first hear about them, in the sixth century, five Ephors ("overseers") were appointed by assembly acclamation for one-year terms from the entire male citizen body. The short list of five candidates, however, was probably drawn up by the Council of Elders, so that the acclamation was a mere formality. A man could be an Ephor only once in his lifetime, so many Spartiates gained political experience in this way. When the five voted, a simple majority won.

7 Plutarch, *Lycurgus* 7.1; Crawford/Whitehead no. 52A.

The office was created to "oversee" the kings, and gained its powers by taking them mainly from the kings. The Ephors' ability to check the kings was symbolized by the fact that they alone were not required to rise to their feet when a king entered the room. By the Classical period, Ephors had wide-ranging powers. Two of them accompanied a king on campaign. At home, they were responsible for internal security, for which they were awarded the power of summary arrest, and could suspend any officer, even a king—and indeed we hear of seven cases of kings being put on trial just between the 490s and 370s. Kings were tried before a jury made up of the Ephors and the Elders, including the other king, and a majority vote won.

The Ephors also had broad judicial responsibilities in civil cases. They were responsible for the *agōgē* and for public finance. They received and negotiated with foreign embassies (and hence were fed at state expense, like the kings), and introduced business arising from these meetings to both the Council of Elders and the assembly, so that they effectively controlled much foreign policy. They convened meetings of the Elders and emergency meetings of the assembly, chaired all assemblies, and issued the orders that executed assembly decisions. In the event of war, they decided which and how many age-groups to call up. But the powers of the Ephorate were limited by the fact that every year it was made up of five different men, so that at times of uncertainty policies could rapidly change, even year by year.

Even if there was a degree of "similarity" among the Spartiates themselves, Sparta was a layered oligarchy. At the top, at least in a titular sense, were the two kings; they were supported by twenty-eight Elders and checked by five Ephors, who kept everyone on the Spartan straight and narrow path. Then there were the thousands of Spartiates who made up the assembly—eight thousand at the start of the fifth century. This was the ruling class, and their subjects were the mass of the disenfranchised or relatively disenfranchised populations of Laconia and Messenia.

The Peloponnesian League

Strengthened by the final acquisition of Messenia and by the new social system, the Spartans went on the warpath. Brimming with confidence, in about 560 they set off north to Tegea, with the intention of turning the Arcadians into helots as well and curbing Argive influence in Arcadia. They were defeated by the Tegeans, however, and this prompted a change of policy, from annexation to subordination by alliance. The change was marked by bringing the bones of Orestes, the legendary Peloponnesian hero (the son of Agamemnon and nephew of the Spartan king Menelaus), from Tegea to Sparta, and the bones of Orestes' son Tisamenus from Achaea to Sparta. The idea was that leadership of the Peloponnese had passed from the others to the Spartans by hereditary right.

By about 550, Sparta had prevailed against the Tegeans and entered into an alliance with them. This seems to have triggered an avalanche, and before long others had agreed to treaties of alliance—above all, Corinth, Elis, Sicyon, Megara, and Epidaurus. The smaller states needed protection, the larger ones the knowledge that their oligarchies would have Spartan support. As the strongest state, Sparta would be the leader of the alliance. The deal was that, in return for Spartan backing for their regimes, they would supply troops for use against external enemies or helots. From 382, however, by which time the hiring of mercenaries was common, they were allowed to supply money in lieu of men, at a rate of three obols for one hoplite or two light-armed soldiers.

The Peloponnesian League, as we call it today, started as a fairly loose arrangement, but this became unsatisfactory from the Spartan point of view, since their so-called friends were not above disobeying Spartan orders or fighting one another. So, seizing opportunities as they arose, they gradually tightened things up until the oath sworn by members of the league obliged them to follow the lead of the Spartans, but the Spartans did not have the same obligation.[8] Each of the member states had an alliance with Sparta, but not with other member states. This left all the league's foreign policy in Spartan hands, although the allies were otherwise self-governing. Only the Spartans could call meetings of the League Congress, but the fact that each member state had a single vote in Congress meant that the vote could go against them.

The league came close enough to uniting the Peloponnese that members felt themselves to be part not just of a distinct geographical entity, but also of a distinct political entity, with its own interests and identity. The chief holdouts from the league, preventing the Spartans from turning the Peloponnese into a federal state, were Argos, the old enemy, and the Achaeans. In 546, the Spartans had another go at taking Cynouria from the Argives; this time they won, and gained much of the southeast coast of the Peloponnese and

8 E.g. Xenophon, *Hellenica* 2.2.20.

the island of Cythera. This was a severe defeat for Argos, which had long been an aggressive and expansive state, and the once-great city took a back seat in Peloponnesian affairs for quite a while afterwards. Its decline was hastened by a further defeat at Spartan hands in 494, in the battle of Sepeia, near Tiryns. Argive losses this time were so devastating that afterwards they had to enfranchise members of their subject populations, just to remain viable as a state.

Cleomenes I, ascending to the Agiad throne of Sparta in 520 or thereabouts, was committed to this policy of Spartan expansion. From early in his reign, he began to target Athens. In 519 the Boeotian town of Plataea approached Sparta for an alliance, since they did not want to get sucked into the orbit of Thebes, which was forming its Boeotian neighbors into a confederacy under its leadership. Cleomenes cunningly refused the alliance and told the Plataeans to ally themselves with Athens instead—which was, of course, far closer. An alliance was duly concluded between the Plataeans and the Athenians—and forever afterwards, unless really drastic circumstances overrode it, the fundamental attitude of the Thebans toward Athens (and vice versa) was one of hostility. Cleomenes had cleverly set two of the most powerful Greek states against each other.

By the time of the Persian invasion in 480, then, the Spartans, with their Peloponnesian allies, were by far the most powerful state in Greece; they had a good battlefield record and were known as professional and disciplined soldiers. They were the natural choice to lead the resistance against the invader.

7

Greek Religion

Although each community developed its own festivals and calendar of sacrifices, although each community was its own religious authority with no higher body set over it, and although different gods and cults were prominent in different communities, it still makes sense to talk of "Greek religion." Here again the Greeks were one and many. By the historical era, much the same set of gods was worshipped with much the same set of practices. There were local differences, but any inhabitant of any Greek state would be able to comprehend and engage emotionally with acts of worship in another community.

Mainstream Greek religion was always a matter of public action as much as it was of faith or belief. There was no sacred text to whose provisions one had to adhere (though early poets were regarded as authorities), no commandments or creed in which one had to believe in order to be "orthodox," no Church to coordinate practice and develop doctrine. Religion was largely a matter of the appropriate performance of ritual. A great deal of religious practice was an obligation one assumed as a member of some community—the state, deme, tribe, regiment, family.

But ritual also rested on a bedrock of beliefs: that the gods exist, that they take thought for us, and that they know more and are more powerful than us. Since belief in the gods was fundamental, atheism and agnosticism, in senses of the words that we would recognize today, were possible positions. They were rare, however; Greek religion was never under any kind of threat from within. The very first attested expression of agnosticism, by the fifth-century philosopher Protagoras of Abdera, is still the best (if somewhat pompous): "Where the gods are concerned, I am not in a position to ascertain that they exist, or that they do not exist. There are substantial impediments to such knowledge: the obscurity of the matter and the shortness of human life."[1] The statement needs no comment, beyond saying that permission to question even firmly held beliefs is one of the most precious legacies passed down to us by the Greeks.

Religion was everywhere; "All things are full of gods," said Thales of Miletus.[2] There was, literally, no significant aspect of one's life that did not have a religious dimension; every meal and every battle and every meeting of a political assembly began with sacrifice and prayer. Then there were sanctuaries, shrines, and sacred objects and places all over the urban and rural landscapes, sometimes in prominent positions, sometimes tucked into the neighborhood. But the pervasiveness of religion extended well beyond these concrete tokens of worship: the gods could appear in different guises, and therefore one might at any moment meet a manifestation of a deity. The gods performed major, public epiphanies once in a while, such as appearing in support of an army in battle, but they could also appear to individuals. It could not have been an ordinary woman of Argos who managed to kill King Pyrrhus of Epirus; she must have been Demeter at the time.[3] If you found a woman sexy, she was, albeit temporarily, an incarnation of Aphrodite. In the biblical Acts of the Apostles, the Lycaonians took St. Paul to be Hermes, for his eloquence, and his companion Barnabas to be Zeus.[4]

The Gods

Greek religion was polytheistic; as in Hinduism today, there were many gods and goddesses, major and minor. Not every deity was worshipped in every state, and not every individual worshipped every deity. In Athens, there were hundreds of cults; it was simply impossible for any single person, however pious, to take part in them all. Polytheism is flexible: if you pray for a while to one deity and nothing happens, you try another one—while making sure not to disrespect any of them. In this way, every individual had his or her personal pantheon. Nor are polytheistic gods jealous, so that there was room for the introduction of new gods into any pantheon, public or private, and for resident foreigners to worship in their own ways.

---

1 Protagoras, F 4 Diels/Kranz.
2 Aristotle, *On the Soul* 411a8.
3 Pausanias, *Description of Greece* 1.13.7–8.
4 Acts of the Apostles 14:8–18.

Figure 7.1. Zeus (or Poseidon). No one quite knows whether this famous bronze statue represents Zeus (hurling a thunderbolt) or Poseidon (wielding a trident). It dates from c. 460, and is somewhat over lifesize. National Archaeological Museum, Athens, X 15161. Photo © Scala / Art Resource, NY.

The Greek gods were thoroughly and regularly pictured in human shape; we hear of gods washing, walking, eating, drinking, sweating, being wounded, and making love. This aspect of Greek religion came under criticism, with Xenophanes of Colophon claiming in the sixth century that men had erroneously made the gods in their own image.[5] It would be

5 Xenophanes F 11, 14–16, 23–26 Diels/Kranz.

wrong, however, to dismiss Greek religious thought as immature. They did not really think that the gods looked like us. Zeus took on human form to impregnate mortal Semele with Dionysus, but when she asked to see him as he was, the sight blasted her to death. When the Greeks portrayed their gods as young and attractive, it was not so much that they thought that they looked like young, attractive human beings as that youth and beauty were qualities that evoked or represented the divine. In many sanctuaries there existed, alongside anthropomorphic statues, older, nonrepresentational statues of the gods: the original cult statue of Hera at the Samos Heraion, for instance, was just a plank of wood with some significant markings. Describing the gods in human terms was, as it always is, a way to make it easier to relate to them.

Many of the Classical Greek gods were also known to the Mycenaeans; there was considerable continuity. By the end of the Archaic period, rationalization had whittled the major gods, who were sometimes imagined as living on the top of Mount Olympus, down to twelve. The number is first attested in the Altar of the Twelve Gods set up in Athens in 522/1. The main deity in the Olympian pantheon was Zeus, the sky and weather god—a version of the old Indo-European sky god Dyaus Pitar (compare the Roman Jupiter). He and his brothers, Poseidon and Hades, divided the three parts of the world between them. Zeus got the sky, Hades the underworld, and Poseidon the surface of the earth, so that he was the god of the sea, but also of earthquakes. The sky is broad and encompassing, and so Zeus was the father and ruler of gods and men. Even Poseidon was thought to live on Olympus with him, though Hades was confined to the underworld. Zeus' wife was Hera, goddess of marriage and childbirth; she shared the latter domain with Apollo's twin, the virgin Artemis, who was also the goddess of hunting and wilderness, and hence her temples tended to be remote from, or on the margins of, human settlements.

Athena, born from Zeus' head, was the goddess of craft and warfare, and was also commonly the protectress of cities. Her approach to warfare was calculating, as distinct from that of Ares, who was the god of warlike frenzy, a useful passion in the kind of hand-to-hand combat in which men of old were engaged. In myth, then, Ares' lover was Aphrodite, the goddess of feminine beauty and sexual passion. Aphrodite was actually the wife of Hephaestus, the lame dwarf-god of metallurgy and volcanoes. Apollo was the god of prophecy and disease/healing, the link being that he suddenly takes hold of a person, but he was also the ever-youthful god of music and culture. Hermes was the messenger of the gods, in charge of travelers, communication, thievery, and magic; the crossing of boundaries is perhaps the common core. Demeter was the goddess of cereal crops and of human and animal fertility. The lists of the canonical Twelve Olympian Gods usually also included Hestia, the goddess of hearth and home.

But although in the myths each of these twelve gods was single, in practice they were multiple, because they had many cult names ("names of invocation" in Greek), each with a different form of worship. There was Zeus the Savior, Zeus of the Hearth, Zeus of the Hilltops, Zeus the Kindly, Zeus the Protector of Stores, and so on. At low-lying, humid Olympia there was Zeus the Averter of Flies. Every major god simultaneously had both local and pan-Hellenic dimensions. The multiplicity of deities made it easy for the Greeks to comprehend other polytheistic systems as well: they simply identified Egyptian Isis with Demeter, for instance, or Phoenician Melkart with Heracles.

Chief among the gods excluded from the Olympian list (though he sometimes replaced Hestia on it) was Dionysus, god of misrule, altered states of consciousness (especially when induced by wine), and patron of dance and drama—a god, despite having a mortal mother. But there were others: Heracles, son of Zeus (but also of a mortal father), lived on Olympus after he had become a god; the Muses dwelt there too. There was Korē or Persephone (the daughter of Demeter and wife of Hades), Pan (a lusty, partly bestial nature god, and the cause of "panic" in goats and men), Asclepius the healer (at whose temples the afflicted came to sleep, and the god revealed their cures in their dreams), the witch Hecate, and countless Nymphs. Earth, Sun, and Moon were deities. There were personifications such as Fortune, Fear, Democracy, Health, and Peace.

As well as gods there were *daimones*, good and bad spirits who intervened in human affairs, reclassified by later Christians as evil "demons." Finally, there were "heroes," who received local worship at their tombs. They had been founders of cities, or men (more rarely women) who had been so outstandingly good at something in their lifetimes, often athletics or war, that they seemed more than human; in a few cases, heroes were former full deities who had been downgraded as the Olympian gods rose to prominence. Taken all in all, the natures, functions, names, and characteristics of the Greek gods and demigods constitute a serious attempt to explain the nature of the universe, seen as a place of power, and all that it contains.

Negotiating with the Gods

The chief means of communicating with the gods were offerings and prayer. Offerings—sacrifices and libations—might be made just as a way of honoring a god, but they were often based on reciprocity: either you were giving to the gods in expectation of a return from them in the future, or you were repaying them for their goodwill. Pure devotion—worshipping a deity out of love—was not a common Greek sentiment.

Animal victims ranged from a bull ox down to a hen or a pigeon. Sacrifices were not tidy—blood was shed and tended to get everywhere, not just in the catching bowl, as the creature resisted its fate; then the corpse was carved up, if it was a large animal, and burned on the fire, sending the offering up as smoke to the gods and cooking the meat for human consumption. The most usual sacrificial victims at public temples were cattle, sheep, goats, and pigs. But these were expensive sacrifices for special occasions; daily domestic offerings involved tossing a bun, perhaps, or a honeycomb, or a handful of grain or frankincense onto the hearth, or pouring a libation at an ancestor's tomb. As Hesiod said:[6]

> Sacrifice to the immortal gods as your means allow
> With holiness and purity, and burn the glistening thigh-bones.
> And at other times propitiate them with libations and offerings,
> Both when you go to bed and when the sacred light appears,
> That their hearts and spirits may be kindly toward you.

In a blood sacrifice, the gods received the inedible bits—the fat and the thigh-bones, the gall bladder and the tail—while humans ate the meat and the edible innards. This seemed strange even to the Greeks, and they explained it by means of a story about an original trick played on the gods by the Titan Prometheus, the fundamental Greek culture hero. Occasionally, the meat was sold by the priest to a butcher for the profit of the sanctuary, but it was often eaten on the spot; many temples had cooking and dining facilities.

Other offerings included first fruits—some of your harvest, or your catch of fish, or whatever it might be, on the understanding that since the gods

---

6 Hesiod, *Works and Days* 336–340.

Figure 7.2. A sacrifice. This fifth-century red-figure vase shows all the essential ingredients of a sacrifice in a compact image. The man is putting offal on the altar for the gods, while the boy behind him is roasting spitted meat for human consumption and the boy to the right of the altar is pouring a libation. Musée du Louvre, Paris, G496. Photo © RMN-Grand Palais / Art Resource, NY.

had given they deserved a portion in return. Whereas blood sacrifices took place at an altar, a first-fruit offering might be left in a sacred place, sunk in a lake, or placed on a table in the temple. Votive offerings were made in consequence of a vow: "If I have a good harvest, I'll sacrifice a piglet to Demeter." Much of the Greek material on display in museums around the world consists of former votive offerings that have been preserved in their sanctuaries. A portion, usually one-tenth, of the booty taken in war was expected to be given to the gods, and this was one way in which sanctuaries such as Olympia and Delphi became hugely wealthy. Girls gave their play-things before they got married, artisans the worn-out tools of their trade, soldiers their swords and shields. Teenagers cut off locks of their hair and gave that piece of themselves to the gods in return for protection in adult life.

Libations and sacrifices were usually accompanied by prayers; music might be played and incense burned, on the understanding that what was

pleasing to humans might be pleasing to gods as well. Prayers could also
be offered up at any time. It is not misleading to think of prayer in ancient
Greece much as we do today, except that if a Greek accompanied his prayer
by a ritual gesture, he would be likely to stand or kneel with arms raised
(straight, or crooked at the elbow), and the prayer was spoken or mur-
mured aloud. Gods were addressed humbly, and in an elaborate prayer one
rehearsed a number of their titles, out of politeness and a natural concern to
make sure one got their attention. You would also mention the deity's obligation to you: you have been a loyal devotee, with a good record of copious
sacrifices, and you expect him or her to answer your prayer in return. The
gods were not always reasonable, but in your dealings with them you acted
as though they might be.

Rituals of purification accompanied most Greek sacral acts. Water was the
main means of purification, with sprinkling more likely than full washing.
Fumigation was occasionally used to cleanse a room. Blood was sometimes
used as a purificatory agent; before the opening of the Assembly in Athens,
for instance, officials carried piglets around, cut their throats, and sprayed
the blood over the seats and the members of the presiding committee. On
the sacred island of Delos, piglet blood was regularly sprinkled around the
margins of the entire island to keep it pure. The practice attracted the scorn
of the prophet–philosopher Heraclitus of Ephesus: "They vainly purify
themselves with blood when they are defiled with it, as though someone
who has stepped into mud were to use mud to wash himself." He added that
praying to a statue was as inane or insane as talking to a house.[7]

Divination

Divination was an important feature of Greek religion. Signs could be
solicited—by looking, for instance, for marks on the liver of a sacrificial
victim—or unsolicited, like the sudden sneeze of a passerby or the pattern
of a bird of prey's flight. Randomness was one way in which the gods drew
mortals' attention to something potentially important. Uncanniness was
another—if, for instance, sweat dripped from a statue. Every lucid dream
was a message from the gods:[8]

---

7   Heraclitus, F 5 Diels/Kranz (late sixth/early fifth century).
8   Xenophon, *Anabasis* 3.1.11.

When at last Xenophon did fall briefly asleep, he had a dream in which thunder rumbled and lightning struck his family home and brilliantly illuminated it all. He woke up terrified. From one point of view, he was inclined to put a positive interpretation on the dream, since a great light from Zeus had appeared in the midst of trouble and danger; but from another point of view he found it alarming.

The problem was interpreting the signs. For this, one might turn to a *mantis*, a seer or diviner. He (female *manteis* were rarer) might be a figure of some standing in the community, perhaps even in the permanent employ of the state or attached to an army. Army seers played a very important part in campaigns, and often had delicate relationships with their commanding officers. Since they were known to be fallible, the final decision was made by the general—most famously by Homer's Hector, the prince of Troy: "One omen is best: to fight in defense of the fatherland."[9]

Many seers were itinerant, however, moving from town to town. They could interpret signs, perform purificatory rituals or sacrifices, and write curses for jealous lovers and worried litigants; they could advise the community how to purge an epidemic or a private client how to make a success of his marriage or business venture. A seer usually claimed to be employing divinely inspired intuition (the word *mantis* is related to *mania*), but some common kinds of divination, such as the examination of livers, were capable of being written up in the form of guidelines. We even hear of a man with no training in seercraft who started practicing as a professional just because he inherited a seer's notebooks.[10]

Since the dead were often the source of the kinds of problems seers were called on to solve, they were experts in how the living should appease the dead. Some practiced necromancy, the summoning of the dead to prophesy or yield up information, as, most famously, in the eleventh book of Homer's *Odyssey*. Although astrology became popular in Greece later, in the Hellenistic period, and although by the Classical period thinkers show awareness of at least some aspects of Babylonian astrological theory, it seems not to have been one of the tools employed by Classical seers. They were more likely to be consulted over an uncanny astronomical phenomenon, such as an eclipse or a shooting star.

9 Homer, *Iliad* 12.243.
10 Isocrates 19.5–6 (*Aegineticus*).

Figure 7.3. Model liver in bronze. This third-century curiosity comes from
Etruria in Italy rather than Greece, but it reflects Mediterranean-wide divinatory
practices. A liver was thought to consist of a number of different areas, each
relating to a different aspect of life; the diviner looked for anything unusual
in a given area and made his interpretation accordingly. Museo Archeologico,
Florence. Photo: Wikimedia.

Clearly, a seer operated in ways that we would call magical. A magi-
cian harnesses occult forces in an attempt to bring about a change in this
world, as a curse is supposed to stir the dead to harm an enemy (and so
Greek curses were buried along with fresh corpses). Magical practices
pervaded Greek religion, but the Greeks expressed distaste for many of
the practices of seers, calling them witchcraft or sorcery—an attempt,
perhaps, to sweep them under the carpet. The fact remained that many in
the Greek world made use of magicians and magical practices.

Consulting a seer at one of the internationally famous oracles was a
major event in a state's or individual's life. The most famous oracles in
the Greek world were at Cumae in southern Italy (Apollo), at Dodona in
northwest Greece (Zeus), at Didyma near Miletus (Apollo), at Claros near
Colophon (Apollo), at Olympia in the Peloponnese (Zeus), and at Delphi
in central Greece (Apollo). It was usually women who spoke for the god,
such as the Pythia at Delphi or the Sibyl at Cumae; their minds were
supposedly more enterable than men's. No drugs or fumes were involved:

the attribution of the prophetess's possession to fumes emerging from subterranean regions was an attempt, started by the Greeks themselves,[11] to rationalize what was happening at Delphi. Of course there are fissures in the rock, but they were covered up when the temple was built. In any case, the Delphians would not have depended on the possibility that sufficient fumes would be produced on any given day for the Pythia to do her work, and even if there were fumes, they would be ineffectively dispelled in the open air. In all the sites we know of, all around the Mediterranean, the prophesying priest or priestess simply went into a light trance, so that she was disassociated from her normal mental state and could contact another layer of her mind. The phenomenon of "channeling," popular in New Age circles in the 1980s, at least showed us how easy this can be for some people.

At Delphi, questions came in two forms: they either required a simple "yes" or "no" response (and in that case a jar with black and white pebbles might be used, or some such device), or they required more complex answers. Questions requiring only a yes-or-no answer could perhaps be handed in on other days, but for more complex questions oracles opened only on specified days of the month. In the Classical period, the Delphic oracle was open only once a month. The queues were such that one of the ways in which the Delphians rewarded benefactors was by giving them the right to move up to the front.

Individuals consulted oracles about a range of personal issues. States consulted oracles when they were planning to found an overseas colony, go to war, make peace, introduce the worship of a new deity or hero, or rid themselves of a drought—these kinds of issues. But there was no obligation to consult an oracle, and in the vast majority of cases no consultation took place. Perhaps the solution was simple or the questioner had no need to shift responsibility for his actions on to a higher authority; perhaps he was economizing, since consultation of a famous oracle such as Delphi was expensive; perhaps the matter was too urgent for there to be time to travel all the way to Delphi or wherever. Questions about foreign policy always greatly outnumbered those concerning internal politics and legislation. In the fourth century, once the Greeks were bound

11 Diodorus of Sicily, *Library of History* 16.26 (first century BCE).

by common peace treaties and more closely unified, state consultation of Delphi dropped off dramatically.

The very act of consultation more or less committed one to agreeing with the oracle's decision. Oracles were consulted, then, so that the state or individual could have the reassurance of knowing that they had the god on their side; it was a way to manage risk and uncertainty, and to gain a weapon with which to quell objections. But sometimes the oracle's answer came in the form of a riddle, as a way of forcing clients to come up with their own interpretation and choice of action. When the Athenians were told by the Pythia in 480 that they would be safe from the Persians if they stayed behind "a wall of wood," they had to decide which wall this was: the old wooden wall of the Acropolis or the metaphorical wooden wall of the fleet.[12]

Civic and Personal Religion

But if, in the civilized communities of Greece, magical practices were marginalized, as they are nowadays, or were safely incorporated within normal religious practice (as they also are nowadays), that was because it was the powers-that-be in any given state who decided what was central and what was marginal. By the historical period, the state was greatly involved in its citizens' religious lives. Lacking a Church, some organizing hand was required, and the state supplied it; presumably, before the emergence of the city-state, individual members of the elite had done the job, in their capacity as priests.

State authorities decided what counted as orthodox and heterodox, and punished transgressors; they decided whether to allow the worship of a new, foreign deity; they arranged for the funding of some festivals by wealthy citizens and funded others themselves; they controlled the sacred treasuries; they filled vacancies in some priesthoods; they authorized the construction and approved the design of sacred buildings; they chose the delegates to accompany the sacrifices they provided for international festivals; they chose the delegates for the amphictyonies of which they were members; they decided when and on what issues oracles were to be consulted; officers of the state performed sacrifices on behalf of the general population.

12 Herodotus, *Histories* 7.142–143.

Many of us today feel that our religious lives are no concern of the state, and we would be disturbed and offended if the state were involved to any significant degree. But perhaps this is because our religions tend to be otherworldly. Greek religion was this-worldly. That is, rather than trying to save a person's soul for the afterlife or the next incarnation, Greeks were concerned with improving things in this world. Religion therefore overlapped the sphere of politics and fell into the domain of the civic authorities. We are used to the separation of Church and State, but the idea was first mooted in the seventeenth century, by the philosopher John Locke; it was unthinkable to the Greeks, who had no Church, only the State.

In any case, there remained opportunities for personal choice. From a modern perspective, it seems remarkable that Greek religion, in its dominant civic and publicly financed form, was more or less uninterested in the souls of its practitioners—in their moral improvement or their status in the afterlife. The basic conception of the soul, throughout the periods covered in this book, is found as early as Homer. In this conception, the soul was a kind of memory of the living person, which after death lived a half-life in the underworld. The soul was closely connected with breath, so that on death it left the body with the last breath or even through a gaping wound, and flitted "gibbering like a bat" down to the underworld.[13] But not everyone died; exceptional men and women were granted eternal life-after-death in the Elysian Fields, a kind of paradise. The worst criminals were thrown into Tartarus, a bronze dungeon in the depths of Hades' kingdom, for eternal exemplary torture.

But if a man did want to improve his soul—perhaps he adhered to the minority view that the soul was the true self, and was the immortal and reincarnating part of a person—there were possibilities. The most esoteric was to become an Orphic, a follower of the teachings and practices ascribed to the legendary musician Orpheus. Orphism was widespread around the Greek Mediterranean, but far from mainstream. It consisted of a set of practices that were supposed to allow the soul to retain or recover consciousness after death, so that it could navigate its way through the underworld and consciously choose a better future.

Another option was more mainstream. Here and there in the Greek world were sanctuaries specializing in *mustēria*, "mystery" cults; the Greek

13 Homer, *Odyssey* 24.5–6.

word implies no more than that they were cults into which one had to be initiated. The two most famous such sanctuaries were that of Demeter and Persephone at Eleusis, in Athenian territory, and that of the Great Gods on the island of Samothrace in the northern Aegean. The rites as they existed in Classical times probably took shape in the sixth century in Eleusis and the fifth on Samothrace, though some form of worship had been going on in both places for a long time—on Samothrace since Neolithic times. Both cults continued until well into the Common Era. The Samothracian cult flourished especially from the late fourth to the second centuries under the patronage of the Macedonian royal family (who wanted a religious center in the north to rival Delphi, Eleusis, and Olympia), and then of the Macedonian dynasties that ruled the great kingdoms of the Hellenistic period, especially the Ptolemies of Egypt.

There were other mysteries, but we know less about them; most were local, a few international like those of Eleusis and Samothrace. Not that we know a great deal about what went on at Eleusis or Samothrace either: initiates were sworn to secrecy and kept their promises. But it is clear that the Eleusinian rites had the ability to manipulate the emotions of the celebrants, moving them from great fear to great joy—perhaps as in the famous myth that accompanied and somehow underpinned the rituals, in which Demeter mourned her lost daughter and rejoiced when at last she was found.[14] Although initiates were not allowed to talk about the details, they could express the profundity of the experience; word of mouth did its work, and over the centuries hundreds of thousands, from all over the Mediterranean, chose to take part, for the startling experience it provided and for its promise of agricultural prosperity in this life and a happier lot in the afterlife.

We know even less about the mysteries of Samothrace than we do those of Eleusis. The sanctuary was sacred to gods known to noninitiates as the Great Gods, though initiates may have known their names; there were probably three of them—a pair of male deities and a single female. The benefit of initiation was said to be safety at sea, but since few initiates were regular sailors, a storm-tossed sea was presumably an allegory of the human condition. It seems safe to conclude that, as at Eleusis, the manipulation of

---

14 See the "Homeric" *Hymn to Demeter* (first half of the sixth century).

emotions played a large part, so that initiates would be left with a sense of a calmer future.

Priests and Temples

Since Greek religion was largely nondogmatic, there was no professional priesthood as we understand it. Although priests and priestesses did perform sacrifices (particularly when a group, such as the community as a whole, had commissioned the sacrifice), any individual could do so on his own behalf, and could pray, pour libations, and so on. Usually, the senior member of a sacrificial party would do the honors. Usually, only a man did the shedding of the blood, while the women present played on the emotions with a kind of cross between a chant and a scream.

So far from requiring a vocation (as in Christianity), in Greece many priesthoods were positions that were passed down within a single aristocratic family or group of families, or were sold by the state, and in democratic states such as Athens some priesthoods (and other religious posts) were assigned by lot from a short list of volunteers. There was no special rite of ordination; the only training was taking advice from a predecessor. Sometimes for no more than a year, and intermittently within that year, a priest or priestess (it usually depended on the gender of the deity) administered the sanctuary along with his or her staff, looked after the cult statue and the temple's finances and treasures, advised worshippers on procedure (for instance, on how to achieve ritual purity before entering the sanctuary), prayed and sacrificed for the welfare of the community, pronounced curses where necessary, presided over the worship at the sanctuary, and played a glorious role in the deity's main festival. He or she was restricted to just the one temple: a Poseidon expert was not considered also to be an Apollo expert. In return for this work, a priest received a portion of meat from every sacrifice, as well as some of the first fruits, and he might also be given the right to sell the hides after a sacrifice. He was unlikely to make money from the job, however, and priests were invariably members of the privileged class who did it out of devotion and for the prestige. It helped them maintain their position as leaders of the community.

Little happened inside most temples. Congregation took place outside, around the altar (often a mound of turf or a slab of natural rock), which was generally placed in front of—that is, usually, to the east of—the temple. Temples were houses for gods, not places of congregation and worship; the word for temple, *naos*, means "dwelling-place." The famous Athenian Parthenon is "the chamber of the Virgin Goddess." As dwelling-places, temples often contained a statue of the deity, and they were also storehouses for the god's valuables, gifted to him in the form of dedications.

Sacrifices provided the gods' food and libations their drink, and many cult statues had special clothes which were ceremoniously washed and re-presented at regular intervals. Slaves, tied to the temple, looked after its grounds and farmed its estates. Valuables were as safe there as anywhere: temple walls were thick and made of stone (unlike house walls, where only the foundations were stone), doors and gates were lockable, and the precious goods were further protected by fear of divine wrath. Every sanctuary was *asulon*. The word designates a place where seizure of goods or persons is forbidden (it is the origin of our word "asylum"), so they were places where

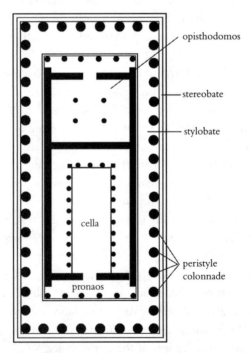

Figure 7.4. Temple ground plan. This plan is of the famous Athenian Parthenon, and is fairly typical. Nearly all Greek temples are oriented with the doorways to the east, so that the cella, which contained the cult statue, received as much light as possible. The other rooms and areas were used chiefly for the storage of valuable dedications. Image: Wikimedia.

people, even slaves in some instances, could go and find refuge from their pursuers, and where travelers could spend an untroubled night.

The Festival of Dionysus at Athens

Greek civic calendars were punctuated by sacrificial festivals. Classical Athens reputedly had more than anywhere else, and several of them occupied a number of days. Many of them involved a procession with the sacrificial animals, the cult statue of the deity, and other sacred or symbolic artifacts; the city, divided into actors and spectators by the procession, was reunited by the sacrifice and communal feasting that followed. Many festivals involved hymn-singing and dancing; several involved at least some of the celebrants staying up all night; several included entertainment, especially athletic, musical, choral, and dramatic contests. Some were just for men, some just for women, but the greatest involved the whole community, including metics and children. Festivals were, apart from anything else, opportunities for a break from work, and they tended to be more joyous than solemn. The Greeks had no weekends, so a holy day was literally a holiday. "A life without festivals," according to the philosopher Democritus of Abdera, "is a long road without inns."[15]

There was no such thing as a typical festival. I have chosen to give a brief description of the City Dionysia at Athens because our evidence for it is good; because it was the most expensive festival in the Athenian calendar, and so tells us something about the uses to which they chose to put public money; and because it was the main festival at which Athenian dramatists displayed their work.

The ninth month of the Athenian year, Elaphebolion (March/April), was dominated by the four days of the City Dionysia—so called to distinguish it from an "Agrarian" counterpart, a one-day winter festival which was celebrated in a number of the larger demes in Attica. At some point toward the end of the sixth century, perhaps at the instigation of the Peisistratids, but probably a bit later, the traditional celebrations involving a procession with phallic poles and a sacrifice were hugely expanded and enhanced, until, without losing their carnivalesque atmosphere, they began to include the performance of plays and choral singing. These were escapist fantasies, and Dionysus was the god of liberation.

---

15 Democritus, F 230 Diels/Kranz (late fifth century).

Part of the southeastern slope of the Acropolis, overlooking the sanctuary of Dionysus, was developed as a theater. In the fifth century, probably only the bottom few rows had seats for dignitaries, while the rest was banked turf; contractors supplied wooden seating in return for a portion of the gate. The theater had a capacity of perhaps six thousand, which was increased in the second half of the fourth century to fifteen thousand or more. The audience was made up of men and boys, certainly, but it is very unclear whether women attended; probably they did, in small numbers, but were seated separately.

By the Hellenistic period, every Greek or hellenized town had a theater; it was as essential to Greek life as an agora and a gymnasium. Anyone who has visited any of the larger theaters, such as the one at Epidaurus, will have been impressed by its sheer size. The *orchēstra* alone—the "dancing-ground" in front of the stage, where the chorus performed—could be up to twenty meters (twenty-two yards) in diameter, which means that even the nearest spectators, in the privileged front-row seats, were already a long way from the stage. It was some compensation that the acoustics in many of the theaters were amazingly good, but, even so, if you were in one of the back rows, fifty meters or more from the stage, the actors would have appeared very small. Acting was therefore very stylized: actors wore masks, made large gestures, and projected their voices. In Athens, prizes were introduced for actors in 449, with the judges paying attention above all to delivery. The mouthpieces of the masks the actors wore were designed to amplify their voices.

Tragedy and Comedy

Drama, expressed in verse, probably developed out of the performance of song and dance during earlier Dionysian festivals—comedy from those that occupied a vulgar register and tragedy from the more elevated kind. The word "tragedy" originally meant "goat song," and that might make sense in the context of a sacrifice; "comedy" might mean "revel song" or "village song." But all early developments are lost: the earliest tragedy to survive (Aeschylus' *Persians* of 472) dates from well after the institution of the festival, and the first complete comedy is Aristophanes' *The Acharnians*, produced in 425, though comedies had been included in the festival since 486. As well as three tragedies, perhaps forming a trilogy, each tragedian also wrote a single satyr-play (in which the chorus consisted of satyrs, lusty followers of Dionysus), which was based, even more loosely than the tragedies, on a mythological story, and was put on after the tragedies as light relief.

At the Dionysia—uniquely to democratic Athens—the plays were entries in a competition; there were judges present, one from each tribe, and it was their job to pick the two winners, one tragedian (out of three) and one comedian (out of five, later three). The first prize was simply prestige. All the playwrights' and producers' efforts, then, were spent on plays that, as far as anyone knew, would be performed once and once only. But repeat performances did take place: the best of the plays were popular outside Athens as well, and in 386 the revival of old plays was introduced as a noncompetitive element in the festival.

The only writer of early comedies some of whose works survive in their entirety is the great Aristophanes; we have eleven of his forty or so plays, and many fragments, some extensive, from his pen and others. The most striking aspect of Old Comedy (as the first phase, down to about 400, is known) is its freedom. First, it had freedom of plot: the playwright made up his own story and set it in contemporary times or in a fantasy-land, rather than in historical or legendary times. The second main freedom was freedom of expression. Some of the characters were well-known figures, especially politicians, either thinly disguised or not at all. They and the other contemporaries referred to in the plays were slandered from all directions. Clearly, there were few or no laws in Athens covering defamation; occasional attempts to impose restrictions were temporarily dictated by circumstances such as war and were not particularly successful. Equally clearly, there was no censorship, since slang, vulgarities, and obscene and lavatorial jokes abound. The actors were costumed so as to be the opposite of the ideal youth: they wore grotesque masks and costumes, padded at belly and rump, with outsized leather phalluses attached.

The three great Athenian tragedians some of whose works survive are Aeschylus, Sophocles, and Euripides. Aeschylus lived from about 525 until 456, and we have six or seven of his eighty plays. Sophocles was born in the 490s and Euripides in the 480s, but both died in 406. We have seven of Sophocles' 124 plays, and seventeen or eighteen of about ninety by Euripides. And, apart from fragments, that is all—unless one of the plays attributed to Euripides (*Rhesus*) is in fact from an anonymous fourth-century pen. Otherwise, the three tragedians' many contemporaries and successors are little more than names attached to a few meager fragments or a bare list of titles.

By the middle of the fifth century, by which time drama had become more or less fixed in form, there could be many nonspeaking characters on the stage, but no more than three had lines. Apart from the actors, there was a chorus of between twelve and twenty-four dancers, who were visible in the *orchēstra* usually from start to finish of the play. The chorus-leader often had a speaking part, and partook minimally in the action of the play, but the chorus's main role was, by means of dance and often poignantly beautiful verse, both allusive and elusive, to comment on what was happening in the play—to give the mythological and ethical background. They were not professional dancers, but (like the actors too, at first) ordinary Athenian citizens who had volunteered for the privilege. And it was a real privilege, since chorus-members were exempt from military service while in training. Adding the choruses of fifty men and fifty boys from each tribe who took part in the choral contest to those involved in the production of the dramas, well over a thousand Athenian citizens were actively involved in the festival every year. And this was not the only dramatic festival; there was also the Lenaea, in the winter (our January), at which, by the last third of the fifth century, further tragedies and comedies were displayed.

The effect on the audience of a tragedy, appropriate for an offering to Dionysus, was supposed to be emotional release. There will be a conflict—of some god against a human being, or between two or more humans. The main character must take a stand on some issue, so that his or her downfall does not come out of the blue. The characters invariably display for us human frailty, and that is their only flaw. And since we are human, that is how their suffering affects us. Not all Greek tragedies have *Hamlet*-type endings in which everybody dies. Sophocles' last play, for instance, *Oedipus at Colonus* (produced posthumously in 401), is a powerful and moving drama, but you would not call it a "tragedy" in the modern sense of the term.

Drama and Society

But there was more to tragedy than immediately meets the eye. For much of the Classical period, drama was still for the elite and sub-elite, or at least for those who felt they could afford the entrance tickets, which were introduced by the mid-410s at the latest. The dramatists, who like all poets considered themselves educators, took on the advisory role performed in earlier centuries by the lyric poets. Rarely were so many influential Athenians in one place together; it was a good opportunity for playwrights not just to raise the kinds of universal questions with which tragedy was directly involved, but also to shed oblique light on contemporary social and political issues, and to reveal some of their complexities.

A debate was a formal part of many plays, so this was a great opportunity for the writers to present views for the audience to reflect on as though they were attending a meeting of some fictional Assembly. About sixty lines of Euripides' *Suppliant Women*, for instance, are devoted to an argument about the advantages and disadvantages of democracy versus monarchy (with the Athenian monarch Theseus championing democracy!). Aristophanes' *Clouds* has a hilarious debate between characters representing traditional thinking and the New Thought, the new modes of thinking and arguing that had become fashionable among the privileged young of Athens.

The last tragedy to have dealt with a piece of real history was Aeschylus' *Persians* in 472 (until the resurrection of historical dramas in the Hellenistic period), and the obliqueness of the tragedians' references to the present was therefore due to the fact that their plays were set in the legendary past, a time of heroes such as Theseus. Still, there is little oblique about Euripides' *Trojan Women*, a heart-rending portrayal of wartime suffering, written in 415, a few months after the Athenians had sacked the island of Melos as savagely as the legendary Greeks had sacked Troy; whether or not Euripides was intending to comment on the Melian affair, people in the audience will have taken the play that way. Interstate relations are prominent in all those plays, such as Aeschylus' *Seven against Thebes*, that involve warfare or the threat of warfare. Then again, all states have to find a balance between individual freedom and conformity, and this was a common tragic plot: the potential for social disruption and even tragedy if the claims of an individual household clash with those of the state is one of the themes of both Aeschylus' *Oresteia* trilogy and Sophocles' *Antigone*. Clashes between citizens and noncitizens are frequent in plays such as Euripides' *Andromache*. Not a few plays, starting with Aeschylus' *Suppliant Women*, produced around 465, at the height of the Athenian leadership of a huge Aegean alliance, revolve around the issue of the protection of the weak.

In short, every tragedy would have reminded at least some members of the audience of at least some issues of concern to the Athenian state, or indeed to any other state. For the plays were staged in other cities, and even at the Athenian Dionysia there were non-Athenians in the audience, resident foreigners and visiting dignitaries. Hence quite a few of the plays are explicitly or implicitly pan-Hellenic in flavor: in Aeschylus' *Persians*, for instance, the Athenians battle the Persians, but are clearly meant to stand for the Greeks as a whole. Countless times in the plays, non-Greek barbarians are held up for inspection or ridicule.

By contrast with the obliqueness of most tragedies, Aristophanic comedy was often blatantly political, in the sense that it held up for ridicule the behavior of contemporary leaders and addressed contemporary issues such as war and peace. The overall tone of Old Comedy is conservative: characters miss the "good old days" before democracy ran wild, charge the Athenian people with being good-hearted but easily duped, criticize contemporary politicians, and ridicule advanced thinkers—all with the aim of raising a laugh. But comedy soon lost its sting; by the end of the fifth century, a gentler comedy of manners was beginning to take over, focused on the household rather than the public life of the city. Apart from anything else, it made it easier for plays to be exported, since an Athenian political setting was irrelevant abroad.

Drama was one of Athens' great gifts to the wider Greek world, and hence to the European tradition, but what it has become should not blind us to its origins. A visit to the theater was not the commonplace event that a visit to the cinema is for us today. Greek drama was not available on a daily basis, but only as part of a religious festival. It was a special occasion, and an emotional high point of the year. The plays were performed to delight the gods as well as to entertain and educate human beings.

8

The Persian Wars

In 549 the Persians (from Persis, now the province of Fars in Iran) under their dynamic king Cyrus the Great rose up against the main Near Eastern power, the Medes, who had in their turn engineered the collapse of the Assyrian Empire just sixty or so years earlier. Within a few years of conquering Media, Cyrus had also taken over the empire of King Croesus of Lydia, which included as tributaries the Eastern Greek cities on the coastline of Anatolia, and some of the Aegean islands. All of them were forced into submission, except for Miletus, which managed to retain the same favorable terms that it had enjoyed under Lydian rule.

In 539 Cyrus annexed Babylon (and freed the Jews from their almost-fifty-year exile), and in 525 Cyrus' son, Cambyses, gained Egypt. All of the main Near Eastern powers had fallen to the Persians within twenty-five years; nothing similar would be seen again until the expedition of Alexander the Great or the Arab conquests of the seventh century CE. Thus was founded the Achaemenid Empire, named for the putative ancestor of Cyrus and his successors. In 517 Darius, who had seized the throne five years earlier, added Samos and more of the Aegean islands, and then Cyrenaica (northeast Libya, in modern terms). In 513 he invaded Europe and occupied Thrace up to the river Strymon, though he was frustrated by the Scythians to the north of the Black Sea. In 512 Macedon too submitted in the required Persian fashion, by offering the king's envoys earth and water. The Persian Empire was larger even than the future Roman Empire; it covered more than 10 percent of the planet.

The Greeks suddenly found themselves within and on the borders of the largest, wealthiest, and most aggressive state in the world, with a population of perhaps forty million souls, and capable of drawing on troops and revenue from Thrace to Afghanistan and from Georgia to Egypt. The story of the clash of cultures was brilliantly told by Herodotus of Halicarnassus, one of the literary geniuses of antiquity. He was writing in the 430s and 420s, but he had traveled extensively and had spoken to people who remembered the Persian Wars.

The Ionian Rebellion

In 507, threatened by the Spartans (pp. 89–90), some Athenians traveled east, to Sardis in Lydia, to ask Artaphrenes, the Persian satrap, for an alliance with his brother, Darius. Whether or not they were an officially sanctioned embassy (whatever that might mean at this time of chaos in Athens), they must have known that the Persians would offer military assistance only if Athens agreed to become a vassal state. And that is indeed what Artaphrenes demanded, prompted no doubt by the exiled Athenian tyrant Hippias, who was living in Sardis. The envoys agreed to Artaphrenes' terms.

As we have seen, however, the Athenians took care of their problem themselves, and in their new confidence they punished the envoys when they came home and risked the wrath of the Great King by refusing to acknowledge that they were now his vassals. And then they further provoked Darius. In 499 the Ionian Greeks rose up in rebellion against Persian overlordship, and, swayed by their appeal to pan-Ionian sentiment, the Athenians agreed to help. Since the Ionians were prospering under Persian rule, the rebellion seems to have been inspired by ethnic considerations, a sense of Greekness, and the desire for freedom soon spread through western Anatolia and Cyprus. This was the moment when "Greek freedom" became a slogan—one that, as we shall see, became endlessly used and abused over the following decades and centuries.

In fact, Athenian aid was somewhat half-hearted. They committed twenty ships—a good portion of their fleet at the time—and the Eretrians of Euboea, also ethnically Ionian, sent another five, but after the allies were badly defeated at Ephesus in 498, on their way back from a not entirely successful assault on Sardis, the Athenians stayed away. By 494, the rebellion was over; one by one the cities, which never fully united, were besieged and captured, or came to terms. The town of Clazomenae moved to a new location on a small island offshore, but even that was little use. The general collapse was hastened by Samian treachery and Greek naval inexperience in a final sea-battle in 494, off the island of Lade near Miletus—the first sea-battle in Greek history to have involved hundreds of ships.

Miletus fell, at the height of its prosperity, and the city was more or less razed to the ground. Much of its population was killed or sold into slavery or resettled in Mesopotamia (modern Iraq); much of its land was granted to Persian noblemen. The city never fully recovered. The nearby oracular sanctuary of Didyma was devastated too, and fell silent for 160 years. Persian control of the Eastern Greek cities became stricter. The Athenians were being shown what they could expect when the Persians got around to punishing them as well.

Miltiades and Marathon

Miltiades had left Athens in 516 to take charge of his family's interests in the Thracian Chersonese, based in the town of Cardia, and his mini-kingdom came to include the islands of Imbros and Lemnos as well. Only a few years after his arrival, the Persians annexed Thrace, and Miltiades had submitted to them, as other rulers and regimes did throughout the area. But then the Scythians, rampant after their defeat of Darius' invasion of their land, approached in force. Miltiades decided to cut his losses, which must have been considerable (his family had ruled the Chersonese for fifty years), and run. Within a few years of his return, once the Athenians had made sure that he did not aspire to monarchy there as well, he had been elected one of the Generals for 490/89.

Meanwhile, Darius had been planning his attack on Greece. A naval expedition in 492 under Mardonius, simultaneously son-in-law, nephew, and brother-in-law of Darius (Persian dynastic politics were complex), was wrecked off the coast of the Athos peninsula by the meltemi, the recurrent northerly summer gale of the Aegean, with the loss of thousands of lives. Mardonius had been sent west to replace Artaphrenes, disgraced because it was on his watch that the Ionian Rebellion had occurred. The following year, envoys were sent to the major Greek states to demand submission to Persia; in Sparta and Athens they were killed as common criminals—an act, close to sacrilege, that was intended to send a message not just to the Persian king, but also to those in both states who were in favor of coming to terms with the Persians.

The sending of envoys all around Greece suggests that Darius' intention was not merely to punish Athens and Eretria. Why else would he demand northern Greek submission when he was not planning to take his forces there? He would devastate Eretria, but he wanted to occupy Athens and install the now aged Hippias as tyrant, so that he would have Attica as a bridgehead in mainland Greece and a launch point for further conquest. By the summer of 490, with Samos as his headquarters, he had assembled a large fleet and an army of perhaps thirty thousand.

The first part of the mission went well. Eretria was betrayed by the pro-Persian faction within the town, and suffered terribly in the ensuing orgy of destruction. Many Eretrians had fled, but many others were made prisoners and eventually resettled deep in Asia. "Farewell, beloved sea!" they wept, in an epigram attributed to the philosopher Plato.[1] From Euboea, the Persians landed on Attic soil at Marathon—exactly where Hippias had landed as a young man with his father fifty-six years earlier. It was early September 490, and the Persians were only forty kilometers (twenty-four miles) from Athens.

The Athenians dispatched a runner to summon Spartan help, but the famously pious Spartans procrastinated: it was the time of an important religious festival, they said. It would have been more truthful if they had said that there were those in Sparta who were not sure that a rapprochement with Persia was not the way forward. Cleomenes, recently dead by his own hand, and his co-king Damaratus had fallen out over this issue—and indeed Damaratus, exiled by Cleomenes' machinations, was made welcome in the Persian court and would accompany the next Persian invasion of Greece, in 480. Even though these two figureheads had departed—Cleomenes was replaced by his half-brother Leonidas—the same factions remained in Sparta.

The Athenian hoplites were joined by lightly armed slaves and a few hundred more hoplites from Plataea. Despite being outnumbered, Miltiades and his fellow Generals chose to march out against the Persian army. We have no idea why they would do this. Ancient accounts of battles are often little more than literary flourishes, and they omit almost all the information we would like to have; since until well into the Hellenistic period even generals led from the front, no one was in a position to see the whole picture. So the course of the battle of Marathon is mysterious to us. The Persians generally relied on their fearsome and numerous cavalry more than their

---

1 Philostratus, *Life of Apollonius* 1.24 (early third century CE).

Figure 8.1. Greeks vs. Persians. This detail from a red-figure cup of c. 480 (the Edinburgh Cup), by the Triptolemus painter, shows a Greek hoplite vanquishing a fallen Persian soldier. Notice the Persian's exotic clothing, including trousers, which the Greeks thought effeminate. National Museums of Scotland A.1887.213. Photo: Wikimedia.

infantry, whose equipment was inferior to that of the Greeks, yet it seems that the cavalry was scarcely used in the battle. Why not? Perhaps they had changed plan and were embarking them on the ships. We just do not know.

Anyway, the Athenians decisively won the battle; the Greek hoplite phalanx had proved its worth against a foreign foe. The Persians sailed around Cape Sunium and anchored close to Athens a day or two later, perhaps hoping to find the city in the hands of their supporters, but by then the Athenian army had also returned, and the Persians retreated. The next day, the Spartan contingent of (only) two thousand finally reached the stinking battlefield.

The Athenians lost 192 men, while the Persians allegedly lost over six thousand; the ghosts of dead men and horses were said in later years to haunt the battleground.[2] The incredible victory enormously raised

2 Pausanias, *Description of Greece* 1.32.4.

Athenian prestige on the international stage. The spoils were enough to pay for not only Pheidias' colossal, triumphalist bronze statue of Athena Promachos on the Acropolis—Athena as the warrior protectress of the city, so tall that she was a landmark for sailors—but also for the construction of the Athenian treasury at Delphi (to store valuable dedications), and more besides.

Themistocles and the Athenian Navy

Darius deeply resented the ignominy of defeat by a flea-sized state just across his borders, and when he died in 486 he bequeathed the task of conquest to his son, Xerxes. But Xerxes was delayed by more pressing engagements, and only in 483 did work begin on a canal through the Athos peninsula, to avoid the fate of Mardonius' fleet in 492; the canal was about 2,200 meters long (2,400 yards) and wide enough to allow two triremes to row abreast. It would take three years to complete. There were no mechanical diggers; this was spade work. Great stores of grain and salted meat and fish were laid down along the route in Thrace, roads were constructed, and the river Strymon was bridged. All this effort proves that the Persians felt they were coming to stay. The Greeks were to become subjects of the empire.

In the 480s, however, a man had become prominent in Athens who would change the course of its history forever. From the time of Themistocles' appearance in Athenian public life, he was concerned to strengthen and maintain Athens' navy. His first major coup, in 493, was to move the center of Athens' seafaring activities a few kilometers north, from the old harbor of Phalerum, where ships had to be beached, to the Piraeus peninsula, which with three natural harbors (one of them very capacious) was better suited to future requirements and was, in addition, easier to fortify. The work took time, of course—building shipsheds and so on is demanding—but Piraeus was functioning as Athens' port by 480.

Miltiades briefly eclipsed his younger rival, but died in 489 of a gangrenous wound, and Themistocles grew in power and stature through the 480s, by means of holding repeated annual Generalships. He was the first to show the political possibilities of the post, the only high-level position that could be held by the same man over and over again. He saw to the ostracism of his rivals, chiefly on the ground that they were prepared to compromise with the Persians, and avoided being ostracized himself, though a large number of *ostraka* have been found with his name inscribed on them.

In 483 he pushed through a proposal that must have required all his eloquence. A rich new seam of silver was discovered underground at Laurium, the Peisistratid-era surface seam having recently been exhausted, and, following standard practice, the Athenians were inclining to share some two and a half tons of silver out among themselves; it would have amounted to a few weeks' wages for each of the poor. Citing the ongoing friction, occasionally worse, between Athens and Aegina over control of the local sea lanes, Themistocles persuaded them to use the windfall to build up the war fleet. Athens had started to add triremes to its bireme (penteconter) fleet around 515, and by then had seventy ships, but Themistocles arranged for another hundred triremes to be constructed. By the time of the crucial battle of Salamis in 480, Athens was able to launch over two hundred ships with experienced crews. Triremes, faster and more maneuverable, had been invented around 560, probably in Phoenicia; they were adopted by the Samians around 525 and were gradually replacing penteconters all over Greece, in a kind of arms race.

Penteconters were rowed by fifty men (with sails for secondary propulsion) and served both commercial and military purposes, since men sailed equally for trade or piracy. A trireme was a dedicated warship with a crew at its fullest of almost two hundred. The advent of the trireme indicates the transfer of naval authority from ship-owning individuals to the state. A fleet of two hundred triremes required forty thousand men, at a cost of more than ten thousand drachmas a day. In agreeing to Themistocles' plan, the Athenians were committing themselves to regular expenditure of vast amounts of money on warfare—on timber and other materials, and on paying large numbers of men to serve as crews and work in the port facilities. They also had to maintain good relations with places such as Macedon, Thrace, and southern Italy, because Attica itself no longer grew ship-quality timber. In the short term, the decision to turn Athens into a naval power meant that for the second Persian invasion all Athenian manpower was committed to the fleet, with little remaining for the land army. In a nice gesture, Miltiades' son, Cimon, led a group of wealthy young men up to the Acropolis, where they solemnly dedicated the bridles of their horses, as a token that in the coming conflict they would be needed not as cavalrymen but as unmounted marines.[3]

The Hellenic League

In the summer of 481, Sparta at last summoned a congress of Greek states. They formed an alliance, which we call the Hellenic League, and bound themselves not just to repel the Persians, but to help one another whatever particular enemy threatened the freedom of the Greek cities. This was a real acknowledgment of a shared Greekness, and a first attempt to unify the Greek states under such a banner. They sent spies to Anatolia to assess Xerxes' strength, and agreed to put aside their mutual and often long-standing differences, such as the conflict between Aegina and Athens. They chose the Spartans, with their military expertise and leadership of the Peloponnesian League, as the overall commanders of the Greek forces. They also threatened to retaliate with ultimate force against any Greek state that "medized," which was the term for collaboration with the Persians (whom the Greeks regarded as just the latest Median dynasty). But since after the war little revenge was taken, the threat was designed more to jolt others into joining before the war than to indicate what they would do after it.

By October, Xerxes had reached Sardis. He sent envoys ahead to receive tokens of submission from the Greek states. Athens and Sparta were excluded from the offer, because of their killing of the envoys in 491. A great many Greek states chose to submit to Persia, which is not too surprising, given that rumor must have been daily exaggerating the number of troops who were on their way, and their ferocity. Herodotus gives the impossible figures of 1,207 warships, 80,000 cavalrymen, and 1,700,000 foot soldiers.[4] Even without exaggeration, with perhaps 150,000 land troops (including 8,000 cavalry) and a navy of about 800 warships, Xerxes' army of conquest was truly formidable.

Thessaly and all of eastern central Greece chose submission, except for Euboea, two Boeotian towns (Thespiae and Athens' satellite, Plataea), Doris, and Phocis. It did not help the Greek cause that the Delphic oracle, convinced that the Persians were going to win, was counseling nonresistance. Sparta was told it would be destroyed, or at the very least lose

3 Plutarch, *Cimon* 5.2–3.
4 Herodotus, *Histories* 7.59–99.

one of its kings (which it did, of course, at Thermopylae); Athens was told to abandon the city and fly to the ends of the earth. The Athenian emissaries to Apollo presented themselves as suppliants in order to get a second opinion from the god, and he told them, famously, that "a wooden wall" would keep them safe. There was a difference of opinion in Athens: some, including the professional seers and interpreters of oracles, held that the reference was to the stockade that had once surrounded the Acropolis, but Themistocles' view prevailed—that the oracle was in fact referring metaphorically to the navy as a wooden wall. The navy would keep them safe.[5]

In the end, only twenty-nine Greek states chose to join Sparta and Athens; as a first attempt to unify the Greeks, the Hellenic League was not a great success. Collaboration with or submission to Persia was not treason or treachery, because there was no Greek nation to betray and pan-Hellenism—a sense of Greek community—was not deeply rooted. In any case, the Persian Empire tolerated cultural diversity, and Xerxes had been making benevolent promises along those lines. So, out of fear and self-interest, the Greeks remained divided. The Greeks in the fantasy of Homer's *Iliad* were more united than the Greeks faced with the reality of the Persian invasion.

The allies invited Argos to join their alliance. The proud Argives refused unless they were given joint command with Sparta, but this was no more than a way to save face, since they were already planning to collaborate with the enemy; Xerxes, claiming legendary Perseus of Argos as the ancestor of his people and therefore kinship, had offered them a prominent role in post-conquest Greece, and they could see the prospect at last of taking the hegemony of the Peloponnese away from Sparta. They stayed aloof from the fighting, but if the Persians had reached the Peloponnese, they would certainly have come in on their side.

Gelon, tyrant of Syracuse and ruler of much of Greek Sicily, also refused to help—but then he knew that the Carthaginians (from modern Tunisia), possibly even at the urging of the Persians, were about to launch a massive invasion of Sicily. The Cretans simply refused, having been warned by Delphi to remain neutral; the Corcyraeans wavered, but eventually withheld their valuable fleet of sixty triremes. In the end, more Greeks fought on the Persian side than fought against it, above all

---

5 Herodotus, *Histories* 7.140–143.

because the Eastern Greeks, as tributaries of the Persians, were required to supply troops.

Thermopylae and Artemisium

In April or May 480 Xerxes was ready to cross over into Europe. He did so with a magnificent gesture, designed, along with the Athos canal, to overawe his opponents. In imitation of Darius' bridging of the Bosporus in 513, for his attack on Thrace and Scythia, Xerxes bridged the Hellespont, which at its narrowest is about 1,500 meters wide, or a bit less than a mile. It was a remarkable feat of engineering, requiring several technical innovations and a great deal of forward planning (it is hard to get hold of mile-long esparto cables at short notice), but the first pair of bridges was destroyed in a storm. Xerxes lashed and shackled the water to bring it to heel, executed the engineers, and the next bridge held. The hulls of 674 warships made up the two pontoons. And so his men reached Europe without getting their feet wet, as though to say that it was all continuous land from Susa to Sparta, and it all belonged to the Great King.

After some hesitation, the Greek allies decided to form two lines of defense: one in the north, directly in the line of the Persian approach, at Thermopylae on land and at sea off Cape Artemisium in northern Euboea, and one to fall back on in the south, around the isthmus to the Peloponnese and the Saronic Gulf. The Greeks sent only a token force to Thermopylae. Once again, the Spartans had or claimed to have religious reasons for not sending their entire army; others too cited local festivals or the imminent Olympic festival as reasons for not sending soldiers. It looks as though Xerxes had timed his arrival well. But the Spartan king Leonidas raised a personal guard of three hundred—the Three Hundred of cinematic fame—and about 3,500 other Peloponnesian troops (including helots, as usual), and they were joined by several thousand more allies. They were enough to hold the narrow pass, if all things were equal, but not enough to inflict a defeat.

At Artemisium, however, the fleet was at strength; perhaps they could check the advance of the Persian forces. Even though quite a few Persian ships had been destroyed during a three-day eruption of the meltemi, the Greeks, with about 275 ships, were still outnumbered. Nevertheless, when battle was joined, they gave as good as they got. But then they learned what had happened at Thermopylae. After three days of fighting, the pass had been turned, the Greek forces (or those that remained, since some had left when defeat became certain) had been annihilated (except that the Theban contingent had surrendered, knowing that their city was poised to medize anyway), and the Persians would soon be marching south. The Greeks disengaged and sailed back to the rendezvous at the island of Salamis, in the Saronic Gulf near Athens. At the pass of Thermopylae, the Spartans later erected a monument with a moving inscription written by the internationally acclaimed poet Simonides of Ceos:[6]

> Go tell the Spartans, thou who passeth by,
> That here obedient to their laws we lie.

The Thespiaeans could have put up an even more poignant memorial; they lost their entire hoplite levy of seven hundred men.

The Battle of Salamis

Nothing could now stop the Persian advance, and the Athenian fleet was used, on Themistocles' orders, to evacuate the city and ferry its inhabitants to safety around the Saronic Gulf. Athenian refugees joined the thousands fleeing the destruction of Thespiae and Plataea, and the devastation of Phocis by another division of the Persian forces. It must have seemed the end of the world: no one knew if he would see his native city again or whether, if they did return, it would be as insignificant members of an increased Persian Empire, slaves (as they saw it) to the Great King. A few hundred diehards remained on the Athenian Acropolis.

Before long, Xerxes' full army entered Attica and his fleet reached Phalerum. The Acropolis, with its fortification walls, proved harder to take than the Persians might have imagined, until some enterprising men scaled one of its undefended faces. The defenders were massacred, the walls toppled, the temples burned to the ground, and their sculptures smashed. The city was put to the torch. The burning of Athens was visible to the Greek forces at Salamis. Many of them, including much of the high command, regarded this as the end of the war on the mainland and were now concerned only

---

6 Herodotus, *Histories* 7.228. The translation is by John Dryden (1631-1700).

to retreat to the Peloponnese and make a last stand there. But Themistocles persuaded them to stay.

The island of Salamis lies deep in the Saronic Gulf, with only two exits out into open water, one to the west of the island and one to the east. One night, Xerxes divided the fleet into two, with each division blocking one of the exits, pinning the Greeks in the water on the eastern side of the island, which had three good anchorages (one is now the largest naval base in Greece). This was an error. Artemisium had shown that the Persian fleet was formidable in open water. Why would Xerxes risk battle in a confined space? He easily outnumbered the 310 Greek ships (most of which were Athenian). His thinking was probably that winter was coming, and he did not want so many thousands of his men lying idle until the next campaigning season. He wanted to end the war, and he arrogantly expected to do so easily.

At dawn, the Greek fleet launched in seeming disarray, with some ships even breaking off north, as if to make for the isthmus. The Persians took the bait and sailed into the narrows; the Greeks backed water to draw them farther in. The tired oarsmen of the Persian ships, who had been up all night struggling to retain formation at the exits, began to lose control in the choppy water. The Greek ships rowed hard into the attack. Many Persian ships immediately chose flight back to Phalerum, while the Greeks encircled and mopped up the rest. In the end, the battle was one-sided: over the course of a long day, the Persians lost over two hundred ships, while the Greeks lost about forty and more than made up for those losses, in terms of hulls, by the numbers they captured.

Xerxes, who had watched the battle and the massacre of his floundering troops from a high point in Attica, waited a few days, undecided whether to continue. But without control of the sea, it would be hard for him to keep the army supplied. It was late in the season, and one morning the Greeks received the news that the enemy had left for winter quarters in Thessaly.

The Persians Repulsed

Salamis returned control of the Aegean to the Greeks, but the Persians were still formidable on land, and perhaps eighty thousand men stayed behind under Mardonius to continue the campaign the following year, while Xerxes took the rest of his men home. Mardonius spent the winter sounding out potential allies in southern Greece and even trying to turn the Athenians with the offer of a privileged position in the future Persian satrapy of Greece. Some in Athens were tempted, but the offer was refused.

In the spring of 479, Mardonius marched south from Thessaly, recruiting more troops on the way from friendly Greek states, and in June Athens was once again evacuated, occupied, and put to the torch. Mardonius then withdrew from Attica and settled in Boeotia, not far from Plataea, preferring this as a battleground. After much prevarication, the Spartans sent north a huge force of combined Spartiates, Peloponnesians, Perioeci, and helots, commanded by Pausanias, regent for the young Agiad king Pleistarchus, the son of Leonidas, the king who had fallen at Thermopylae. He was joined by a substantial Athenian contingent, and they marched to face the Persians.

Each side chose terrain suitable for their own army—the Greeks privileging their hoplites with a gentle downward slope, the Persians their cavalry (which had been entirely useless the previous year) with open ground—and waited, hoping to tempt the other side off its strong point. The waiting game continued as the month of August progressed, and troops continued to flood into the Greek camp, until they numbered perhaps sixty thousand, but then Mardonius went on the offensive. He was finding it hard to supply his enormous army and needed to wrap things up.

His cavalry succeeded in blocking the Greeks' best water source and capturing a train of five hundred mules laden with supplies; over the following days no further supplies reached the Greek camp. Foreseeing future difficulties, Pausanias decided to move closer to Plataea, where there was water and provisions stood a better chance of getting through. But when the Greeks began this maneuver—could this have been Pausanias' plan?—Mardonius took the withdrawal to be a disorderly retreat and gave the order for a general attack.

Believing victory to be theirs, the Persian army streamed after the Greeks, in some disarray themselves and in terrain where their cavalry would be of limited use. The Greeks turned to face their foes. The battle—which was more like several different battles, as the Greek contingents were separated—was extremely hard and closely fought. But the Persian infantry was no match for their hoplite opponents, and when Mardonius himself was killed, even the cavalry fled the field. In the rout, the Greeks slaughtered thousands.

Meanwhile, the Greek fleet was at Delos, waiting to take on the Persian fleet, stationed at Samos. Once they had been joined by the Athenians, who turned the soldiers who had fought at Plataea into sailors, the Eurypontid king of Sparta, Leotychidas II, set sail for Samos, only to find that a reduced Persian force—the Phoenicians having sailed home—had retreated across the strait to the coast below Mount Mycale and built a strong stockade around their position. They had also disarmed their Greek allies, who they feared would change sides.

Leotychidas came to land beyond the Persian position and led the Spartan contingent in a circuitous route to come at them from behind, while the Athenians, led by Xanthippus, led the frontal attack. This direct attack was so successful—aided by the fact that the Samians did indeed snatch up weapons inside the camp and fight for the Greek cause—that there was little for Leotychidas to do when he arrived apart from take prisoners and cut down a few last resisters.

For the time being, at least, the Persian invasion had been repulsed. The final battle had been nicely coordinated between the Athenians and the Spartans, and it suggested a new direction for the Greeks. Over the course of the past two years, Athens had proved itself the equal of Sparta and had risen to international prominence. A new era now seemed possible, in which others would line up behind the leaders of the resistance. Under the dual leadership of Sparta and Athens, all Greeks everywhere could unite and cooperate. Those who entertained this dream were to be sorely disappointed.

9

The Greeks at War

The Greek world was made up of hundreds of independent city-states, often situated quite close to one another and competing for limited resources. Under these circumstances, conflict is inevitable, and it is less surprising that warfare was a wretchedly regular occurrence. The Greeks recognized that peace is or should be the normal condition, but their history is often the history of their wars. A large and ambitious state such as Athens found itself at war, throughout the Classical period, more often than not. Campaigning seasons tended to be short up until the last quarter of the fifth century, but even so war was on everyone's minds, whether they were scheming politicians or fearful mothers.

The Greeks went to war for all the normal reasons: fear, self-interest, greed, vengeance, self-defense, the defense of friends and the oppressed. In the rhetoric about warfare, however, glory and prestige were stressed more than would be usual nowadays. There was, as we shall see, a slightly ritualized aspect to some Greek warfare—though no more than in other premodern forms of warfare—and in addition to the usual material advantages of victory there was also the knowledge that victory moved the winning state up the pecking order, as the loser moved down. The pecking order was established and maintained in many ways: ancient glory, monumental temples, and Olympic victors all counted, for instance, but present power counted most, and that was proved and increased by warfare.

Land Battle

For much of the Archaic period, warfare was not publicly funded, and wars were typically initiated by members of the elite acting as private individuals, or representing the state as Polemarchs. Most fighting was piracy or cross-border raiding, undertaken for profit and occasionally for an extra bit of land. Subjugation of the enemy was rarely the objective. Throughout the seventh and sixth centuries, there were only about a dozen major campaigns. But toward the end of the sixth century, warfare came under state control (it long had been in Sparta), and soon all the great states had the ability to field large numbers of troops.

Hoplites, heavy infantry, were not alone on any Greek battlefield. Lightly clad and lightly armed troops always played a part, and a prominent part in those battles that were not set pieces involving two hoplite phalanxes. In the hoplite era of fifth-century Greece, mobile troops were used chiefly for foraging and the destruction of enemy farmland, but their value on the battlefield began to be rediscovered toward the end of the century. No hoplite could catch them, so they could run up in open order, discharge javelins or stones, and run away again, or fire arrows and slingshot from afar. They were even more effective if the formation they were attacking had been immobilized first by their own heavy infantry. Only in the fourth century, however, were they organized into their own regiments and used regularly for battle, or interspersed within a hoplite phalanx.

There was also little use of cavalry in the Archaic and Classical periods. The terrain of Greece, and the lack of saddles and stirrups, discouraged cavalry engagements, and numbers were usually few, since only the rich could afford horses. The cavalry was the elite branch of the forces, as in all premodern states: think of the *equites* of Rome and the *chevaliers* of France. Athens had organized a substantial cavalry force of 1,200 by the third quarter of the fifth century, but, outside of a few horse-breeding places such as Macedon and Thessaly, that was very unusual. Cavalry was used more for scouting, skirmishing, protection, and pursuit than as a strike force in its own right or in coordination with the infantry; combined cavalry and infantry assaults were an innovation of the fourth century. The basic offensive tactic was to swoop in, discharge javelins, and wheel away to safety—like mounted light-armed troops, though some cavalrymen wore armor. Cataphract cavalry—where the horsemen were covered from head to foot in armor—was an invention of the Hellenistic period, learned from the Persians.

Siege warfare was hampered, until the fourth century, by lack of effective technology. By the middle of the fifth century, attackers knew how to imitate a tortoise and hold a protective shed over their heads, and they knew how to undermine walls, or scale them, or batter them down, but all these tactics were highly dangerous. Direct assault was rare until artillery was invented. Nontorsion artillery (a large crossbow) was first used at the very beginning of the fourth century, and torsion artillery, capable of hurling stones as well as sharp missiles, about fifty years later. Now lofty siege towers could bring powerful weaponry into play, to clear the walls of defenders while ground troops brought up ladders or rams. Fortification design necessarily improved to meet these technological advances, and some towns even changed location to more defensible sites.

Before the fourth century, towns were regularly put under siege, but they were passively blockaded rather than actively attacked, and sieges failed as often as they succeeded. The basic passive technique—enormously time-consuming—was to surround the town with palisades, trenches, and ramparts, so that no one could get out and supplies could not get in, and then just wait for fear, hunger, and thirst to do their business. Besieging port towns was especially difficult, unless one had control of the sea. Throughout Greek history, the most effective method of breaking into a town was to suborn some of the inhabitants and gain entry by treachery. And, given the factionalism of Greek political life, this was often a relatively easy thing to achieve. In the opinion of Philip II of Macedon, any fortress could be taken provided a donkey laden with gold could make its way there, and in the opinion of Aeneas Tacticus, a fourth-century writer on siegecraft, the best defense in a siege was harmony among the citizens.[1]

Hoplites

Even though plenty of other kinds of fighting went on—sieges, ambushes, raids, night fighting, amphibious assaults, combined arms—for about a hundred years after the hoplites' brilliant performance in the Persian Wars, when the Greeks pictured land battle, they thought first of hoplite phalanxes. This was a spectacular form of warfare, involving thousands of soldiers, many of them clad in gleaming bronze, and the Spartans in scarlet cloaks as well. It required incredible courage, because, in order to kill, a hoplite had to risk being killed himself. It therefore gained enormous prestige, and other forms of fighting, mounted or unmounted, that involved long-range weaponry such as arrows, slings, or javelins were considered less glorious.

---

1 Philip: Cicero, *Letters to Atticus* 1.16.12. Aeneas Tacticus, *On Siegecraft* 14.1.

Figure 9.1. Hoplite. This late-sixth-century bronze statuette gives an excellent impression of a hoplite's fighting stance and fearsome appearance. Notice the Boeotian style of shield, which proves that hoplites did not always pack in tight behind big, round shields. Berlin, Staatliche Museen Misc7470. Photo © bpk Bildagentur / Art Resource, NY.

We have already looked at hoplite equipment. The implication of it is that a hoplite phalanx was most effective if the soldiers could stay so tightly packed that their shields overlapped their neighbors, so that the enemy would be faced with an impregnable fence of spear points. The length of the spears (about two meters/6.5 feet) meant that even those of the second rank would be in play. But such tight packing—each man would have to occupy forty-five centimeters (eighteen inches)—is impossible to achieve except when immobile in defense.

A phalanx favored level or undulating terrain, and it is noticeable how many hoplite battles came to be fought in places like Boeotia (the plain there was "the dancing-ground of war," according to Epaminondas of Thebes),[2] but there is no terrain in Boeotia or anywhere else that is so flat and free from obstacles that an advancing phalanx of relatively untrained men could retain a really tight formation. Hoplites often charged over the last stretch of the advance, and that would open up the formation even more, as Thucydides remarked from his own experience.[3] The Spartans were famous for advancing at a constant, measured pace, to the sound of pipes, precisely in order to retain formation; others were not so good at it. Phalanxes were subdivided into smaller tactical units which, to a certain extent, could act independently to counter developing situations, and this too shows that phalanxes were not always supposed to be tightly cohesive.

Hoplites needed a zone in which to fight, to wield their spears (or swords, once spears broke) and move their shields in defense. Overlapping shields would have impeded them. Even doubling the interval, so that the edges of the shields almost touched, would have made little difference. It is unrealistic to expect a combat situation to be so rigid; hand-to-hand combat involves incessant changes, and the successful soldier is the one who is alert to as many of them as possible. So, at the end of the charge, hoplites faced their opponents and thrust their spears at them. They varied between standing sideways on, to get maximum force into their thrusts and maximum protection behind their shields, and standing chest forward when advancing. They stood several feet apart from their neighbors, with room to swing a shield. Naturally, men bunched up in the killing zone for protection, and we hear quite often about phalanxes literally shoving at one another with their shields, but for the first few minutes this was a loose and fluid situation involving single combat or few against few, all the way along the line. After the battle, awards were given for individual valor, proving that hoplites were not just cogs in a machine.

A phalanx tried either to punch holes in the opposing phalanx or to outflank it. The first tactic required a deeper phalanx, with a large number

2 Plutarch, *Moralia* 193e (*Sayings of Kings and Commanders*).
3 Thucydides, *History* 5.70.

of ranks, less space between individual soldiers, and a shorter front, so that it risked being outflanked by its opponents. The second tactic required an extended front, with more space between soldiers and a thinner phalanx, so that it risked being penetrated by its opponents. Phalanxes were regularly deployed eight or more ranks deep. Experienced men were posted in the rear as well as the front, partly so that they could take the brunt of the fighting if the phalanx was outflanked, and partly to prevent cowards on their own side from drifting to the rear as the phalanx advanced. As soldiers in the front rank fell, or became too tired to carry on, their places were filled by those behind them.

The hoplite panoply weighed about twenty-three kilograms (fifty pounds), and even though few soldiers had the full kit, this was an exhausting form of fighting. Armor was fairly effective, but uncomfortable. Many hoplites preferred lighter headgear to a heavy bronze helmet. Felted linen corselets were more common than bronze ones, and tests have shown them to be effective; leather was an alternative material. The neck, thighs, and groin were the most vulnerable parts. Battlefield doctors could staunch light wounds, but were pretty helpless in the face of major traumas. Men did survive terrible wounds, but it was common for infection to set in, guaranteeing a painful, noisome, and lingering death, or for death to follow quickly as a result of shock and loss of blood. Tyrtaeus of Sparta sang of the death of an elderly hoplite, "gasping his brave last in the dust, hands clasping blood-soaked genitals, body stripped of armor."[4]

Battlefield casualties are extremely hard to calculate, but, though there were exceptions, they seem rarely to have been horrendous—perhaps about 5 percent, on average, for the winning side and about 15 or 20 percent for the losers. Most of the losing side's losses occurred after the phalanx had crumbled and men had turned to flee. Flight made a man vulnerable, and in his heavy armor he could be outrun by light-armed troops or horsemen. The first thing a fleeing hoplite did was discard his cumbersome shield: hence the famous instruction of a Spartan mother to her son, to return "either with your shield or on it."[5] But even 5 percent is a grim number for a class of men who were likely to have to repeat the experience the following summer. At that rate, and given that hoplites were liable to

4 Tyrtaeus F 10.23–27 West.
5 Plutarch, *Moralia* 241f (*Sayings of Spartan Women*).

call-up until their sixtieth year (though the likelihood decreased the older a man got), the chances of death in battle for any individual were high.

Phalanx Etiquette

Of course, battlefield massacres occasionally happened. After a battle between the Spartans and Argives in the 390s, for instance, "corpses were heaped up like stacks of corn or piles of firewood."[6] But generally the casualty rate was relatively low. This was due in part to common sense. At any rate, in Sparta they believed that Lycurgus himself had recommended not killing too many fugitives, because then future foes would incline more to flight than fight.[7] The short duration of hoplite battles was another factor. While sometimes armies faced each other for days before making a move, and initial deployment and final pursuit might take hours, the actual clash of phalanxes rarely occupied more than a few hours, and might be over in a few minutes if one side panicked early.

But the relatively low casualty rate was also due to the fact that hoplite battles of Greeks versus Greeks were fought according to certain conventions. I do not mean all the religious rituals that surrounded battle, from consulting an oracle to pre-battle sacrifices: that is just the way the Greeks went about everything. Nor do I mean that, for instance, they usually obeyed truces and avoided killing children or damaging sanctuaries or mutilating the dead; these conventions are common to all humankind.

The most interesting conventions governed engagement and disengagement. Battles began when one side deployed in battle formation. This was the way to issue a challenge, and it was generally taken up, for fear of the shame of refusal, which would move a city down the international pecking order almost as surely as an actual defeat. So the other side then deployed as well, without interference from their enemies, and when they were ready battle was joined. There were of course exceptions to this formal procedure—at the battle of Sepeia in 494, for instance, the Spartans attacked the Argives while they were eating breakfast—but this was unusual.

In a traditional hoplite battle, neither side had reserves, and few fleeing armies ever managed to rally and reform. So the winner was whoever

---

6 Xenophon, *Hellenica* 4.4.12.
7 Plutarch, *Moralia* 228f (*Sayings of Spartans*).

still held the field once the other side had fled, and when the losing commander applied for a truce during which his dead could be collected, that
counted as an official admission of defeat and the battle was over. Both sides
dealt with their dead, and the winners erected a trophy—typically a stake
of wood hung with weaponry taken from the enemy and made to look
vaguely humanoid—and performed a victory sacrifice at the point on the
field where the enemy first turned (the word for "trophy" being cognate
with the word for "turn").

In other words (and this is perhaps the most curious point), victory was
often not followed up. This was not all-out war. Until late in the fifth century,
there was rarely any attempt to pursue the enemy back home, and then to
besiege his town and subjugate the entire state or impose a regime change;
warfare was mostly seasonal, restricted to a few weeks in the early summer.
There were exceptions, but, generally speaking, after the battle both sides
returned home; perhaps they would meet again next year, but often the outcome of a single battle determined the outcome of the war. The winning
state had proved its prowess and gained plunder, and that was enough.

Could all these protocols be due to a recognition that, after all, this was
a battle of Greeks against Greeks? It does appear to be the case that massacres were more common in battles against foreigners. In the fourth century, Plato wrote that Greeks should aim for victory when fighting other
Greeks, and for destruction only when fighting non-Greeks.[8] And, as I have
mentioned, after the Persian Wars the practice of dedicating trophies at pan-
Hellenic sites to commemorate victories over fellow Greeks died down,
possibly by official edict. Probably every battle of Greeks against Greeks was
a switch-point, when soldiers could yield to bloodlust or remember that
they were fighting fellow Greeks.

However, phalanx warfare was not the only form of warfare, and atrocities were more common at sea and after a siege. Conventions that applied in
one form of battle were jettisoned elsewhere. Many is the time we read of
floundering sailors being deliberately drowned, or captured oarsmen having
their right hands cut off, or all the adult males of a town being slaughtered
after its capture, with the rest of the population sold into slavery or abandoned to die. Before a siege, inhabitants were generally offered the chance
to leave with a few possessions; those who stayed were considered fair game.
Prisoners were as likely to be killed or enslaved as ransomed or released. The
treatment of female prisoners may be imagined. Atrocities did not happen

8 Plato, *Menexenus* 242d; see also *Republic* 469e–470a.

every time—far from it—but they could take place when the attackers felt they had particular reasons for revenge, such as that the crew of one of their ships had been murdered, or they had been forced to undertake a long siege, or simply if they had good enough strategic reasons.

Changes in Tactics

The Peloponnesian War (431–404) accelerated trends that were already in motion. This was a new kind of war, not one that could be decided by a single battle. Set-piece battles by mutual consent on suitably level terrain were outnumbered by other forms of engagement, and battles were fought farther away from home than the borderlands. Reserves began to be used. Different terrains brought light-armed troops and cavalry into greater prominence. The hoplite panoply became lighter as mobility came to seem as important as protection.

Armies now did not necessarily return home at the end of the campaigning season, and so the convention arose that land occupied by force, "spear-won" land in the Homeric phrase, belonged by proprietary right to the conquerors, just as any kind of booty did. Garrisoning occupied towns therefore became common. Extended campaigns meant that professionals, mercenaries, began to be used more and more, to prevent the domestic economy from collapsing; citizens could stay home and tend their farms or businesses. By the Hellenistic period, tens of thousands of mercenaries were employed around the Greek world.

Greeks had fought as mercenaries abroad for as far back as the record goes, but now mercenaries began to be used more regularly in Greek wars too. Supplementing citizen troops with mercenaries made it easier for states to fight on more than one front simultaneously; citizens still fought in the fourth century in large numbers, but mercenary contingents were invariably employed as well. Generalship became more than just a matter of deciding where to place your various units in the line. Other states began to take training and drilling as seriously as the Spartans, and in the fourth century several developed standing corps of trained men, of which the most famous was the 300-strong Theban Sacred Band, formed, some said, entirely of homosexual couples, who would never let each other down.[9] Warfare became more professional. Technical treatises were written, of which we have two extant

9 Plutarch, *Pelopidas* 18.1; Crawford/Whitehead no. 271.

from the fourth century: Xenophon's *The Cavalry Commander* and Aeneas Tacticus' *On Siegecraft*.

At the same time, however, warfare became less prestigious—another reason why citizens were increasingly happy to make use of mercenaries and slaves. In the fourth century, long-range weaponry was used far more extensively—the slings, arrows, and javelins wielded by mobile troops, the missiles launched by siege artillery. Less and less was it a matter of face-to-face combat among social equals with the same value system. When Archidamus III (Eurypontid king of Sparta 360–338) first saw an artillery missile, he said: "So that's it for manly courage!"[10]

Naval Warfare

The most important aspect of naval warfare was how much it cost. Leaving aside the substantial startup costs, just paying crews cost a talent per trireme per month, and a sailing season might last for several months. The reason this is important is that it created a vast disparity among the Greek states. The smaller states could not afford war fleets, so they were always outgunned by those that could. And this meant that, from the time of the introduction of the trireme onward, alliances became absolutely and essentially a feature of Greek interstate relations. Smaller states needed the protection of large ones and accepted that their independence might be somewhat compromised.

In a naval context, there was another reason why alliances were important. Even apart from the necessity of havens in bad weather, ancient ships could not stay long at sea. They had to be beached frequently, to forage for supplies (warships had little spare room), to allow the oarsmen to rest, to dry out the insides of the ships, and to kill the teredo "worm" (a kind of boring mollusk). It was essential for a naval power to have allies or at least neutral states around the coastlines.

We cannot be sure that any state had a navy before the middle of the sixth century. What they had was rich men who owned ships that could be requisitioned for military purposes. But then quite a few substantial fleets emerged quite quickly, chiefly in response to the threat of Persia or Carthage. Corinth, Samos, Syracuse, and Athens led the way. After about 540, we hear of an increasing number of sea battles involving Greeks. Before

---

10 Plutarch, *Moralia* 219a (*Sayings of Spartans*).

Figure 9.2. The trireme *Olympias*. This reconstruction of the most famous class of Greek warship, the trireme, was built and tested for seaworthiness in the 1980s in Athens. With a heavy bronze ram, a trireme was essentially a maneuverable ramming machine. Its light weight meant that a trained oar-crew could reach a speed of up to fifteen knots. © RMN–Grand Palais / Art Resource, NY.

that, the main military use of ships had been to transport men to a land battle, with oarsmen doubling as fighters. If such ships met at sea, the fighting imitated a land battle: ships drew as close to one another as they dared and fired arrows and javelins at the enemy, rather than performing the riskier maneuvers required for ramming.

The introduction of the trireme toward the end of the sixth century forced the Greek states to adopt a more professional approach to naval warfare, as we have seen in the case of Themistoclean Athens. Triremes were so superior to penteconters as warships that no state with ambitions could afford to be without them. Crews, two hundred to a ship, were drawn largely from poorer citizens, but also foreigners (the Aegean islands were a good source), slaves, and metics. These made up the 170 rowers (though not every ship went to sea with a full complement, since top speed was necessary only for battle), and then there were the ship's captain, helmsman, and other seamen, and a dozen or so archers and hoplite marines. The marines and those on the upper deck were the elite, and they, along with the upper level of oarsmen, tended to be citizens. Rowing a warship was difficult, dangerous, and squalid. Those on the lowest of the three levels were dripped on by the sweat, if nothing worse, of those above them and their feet were close to the bilge water; they could see nothing, and in battle lived in terror of an enemy ram suddenly crashing through the timbers below them.

In preparation for battle, sails and mast were lowered, so that the ship could rely for maneuverability on its rowers and the deck was cleared for the fighters. Ships usually took up a single line, each side facing the other. The basic tactic was to get into a position to disable an enemy ship by ramming (with or without subsequent boarding by marines) or by breaking its oars and oarsmen. Triremes were highly maneuverable; equipped with bronze rams, they were used rather like guided missiles. A few ships, working together, tried to break through the enemy line, and then they would individually turn and ram the defenseless side or rear of the enemy. This required great skill from the helmsman and oarsmen; for instance, maximum forward effort was required from the oarsmen during a ramming run, but as soon as the ram had struck, they had to back water to prevent the two ships from becoming wedged together. A naval battle often resembled a slow-motion aerial dogfight, as ships tried to ram while avoiding being rammed. Another common tactic—the pirate's favorite, because it preserved cargoes—was for several ships to gang up and harry an enemy vessel onto shore. Because of the numbers—in a battle of three hundred ships, sixty thousand men might be involved—losses in sea battles could be appalling.

Interstate Relations

There were a number of channels of communication between states. From the early sixth century, many states that we know of had at least one *proxenos* resident in other states. For instance, in the mid-fifth century a Spartan called Lichas was the *proxenos* of Argos at Sparta. He was a citizen of Sparta, but he undertook to represent Argive interests. This was a development of the earlier situation when communication between communities was effected by elite individuals who were bound by ties of *xenia* (p. 52); in effect, a *proxenos* was expected to do for a state what a *xenos* had done for individuals. A man was made a *proxenos* by the powers-that-be in the state he was to represent, so it was a way of honoring him (and, by the fourth and third centuries, it had become rather an empty gesture). It was his job to look after visitors from the state he represented, and introduce them to the council or do whatever was needed to make their visit a success. He did not have to be in sympathy with the state he represented.

Proxenia was just one way in which communities declared themselves friends and strengthened their relations. One state might guarantee another certain privileges, of which the most important was the promise not to harm it in any way—that is, granting it *asylia* ("inviolability," an extension of the natural inviolability of temples), a guarantee that none of their citizens would harm it. In the Hellenistic period, two states might even enter into *isopoliteia*, whereby men living in one city could take up citizenship rights in another city, if they chose to move there; even stronger forms of this were *sympoliteia*, when two neighboring states merged their political institutions into one, and *synoikismos*, when two or more communities merged physically as well as constitutionally.

Other channels of communication existed for nonroutine business. If a state had an urgent message to convey to another state, it would send a herald, who was considered to be sacrosanct; instantly identifiable by his special winged staff with its entwined snakes (showing that he was under the protection of Hermes), he was not to be molested in any way. It was his job to deliver a declaration of war, for instance. On the other hand, if there were negotiations to be undertaken or a dignitary to be greeted with gifts and flowery speeches, the state would send an embassy made up of *presbeis*, literally "elders," who were respected, but not strictly sacrosanct. Finally, states might entrust particularly delicate negotiations and mediations, especially those that might end war, to a neutral third party—a suitable individual or another state.

Treaties of friendship and/or alliance followed, usually (up until the fourth century) for a specified period of time:[11]

> This is the covenant between the Eleans and Heraeans. There shall be an alliance for a hundred years, starting with this year. If anything is needed, in word

11 Meiggs/Lewis no. 17 = (translated) Fornara no. 25; Rhodes no. 435; Crawford/Whitehead no. 85 (c. 500 BCE).

or in deed, they shall stand by each other in all matters and especially in war. If they fail to do so they shall pay a talent of silver to Olympian Zeus, to be used in his service.

Like all other ancient Greek contracts, treaties were sealed by solemn oaths. Treaties were typically either both offensive and defensive (that is, the parties swore to have the same friends and enemies), or only defensive, so that it was only if one of the parties was attacked that the other party was required to help. A treaty might treat the parties involved as equals, or subordinate one party to the other by means of obligations. Treaties with kings were made with the king in person, so that every time one died there was a flurry of diplomatic activity from states anxious to renew a pact with his successor.

However much work had gone into hammering out the precise details of the pact, and however strictly the treaty was bound by oaths and the threat of penalties, states invariably anticipated conflict, and many treaties were broken before their expiration date, though a breach was understood to be risky, since it might offend the gods. In short, treaties were considered declarations of intent as much as they were workable agreements. The reason why treaties commonly paired "friendship and alliance" was that the affective relationship of friendship was meant to shore up the legal relationship of alliance and make it more enduring. Claims that the two parties were ancestral kin had the same purpose.

If all these systems for interstate communication seem rather ad hoc, that is because they were. In the days before the existence of an internationally constituted body such as our United Nations, international law was a matter of custom rather than enforcement. In the treaty translated above, for instance, between Elis and Heraea, who—or what, apart from religious scruple—was to see that the fine of a silver talent was paid? There were the unwritten "laws of the Greeks,"[12] largely religious or commonsensical in origin, which urged fairness and restraint from violence in various ways, endorsed the principle of aiding the weak, and even recognized a distinction between ownership of land and its mere possession by conquest—but, unless the offending state was a member of a grand alliance with a council, or unless the Amphictyonic Council chose to get involved (as it occasionally did, if any of its own councilors brought charges), there was no body to enforce respect for these unwritten laws when states chose to ignore them.

12 E.g. Thucydides, *History* 4.97.2–3; Diodorus of Sicily, *Library of History* 19.63.5; Rhodes/Osborne no. 35 (translated, Rhodes no. 479).

That left it up to other states to try to punish the offender in some way—and that of course reintroduced the punishing state's own self-interest. Despite regular reassertions of the principle that disputes should be dissolved by arbitration or mediation rather than by fighting, it was commonly held that not to fight for one's claim was a sign of weakness. Instead of international law, it was generally true in the Greek world that "the strong lay down the law for the weak."[13]

However, even if these unwritten laws were frequently violated or were hard to apply, they did form a bedrock of moral principles which were at least supposed to guide interstate relations. The first of these was reciprocity—that one should repay good with good, but also harm with harm; a fundamental form of interstate relation was the right to reprisal if a state felt it had been harmed by another. Another principle was pan-Hellenism—that one should treat Greeks better than barbarians. Another was that all states, whatever their size, had an equal right to self-determination. But it is impossible to draw up a list of such principles, because the basic idea was that the same moral code that governed relations between citizens of the same state should also govern relations between states. Every Greek state regarded itself, however faintly, as a member of the society of Greek states and was aware of the code that was meant to apply. At every moment in interstate relations there was a fork in the road, and a state could choose cooperation or competition.

13 Demosthenes, 15.29 (*On the Freedom of the Rhodians*).

ACT II

The Classical Period
(479–323)
A Tale, Mainly, of Two Cities

10

The Delian League

By 479 Athens was ready to challenge Sparta for the leadership of Greece. For the next seventy-five years, Greek history is very largely Spartan and Athenian history. They became the focal points, and the history of the Classical period can therefore seem narrower than what came before or what would follow after. Smaller states tended to get drawn into the orbit of one or the other of these two leaders; much the same was happening in Greek Sicily as well, with Syracuse the center there. Smaller states were extras to the lead roles of the major states on the Mediterranean stage.

The Classical period (479–323) is bracketed by two world-changing invasions: the Persian invasions of Greece and Alexander the Great's invasion of Asia—the latter presented as retaliation for the former. Alexander's invasion brought the Achaemenid Empire to an end and the constant possibility of Persian intervention in Greek affairs. Immediately following the Persian Wars, it still might have been possible for the Greeks to unify in the face of the threat from the East, but that did not happen. An account of Greek history in the fifth and fourth centuries is bound to read at times like a litany of inter-Greek warfare. Orators spouted pan-Hellenic sentiments, but the ideals were not deeply enough rooted to overcome the ancient particularism of the Greeks; pan-Hellenism was propaganda rather than practical politics. It is ironic that Athens and Sparta, the two states that were chiefly responsible for repelling the Persians, were also principally to blame for keeping the Greek states disunited and weak, and therefore vulnerable, ultimately, to a second invasion, by the Macedonians. The mainland Greeks had avoided becoming part of the Persian Empire, but in 338 they fell instead under what would become the Macedonian Empire.

The Downfall of Pausanias

In Athens, following the defeat of the Persians, two tendencies emerged. Themistocles championed the idea that Athens should establish itself as the supreme power in Greece and prepare, therefore, for conflict with Sparta. In keeping with this view (and in case of further Persian invasions), he ensured that the city's defensive wall was rebuilt, often with rubble salvaged from the ruins, and that Piraeus was properly fortified. Men, women, and children helped to raise the fortifications in record time. The new wall—frequently

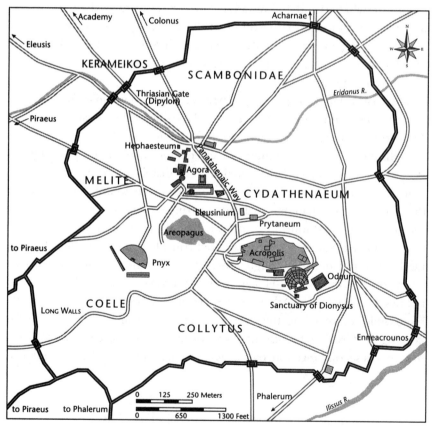

Map 10.1. The Themistoclean Wall, showing the city demes.

repaired, of course—determined the size of the city for almost a thousand years. It was about 6.5 kilometers long (a little over four miles), and the total area enclosed was about four hundred hectares (about 1.5 square miles or a thousand acres); there were suburbs, of course, but the city of Athens was about the size of Golden Gate Park in San Francisco. Sparta protested at the building of the wall; it tried to argue that under its protection no Greek state needed a defensive wall, but Themistocles wanted to see Athens independent.

Cimon, the son of Miltiades, led the other faction. He saw the future of Greece lying in a more pan-Hellenic direction, with Sparta and Athens sharing the leadership. He argued that unless the two worked together, Greece was "lame."[1] This was a critical moment—a switch-point at which Athens could have followed Cimon's lead and the Greeks would have moved toward greater unity. But Cimon was soon thwarted. For the first few months, the Spartans and Athenians did indeed share the task of protecting the Eastern Greek states, which were now in rebellion against Persia, and they made vital gains: by subduing much of Cyprus (no Greek war fleet had ever ventured so far) and retaking Sestus in 479 and Byzantium in 478, they secured the southern and northern approaches to the Aegean. Meanwhile, on the mainland, some of the states that had medized were punished, but care was taken not to make this the kind of crusade that would destabilize Greece. The full punishment of Thebes was delayed, in fact, for almost 150 years.

But Pausanias, the Spartan regent and still the commander-in-chief of the Hellenic League, displayed such arrogance about his role in the war and, based in Byzantium, began to draw close to his supposed enemies to such a degree that the Eastern Greeks could not see him as their savior. When he was recalled to Sparta, they refused his replacement and entrusted themselves to the Athenians. In the background of all this was their anger that, at one point, the Spartans, rightly regarding the Eastern Greek cities as permanently vulnerable, had recommended relocating them elsewhere in the Mediterranean. The Athenian takeover was perhaps inevitable, given the importance of naval strength to the security of the Aegean, but it had come about under circumstances that deeply embarrassed the Spartans.

Pausanias fell due to arrogance, but arrogance was the order of the day. Even though they had long been in contact with foreigners of every stripe, the shock of victory—they had twice defeated the best that the non-Greek

---

1 Plutarch, *Cimon* 16.10.

world could throw against them—left the Greeks supreme and with supremacist attitudes toward all the peoples they called "barbarians," especially the
Persians. The polarity was perpetuated by the Athenians above all, because
they were the ones who were continuing the fight, and so for propaganda
purposes they portrayed the Persians as alien.

Other views of the Persians were current—more nuanced, less prejudiced—
but for a while in the fifth and fourth centuries, a set of stories the Greeks told
themselves portrayed Persians as the physically and mentally weak slaves of a
despotic master, and themselves, by contrast, as tough and free. This was not a
completely black-and-white opposition: both Greeks and Persians had a long
history of learning from the other side, and after the wars not a few Persian
artifacts and clothing styles were adopted by fashionable Greeks. But there was
an underlying assumption on the part of the Greeks of cultural and physical
supremacy. They even found a "scientific" way of explaining this: character is
the product of climate, and the climate in barbarian countries enfeebles them.[2]

In a way, then, even though the Greeks had scarcely united to defeat the
Persians, in the aftermath of victory—once it became clear that the battles of
479 did constitute some kind of victory, or at least a lull in the fighting—the
common enemy brought them closer to a kind of unity, a stronger sense of
Greekness. They imagined the war as a rerun of the Trojan War, when the
Greeks in Homer's poem had been genuinely united. Even though we do
not know how long it lasted or how effective it was, a tribunal was created in the 470s, based for good pan-Hellenic reasons at Olympia, to arbitrate disputes between Greek states before they fell to fighting. In the words
Herodotus puts into Athenian mouths not long before the battle of Plataea:
"We Greeks are in blood and one in language, and we have temples to the
gods and religious rites in common, and a common way of life."[3] This is in
many ways a problematic assertion, but it shows what the Greeks felt, or felt
they should feel, in the face of the enemy.

A Grand Alliance

Early in 477, the Athenians took a great step forward and formed states
all the way around the Aegean and Black Sea coastlines into a military

---

2 Especially pseudo-Hippocrates, *Airs, Waters, Places* 16; Aeschylus, *Suppliant Women* 497–498;
  Aristotle, *Politics* 1327b19–36.
3 Herodotus, *Histories* 8.144.2.

alliance. Unlike the Peloponnesian League, all the members were allied with one another, not just with Athens. As in the Peloponnesian League, only foreign policy was at issue and the allies were otherwise supposed to be self-governing. The purpose of the league was to free those Greeks who remained under Persian sway and to keep them free forever, and to compensate themselves for losses sustained in the war. It was a continuation, then, of the Hellenic League of 481, with the exclusion of the Peloponnesians. There was a league council, chaired always by an Athenian, at which each member state had a single vote. Delegates probably voted in accordance with decisions taken by their home authorities.

Greek wars so far had always been fought on an ad hoc basis, with both funding and men raised when the need arose. The Athenians, seeing no immediate end to the conflict with Persia, and in view of the enormous expenses involved, asked their allies for regular annual tribute. Ironically, the precedent for this was Persian: that was how the Achaemenid Empire was run, with each satrapy assessed at a certain level of tax, which was paid yearly to the king. In the case of the new Greek league, the allies were required either to supply ships and their crews or to contribute money toward the costs of the allied fleet. They were also obliged to supply troops for allied campaigns. Most of the allies, those that were small, chose to provide money rather than ships, so that the allied fleet was in practice largely Athenian. The money was, in effect, protection money: the Athenians were being paid to keep the Aegean safe.

The setup sounds more egalitarian than it was. It was the Athenians who assessed the tribute and provided officers, called *Hellēnotamiai* (Treasurers of the Greek Funds), to manage it; the allies had no direct access to allied funds. It was Athens that led the way in terms of policy, because many of the member states were too small to do anything but follow its lead. And it was Athens that supplied the generals who mustered and led expeditionary forces, and who were elected by and answerable to only the Athenian people. In inscriptions, the league is not referred to as a league of equals, but as "the Athenians and their allies," and even as "the cities which the Athenians control."[4] The Athenians intended, right from the start, to use their leadership of the league to make their city wealthy and powerful.

---

4 "The Athenians and their allies": Meiggs/Lewis no. 40 = (translated) Fornara no. 71; Rhodes no. 360. "The cities which the Athenians control": *IG* i³ 19 or 27.

The level of tribute for the first member states was fixed by the Athenian statesman Aristeides. Since we hear of no complaints—and since Aristeides gained the nickname "the Just"—member states clearly felt they could afford what was asked of them; in many cases, it was probably much the same tribute that they had been paying the Persians. By the time we have evidence, the amounts paid by those who were providing money rather than ships ranged from less than a talent a year to thirty talents for the most prosperous, such as Aegina and Thasos. The league treasury was established on the island of Delos, where league meetings were also to be held, and so the alliance is known nowadays as the Delian League. Delos was chosen not just because it occupied a central position in the Aegean and had a good harbor, but also because it was sacred to Apollo, the father of Ion, the eponymous ancestor of the Ionians, who were early members of the alliance, and whose mother city Athens professed to be. Though many members were not Ionians, the league was the Ionian response to the Dorian Peloponnesian League.

The allies had some early successes, but their goals were set by the Athenians and served Athenian economic interests. It was important to throw the Persian garrison out of Eion in Thrace, but the Athenians immediately occupied it for themselves, to exploit the local timber and mineral resources. Then, in about 475, Cimon attacked the island of Scyros, claiming to act on behalf of the Delphic Amphictyony, which had condemned the islanders for their piracy. He sold many of the inhabitants into slavery, and, continuing the policy begun at Chalcis and Salamis thirty years earlier, brought in Athenian cleruchs to populate the now deserted island. It was certainly no coincidence that the island commanded two naval corridors to Athens, from the Hellespont and from the Thraceward region. Before long, Carystus in the south of Euboea, also critically placed for Athenian shipping, was forced to join the league. Up until then, membership had been voluntary.

An oracle had also instructed Cimon to find on Scyros the skeleton of the Athenian founder hero Theseus, who in legend had died there. And indeed a large skeleton was discovered, perhaps a warrior grave from the Mycenaean period. The bones were conveyed to Athens, where they were reburied in a glorious new tomb and a hero cult was instituted. Theseus had risen from obscurity late in the sixth century when the Peisistratids began to promote him as a hero for all Athenians, and the new democracy used him in the same way, as a symbol of Athenian strength and unity. Images of Theseus proliferated in all artistic media. This was a powerful moment, and Cimon's prestige soared.

By the end of the 470s, Themistocles had fallen victim to an ostracism. Cimon's faction, for whom Persia was the main enemy, not Sparta, was in the ascendant. Themistocles began his exile in Argos, but while he was there the Spartans accused him of having collaborated with the Persians. He was hounded from place to place in Greece, and by 463 had stealthily made his way—no doubt to his enemies' delight—to the Persian court. There was a new king on the throne, Artaxerxes I, and he received Themistocles kindly. The man who had made Athens great by arming it for the fight against the Persians ended his days as an honored guest of the Persian king.

Athenian Leadership of the League

There must have been rumbles of discontent from league members, but Athenian authoritarianism continued unabated. If the Carystians demonstrated that joining the league was not necessarily voluntary, in the early 460s the Naxians discovered that leaving it was not up to them either. They were besieged into rejoining. And the rumbles surely increased in volume after Cimon's stunning success, perhaps in 466. The Persian army and navy were assembling for a fresh offensive at Aspendus, on the Eurymedon in Pamphylia (central southern Turkey today). Cimon caught them unprepared, before the full force had mustered, annihilated their fleet, and decimated the army.

Cities on the southern coastline of Anatolia rushed to join the Delian League, but from another point of view there was considerably less need for the league now that the Persians had been so thoroughly humbled. The next to attempt to secede was Thasos, in 465. The trigger in this case was the Athenian occupation of Eion, which was in Thasian territory. A few years after taking Eion, the Athenians had also tried to establish a colony at Ennea Hodoi (Nine Ways), a few kilometers north of Eion. The settlers had been wiped out by local Thracians, but even the attempt must have worried the Thasians. They had long had a monopoly on trade in the area in timber and minerals; they could not sit by and watch their

economic base being undermined. The Athenians, led by Cimon, demonstrated their determination by devoting three years to the subjection
of the island. The harsh terms imposed when the Thasians capitulated
included the surrender of their fleet to Athens and a large indemnity. And
the Athenians took over all of the mainland territory that had belonged
to Thasos, the resources of which would constitute a considerable boost
to their revenues.

It would not be fair to say that it was now fear of Athens that held the alliance together. New members were joining of their own accord, and on the
whole the Athenians acted with decency toward their allies. At its height,
the league consisted of at least 190 states, but possibly over 300 (small places
were not always listed separately), and while disaffection was depressingly
regular, especially in the late 450s and early 440s, it was never concerted
until toward the end, in the 410s and 400s, by which time the downfall of
the league had become inevitable. And when, for instance, Methone on

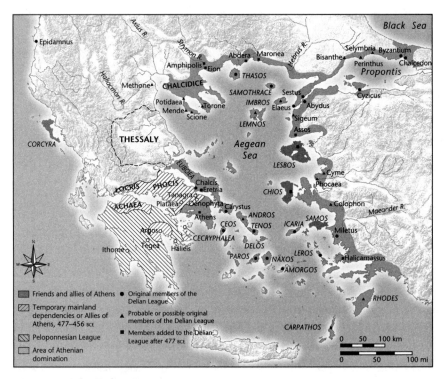

Map 10.2. The Delian League.

the Thermaic Gulf failed to pay its tribute one year, Athens appreciated its special difficulties and tolerated late payment.[5]

But it looks as though the Athenians behaved decently only when their own interests were not threatened. Methone on its own was no threat at all. A door had opened for the Athenians, and wealth and power beyond their dreams beckoned from the other side. The Spartans looked on the Delian League with increasingly justified suspicion. Disturbingly, there had been talk in Sparta of going to help Thasos, but in the event nothing happened, because in 465 a major earthquake and its aftershocks flattened Sparta, with terrible loss of life among the Spartiates, and thousands of helots, along with some Perioeci, seized the opportunity to revolt.

The Third Messenian War occupied all of Sparta's military efforts for some years, up until 460 or even later, since the rebels dug in and were well supplied at Mount Ithome in Messenia. The Spartans were so desperate that they called for help not only from their friends, but even from the Athenians, who were perhaps obliged to help under the terms of the Hellenic League, which still technically existed. A force of Athenians raised by Cimon went there in 462, but after a while the Spartans dismissed them. The Athenians later claimed that this was because the Spartans were unsure whether, as democrats, they might not have sided with the revolting helots. This might make sense if news had reached the Spartans already of the distinctly anti-Spartan mood that had swept Athens in Cimon's absence, but the real reason was probably that the Athenians had been called in as experts at siege warfare, and yet had failed to dislodge the Messenian rebels from Ithome. Tension between the two states increased.

While Cimon was in Sparta with his upper-class volunteers, helping their peers in another state against their underclass, the leading democrat, Ephialtes, son of Sophonides, seized the opportunity to launch his reforms (p. 209). When Cimon returned, he did his best to resist, but earned himself only ostracism. Moreover, the Athenians formed alliances with Sparta's enemies, especially the Thessalians and Argives. This was a disturbing move by Athens, the leader of an anti-Persian league: both the Thessalians and the Argives had medized in the war. Clearly, the Athenians regarded the Hellenic League as defunct, so that new loyalties could replace old ones.

Next, the Athenians managed to exploit friction between Corinth and Megara to detach Megara from the Peloponnesian League. This was a

5 Meiggs/Lewis no. 65 = (translated) Fornara no. 128; Rhodes no. 430.

very valuable prize, since Megara formed an easily defensible land buffer between them and the Peloponnese, and was essential for Spartan communication with Boeotia. The Spartans were too busy with the helot revolt to respond.

The First Peloponnesian War

Warfare was now the only possible outlet for the tension that had built up between the Athenians and the Peloponnesians, and between 461 and 446 there were enough clashes, in enough theaters, for us to include them under a general umbrella and call them the First Peloponnesian War. The immediate triggers were the Megarians' decision to change sides, and the Athenians' Long Walls. These massive walls, begun in the late 460s or early 450s, joined Athens securely (in the days before siege artillery) to the sea, with one leg going down to Phalerum and the other to Piraeus. Each of them was about six kilometers long (almost 3.75 miles), nine meters high (thirty feet), and four or five meters wide at the top (up to sixteen feet). They had only one function: to make it possible for Athens to continue to be supplied by sea if it was blockaded by land. The only candidate for an enemy who would attack them by land was the Peloponnesian League, so no one had any doubt that Athens was positioning itself for the war that would come.

The Athenians continued to pile pressure on Corinth. They took Naupactus, which commanded the entrance to the Gulf of Corinth, from the Western Locrians and populated it with former helots from Messenia, who had been allowed to leave unharmed at the conclusion of the Third Messenian War. They made an alliance with the Achaeans on the south coast of the gulf. They defended Megara against a Corinthian assault in 459, and were simultaneously supporting the Argives in their conflict with Corinth. Next, threatening Corinth's southern approaches, they annexed the island of Aegina. This was not league business (though league troops were used), but just a manifestation of Athenian aggression. As well as ring-fencing Corinth, perhaps with the intention of forcing it and its navy out of the Peloponnesian League, the Athenians' second purpose in the war was to take central Greece for themselves before the Spartans did. In 457, they succeeded in this, when the Athenian General Myronides gained for the Delian League all Phocis and Boeotia except for Thebes.

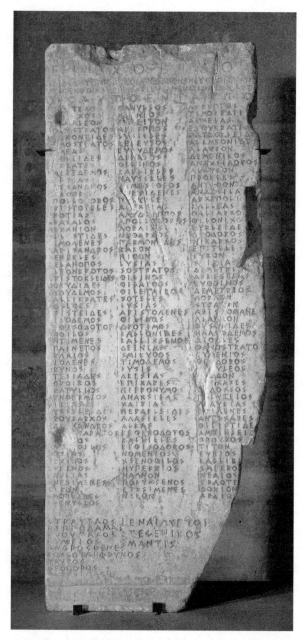

Figure 10.1. Athenian war dead stele. This is a typical commemorative stele: a block of stone (in this case marble) with an inscription. This one bears the casualty list of the Athenian tribe Erechtheis for the year 459/8. Musée du Louvre, Paris. Photo © RMN-Grand Palais / Art Resource NY.

A vivid sense of how many separate campaigns the Athenians were fight-ing is provided by a surviving list of the war dead of one year (probably 459/8) for just one of the ten tribes: 177 men died "in Cyprus, in Egypt, in Phoenicia, at Halieis, on Aegina, and at Megara."[6] The Athenians and their allies were continuing the attempt to recover Cyprus town by town, and while they were there they were approached for help by Inaros, who had stirred the Egyptians into rebellion against Persia. The Egyptian campaign continued for some years, but it ended, perhaps in 454, with the loss of per-haps forty or fifty Athenian ships and thousands of lives—such a thorough payback for Eurymedon that references to the disaster are always muted in our Greek sources. However, the Athenians managed to turn the affair to their profit. On the grounds that the Aegean was now unsafe, the league treasury was moved from Delos to Athens.

The First Peloponnesian War trickled on, until in 451 another build-up of Persian forces, this time in Cilicia, prompted a token peace treaty of five years between Athens and Sparta. Cimon had returned from exile on his family's estates on the Thracian Chersonese, and as soon as he had finished negotiating the terms of the treaty, he was dispatched to Egypt and Cyprus. He managed to further deter the Persians, but lost his life in the process. Cimon was the last of the old-style political leaders of Athens, who main-tained their power by ostentatious acts of generosity toward the city and by personal patronage of the poor. With the death of this staunch enemy of the Persians, some of the steam left the anti-Persian cause.

Before long, the fragile peace between Athens and Sparta was threatened by the Second Sacred War, which broke out in 449 over the control of Delphi. It was a futile affair. The Athenians had supported the Phocians in their desire to take over control of the sanctuary from the Delphians; the Spartans drove the Phocians away, and a few months later the Athenians restored them. The peace remained in place only because the two main protagonists had not actually met on the battlefield.

In 447 the Athenians' ten-year hegemony in central Greece came to an end when the Boeotians reunited and drove them out. The Athenian defeat induced Euboea to secede from the league, and at more or less the same moment the Athenians heard that the Megarians had risen up against their garrison. A force was sent to retaliate, but found itself confronted by a large Peloponnesian army. A deal was rapidly struck, whereby Athens would renounce its claim to Megara if the Spartans left them Euboea, and the

6 Meiggs/Lewis no. 33 = (translated) Fornara no. 78; Crawford/Whitehead no. 127.

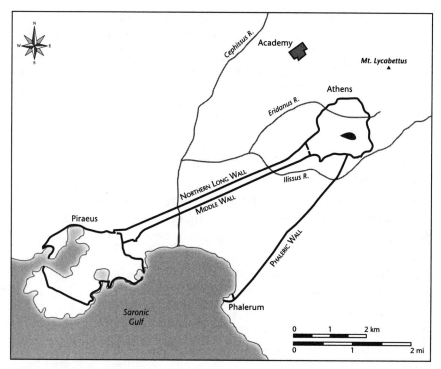

Map 10.3. The Athenian Long Walls.

Spartans withdrew. Euboea was then quickly recovered, and each town was made to swear an oath of loyalty to Athens. Histiaea suffered worst: the town was ruthlessly depopulated, and the place was renamed Oreus and taken over by Athenian cleruchs. Chalcis and Eretria received cleruchies as well, so that Euboea was thoroughly garrisoned.

At this point, in 446, the two sides came to the negotiating table and entered into a thirty-year peace, which essentially recognized Spartan hegemony on the mainland and Athenian hegemony in the Aegean. Neither was to intervene in the affairs of the other's allies, which were the sole responsibility of the leader of that alliance. The Greek world was effectively divided between the two superpowers.

But the Athenians lost the First Peloponnesian War, as they would lose the second; they had succeeded neither in detaching Corinth from the Peloponnesian League nor in holding Megara, Phocis, and Boeotia. Having been forced out of central Greece, they now withdrew from the Peloponnese, where the situation was not favorable to them anyway: in

450 Argos had entered into a thirty-year peace accord with Sparta, leaving Athens with no strong friends there. But around 445, the Athenians improved their Long Walls by building a middle wall, closer to the northern wall, so that if either of the other two walls was breached, they would still have a corridor to and from Piraeus. This was not the action of people who expected the peace to last, and they were right.

Athenian Outreach

Throughout the period of the Delian League, Athens continued to extend itself. It sent settlers, often cleruchs, out to the Thraceward region, the Thracian Chersonese, Euboea, Scyros, Naxos, Andros, Imbros, and Lemnos—anywhere that was restive or of strategic or economic importance. On two occasions, substantial Athenian fleets sailed into the Black Sea and Athenian settlers, again probably cleruchs, were dropped off in this town, and that as a way of gaining new allies and ensuring smooth passage for the shipping that was supplying Athens with commodities. These cleruchies were, as usual, made more acceptable by reductions in tribute payment, to compensate for the loss of income from the confiscated land.

But it was not always league business that took Athenians abroad. In 444/3 they played a major role in establishing a new colony in southern Italy, at Thurii; the new settlers included the historian Herodotus of Halicarnassus. Diplomatic negotiations also culminated in 433/2 in alliances or renewed alliances with towns in Greek Italy, with the Messapians (the local enemies of Tarentum, a Spartan foundation), and with Sicilian Leontini. In 427, during a mission to help Leontini against Syracuse, the Athenians also entered into an anti-Syracusan alliance with Rhegium on the toe of Italy and, in western Sicily, with Egesta, a non-Greek (Elymian) town.

In 441 the Milesians appealed to Athens for help against the Samians, who were expanding on the mainland into territory the Milesians considered theirs. Both were members of the Delian League. Pericles, holding his eighth Generalship, agreed to help the Milesians—and made himself the butt of all kinds of jokes, since he had just recently set aside his Athenian wife in favor of his Milesian partner, the famously alluring Aspasia. In the summer of 441, the Athenians expelled the Samian oligarchs, imposed democracy, and sailed away again. But the oligarchs raised a mercenary force and returned, and seceded once more from the league. The Athenians returned in force in 440: Samos was a critical naval base for the league, right off Anatolia, and it could not be allowed to fall into the wrong hands. The Peloponnesian League voted—but only just—not to invade Attica in support of the Samians, who surrendered early in 439 and paid the usual penalties, including the imposition of a cleruchy. The long and glorious history of Samos, one of the greatest states of the Archaic period, was brought to an abrupt halt, and the island became dominated by outsiders for 150 years. Of the allies, now only Lesbos and Chios still paid a tribute of ships rather than money—but most of the Lesbian cities would lose theirs in a failed rebellion in 427, and the Chians came close to losing theirs in 424.

In 437 an expeditionary force under Hagnon returned north to renew the attempt to found a colony in the Thraceward region. This time it worked, and the Athenians refounded Ennea Hodoi as Amphipolis. It was an allied foundation, not purely Athenian, but perhaps only because the Athenians did not have enough men to spare. At any rate, the Athenians always acted as if it were their own, and Hagnon was honored for a while as the founder. This time the Athenians appeased the Thracians, who had massacred the previous colonists, by finding and reburying in Amphipolis the bones of the legendary Thracian king Rhesus, thus demonstrating that they had his approval.

An Athenian Empire?

After a final defeat of the Persian fleet off Cypriot Salamis in 450, we hear of no more major offensives against the Persians, and most fourth-century writers attribute this to a formal peace treaty, named the Peace of Callias after the alleged Athenian negotiator. But neither of our two fifth-century historians, Herodotus (writing in the 420s) and Thucydides (died c. 400), mention any such treaty, when both of them had opportunities to do so. It may simply be that neither side saw any point now to open warfare, especially after the death of Cimon in 451. In our day, the two Koreas are still officially at war, though they do little about it. Seeing the hostility growing between Athens and Sparta, Artaxerxes may have decided to pull back and let the two Greek superpowers wear each other down. But, if there was no peace treaty, the Persians never formally renounced their claim to the Eastern Greek cities.

The cessation of hostilities meant that there was now little justification for the league, and indeed we hear of no more league meetings. The Athenian

Assembly took over responsibility for league policy. This was one of a number of imperialistic changes. The Athenians confiscated land for cleruchies and for sanctuaries for their own goddess, Athena (as "Athena, Mistress of Athens"), so that the rents from it came back to her treasury in Athens. They were prepared to impose democracy by force on their allies, most strikingly at Erythrae in 452.[7] The autonomy of allied states was further compromised by the presence in them of Athenian officials to look after Athenian interests. Certain classes of legal suits had to be heard in Athenian courts before Athenian juries, so that the allies were denied full judicial independence. Not only did the Athenians use league forces for specifically Athenian projects, but they spent league money on them too. Large sums were transferred from the league treasury to the Treasury of Athena in 447 and 432, the first for the Acropolis building program and the second for the imminent war against the Peloponnesian League.

They eliminated the navies of potential rivals among the allies. They punished rebellion or even provocation ruthlessly, especially when under pressure during the Peloponnesian War. They reserved a sixtieth of the tribute for their own Treasury of Athena. In the 420s, they tried, with limited success but an imperious tone, to get all member states to adopt Athenian weights, measures, and coin standards.[8] They required the allies to be represented at the three most important Athenian festivals and to support them with gifts—the Greater Panathenaea with a cow and panoply, the City Dionysia with a model phallus, and the Mysteries at Eleusis with first fruits (1/1200 of their wheat and 1/600 of their barley). This might have been intended as a gesture of inclusion, but, writing in the middle of the fourth century, the orator Isocrates thought that the opposite reaction was likely: "So exactly did the Athenians of that time gauge what arouses hatred in people that they voted to divide the surplus of the allied tribute into piles of one talent each and display it on stage when the theater was full of allied representatives during the Dionysia."[9]

The Athenians regarded the Delian League as a huge extension of the Athenian hinterland. Just as they expected people throughout Attica to give preference to Athenian coins, so they expected people throughout the Aegean to do the same. Just as they expected the demes of Attica to make

7 Meiggs/Lewis no. 40 = (translated) Fornara no. 71; Rhodes no. 360.
8 Meiggs/Lewis no. 45 = (translated) Fornara no. 98.
9 Isocrates, 8.82 (On the Peace).

first-fruit offerings to Demeter, so the allied states were required to as well. And why should they not embellish their city, which they saw as the capital city of the entire Aegean? Why should they not centralize legal processes, just as any state does? Even if all this was high-handed behavior, there were clear benefits for the allies. Bickering between states died down; trade was enhanced by the suppression of piracy and Persian shipping, and by the standardization of weights and measures around the Aegean and the centralization of commerce on Piraeus.

So what do we call the Delian League? It is commonly said that, at some point in the decades following its inauguration, the Athenians changed a league into an empire, and in tandem changed the league's aim from keeping the Persians at bay to keeping the Athenians in style. The original author of this view was Thucydides, who went so far as to describe Athenian power as a form of tyranny.[10] But it seems to me that the Athenians never intended the league to be a league of equals; they were in it for the money and power right from the start. In any case, I want to withhold the title of "empire" on a technicality. It is true that "empire" and "imperialism" are broad concepts, covering different kinds of dominance, as we shall see later in this book when we come to the Roman treatment of Greece. But there was a key element of empire missing from the Delian League, and that is the control of people who are in certain respects different from oneself: they live far away, speak a different language, have a different culture. An empire must be a multiethnic and multicultural state. The Delian League lacked this feature. Athenian subjects were other Greeks like themselves, and many of them were Ionians, with Athens as their ancestral mother city. Athens was the spider at the center of a hegemonial network, but not quite an imperial queen.

10 Thucydides, *History* 2.63.2, 3.37.2; Crawford/Whitehead nos. 208, 210B.

II

The Economy of Greece

The Greeks had no word for, and no concept of, "the economy" as a whole, as the aggregate of all economic activities, markets, or sectors; the word *oikonomia* ("household management") was never generalized in that way and essentially covered no more than budgeting. This does not mean that individuals did not behave as rational economic agents when they could afford to (those who could not practiced risk-management rather than profit-making), and the ancient economy is largely comprehensible in modern terms. The main nonrational aspects of the Greek world were that honor was found almost as desirable as profit, that people clung on to their farms and homes for social rather than economic reasons, and that a certain amount of goods were exchanged as gifts rather than traded for profit.

In theory, economic history should reveal both the structures and the performance of the economies it studies. In the case of ancient Greece, it is almost never possible to assess performance, because we do not have the numbers. In ancient Babylon, scribes often correlated the prices of commodities to the movements of the heavenly bodies that they so meticulously recorded, but we have no such archive for Greece. The island of Delos in the Hellenistic period supplies some useful information, but otherwise we have to rely on scattered and decontextualized information, and much of it comes from Athens, which we know to have been economically exceptional—larger and richer than normal. We can, however, say—safely, if vaguely—that, over the periods covered in this book, there was healthy growth in both agricultural and nonagricultural production, in standards of living, in wages (both nominal and real), and in per capita consumption of goods.

Even if precision is unattainable, many features of the ancient Greek economy are relatively clear to us. The fundamental economic sequence where goods are concerned is production, distribution, and consumption. A sketch of these three elements will afford an overview of economic activity in Greece.

Production

Farming, of course, was fundamental. As we have already seen, many farmers remained at the subsistence level, producing little for the marketplace, while others produced surpluses for the market. In Athens, the wealthiest 7.5 percent of the population owned about 30 percent of the available farmland (which constituted about 40 percent of Attica), so they controlled a lot of the food supply. Ownership of a good estate in Attica made a good foundation for more lucrative enterprises, such as buying land abroad, interest-bearing loans, renting property to metics, taking out a lease on mining concessions, tax-farming, quarrying, forestry, owning slave-operated workshops, or hiring out slaves. The elite continued their involvement in long-distance trade as well, though they were more likely in the Classical period to invest in it rather than actually to captain a ship, as they had earlier. Much trade, both local and long-distance, was now in the hands of a middle-income group.

We also saw the kinds of foods Greek farmers were growing. Here we just need to take account also of the market for secondary agricultural products, such as wool and leather, and for the products of other forms of land use, especially wood, stone, metals, and clay. There were three contexts for these raw materials to be turned into finished objects. First, some items were made within the home for domestic use, not for sale. Spinning, weaving, and basketry, for instance, were done by the womenfolk of a household; there were retail outlets chiefly for nonordinary items, such as silk clothing. The turning of cereals into food was also largely a domestic job; we do hear of successful bakers, but they were probably specializing in sweet pastries, for which Athens was famous. Second, there were workshops, staffed mainly by slaves and doubling as retail outlets, that were detached from the home; and, thirdly, there were domestic workshops, involving perhaps just the head of the household, his wife and son, and a slave or two.

Typically, a detached shop was owned or rented out to a metic by a citizen member of the wealth elite, and staffed by slaves with a slave or free man as a foreman. The father of the orator Demosthenes left a substantial bequest:[1]

> One workshop had thirty-two or thirty-three knife-makers, worth on average five or six minas apiece, with none worth less than three minas. This workshop made him a net profit of thirty minas a year. The other had a total of twenty bed-makers, who were security for a loan of forty minas, and made him an annual profit of twelve minas.

In Athens, we hear more often of medium-sized workshops with a dozen or so slaves than we do of large ones, such as the shield-making factory owned by the father of the speechwriter Lysias, to which 120 slaves were attached. Larger workshops, large enough to count as factories, did not generally appear before the Hellenistic period. In Athens, the crafts which evolved out of the home were naturally those, such as metalworking, that benefited from the input of more than one expert and a foreman to coordinate the work.

Production requires labor. In economic terms, labor was scarce in Greece. Most men were unavailable because they were too busy working to put food on their own tables; nearly all women were confined to working in the home; and slaves belonged to their owners. Moreover, many Greeks hated working for others; it was felt to be demeaning. The gap was filled by resident foreigners and by unfree laborers (serfs or slaves). Temporary labor markets were created by large-scale public building works, but basically this was not a flourishing sector of the economy.

Finally, production requires capital, in the form of assets, such as buildings and machinery, and of cash. States raised money in all the usual ways, chiefly by taxation, leasing public land, and fines. Although their intention was rarely to help local business, states also supplied the basic infrastructures such as roads, bridges, harbors, and marketplaces, and they put money into circulation. Money supply was straightforward, consisting largely of coins/bullion and loans. Resources could also be acquired by violence—by piracy and brigandage (more common in the Archaic period than later), or by warfare. For lack of precise figures, it is impossible to quantify the impact of

---

1 Demosthenes 27.9 (*Against Aphobus I*); Crawford/Whitehead no. 278.

capital on the Greek states, but we can safely say that businessmen had the means to increase their productivity.

Distribution

The price of any given item is determined by its production costs and transaction costs, the degree of competition, and the level of demand. Transaction costs—the total costs of buying or selling things—were high in the ancient world, largely because of the slowness of communication and transport. One of the reasons Piraeus, Athens' port, was so successful as a commercial hub was that sellers and buyers were more likely to find one another there than anywhere else. At Piraeus in the Classical period, traders encountered the largest consumer market in the Aegean; in fact, it is no exaggeration to say that Athens in the fifth and fourth centuries was the driver of growth all over the Aegean, as the island of Delos would be in the second and first centuries.

Some goods were moved short distances by land (by mule or oxcart), but far more goods were transported by sea. It was cheaper that way, because the larger volume of goods being transported meant that the cost per unit was decreased ("economies of scale"); merchantmen of the Classical period carried between twenty and seventy tons of cargo. Archaeology confirms the importance of trade by sea by a simple equation: the farther inland sites are, the less imported pottery is found. Trade always flourished in the Greek world. Its volume is impossible to estimate (though recent advances in finding and working with ancient shipwrecks are helping), but throughout the centuries covered by this book, luxury goods, staples, and everything in between were moving around the Mediterranean in increasingly large quantities. The trade in luxuries was very small, although it involved a considerable transfer of capital. Consider how much a two-ton *kouros* statue, perfectly executed in fine marble, must have cost to make and transport.

States never developed merchant fleets; this was private enterprise, and financial instruments were developed to make it easier. One was the bottomry loan, a short-term, high-value, high-interest loan taken out with collateral provided by the "bottom" or keel of a ship, or its cargo or some portion of it. Interest rates were not set by a central bank, but were negotiated between lender and borrower. Sea voyages were hazardous in the

Figure 11.1. A *kouros*. The stance is typical, but not all *kouroi* were as tall as 4.8 meters (almost 16 feet). Inscribed on the left thigh of this statue, which was originally one of a pair, is "Isches," the name of the man who dedicated it in the Samos Heraion early in the sixth century. Samos Archaeological Museum no. 840. Photo © Kathryn Waterfield.

ancient world. The chances of a ship being wrecked or attacked by pirates were not negligible. Bottomry loans acted as a kind of insurance for the borrower, because if the cargo was lost, he kept the money and did not have to pay any of the interest either.

But the hazards meant that long-distance traders tended toward conservatism: they stuck to tried-and-tested routes where they knew their customers and there was less risk of running into a pirate fleet, and cargoes tended to consist of goods known to be saleable, with a small admixture of higher-risk items. They tried to keep their voyages short: the Mediterranean fell into fairly distinct trade areas—the far west, centered on Massalia; Italy, Sicily, and the Adriatic; the Aegean; the Black Sea; the southeastern Mediterranean—and traders tended to travel only as far as the neighboring area, and leave it up to others to move the goods onward.

The state became involved in trade in a number of ways. The evidence, as usual, is largely from fourth-century Athens, but enough inscriptions are extant from other places for us to be certain that the same practices were widespread. In Athens, the state provided permanent and temporary markets; it provided legal protection and, because large sums of money were often involved, it made sure that disputes relating to maritime trade were heard promptly; it minted the coins that simplified transactions and guaranteed their purity; it insisted on its own weights and measures being used within its own marketplaces, as a defense against chaos and cheating; it made laws to prevent shady dealing, and backed them up with officials, such as the *agoranomoi* ("market superintendents"), who checked the quality of goods being sold and negotiated with traders to fix the prices of commodities for each day; it made laws about how contracts were to be written in order to be valid.

All these institutions were intended to make life easier and fairer for both buyers and sellers, and to make it possible for people to trade with confidence with strangers; that is what a market does. But Greek states set up these institutions not so much for economic reasons, such as stimulating trade, as for political reasons, such as gaining the goods and services they required to function and to keep their populations happy. The importing of grain was absolutely essential to Athens' survival, yet almost all the grain business in fourth-century Athens came to be funded and underwritten by private banks, without state involvement. In fact, states also intervened in ways that decreased profits. In the first place, they levied duties (of

1 percent, later 2 percent, in Athens) on all imports and exports. Sometimes they controlled the price of grain (but only of grain); it was understood that at a time of shortage prices would rise, but states still expected traders to keep their prices low, and they might restrict the dealers' profits to, say, one obol in the drachma.

In the fourth century, the Athenians required all cargoes of grain that arrived in Piraeus to be sold in the retail market in Athens and the wholesale market in Piraeus; they required traders resident in Attica who had taken out a loan for a grain shipment to bring the cargo back to Piraeus; and the Assembly was allowed to decide the price at which grain taxed from Athenian cleruchies on Lemnos, Imbros, and Scyros would be sold to the people.[2] As a result of the first two of these measures, it is not impossible that Athens may in some years have been a net exporter of grain, despite its chronic shortage. In the Hellenistic period, it was common for kings to give cities gifts of grain not just to alleviate hunger, but for resale or investment. Eumenes II of Pergamum, for instance, once gave an enormous quantity of wheat to Rhodes, with instructions that it was to be sold, and the interest on the money raised was to be used to found schools for children; it was often easier for kings and states to give in kind rather than cash.[3]

Consumption

The term "consumption" refers to the quantity of goods consumed in a given economy by both individuals and governments. Lacking precise figures, we are incapable of assessing levels of consumption, and therefore of answering with any degree of precision questions such as whether, when, and where standards of living improved or declined. But a couple of generalizations are safe.

First, the consumption of goods produced locally was always more prevalent than the consumption of imports. It is clear that Athens was exceptional in the quantity and quality of the imports it consumed; the importance of Piraeus meant that far more goods were available there than elsewhere. We

2 Phillips nos. 322–328.
3 Polybius, *Histories* 31.31.1.

happen to know that the tax-farmers who in 401 bought the right to gather the 2 percent tax on imports and exports made a little over 36 talents, so that the value of the imports and exports was around 1,800 talents—a very large sum indeed. The Old Oligarch (as the author of a late-fifth-century pamphlet is known) said: "Every delicacy to be found in Sicily, Italy, Cyprus, Egypt, Lydia, Pontus, the Peloponnese, or anywhere else—all these things end up together in one place thanks to the Athenians' rule of the sea."[4] But the prosperous Athenians were exceptional in developing such extensive demands.

Second, even if quantification eludes us, it seems clear that people's living standards did improve over time. Thucydides remarks how maritime trade in the Archaic period increased the wealth of communities.[5] Skeletal remains show that, over the periods covered in this book, health improved and the average heights and ages at death rose, more for men than for women. The average size and cost of houses increased dramatically. Cities grew in size and in magnificence. More and more land was brought under cultivation.

Nominal wages in Athens were always variable, but increased from an average of one drachma for a day's manual labor toward the end of the fifth century to 2.5 drachmas toward the end of the fourth century. Within much the same period, pay for Assembly attendance in Athens rose from three obols to six obols. There were fluctuations, but overall inflation was low, so this represents a rise in real wages too; taking account of the price of wheat at these two points in time, we still see a rise of over 50 percent. Although these are only two dots on a graph that must in reality have been far more complex, there was clearly an overall improvement.

In every state that we know of, land was alienable, but there was not much of a land market, because more was inherited than sold. Land came on the market as a result of state confiscations, and some land was certainly traded, but it was nowhere near as significant an element of the ancient Greek economy as it is for us nowadays. In this sector, the economy was constrained by social factors. Landownership was a sign of status, and in many places a precondition of citizenship, so that people were reluctant to sell. Families were also bound to their land by the fact that their ancestral shrines and tombs were on it.

---

4 Tax-farmers: Andocides 1.133–134 (*On the Mysteries*). Old Oligarch: pseudo-Xenophon, *The Constitution of the Athenians* 2.7.
5 Thucydides, *History* 1.13; Crawford/Whitehead no. 81.

Slavery

The Greeks employed slaves in large numbers. Could this have been a brake on the economy? Consider this imaginative passage from Aristotle: "Suppose that each instrument could do its own work on command or by anticipation . . . Shuttles would weave all by themselves, plectrums would make music all by themselves, and then foremen would need no underlings and masters would need no slaves."[6] If slave labor is an alternative to mechanization, perhaps reliance on slaves blinded the Greeks to the possibilities of technological innovation.

Saying this, however, depends on a tacit comparison with the pace of technological advancement today. But it is we who are exceptional, not the ancient Greeks; preindustrial, agricultural economies, largely dependent on empirical knowledge and powered mainly by human and animal muscle, have always moved slowly. In order to increase production or distribution, the Greeks invented or saw the advantages of the water wheel, the force pump, and the Archimedean screw for raising water; the lever press for olives and grapes; the wedge press for small quantities of liquids; the rotary mill for flour (replacing, toward the end of the Hellenistic period, the hopper mill); possibly the water mill (though it only came into common use in Roman times); and the pulley hoist, cogged gears, and a connecting rod transferring circular energy to rectilinear energy, so as to drive a large saw, for instance. This list compares well with other similar societies over the same span of centuries. And, of course, small incremental improvements were constantly being made to machinery and methods.

However, while the situation of small communities is unclear, for lack of evidence, the economies of all the large Greek states did depend crucially on unfree labor. Once Greece as a whole became wealthier in the sixth century, slavery took off. In Athens, in about 430, there were perhaps ninety thousand slaves, serving a total population of 340,000. Of these slaves, about fifteen thousand worked at peak periods in the Laurium mines and washeries; about fifty thousand in Athens, Piraeus, and the other Attic towns; and the rest in the countryside, in villages, on farms, and in mills and quarries.

If these numbers are correct, Athens may be called a slave society (like the Empire of Brazil and the southern states of America in the eighteenth and nineteenth centuries), not just a society with slaves. In a sense, in fact,

6 Aristotle, *Politics* 1253b–1254a.

Figure 11.2. Quarrying. This Corinthian black-figure plaque from c. 575–550 shows male workers extracting clay from a pit and passing it up in baskets to their female colleagues on the lip of the pit. It was hot work, and they have hung their water flask nearby. Berlin, Staatliche Museen F 871. Photo © bpk Bildagentur / Art Resource, NY.

Athens was more of a slave society, in that ownership of slaves was widespread throughout all strata of society, not largely restricted to the rich. The same certainly goes for many other Greek states. Sizeable estates on Chios and Aegina were worked by slaves, and their navies were manned by slaves; the gold and silver mines of Thasos and Siphnos must have required large labor forces.

Throughout Greece, hundreds of thousands of slaves took on the most dull, dirty, dangerous, and degrading jobs. Not everybody owned a slave, but everybody wanted to. It cost money to buy and maintain a slave, but they were worth it; slave-ownership was regarded as a practical necessity, not as a luxury. Slaves provided both skilled and unskilled labor in the mines and quarries, and on the farms of rich and poor alike. In the fields, they did the regular work and were supplemented by free labor at peak times such as harvests. If their masters were of the hoplite or cavalry classes, they often accompanied them to war as batmen. In town, they worked as assistants to every kind of business, but also as managers of businesses when the owners chose not to be directly involved, and they worked in domestic service and for the state. Domestic slaves might do productive work (such as shopping, cooking, or weaving), or, in richer households, nonproductive work as *paidagōgoi* ("child-minders," who accompanied children in public), hairdressers, doorkeepers, or maids, but few slaves had only one job.

The thousand or so public slaves in Classical Athens were used as manual laborers for repairing roads and so on, but also as civil servants—as assistants to the various committees, for instance, and as a rudimentary police force, responsible for keeping order in public meetings and collecting the corpses of those who died in the streets. Some had very responsible jobs, such as keeper of the state archives or state accountant; slaves managed the mint and even oversaw elections. These jobs were given to slaves rather than citizens because politicians did not want to see them in the hands of their rivals. Slaves were not supposed to develop special interests but to be loyal to the hand that fed them, in this case the state.

Foreign slaves could come from anywhere, but the main sources in Europe were Scythia, Thrace, and Illyris, while Asian slaves came largely from Syria and from non-Greek areas of Anatolia such as Paphlagonia, Caria, Lycia, and Phrygia. Black African slaves were rare in the Classical period, and it was considered rather chic to own one. After Alexander had conquered the East and Greek immigrants had introduced chattel slavery there, slaves came from as far east as India, and African slaves became common in Greek Egypt.

Slaves might be children born of slaves, metics who had been demoted for some crime, or even abandoned babies taken into another household, but more commonly they were bought from abroad, or taken in war or by pirates (who thus played a role in the Greek economy). Many of those captured were already slaves, who were simply recycled to new locations, but some were free, and in the Classical period they were mostly women, since male captives were killed or ransomed or exchanged for prisoners, and children and the elderly were frequently left to fend for themselves, as slave traders had no use for them. Buying in was not necessarily the more expensive option, since the owner avoided the costs of rearing a nonproductive slave child.

The purchase price in Athens (for which we have figures) varied greatly according to age, physique, appearance, and especially skill, since an owner could recover his outlay by hiring out a useful slave. A third-rate slave might cost only seventy or so drachmas, but a very wealthy Athenian, Nicias of the deme Cydantidae, is said to have paid six thousand drachmas for a good manager of the slaves who worked his silver mines.[7] The average price was between a hundred and fifty and two hundred drachmas; since a low annual income was about four hundred drachmas, slaves were rather expensive.

In talking about the cost of slaves, we are getting to the nub of the matter: slaves were chattels, bought by a master and belonging as entirely to him as any other purchase. Aristotle even defined a slave as an "animate tool."[8] By law, slaves could be bought, sold, and bequeathed; their children were routinely taken from them and sold elsewhere; female slaves were regularly obliged to have sex with their owners—which is to say they were regularly raped. Slaves were so commonly thrashed that Aristophanes joked that the reason they were called "boy" (*pais*) was because they were so often beaten (*paiein*).[9] At nighttime, agricultural slaves might be locked inside secure towers to prevent them from running away. Owners had great power over their slaves.

Domestic slaves were on the whole quite well treated; a familiar character from Athenian drama is the loyal old retainer, and women could become close to their maidservants. Farm or workshop managers might become indispensable to their owners, and many a small farmer must have worked peaceably in his fields alongside his slaves. Early in the fourth century, a prominent banking family trusted their slave accountant, Pasion, enough to free him and elevate him to ownership of the bank. These instances remind us that even slavery was a negotiated relationship, a two-way street. But the relationship between master and slave could be uneasy. It was a common belief that the only reason slaves did not kill their masters was fear of the consequences.[10]

On the whole, however, slaves resorted only to the minor strategies of resistance that were available to them: laziness, theft, breakage, running away. In Athens, a slave could take refuge at the altar of the Furies, or that of

---

7   Xenophon, *Memoirs of Socrates* 2.5.2.
8   Aristotle, *Politics* 1253b–1254a.
9   Aristophanes, *Wasps* 1297–1298.
10   Plato, *Republic* 578d–579a; Xenophon, *Hiero* 4.3; Lysias 7.35 (*On the Olive Stump*).

Theseus, and ask to be bought by someone else, but this had the obvious drawback that he had just proved himself "untrustworthy" and was therefore unlikely to be bought. It was a feature of Athenian law that, for the majority of court cases, a slave's testimony was not considered valid unless he or she had been tortured. Perhaps the only point of this was to emphasize the distinction between slaves and others, who would never have to undergo such a trial. In any case, the torture of slaves seems to have been rare.

Helot revolts were not unknown in Sparta, as we have seen (though helots were not exactly slaves), but otherwise there were few occasions in the history of any Greek state when there were collective slave actions, and even fewer of them escalated into the kind of armed rebellion that Sparta or Rome witnessed. The only certain such rebellion—a late source also talks vaguely of something similar on Samos[11]—took place on Chios in the third century, when a man called Drimacus, a kind of Robin Hood character who attracted fabulous stories, took to the hills with a large number of slaves and formed a breakaway mini-state which negotiated a modus vivendi with the authorities in Chios town and lasted until he was murdered a few years later by one of his followers.

In Athens, toward the end of the Peloponnesian War, a great many slaves seized an opportunity to abscond. Thucydides says that they numbered over twenty thousand and implies that the majority of them were mine-workers at Laurium.[12] We should trust him, since the extraction of silver-bearing lead ore was by far the largest Athenian industry. It takes sixteen kilograms (over thirty-five pounds) of ore and a great deal of processing to produce one drachma's worth of pure silver—4 grams/0.15 ounce—and millions of coins were made in Athens every year. There were two other occasions when slaves escaped from Laurium in large numbers, toward the end of the second century. The reason why Laurium was at the center each time is that it was one of the very few places in the Greek world where there were enough slaves for them to organize. In all these cases, however, the revolts were unsuccessful, in the sense that the great majority of the slaves were recaptured, punished, and returned to work.

Slaves were routinely punished, as I have already mentioned. Masters employed the carrot as well as the stick, however. The ultimate inducement

11 Athenaeus, *Wise Men at Dinner* 267a–b (second/third century CE).
12 Thucydides, *History* 7.27.5, taken with 6.91.7.

was the promise of freedom. Both individuals and states emancipated slaves—the former, however, often only when the slaves were elderly, and the latter often only if they had risked their lives as soldiers. Slaves might be freed unconditionally or with conditions attached, such as the obligation to continue to work for their former master. In Athens and elsewhere, a freed slave, since he was a foreigner, gained metic status.

Slaves might also buy their freedom. One of the ways owners made money was by setting slaves up in business—as a prostitute, perhaps, or a charcoal-maker, or as the manager of a workshop. Slaves from this privileged class sometimes even had family lives. Or he might hire slaves out to the mines, or as laborers for the state; in these cases, they were paid at the same rate as free men. Owners kept some of their pay, but slaves could slowly put money aside for emancipation.

Greeks too were enslaved by Greeks, especially as a result of warfare, but in far smaller numbers than foreigners, and Greek slaves tended to be women, as I have already mentioned. Fluency in Greek would be appreciated in the kinds of work they were required to do. After Solon's reforms, no Athenian was a slave within Athenian territory, and by the Classical period we can say that other states also drew the line against enslaving fellow citizens; the Cretans were a backward exception. However, in a number of places—Sparta most famously with its helots, but also Thessaly, Argos, Sicyon, and Epidaurus, among others—Greeks had been turned by conquest into serf-like populations, working for other Greeks.

Some qualms were expressed about this. Two Spartans—Callicratidas, admiral in 406, and King Agesilaus II—seem to have refused to enslave Greeks taken in war (one wonders what they thought about their helots). Plato too thought it wrong. In Athens, the leading statesman of the 330s and early 320s, Lycurgus, had a law passed that made it illegal "for any Athenian citizen or resident of Athens to purchase any [Greek] prisoner of war of free birth for the purposes of enslavement, or any slave without the consent of his former owner," and there was a similar ruling in a late-third-century treaty between Miletus and Cnossus in Crete.[13]

---

13 Callicratidas: Xenophon, *Hellenica* 1.6.14; Agesilaus: Xenophon, *Agesilaus* 7.6; Plato, *Republic* 469b, 471a (see also Herodotus, *Histories* 8.3); Lycurgus: pseudo-Plutarch, *The Lives of the Ten Orators* 841f–842a; *IC* Cnosos 6.

These were steps in the right direction, but it was a very rare voice that went that far, let alone farther. In a pamphlet composed in the first half of the fourth century as if it were a speech to the Spartans on the subject of their subjection of the Messenians, the orator Alcidamas of Elaea declared: "God has set all men free; nature has made no man a slave"—a direct contradiction of the central, supremacist tenet of pan-Hellenism, that foreigners were natural slaves.[14] But these qualms were restricted to the few. Intellectuals worried about slavery throughout antiquity, but no one took much notice.

---

14 Alcidamas, F 3 Avezzù.

12

Athens in the Age of Pericles

A thens prospered in the decades following the Persian Wars. It became the city celebrated by the Boeotian poet Pindar as "radiant, violet-crowned, famed in song, the bulwark of Greece."[1] Piraeus grew from a village to a planned city. Metics poured in to take advantage of the business and employment opportunities, the citizen population increased as it does at times of prosperity, and more and more slaves were bought or reared to cope with the increased labor requirements.

The combined population of Athens and Piraeus rose fast in the fifty years between the Persian Wars and the Second Peloponnesian War. Athens became, and remained, the most populous state in Greece, though Syracuse was a close second. By 430 the total population was about 340,000, double what it had been fifty years earlier—these numbers are of course no more than informed guesses. Of these, 50,000 were adult male citizens, 175,000 their wives and children, 90,000 slaves, and 25,000 metics and their families, either immigrants or freed slaves. About half the adult male population were rich enough to serve as hoplites. Urbanization proceeded apace, until (uniquely in Athens) only about half the adult male population made a living from the land. Athens had a very well developed market economy, or at least an economy with markets.

The rise in population had a critically important outcome, which was to affect the foreign policy of Athens for the rest of its existence. The populace could no longer be fed on homegrown produce alone; from the 470s onward, in addition to all its other requirements (especially timber and

---

1 Pindar, F 76 Snell/Maehler.

minerals), every year Athens had to import grain (usually wheat, because it grew barley) to supplement its domestic production. In fact, shortage of grain had been dictating some elements of foreign policy since the late sixth century; the gradual annexation of Euboea from the time of the first cleruchy at Chalcis in 506 was largely motivated by the desire to make the island an Athenian breadbasket. The Athenians clung on through thick and thin (as we shall see) to the islands of Lemnos, Imbros, and Scyros, which were all important sources of grain, and by populating them with cleruchies made them extensions of Athenian territory. One of the primary reasons for the Delian League was that control of the Aegean helped Athens feed its bloated population. The same goes for the Second Athenian League in the fourth century; by the time the population recovered from the Peloponnesian War, it stood at about 220,000, and the importing of grain remained critical.

A report was given to every main meeting of the Assembly about the grain situation. If there was a crisis, in the fourth century individuals were appointed to sort it out, but early in the third century a board was created of annually elected Buyers of Grain, one per tribe, to try to ensure a regular and adequate supply from abroad and its equitable distribution at home. We cannot quantify Athenian imports, which will in any case have varied year by year, but in competition with others who were in a similar position, Athens had to forge and maintain good relations with grain-rich parts of the world where it was not going to be able to impose cleruchies, such as Thessaly, Sicily (but much of the island was Dorian and likely to be unfriendly), Egypt, Cyrene, Cyprus, Macedon, Thrace, Italy (both the Celtic north and the Greek south), and the northern Black Sea coast. And then, from the end of the fourth century onward, it was the Hellenistic kings who controlled much of the production of grain in the Mediterranean, and whose benevolence had to be petitioned.

By far the most important source of grain for the Athenians was always the northern coast of the Black Sea (Ukraine and Crimea in today's terms). But this meant that grain ships had to pass through the long narrows of the Bosporus, Propontis, and Hellespont before reaching the relative safety of the Aegean Sea. Reliance on imported grain, combined with dependency on a single source, was the Athenians' weakest point. Anyone who could gain control of the narrows could bring them to their knees.

It was always crucial for the Athenians to have plenty of friends and allies in the region.

Democracy Radicalized

The ebb and flow of power between oligarchs and democrats that characterized the 470s and 460s erupted into open hostility in 462/1, when the democrats—chiefly Ephialtes (an obscure figure to us)—took advantage of the absence of Cimon and many members of the hoplite class in Sparta to draw the political teeth of the Areopagus Council, populated by rich ex-Archons and sympathetic to Cimon's policy of partnership with Sparta. Ephialtes removed the council's last political function, that of assessing the conduct of office-holders, and gave it to the people. Now officers of the state, who tended to be members of the wealth elite, would be assessed by the people, not by other members of the elite. The Areopagus Council was left with a reduced set of purely judicial, nonpolitical functions; it remained a prestigious institution, but the exclusiveness of its membership was somewhat diluted a few years later, when the Archonship was opened up to the third of Solon's property classes, the Zeugitae.

At the same time, the popular courts were made courts of first instance rather than just appeal courts. The Heliaea was refashioned as a number of separate jury courts (and was renamed the *Dikastēria*, the People's Courts), each to hear different kinds of cases, and it was now the relevant Archon's job simply to pass all those cases he deemed viable on to the relevant court, without making any further judgment himself. The people sitting as the Assembly and the people sitting as jurors were now seamlessly the same. They were different institutions, with different jobs; the courts could even annul a piece of legislation passed by the Assembly. But in practice each supported the other; the Assembly passed laws, and the courts made sure that the democracy's officers always worked in the people's best interests. The Athenian people had effective control of all important political and judicial matters.

Disgruntled oligarchs had Ephialtes murdered, and Pericles, the son of Xanthippus, took over Ephialtes' role as the champion of the people. Above all, in the late 450s he introduced pay for jurors, so that people would not be debarred by poverty from serving. This was a crucial move for the democracy; Cleisthenic theory was now put into practice. The pay was two obols a day, raised to three in 425; it was just enough to supply a small family with its daily barley and to decrease dependency on the patronage of the rich. The poor (that is, in Greek terms, everyone who had to work for a living) soon came to dominate Athenian juries, and speakers learned to adjust their delivery accordingly. Later, perhaps in the 440s, pay was also introduced for military service; somewhat later again, pay for councilors was introduced, at a rate of three obols a day.

The ancient Athenians had the most radical democracy the world has ever known, because, in theory, every single citizen had the right to make a direct contribution to the running of the state. Modern democracies in large nation-states are representational: we elect people to represent us in government. The closest we get to direct participation is through referendums. But in Athens, "we the people" *were* the government. Of course, the democracy can be criticized for excluding women from the vote (let alone slaves and foreigners), but this would be anachronistic, since the first time that women gained the vote was 1893, in New Zealand. The pressure that gave Athenian democracy its radical turn probably came from below, from the people themselves, or at any rate from their leaders. It made no sense for the defense of the city to depend critically on the thousands of poor men who crewed the warships if they did not also have a say in the future direction of the city.

Administration of the democracy and leadership of a sprawling alliance made heavy demands on the Athenian people. At the beginning of every year, a panel of six thousand jurors aged over thirty was enrolled, to be distributed as required among the courts, which met perhaps twelve or fifteen times a month, with juries for some cases numbering 201, 401, 501, or even in the thousands, depending on the seriousness of the crime. Several thousand aged over twenty attended Assembly meetings, of which there were by the mid-fourth century forty a year, lasting (usually) no more than several hours in the morning. Then there were five hundred councilors and at least seven hundred other political and bureaucratic positions, and several hundred more Athenian officials served abroad in the cities of the Delian League. Many men, not just the big-name politicians, were concerned and courageous enough to address the Assembly and propose decrees. Athenians responded positively to the fact that their futures were in their own hands.

They expressed their commitment to democracy also by their extensive use of sortition (with its implication that everyone was equally capable of doing the jobs for which this method of selection was used), and by systematically denying the majority of their officers, apart from Generals and financial controllers, the ability to develop a personal power base.

The relative powerlessness of officers is one of the hallmarks of Athenian democracy—and a source of inefficiency, according to its critics. Nearly all posts were subject to annual election or sortition, and could be filled by the same man only once in a lifetime; most posts were not individual, but entailed membership of boards or committees; all officers were accountable and subject to ongoing scrutiny; and then there was always the threat of ostracism or of an indictment for having made an illegal or inappropriate proposal. The people knew their strength; if any of their leaders abused his position, they could rapidly bring about his downfall.

Public Finance and Taxation

As usual, we know little about the public finance systems of states other than Athens; we read incidentally in literature and fragmentary inscriptions from other states about a wide variety of taxes—enough for us to be certain that this was an area in which states exercised considerable ingenuity in finding new assets, services, and products to tax—but it is hard to gain a coherent picture. In the mid-430s, Thucydides assures us that Athens had accumulated a reserve of 9,700 talents, the equivalent nowadays of several billion dollars—not bad for a premodern state the size of Luxembourg.[2] From one point of view the scale of Athenian finances was greater than that of any European state for well over two thousand years. In the 330s and 320s, Athens was spending an average of about 40 metric tonnes of silver a year; the population in those days was perhaps 250,000, so that makes about 160 grams per person. This relative quantity was not overtaken until the Industrial Revolution rocketed Great Britain into the fiscal stratosphere over two thousand years later.

The sources of Athens' income in the later fifth century were both foreign and domestic. Tribute and other proceeds from the allies, such as rents and indemnities, amounted to about six hundred talents a year. Domestic revenues are hard to calculate. The discovery, not long ago, of a cache of records of state finances at fourth-century Argos shows how even small transactions could be liable to tax;[3] there are bound to be many aspects of the Athenian system that are invisible to us. The main sources of income were a very few direct taxes (such as those paid by metics and sex workers),

---

2 Thucydides, *History* 2.13; Crawford/Whitehead no. 194B.
3 *SEG* 54 2004 427.

selling to tax-farmers the right to collect taxes, harbor dues and market fees, legal fines and confiscations, leases on state-owned mines and quarries, profits from coining, rents, and the sale of wartime booty. All this probably brought in about four hundred talents a year. Since Athens' expenses were undoubtedly more than four hundred talents a year, it follows that it could not have become the magnificent place it was without the tribute of the Delian League.

The Athenians' three main areas of expenditure were warfare, religious festivals, and pay for public and military service. Warfare costs naturally varied year by year, but could be as high as about 1,500 talents a year, which was the annual average from 432 to 423; we have seen how expensive it was to run an ancient fleet, and exceptional campaigns, such as a long siege, could rapidly drain the exchequer. Festivals cost a hundred talents a year and pay for public service, by the late fifth century, about 150 talents.

Private citizens were required by law to help out with public expenses. There was no regular system of income tax, but Athens (and some other states) had in place two wealth taxes that were levied as and when necessary. The first was the *eisphora* ("paying in"), an occasional tax first attested in the early 420s, and designed to raise several hundred talents for military purposes. The second form of wealth tax was the liturgy system (*leitourgia*, "public service"). In the Archaic period, members of the privileged class took it upon themselves to help out: they might provide a ship for the state fleet, embellish a public park, or refurbish a temple. They were glad to do it—to trade monetary capital for symbolic capital. The liturgy system was an institutionalization of this Archaic voluntary benefaction. There were ninety-seven liturgies in a normal year, and 118 every fourth year, when the Panathenaea festival was celebrated with extra splendor.

In Classical Athens there were perhaps two thousand men, metics or citizens, who were rich enough to be liable to liturgies, and of the two thousand a super-rich element of perhaps three to four hundred who were liable to the most costly liturgies. Liability was usually by voluntary self-declaration or by inheritance, but we hear also of reports to the authorities by neighbors, and of legal challenges, because the rich were commonly suspected of disguising their wealth. But the liturgy system was not intended to be a leveler, a way to reduce the wealth of the rich—even though, in some cases, it seems to have caused actual hardship, or at least a liquidity crisis—because the democracy continued to need rich men to serve the state.

The liturgy system in Athens—something similar was in place in many other states—was used to raise money for both military and religious purposes. A trierarch, for instance, was required to man, equip, and maintain a trireme for a year, the hull of which was provided by the state. Until about 360, he was also required to captain the ship, even though it was understood that he was supplying money, not expertise, which was up to the senior members of the crew he hired. The most expensive religious liturgy was the *chorēgia*, which involved recruiting a chorus for a dramatic or choral festival, and paying for the trainers, the training, the rehearsals, the costumes, the scenery, and the equipment.

The speaker (we do not know his name) of a speech written by Lysias shows how liturgies could add up:[4]

> I came of age in [411/10], and was appointed *chorēgos* for tragedies and spent thirty minas. Two months later, at the Thargelia, I was victorious with a men's chorus at a cost of two thousand drachmas. In [410/9], I spent eight hundred drachmas on pyrrhic dancers for the Great Panathenaea, and in the same Archonship I was also victorious with a men's chorus at the Dionysia, and my expenditure, including the dedication of the tripod, was five thousand drachmas. In [409/8], I spent three hundred drachmas on a cyclic chorus for the Little Panathenaea. In the meantime, I was trierarch for seven years, at a cost of six talents.

As if liturgies were not costly enough already, the competitive rich often spent more than was necessary to make their contribution especially splendid and memorable. Before the Sicilian Expedition of 415, for instance, each trierarch "spared no effort to make his ship stand out from the rest for its very magnificence, as well as for its speed."[5] But no one was required to undertake expensive liturgies year after year (unless they chose to, as did the speaker above), and at the lower end of the scale there were cheaper ones, such as paying for the upkeep of four young girls who were consecrated to Athena and lived for a year, dressed in white, in a special apartment on the Acropolis, complete with its own playground.

The Peloponnesian War exposed one of the chief weaknesses of the system, because the state had to go on demanding liturgical contributions from the rich just when they were cut off from the sources of much of their wealth. Resentment built up, and in the fourth century we hear increasingly

4 Lysias 21.1–2 (*Against a Charge of Taking Bribes*).
5 Thucydides, *History* 6.31.3.

about men deliberately concealing their household's wealth in order to avoid undertaking liturgies. It had probably happened before; it is not hard to do in a paperless society. Steps were therefore taken to make the system less burdensome for the rich and to coerce the unwilling to play their part.

Legal coercion was supplemented by ideological coercion, so to speak. Since honor was now in the gift of the people, *philotimia*, the aristocratic, selfish, competitive desire for glory, was redefined under the democracy until it meant a zealous desire to do the community good, particularly by performing liturgies or making voluntary cash contributions to the state. Competitive values were usurped by the democracy and put to cooperative uses.

Pericles' Citizenship Law

On Pericles' initiative, in 451/0 a law was passed restricting an Athenian's choice of marriage partner. This was the first law of its kind anywhere in Greece, but not the last. Previously, by unwritten custom a child was an Athenian citizen if his father was one; but under the new law both parents had to be Athenian citizens. Any citizen who broke the law would be liable to a hefty fine, and the non-Athenian partner might be sold into slavery.

Presumably, the reason for wanting to restrict the number of citizens was that citizenship was a valuable possession. As it happened, one of the advantages was demonstrated just a few years later, when a generous gift of grain from the Egyptian rebels was to be distributed among the citizenry; we are told that almost five thousand people who had been thought to be citizens were now deemed not to be.[6] Metics were further marginalized by the law: they might have hoped for citizen grandchildren, if their daughters married Athenian men. The first result of Pericles' law was that Athenian women became more desirable as wives.

Although there is no direct evidence, the law was probably somewhat softened in 430, by the addition of a rider, at Pericles' insistence, to the effect that a man with no legitimate heirs could adopt a son of his born of a non-citizen mother. The law needed changing just then, because the epidemic of typhoid fever that was decimating the Athenian population had made it unrealistic. The change worked well for Pericles himself, because he lost

---

6 Plutarch, *Pericles* 37.4; Crawford/Whitehead no. 128.

both his legitimate sons to the plague, but was able to adopt his son (another Pericles) by his partner Aspasia.

The law accelerated the Athenian habit of seeing themselves as special, as possessing certain characteristics that distinguished them from others, even other Greeks: they were resourceful, adventurous, industrious, argumentative, natural democrats, defenders of the oppressed. Politicians and playwrights reinforced the message—Pericles above all, by telling Athenians in speech after speech how they should think of themselves—while annual funeral speeches delivered over the year's war dead painted idealized portraits of the perfect Athenian citizen. A certain narcissism characterizes the era when Pericles was dominant in Athens.

This was an accidental outcome, however. In itself the law was not really an attempt to guarantee ethnic purity; after all, there was foreign blood in many Athenians' veins, even if it became more diluted after 450. Wealthy Athenians had traded daughters with their friends abroad (especially in the Archaic period), poor Athenians had married their metic peers, and cleruchs had taken wives wherever their farms were. Moreover, the Athenians had the habit of awarding citizenship to foreigners as a way of honoring them; not all the grants were full citizenship, but it shows that citizenship did not necessarily entail ethnic purity. Athens was a more open, permeable, and heterogeneous society than that. By the end of the fifth century, for instance, all Euboeans had the right of *epigamia*—the right to contract legally valid unions with Athenians.

Pericles' law was a way of saying that all Athenians, in so far as they were Athenians, were equal, and it was a way of distinguishing them from all the foreigners and slaves who had been flooding into Athens. It was an attempt to unite the Athenians after the turmoil of the First Peloponnesian War, which had just been brought to a conclusion (though only tentatively, for five years), and in preparation for the war that was coming.

Pericles and Athens

Pericles, whose Alcmaeonid mother was a niece of Cleisthenes (and whose wife may have been an Alcmaeonid as well), came to the fore, as we have seen, in the 460s and 450s, as an able military commander, a committed patriot, a passionate advocate of democracy, and firm to the point of harshness in maintaining Athenian domination of the allies. His first

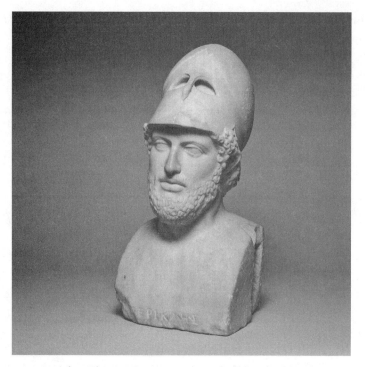

Figure 12.1. Pericles. This is a Roman copy in marble of a fifth-century Greek original by Cresilas. Pericles seems both serene and stern, and wears his helmet pushed back on his head, as though to signify that he was both a man of peace and a man of war. British Museum, London, 1805,0703.91. Photo © The Trustees of the British Museum / Art Resource, NY.

certain Generalship came in 455/4, with another in 451/0, but then they came thick and fast until 429/8, when he died in office. Thucydides wryly commented that "Athens, in theory a democracy, was on the way to being ruled by the leading man." The comic poets waded in too, calling him "Olympian" and all-powerful, and claiming he looked just like the tyrant Peisistratus.[7]

But these gibes were exaggerated. Pericles did nothing unconstitutional, and his career was marked by support and increase of democratic institutions, not by any impatience with them. Moreover, at every point in his career as General he was one of a board of ten, whose decisions had to be consensual; he was liable to assessments before and after every term of office,

7 Thucydides, *History* 2.65.9; Plutarch, *Pericles* 3–9.

and to votes of confidence at any point during the year; and he had to seek re-election every year. At every point of his career, the people could have ousted him if they did not like what he was doing—as they did, briefly, in the last year of his life—or even ostracized him. Perhaps in order to lessen that risk, he quite often used his associates as front men, getting them to propose his policies in their names, reserving himself for the most important and solemn occasions.

He certainly had opponents. In fact, the conflict between him and his greatest rival, a relative of Cimon's called Thucydides, the son of Melesias (not the same man as the historian, the son of Olorus), reached such a pitch that Thucydides was ostracized in 443/2. Thucydides chose to make his stand on Pericles' allegedly immoral use of allied tribute for the building program—not that there was much of an issue to be made of this in itself, as far as the Athenians were concerned, but presumably he made it out to be a symptom of Pericles' untrammeled personal power. Pericles' conduct of the savage little Samian war (pp. 186–7) also came in for criticism.

Ancient Greek politics was a game of factions, small groups of like-minded people united by shared interests, and often by kinship, patron–client relationships, and religious ties as well. These factions, which might form around a single leader, lasted as long as they felt they had work to do and collaborated with other such factions when they had common interests. In Athens, in the last quarter of the fifth century, some of the "clubs" (*hetaireiai*—"groups of companions," or fellow symposiasts) had become politicized and were used for the promulgation of oligarchy—until they were banned by the restored democracy in 403. Achieving dominance is infinitely more difficult in such a situation of fragmentation and flux than in, say, a two-party democracy. Pericles' success was due in part to his interpersonal skills: he could get more of these factions to line up behind him than any of his rivals could. Athenian democratic politics was always a matter of who one's friends and enemies were.

But Pericles' influence extended more widely than the field of politics. He epitomized Athenian culture by surrounding himself with artists and intellectuals, and by pursuing the building and rebuilding program which, along with democracy, has secured Athens' fame for all time. It was certainly one of Pericles' intentions to impress his fellow Greeks with Athenian splendor, and he succeeded; it is not just we moderns who marvel at Athenian remains—the Greeks themselves considered Athens to be the leader in all cultural fields. Rivals emerged in the Hellenistic period, but until then

Athens was "the school of Greece," as Pericles himself put it.[8] Almost every contemporary artist, sculptor, philosopher, poet, and prose writer of any standing in the Greek world was either a native Athenian or lived for a while in Periclean Athens.

The period of Pericles' dominance, and even the years immediately after his death, was a time of great confidence in Athens, despite the Peloponnesian War. Educators were sure that they were offering the best education ever; the art of rhetoric was being developed; sciences such as astronomy and medicine made great progress; artisans and craftsmen were producing unparalleled works. Artists and their clients valued the new: "I do not sing old melodies," boasted Timotheus, the most popular of the new musicians and a friend of Euripides, who was testing the limits of tragedy.[9] Athenians were proud of their adaptability, compared with Sparta's traditionalism. It seemed that there was nothing that humans could not achieve—as long as they had an Athenian upbringing.

Pericles' Building Program

We have seen that, financially speaking, the building program undertaken in Pericles' time would have been impossible without allied tribute. Whatever the morality of that decision, an intense program continued, with occasional wartime interruptions, for over forty years, during and past the time of Pericles' preeminence. Nor was it just Athens itself that was embellished. This was the time when the famous temple of Poseidon at Cape Sunium was built, for instance, and the Artemis temple at Brauron was rebuilt; considerable work went on here and there in Attica. In these forty years, Athens spent as much and built as much as other major cities had achieved in hundreds of years. For monumental temples, only Acragas in Sicily came close.

One of the popular benefits was that large numbers of Athenian and foreign craftsmen and laborers (including slaves) were kept in employment for so long—not just those who worked on the sites, but all those who supplied and transported materials. But the main benefit was intangible: the new buildings taught Athenians to regard their city as the world leader. As the al-Qaeda terrorists well knew on September 11, 2001, buildings are

8   Thucydides, *History* 2.41.1; Crawford/Whitehead no. 149.
9   Timotheus, F 7 Diehl.

potent symbols. That is also why for over thirty years the Athenians had let the Acropolis remain in ruins, just as the Persians left it in 479—a smoke-blackened and grim memorial. The only substantial work in these decades on the Acropolis was the repair of the gateway and the building of walls.

But Periclean Athens resounded with the din of construction. Magnificent ship sheds and a mercantile center were rising in Piraeus, and the Odeon, a huge concert hall, was being built next to the Theater of Dionysus on the southeastern slope of the Acropolis. The Hephaesteion (a temple to Hephaestus and Athena, still wrongly described to tourists as a temple of Theseus), overlooking the Agora from its northwest corner, was also possibly started in the 440s. A couple of decades later, two great colonnades—the Stoa of Zeus the Liberator and the South Stoa—arose on the edges of the Agora.

The most famous Periclean constructions, however, were religious in form and located on the Acropolis—and of these the best known is the Parthenon, the home of the virgin goddess Athena, widely regarded as one of the most perfect expressions of Greek architecture. Work began in 447, and proceeded in the years of relative peace that followed. This was the only one of "his" buildings that Pericles lived to see completed. The bulk of the largely Doric temple was finished by 438, when the cult statue, the work of Pericles' friend Pheidias, was installed and dedicated; the sculptures that adorned the pediments, panels, and friezes of the temple took a further two or three years from 434. Following Pheidias' success in Athens, he was commissioned to make the even greater statue of Zeus for Olympia, considered to be one of the wonders of the ancient world. Gold-and-ivory statues became something of a rage among states that could afford them, but Pheidias' Parthenos was the first.

The Parthenon (which replaced an older temple of Athena that was begun in the 480s but destroyed by the Persians, still uncompleted) was a proclamation of the glory of Athens and a visual confirmation of the success of Pericles' policies. Aesthetically, it is an extraordinary piece of work, and the precision of its architecture is astounding; the architects wrote a handbook, explaining all their calculations, but it is lost. Every one of the thousands of blocks, weighing in total 100,000 tons, was made with local materials, out of white marble from nearby Mount Pentelicon, before being painted in vivid primary colors.

Over the subsequent decades, apart from minor projects, the Acropolis gained its proud Propylaea ("gateways")—a five-gated entrance with wings

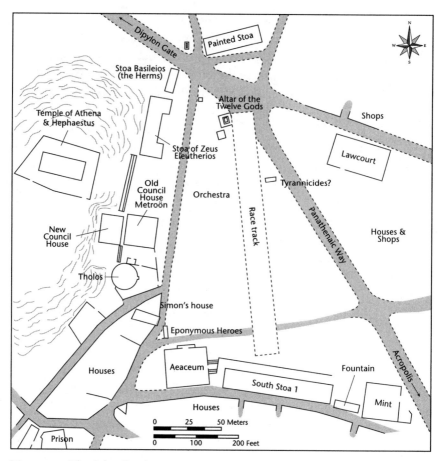

Map 12.1. The Athenian Agora, c. 400.

on either side—and the small temple of Athena *Nikē* (Athena as Victory), which stood on a bastion at the southwestern corner of the hill, and the so-called Erechtheum, famous for its South Porch, where statues of young women (called caryatids) serve as pillars. This was a multipurpose building—hence its lack of symmetry, very unusual for a Greek sacred building—that housed Athena Polias' most ancient cult statue, as well as other shrines relevant to Athens' origins. After several interruptions, it was finally completed in 405—so that, ironically, the Periclean building program was completed just in time for Athens' defeat in the war that he had started, or at least had not avoided.

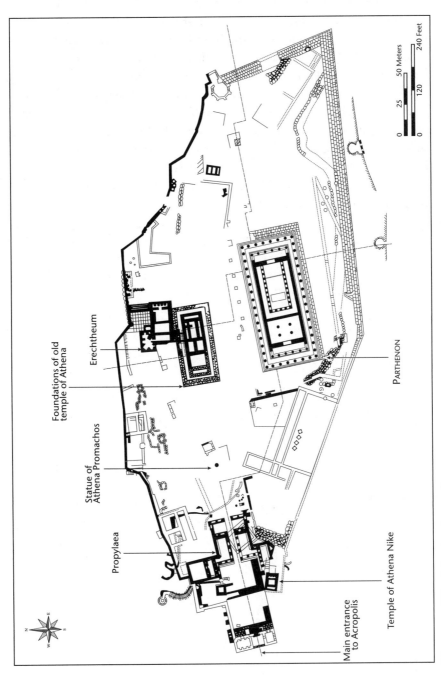

Foundations of old
temple of Athena

Erechtheum

Statue of
Athena Promachos

Propylaea

PARTHENON

Main entrance
to Acropolis

Temple of Athena Nike

N
E
S
W

0   25   50 Meters

0   120   240 Feet

Map 12.2. The Athenian Acropolis, c. 400.

The most dominant theme of the sculptures of the Acropolis is victory—
of rationality over chaos, of man over monster, and of Athenians over everyone. Again, it is hard not to see the imprint of Pericles here, seeing that as
General he had helped Athens reach this position. It was also a morale-
booster for troubled times: we are the greatest; we will overcome the enemy.
In fact, it may be more accurate to think of the Parthenon as a victory monument than as a temple: it housed the spoils of war, its sculptures celebrated
conquest, and, oddly, despite the presence of Pheidias' statue, we never hear
of a priestess being attached to the temple; nor did it have its own altar, but
borrowed that of the Erechtheum. In later centuries, it certainly became a
place of worship—first as a Christian church, and then as a mosque—but its
original function is not entirely clear.

13

Women, Sexuality, and Family Life

Reconstructing the kind of private matters that I want to touch on in this chapter is often a delicate matter. One has to read between the lines of the literature, bearing in mind that it was written by male members of the wealth elite for whom there was often a lot at stake, and who had firm ideas about how such things were meant to be. Then again, another important source is the corpus of surviving law-court speeches—but in their case one always has to remember that the speakers were trying to win a suit, even to save their lives, and that they were bound to have put a certain spin on their presentations. Archaeology is some help, in the sense that, say, house designs can tell us something about women's lives, but generally one has to supplement literature with cracking the codes of vase-painters, who allow us invaluable but tantalizing glimpses of domestic life, as though we were pedestrians briefly passing a window open to our gaze.

Athenian Women

In one of Xenophon's books, written in the first half of the fourth century, the wealthy Athenian landowner Ischomachus explains the facts of her new life to his young bride. She will work indoors, while he is outside, in the fields or in town, doing men's work in public. This is divinely ordained, he explains: the gods have made men's bodies and minds suitable for outdoor work, and women's weaker bodies and less sturdy minds suitable for indoor work.[1] The idea is founded, of course, on a basic fact of agriculture—that field work commonly requires male muscular strength.

The vast majority of Greeks believed unquestioningly in this separation of the male and female spheres. Some women even cultivated indoor pallor, and used powdered white lead as a cosmetic. When Herodotus wanted to convey the topsy-turviness of the Egyptian way of life, he gave as one example the fact that "women go out to the market and engage in trade, while men stay at home and do the weaving."[2] Essentially, a woman's job was to practice the virtue of self-effacement, to raise children, and to keep house. Women were supposed to find fulfillment in marriage and motherhood as men did in war and politics. The idea that women could play a part in politics was so fantastic that Aristophanes used it twice (in *Lysistrata* and *Assemblywomen*), to raise an immediate laugh. The Greek polis was a men's club. In public speeches, women were rarely named; instead they were called so-and-so's wife or daughter.

Women had a bad press. In Greek myth, the gods, wanting to punish men for their sins, created Pandora, the first woman, and gave her a desirable body and a deceitful mind; she released all evils into the world. Helen, Clytemnestra, the Amazons, the Maenads, Phaedra, Deianeira, Circe, Medusa, Medea—in the myths, women who threaten the world of men with their sexuality, moral weakness, or irrationality outnumber and outweigh meeker souls such as faithful Penelope and self-sacrificing Alcestis. Then the poets taught men to regard women as oversexed, drunken shrews, and Semonides of Amorgos likened women to animals—the dirty sow, the cunning vixen, the sluttish bitch, the lazy donkey, and so on, with only the woman who resembles the industrious bee coming in for praise.[3]

Given these preconceptions, men liked to have the controlling hand. Although they regarded their wives as among their greatest assets, for the productive work they did and for their perpetuation of the household into the next generation, the leading male was very much the paterfamilias; theoretically, his were the final decisions, in everything from household finances to how much makeup his wife should wear. The fact that his wife came to him as a teenager, who had spent most of her life indoors, while he

1 Xenophon, *On Estate-management* 7.10–43.
2 Herodotus, *Histories* 2.35.
3 Semonides of Amorgos, F 7 West (mid-seventh century).

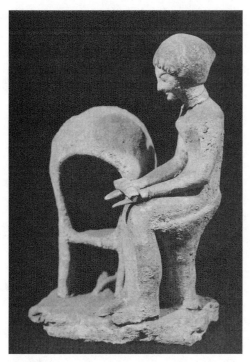

Figure 13.1. Bread-making. It was a woman's job, as in this statuette, to make bread in the home. Here she is about to place her rolled dough into the oven. This crude statuette—a plaything?—dates from the Mycenaean period. Strasbourg Archaeological Museum. © De Agostini Picture Library / G. Dagli Orti / Bridgeman Images.

was likely to be in his late twenties gave him a distinct advantage when it came to dictating the terms of their relationship.

The only full citizens of Athens were adult males. Athenian women were not enrolled on the deme registers and had few rights under the law. In particular, they were not allowed to own or inherit property, bring prosecutions, or vote. A child was legally an orphan if his father was dead, even if his mother was still alive. Like slaves and metics, women were legal minors, in that their interests had to be represented by a male guardian. This would typically be the father until the girl was married, when her husband took over.

Since under Athenian law only males could own property, there were hoops to be jumped through when, as commonly happened, a man died leaving only a daughter. In order to keep the property within the family, a male guardian had to be found from among her close kin on her father's side, descendants of a common great-grandfather. If she was unmarried, her new guardian married her, in the hope that she would in due course give birth to a son who could inherit the family property. If either she or her new guardian were already married, they were supposed to get divorced so that they could marry each other. If she already had an adult son, he could act as her guardian; if she had an underage son, the arrangements would keep the property in the family until he could inherit.

All Greek communities were concerned to maintain the number of citizens and therefore soldiers, and this meant that many of them had laws forbidding the sale of the family estate to non-family members. The same thinking lay behind these regulations about women: it was their job to transmit property from one male member of the family to another, to preserve the family and its estate. Something similar went for their dowries. A dowry was the woman's share of her birth family's estate, and she held it in trust for her children. While she was married, her husband had free use of it, but it was not his—but then it was not hers either: it belonged to her future children. In the event of a divorce, it had to be returned to her father or guardian in full.

Women had a clear civic duty—to produce the next generation of citizens. One of the ritual sentences pronounced at an Athenian betrothal ceremony (a formal pledge in front of witnesses) by the future bride's father was: "I give you this girl for the plowing of legitimate children."[4] If a woman failed to produce a male heir, she might face divorce; if she did produce a male heir, she might receive more respect from her husband, and perhaps correspondingly more freedom. Once established within a household, it became her domain, but she had to be careful not to enter into any commercial transactions over the value of one *medimnos* of barley (no more than a few drachmas), unless she had her husband's permission, because otherwise he could invalidate the transaction.

Wider Horizons

There is no doubt that Athenian women lived restricted lives. "The greatest glory," Thucydides has Pericles say, "will accrue to the woman who is talked about least among men, whether for good or ill." Or, as Sophocles pithily

---

4 Menander, *The Grump* 842; *The Short-haired Girl* 1013–1014; and elsewhere.

put it: "A modest silence is a woman's crown."[5] But there were opportunities for wider horizons. For one thing, it was upper-class women who were more likely to live with such restrictions; in poorer households, with fewer or no slaves, women had to do more and get out more—and it should be remembered that poorer households were the vast majority. Many small businesses, run from the home, must have been managed or comanaged by women, especially when the menfolk were away at war. Many women certainly knew as much about the household finances as their husbands.

It was considered vulgar for a woman to be seen in public without being modestly veiled and accompanied by a slave or a friend, but even under these conditions there were opportunities for interaction with the wider world. The restrictions were applied more in town than in the country. But, in both town and country, older women worked as midwives and younger women as wet nurses; women of all ages worked in the fields, especially at harvest time, or went out collecting wild greens. They visited neighbors and seers and husbands in prison, fetched and carried water at the public fountains, washed clothes in the river, joined in funeral processions, went to the public baths, attended certain public gatherings, played a part in many religious festivals, went shopping in the Agora. Once in a while, a woman might have to go to the office of some public official, to register her divorce, for instance. Poor women worked in the Women's Market section of the Agora as shopkeepers, selling mainly food and textiles, products for which they could put to use expertise acquired at home.

Religion was the domain where women gained the greatest freedom in the Archaic and Classical periods. The Thesmophoria, for instance, was a festival that was widely celebrated throughout Greece; in Athens and some of the outlying demes, it was held in the middle of the fourth month of the Athenian year, Pyanepsion (October/November). Given the time of year, and the fact that it was held in honor of Demeter and Persephone, it seems to have been a way of marking or anticipating the return of Persephone from the underworld to the upper world and the resumption of growth in the fields after the heat of summer. The festival was for women only (they had to be married, and citizens rather than metics), and men were strictly excluded, on pain of severe punishment. It lasted for three days in Athens, but up to ten days in some Sicilian towns, and for that period of time the women left their homes and camped out in makeshift huts in the precinct

5 Thucydides, *History* 2.45.2 (Crawford/Whitehead no. 163B); Sophocles, *Ajax* 293.

of the Two Goddesses. Probably no more than a few dozen women were involved, because they all had to fit inside the precinct and keep what was going on secret.

In the summer, about three and a half months before the Thesmophoria, women threw various offerings—piglets (representing female genitalia) and cakes in the shape of male genitalia and other phallic symbols—into pits (natural or excavated) in the ground, symbolizing the underworld. The central act of the festival was the bringing of this rotten mess, the *thesmos*, back up to the surface, while chanting the ritual words. The remains were then consecrated, and would later be mixed with seed and ritually sprinkled on the three sacred fields of Attica, which had previously been ritually plowed, to promote fertility throughout the land.

This festival was far from being the only religious occasion when women gained more freedom than usual. They were allowed to play important roles in religion and in mourning because they were considered less rational than men, and more prone to express emotion. This is also why there are so many prominent female roles in Greek tragedies (even though actors were always male). Women gained a kind of equality in the household and in religion, but it was men who dictated the terms.

Spartan Women (and the Shortage of Spartan Men)

The above sketch applies to the women of Athens, and probably to those of many other Greek states as well, but it did not apply universally. In Sparta and a few other places, women had more freedoms. In Sparta, this was originally due to the fact that, up until the age of thirty, Spartiate men did not spend time at home, but in barracks along with their peers, and even after that age the mess, not the household, remained the center of their world. Their womenfolk were therefore largely responsible for their households, disposed of large sums of money, and were not restricted to chores such as weaving and kneading dough, which were taken on by helot women or slaves. Spartan women were allowed to dress lightly, in a way that seemed immodest to other Greeks, who called them "thigh-flashers."[6]

---

6 E.g. Ibycus F 65 Edmonds.

The crucial difference from Athens was that Spartan women could own property, which came to them as a dowry or by inheritance. On the death of her father, if a Spartan woman had a brother or brothers, she received half the amount of land that he or they did; otherwise she inherited the lot, or shared it with a sister or sisters. Over the course of the Classical period, male Spartiate numbers went into a steep decline, so that there came to be many husbandless Spartan women, with even more responsibilities and public duties. By the middle of the third century, the richest people in Sparta were women, and they wielded considerable influence through their many male clients, despite their inability to hold political office or vote. Many Greeks, especially Aristotle, were shocked at the license allowed Spartan women and saw it as a real flaw in their system. If women have wealth, they gain influence over the male leaders of the community—and so Aristotle asked scornfully: "What difference is there between women ruling and rulers being ruled by women?"[7]

Spartan women were just as important in the religious sphere as women all over Greece—especially unmarried women, as choral dancers—but they were also, to the astonishment of other Greeks, educated to a certain extent. Girls elsewhere might be taught at home to read and write to a basic level, but otherwise their education mainly concerned the domestic work they would have to do as wives. Spartan girls not only learned their letters at home, but they went to school in age-groups to learn singing and dancing and sports, just as their brothers did (though far less intensively, and for far fewer hours). All in all, it was probably better to be a woman in Sparta than in Athens.

However, the freedoms allowed Spartan women opened a calamitous flaw in the system. Because women could inherit, in some cases—in increasingly many cases—despite the enormous amount of land available, the sizes of farms that men inherited shrank until they could no longer contribute to their messes, which meant that they lost their citizenship. The women, meanwhile, continued to accumulate property. The process was accelerated by the concentration of wealth in fewer and fewer families, as already wealthy men and women combined their estates, and then had few children so that they would not have to divide the estate too much. Spartan society was ruined by greed.

---

7 Aristotle, *Politics* 1269a–1271b; the quotation is from 1269b32–34.

In 479, there were eight thousand Spartiates, full Spartan citizens; by the middle of the fourth century, there were perhaps a thousand. The problems created by the inheritance rules and greed were accelerated by the catastrophic earthquake of 465, and then the Spartans were almost continuously at war for sixty years from 431. In military contexts, they could often make up the shortfall by recruiting helots, Perioeci, allied troops, and mercenaries, leaving senior posts and homeland defense to Spartiates, and making sure that Spartiates did not bear the brunt of the fighting. The army with which Agesilaus invaded Anatolia in 396, for instance, included only thirty Spartiates, his staff officers. But in political terms, by the middle of the fourth century Sparta was dominated by a relatively small elite of rich men and women.

Why did they not correct the situation? Why did they not extend citizenship to a larger number of men? Some remedial steps were taken. Around 500 it became the custom to treat unmarried Spartiate men with insulting disdain; only men with sons were allowed to go and die at Thermopylae in 480; a regulation was introduced after the earthquake of 465 exempting a man from military service if he fathered three sons and from all taxes if he fathered four. But these were band aids, not solutions. The same goes for wife-sharing (p. 110).

It was probably pride that stopped them taking the necessary steps—the same sort of pride that kept them from fortifying their city with a defensive wall until the cusp of the third and second centuries. As fourth-century Agesilaus is reputed to have said, pointing to his troops: "These men are the Spartans' walls."[8] So, I think, they were proud of their ability to maintain their position high in the pecking order of states even with fewer citizen soldiers than their rivals. It was only once the Peloponnesian War had exposed the inefficiency of this attitude that Spartan society reached its crisis point.

Marriage and the Household

A household (*oikos*) was constituted by marriage; it consisted, normally, of a man and his immediate family—wife and children, but possibly siblings and members of the previous generation too, on both his and his wife's

8 Plutarch, *Moralia* 210e (*Sayings of Spartans*).

side—and his slaves, livestock, and property. But a household was also seen, in a more four-dimensional fashion, as the family as a whole, including its past and future members. For citizens, the household was therefore the way in which their citizenship was passed on to future generations of legitimate heirs. The current inhabitants saw themselves as custodians, keeping the household and citizenship in the family. The *oikos* endured, but its members changed generation by generation.

Marriages were arranged—that is, the betrothal took place—between the husband-to-be and the father or guardian of the girl. By the time the couple got married, he was in his late twenties or early thirties, and she was aged fourteen or fifteen—so, soon after she became fertile, she was safely confined within legitimate marriage. A poor man was looking chiefly for a helpmate and someone to bear him sons to carry on his profession. A rich

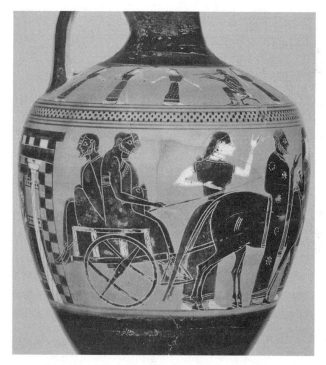

Figure 13.2. Wedding scene. Here we see a bride riding on a mule-cart to her new home, with the groom seated beside her. She has removed her crown and veil, ceremonially exposing her face to her husband for the first time. This lekythos was painted by the Amasis Painter in the middle of the sixth century. Metropolitan Museum of Art, New York, 56.11.1.

man wanted the same, but he was likely also to be seeking political or economic advantages from the union. Commonly, he married close kin, as we have just seen, in order to preserve property within the family.

Marriage was for reproduction, rarely for love; there was no premarital dating, and, especially given the age gap between them, husbands and wives rarely went out together for social occasions or engaged in intimate conversation as equals. Married couples had sex, but rarely slept together. An upper-class man was more likely to experience passion with his boyfriend or mistress. It was apparently worthy of note that, once he had got rid of his wife and installed his partner Aspasia in his house, the Athenian statesman Pericles used to kiss her on leaving her side in the morning and on returning after work.[9] For his wife, an upper-class man felt *philia*, "affectionate friendship," but rarely *erōs*, "passionate love." In fact, according to the fourth-century Athenian speechwriter Isaeus, a man who displayed too much affection for his wife was inviting gossip-mongers to regard her as a prostitute.[10]

Divorce, the dissolution of the household, was straightforward, as it had to be, given that one was even obliged to divorce under certain circumstances. Divorce was a matter simply of the husband sending his wife (and her dowry) back to her father or her father's heir, or of the wife leaving the married home and registering the separation with the appropriate official. There was stigma attached for the woman, so it was more common for the man to initiate proceedings. On one notorious occasion in late-fifth-century Athens, the wife of Alcibiades tried to initiate proceedings by going to the Archon's office to register the divorce—she was fed up with his multiple affairs with partners of both sexes—but Alcibiades dragged her back to his house.[11] Known grounds for divorce (apart from the legal complexities surrounding heiresses) include childlessness, nonpayment of a dowry, and adultery.

Sex and Sexuality

Sex was *ta aphrodisia*, "the rites of Aphrodite." Greek marriages were monogamous—were, indeed, the origin of the European tradition of

9 Plutarch, *Pericles* 24.6.
10 Isaeus, 3 13–14 (*On the Estate of Pyrrhus*).
11 Plutarch, *Alcibiades* 8.3–4.

monogamy—but while women had to be sexually faithful to their husbands, the men suffered no such restrictions. A man could have sex with his slaves, there were plenty of prostitutes in every town, he might have a boy lover, and he could keep a mistress.

Nearly all prostitutes were slaves or metics. If a citizen woman worked as a prostitute, she made herself unclean and was not allowed to enter sanctuaries. There were various categories of prostitute, from cheap brothel-workers and streetwalkers (*pornai*, the general word for "prostitutes"—hence our "pornography") to expensive courtesans (*hetairai*, "companions"). Some whores traveled around from town to town in troupes with their keeper; many followed armies. Piraeus, naturally, down by the docks, was one place to go to find sex, and another was the Cerameicus district, straddling the northwestern stretch of the city walls. Archaeologists have uncovered one twenty-room brothel there, but *pornai* also worked outside, up against a wall or a tombstone.

Another category of prostitute, though no doubt with considerable overlap of personnel, doubled as entertainers at symposia. Many prostitutes, apart from the very cheapest, were expected to entertain their customers in some way. Men were spending extended time with prostitutes—eating and drinking, making conversation, making music together—and since prostitutes were less bound by conventions than their wives, it is understandable that men fell in love with them. They were expected to be sexy, but wives were not; *hetairai* were expected to be cultured, but wives were not. And so prostitutes were hired for longer-term associations—traveling abroad with a client, perhaps, or even cohabiting on a permanent or semipermanent basis. Some prostitutes were bought from their owners by one or more men with exclusive rights, and set up in their own apartment.

Although we do not quite know the background of Aspasia of Miletus, Pericles' partner, it is possible that she started as a prostitute, until Pericles took up with her. Often, as in Pericles' case, this was something a man would wait to do until his citizen wife had given him a son or sons. But the other main market for *hetairai* consisted of elite young men, sowing their oats before taking a citizen wife. A talented *hetaira*—good-looking, intelligent, cultured, good in bed—could make a lot of money. We hear of fees in the hundreds of drachmas, to be compared with half a drachma for quick relief from a streetwalker. In fact, a successful *hetaira* could earn herself the right to set up house on her own (as respectable women could not and would not) and choose her customers.

Figure 13.3. Aphrodite of Cnidus. World-famous for its beauty, the original of this famous statue by Praxiteles of Athens has not survived, but many copies were made, showing the goddess in a variety of slightly different poses. Staatliche Antikensammlung, Munich, 258. Photo © bpk Bildagentur / Art Resource, NY.

Along with Aspasia, the most famous *hetaira* in Athens was the beautiful Phryne, who modeled for the best artists of the day (around 340): Praxiteles sculpted her in marble as the first fully nude female sculpture in the West, the famous "Aphrodite of Cnidus"—an image of the goddess bathing— while Apelles of Colophon painted her as "Aphrodite Rising from the Sea." Another Athenian beauty, Thais, became the wife of Ptolemy, the first Macedonian king of Egypt.

Male prostitutes, a rarer breed, occupied the same range from cheap to expensive. In upper-class Athenian society, "Greek love" (a term for homosexuality coined in the eighteenth century) was not regarded as perverted, against a standard of heterosexuality as normal. But outside of that social circle, homosexual relationships were not widely approved, and in some states they were illegal. Although men did sometimes become long-term lovers (as were the Athenian playwright Agathon and a man called Pausanias, both of whom appear in Plato's *Symposium*), the most common form of homoeroticism was, literally, pederasty—"sexual desire for boys" from about the age of fourteen. It was accepted that a noble youth had a kind of beauty, and that older men would be attracted to him and would try to win honor by winning his favors. But a man's attraction to a boy or to another man said nothing, in our terms, about his "sexuality"; it did not make him gay as opposed to straight. When Greeks thought about sex, they focused less on the genders of the people involved than on who was doing what to whom—who was the penetrator and who was penetrated.

Athenian homoeroticism was, as far as we can tell, largely an upper-class phenomenon. The gymnasium (where boys and adult men alike exercised naked) and the symposium, both elite venues, were common settings for homosexual activity. "Happy the lover," sang Theognis, "who exercises in the gymnasium and then spends the rest of the day at home in bed with a beautiful boy."[12] But the older man was expected to cultivate the boy's mind as well—to be a kind of godfather.

If an affair took place, the partners would likely be faithful to each other and would typically stay together for a few years, while the boy was still beardless. What the boy got out of the affair—and this too is why it was an upper-class phenomenon—was a form of patronage. In return for "gratifying" his lover, as the Greeks rather delicately put it, he would expect the older man to act as an extra guardian in public life, to introduce him to the best social circles, and later, perhaps years after the sexual side of the affair was over, to help him gain entry into the political life of the city. Hence the comic poet Aristophanes characterized politicians as "wide-arsed"—as having been thoroughly buggered in their youth.[13]

12 Theognis, *Elegies* 1335–1336.
13 Aristophanes, *Acharnians* 716, *Clouds* 1088–1094.

Female homosexuality certainly existed as well, but we know less about it. Men tended not to talk about it, because it disturbed their gender categories, and women rarely had the opportunity to write down their experiences. The most famous traces of love between women were written in the Archaic period. It seems that on Lesbos groups of unmarried women met in a kind of school, where they were groomed by older women in the feminine arts and crafts. Within these circles, love could blossom, and it apparently did in the heart of one of the teachers, Sappho:[14]

> Whenever I catch a brief glimpse of you, my voice fails me,
> My tongue mangles words, at once a subtle fire runs under my skin,
> There is no sight in my eyes, my ears ring, and I drip with cold sweat.
> I am seized with trembling all over, I am paler than grass.

14 Sappho, F 31, 94 Lobel/Page.

14

The Peloponnesian War

Tension between Sparta and Athens was scarcely relieved by the thirty-year peace treaty of 446. The final insults blew up in the 430s, with Corinth once again the target of Athenian maneuvering. First, the Athenians sent help to Corcyra (modern Corfu), a democratic Corinthian colony that was in bitter dispute with its mother city and possessed a substantial fleet. Then, while trying to recover rebel Potidaea, a strategically placed town in the northern Aegean, they trapped a force of Corinthian volunteers inside the town, who had come to help their former colony secede from the Athenian alliance. Another Spartan ally, Megara, was suffering from economic sanctions imposed by Athens after a diplomatic row. The Spartans had no choice but to protest, since the Corinthians had the best fleet in the Peloponnese (though no match for the Athenians) and they needed to secure the loyalty of the Megarians, who had been allies of the Athenians only fifteen years earlier. The Athenians offered to allow a neutral state to assess the Spartan complaints, as they were obliged to by the terms of their treaty, but the Spartans refused: they could not afford to risk losing the case. Besides, who would dare arbitrate such a major dispute between the two Greek superpowers, and who would enforce whatever decision the arbitrator arrived at?

By the autumn of 432, the Peloponnesian League had voted for war, but nothing happened for some months except more futile diplomacy. Every Spartan approach was brushed aside by Pericles. A flashpoint was all that was needed, and it was the Thebans who supplied it, with a surprise attack in March 431 on Plataea, an Athenian ally and the only Boeotian holdout from their confederacy. The attack failed, but it was taken by all parties to have been the first act of war.

At the start, the Spartans could count on allies from all over the Peloponnese, Megara, and much of central Greece, but one of the Athenians'

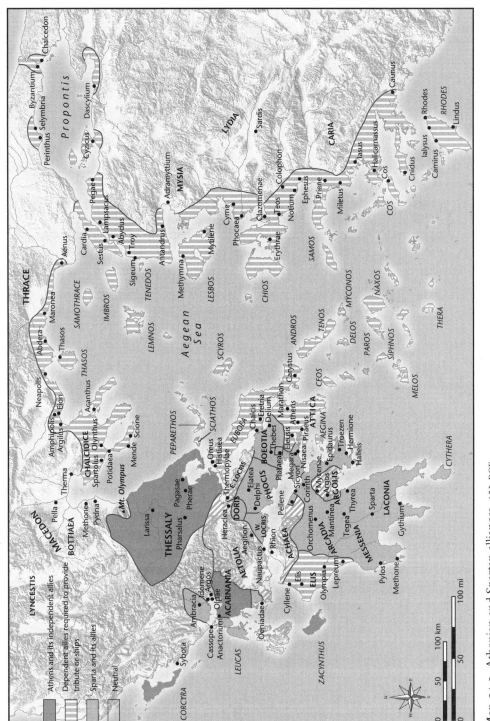

Map 14.1. Athenian and Spartan alliances, 431 BCE.

first acts was to clear the island of Aegina of its residents and repopulate it with Athenians, using a past religious crime as an excuse. The Athenians had as allies the two hundred or so states of the former Delian League, the Thessalians (with their magnificent cavalry), Corcyra, Zacynthos, and (since the late 450s) Acarnania—useful allies for a naval power, and the island of Cephallenia was taken from the Corinthians in the first year of the war. The Greeks of Sicily and southern Italy were divided fairly evenly between the two sides. With the Greek world effectively falling into two camps, this was set to be the greatest war ever of Greeks against Greeks.

Sparta's avowed intention was to put an end to the Athenian alliance, which was portrayed as a form of enslavement of fellow Greeks. In fact, as everyone knew but no one could admit, this was a war to determine which of the two states would be the leader of the Greeks. Liberation was just a cynical watchword.

The Archidamian War

The Peloponnesian War fell into distinct phases—so distinct that it is far from clear that we are dealing with a single war. But it is traditional, following Thucydides, a contemporary of the war and its greatest historian, to see the phases as parts of a single action. The first ten years of the war are called the "Archidamian War," after the Eurypontid king of Sparta, Archidamus II.

Lacking an effective fleet—the Spartans requested naval help from the Syracusans, but local conflicts made it impossible for them to comply—Archidamus was confined to land. The strategy he chose was to invade Attica in order to devastate the farmland and provoke the Athenians into giving battle—a battle he was confident he could win. This was, above all, psychological warfare, and it nearly worked: Pericles had difficulty restraining the Athenians when they saw the damage being done to their land. But restrain them he did, and so Archidamus tried again the next year, and in several of the subsequent years. The Spartan army arrived when they expected the cereal crops to be ripe enough for them to steal or burn, and stayed for a few weeks at the most, doing as much damage to farmland as possible.

Pericles' strategy was to let Peloponnesian energy exhaust itself against the city's defenses; the Long Walls and Athenian control of the sea meant that they could still be supplied. The Athenian cavalry emerged to protect the farmland around the city, and the navy was used for very effective raids on the Peloponnesian coastline. These naval expeditions were generally timed to coincide with the Peloponnesian invasions of Attica, so that there would be fewer people cooped up inside the city and the Peloponnesian forces would be encouraged to leave sooner. Until 424, the Athenians also invaded Megaris twice a year, to disrupt sowing as well as the harvest, but if the intention was to force Megara back into alliance with Athens, it was ineffective. Megara had its own Long Walls, built, ironically, with Athenian help when they were allies, and they kept the town safe.

The Peloponnesian invasions of Attica caused little material harm, as we are assured by an unknown fourth-century historian.[1] They did not penetrate far into Attica, and the damage they did, though serious for the farmers whose land suffered, had no broader economic significance. But the invasions had an unexpected side effect. Everyone who had no other place of refuge (in the hills or a fortress) camped within the walls of Athens— inside the city itself, and along the corridors of the Long Walls. There were perhaps 100,000 extra people stuck inside the city in crowded and unsanitary conditions. In 430 a plague (now securely identified as typhoid fever)[2] reached Athens by ship from Africa. Over the next three years, it ravaged the city and wiped out perhaps a third of the population. The northern army, besieging Potidaea, became infected too, and a thousand men died there in a month.

The plague succeeded where the Spartans were failing. The Delphic oracle had come out on Sparta's side at the beginning of the war, so this was a second blow from Apollo, the god of epidemics as well as prophecy— and superstition was further stoked by the fact that, by some miracle, the plague never infected the Peloponnesians or their allies. The Athenians made an attempt, a few years later, to recover the god's favor by purifying his sacred island of Delos, but in the meantime, with their morale plummeting, in 430/29 they charged Pericles with embezzlement and suspended his Generalship. He was reinstated at the beginning of 429/8, but the elderly statesman died only a few weeks later from the plague.

After Pericles' death no single politician stood out for a while. Since their leaders were more nearly equals, the Athenian people acquired a reputation for fickleness, as they followed the advice of whichever populist speaker they happened to find persuasive on any given day or issue.

---

1 *Hellenica Oxyrhynchia* 17.5.
2 http://www.scientificamerican.com/article/ancient-athenian-plague-p/.

In 427, for instance, after the rebel Mytileneans had been besieged into surrender, the Athenians first voted to make an example of the town, the largest on the island of Lesbos, by killing all its male citizens and enslaving the women and children—but then the very next day they changed their minds. Utter atrocity was commuted to the execution of a thousand men, thought to be the ringleaders of the uprising, and the Athenians hamstrung the Mytileneans in the usual way by denying them a fleet and city walls.

The End of the Archidamian War

It was proving hard for either side to gain an advantage. The Boeotian Confederacy completed its tally by taking Plataea in 427, after a two-year siege—but the Athenians had more or less evacuated the town before the siege began. The Boeotians destroyed it anyway. On Corcyra, democrats and oligarchs massacred one another, with the democrats finally proving the more successful and the more bloodthirsty. The Athenians made an attempt to widen their alliance in Caria and Lycia. Suspicious of the Chians, in 424 they ordered the demolition of their fortifications.

In 427 the Athenians' Sicilian allies sent no less a person than the world's greatest orator, Gorgias of Leontini, to plead their cause, and in response the Athenians achieved some success in preventing the spread of Syracusan influence and fortifying Ionian states there against their Dorian neighbors (the Dorian–Ionian polarity was sharper—or at any rate exploited more—in Sicily than elsewhere). In 424, however, a general peace among all the Sicilian Greek cities, the Peace of Gela, brought to an end the Athenians' campaign and any further ambitions they might have entertained about Sicily. The Spartans carried out their usual invasions of Athenian territory, and the Athenians attacked Melos and Boeotia in 426, along with their regular invasions of Megaris. The Athenians, who had stationed a fleet at Naupactus in the Corinthian Gulf in 430, beat off several assaults from the Spartans or their allies in the region, with their Generals Phormion and Demosthenes doing sterling work. An indecisive state of affairs, on both Sicily and the mainland—but the scales were about to tip in the Athenians' favor.

In 425, on the initiative of Demosthenes (though he was not in office that year), the Athenians landed a force on the Messenian peninsula of

Pylos in the southwest of the Peloponnese, threw up a fortress, and filled it with Messenians from Naupactus. It was to serve as a base for disaffected Messenian helots to stir up rebellion and wage guerrilla warfare. This was a good plan in itself, but it proved even better than expected when, in the course of trying to drive the Athenians off the peninsula, a force of several hundred Spartans became stranded on the islet of Sphacteria, just off the coast. They held out better than expected, but the Athenians eventually overran the island, and the remaining Spartans surrendered—to everyone's surprise, since Spartans were not supposed to surrender. Two hundred and ninety-two prisoners, among them 120 Spartiates, were taken to Athens. The prisoners must have included men of very high rank, because, fearing for the hostages' lives, the Spartans put an end to their annual invasions of Attica.

The Athenians were in a very strong position. They undertook a radical upward revision of the allies' tribute, greatly increased the number of places they expected (in some cases unrealistically) to pay tribute, and tightened up the procedures for tribute collection. In 424, however, despite further gains (the island of Cythera, and Nisaea, the nearby southern port of Megara), the pendulum swung back against them. A bold, two-pronged invasion of Boeotia was bungled, and the Athenians were badly mauled at the battle of Delium, the first major land battle of the war.

Next, overcoming Spartan aversion to fighting far from home, their general Brasidas, who had just foiled the Athenians' latest attempt on Megara, was sent to northern Greece. With a combination of diplomacy ("he was a pretty competent speaker, for a Spartan," said Thucydides)[3] and the threat of force, Brasidas succeeded in persuading several smaller towns in the Thraceward region to leave the Athenian alliance, and then he laid siege to Amphipolis. Before an Athenian fleet, commanded by the future historian Thucydides, could bring help, pro-Spartan Amphipolitans had surrendered the town to Brasidas. The Athenians never recovered this outpost, though they tried many times. Thucydides' failure at Amphipolis led to his prosecution and lifelong exile. He retired to his estates in Thrace, from where he could survey the war, keep in touch with men from both sides, and work on his history.

With the Athenians in their turn demoralized, the Spartans seized the opportunity to sue for peace. There seemed little chance of the two sides

3 Thucydides, *History* 4.84.2.

Figure 14.1. Pylos shield. The inscription on the inside of this shield, a
real piece of tangible history, reads: "The Athenians [took this] from the
Lacedaemonians at Pylos." It may even be the shield mentioned by the historian
Thucydides (4.12) that the Athenians used as a trophy of their victory. Agora
Excavations 2008.19.0020.

coming to an agreement, however, until by chance both Cleon of Athens
and Brasidas of Sparta, the two fiercest hawks (the mortar and pestle of
war, Aristophanes called them),[4] died in a single battle at Amphipolis.
The Spartans were particularly anxious for peace, not just to recover their
POWs, but also to secure the Peloponnesian League: the old Arcadian rivals,
Mantinea and Tegea, were fighting each other, there was internal conflict in
Elis, and several member states were unhappy about the idea of rapprochement with Athens. And then there was the prospect of the expiration in 420
of the thirty-year treaty with their old enemy the Argives, who had already
made it plain that they were planning to challenge Sparta once again for
leadership of the Peloponnese.

4 Aristophanes, *Peace* 268–284.

The treaty that was drawn up in 421 recognized, with minor exceptions (the Athenians kept Nisaea and the Boeotians what was left of Plataea), the status quo that had existed before the start of the war. Athens had clearly won the war, or at least not lost it, because its alliance was still intact. The peace was to be binding not just on the protagonists but on all their allies too, and was to last for fifty years. The war seemed to be over. But the series of rebellions in the north had rattled the Athenians and they made Scione the deterrent to further uprisings. In a nasty coda to the war, the fate that the Mytileneans had narrowly avoided was meted out to this small town, which had opened its gates to Brasidas: all the men were killed, while their womenfolk and children were abandoned or sold into slavery.

The Years of "Peace"

The Peace of Nicias (named after the chief Athenian negotiator, the successful General and businessman, Nicias of Cydantidae) was a farce right from the start. Several member states of the Peloponnesian League were unhappy with it. When the Spartans demanded that the Boeotians hand over an Athenian fortress they had captured so that the Spartans could exchange it for Pylos, as stipulated by the treaty, the Boeotians demolished the fortress instead. So the Athenians held on to Pylos, but they had already dutifully returned the POWs. Then the commander of the Spartan garrison in Amphipolis refused to restore the town to Athens. Since the Spartan authorities did not punish him, and even entered into a fresh military alliance with the Boeotians, it was clear that their commitment to the peace was fragile.

The peace policy fell into disrepute in Athens too. The Athenian hawks, led by Hyperbolus and Alcibiades, took advantage of the fragility of the Peloponnesian League to arrange a 100-year alliance with the three democratic Peloponnesian states, Argos, Elis, and Mantinea. Alcibiades, son of an Alcmaeonid mother and, until he came of age in 432 or thereabouts, a ward of Pericles (Alcibiades' father had died in 447, during the First Peloponnesian War) was a rare individual. By charm and eloquence, he manipulated and influenced everyone and everything around him throughout his colorful life. Flamboyant, passionate, egotistical, opportunist, extremely wealthy and ambitious, he pursued a course of self-interest with great determination. Above all, Alcibiades was an old-style aristocrat, at odds with the collectivism of Athenian democracy; he was more concerned with the old heroic values of competition than the quieter virtues of cooperation.

In 418 the Tegeans appealed to Sparta for help against the Athenians and their Peloponnesian allies. The Spartans brought the allies to battle on the plain near Mantinea and won. The Peace of Nicias should have been one of the victims of the battle, but everyone carried on as though it were intact—as though the Athenians and Spartans had not just clashed once again on the battlefield. The new Athenian alliance was another casualty: it fell apart in disarray, with the Argives themselves—under a renewed oligarchy—the first to ally themselves with Sparta. Within a year, democracy had been restored at Argos with Athenian help, and the Argives were back in the Athenian camp, but the Spartans could still congratulate themselves for having repaired the Peloponnesian League.

In Athens, the hawks were in the ascendant. Hyperbolus' exile in 417 or 416, in the last ostracism ever held, left Alcibiades and Nicias as rivals, championing war and peace respectively. The Athenians continued on a belligerent course. Despite its relative insignificance, the Dorian island of Melos had long irritated them, not least because it was the only Aegean island not in their alliance. Since Nicias' invasion of the island in 426, the Athenians had considered it part of their league, but the Melians clearly thought otherwise and had not been paying tribute. In 416 the Athenians launched a large expedition. The Spartans were too afraid of the Athenian navy to send help. The Melians resisted until they were starved into submission. In an act of sickening familiarity, all the men the Athenians could lay their hands on were killed, and the women and children were enslaved. The island was repopulated with Athenian cleruchs. Thucydides marked the terrible occasion with a brilliant debate between the Athenians and the Melians, in which the Athenians cynically justified their actions by the doctrine that might makes right.[5]

The Sicilian Expedition

In 415 the Athenians launched their most ambitious campaign yet—a full-scale invasion of Sicily. The Peace of Gela had broken down, and Athenian allies in Sicily again needed assistance. After considerable debate, the

5 Thucydides, *History* 5.84–113.

Figure 14.2. Herm. A late-sixth-century herm from the island of Siphnos. The erect phallus was apotropaic: herms warded off bad luck and so ensured the prosperity of the building or street or district they guarded. National Archaeological Museum, Athens, 3728. Photo: Wikimedia.

Athenians converted what might have been a relatively small-scale venture into an attempt to defeat Syracuse and take over the resources of the island. The idea had been floated before, in the 420s, but had been foiled then by the outbreak of peace on the island. The excuse in 415 might have been that this was a preemptive strike, against the probability that the Syracusans would soon be free to come and help their Spartan allies. But it was utterly unrealistic to expect to be able to rule as troubled and as large an island as Sicily from distant Athens.

One night in late May or early June, just as the armada was poised to sail for Sicily, a terrible act of sacrilege took place. Herms were distinctively Athenian boundary-markers, placed at crossroads and at the entrances to streets, neighborhoods, and homes; they were busts of the god Hermes on top of plinths, each with a prominent erect penis to ward off evil. On that night, the noses and penises of dozens of these statues were hammered off.

Hermes was the god of travelers. This was clearly an attempt to jinx the expedition by men who were opposed to it. In the heat of the moment, the affair, with its "undemocratic contempt for the laws," was taken to be "part of a conspiracy to bring about a revolution and to subvert the democracy."[6] It was the scale of the planning: a lot of people must have been involved, too many for it to have been merely a drunken prank. And it was obviously members of the elite who had done it. The thinking, presumably, was that oligarchs might want to stop the expedition because, if successful, it would hugely strengthen the democracy.

A witch-hunt ensued, with generous rewards offered for information. Armed citizens patrolled the streets and fortifications of Athens and Piraeus. The Peloponnesians and Boeotians massed on the borders of Attica. Had they been expecting to find oligarchs in control of Athens? And then, at the height of the hysteria, Alcibiades and certain of his friends were denounced not for the mutilation of the herms, but for a different sacrilege: perhaps as a form of initiation into a club, they had put on a version of the sacred and secret Mysteries of Eleusis in a private house, with noninitiates present.

The Athenians might have been inclined not to take this overseriously, were it not for the fuss over the herms and the fact that Alcibiades' contempt for democracy was well known. Olympic victory was a traditional stepping-stone to personal power, and the previous year Alcibiades had achieved a unique success. It was not just that he had unprecedentedly entered no fewer than seven teams in the four-horse chariot race, and had come first, second, fourth, and seventh (the other teams presumably crashed), but also that, in doing so, he had ended a long run of Spartan victories in this prestigious event. Back home he celebrated his victories with equal ostentation, commissioning no less a person than Euripides to compose a celebratory epigram and famous painters to glorify his victories.

The authorities in Athens soon learned the names of those responsible for the mutilation of the herms, and at least sixty-five men were put to death or fled into exile; these included some of the wealthiest men in Athens, and the sale of their confiscated property refilled the Athenians' coffers. But by then the armada had already set sail for Sicily: 136 ships (rowed by men who would double as soldiers on land), over five thousand hoplites, a small cavalry troop, and plenty of light-armed soldiers. A ship was dispatched to bring Alcibiades back from Sicily to face trial. He agreed to return, but he and his closest friends

6 Thucydides, *History* 6.27.3, 28.2; Crawford/Whitehead no. 214.

escaped in southern Italy. In Athens, he was found guilty of sacrilege and condemned to death in absentia, but by then he had made his way to Sparta, where influential men were his friends. The Spartans welcomed such a high-profile defector, and listened as he advised them to send aid to Syracuse and added his weight to the idea, long discussed in the councils of the Peloponnesian League, that the Spartans should occupy some location in Athenian territory, to match the Athenian and Messenian occupation of Pylos.

The campaign in Sicily continued for another two grueling years. Before the Spartans sent reinforcements in 414, the Syracusans were on the ropes; afterwards, with their confidence raised, they never lost the initiative. In 413, facing certain defeat and having lost access to the sea, the Athenians tried to escape by land. There were forty thousand of them, soldiers and sailors. But the Syracusans had placed men in ambush along the various routes. On the sixth day of the retreat, one division of the Athenians surrendered; their numbers had been reduced from twenty thousand to six thousand by constant enemy harassment, and their General, Demosthenes (who had come out with reinforcements earlier that year), gave up. On the eighth day, the other half, under Nicias, was massacred, leaving only a thousand survivors. The two Athenian Generals were executed, while their men were kept captive in quarries, and those who did not die of starvation or exposure were ransomed or sold into slavery.

Decelea and the Ionian War

By now, Athenian manpower had been reduced to about a third of its prewar level. But this was still enough to fight on, albeit with increasing desperation and recruitment of slaves and mercenaries. Money was a big issue. Earlier in 413, the Athenians had canceled the allied tribute system and replaced it with a 5 percent tax on goods passing through all the harbors under its control. This would make life easier for the rich throughout the alliance, who were shouldering much of the burden of the tribute, and allow the Athenians to assess their income more accurately, given the increasing likelihood of the allies defaulting on their tribute payments. It is a testament to the density of seaborne traffic in the Aegean even at a time of war or impending war that the Athenians thought that this was the way to stabilize and improve their income. Part of the plan was to make Piraeus a more attractive destination for traders, since the equivalent tax there remained at 2 percent.

In the spring of 413, the Spartans prepared to invade Attica and renew the war in Greece. The year before, the Athenians had joined the Argives in raiding Laconia itself, and this blatant violation of the phony peace gave the Spartans their excuse. But this time ravaging the countryside was not the purpose of the invasion. They occupied the village of Decelea, fortified it, and stocked it with troops (mainly Boeotians), under the command of one of the kings. Now they had a permanent force about twenty-two kilometers (thirteen miles) from Athens, and this gave them the ability to wage economic war on the Athenians by getting slaves to abscond, by being a permanent presence in Athenian farmland, and by interrupting the overland route from Euboea, which was not only a source of grain, but was where much Athenian livestock had been kept since the start of the war. Supplies from the island now had to be ferried around Cape Sunium, and the fortifications there were duly improved. The mines at Laurium virtually ceased operating, and silver coinage did not resume until the late 390s. The writing was on the wall for Athens.

Given current Athenian weakness, the Spartans were approached in 412 by several Athenian allies—including the big three: Lesbos, Chios, and Euboea—who wanted guarantees of support if they defected. In the north, league members from Byzantium to the Hellespont also sent envoys. Ominously, the delegations from western Anatolia were accompanied by representatives of the two Persian satraps, Tissaphernes and Pharnabazus. In 422, not long after the new king, Darius II, had come to the Persian throne, the Athenians had entered into a nonaggression pact with him. But as far as the Persians were concerned, the Athenians had trampled on this agreement when, in 414, they had helped Amorges, a Persian rebel in Anatolia. Besides, urged on by their king, the satraps wanted a return to the situation before the Persian Wars, when all the Greek cities of Anatolia had been tributaries of the Persian Empire. For their part, the Spartans were now prepared to cede the forty or so Eastern Greek cities in return for Persian cash, a decision that exposed the hollowness of their claim to be liberating Greeks. The entrance of Persia into the war doomed Athens; they made a fatal mistake when they allied themselves with Amorges.

The two satraps were not working in concert, and the Spartans chose the Aegean and Tissaphernes over the Propontis and Pharnabazus; they had an urgent need of Chios' fleet of sixty warships, and Alcibiades had useful contacts among the oligarchs on the island. Once the Chians had declared for Sparta, Alcibiades used the island as a base from which to stir up rebellion in Ionia. Tissaphernes paid for the campaign. A measure of Athenian alarm at these developments is that they chose to break into a special fund of a thousand talents that had been set aside at the beginning of the war for use only in the direst emergency. They sent ships out to the Aegean in increments, until there were over a hundred at Samos.

In short order, the Athenians succeeded in undoing some of the Spartan gains. Chios descended into civil war for a few years. The Athenians lost Rhodes, however, another critical island, to an oligarchic coup. The Spartans endeared themselves to Tissaphernes by capturing the rebel Amorges and handing him over for punishment, but in 411 they abandoned Tissaphernes, who was proving slow with his payments, and moved north to Pharnabazus' territory on the Hellespont, where they made Abydus their base. They were now in a position to support rebellion in the region and threaten Athenian shipping through the Hellespontine bottleneck. The Athenians had no choice but to follow them north.

Oligarchy in Athens

By 412 Alcibiades had made himself unwelcome in Sparta. It was widely known that he had had an affair with the wife of Agis II, the Eurypontid successor of Archidamus, while Agis was stationed at Decelea. He needed to find a way back home to Athens. Meanwhile, he left Sparta for Tissaphernes' court in Sardis. From there he opened negotiations with the Athenian fleet on Samos, holding out the prospect of bringing Tissaphernes over to their side if they would sponsor his return to Athens. The condition was that the democracy which had expelled him would have to go.

There were two principal Athenian factions on Samos, and both were ready to listen to Alcibiades. One was led by Thrasybulus of Steiria, who, although a democrat, was prepared to accept a moderate, broad-based oligarchy, formed by limiting citizenship and office-holding to a few thousand men, if that was what it took to gain the Persian cash that would save Athens. The other faction on Samos was led by the famously corpulent Peisander. On the face of it, he agreed with Thrasybulus, but in fact he was committed to a narrower oligarchy. And it was he who went to Athens in the December of 412 to try to bring about the revolution that would restore Alcibiades.

Peisander's ostensible mission in Athens went well: there was opposition, but in the end the Assembly, chastened by the disastrous failure in Sicily, was prepared to entertain the idea of "a different kind of democracy" in order to avoid the destruction of the city, even at the cost of allying themselves with the hated barbarians and recalling Alcibiades.[7] Peisander hinted that such measures would be temporary, and that when the war was won with Tissaphernes' help, full democracy would be restored. In any case, Athens was already a little less democratic than it had been; in 413 a special board of ten elders called Preliminary Councilors (Hagnon and the playwright Sophocles were two of them), appointed for an indefinite period, was created to make it less easy for the Athenians to make the kind of decision that had led to the Sicilian expedition. Presumably they vetted proposals before passing them on to the Council.

Peisander's covert mission was also successful. The rich were hurting: the state was increasing its financial demands on them just when the war was slashing their profits. So it was not hard for him to find sympathizers, and he went the rounds of the politicized clubs, urging them to action. In the spring of 411, while these men published their oligarchic manifesto and created a climate of fear in Athens by assassinating a few of their opponents, Peisander visited Tissaphernes and Alcibiades in Sardis to report on progress and to negotiate the precise terms of Persian support. To his dismay, he found that Alcibiades did not have the influence over Tissaphernes that he had claimed, and that Tissaphernes was in fact not interested in helping the Athenians at all.

Peisander and his supporters on Samos decided to go ahead without Alcibiades. They stirred up oligarchic revolution on the island, and sent envoys out to do the same elsewhere. Returning to Athens, Peisander found the Assembly, ignorant of the fact that Tissaphernes was not coming in on their side, amenable to his plans. Before long, Peisander and his cohorts had pushed through their oligarchic reforms. The Council was to be replaced by a new Council of Four Hundred, the members of which were all oligarchic sympathizers and were not subject to annual re-election. The Assembly would be convened by this council as it saw fit, and officeholders would be selected from a pool of the five thousand wealthiest men of Athens. Pay for public service was suspended. A special committee was formed to conduct the census that would lead to the list of the Five Thousand, but only the moderates among the oligarchs—led by Theramenes, the son

7 Thucydides, *History* 8.53.1.

of Hagnon—wanted to see the process completed. Peisander and the rest wanted the Four Hundred to constitute a new start for Athens.

The Athenians on Samos were appalled by what was happening back home. They refused to recognize the legitimacy of the oligarchy and set themselves up as the democracy in exile. Thrasybulus was elected General, and Alcibiades, to his relief, was invited back and honored in the same way. There was some talk among the troops about sailing to Athens and forcibly restoring democracy, but that would have meant abandoning the eastern Aegean to the enemy, and Alcibiades curbed their haste. "On this occasion, at least," Plutarch commented drily, "he proved to be the savior of the state."[8]

Still, the Athenian oligarchs were thrown into disarray by the combination of the threat from Samos and Spartan successes in the Hellespont, where enough Athenian allies had defected for the grain route from the Black Sea to be in severe danger. None of the oligarchs' plans had succeeded, they had alienated Theramenes and the moderates, and their only hope for remaining in power lay in rapidly negotiating peace. They sent an embassy to Decelea, but Agis was committed to using military force to bring Athens to its knees. On his return, Phrynichus, one of the oligarchs who had gone to negotiate with Agis, was stabbed to death in the Agora. When democracy was restored, his assassin, an Aetolian, was rewarded with citizenship and a golden crown worth a thousand drachmas "in return for the good he has done the city and the Athenian people."[9]

But now the Athenians lost patience. Many of them were employed just then in Piraeus, fortifying for the oligarchs the Eetionea headland—preparing it, perhaps, for a Peloponnesian garrison. They downed tools and, with Theramenes' encouragement, formed a mob and marched on Athens to force the Four Hundred to keep their promise of establishing the Five Thousand. The rioting, and the unpopularity of their underhand attempt to treat with the Spartans, made the regime of the Four Hundred untenable, and the final blow came with the defection of Euboea, encouraged by a Spartan fleet which the Athenians were helpless to resist.

On Theramenes' initiative, power was transferred to the Five Thousand, defined now not just as men of means, but as all those who could afford their own hoplite equipment (who probably numbered quite a bit more than five

8 Plutarch, *Alcibiades* 26.4.
9 Meiggs/Lewis no. 85 = (translated) Fornara no. 155; Rhodes no. 165.

thousand, in fact). Peisander and the main oligarchs fled to Decelea; those who remained were executed. The rule of the Five Thousand lasted only a little longer before succumbing in the summer of 410 to pressure from the democrats on Samos. Naval victories in the Hellespont reminded them that a constitution that excluded the Thete rowers of the fleet was not sustainable. Full democracy was restored. Athens had survived its worst constitutional crisis since the foundation of democracy a century earlier.

War in the Hellespont

One of the first things the Five Thousand did was pardon Alcibiades. But he chose not to come home immediately: Athens was still in turmoil, with the trials going on of men whose conspiracy he had arguably instigated. So, despite lacking any official position, he continued to serve the Athenian cause, but as a maverick—as a kind of privateer who accepted orders from Athens, as Walter Ralegh did from Elizabethan England.

The years from 411 to 408 were the climax of Alcibiades' military career. Victories in the Hellespont, culminating with the annihilation of the Spartan fleet at Cyzicus, secured the grain route for the foreseeable future. Money was hardly forthcoming from Athens these days, but Alcibiades proved good at extorting cash from Athenian allies, and his men plundered Pharnabazus' territory as well. They garrisoned Chrysopolis on the Bosporus and instituted a tax of 10 percent on freight. Though there may have been a toll station there earlier, its legitimacy is unclear; when the Byzantines did something similar in 220, the Rhodians (who had by then inherited the Athenians' naval dominance) were so alarmed about the possible damage to their and their friends' profits that they declared war.

On the strength of these successes, Alcibiades at last returned to Athens in 408. The Athenian people had short memories: without a doubt his advice to the Spartans was partly responsible for their terminal condition, and he had fought well for the Spartans in Ionia. But he paved the way for his return by sending a large number of captured enemy ships to Piraeus, laden with prisoners and booty. The Athenians revoked all the charges against him, had the priests undo the curses they had pronounced after the affair of the Mysteries, elected him General with special powers, and sent him back to Samos to regain control of the Aegean as he had of the Hellespont. Before his departure, he stage-managed a great symbolic coup by providing a military escort that allowed the traditional procession from Athens to Eleusis for the Mysteries—the same Mysteries he had been accused in 415 of mocking—to take place for the first time for five years, since the Spartan occupation of Decelea.

Lack of resources, however, made it impossible for the Athenians to fight successfully on several fronts. They had to concentrate on the Hellespont and the Aegean, for the sake of their alliance and their grain—and on the mainland Nisaea, Cythera, and Pylos were all retaken. Then decisive disaster followed: the Spartans had bypassed the self-serving satraps and entered into an agreement with Darius himself. The king's younger son, Cyrus, was due to arrive in Anatolia with a mandate to support the Spartans with both men and money. Gone were the Athenians' last hopes of securing Persian funds for themselves, or even Persian neutrality. Ironically, the Athenians heard the news when their own ambassadors, on their way to Susa to try to negotiate some such deal for themselves, met the Spartan delegation on its way back.

The Surrender of Athens

Alcibiades found his match in the new Spartan commander in the Aegean. As bold as Brasidas, Lysander burned not just to see the Athenians crushed, but to see Sparta elevated to their position in the Mediterranean—with him at the helm. Lysander was the son of a Spartan Inferior (and so had been sponsored through the Spartan *agōgē* by another family), and he seems to have longed to prove himself greater than true Spartiates. The young Persian prince Cyrus, aged fifteen, could have found no better shoulders on which to lay responsibility for the war in the Aegean.

Cyrus took up residence at Sardis in the spring of 407. Lysander spent much of the year, based at Ephesus, training and preparing his men. He assiduously avoided battle with the Athenians; he built relationships with the Eastern Greek oligarchs (whether or not they were currently in power); and he flattered his way into Cyrus' favor and coffers, receiving over time as much as five thousand talents. The friendship between the two men was entirely self-serving on both sides: Lysander wanted Persian cash, and Cyrus knew that he would one day be in need of Spartan hoplites. His elder brother was the heir to the Persian throne, but Cyrus wanted it for himself.

Alcibiades' fall was sudden, burdened as he was with Athenian expectations. In the summer of 407, his fleet was defeated by Lysander off Notium, the port of Colophon, while Alcibiades himself was away, perhaps irresponsibly. The Athenians did not choose him as one of the Generals for the following year. Rightly fearing prosecution back home, Alcibiades withdrew to a private fortress on the Thracian Chersonese. He never saw Athens again. Conon of the deme Anaphlistus, an experienced General, was sent out to Samos to replace him as commander of the demoralized fleet.

In the campaigning season of 406, the Spartan fleet of 140 ships, led this year by Callicratidas, was more than twice as large as that of the Athenians and dominated the Aegean. Following a stunning victory at sea, in which thirty Athenian ships were lost, Callicratidas managed to trap Conon with forty remaining ships in the harbor of Mytilene. In a last desperate effort, the Athenians manned their ships with untrained men from every walk of life and stratum of society. In July this motley fleet of 110 ships set sail from Athens, under the command of no fewer than eight of the ten Generals for that year. At Samos, they were joined by an allied flotilla and the remains of the Aegean fleet, and they sailed to relieve Conon. Callicratidas left ships to enforce the blockade and set out with the rest to intercept them. The battle, off the Arginusae islands, east of Lesbos, was long and hard, but in the end the Spartans were well and truly beaten, losing seventy-seven ships to the Athenians' twenty-five. The Spartan dead included Callicratidas.

In the emotional seesaw of these closing months of the war, Athenian hopes were again high. They had defeated a triumphant Spartan fleet and they stood a chance of regaining their Ionian losses. But they threw it all away. First, they condemned to death all the Arginusae Generals, despite their great victory (and despite the misgivings of the Assembly chairman for the first day of the trial, the philosopher Socrates), for having failed to pick up over two thousand of their own sailors who were floundering in the water and subsequently drowned. Two of the Generals had disobeyed the summons home, but the other six, including the younger Pericles, were executed. The Generals explained that a rising storm had made it impossible for them to rescue the men, but the Athenians wanted blood. The poor had borne the brunt of the fighting in the Ionian War; the battles had taken place at sea, so that losses among the hoplite rich had been negligible. They had had enough, and the Generals were suitable scapegoats.

Cyrus was obliged to return east for a long while to attend the deathbed of his father and the accession of his brother as Artaxerxes II. Lysander's men saw some action on the coast of Anatolia in the summer of 405, and they even raided the coast of Attica, but his main target was again the Hellespont and the Athenian grain supply. The Athenians had no choice but to follow him there. They beached their ships at Aegospotami, so that they could keep an eye on the Spartans on the other side of the Hellespont at Lampsacus, but they had to forage widely for provisions. It so happened that Alcibiades was nearby, and he still felt sufficient loyalty to the Athenian cause to warn the three Generals at Aegospotami of the weakness of their position. But they rudely sent him packing: "Others are in command now, not you."[10] This was Alcibiades' last appearance on the public stage: he was assassinated in 404, seemingly by Pharnabazus, to gratify the Spartans.

When Lysander's attack came, the Athenians were entirely unprepared and he caught most of the ships still drawn up on the shore. All but ten or twelve ships were captured or destroyed, and thousands of men lost their lives, since Lysander had given the order to take no prisoners. Conon was one of those who escaped. In Athens, they prepared for siege. Lysander speeded up the process of starving them into submission by sending every Athenian he found in the Aegean back to Athens—all the thousands of cleruchs and garrisons, for example.

Within a very few weeks, the entire Athenian alliance had fallen apart. All over the Aegean, Lysander and his men were made welcome, democrats were cruelly massacred, and narrow oligarchies imposed instead, supported by a garrison under a Spartan governor. Democracy was truly under threat. These oligarchs were the men whose friendship Lysander had cultivated over the previous years; in effect, he was creating a personal empire. The towns, now subject to Sparta, were required to continue paying tribute, disguised as contributions to the war effort. Only the Samians held out for a while, and were rewarded with a grant of Athenian citizenship, should any of them choose to live in Athens—an empty gesture at the time, since Athens was staring defeat and possible destruction in the face. After settling affairs in the Aegean, the Spartans sailed for Athens in October 405.

Lysander ravaged Salamis and blockaded Piraeus with 150 ships, while Pausanias, who had come to the Agiad throne of Sparta in 409, invaded from the Peloponnese and camped right outside the city, and Agis' forces hovered nearby at Decelea. Starved of both food and allies, the Athenians were soon forced to negotiate. Remembering how they had slaughtered or expelled whole populations, they miserably expected the same treatment themselves. There was a division of opinion among the Spartan allies;

10 Plutarch, *Alcibiades* 37.1.

Lysander wanted to destroy Athens, and some of the allies agreed with him. But the stated purpose of the war had been the ending of the Athenian alliance, not the destruction of Athens, and after prolonged negotiations, in 404 Athens surrendered not all its fortifications, but only the Long Walls and the Piraeus defenses. The war fleet was limited to twelve ships; the Delian League was formally dissolved, and Athens was effectively incorporated into the Peloponnesian League. The fortifications were demolished amid scenes of celebration: "People thought that this day marked the beginning of freedom for Greece."[11] They were wrong.

11 Xenophon, *Hellenica* 2.2.23; Crawford/Whitehead no. 240.

15

The Instability of Syracuse

When the Greeks arrived in the eighth century in Sicily, rich in timber and fertile volcanic soil, they found two main native peoples there, and some minor ones. The Sicels (after whom the island was named *Sikelia*) occupied the territory to the east of the Halycus River, and the Sicanians lived to the west of it. Both these peoples were agriculturalists and pastoralists rather than town-dwellers. There were also a couple of nonnative peoples, of whom the most important were the Phoenicians. The Phoenicians had long had trading contacts on the island, and at much the same time that the Greeks were settling in the east and spreading west, the Phoenicians were doing the same from the other direction. They came especially from what is now Tunisia in North Africa, where there was the great Phoenician-founded city of Qart Hadasht ("New City")—Carthage to us.

The presence of the Carthaginians determined much of the course of the history of the island. Carthage was a commercial powerhouse, and at times of peace Sicilian Greeks and Carthaginians happily traded together, but they were often at war. So much of the energy of the Greeks was absorbed in fighting with the Carthaginians, and not infrequently among themselves as well, that they rarely became involved with the affairs of the mainland Greeks to the east. They had strong trade links, particularly with the Peloponnese and the Adriatic, but no Sicilian warships sailed as far east as the Aegean until a late stage of the Peloponnesian War, toward the end of the fifth century, and rarely thereafter. These ships belonged to Syracuse, which was more or less the hegemonic power in Greek Sicily, and on which, therefore, the Greek historians focused, to the detriment of our knowledge of other Greek states. It makes sense, then, to devote a separate chapter to a brief account of Syracusan history.

Thucydides has a Syracusan politician express regret "that Syracuse is only rarely in a condition of internal peace,"[1] and we will find this contention amply borne out. Syracuse and the other Sicilian Greek cities (but especially because of Syracusan influence and meddling) were extremely unstable societies. This reminds us that, as far as we can tell, many other Greek cities were pretty unstable as well, racked by what the Greeks called *stasis*, fighting between different political factions which, at its worst, constituted civil war. Athens, however, was different; there were only two periods, neither of more than a few months in duration, when democracy was replaced by oligarchies, and it is a good historical question to wonder why that should be so: what was it about Athenian society, compared with Syracuse, that made stability possible there?

Archaic Syracuse

By the sixth century, much of Sicily had been divided up by Greeks. In some cases, the process had involved hostilities with the natives, but in others peaceful cooperation. The site of Syracuse, a Corinthian foundation of 734 on the offshore island of Ortygia (Quail Island), was chosen above all for its magnificent harbors, fertile farmland, adequate rainfall, and bountiful freshwater spring, the famous Arethusa (whose eponymous nymph was said to have fled to Sicily from Greece to avoid being raped by a river god).

The Greek newcomers destroyed the native settlement on Ortygia and drove off the inhabitants; by the middle of the sixth century, the island had been linked to the mainland by a causeway, and the city rapidly grew. Over the years, Ortygia was turned into a virtually impregnable citadel, one of two that the city boasted. The Syracusans came to control much of the southeast of Sicily, with their territory bordered by two other Greek cities, powerful Gela to the west (a Rhodian foundation) and Leontini to the north, settled by Chalcidians from an earlier Sicilian foundation. The first of the great Doric temples for which Sicily is famed was built in Syracuse in about 575; it was made of sandstone and dedicated to Apollo. The Greek cities of Sicily soon became the wealthiest in the Greek world thanks to their grain and timber, and their temples bear witness to their pride. There is a nice foundation story for Syracuse, in which two Corinthians go to Delphi

1   Thucydides, *History* 6.38.3.

Figure 15.1. Temple of Concord, Acragas. This beautifully proportioned Doric temple from Sicily is one of the finest to survive anywhere in the Greek world. It was built in the third quarter of the fifth century. The attribution to Concord is not much better than a guess. The columns have a height of 6.7 meters (22 feet). Photo: Wikimedia.

to inquire about founding a settlement somewhere overseas. The oracle asks whether they want health or wealth, and the one who founded Syracuse (a man called Archias) chose wealth, while his friend chose health and was assigned Croton in southern Italy.[2]

Syracuse's huge territory, amounting at this time to at least three thousand square kilometers (1,150 square miles) was held with the help of different forms of subordination. The local Sicels had been reduced to serfdom, like the Spartan helots, and outlying villages and towns were dependencies of Syracuse, somewhat like the Spartan Perioeci. Only the inhabitants of the city and its immediate hinterland were full citizens, somewhat like the Spartiates. By the middle of the sixth century, other Greek communities on the island were beginning to clash not just with the natives but with the Carthaginians as well, but in the east of the island Syracuse was remote from these conflicts, and its progress was relatively unimpeded.

2 Strabo, *Geography* 6.2.4.

So far, so typical: apart from its unusual size, Syracuse could be any Greek city anywhere. But the Sicilian Greek cities were plagued by internecine feuding of a more persistent kind than the cities of Old Greece, and several of them fell under tyrannies relatively soon after their foundations. The mainland Greek ideal of republicanism seems not to have sunk deep roots in Sicily. Tyrannies remained very common throughout its history. Perhaps the constant threat of the Carthaginians, and frequent warfare among the Greeks themselves, made warlords seem desirable leaders; perhaps, also, it was due to the fact that the Sicilian tyrants were commonly far more oppressive rulers than the Archaic tyrants of mainland Greece and Anatolia. They never gave the republican spirit a chance to flourish.

Syracuse was ruled for a long time by an elite group called the Gamoroi, "the landowners," descendants of the original settlers. They seem to have been typical landowning aristocrats, and the lifestyle they developed was hardly different from that of their friends in Old Greece: they spent their wealth ostentatiously, lived luxuriously, took part in international games and international trade (exchanging grain and timber for minerals, of which the island was short), and networked with their peers abroad. Curiously, for all their great wealth, the Sicilian and southern Italian Greeks never developed their own international games, although they had plenty of local festivals. They preferred to go to the trouble of taking part in mainland Greece, because it kept them in the mainstream of Greek life.

Tyranny in Syracuse

The Gamoroi were briefly ousted late in the sixth century, though it is not clear what kind of constitution replaced them; it was possibly some kind of democracy—and the Athenian democracy was taking off at much the same time—since they were ousted by a coalition of ordinary citizens and serfs. In any case, the replacement did not last long. The exiled aristocrats joined forces with Gelon, the tyrant of Gela, and returned in 485 to install him as ruler of Syracuse as well, with themselves holding all the privileged positions under him. The political unification of Syracuse and Gela created by far the largest and strongest bloc on the island, and Gelon also entered into a marriage alliance with Theron, the ruler of Acragas. Gela, Acragas, and Syracuse were all Dorian cities. But despite this auspicious beginning, Gelon's Deinomenid dynasty (named after his father) would rule

Syracuse for only twenty years before being swept away in another of the great upheavals that characterize Syracusan history.

Gelon died in 478, but in his short reign he made Syracuse the dominant military and cultural force in the whole of Sicily—a position the city retained, with few interruptions, for the next two and a half centuries. He developed a war fleet of some two hundred triremes, easily outnumbering any other city on the island. He initiated a program of monumental building that made Syracuse the most beautiful city in the Greek world (before the development of Athens later in the century), and sponsored artists and intellectuals. He made himself the most powerful ruler in the Greek world at the time—perhaps even the most powerful man in Europe—but his methods were sometimes drastic. For instance, he greatly expanded the city beyond the original settlement on Ortygia and filled the new suburbs with former inhabitants of Gela and elsewhere—towns that were ruthlessly reduced and depopulated. He cleared Syracuse of its urban poor by selling them into slavery, and the city was remodeled as an elite enclave, like Sparta.

The Sicilian tyrants rarely did things by halves, and Gelon was not alone in instituting massive relocations of people. Since the tyrants rarely dared to arm the rural and urban poor—that would have been asking for trouble—they employed mercenaries in large numbers. A chief purpose of these relocations, then, apart from the assertion of dominance, was to free up land—especially land close to the Carthaginians—with which to reward mercenaries and friends. We know of thirty such forced relocations in Sicilian history, about as many as we know from the rest of the Greek world in total; sometimes whole towns simply ceased to exist, or were reduced for decades.

But Syracuse's newly augmented power attracted the attention of the Carthaginians in the west of the island. At the battle of Himera in 480 (which took place, some said, on the same day as the battle of Salamis in Greece), Gelon and Theron decisively defeated the Carthaginians, who had invaded ostensibly in support of Greek enemies of Syracuse, and six years later, Gelon's brother and successor, Hieron, overwhelmed the Etruscans, who had been the allies of Carthage, at sea off Italian Cumae. These two victories temporarily secured almost the entire island against the Carthaginians, and left the tyrants of Syracuse and Acragas in control of most of Greek Sicily. With monuments at sites such as Olympia and Delphi in Greece, the Deinomenidae portrayed the victories as the defeat by Greeks of barbarians, just as the Greeks were doing for their victory over the Persians. In a poem written for an athletic victory of Hieron's, Pindar equated the battle of Cumae with Salamis and Plataea.[3]

The twelve-year reign of Hieron was marked or marred by further extreme acts of violence, further movements of populations, and further expansion of Syracusan power and influence. On his death, Syracuse descended into relative chaos, with power contested among democratic elements, Hieron's brother, his son, and his numerous former mercenaries, who were being denied full citizenship by the "old citizens," those who had gained citizenship under Gelon rather than Hieron. Even the Sicels and some of the other Sicilian Greek cities became involved. It is not clear what the primary cause of the troubles was—mercenary rioting, resentment that had been building up against the tyrants, or some combination of factors. At any rate, the common people, or their champions, won, and in 465 Syracuse gained a democratic constitution and marked the occasion by instituting the cult of Zeus the Liberator. Other cities in Sicily were undergoing similar violent transitions, or shortly would be under pressure from the Syracusan democrats. Anyone looking at Sicily in the 470s would have said that the tyrants' positions were secure, but by 460 they had all died or been swept away, the victims of civil wars and internal dissent, and every Greek city in Sicily was a republic.

Democracy and Dionysius

The Syracusan democracy, based on a citizen population of about twenty thousand, gave legislative power to the popular assembly, but it is not clear whether it had an Athenian-style council, tasked with preparing the agenda for the assembly, or whether the board of Generals simply presented issues to the assembly for acclamation. Aristotle hesitated to call the Syracusan constitution at this time a democracy,[4] but there is evidence to support the view that Syracusan democracy was actually quite close to the Athenian version, and possibly even modeled on it. For a few years, for instance, until the protests of the rich secured its demise, they had available an institution resembling ostracism, so that they could remove anyone who seemed to be

---

3 Pindar, *Pythian Odes* 1.75–80; the sentiment was repeated by the fourth-century historian Ephorus of Cyme, *FGrH* 70.186.
4 Aristotle, *Politics* 1304a.

aiming for tyranny. The institution was called *petalismos* after the leaves on which the names of the offending men were written; whereas ostracism sent an Athenian into exile for ten years, in Syracuse the penalty was five years. Moreover, Thucydides tells us that in 414 the Syracusan people sacked the entire board of Generals, which implies that they were not just formally sovereign but had real power, or at least took it on this occasion.[5] We hear also of occasional assemblies at which the people displayed sufficient confidence to shout down speakers.

The art of persuading mass audiences—that is, the art of rhetoric—was being developed at this time in Sicily, and in Syracuse in particular; we know little about its beginnings, but from the second generation we have several works from the pen of Gorgias of Leontini, whose style, far too florid and artificial for our tastes nowadays, was greatly admired in his own day (c. 480–380—he had a very long life). Rhetoric is such an essential tool of Athenian-style democracy that it could surely only have flourished like this under a democratic regime. On balance, it seems best to conclude that for several decades of the fifth century Syracuse did have a real democracy, tempered, perhaps, in certain ways by the powers of the board of Generals.

The power vacuum that followed the fall of the Sicilian tyrants in the 460s allowed the indigenous Sicels to form their own state (probably federal in nature) under a warlord called Ducetius, the only leader of the Sicels whose name we know. This bid for ethnic freedom was crushed by the Syracusans in 440, however, and Syracuse became the leader of the Dorian communities in Sicily, which had been chiefly threatened by Ducetius. Tension built up between the Dorian and Ionian cities, and in the 420s, as we have seen, the Athenians decided to intervene. They had assumed championship of the Ionian states that formed the majority of the Delian League, and had gained quite a few allies among the Ionians of Sicily and southern Italy. In 427 they sent a large force to help the Ionians against the Dorians. A peace accord hammered out at the Congress of Gela in 424 brought this war to an end and temporarily united the Sicilian Greek cities, but in 415 Alcibiades renewed the fight. As we already know, the Athenians' Sicilian Expedition came to a catastrophic end in 413.

But now it was the Carthaginians' turn. Between 409 and 406, they overran much of Greek Sicily, committing terrible atrocities, and even put Syracuse under siege. The terrified Syracusans abandoned

5 Thucydides, *History* 6.103.4.

democracy (they had instituted a more radical version following their victory over the Athenians) and put themselves in the hands of a new tyrant, Dionysius I. Once he had overcome a couple of rebellions against his rule, he dominated Sicilian affairs for forty years and acquired an undeserved reputation as the archetypal fierce and paranoid despot, and therefore liable to absurd stories such as that he had a trench dug around his bed to deter assassins.[6] He was certainly ruthless—though no more than other Sicilian tyrants—but his son attracted the hostility of the Athenian philosopher Plato, whose prejudices have tainted the tradition about the father as well. Dionysius was apparently born in relatively humble circumstances, but his military skills in the war against the Carthaginians brought him to the fore. Tyrants reappeared in other Sicilian cities too at much the same time; it seems that the Carthaginian war destabilized the whole island.

The Carthaginians had intended to sweep the Greeks off the island altogether, but their attack fell apart as their army succumbed to disease. Dionysius settled with them, but only to buy time to prepare to renew the war. In 397 he was ready. While driving them back (and paying them back in kind for their earlier atrocities), Dionysius seized the opportunity to expand Syracuse again at the expense of the weakened Greek states. By the time he died in 367 (apparently after over-indulgent celebration of the victory of a tragedy he had written for the Athenian Lenaea festival), after the longest reign of any tyrant in the Greek world, Syracuse controlled an empire consisting largely of Greek cities in Sicily and southern Italy, and his court was famed all over the Mediterranean. His only failure was that he had not driven the Carthaginians entirely from the island, as he had intended, but had settled for a negotiated peace that left the "barbarians" as a strong presence on the island. The fundamental dynamic of the island, Greeks versus Carthaginians, remained in place.

Stability and Instability

What emerges from the story of Archaic and Classical Syracuse and Sicily is that events moved on a large and violent canvas there. It is not just that the Sicilian communities suffered a far greater degree of internal turmoil, often

6 Cicero, *Tusculan Disputations* 5.20.

apparently manifesting as class warfare, so that Syracuse and other places swung violently from monarchy to democracy (or something like it) and back again. It is also the scale of events. Virtually the entirety of the island was won or lost in wars against the Carthaginians and in wars of Greeks against Greeks, with tens of thousands of battlefield losses. In the course of these wars whole cities were devastated, and populations were left to find new homes or were forcibly resettled; Syracuse was one of the very few Sicilian cities that was never destroyed at any point in its history, even during the Roman sack of 212. The Sicilian tyrants operated with an astonishing freedom that would not be matched for many years, until the rise of the Hellenistic monarchs.

Aware, perhaps, of this difference between themselves and the mainland Greeks, members of the Sicilian Greek elite spent vast sums of money presenting themselves back in Old Greece as holders and perpetuators of traditional values. Pindar and Bacchylides were employed over and over again to laud Sicilian victories in the international games; costly statues in marble and bronze, erected in Delphi and Olympia, announced to the Greek elite that their peers in Sicily were just like them, and then a little better. One of the most famous of these statues is the bronze charioteer in the Delphi Archaeological Museum. This was originally part of a typically extravagant statue group: a lifesize bronze chariot, with four horses and a charioteer, flanked on either side by two other horses, each with a jockey or groom. Even Delphi had never seen anything like it. The work was commissioned by Polyzalus, the last of the Deinomenid dynasty, in 466, just before the democratic revolution, to commemorate his brother Hieron's victories at the Pythian games. It was probably an attempt to patch up one of their interminable quarrels, which were exacerbated by the fact that Gelon had divided his rule, leaving Hieron as civic governor, but Polyzalus in command of the armed forces.

Syracuse alone suffered around twenty serious uprisings in its history, and the same could be said of most of the other Sicilian Greek states—as it could of many states in Old Greece too. But not Athens. Syracuse had two or perhaps three periods of democracy, one lasting several decades in the fifth century, but democracy always gave way to violence and tyranny. By comparison, the stability of the Athenian democracy seems remarkable: in two hundred years, there were only two serious disruptions (one in the last chapter, one in the next), and both were short-lived and due to extraordinary wartime circumstances.

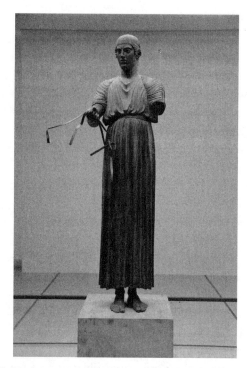

Figure 15.2. Delphi charioteer. This lifesize bronze statue is one of the most famous to have survived from the ancient world. The eyes are inlaid in glass and stone, copper was used for the lips and eyelashes, and silver for his headband. His calm expression and rigid pose are typical of the artwork of the time (the 460s). Delphi museum, 3520, 3485, 3540. Photo © Gabriella Irvine.

How do we explain this? An element of Athenian history that was evidently missing in Syracuse was the emergence of people such as Solon and Cleisthenes, men who could rise above social divisions and work for the good of the community as a whole; Syracusan leaders seem always to have preferred self-aggrandizement and self-interest to the common good, and it was a telling feature of their regimes that they used all forms of propaganda (such as coins, victories, and building programs) to develop cults of themselves as notable personalities. Moreover, we could speculate that the frequent changes of population in Syracuse, especially as successive dynasts installed their friends and the mercenaries that had worked for them, ejecting their enemies and the previous dynast's mercenaries, made it hard for Syracusans to attain the sense of identity and belonging that Athenians had, and which helped to unify them.

But the overriding factor was, I think, communication or its absence. Communication among separate interest groups is vital for successful political systems, but it seems clear in the case of Syracuse that there was rarely, if ever, any effort to reconcile the interests of rich and poor, so that the city lurched between one and the other. Rich and poor were frequently at loggerheads, and even if the poor had the numbers, the rich had the money and the weaponry (that is, they could afford to hire mercenaries), and usually won. In Athens, on the other hand, there was a broad consensus of rich and poor, based on the fact that the rich were allowed social power as long as the poor retained political power. In Athens, that is, the poor accepted that they needed the rich to lead, because the rich had the time, education, and money to do so (and maybe the expertise too), and so the poor tolerated the privileges of the rich and rewarded them for their leadership. Isocrates, though hardly sympathetic to democracy, summed it up well in the fourth century:[7]

> Our forebears resolved that the people should, tyrant-like, appoint officers, punish failure, and adjudicate disputed cases, while those citizens who had the time and sufficient means should be responsible for the state as servants of the people. If they did their jobs honestly, they should receive a vote of thanks and be content with that honor. If they proved to be bad administrators, they should receive no mercy and be liable to the severest penalties. How could one find a more stable or more fair democracy than this, in which the most competent are appointed to office, but authority over them is wielded by the people?

The poor agreed to let the rich lead, and the rich agreed to adjust their values to democratic ideals. In their speeches to the Assembly and the law courts, the rich de-emphasized their advantages and presented themselves as true democrats and their enemies as motivated by self-interest. They made a real effort to meet the democracy halfway—even if sometimes out of fear of the consequences of not doing so.

At the same time, the poor channeled the status-seeking of the rich in democratic directions. The rich wanted to be *kaloi k'agathoi*, the beautiful and the good—so let them use their graces in the service of the democracy. The rich were in perpetual competition to outdo one another—so let them compete with the splendor and generosity of their work for the democracy. And the rich, or most of them, were happy to do so. It was only when times got tough in the Peloponnesian War—when their livelihoods were

---

7 Isocrates 2.26–27 (*Areopagiticus*).

threatened and they could see their peers losing fortunes all around them—
that the rich sought an alternative to democracy. Nor was their usual acceptance of democracy a sham, since they understood that the way for them
to retain authority was to accept the restrictions imposed on them by the
democracy. They accepted that the good of the community as a whole took
precedence over the good of any individual or class. The sense of community was greater in Athens than elsewhere, and that acted as a kind of fixa-
tive. Stability comes from collective power or a general acceptance of the
depersonalized rule of law, while instability comes from personalized power.

This is not to say that all was peace and love and harmony in Classical
Athens. Far from it. Rich were set against poor, old against young, hoplites against oarsmen, city-dwellers against countrymen. There were vigorous and passionate disputes at very many Assembly meetings, and the
dichotomies remained potentially harmful. A far greater degree of "popular
justice," such as the spontaneous stoning of wrongdoers or forms of ritual
humiliation, was tolerated than we would find acceptable today, and these
were often targeted by the poor against the rich. For example, after the restoration of democracy in 403, a man called Callixeinus returned to Athens,
assuming that he would be forgiven for allegedly having misled the people
a few years earlier; he had been the chief instigator of the mass trial of
the Arginusae Generals, and when the Athenians came to regret this decision, they had made him their scapegoat. But he was not forgiven. He was
shunned so thoroughly and successfully that he starved to death, having
not even been allowed access to food. The trial of the Arginusae Generals
in itself is another clear example of the poor reacting unconstitutionally
against the rich. But such episodes were never allowed to get out of hand.
The majority agreed that debate was the way forward and concord the goal.

It was this consensus that was lacking in Syracuse, this blend of elite and
nonelite values, which can occur only if the channels of communication are
open and if the majority are allowed an equivalently major part in politics.
In Syracuse, the gulf between rich and poor was such that they could never
communicate in this way. At times in the city's history, the rich were even
physically separated from the poor: they occupied Syracuse, and the poor
were relocated outside. The towns dependent on Syracuse, and the suburbs
of Syracuse itself, were ghettoes. In Athens, on the other hand, rich and poor
mingled on a daily basis, in the law courts, in the Assembly, in the Agora,
and in the course of their festivals and other collective practices. Athens had

more festivals and more Assembly meetings than any other city, and they were major unifiers of the social fabric.

Under Syracusan circumstances, communication and consensus are bound to be distant goals. There were far fewer assemblies in Syracuse, and far fewer politically motivated court cases, so that the two sides had little chance to hear and understand each other's concerns. Moreover, all the forced relocations of populations made it impossible for the poor to cohere as a political body and develop their own agenda in a reasonable fashion, so that violence seemed the only possible way to gain power. The assumption in democratic Athens was that, at a time of looming trouble, consultation and the collective wisdom of the Assembly were the best tools for dealing with it. In Syracuse, they turned to strong individuals instead, because the people had never been allowed the opportunity to demonstrate their collective wisdom.

16

Socrates and the Thirty Tyrants

In 399 the Athenian democracy condemned the elderly philosopher Socrates to death. He famously died by drinking a preparation of the poisonous plant hemlock, which was a standard method at the time; it was not a particularly gruesome way to go, and it was held to absolve the community from the pollution of taking a life because it was self-administered and involved no shedding of blood. He was sixty-nine or seventy years old. As he himself is reported to have said in his defense speech, why bother? He was likely to die soon anyway.[1] As a matter of fact, as we shall see, by their lights the Athenians had sufficient reasons for killing him. The affair will tell us a lot about Athens at the time.

The Thirty Tyrants

Terror and starvation stalked the streets of Athens following its surrender in 404. Land had been devastated, overseas properties lost, livelihoods destroyed or undermined; families had been decimated, and slaves had absconded or been rewarded for their military service by being promoted to metic status; the silver mines would not return to full operation for fifty years, and there were no longer any revenues coming in from the allies. There was greater tension between the poor and the rich than ever before, and the practice of politics over the next couple of decades was decidedly rancorous.

Cleophon, the leading democrat for the past decade, was arrested on a trumped-up charge at Lysander's orders and put to death. Lysander's wishes were relayed to the people by Athenians who were close to him, such as Theramenes, who had spent several weeks in Lysander's company during

---

1 Plato, *Apology of Socrates* 38c.

the siege of Samos at the end of the war. Other Athenian oligarchs had been there as well, deciding the city's future. One of those present was Critias, a cultured intellectual, one of many who returned to Athens from voluntary or enforced exile once the democracy was abolished. Another was Charicles, and all three of these men were to play significant roles in the months that followed.

In August, several months after the city had fallen, the democratically elected Generals were deposed, on Lysander's orders, and a temporary board was formed of five Ephors ("overseers") to act as an interim administration. Then Lysander arrived in person in September and used the pretext of Athenian tardiness in carrying out the terms of their surrender to impose an oligarchy of thirty men. At the Assembly that instituted the regime of the Thirty, Theramenes chose ten of the men, Critias and his fellow Ephors chose themselves and five others, and the final ten were chosen from among sympathizers present. Most of the Thirty were politically experienced men, and not a few of them had played some part in either the scandals of 415 or the oligarchy of 411. A permanent Council of Five Hundred was appointed, but its members came from a select list of only a thousand men, essentially the cavalry class, rather than from the entire citizen body; its job was to ratify the measures proposed by the Thirty, and the Thirty also gave this Council supreme judicial power, removing it from the popular courts. Piraeus for the first time received its own administration: it was placed in the hands of a board of ten headed by Charicles. The Eleven (the Athenian officers responsible, with the aid of public slaves, for arrests, prisons, and executions) were freshly chosen henchmen, supported by a volunteer police force of three hundred Knights, and all other offices were given to oligarchic sympathizers. Once the new regime seemed reasonably stable, the Spartan army departed.

The Thirty started slowly. They set about demolishing the Piraeus ship sheds, now redundant, and a symbol of the democratic power of the Athenian oarsmen. They tidied up some ambiguities in the laws. They indicated that they planned to give the Areopagus Council back its old powers and that they would reduce taxation of the rich. They cracked down on abuse of the system whereby any citizen could bring a public suit against any other citizen; the main abuse was using the threat of prosecution to obtain out-of-court payments from the rich. They banned the teaching of rhetoric, which was felt to enable a man successfully to argue a morally weak case (and besides, debate was an essential tool of democracy). These measures were portrayed as the first stages of the moral rearmament of Athens, a purging of the city.

The Thirty did little in the way of legislation, because they wanted to see Athens as the kind of place where less legislation was needed—where the good men and true were in power, who instinctively knew about such things. It was democracy, with its moral ambiguities, that needed written law. This kind of government by principle rather than precedent was how things were done in Sparta. In fact, it seems distinctly possible that the Thirty were intending to establish a Spartan-style constitution in Athens. Sparta too had five Ephors, a powerful council of thirty, and a general assembly of a limited number of privileged citizens, with limited powers. Such thorough social engineering, almost certainly the brainchild of Critias, a published admirer of Sparta, was bound to meet with opposition. As a precaution, the Thirty asked the Spartans to send a garrison.

Money was the critical issue. The Thirty chose to raise it by killing or banishing men of property, especially wealthy metics and anyone they judged to be a potential opponent, and reselling their property to other Athenians—an ugly program. Inevitably, as soon as they embarked on this course, they were less concerned with constitutional reform than with maintaining their position in the face of escalating abhorrence and resistance. Before long, their reign of terror earned them their familiar title: the Thirty Tyrants. They go down in European history as the first to make fellow citizens live in fear of the pre-dawn raid. In one of his speeches, the orator Lysias gives a vivid description of how he escaped from just such a raid, although his brother was arrested and put to death.[2] We hear that, in all, fifteen hundred people were killed in just a few weeks.[3] Others chose exile before death and were taken in by Spartan allies, despite the fact that the Spartans had ordered all their friends to treat refugees from the Thirty as the common enemies of all Greeks. It seems that the Spartans were right to see the integrity of the Peloponnesian League as precarious.

Once there was no longer much chance of opposition, the Thirty published the list of the three thousand Athenians who were to count as full citizens and members of the Assembly. Only they had legal rights; only they could bear arms, while the rest were disarmed by the Spartan garrison; only they could own property, while the rest were to be resettled, chiefly in

---

2 Lysias 12.4–23 (*Against Eratosthenes*); Crawford/Whitehead no. 244C.
3 Isocrates 7.67 (*Areopagiticus*); pseudo-Aristotle, *The Athenian Constitution* 35.4.

Piraeus. Those in Piraeus were to be the businessmen of Athens (the equivalent of the Spartan Perioeci), while the Three Thousand, like the Spartiates, were to be supported by their slave-run farms, the former owners of which had been uprooted or killed. Foolishly, the Thirty filled Piraeus, the second largest conurbation in Attica and its commercial hub, with men who had cause to resent them and needed only someone to organize them.

Civil War and Reconciliation

The resistance movement began in earnest early in 403, when Thrasybulus, earlier banished by the Thirty, reappeared from Thebes with a small band and occupied a steep, defensible hill near the village of Phyle in the hill country between Boeotia and Attica. The oligarchs' first attempt to dislodge them was foiled by a wild snowstorm. The city was thrown into crisis, and Theramenes, suspecting that the days of the Thirty were numbered, began to distance himself from the other oligarchs—just as he had in 411, and again probably in an attempt to save his skin.

Feeling increasingly cornered, and in need of a pledge of loyalty to cement their ranks, the Thirty made it a condition of membership that each of them should personally undertake at least one assassination. Theramenes refused. Critias publicly denounced him and, with armed Knights standing by in case of resistance, removed him from the list of the Three Thousand. Since the Thirty had the power of life and death over anyone not on the list, in the same breath Critias condemned Theramenes to death. More killings followed. But the oligarchs were rattled, and they moved their base of operations to Eleusis, after killing those whose houses they wanted to occupy. Eleusis was easier to defend, had direct access to the sea, and was just that bit closer to Sparta.

Meanwhile, however, Thrasybulus' force had grown to a thousand men—Athenians, metics, and mercenaries. The chance survival of an inscription allows us to see that ordinary men were involved in the fight for democracy: Leptines the cook, Demetrius the carpenter, Euphorion the muleteer, and many others.[4] Their morale had been boosted by the successful repulse of a second assault on Phyle, in the course of which over a hundred of the

---

4 Rhodes/Osborne no. 4 = (translated) Harding no. 3.

Peloponnesian garrison were killed. Thrasybulus felt confident enough to move his base of operations to Piraeus, where he would find a fresh pool of recruits. The Thirty immediately marched against the harbor town, but they were defeated in a gruesome little battle. Among the seventy or so casualties on the oligarchs' side were Critias, one other member of the Thirty, and one of the Piraeus Ten. The rest fled to Eleusis. Piraeus became a democratic enclave, and the democrats attracted metics to their ranks with the promise of citizenship under the restored democracy, and slaves with the promise of freedom.

In Athens, the Three Thousand appointed a board of ten Archons to replace the Thirty. But, alarmed by the continuing violence throughout the spring of 403 between the respective troops of Piraeus and Athens, the Ten joined the oligarchs in Eleusis in appealing to Sparta for help. The Spartans gave the oligarchs a loan to hire mercenaries, and Lysander permission to go and see to the defeat of the democrats. But a change of policy in Sparta meant that Lysander had not been in Athens long when the Agiad king Pausanias arrived at the head of an army (in which the Corinthians and Boeotians refused to take part) and relieved him of his command. Pausanias continued the fight against the Piraeus democrats, but only to soften them up and make them amenable to diplomacy. Once the two sides had agreed to a truce, he withdrew (taking Lysander with him), guaranteeing no further Spartan intervention and enabling the restoration of democracy throughout Attica—except for Eleusis, which was hived off as an oligarchic mini-state in its own right. For this—for enabling a regime that was bound to be hostile to Sparta—he got into trouble back home and was only just acquitted of wrongdoing.

There was clearly a division of opinion in Sparta, because Pausanias had in fact been carrying out the Ephors' orders. Remembering at last that they were supposed to be liberating the Greeks, they had ordered the removal from the Eastern Greek cities of the oligarchies and garrisons Lysander had established, and their replacement with the appropriate "ancestral constitutions," a vague term that meant whatever anyone wanted it to mean. Lysander's personal empire was dismantled, but he had one more trick up his sleeve: he would turn kingmaker (p. 290).

The chief provisions of the agreement between the Athenian oligarchs and democrats were that, subject to arbitration, all the visible property (land and houses, but excluding things like slaves, textiles, and furniture) that had been confiscated and sold by the Thirty was to be returned, or its cash value; and that anyone who wished could withdraw unharmed to the oligarchic enclave at Eleusis. As for reprisal, the survivors among the Thirty, the Piraeus Ten, the Eleven, and the ten Archons, if they stayed in the city, would face an investigation of their conduct, but only the most egregious crimes such as murder would be punished. Otherwise, there were to be no reprisals. In a generous gesture, it was decided that any trials that did take place would be before juries formed from the better-off members of society, those who had been among the Three Thousand, to prevent vindictive action from enemies of the Thirty.

In late September 403, the democrats processed in splendor and solemnity from Piraeus back to Athens to sacrifice in gratitude to Athena on the Acropolis. When the meat of sacrifice was shared among them, it must have been a powerful moment, binding them in their desire to make the city anew. In gratitude to Pausanias, the Athenians erected a magnificent tomb, the remains of which can still be seen, for the thirteen Spartans who had fallen during his expedition. An interim board oversaw the process of restoring full democracy. There was friction, but the Spartans held back from interfering—even when, in 401, the democrats decided to reunite Eleusis with Athens. On the pretext that the oligarchs were hiring mercenaries and planning to retake Athens, they invited the leaders of the oligarchs to a conference and massacred them.

Scars remained, naturally, and in the decades following the civil war, despite the amnesty with its "no reprisals" clause, the Athenians constantly judged their friends and enemies according to their or even their relatives' behavior during the time of the Thirty. Plenty of speakers in court cases from the following decades accused their opponents of having been close to the Thirty, but, because of the amnesty, it was never the stated reason for taking anyone to court. Nevertheless, the Athenians achieved something remarkable in reconciling the rich to the restored democracy, and writing some decades later Xenophon could say that "to this day both parties live together as fellow citizens and abide by the oaths they swore."[5] Only a few intellectuals, such as Plato and Isocrates, continued to write antidemocratic treatises, but little notice was taken of them; otherwise, there were effectively no oligarchs in fourth-century Athens prior to the Macedonian

5 Xenophon, *Hellenica* 2.4.43.

conquest. The democrats had freed Athens, and from then on the concepts of democracy and freedom were inextricably intertwined.

Education and the New Thought

What had Socrates to do with the Thirty? Perhaps little or nothing—but he exposed himself to his enemies' calumnies, as we shall see. But first, since Socrates was a teacher, we need some understanding of education as practiced in Athens at the time.

Greek education was not designed to develop critical thinking, but to socialize children—to indoctrinate them into the values of their society. Even then, schooling was far from universal: there were not many students, and they were not required to do much. Some upper-class girls were taught at home to read and write, as skills necessary for the management of their future husband's household, but literate women in Athens were likely to be foreigners, especially high-class courtesans. Boys who were destined for no more than apprenticeship to their father's or another trade also learned a bit of writing and arithmetic at home. The more fortunate spent some time out of the home in schools.

Schooling began in Athens around the beginning of the fifth century, but schoolteachers remained few and underrated in the Classical period, and unsupported by the state. Even in 330, Demosthenes could use the fact that his rival Aeschines' father had been a schoolteacher as a slur and a suggestion of low birth.[6] Schools were not institutions separate from the teachers who ran them, that could outlast a teacher's death, nor were they necessarily housed in dedicated buildings or rooms. Schools were generally many and small in cities like Athens, but few and large in smaller places: hence we hear of 119 schoolchildren dying when a roof collapsed on the island of Chios.[7]

Boys who were lucky enough to gain an education attended in a sporadic fashion, for a few weeks or a few years, three kinds of school. A *grammatistēs* taught them to read and write and do their sums, and made them study and even learn substantial chunks of epic poetry, since Homer, especially, was regarded as wise in a large number of areas. This skill set was so fundamental that probably the sons of poorer families also attended this kind of

---

6 Demosthenes 18.129, 257–258 (*On the Crown*).
7 Herodotus, *Histories* 6.27.2.

Figure 16.1. School scene. In the center, a seated teacher checks the recitation of the pupil standing before him. Behind the boy is seated a slave who accompanied him in public—a *paidagōgos*. To the left, another boy practices his lyre. Berlin, Staatliche Museen F2285. Photo: Wikimedia.

school; it cost no more than an obol or two a day. The other two schools were more specialized, and more aimed at elite children. A *kitharistēs* taught music, singing, dancing, and the lyric poets, so that the boys would be able to hold their own in the contests of the symposium and at choral festivals. A *paidotribēs* supervised their physical education at a gymnasium (likely to be publicly owned) or palaestra ("wrestling-ground," likely to be privately owned), to prepare them for all forms of athletic contest and for warfare.

School education was seen as supplementary to the company of adults, from whom one could learn the behavior and patterns of thought that were expected of a citizen. In Athens, attendance at the dramatic festivals, which focused on cultural tensions, was therefore another part of a boy's education—and perhaps one of the few that gave him some notion of critical thinking. Equally important was attending to the decisions of the people in the Assembly and the law courts, and listening to gossip and conversation in the Agora, to see what earned communal praise or dispraise. A few boys, only from the aristocracy, were further socialized by being taken under the wing of an older lover (p. 235).

How effective was this educational system? Literacy levels are very hard to assess. The urban population was likely more literate than country-dwellers; full literacy was restricted to members of the wealthier classes and educated slaves with responsible jobs in the Athenian bureaucracy. But quite a high degree of literacy was required to serve on the Council, and very many

Athenian citizens served on it at least once in their lifetimes. Athens was certainly more thoroughly literate than other states. Literacy was required for certain jobs at the deme level as well.

Education in Athens, then, was haphazard and pretty basic. By the third quarter of the fifth century, however, a new breed of teachers began to arrive, to supplement what was available. Many of the sophists (as they came to be called, but the single label disguises their specific differences) were itinerant teachers, though several of them settled in Athens for stretches of time; they taught a wide range of subjects—from mathematics to martial arts, and from history to music—with different topics being more popular in different places. Most of their teaching was less theoretical than practical. This is the most important way in which their contemporary, Socrates, differed from the sophists: if Plato is to be trusted (and his picture of Socrates is very different from that of our other main source, Xenophon), Socrates had an interest in ethical and metaphysical theory, as well as developing a method of argument and enquiry.

The kind of success the sophists were offering was very different from that which had been valued before, based on military prowess, athleticism, and good looks. Essentially, what a man needed now to be successful in Athens (and elsewhere) was the ability to speak well. The democracy generated a verbal culture, and a politician's very life, let alone his career, could depend on his ability to deliver a persuasive speech in the Assembly or law courts. Some of the sophists, then, were teachers of rhetoric and disputation (and hence of grammar, terminology, logic, and other subjects that support rhetoric and disputation). For argumentative purposes, they relied above all on probability arguments: "Is it likely that a small man such as I would have assaulted a big brute like my opponent?" By these means, they taught their students to argue both sides of a case with equal plausibility, contrary to the unreflective view that truth must lie only with one side or the other.

This higher education was designed only for the rich, since the sophists tended to charge large fees, but it was a step in the right direction, and as well as teaching in select seminars, they also gave displays of their learning or speechifying to wider audiences. Plato and Aristotle made "sophist" a term of reproach, on the grounds that their arguments were often invalid (Aristotle) and that they were concerned only with winning arguments rather than improving people (Plato). But originally the term had more or less the same implications as our "expert": sophists were clever men who were prepared to impart their skills, information, or theories to others.

The sophists latched on to and made extensive analytical use of the opposition between nature (*physis*) and convention (*nomos*—the same word means both official "law" and unofficial "custom"). Did the gods exist in reality or were they human inventions? How much trust can one put in man-made laws, seeing that they are readily changed and repealed, and differ from culture to culture? Was there such a thing as natural law instead, whose demands were more binding on men? Is it a natural law, which it is only realistic to recognize, that the stronger state or individual will rule the weaker, or should the strong restrain themselves and deny their self-interest in accordance with conventional justice? But does this not make human law a kind of tyrant? And so on.

The sophists were suspect for a number of reasons, then. They were feared as slick—as *deinos*, a word that simultaneously meant "clever" and "formidable." The most famous orator of them all, Gorgias of Leontini, did nothing to allay such fears when he likened speech to a powerful drug that operated by a kind of deceit or bewilderment to stir or pacify emotions and change men's minds.[8] There was potential here for real conflict, but it is not certain how far it went. The Thirty, as I have mentioned, banned the teaching of rhetoric, but there are traces of attacks on intellectuals earlier as well.

It seems that around 430—a time when it was critical for the Athenians, newly struck by the plague, to have the gods on their side—a decree, proposed by a man called Diopeithes, was passed to the effect that "anyone who did not pay due respect to divine phenomena or who offered to teach others about celestial phenomena should be impeached."[9] In itself, this was aimed at scientists rather than sophists, and was perhaps a way to get at Pericles, who counted the scientist Anaxagoras of Clazomenae among his close friends and was himself known for his rationalism. But the case seems not to have come to court, and Anaxagoras simply left Athens to avoid trouble. Protagoras of Abdera, the first and greatest of the sophists, also seems to have come under attack, but again the evidence does not allow us to conclude that any case came to court. On the other hand, it is certain that another of Pericles' associates (a kinsman by marriage), the Athenian musicologist and political theorist Damon of Oa, was ostracized "for seeming to be too much of an intellectual."[10] And Diagoras of Melos, a poet of otherwise little consequence, fled into exile to avoid a trial for atheism.

8 Gorgias, *In Praise of Helen* 8–14.
9 Plutarch, *Pericles* 32.1; Crawford/Whitehead no. 157.
10 Plutarch, *Aristeides* 1.7.

There was clearly a degree of intolerance in Athens during the Peloponnesian War, but a few near-prosecutions do not add up to persecution, and wealthy, leisured Athens was still a congenial culture for artists and intellectuals. They got into trouble only on those very rare occasions when they were felt to be politically undesirable or (what came to the same thing) to be in danger of offending the gods. They were not liable to prosecution if their behavior affected only individuals, but were if the state felt threatened. The legal instruments that were available to be used against them were either Diopeithes' decree or the more flexible charge of impiety.

The Practice of Law in Classical Athens

We are unusually blessed with evidence for how lawsuits were conducted in Athens, with over 150 extant speeches, from late in the fifth century until latish in the fourth century. We generally hear only one side of the case, however, and some of the speeches certainly received later polishing for publication. Nor do we know, in most cases, whether the speech was decisive; scholars tend to assume that, if the writer wanted the speech published, it was a winner. But we cannot be sure. Socrates' unsuccessful defense speech is another matter; Plato's and Xenophon's reasons for writing down their versions of it were not purely commemorative.

In so far as, from scattered references, we can reconstruct the law about impiety, relevant to Socrates' case, it read as follows: "If a man is guilty of impiety, he is to be tried in the court of the King Archon and made liable to death or confiscation of property. Any citizen who so wishes may bring the prosecution." In some areas of law, clear definitions were felt to be important, but social crimes such as impiety were deliberately left vague; as here, the focus was on procedure rather than on defining the crime. Precise definition was felt to be undemocratic, in that it would favor the legal expert rather than the common man's understanding of right and wrong. Athenian courts were more concerned to settle disputes without violence than to deliver objective justice.

Impiety cases were *graphai*, "writs," so that it was up to the community itself to bring the prosecution (in the person of the citizen prosecutor or prosecutors), as well as (in the many persons of the jurors, 501 in Socrates' case) to interpret and apply its moral code in reaching a verdict and choosing a penalty. Although the jurors swore to assess the case in accordance with the laws, there was no judge or other legal expert to instruct them;

laws were regarded more as a kind of evidence, to be wielded as instruments of persuasion, than as the system of regulations on the basis of which a verdict should be reached. A verdict was reached by a simple majority vote, by secret ballot. There was no right of appeal, because the case had already been heard by the ultimate authority, the Athenian people.

Though speakers often referred to precedents and argued that the correct verdict would deter crime in the future, in the absence of thorough records and legal experts, consistency was hard to achieve. Complex issues tended to be skated over, since the jurors were largely uneducated men. In his play *Wasps*, Aristophanes likened them to insects who sting their victims sometimes for no good reason. There was no police force to gather evidence, and there were no professional barristers to present it in court; it was presented, within the space of a few hours at most (with no trial lasting longer than a day), in an exchange of speeches by the two parties (prosecutor first)—the speeches having been either composed by the litigants themselves or bought, at considerable expense, from a professional speechwriter such as Lysias, Isaeus, or Demosthenes. Socrates allegedly spoke off the cuff.[11] Evidence was invariably circumstantial, backed up by arguments from probability. Witnesses (whose statements were read out by the slave Clerk of the Court) were of course expected to tell the truth, but their testimony was very secondary to argument, and they were brought in only to confirm some point, not to give lengthy statements themselves.

Argumentation that we would consider entirely inappropriate to a courtroom was common. Appeals for pity were frequent, as were digressions on the remote background of the case, but most common of all were outrageous slurs or innuendos against one's opponent and his family and friends. In the higher courts, from which come all the extant speeches that we have, trials were literally *agōnes*, "contests" between two members of the wealth elite trying to gain or regain individual honor while appealing to the communal and cooperative values of the ordinary juror.

The tactic of insult was frequently exploited in all cases involving vague charges such as impiety. There were very few restrictions; the most popular accusations included foreign or servile birth and deviant sexual behavior, while the litigant presented himself as a true bearer of the most noble Athenian characteristics. There was no need to prove these slurs, and they were introduced whether or not they were relevant to the case—or, rather,

11   Plato, *Apology of Socrates* 17b–c.

the Athenians had different standards from ours of what counted as relevant. For us nowadays, the fact that the defendant needs a shave and a haircut should have no bearing on the question of his guilt, but for Athenian jurors it was precisely relevant. It was a form of probability argument: "Compare the two of us. Who is more likely to be a criminal?"

In a society that is not wholly literate, arguments may be suspect, so it was up to the litigant to present himself as a *character* the jurors could trust. Greek law had always been very interested in people's motives, which is one reason why offenses such as impiety were not defined: the focus was on the criminal, not the crime. Each time afresh, the jurors had to divine the intent of the law; since it was assumed that the laws were beneficial to the state, then the question became which of the two litigants was beneficial to the state. Hence the value of insulting your opponent.

All this might strike one as inefficient and amateur, and these charges have often been brought against the Athenian administrative system as a whole, but efficiency was not the point. The Athenians decided on guilt or innocence by conformity with everything covered by the term *nomos*—not just law, but also custom and tradition. The openness with which trials were conducted was exactly the point, because it gave the jury the discretion to judge the plausibility of litigants' claims to be true democrats and good citizens. And the Athenian system was considered admirable: when Alexandria was founded in Egypt toward the end of the fourth century, its legal system was substantially based on that of Athens.

The Athenians are often accused of failing to distinguish between unlawful behavior and failure; that is why they so often prosecuted Generals for unsuccessful missions, and politicians for decisions that happened later to turn out to be calamitous. But in a system where loyalty to the democracy was the prime determinant of guilt and innocence, failure is a kind of unlawful behavior. Every route by which we approach Athenian law brings us sooner or later to the same realization: precisely those aspects that we might see as deficiencies are what enabled the legal system to be a powerful tool of the democracy.

Socrates' Trial

When Socrates got to his feet in 399 to deliver his defense speech, he was a well-known figure. Athens was too large to be a face-to-face society, but its prominent personalities were widely familiar, and, apart from many more incidental mentions by comic poets and other gossip-mongers, Socrates had featured as a character in two of the comedies put on at the City Dionysia in 423, Aristophanes' *Clouds* (extant in a revised edition) and Ameipsias' *Connus* (lost).

We are lucky to have the actual wording of the charges against Socrates, preserved in a late writer who drew on a reliable source: "Socrates is guilty of not acknowledging the gods the city acknowledges, and of introducing other new deities. He is also guilty of subverting the young men of the city. The penalty demanded is death."[12] There are a number of oddities about this. Given the nature of Greek religion, with its emphasis on practice over belief, it would be virtually impossible to make a charge of heterodoxy stick. Socrates certainly expressed doubts about certain aspects of Greek beliefs—especially the view that gods could do bad as well as good—but radical views were not uncommonly expressed in Athens at the time. Euripides, for instance, peppered his plays with outrageous remarks about the gods and everything else under the sun.

The charge of "introducing new deities" is even stranger. Many new deities and heroes received cults in Athens in the decades preceding Socrates' trial, and the process continued in the fourth century as well. The only "new god" it could have been referring to was what Socrates called his spirit guide—a signal, so to speak, inside his head which occasionally seemed to offer him preverbal advice. He understood it as a kind of *daimōn* (p. 123). In one sense, there was nothing unacceptable about this: it was no more than a form of divination. But it was private to Socrates alone and excluded others in a most undemocratic fashion; nor was it the kind of deity that could be properly introduced into Athens after debate in the Assembly.

Still, the case was not going to be won on these charges alone. The reason the prosecutors introduced them was to remind the jurors of certain prejudices about Socrates. In *Clouds* Aristophanes had used him as a figurehead for all kinds of pseudoscientific and sophistic ideas, and to the ordinary man "scientist" meant "atheist" and "sophist" meant "subversive." The arousal of prejudice was, as we have just seen, one of the primary objectives of courtroom speeches.

The meat of the charge was the third bit, about corrupting the youth of Athens. Throughout his life, from about 440 onward, Socrates had surrounded himself with groups of wealthy young men who discussed his

---

12 Diogenes Laertius, *Lives of Eminent Philosophers* 2.40 (early third century CE).

methods and ideas, and these groups coincided to a very large degree with those that had been involved in the sacrileges of 415 and the oligarchies of 411 and 404. It was known that they associated with Socrates because they were seeking political education from him: that is the premise of two fourth-century Socratic dialogues, both possibly written by Plato, *Alcibiades* and *Theages*, while Xenophon includes, among the primary subjects Socrates taught, "what is a state, and who is a statesman; what it is to rule over men and who is capable of doing so."[13] Since many of his followers were known for their oligarchic and pro-Spartan sympathies, and since it is commonly believed that students gain their ideas from their teachers, Socrates became tarred with the same brush.

Here the prosecutors did have a good case, even if a circumstantial one. This is what they would have reminded the jurors. Socrates was known to be unsympathetic to democracy and its egalitarian values. Above all, he wanted to see the city run by experts, not by more or less random people chosen by sortition. Since such experts would necessarily be few, Socrates inclined toward oligarchy. Add to this the fact that, for a few years in the late 430s and early 420s, Socrates had been close to and probably the lover of Alcibiades, who had been cursed for his sacrilege, had defected to the enemy, and was suspected of harboring hopes of tyranny. Add, again, the facts that several members of the Thirty had been in Socrates' circle, including Critias himself, and that since Socrates was not removed from the city during their regime he was probably one of the select Three Thousand who were permitted citizenship, and could even be made out to be the éminence grise of the Thirty. It is true that Socrates had also risked the wrath of the Thirty by refusing to obey an order to arrest a prominent former democratic General, but, still, his links to the Thirty must have seemed overwhelmingly strong.

It is not hard to see how, in a legal system such as that of ancient Athens, the prosecutors could have secured a conviction. Socrates probably did not help matters by speaking uncompromisingly and arrogantly at his trial. But why take the elderly philosopher to court just then, in 399? He had been known as a teacher of upper-class young men since the 430s; it was twenty-four years since Aristophanes and Ameipsias had made him the most notorious intellectual in Athens. As was the case for other intellectuals, Socrates became a target only once he was perceived as a threat to public order. His links to the Thirty changed his status from harmless eccentric to

13 Xenophon, *Memoirs of Socrates* 1.1.16.

undesirable. Granted, the amnesty was in place, but we have seen that this only prevented reference to the Thirty in the main charge, and did not stop speakers accusing their opponents of working with the Thirty. No doubt Socrates' accusers (whose speeches have not survived) did just that. Some fifty years later, in 345, the politician Aeschines said: "Athenians, you had the sophist Socrates put to death because he seemed to have been the teacher of Critias, one of the Thirty who destroyed the democracy."[14]

Socrates had been living on borrowed time ever since the defeat of the Thirty in 403. This is not to say that the charge of impiety was, in some Stalinist sense, just a cover for a political trial: religion and society were so intertwined that to charge Socrates with impiety was already to accuse him of being an uncommitted citizen. The general atmosphere was not at all conducive to Socrates' acquittal. As might be imagined, after the war and the fall of the Thirty, a great deal of energy was spent in re-establishing and shoring up the democracy. The buildings that were built and the locations they were put in, the inscriptions that were erected for display, the sentiments that were expressed in speeches—all declared the city to be a forcefully renewed democracy, with no taint of the Thirty remaining. It is no coincidence, then, that the three prosecutors who made up the team against Socrates were all (as far as we can tell) prominent democrats. One of them, a man called Anytus, had even been one of the heroes of Phyle, along with Thrasybulus. Socrates was an undemocratic stain on the new Athens.

14 Aeschines, 1.173 (*Against Timarchus*).

17

The Futility of War

For the first time in Greek history, a single state was dominant, but Sparta's position as leader of the Greeks did little to unify them, and in fact did not long remain unchallenged. The refusal of members of the Peloponnesian League to obey Spartan orders over Athens in 404–403 was a foretaste of the future. Within just a few years of the end of the Peloponnesian War, several of Sparta's former allies had joined forces instead with a resurgent Athens and were waging war against Sparta and its remaining allies. The extent of the turnaround may be measured by the fact that the Athenians allied themselves with those who had demanded the destruction of their city in 404 against those who had argued for its preservation.

The major players continued to pursue the elusive goal of ascendancy over other Greeks—and pursued it, paradoxically, under the banner of liberating them. The Ionian–Dorian division of the fifth century was dropped as a diplomatic tool, since it no longer reflected reality in a world of shifting alliances. But this struggle was ultimately futile, since it only helped a new power grow in the north. "For all their attempts to impose their rule on one another, they succeeded only in losing their ability to rule themselves," was a late historian's somber but accurate comment.[1] In 338, at the battle of Chaeronea, the Macedonians under Philip II defeated the Greeks and curtailed their cherished freedoms forever.

The Spartans also managed to irritate Artaxerxes of Persia enough for him to get involved again in Greek affairs. First, they supported the attempt of his younger brother, Cyrus, to take his throne (a young Athenian called Xenophon joined the expedition and memorably recorded the march of the "ten thousand" Greek mercenaries in his *Anabasis*), and then they invaded

---

1 Justin, *Epitome of the Philippic History of Pompeius Trogus* 8.1.1 (a third-century CE epitome of a first-century BCE work).

Anatolia in an attempt to keep the Eastern Greek cities out of Persian hands. Since the Spartans had recognized the Persians' right to these cities in 411, this was treachery, but there had always been those in Sparta who saw the subjection of the Eastern Greeks to Persia as a temporary measure, to be revisited after the war.

The Greeks found it impossible to live at peace with one another. Internally, communities continued to be racked by conflict between oligarchs and democrats, which increasingly came to mirror tension between rich and poor. Externally, the most successful peaces of the fourth century were imposed by outside powers, while most Greek attempts at reconciliation were derailed by self-interested parties. Each of these peace treaties constituted a switch-point when the Greeks could have moved toward greater unity, but competitive belligerence and self-interested particularism were built into the fabric of Greek statehood, and the opportunities were never fully grasped. The fourth century showed that the polis system had run its course, because it was no longer capable of serving the Greeks' best interests.

The Corinthian War

The Spartan forces in Anatolia at first achieved little. Their main weakness was at sea, so Pharnabazus, with Artaxerxes' blessing, raised a large fleet and appointed as his admiral the Athenian Conon, who was working for Evagoras of Salamis, a Persian vassal king on Cyprus. By the summer of 396, Conon had won over the Rhodians and acquired a base in the Aegean. In response, the Spartans sent reinforcements east, and a fresh commander—King Agesilaus II, with an entourage that included Lysander. The Persians in their turn responded by sending money to political leaders in Greek states known to be hostile to Sparta, urging them to war.

Lame Agesilaus had come unexpectedly to the Eurypontid throne in 400. He was already over forty years old, since he succeeded his half-brother, Agis II, when on Agis' death his son was refused the kingship on the grounds that his father was probably Athenian Alcibiades. It was Lysander, formerly Agesilaus' "inspirer" (pp. 109–10), who had been the prime mover of his elevation, in the expectation that it would allow him to retain power. But in Anatolia, Agesilaus, eager for his own glory, made it clear that he was the king and that Lysander was just one of his advisers. In the end, however,

Agesilaus was scarcely more effective than his predecessors in Anatolia, but only because in 394 he was recalled to mainland Greece for the Corinthian War, just as he was poised to push deep into Persian territory. He left garrisons to protect the Greek cities, and obeyed the command to return.

The point of the Corinthian War (395–386) was to curb Sparta. It achieved exactly the opposite; at the end, Sparta was more dominant than ever. All over the Mediterranean, the Spartans had been settling matters to their liking, just as the Athenians had before them. In the 400s, they campaigned in the northern Aegean, in Sicily, and even in Egypt, which was once again in revolt from Persia, and would remain so until 343. Then in 400, at the conclusion of a two-year war with Elis, in which the Eleans had suffered terribly, the Spartans deprived them of their democracy and over half their territory, the inhabitants of which promptly formed themselves into confederacies, and in the same year they advanced into Anatolia. Sparta had to be stopped before it got too powerful.

It was the Boeotians who started the war, just as they had in 431. They provoked a border incident between the Locrians (their allies) and the Phocians (Spartan allies), knowing that the Spartans would retaliate, and formed an anti-Spartan alliance made up of their central Greek friends, along with Athens, Corinth, and Argos. The Spartan invasion of Boeotia in 395 was not a great success. Lysander succeeded in getting Orchomenus, which had long been an unwilling member of the Boeotian Confederacy, to secede from it, but he was too impatient to rendezvous with Pausanias as planned, and he lost his life trying to defeat the Boeotian forces by himself. How are the mighty fallen! On his return, Pausanias was prosecuted— for a crime for which he had already been acquitted once, that in 403 he had allowed the Athenian oligarchy, friends of Sparta, to be replaced by democracy—and went into exile. He was replaced by his son, Agesipolis.

After this failure in Boeotia, the war developed two main fronts: on land around Corinth (hence the name of the war) and at sea in the Aegean. Two major battles were fought on land early in the war: the Spartans won (just) at the Nemea River, near Corinth, in 394, and then again a few weeks later at Coronea in Boeotia, when Agesilaus, marching his men home from Anatolia, overcame an attempt to halt his progress. But after that the land war settled down to a stalemate. The allies dug in at Corinth and the Spartans did the same at neighboring Sicyon, and a war of skirmishing dragged on for another seven years. It was most significant for the demonstration the Athenian General Iphicrates gave of the effectiveness of light-armed troops, when he used lighter-armed hoplites (known as "peltasts" because of their crescent-shaped *pelta* shield) to sow death and panic in a Spartan troop of six hundred heavy hoplites.

At sea, the Spartans were thoroughly humiliated. In 394 their fleet of 120 ships was annihilated by Conon and Pharnabazus. The Eastern Greek cities celebrated the ending of Sparta's ten-year dominance of the Aegean

Figure 17.1. Dexileos monument. The inscription that accompanies this Athenian grave marker announces that Dexileos died aged twenty, fighting in the Corinthian War. It was extremely rare for ages to be recorded on grave markers, but men of Dexileos' class had served the Thirty Tyrants, and his family wanted it to be clear that he was too young to have done so, and died fighting loyally for the democracy. Kerameikos Museum, Athens, P 1130. Photo: Wikimedia.

by mass defection. Then, early in 393, the Persian fleet freed the Cyclades from Spartan control, ravaged the coastline of Laconia, and occupied the island of Cythera. The Spartans could do nothing. Pharnabazus soon sailed home, but he left the fleet and Conon at the allies' service and distributed large amounts of money, which the allies spent on hiring mercenaries, and rebuilding their fleets and their fortifications. Only ten years after its fortifications had been demolished, Athens was secure again.

The Spartans tried to end Persian aid to their enemies by arguing (or pointing out) that Conon was now plainly working for the Athenians, not the Persians. Tiribazus, the Persian satrap in Lydia, imprisoned Conon, but Artaxerxes was still angry with the Spartans and he ordered him released. Conon died shortly afterwards, but he had done his job and returned the Aegean to Athenian control. He was the first Athenian to receive the singular honor of a statue in the Agora in his own lifetime.

The Athenians' recovery had been remarkable, and they began to wonder whether they could not regain, in some form, their grand naval alliance of the previous century. In 390 Thrasybulus took a step in that direction when he entered into a series of alliances with Greek cities and Thracian kings from Thasos to Byzantium, and resuscitated the questionable 10 percent tax on shipping passing through the Bosporus (p. 253). Since Athens was no longer the wealthy superpower it had been, Athenian Generals were frequently short of money in the fourth century, and they found creative ways of raising it—even hiring their men out as laborers at harvest time. Thrasybulus extracted some from his new friends, but more was needed, and he went to southern Anatolia to try his luck there. At Aspendus, however, some of his men got out of hand, and the furious inhabitants stormed his camp one night and killed him. It was a sorry end for the Hero of Phyle.

The King's Peace

The Athenians' successes in the Hellespont, where their forces were now commanded by Iphicrates, alarmed Artaxerxes, and he ordered his satraps to do what they could to check him. Sensing a change of heart, in 388 the Spartans sent Antalcidas, who had a long history of negotiating with the Persians, to Susa to secure peace on favorable terms. Artaxerxes was persuaded. His most pressing problem was the ongoing rebellion of Egypt, his most valuable province. He wanted his army of invasion to be spearheaded by Greek mercenaries, the best soldiers in the known world. He needed the Greeks to stop fighting so that the mercenary market in Greece could revive. So, in the spring of 387, Antalcidas returned with Artaxerxes' terms.

There had been multilateral treaties before, but for the first time this peace was to be binding on all Greek states equally—a common peace, not restricted just to the belligerents and not limited in time. The Greeks were recognized as a people in their own right; finally, the futility of war taught the Greeks to accept a kind of unity. The principle that states should be allowed to govern themselves, free of external influence, was enshrined in the requirement that all states were to respect one another's autonomy and territorial integrity, and were jointly to retaliate against any state that breached the treaty. There was very likely a clause stipulating the use of arbitration rather than military action as a way of resolving conflicts. The Eastern Greek states were ceded to the Persians, of course. But there was a stinger: any state that did not accept these terms would face the king's wrath in military form. And who would police the Greeks for the Persian king? The Spartans, naturally. It would be up to them to decide what counted as autonomy and make sure that the Greek states obeyed.

It was likely that some parties would need persuading. The Spartans used the threat of force to break up the Boeotian Confederacy so that a weakened Thebes would toe the line, and also to dismantle the union of Argos and Corinth (the two states had surprisingly and uneasily joined together in 392, in an anti-Spartan democracy). As for the Athenians, on his return from Susa, in a brilliant campaign Antalcidas undid all of Thrasybulus' and Iphicrates' gains in the Hellespontine region, and trapped the grain ships bound for Athens in the narrow Bosporus. As at the end of the Peloponnesian War, the Spartans were now funded by Persia, and the Athenians were faced with real difficulties if the grain ships could not deliver. The King's Peace, or the Peace of Antalcidas, was accordingly sworn into existence in 386.

So far from having been laid low by the war, Sparta's position as mistress of Greece had been confirmed. The cost was high, however. Agesilaus might quip that it was not so much that the Spartans had medized as that the Persians had laconized[2]—that the Persians had helped the Spartans more than the other way around—but in fact the Spartans had betrayed the Eastern Greek cities. The Persians at last regained their long-lost subjects, and by 381 they had also brought Evagoras to heel on Cyprus, where he had

2 Plutarch, *Agesilaus* 23.4, *Artaxerxes* 22.4.

been trying for ten years to make himself master of the entire island. They made no claim to any of the Aegean islands, so Athens kept Scyros, Lemnos, and Imbros, but lost the prospect of increasing its influence in general, since that would now be understood as impinging on others' autonomy.

The Boeotian War

Ignoring their own oppressed and unfree populations, the Spartans drove the Olynthians out of Macedon, as a favor to King Amyntas III of Macedon, and broke up their new Chalcidian Confederacy on the grounds that it denied its members their autonomy. Without even the excuse of the autonomy clause, they also punished Mantinea and Phleious, former allies who had betrayed them. Mantinea had its walls demolished, and was broken up into villages, each ruled by an aristocratic, pro-Spartan family. The Spartans' power was at its height, but they were using it in ways that worried their enemies and alienated some of their friends.

The most significant act of Spartan aggression took place in 382, when their general Phoebidas, ostensibly leading an army north to help Amyntas, accepted an invitation by pro-Spartan Thebans to seize and occupy the Cadmea, the Theban acropolis. This was a blatant breach of the principle of autonomy and the Spartans were compelled to punish Phoebidas, but he was Agesilaus' man, and this was Agesilaus' Sparta. So he received a fine rather than the death penalty—and the garrison remained in Thebes. The rest of the Greek world expressed shock, but did nothing except take in Theban exiles. Their leader, Pelopidas, was made welcome in Athens.

In the winter of 379/8, Pelopidas and a band of exiles slipped into Thebes and linked up with their friends inside. They assassinated the leaders of the pro-Spartan faction, released political prisoners, reclaimed the city, and instituted democracy. The Athenians broke out of the general passivity that had followed the King's Peace and supported the conspirators with a small force, which was especially useful in besieging the Spartan troops on the Cadmea into surrender—just in time, because Cleombrotus (who had come to the Agiad throne in 381 on the death of his brother Agesipolis) was only a day or two away with a relieving force. In the event, Cleombrotus was foiled by wintry conditions and achieved little.

The Athenians were naturally frightened that they might have provoked the Spartans to action against them, but the reaction, when it came, early in 478, was half-hearted. The Spartans had occupied Thespiae in Boeotia, and their general there, Sphodrias, marched into Attica and plundered the countryside near Eleusis. This was an act of war, but, not wishing to come to blows, the Athenians indicated that they would be satisfied if Sphodrias were suitably punished—but, just like Phoebidas a few years earlier, and again at the urging of Agesilaus ("the city needs men like him"),[3] Sphodrias was scarcely punished. So the Athenians reaffirmed their support for Thebes, and stepped up their rearmament program.

They also decided to secure themselves by forming another grand alliance. They already had a few alliances here and there, and had been careful to make sure that the terms never transgressed the King's Peace: "The Chians shall be treated as allies on terms of freedom and autonomy."[4] Now they decided to offer this kind of alliance to the Aegean world at large, along with an anti-Spartan stance. This was the beginning of the Second Athenian League, which would endure, somewhat shakily, until 338.

The league was announced in the summer of 378 with a manifesto that survives on an inscription published a year or two later.[5] As well as keeping safely within the guidelines of the King's Peace, the manifesto was careful to suggest that this new alliance would be nothing like the Delian League of the fifth century. Allied states would pay no involuntary tribute and would have access to league funds; Athens would not take over allied court cases; the allies would retain their autonomy and receive no garrisons or Athenian officials; and so far from having cleruchies imposed on them, no Athenian would be allowed to own land in any allied state at all. The allies would have their own council, which met in Athens, where their delegates could debate and vote (one vote per state) on league business without Athenian influence, before putting a proposal to the Athenian Assembly.

The Spartans kept hammering away at Boeotia with annual invasions, but they achieved little, and the Thebans began the process of recovering for their confederacy the Boeotian towns the Spartans had garrisoned. This renewed confederacy was to be democratic, but with Thebes firmly and forcefully at its head, and this was an embarrassment to their allies, the Athenians, who were promising prospective members of their new alliance autonomy. Having failed on land, the Spartans turned to the sea, but were

---

3 Plutarch, *Agesilaus* 25.4.
4 Rhodes/Osborne no. 20 = (translated) Harding no. 31.
5 Rhodes/Osborne no. 22 = (translated) Harding no. 35; Rhodes no. 431; Crawford/Whitehead no. 269B.

twice thoroughly defeated by the Athenians. Athenian control of the sea was re-established, and would endure for the next few decades before being brought to a final end. A peace conference in Sparta in 375 was ineffective, except that, in adhering to the principle that everyone could keep what they had, the Athenians gained official recognition for their new alliance.

The Humbling of Sparta

In 371 the states made another attempt to bring the Boeotian War to an end. But instead of peace, the conference, in Sparta, led within twenty days to further fighting. The Spartans snubbed the Thebans by refusing to let them swear the oath for the Boeotians as a whole; they refused to recognize the Boeotian Confederacy and wanted each Boeotian town to swear separately. Showing the way—and revealing the Athenian drift toward friendship with Sparta rather than Thebes—every member present from the Athenian alliance swore separately. But the Thebans, led by their dynamic general Epaminondas, argued that the Spartans should free their Perioecic communities before the Thebans dissolved their confederacy, and the meeting broke up in rancor. The Spartans already had an army near Boeotia in Phocis, to protect the Phocians against Theban attacks, and Cleombrotus now delivered the Thebans an ultimatum: free the Boeotian towns or face the consequences. The Thebans refused, and Cleombrotus invaded.

The Spartan army well outnumbered the Thebans, but Cleombrotus was up against the two best tacticians of the era: he was outgeneraled by Epaminondas, and his men were outclassed by the Theban elite corps, the Sacred Band, commanded by Pelopidas. The battle of Leuctra (a village near Thespiae), fought in June 371, was won by Epaminondas' brilliant use of cavalry and infantry working together, and it was a decisive victory for Thebes. Leaving aside other casualties, four hundred out of the seven hundred Spartiates present lost their lives, including the king, and they constituted at least a quarter of the existing Spartiate population. It was the first formal infantry battle that the Spartans had lost for three centuries.

The Athenians greeted the news with dismay, knowing that it heralded Theban ascendancy in Greece. They arranged a conference at which the Greek states reaffirmed their allegiance to the King's Peace, and to the principle that each state was to rest content with what it had, or face obligatory retaliation from all the other signatories. It was a warning against Theban expansion. The Eleans, however, refused to take the oath, because the treaty recognized the independence of the Triphylian Confederacy; they had recovered some of the dependent communities they had lost in 400, but the Triphylians remained stubbornly independent for over a hundred years.

The Athenians, leaders of an expressly anti-Spartan alliance, were now paradoxically drawing closer to the Spartans. Thebes dropped out of the Second Athenian League and formed its friends, effectively all of central Greece, into an alliance of its own. In theory, this was an alliance of equals (and therefore not in breach of the King's Peace), but in practice Thebes was dominant.

Theban Ascendancy

After Leuctra, the Boeotians wanted to finish the Spartans off once and for all, but their ally, Jason of Pherae in Thessaly, persuaded them to be content with driving them out of Boeotia, just as he would shortly drive them out of their last outposts in Thessaly. He might well have thought that the Spartans would destroy themselves. Strictly, all the Spartiate survivors of Leuctra should have lost their citizenship and been treated with contempt for the rest of their lives, as those who did not die or win in battle traditionally were. But the reduction in citizen numbers would have threatened Spartan society with collapse, so Agesilaus "allowed tradition to sleep for that day."[6]

Jason was one of a new breed of warlords, lurking on the margins of the Greek world and poised to expand into it if the opportunities presented themselves; Evagoras of Salamis and Mausolus of Caria were cut from the same cloth, and the most successful of them all would turn out to be Philip II of Macedon. Over the past few years, Jason had, by force and intimidation, united much of Thessaly under his rule, and even extended his influence into Macedon. No doubt his advice to the Boeotians was self-serving: he wanted hostility to continue between them and the Spartans so that he would remain unmolested. On his assassination in 370, however, the Thessalian cities returned to their habitual internecine strife. But Jason's successor (after another assassination or two), his nephew Alexander, inherited not just his position, but also his ambitions.

6 Plutarch, *Agesilaus* 30.6.

Spartan weakness instigated a period of turmoil throughout the Peloponnese, as helots and Perioeci rose in rebellion and anti-Spartan factions seized the opportunity to gain or regain power in the cities. Much blood was shed in the process, especially in Argos, where the poor rose up against the rich, killed them (even the democrats among them), and seized their land. More constructively, in 370 Mantinea was reformed as a polis, and along with its old rival Tegea formed an Arcadian Confederacy out of the Arcadian and Triphylian communities; the confederacy had a democratic constitution, and was to be centered on a new city called Megalopolis ("Great City") in southern Arcadia, so as not to privilege any of the existing cities. Megalopolis incorporated the populations of forty previous towns and villages.

The Spartans declared war on the Arcadians, and the Arcadians appealed for help from Thebes. Epaminondas raised a large army from central Greece, which was further swelled by contingents from Elis and Argos. In the winter of 370/69, they launched a massive invasion of Laconia. Never before, as Agesilaus had boasted, had the women of Sparta seen the smoke of an enemy campfire.[7] By dint of offering freedom to helots, the Spartans raised a large enough army to save Sparta itself, but the invaders then crossed into Messenia and liberated the helots and Perioeci, founding the city of Messene on Mount Ithome and creating Messenia for the first time as a political entity in its own right. Expatriate Messenians flocked home in joy.

The removal of fertile Messenia, the source of Spartan prosperity—the foundation of its culture, in fact—was a terminal blow. At a stroke, and within a generation of reaching the apex of its power, Sparta was greatly reduced. The Peloponnesian League was effectively defunct, after about two hundred years of existence. The previously unthinkable happened, and there was unrest even among the Spartiates themselves, a number of whom had to be executed. It was not a serious uprising, but what is remarkable is that it happened at all. The Athenians (who must, for historical reasons, have been not displeased by the reduction of Sparta) declared their opposition to the Thebans by harassing their army as it returned from the Peloponnese.

While warfare between Thebes and Sparta continued in the Peloponnese, the Athenians, who had gained recognition that Amphipolis was rightly theirs—assigned to them by the Peace of Nicias in 421, but not yet recovered—turned their attention Thraceward and renewed their attempt to secure

---

7 Plutarch, *Agesilaus* 31.5.

Figure 17.2. The Arcadian Gate of Messene. As a deliberately designed new city, Messene was filled with beautiful open spaces and magnificent structures. Here we see the remains of the northern or Arcadian gate. The wall was between seven and nine meters high (between twenty-two and thirty feet) and ran for nine kilometers (over five miles) around the city. Photo © Peter Eastland / Alamy Stock Photo.

easy access to northern minerals and ship-quality timber. But obsessively repeated efforts in the 360s came to nothing, as the crafty Amphipolitans entered into alliances with the two strongest powers in the region—first with Macedon, then the Olynthians (whose Chalcidian Confederacy had reformed as Spartan power waned), and then Macedon again. The Athenians were scarcely more successful on the Thracian Chersonese, where possession of the towns was being contested by several powers—especially the kings of the Odrysians, the most powerful Thracian people—and the Thebans and Alexander of Pherae were doing their best to interrupt Athenian efforts there as well.

But the Athenians gained a number of new allies in the north, including Potidaea, which received a cleruchy at its request, as a defense against Olynthus. This was the second cleruchy to be established in just a few years. In 366, in support of a rebel Anatolian satrap, the Athenians, after a ten-month siege, had driven a Persian garrison off Samos, which had been annexed by Mausolus, the aggressive satrap of Caria. The Persian garrison infringed the terms of the King's Peace, but it was clear to everyone that the Athenian action was not disinterested. They wanted Samos for its fertile fields and its harbor (it once again became the Athenians' main naval base in the Aegean), and they established a huge Athenian cleruchy on the island, partly made up of restored Samian democrats.

While Epaminondas had been leading the Thebans' campaigns in the Peloponnese, Pelopidas was responsible for their attempt to regain influence in Thessaly, which meant checking their former ally, Alexander of Pherae. In 364, after several attempts, Pelopidas invaded in greater force, only to die in battle—but his troops and their Thessalian allies succeeded in confining Alexander to Pherae itself. But Alexander was assassinated in 358, Thessaly returned to impotent chaos, and the Thebans never tried to revive their control there.

In the Peloponnese, a critical point had been reached. Despite a crushing defeat by the Spartans in 368 (in the Tearless Battle, so called because there was no loss of life on the Spartan side), the Arcadians had gone to war with the Eleans over the Triphylian issue. But the war, which lasted from 366 to 362, had fractured the young Arcadian Confederacy along traditional fault lines (Mantinea versus Tegea), and in the end the Thebans, as current protectors of the King's Peace, had no choice but to return to the Peloponnese to impose order. The Thebans and their central Greek allies were joined in the Peloponnese by the rump Arcadian Confederacy, Argos, and Messenia. They were opposed by the Mantineans, Spartans, Eleans, Achaeans, and Athenians, under the command of octogenarian Agesilaus. The Corinthians had adopted a policy of neutrality a few years earlier, and stuck with it, but otherwise this was close to being a pan-Greek war.

In 362 the two sides met at Mantinea, for the battle that was supposed to decide the question of which of the two alliances would be the leaders of the Greeks. But it did no such thing. The Thebans won—but Epaminondas was killed, and with Pelopidas dead as well there was no longer a strong hand on the Theban helm. Since Theban leadership outside of central Greece depended not on its institutional position in any league but on its prestige and ability to win battles, and since Pelopidas and Epaminondas had been chiefly responsible for both of these factors, their deaths spelled the end of the brief Theban ascendancy. With nothing resolved, the exhausted

Greeks made peace, but Sparta refused to sign, since the only issue in which it was interested—the autonomy of Messenia—was not up for negotiation. But within a few years, one of the chief belligerents, Agesilaus, was dead. He died in 359 on his way home from Egypt, where, despite his advanced age, he had been working as the commander of a mercenary force, aiding the rebels against the Persians.

The Social War

By 375, the Second Athenian League, with over seventy members and a modest annual income of about sixty talents, was an entity of some strength and importance. All had joined of their own accord, voluntarily or by invitation, without apparent Athenian coercion. But it was primarily an anti-Spartan coalition, and after Leuctra it lost purpose and direction, not least because it was the Thebans who had humbled Sparta, not the Athenian alliance after all. Some members drifted away, and new allies were not required to join the league.

But Athens never gave up seeking to renew its influence in the Aegean. And, gradually, some of the old fifth-century habits re-emerged. League money was used to pay for specifically Athenian ventures in the north (the obsession with Amphipolis); rather than being ad hoc payments to cover the costs of particular campaigns, the Athenians wanted to introduce fixed annual payments—tribute, by any other name. Attempts by allies to secede—Ceos in 364, Euboea in 357—were suppressed. At least there were no cleruchies on allied land; the Athenians had kept their promise in that respect. But there were cleruchies on Scyros, Lemnos, Imbros, and Samos, and at Potidaea and Sestus, and it must have seemed that it was only a matter of time before one was planted on allied territory; after all, they had been promised no garrisons, but the Athenians had had no choice but to garrison towns temporarily that were near war zones, even if this was done "in accordance with the resolutions of the allies."[8] As Xenophon said, Athenian poverty was forcing them to treat their allies "with less than total fairness."[9]

Nevertheless, everyone could see that Athens did not have the strength to be as dominant as it had been in the past. And some Athenian allies

---

8 Rhodes/Osborne no. 52 = (translated) Harding no. 69.
9 Xenophon, *Ways and Means* 1.1; Crawford/Whitehead no. 286.

therefore concluded that they would be better off in a different alliance. It was this, rather than concerns about Athenian abuses, that led a number of important allies—including Rhodes, Chios, and Byzantium (the last two founder members of the league)—to rise up against Athens in a "social" (allied) war in 357.

The Athenians had a large fleet of almost three hundred ships, but lacked the resources to man more than a few dozen at a time, and they suffered a series of naval defeats, which drove home the fact that others had acquired the skills that once had been virtually an Athenian monopoly. Once again, it was Persian intervention that brought the war to an end. At one point, the Athenian General Chares was forced by lack of money to work for a rebel Persian satrap in Anatolia. The Persian king responded by threatening to enter the Social War on the side of the rebels, and so the Athenians recalled Chares and accepted defeat. A number of former allies gained their independence or were absorbed by, chiefly, Mausolus or Philip of Macedon, leaving Athens with only a rump alliance. Athens accepted the necessity of pursuing a more cautious and defensive foreign policy, suitable for its limited resources.

Athenian Democracy in the Fourth Century

Against the background of the futile fighting of the fourth century, the Athenians made certain institutional changes designed, above all, to increase efficiency. One major area of inefficiency was the legal code, which had grown haphazardly throughout its history, until it was hard to determine the order in which laws had been made, or where they were stored, or even if they had been written down at all. Some laws contradicted others; many had become redundant. The redundancies led to the important distinction between "laws" (nomoi), which were binding on everyone and assumed to be permanent, and "decrees" (psēphismata), which applied to particular people or situations, and so could become redundant:[10]

> The authorities are not to use an unwritten law in any case. No decree of either the Council or the Assembly is to be more authoritative than a law. It is not permitted to make a law for an individual if the same law does not

10 Andocides 1.87 (On the Mysteries).

extend to all Athenian citizens and if it is not voted by six thousand people, in a secret ballot.

A committee had been formed in 410 to collect and collate existing laws. The work was interrupted by the Thirty, and then in 403 two boards of Legislators (*nomothetai*) were established. The job of the first was to complete the collection and collation, while the second, which had five hundred members, was to scrutinize every single existing law and decide whether or not it should go forward as part of the legal code for the renewed democracy.

Once the Legislators had fixed the code, the two boards made way for one, and no law could be made, repealed, or amended without the approval of this board, which was given only after a deliberately complex and lengthy review (the process was later somewhat simplified). Board members were chosen from the six thousand jurors empanelled for that year, because the oath the jurors had sworn was taken to apply also to this kind of work. The Thesmothetes were given the job of regularly reviewing the laws and reporting problems to the Assembly.

None of this was much of a restriction on the Assembly, since few new laws were made, and most business, including all foreign-policy decisions, was conducted by means of decrees. In 362 the Assembly had its judicial function—trying Generals and politicians for crimes against the state— removed and given to the courts. Since the courts were just the people sitting in another context, this was not felt to be a restriction either. It was a cost-cutting exercise, so that hundreds of jurors rather than thousands of assemblymen would be paid. And the number of cases heard by the courts was reduced by another frugal measure, the ruling that certain cases had to be heard first by an arbitrator (a senior man, in his sixtieth year), and would go to court only if the litigants disagreed with the arbitrator's verdict.

Yet another cost-cutting exercise was the reduction of the number of Assembly meetings from four a month to three, although that was offset by the sensible decision to allow important debates to be carried over for a second day's discussion. The Areopagus Council seems to have been resurgent or potentially resurgent in the 340s and 330s, but it was kept in its place by a tough law in 336 that made it impossible for the council to usurp the place of the democratic Council in the event of a temporary lapse of democracy in Athens—that is, an oligarchic coup: "They shall not deliberate, not even about one matter."[11]

11 Rhodes/Osborne no. 79 = (translated) Harding no. 101; Arnaoutoglou no. 65.

So the Assembly's powers remained pretty much as they had been, and in other respects Athenian democracy was extended, not curtailed. In 403 the Pnyx, the meeting-place of the Assembly, was enlarged and improved, and before long pay for attendance was introduced, since entrance to the Pnyx could now be controlled. This was a bold move, showing great commitment to democracy at a time when Athens had lost the resources of the Delian League and its financial situation was precarious. The rate was one obol a day, but that was soon raised to three; by the 320s it was one drachma (six obols) for the two less important meetings per prytany, and nine obols for the principal meeting. Remuneration was introduced not just as an affirmation of democratic principles after the regime of the Thirty, but also as a way to encourage attendance (and punctuality) when the population was low as a result of the Peloponnesian War, and as a form of poor relief.

In the fourth century, the Athenians were not turning their backs on democratic principles so much as refounding Athens after the horrors of civil war. The democracy was more self-conscious, not less democratic. Other current debates point in the same direction. I mentioned earlier that Thrasybulus had offered the slaves and metics in his rebel army citizenship when the democracy was restored. When the matter came up for debate in 403, Thrasybulus' proposal was more or less shot down. This seems unfair, but it was the result of an intense discussion about citizenship. Thrasybulus' proposal came to nothing, but neither did an alternative proposal, that, as in many other states, citizenship should be restricted to landowners, which would have disenfranchised several thousand of the poorest Athenians. And another outcome of the debate was the reinstatement of Pericles' strict citizenship law of 451/0, which had lapsed during the manpower shortage of the last decade of the war. In fact, the law was soon strengthened by an outright ban on a male citizen's marrying a female noncitizen. The effect of all this was to bolster the democracy by creating a sense of insiders and outsiders, and the effect was enhanced by the prominent placement of inscriptions honoring those who had supported the democracy in one way or another.

A New Professionalism

Lack of allied tribute left fourth-century Athens strapped for cash and heavily reliant on its wealthy citizens, who naturally protested. They were not as well off as their predecessors in the fifth century. The whole financial system needed taking in hand. In the first place, a census was taken of the value of every landowner's property, so that taxation could be fairly distributed. Then, by the 350s, there were two powerful new treasuries, the Military Fund and the Theoric Fund (which was, in origin, a fund to pay for citizens' attendance at festivals and public entertainments). A new form of budgeting had been introduced a decade or two earlier, whereby every spending authority was allocated a fixed proportion of the money available for each prytany, depending on projected needs—a rather rigid system, which tended to leave the boards short of money in those years (and there were many of them in the fourth century) when Athenian revenues were low. In the 360s, trials sometimes had to be canceled for lack of money to pay jurors.

If there was any surplus, at a time of peace it went to the Theoric Fund, and at a time of war to the Military Fund; both funds received their own regular allocations as well. The Military Fund was always controlled by a single official, and the post was elective, not subject to sortition, and could be repeated year after year. Just as ambitious men in the fifth century had exploited the fact that the Generalship was an elected post to gain personal power, so financial managers now began to exploit the same feature of their posts. The Theoric Fund was originally run by a board of ten, but in the 340s a single treasurer began to be elected for this fund too. Both funds—sometimes in parallel, sometimes alternately—grew to be very rich, and their treasurers correspondingly powerful. The Treasurer of the Theoric Fund at some point gained control of all the former financial committees of the Council as well. But his power no more threatened democracy than Pericles had in the fifth century. These men could always be brought low if they behaved irresponsibly. Eubulus of Probalinthus, re-elected as financial controller almost every year from 353 to 342, used his authority to introduce a greater degree of fiscal caution.

In the military sphere, Generals continued the trend begun during the Peloponnesian War and tended to specialize in military matters more than politics, just as Eubulus and other specialized in politics. Athenian Generals even hired themselves out abroad, in between their appointments in Athens. The age of the amateur was passing. Another important step toward professionalism was taken by the development of the *ephēbeia* (the Cadet Corps—literally, "those on the threshold of adulthood"). This was a corps of young men who, at the age of eighteen, embarked on two years of disciplined training, as a kind of National Service; the practice came to be imitated by many other states. They took an oath to defend the fatherland, obey the laws and the authorities, and honor the state's cults.[12]

In the first year, which consisted largely of basic training, they were posted in fortresses in Piraeus; in the second, they were based in fortresses out in the Attic countryside, with the job of patrolling the borders against enemy incursions and runaway slaves. They were trained to fight both as hoplites and as light-armed troops. As in the Spartan *agōgē*, the young men were bound together by athletic competition, communal dining, and shared performance at religious festivals. Each ephebe received a stipend, and at the end of the first year of training he was given a shield and a spear by the state. In Athens, for the period when the *ephēbeia* was funded like this by the state (335–322), it seems that over half of the available eighteen-year-olds joined up, between five and six hundred a year, giving the army a good core of trained soldiers but not reaching out to the poorest families. But when the ephebate was revived in 306, it was reduced to one year and, with a focus on cultural as well as military activities, it gradually became a kind of finishing school for a few dozen sons of rich households.

The new professionals of the fourth century were staking out their fields. Technical treatises were written on medicine (the ample corpus of works attributed, nearly always wrongly, to fifth-century Hippocrates of Cos), architecture, siegecraft, rhetoric, music, town-planning, art theory, and the theater. In his earliest works, written in the 390s and 380s, Plato had his mentor, Socrates (or a fictionalized version of him), engage with a wide range of experts—poets, sophists, orators, Generals, and politicians—and show them all up as ignorant about the fundamental issues of their work. Plato was trying to demonstrate that philosophy as he understood it, or rather as he was in the process of inventing it, was the only true source of education and even of self-perfection. Meanwhile, Isocrates, with his school of rhetoric, was making the same educational claim for what *he* called "philosophy"; the details are unknown, but he had a method designed to inculcate appropriate (by his lights) moral and political views in his students. Aristotle, who came to Athens from Chalcidice in 367 to study at Plato's Academy, marks the culmination of this trend toward the systematization of knowledge. Starting from a few principles (but otherwise rejecting the kind of theoretical speculations that characterized the Academy), he intended to

12 Rhodes/Osborne no. 88 = (translated) Harding no. 109; Crawford/Whitehead no. 306.

say the last word on everything from the ideal political constitution to the nature of God.

The fourth century was the time when philosophy as we understand it was invented; between the time of Socrates and Aristotle, the fundamental rules of logical reasoning were laid down, and great advances were made in every other branch of philosophy as well, from epistemology to ethics. It was the time when the rules of elegant and persuasive speaking and writing were developed, culminating in Aristotle's *The Art of Rhetoric*, in which the three main kinds of public speaking are identified (speaking for display, or in the law courts, or in a mass political assembly) and the manner of speaking appropriate to each kind is thoroughly explained, as well as the general principles of rhetoric. Poets and playwrights differentiated themselves to an increasing extent from prose-writers by focusing more on entertainment than instruction.

Lysippus of Sicyon, who was working between about 370 and 310 (and who was to become the favorite sculptor of Alexander the Great, the one who portrayed him as he liked to be seen), invented a new canon for portraying the human body:[13]

> He made the head smaller than his predecessors had, and the body more slender and firm, so that his statues appeared to be taller than they were.... He used to say that he made men as he visualized them, whereas his predecessors made them as they were.

Despite this final quip, realism was Lysippus' object: the new canon, for all its slight distortions of the human body, allowed statues to be more lifelike to the viewer. Artists were still portraying men as generalizations—man of courage, man of destiny, king—but as the century progressed individualization made more of a mark on their work, and we will see this blossom within a few decades. The fourth century was a time of futile and brutal warfare, but it was also a time of great inventiveness and creativity, when human knowledge was being systematized even as new fields were being opened up.

---

13   Pliny, *Natural History* 34.65.

18

The Macedonian Conquest

Greeks and Macedonians were kin. Macedonian was largely an unwritten language, so our evidence is slight, but it appears to have been an obscure dialect of Greek (with Illyrian and other influences), and Macedonians were slotted into the Greek genealogy by being made descendants of either a nephew or a grandson of Hellen (pp. 31–2).[1] The Macedonian elite had long spoken Greek, dressed like Greeks, held Greek-style athletic competitions, and worshipped Greek gods alongside their own. The right of Macedonian royalty to take part in the Olympic and other pan-Hellenic games was recognized at least from 356, when Philip II won the four-horse chariot event, and later in the fourth century even nonroyal Macedonians were taking part. By the end of the third century, the Macedonian language had become extinct and been replaced by Greek.

Archelaus (413–399) relocated his court from Aegae (which remained a ceremonial and royal burial center) to Pella, which became the first real city in Macedon, and managed to entice major celebrities there, including the Athenian poet and playwright Euripides and the best painter of the day, Zeuxis of Heraclea (in southern Italy), who decorated the new palace. But when Archelaus was assassinated—a far from uncommon event in the Macedonian court—the country reverted to relative chaos for a few decades and in its weakness endured constant interference by Athenians and other Greeks, who already had no fewer than seventeen settlements on the Macedonian coastlines, occupying all the good harbors. Philip II, a Machiavellian prince if ever there was one, ascended to the throne of a fractured Macedon in the late summer of 360. By the time of his assassination twenty-four years later, he had eliminated the southern

---

1 Pseudo-Hesiod, *The Catalog of Women*, F 7 Merkelbach/West; Hellanicus *FGrH* 4 F 74.

Greek presence from his land and made Macedon the greatest state in the Aegean basin.

Macedonian Monarchy

Previously, Macedon had been considered backward by Greeks. Mountains and rivers divided both Upper and Lower Macedon into distinct cantons with little mutual communication. Urbanization was late in coming; for a long while, the people were mainly village-dwelling farmers and pastoralists (mostly of Macedonian stock, but with an admixture of Illyrians and Thracians), until the local Greek cities were absorbed and kings began to found cities—Philippi in 356 (in Thrace, strictly, but it soon became part of Macedon), Cassandreia (formerly Potidaea) and Thessalonica in 316, Demetrias in Thessaly in 293. But the contempt of the polis-centered Greeks was somewhat unfair. Macedonian development was retarded, despite its fabulous natural resources, by the fact that it was a frontier state. The peoples to the west, north, and east were warlike tribes, given to attacking in vast numbers. Beyond them were the Celts of central Europe (some of whom had sacked Rome in 386), and to the northeast the nomad Scythians, no less belligerent and numerous. For centuries—as was recognized by intelligent men such as the Roman general Titus Quinctius Flamininus[2]—Macedon had been a buffer against these peoples, absorbing or repelling waves of attackers and preventing them from reaching the southern Greeks. Hence the military nature of the Macedonian monarchy.

But the Greeks thought little of monarchy, and the Macedonian monarchy was of an especially old-fashioned, almost Homeric kind. All natural resources were owned by the king, and so was all the land (though its holders could sell it and bequeath it), so that his subjects were his tenants and owed him loyalty, taxes, and military service. All treaties and agreements were made with him in person, rather than with "the Macedonians." The king was the leader of the army and the sole decision-maker in all matters of importance, but he had an advisory council of aristocrats, who, as great landowners and princes in their own right, formed the basic military and administrative structure of the state.

2 Polybius, *Histories* 18.37.8–9.

Macedonian kings always preferred this personal, charismatic style of monarchy to anything more institutionalized; they liked to establish relationships with individuals and get business done that way. The king and those who were close to him hunted together, dined together, and got drunk together. They were a cavalry elite, some of them considered royal in their own cantons, and they were allowed to speak freely to the king. A king in the Macedonian mold had no constitutional restraints, but without the goodwill of these Companions or Friends, he could hardly function. When Ptolemy IV of Egypt "made himself inaccessible to his courtiers and everyone else who was responsible for the administration of Egypt," he soon found himself enmeshed in a whole series of conspiracies against his life; when Attalus II of Pergamum met opposition from his Friends to one of his plans, he sensibly gave in.[3] In this sense, Friends could limit a king's ability to act, and did so if they felt their interests were at risk; and so, later in the Hellenistic period, kings began to introduce their favorites into their courts, as a way of breaking the Friends' monopoly.

But a Macedonian king selected many members of this council himself, all those he did not inherit, and he bound them to himself with generous gifts, by promoting them to high office, and by leading them to profitable victory. His court—and subsequent courts in the Hellenistic period—subsisted on something very like *xenia*, except that what the king expected in return for his generosity was loyalty rather than gifts. On public occasions, the king, magnificently attired, appeared surrounded by his scarcely-less-impressive Friends; it was one of their jobs to enhance his majesty.

At the lower end of the scale, every man bearing arms had the right to assemble, but the Macedonian assembly had no independent power; it met at the ruler's behest, and its job was to approve his decisions. As much as anything, convening an assembly was a way for a Macedonian king to show that he had public support. A typical use of such an assembly was that of Alexander the Great after he had killed his friend Cleitus; he convened an army assembly for a show trial of the dead man on the charge of defamation of the king, so that his murder became justified. As with the Spartan assembly, protest was possible, but rare. Succession to the throne depended on a number of factors: birth into the Argead house that had ruled Macedon for hundreds of years, nomination by the outgoing king, the agreement of the king's inner circle, and the approval of the assembled Macedonians, expressed by acclamation. But only the first of these factors

3 Polybius, *Histories* 5.34.4–10; Welles no. 61.

was more or less cast in stone; the others might be jettisoned if political realities demanded it.

Macedonian monarchy was only slightly tempered, then; the king listened to his advisers and was expected to behave in certain ways, but the final decisions were his alone. He was the executive head of state and the chief religious official. Matters of policy, both foreign and domestic, were his responsibility; it was his right to form and break alliances and to declare war and peace, and he was commander-in-chief of the armed forces. He could promote and demote men as he liked, and failure or success depended only on his opinion. He was also the chief judge, with the power to decide whether or not to hold a trial in any given situation, or even whether to order a summary execution. Above all, he had to be strong and be seen to be strong—the best warrior and the best hunter, with the greatest appetite for drink. His court was simultaneously the political and administrative center of the realm and the stage for displays of kingly power. This was the style of kingship that Philip inherited and would in due course pass on to his son, Alexander the Great.

Philip II of Macedon

Philip's first priority, when he became king in 360, was to secure his borders. Fortunately, the Illyrians, who had just killed his predecessor (his brother) and inflicted enormous losses on the Macedonian army, failed to follow up their victory and rested content with their occupation of Upper Macedon. Philip kept them happy with a treaty sealed by his marrying the granddaughter of the aged Illyrian king. The Paeonians (from, in modern terms, the Republic of Macedonia), another constant thorn in Macedonian flesh, were poised to invade, but they were only after plunder, so Philip bribed them to stay away, and did the same with the Thracians.

With his borders secure for the time being, Philip turned to a much-needed reform of the Macedonian military. The Macedonians relied chiefly on their formidable elite cavalry, while foot soldiers were mostly recruited from the peasantry as and when needed, or by hiring mercenaries. Philip now greatly expanded the infantry, and created a standing army by paying his men and providing their equipment where necessary. By recruiting troops from every canton, both the army and the country were simultaneously bound together.

The cavalry was restructured into heavy and light regiments, and both cavalry and infantry were rigorously trained. The Macedonians soon came to specialize above all in combined cavalry and infantry operations. By 350 a specialist engineering corps had also been created to develop and build siege devices and artillery. In 338 Philip, with minimal reliance on mercenaries, was able to lead over thirty thousand trained Macedonians south against the Greeks, and four thousand horsemen. His army was the best in the world and, recognizing this, over the following decades every other major power in Greece created a corps equipped in the Macedonian fashion. Otherwise, they would face either defeat by or dependency on Macedonian military muscle.

Philip lightened Greek hoplite armor, especially by reducing the size of the shield, but armed his foot soldiers with an exceptionally long, sturdy pike called a *sarissa*. This could be five meters long (sixteen feet or more). Macedonian phalangites took up as tight a formation as possible, and the length of the pikes meant that those of the first five rows projected out beyond the front rank. The pikes had butt-spikes, so that they could be planted securely in the ground. In defense, then, a solid phalanx was more or less invulnerable to anything except long-range weaponry, scythed war chariots, or elephants (first encountered by Greeks during Alexander the Great's campaigns in the East). In attack, provided the phalanx remained solid, it was equally hard to defeat. If it came to hand-to-hand fighting, each phalangite had a short sword. Philip also created a standing brigade of soldiers armed more like Greek hoplites, and he employed foreign mercenaries, especially from Thrace, as his light-armed troops.

Next, he put his new army to the test. He crushed the Paeonians and incorporated Paeonia into Macedon, and then drove the Illyrians out of Upper Macedon. Out of gratitude for the removal of the great threat, and recognizing that unity would bring strength, the kings of the Upper Macedonian cantons allowed the incorporation of their territories, so that Upper and Lower Macedon were united under a single rulership. Orestis to the northwest, previously part of Illyris, was also incorporated. Every new territorial acquisition swelled his army, since citizens were obliged to serve. Philip had arguably created the first nation-state in Europe, with a population of perhaps a million. He would next create Europe's first empire.

Philip further developed an old system, borrowed from the Persians, whereby the sons of high-ranking Macedonians would come and live in the royal court in Pella during their teenage years as Royal Pages, to serve as the king's attendants and to be the friends and the future Friends of the heir apparent, who was educated with them. The boys, some of them his own relatives, were being trained for high office as generals and governors, but they were also hostages for the loyalty of their fathers and tokens of their fathers' recognition of the supremacy of the Argead house. In the extravagant royal courts of a later period, there might be several hundred Royal Pages, but at first there were no more than a dozen or so.

Macedonian kings were polygamous and—to the horror of the Greeks—Philip ended up with seven wives. Philinna of Larisa bore him a son called Arrhidaeus, perhaps in 357, but he suffered from some form of mental impairment which, under normal circumstances, would have ruled him out as a candidate for the throne. Olympias of Molossis (part of Epirus) bore him Alexander in 356 and a daughter, Cleopatra, a year or two later. Other wives bore him another three daughters.

Philip next turned to the Greek towns of the northern Aegean, and by the mid 350s the only holdout of any importance was the Chalcidian Confederacy. Athenian attempts at containment were futile. Philip first took Amphipolis and then, when the Athenians declared war, the state of open hostility made it possible for him to take Pydna, Methone (the siege cost him his right eye), and Potidaea from them as well. The Athenians were too tied up with the Social War to respond effectively. From the Thasians he took the rich mining town of Crenides, which he renamed Philippi, and he drained the marshes there to create new farmland. He imported populations from elsewhere (such as twenty thousand Scythians in 339) to farm the new land at Philippi and elsewhere and to occupy the cities he founded or enlarged.

In the absence of the Athenians, Philip went on to take over much of Thrace, again conquering Athenian allies in the region. His expansion into Thrace was greatly eased by the quarrelsome division of the most powerful kingdom, that of the Odrysians, among the three sons of the former king. Philip was drawing ever closer to Athenian territory in the Thracian Chersonese, currently populated by thousands of cleruchs, who had been sent there in 353 to secure the region.

The Third Sacred War

Philip had plans for Greece, and soon another Sacred War, the third (355–346), gave him his great opportunity. In 356, the Thebans got the Amphictyonic Council to impose a hefty fine on the Phocians on the (probably specious) charge of having cultivated land that was sacred to Apollo. The Phocians, allies of the Athenians, reacted by seizing and occupying Delphi. At first, the

Amphictyonic Council scarcely responded. But the following year, when it became clear that Athens was going to lose the Social War and would be in no position to help, the council declared war on Phocis. Greece was once again divided into two camps, with the northern and central Greeks choosing to defend the oracular shrine and the Phocians, isolated in central Greece, finding allies in the Athenians, Spartans, and other Peloponnesian states.

The rising costs of the war pushed the Phocians into an almost unthinkable act of sacrilege: they began to turn Delphian treasure into coin to hire mercenaries, and by dint of offering extravagant wages gathered a formidable force. To the alarm of the rest of the Thessalians, they allied themselves with Pherae, ruled at that time by Jason's sons. Uncertain that they could do the job on their own, the other Thessalians asked Philip of Macedon for help. Philip leaped at the chance. As it happened, he was at first badly beaten by the Phocians, thanks to their financially motivated mercenaries—the two most serious defeats of his life. But he persevered, and in 352 he gained his revenge by annihilating a Phocian army in Thessaly. The victory gave him Pherae, with its excellent port at Pagasae (modern Volos), and within a few years Thessaly had become, as it usually remained, little more than a satellite of Macedon. When the Thessalians elected Philip their Archon, he had legitimate rank in the Greek world.

Philip advanced his army up to Thermopylae, the gateway to the south, but the Athenians had blocked his passage and he let the Phocians be for a while. In Athens, Demosthenes, still rather obscure as a politician, though a well-respected writer of courtroom speeches, stepped up the stridency of his warnings about the threat Philip represented and began to distance himself from Eubulus' pacifist platform. The war became stuck in a series of indecisive battles between the Thebans and the Phocians, with the latter generally doing better; at one point they had created a kind of Greater Phocis by taking over much of central Greece. Looking for a way to tip the scales in their favor, in 347 the Thebans approached Philip for help. They must have been desperate; they must have known the risk they were running, having witnessed the subjection of the Thessalians after they had called Philip in.

The previous year, Philip had destroyed Olynthus, using the excuse that it was sheltering pretenders to the Macedonian throne, and completed his takeover of the Chalcidian towns, so that all the Thraceward region was under his control. The Athenians, suffering from bad luck and bad weather, had failed to supply Olynthus with adequate help. Despite Demosthenes' warnings in his *Olynthiacs* (delivered in 349/8), his fellow citizens had focused more on preventing a Macedonian takeover of Euboea than on defending Olynthus. In the event, Euboea passed largely out of their hands, although at least it did not fall entirely into Philip's.

Now, having failed to stir the other Greeks to war against Philip, the Athenians were opening peace negotiations with the Macedonian king, who had let them know, in his usual suggestive fashion, that he was interested. By this ploy, Philip took the Athenians out of the game; not wanting to jeopardize the prospect of peace, they would not interfere if Philip helped the Thebans, and he would gain international kudos if he rescued sacred Delphi from the Phocian marauders.

The way to peace was not yet entirely clear, however. Any treaty between Philip and the Athenians would have to include their allies as well—and among the Athenian allies were the Phocians. After intense debate in the Athenian Assembly, and several embassies back and forth, Philip got his way and the Phocians (and others) were excluded by the device of limiting "Athenian allies" to the few remaining members of the Second Athenian League. Only they would be included in the formal treaty. The Athenians had abandoned the Phocians, but their ambassadors received verbal guarantees from Philip that the Phocians would be treated well.

This was not the first time Philip had made promises to the Athenians; he had promised them Amphipolis in exchange for Pydna, but then just took both places for himself. It is true that he had kept his promise to the Olynthians and given them Potidaea, but still, to believe his promises, the Athenians must have been desperate for peace. It seemed the only way to stop him advancing closer to the Hellespont and threatening their grain route, or even advancing on Athens itself, and he was also offering to return Athenian prisoners of war. And so in 346 the Peace of Philocrates, named after the chief Athenian negotiator, was sworn into existence.

The Phocians, deserted by their allies and deeply divided among themselves, had no choice but to surrender, and the Sacred War was over. In punishment for their looting of Delphi, Philip oversaw the leveling of the Phocians' towns. After its brief prominence, Phocis was permanently reduced. The entire population was disarmed (their weapons were considered polluted by their sacrilege) and resettled in villages in the countryside. They were expelled from the Amphictyonic Council (their votes were given to Philip personally), and they were required to repay the cash equivalent of the valuables they had stolen from Delphi. Since the villages could afford only ten talents a year, it was going to take a very long time. The grateful Amphictyonic Council, responsible for the administration of Delphi, gave Philip the enormously prestigious job of presiding over that year's Pythian Games.

The Conquest of Greece

Demosthenes had originally supported the peace treaty, but he soon saw that the Athenians had been duped into shamefully abandoning their allies and massively strengthening Philip's position. Eubulus' popularity waned as he argued that they should keep the peace, but Demosthenes and others already saw it as temporary. And with every further eastern step Philip took in Thrace, the war party in Athens gained supporters. With the final defeat of the last of the Thracian kings, Thrace became a province of Macedon, with its own governor, and Philip's kingdom now bordered Athenian territory in the Chersonese and was starting to threaten their grain route.

For a couple of years of skirmishing in the region, the two sides pretended that they were not yet at war, but eventually Philip lost patience. He probably had already decided to invade Anatolia, so he badly needed the coastline of the Chersonese and the Propontis as his launching pad. In 340, with fighting between his ally, the town of Cardia, and the Athenians as his excuse, he left sixteen-year-old Alexander in Macedon as his viceroy and marched to the Propontis, where he attacked Perinthus and Byzantium. The Athenians broke up the stone on which the Peace of Philocrates was inscribed and sent a force north. At this, Philip seized 180 grain ships that had been bottled up in the Bosporus by the fighting, sold the grain (which had been destined for Athens), and destroyed the ships. The Athenians in their turn trapped Philip in the Propontis, but he extricated himself by means of a ruse, or perhaps a truce, and marched north to extend his empire all the way to the Danube. The Athenians had temporarily saved the day, but Philip was otherwise unstoppable.

Early in 338, the Amphictyonic Council, now effectively Philip's puppet, called on him to take command of another Sacred War. The issue was again the cultivation of sacred land, with the offense this time committed by the Locrians of Amphissa. But by the time he had reached Elatea in Phocis, it became clear that Athens, not Amphissa, was Philip's objective. With his star shining brightly in this hour of darkness, Demosthenes persuaded the

Figure 18.1. The Lion of Chaeronea. This funerary monument was allegedly erected on the very spot where the Theban Sacred Band was wiped out during the battle. The original was broken up early in the nineteenth century, but has since been restored. It stands six meters or twenty feet tall. Photo © Philipp Pilhofe.

Thebans to ignore Philip's threats and blandishments, and the Athenians to enter into a last-minute alliance with their old enemies. Others flocked to the Athenian–Theban banner, but they were not enough. Too many of the Greeks wanted peace, almost at any cost; too many Greek politicians had been the recipients of Philip's gifts.

After some feints and maneuvers, the two sides met on August 2, 338, at Chaeronea in Boeotia. Philip faced the largest Greek army that had been put together since Plataea in 479—even the Corinthians came out of retirement—but numbers were about even. The hard-fought battle was won when Philip feigned retreat from an oblique battle line, only to have his superbly trained troops turn and smash into the Greeks with, especially, his heavy infantry and heavy cavalry working together. The right wing, under the command of Alexander, wiped out the renowned Sacred Band of Thebes almost to a man. As the Athenian politician Lycurgus melodramatically remarked, Greek freedom was buried along with the corpses of those who fell.[4]

The Settlement of Greece

This was different from earlier defeats. This was not a case of the reduction of just one or two states, or the few members of an alliance, but of all the mainland Greeks collectively. It was Philip's intention to keep them quiescent. He did not want to be distracted by trouble in his rear when he invaded Anatolia. Chaeronea had pacified the central Greek states, but the Peloponnese needed some attention. Although the Spartans had not joined the other Greeks at Chaeronea (for no better reason than that they hated the Thebans), Philip invaded Laconia, and while he chose not to attack Sparta itself, he forcibly rearranged the borders of Laconia in favor of its neighbors, in order to leave no Peloponnesian state powerful enough to dominate the others. He also left a strong garrison in Corinth, as he would also in Ambracia and Chalcis, securing these important ports.

It was probably the same prospect of eastern conquest that determined a policy of clemency after Chaeronea. In Thebes, he established an oligarchy of three hundred and installed a Macedonian garrison. Despite the panic that the defeat triggered in Athens (emergency work on the fortifications, plans to arm slaves and metics), the Athenian General Phocion, known for his conservatism and integrity, managed to secure favorable terms. Philip left the city intact, and even generously returned two thousand POWs. He was probably thinking that he might need the Athenian navy at some point in the future; he certainly did not want to spend time over a long siege. From the Boeotians, the Athenians gained Oropus, a border town (and important

---

4 Lycurgus, *Against Leocrates* 50.

religious center) that regularly changed hands from one to the other. But the Second Athenian League was brought to an end, leaving Athens with just its core islands, mostly populated by cleruchs: Salamis, Lemnos, Imbros, Scyros, Samos, and Delos, so that they lost the Chersonese and everything else. Aegina had been cleared of Athenian cleruchs at the end of the Peloponnesian War by Lysander, and returned to the original islanders, or as many of them as still survived.

In 337 Philip organized a conference at Corinth at which he bound the Greek states together in a common peace, similar to the King's Peace of 386. The Greeks were to respect one another's autonomy and territorial integrity, and act in concert against any offenders; they were also to avoid internal strife. Transgression would draw the armed might of Macedon. All the mainland Greek communities, except Sparta, which remained outside ("It is not our custom to follow others, but to take the lead ourselves"),[5] were also bound into an alliance, modeled on the Second Athenian League, which is nowadays called the League of Corinth. Philip, and then his heirs, were to be presidents for life—almost kings of Greece—and every Greek state had to swear an oath of personal allegiance to him:[6]

> I swear by Zeus, Earth, Sun, Poseidon, Athena, Ares, all the gods and goddesses: I shall abide by the peace, and I shall neither break the agreement with Philip nor take up arms for harm against any of those who abide by the oaths, neither by land nor by sea; nor shall I make war on and take any city or guard-post or harbor of any of those participating in the peace, by any craft or contrivance; nor shall I overthrow the kingdom of Philip or his descendants, nor the constitutions existing in each state when they swore the oaths concerning the peace; nor shall I myself do anything contrary to these agreements, nor shall I allow anyone else to do so, as far as is in my power.

The states were allotted votes on the league council on some proportional principle (perhaps military capacity) that gave Macedonian dependencies such as Thessaly a generous number, even though the council meetings excluded Philip. But only Philip, not the council on its own, could mobilize troops for war.

Over the past decades, common peaces had proved hard to sustain. Circumstances changed and made them redundant or destroyed them. They

---

5 Arrian, *Anabasis* 1.1.2.
6 Rhodes/Osborne no. 76a = (translated) Harding no. 99A; Rhodes no. 444; Crawford/Whitehead no. 350C.

tended to devolve power onto a single leader, or onto a dominant state, with the result that they never lasted beyond the point at which that particular leader or state lost dominance. But the combination with an alliance such as the League of Corinth, which provided a meeting-place where the Greeks could negotiate their differences, made this one far more solid. It helped that the league council had real decision-making power; it was not just an empty shell. The league imposed by Philip more nearly united the mainland Greeks and brought peace than at any time before in their history; in fact, the name "League of Corinth" is a modern invention, and to the Greeks it was "the League of the Greeks."

Under the terms of the league, all the Greek states were to keep their existing constitutions—but in the aftermath of Chaeronea many states had already fallen into the hands of Philip's supporters, and the treaty specifically banned any radical popularist moves such as the cancellation of debts, the redistribution of land (a slogan that always meant the redivision of all farmland into equal or at least equitable allotments), or the arming of slaves for the purpose of revolution. In Philip's vision of the future, the Greeks were ruled by a wealth elite, and the poor were kept in their place.

Eastern Promise

One of the first acts of the League of Corinth was to appoint Philip commander-in-chief for a war to free the Eastern Greek cities from Persian rule and to seek revenge for the Persian Wars of the early fifth century, almost 150 years previously—despite the awkward fact that, at the time, Macedon had been part of the Persian Empire. Greeks still felt strongly about Persians, who had remained influential in their lives since the Persian Wars and whose iniquity was a frequent theme of political speeches and pamphlets. Until well into the fourth century, in a practice that had been instigated immediately after the Persian Wars, every meeting of the Athenian Assembly included in its preliminaries the recital of a curse on anyone suggesting peace with the Persians. The Persian Empire was the kind of bogey that the Soviet Union was to westerners during the Cold War of the 1950s. There was a degree of hypocrisy involved; in a speech delivered in 354, for instance, Demosthenes was still calling the Persian king "the common enemy of all Greeks," despite the fact that for the past sixty years the Greeks on numerous occasions had tried to win the king's favor and financial support, and had never fought him, while fighting one another constantly.[7]

It suited Philip to harness this energy for a crusade. Isocrates even wrote him an open letter in 346, calling on him to unite the Greeks and lead them to eastern conquests. Orators had long been belittling Persian military resources by pointing to their reliance on Greek mercenaries. They cited as evidence of Persian weakness the Great Satrapal Rebellion of the 360s, when several satraps in Anatolia and farther east had risen up simultaneously. They cited the famous trek of the "ten thousand" Greek mercenaries who had returned in 400 from Iraq to Greek lands under the command of Xenophon, as if that showed that a Greek army could go where it willed in Persian lands. Xenophon fueled these dreams by writing, about his men, "For all our small numbers, we made the king a laughing stock."[8] The main dreamers before Philip II seem to have been Agesilaus of Sparta and Jason of Pherae. We hear that both of them, as well as Philip, were inspired by the Ten Thousand to plan eastern conquests, though neither of them was able to put these plans into effect.[9]

Granted that liberating the Eastern Greeks and punishing the Persians were pretexts, what were Philip's real reasons for the invasion? Persian opposition to Philip had been very slight, though Alexander would later cite it in partial justification.[10] Most likely, Philip wanted glory and plunder—the glory of being the greatest man not just in Europe but in the world, and plunder to replenish his empty coffers. His revenues were great—a thousand talents a year from the Philippi mines, for instance—but his expenses constantly drained his treasury; he had undertaken extensive building projects, he was very liberal with his gifts (or "bribes") to Greek statesmen, and he had a majestic court and a large army to maintain. So, although his empire already stretched from the Danube to southern Greece, he wanted more. How much more he wanted, we shall never know.

The Accession of Alexander

There was trouble in Philip's court. Alexander had long been designated Philip's heir in the time-honored fashion, by being promoted in various

7 Demosthenes 14.3, 36 (On the Symmories); Crawford/Whitehead no. 340.
8 Xenophon, Anabasis 2.4.4.
9 Xenophon, Hellenica 3.4.2–3, 6.1.12; Isocrates 5.119 (Philip); Polybius, Histories 3.6.10–12.
10 Arrian, Anabasis 2.14.5.

ways and by receiving no less a person than Aristotle as his tutor, but as the preparations for eastern war progressed, Alexander felt increasingly marginalized. He was due to stay at home; he would be Philip's viceroy in Macedon, but he wanted the glory of victory, and it is likely that he watched with envy as his father drew closer to his generals. Philip even married the niece of one of them, and for a while, following a bitter drunken argument, both Alexander and his mother found it prudent to absent themselves from Philip's court, where the talk was of how the king could now produce a purely Macedonian heir, not a half-caste like Alexander (Olympias being Epirote). Of course, it would take some years for such a rival heir to be born and grow up, so Alexander's position remained secure for the time being, but seeds of dissension were being sown. Alexander and Olympias soon returned to Macedon, but the court remained divided.

In the spring of 336, Pella was bustling with preparations for eastern war. Philip sent an advance force over to Anatolia, commanded by his most trusted generals, Parmenion and Attalus (the father of his latest bride), with the job of establishing a bridgehead and liberating as many of the Greek cities as they could. Preparations were also under way for the marriage of Philip's daughter Cleopatra, Alexander's sister, to her uncle, Alexander of Epirus, the brother of Olympias. The Epirote king had been offended by the breach between Philip and his sister, and the marriage was Philip's way of placating him.

But Philip was assassinated during the wedding celebrations. As the royal party entered the theater at Aegae, the old capital of Macedon (newly adorned with a grand palace), to show themselves before the assembled dignitaries from all over Greece, one of his bodyguards struck him down. So died the man who laid the foundation for Alexander's great achievement. The story that circulated after the assassination was that it had been a purely personal matter—that the killer was a former lover of Philip's who had been brutally treated by him. But this may have been Alexander's attempt to offset the other main rumor—that he and his mother were behind the killing. After all, his father was about to leave him behind and deny him the glory of the eastern expedition.

So, at the age of twenty, Alexander became Alexander III, king of the Macedonians, and he and Olympias set about getting rid of their rivals in court: Attalus was killed in Anatolia, and his daughter and baby granddaughter, Alexander's half-sister, were killed in Macedon. Dozens of others were also done away with, especially anyone who might have a claim

Figure 18.2. *Larnax* from Vergina Tomb II. Scholars dispute whether it was Philip II who was buried in this tomb, but no one disputes the regal magnificence of the artifacts that were buried with him. This solid-gold *larnax* contained the bones of the deceased, charred from the funeral pyre, and wrapped in precious purple-dyed cloth. Museum of the Royal Tombs, Aigai/Vergina. Photo © DeA Picture Library / Art Resource, NY.

to the throne. This degree of savagery was not untypical of Macedonian royal accessions. Philip was buried in the royal cemetery in Aegae (modern Vergina), and there are many who believe that the bones recovered, along with fabulous treasures, from one of the grand tombs there are his. Alexander was now the king, with no more time for education, so Aristotle returned to Athens, where he opened his world-famous school at the Lyceum gymnasium.

Alexander was immediately faced with a number of threats. The least serious, and the one that he turned to first, was the possibility of rebellion among the Greeks. The news of Philip's assassination had been greeted with joy, and there was unrest here and there—more at the level of words than action—but as Alexander marched south, all the Greek states recognized his inheritance of his father's positions on the Amphictyonic Council, as Archon of Thessaly, and as life president of the League of Corinth, and pledged allegiance accordingly.

This left Alexander free to quell trouble on his northern borders. But the Theban rebellion was not over, and in 335, on hearing a rumor that Alexander had died fighting in Illyris, they overthrew the oligarchy imposed by Philip and called not very effectively upon the other Greeks to throw off Macedonian rule. Alexander marched south with astonishing speed. He besieged the city to surrender and then cynically got the League of Corinth (especially the other Boeotian communities, which were delighted to be free of Theban control) to condemn it for having medized during the Persian Wars. Thebes, one of the great cities of Archaic and Classical Greece, was razed to the ground, and only the temples and the house where the poet Pindar had lived were spared. A few decades later, the historian Hegesias of Magnesia-by-Sipylus said that it was as though Zeus had removed the moon from the sky, leaving only the sun (which in his image was Athens).[11] Six thousand Thebans died in battle, and another thirty thousand were sold into slavery. Alexander established his authority over the Greeks by an act of singular violence, and any chance he had in the future of trusting them was destroyed along with Thebes.

Demosthenes had spoken out in support of the Theban rebellion, and Alexander demanded his surrender and that of a number of his colleagues, but somehow he was persuaded to relent. Perhaps he had slaked his thirst for vengeance on Thebes. Having settled Greece and defended his northern borders, he returned to Pella to plan the invasion of the Persian Empire, now scheduled for 334.

Athens after Chaeronea

Defeat at Chaeronea threw Athenian political life into chaos. Presumably the same was happening elsewhere as well. Demosthenes' war faction had been in the ascendant since about 345, and he and his colleagues were now blamed for the defeat: "I was on trial every day," he said later.[12] Nevertheless,

---

11 Hegesias of Magnesia, *FGrH* 142 F 12.
12 Demosthenes 18.249 (*On the Crown*).

the Athenians affirmed their support for his position by choosing him to deliver the funeral speech over the battle dead. He and his group survived the onslaught and shared power for a few years with their opponents.

Peace and prosperity returned to Greece while Alexander was campaigning in the East, and Athens regained a good degree of financial stability, especially when Lycurgus of Boutadae took over the Theoric Fund. In fact, the years of Lycurgus' administration can be regarded as a new age of glory for Athens—a silver age, if we reserve gold for Periclean Athens. His authority lasted a full twelve years, from 336 to 324, and was massively increased when he gained effective control of the Military Fund as well as the Theoric Fund. He restored Athens' revenues to the level they had attained a hundred years earlier, just before the Peloponnesian War.

Lycurgus undertook a thorough overhaul of the Athenian financial system, but he also found less orthodox ways of raising money. He was famous for his dogged pursuit of malefactors in the courts (unfortunately, only one speech of his survives complete), at least in part to raise money for the state from fines and confiscations of property. He was said to write these speeches with a nib dipped not in ink, but in death.[13] And he also raised a lot of money by institutionalizing the request for "voluntary" donations from wealthy citizens, paving the way for the increasing dominance of the wealthy in subsequent decades and centuries. Pirates had been interrupting commercial shipping in the Adriatic, and under his auspices, as we know from a surviving decree, in 325 a new settlement was planted there, in some unknown location.[14]

Lycurgan Athens was driven by a sense of what it had lost. Orators harped constantly on the glories of the city's fifth-century past. Its renewed wealth was spent largely on projects that combined nostalgia with some practical purpose: the Panathenaic stadium was dressed in marble, the Lyceum gymnasium gained a splendid wrestling-ground, the Pnyx was greatly improved and enlarged (a testament to the number of citizens who attended Assembly meetings). The old wooden Theater of Dionysus was massively enlarged and dressed in marble, especially to accommodate revivals of the great tragedians of the fifth century—Aeschylus, Sophocles, and Euripides, whose heroized statues in bronze now adorned the theater, and whose texts were edited into standard versions, which actors were henceforth to follow, without

13 Pseudo-Plutarch, *Lives of the Ten Orators* 841e.
14 Rhodes/Osborne no. 100 = (translated) Harding no. 121.

ad-libbing or adding their own interpolations. Many lesser projects were undertaken too. The very intensity of the building program was an echo of Periclean Athens. The *ephēbeia* was instituted (pp. 306–7) in part as an attempt to restore Athens' military pride.

In Piraeus, the largest secular building in the Greek world at the time, the arsenal, was completed, to store naval equipment. Triremes were now being supplemented by quadriremes and quinqueremes, first developed in Syracuse, and the Athenian fleet was built up to almost four hundred ships, the ship sheds destroyed at the end of the Peloponnesian War were rebuilt, and the harbors and docks were enlarged and fortified—unmistakable references to the naval dominance of fifth-century Athens. And naval dominance meant that trade increased. Lycurgus, himself a member of an old noble family that supplied not only the priest of Poseidon Erechtheus but also the priesthood of Athena Polias, the two most prestigious such posts in Athens, also tried to lure the gods back to Athens. He made sure that all the major Athenian festivals, sacrifices, and religious embassies were carried out in at least as splendid a fashion as in days past.

There was a downside to the Lycurgan reforms, however. Stable finances and a massive navy stoked Athenian pride and aggrandized their dreams. No sooner had Philip died than they were in touch with Attalus in Anatolia, knowing his hostility toward Alexander. By 330, they were provocatively honoring enemies of Macedon, and Demosthenes was delivering his most famous speech, *On the Crown*, which is replete with anti-Macedonian sentiment. By the time Lycurgus died in 324, the Athenians imagined themselves great enough to lead resistance to Macedonian rule, and they were already extending feelers to other Greek states, to see what enthusiasm there might be for rebellion. The delusory nature of such dreams would rapidly be exposed.

19

Alexander the Great

In 334 Alexander left as his viceroy in Macedon an old and trusted general of his father's called Antipater and led an army across the Hellespont into Asia, opening the final chapter in Greece's long relationship with the Persian Empire. He was twenty-two years old. By the time of his death eleven years later, his empire of about five million square kilometers (almost two million square miles) stretched, albeit somewhat patchily, from the Danube to the Nile to the Indus.

Alexander represented the expedition not just as pan-Hellenic payback for the Persian invasions of 490 and 480, but also as a continuation of the Greek war against Troy, the first war of Europeans against Asians, and he represented himself as Achilles, the hero of that legendary war, from whom he claimed descent. However, right from the start this was not just a war of revenge, but of conquest. Alexander's first act on reaching the Asian shore was the Homeric gesture of casting a spear into the soil to indicate that Asia was to be "spear-won" land, his by right of conquest. Almost his second act was a visit to Troy to honor Achilles and other legendary Greek heroes. The bargain Achilles had been offered by the gods was that he would win eternal glory, but at the cost of dying young. Alexander blazed with the same brief light.

Casting a spear into the soil was good copy; Alexander was a master of the dramatic gesture for publicity purposes, and many of the most famous stories about him tell of just such gestures. For instance, he made a long detour early in his journey east just to visit Gordium, the old capital of Phrygia, where there was an ancient wagon, the yoke of which was joined onto the shaft with knotted straps, impossible to untie. There was a prophecy to the effect that whoever undid the knot would rule all Asia. Many had tried, but none succeeded—until Alexander came and arrogantly sliced it through with his sword. Good copy—but also meant to frighten any Achaemenid subjects who were inclined to believe the prophecy.

Antipater's two main jobs were somewhat incompatible: to protect the kingdom and to send Alexander reinforcements as ordered. Throughout his eastern expedition, Alexander hemorrhaged men, not just as casualties of war, disease, and exposure, but also because he had to leave dozens of garrisons along his route. In a series of amazing and closely fought battles, he crushed the Persians and took control of their empire. He never lost a major battle, and there were very many of them. He was a master of bold strategy and flexible tactics; his army contained contingents of just about every possible variety of soldier, mounted and unmounted. In the tradition of Greek generals, he led from the front and his life was often in danger. But that was Alexander's nature—to push both himself and his men to the limits of their abilities. What ordinary men called recklessness was Alexander's way of life, and without it he would never have conquered the Persian Empire and earned his posthumous sobriquet "the Great."

Anatolia

Parmenion, in command of the Macedonian forces in Anatolia, had gained ground and then lost it again to Memnon of Rhodes, the formidable commander of the Persian army in Anatolia. Parmenion had found, as Alexander would too, that the Eastern Greeks did not welcome him with open arms. They had learned by now that their fate was never to gain true freedom, but only ever to change masters. But Parmenion still held a bridgehead at Abydus, and that was where Alexander linked up with him. Between them, they had some forty thousand foot and six thousand horse. They were largely Macedonians and mercenaries; Alexander rightly doubted the loyalty of the Greeks and tended not to use them in his army except as mercenaries. The Thessalian cavalry was very important to him, but Thessaly was almost part of Macedon anyway. At the start of his expedition, many more Greeks were serving as mercenaries on the Persian side than on Alexander's.

Memnon and the Persian satraps decided to make a stand at the Granicus River, and Alexander marched to meet them. In the first phase of the battle, the Macedonians were hard pressed, since they had to force a strongly defended river crossing, but once they were across they made fairly short work of the enemy. On the right wing, Alexander led his cavalry well over to the right, drawing the Persian cavalry away from the infantry they were supposed to protect. By the end of the day, the Anatolian satraps were dead or cowed, and the remaining Persian forces scattered. Disturbingly, however, Alexander very nearly lost his life early in the battle; had he died, the whole campaign would have stalled at the very beginning, and there was no obvious successor to the throne. He was saved in the nick of time by his friend Cleitus.

Following the battle, Alexander appointed his own satraps for Anatolia, revealing that he planned to retain the efficient Persian system, and converted huge swaths of territory into his personal property. His most successful appointment was that of his general Antigonus Monophthalmus (the one-eyed) as satrap of Phrygia, in which capacity he mopped up the remnants of Persian resistance in Anatolia and fought at least one major battle to defend Alexander's rear. Alexander declared the Eastern Greek cities free and canceled their tribute payments, and the Persian-supported oligarchies were deposed in favor of democracies. Alexander would have preferred oligarchies, such as those he was supporting on the Greek mainland, but it was more important for him to mark the change of regime. In one way, however, there was little difference: the newly freed Eastern Greeks were still required to pay "contributions" to Alexander's war chest, and they were liable to taxes.

Alexander was slightly delayed by the necessity of having to besiege Miletus, and then delayed for several months by the siege of Halicarnassus, where Memnon was in command. The city, which had massive walls, was strongly defended, because it was supposed to be the landing point in western Anatolia for Persian troops sent against Alexander. It fell late in the autumn of 334, but Memnon escaped.

At Miletus, Alexander had dismissed most of the Greeks from his fleet; as a result of his suspicion of them, he abandoned the sea, and chose "to conquer the Persian fleet from dry land"[1]—that is, by gaining control of all the harbors and havens it might have used. But Memnon now set himself up in the Cyclades, trying to stir rebellion, and succeeded in winning over some of the islands. He even raided the coastline of Macedon. His death in 333 of an illness was a real stroke of luck for Alexander, and over the next few years—while Alexander did indeed gain control of all the ports of the eastern Mediterranean—his men were able to recover the islands and secure

---

1 Arrian, *Anabasis* 1.20.1.

Alexander's supply lines across the Aegean and the Hellespont. One upshot was that Memnon's half-Iranian widow, Barsine, became a refugee and came to the attention of Alexander. Their affair lasted for several years, and in the early 320s she bore him a son named Heracles.

Syria and Egypt

After conquering mountain-girt and mineral-rich Cilicia (and suffering from a mystery illness in Tarsus, possibly malaria), Alexander swept into Syria. This time he would meet the Great King himself, not just his satraps. Darius III, who had come to the throne in 336, skillfully got behind Alexander in the Amanus mountains, cutting him off from his supply line back to Anatolia, but then found himself forced to fight on a narrow coastal strip rather than in an open plain where he could have exploited his numerical advantage. The battle of Issus was a good example of Alexander's preferred tactics for pitched battles: he massed his cavalry on his right wing, leaving the left (commanded by Parmenion) relatively weak. While Parmenion's cavalry and the infantry battalions in the center held their ground (just), and drew off as many of the enemy as possible, Alexander led his cavalry in a ferocious charge against the Persian left, and then turned and pushed for the center, where the king was stationed. Darius fled.

The battle of Issus was fought in November 333, and after it Darius could no longer pretend that the world had not shifted. Alexander agreed: it was only after Issus that he felt confident enough to start minting coins for his new Asian territories. Darius' losses in the battle were great, and afterwards eight thousand of his Greek mercenaries went over to Alexander's side. Just as importantly, some members of Darius' immediate family had accompanied him, in the manner of the Achaemenid court, and they fell into Alexander's hands. Their importance to him was not as bargaining counters; he turned down every such offer from Darius, however generous. Their importance was that keeping them with him and treating them well would win him allies among the Persian nobility, their friends and relatives.

As Alexander marched down the Phoenician coastline after Issus, he met little resistance, except at Tyre. It took him seven months to take the island city, but he could not afford to leave it in his rear. Much of that time was spent in building a causeway out to the island, which was a bit less than a

Figure 19.1. Alexander coin. This is a typical four-drachma piece of Alexander the Great. On the obverse, the king sports a lion's-mane headdress in imitation of Heracles; on the reverse are Zeus and an eagle, symbols of power. © Trustees of the British Museum.

kilometer from the mainland (about half a mile), so that he could bring up siege engines, but the Tyrians still had a strong fleet of eighty ships, and Alexander was able to surround the city only when the remnants of the Persian fleet, returning from the Aegean, had willy-nilly come over to his side, since he occupied their home ports. Farther down the coastline, Gaza lasted only two months. At both Tyre and Gaza, Alexander's savage side was on display: the punishment of Tyre included two thousand crucifixions, and at Gaza, Alexander had the garrison commander dragged to a gruesome death behind a chariot. This was presumably an imitation of Achilles' treatment of Hector's body in the *Iliad*—but a more brutal imitation, since in Homer's poem Hector was already dead before being hitched to the chariot.

After a long rebellion, the Persians had recovered Egypt (along with Phoenicia and Cyprus) only recently, in 343. It remained restive, and when Alexander arrived in November 332 the Persian authorities there simply surrendered and withdrew. While in Egypt, Alexander endeared himself to the priestly authorities by authorizing the rebuilding of several temples, and he oversaw the initial planning stages of a magnificent new foundation on the Mediterranean coast, the city of Alexandria, the greatest and most splendid of the dozen or so cities he would found and name after himself. Most of Alexander's new foundations, whether Alexander-cities or not, were actually refoundations of Achaemenid settlements, to mark the change of regime; they defended sensitive locations, kept local populations in their place, and facilitated the collection of agricultural taxes. Alexandria would grow to be the greatest city in the Greek world.

Founding cities with one's own name or the name of a close family member was new, a startling declaration of authority learned by Philip from Persia. But Alexander had arrogance to spare for such an enterprise. His achievements were already miraculous, and he was beginning to feel himself more than human. Way out west in the Egyptian desert, there was an oasis city called Siwah, with an oracle of the Egyptian god Ammon, that was already well known to the Greeks; there was even a branch temple at Aphytis in the Chalcidice. Alexander made the long trek there with a question about his parentage. "He consulted the god and received the answer that his heart desired"[2]—that is, he was assured that he was the son of Ammon, the Egyptian equivalent of Zeus. Alexander had taken the first step toward establishing his divinity—either because he truly believed it or because it was a useful tool of subjection.

Alexander's divine parentage was confirmed more or less simultaneously by two other oracles, and stories soon emerged about how Olympias had been impregnated by the god in the form of a snake.[3] But Alexander also never denied that his father was Philip; like Heracles (one of the deities with whom Alexander identified), he would have both a mortal and an immortal father.

The End of the Achaemenid Empire

By the time Alexander marched east again in the spring of 331, Darius had had almost two years to prepare, and he had gathered a mighty army. Battle was joined near the village of Gaugamela, close to the Tigris in what is now northern Iraq, on October 1, 331. The details are unclear, which is particularly unfortunate for the battle that would effectively deliver the Achaemenid Empire into Alexander's hands, but it seems to have gone according to Alexander's usual plan. Darius and his cousin Bessus, satrap of Bactria, fled east to Ecbatana in Media; others made their way to Babylon, or vanished into the nearby mountains.

2 Arrian, *Anabasis* 3.4.5; Austin no. 9.
3 Plutarch, *Alexander* 3.2.

There was nothing to stop Alexander advancing southeast into the heart of the empire. Great Babylon, the most prosperous city in the Near East, opened its gates without a fight, surrendering its forces and immense treasures, just as it had two hundred years earlier to Cyrus the Great, and two hundred years before that to Sargon of Assyria; this was policy, not cowardice. They knew that their agricultural wealth made them desirable, and hoped that, as a sacred site, they would be well treated. Susa surrendered too, and Alexander marched on toward Persepolis, Darius' capital, but the satrap of Persis had occupied the pass at the Persian Gates, and Alexander's first assault was repulsed. But captives told him of a circuitous path that would bring him out behind the enemy. He attacked them from the front and rear simultaneously and massacred them—as though he were paying them back for the battle of Thermopylae in 480, when a circuitous path had worked in their favor.

Persepolis too opened its gates to Alexander, but it did not receive the same respectful treatment as Babylon and Susa. It was thought to be the wealthiest city in the world, and Alexander allowed his men to plunder at will, as long as they did not touch the royal palace built by Xerxes, for which he had plans. He arrived in January 330 and stayed for three months, looting, laying in stores, resting his men, and waiting—for Parmenion to arrive with the slower baggage train, for news of the outcome of a Spartan rebellion in Greece, and for the warm weather to clear the high passes toward Ecbatana, where Darius was holed up. Toward the end of their stay, once he was sure that the enormous palace had been cleared of all its valuables, he burned it to the ground. This was a cold-blooded act, not the result of a drunken revel as some of the sources famously say; Alexander had presented his expedition as a war of revenge against Xerxes, and burning Xerxes' palace was the perfect symbolic capstone. "No city," he said, "was as hateful to the Greeks as the capital of the ancient kings of Persis, and it had to be eliminated."[4]

In the spring of 330, Alexander marched on Ecbatana, seeking the final showdown, but Darius had not been able to gather enough troops over the winter and he fled, hoping to make a last stand in the eastern satrapies. Alexander divided his forces, sending Parmenion on to Ecbatana with sufficient men to guard all the booty and pacify Media, and set off himself with about twenty thousand men after Darius. Deserters from the Persian camp kept him informed about what was going on. Just as in Macedon, Persian

4 Curtius Rufus, *History of Alexander* 5.6.1.

kings had to be strong to survive, and Darius had not done well. He was bound in chains, and Bessus took over command of the forces that were left to him. When Alexander caught up with the fugitives, Bessus had Darius killed and left his body in a cart by the roadside to slow the pursuit.

At Hecatompylus, Alexander gave Darius an honorable funeral, and proclaimed himself King of Asia. The Persians now had only the armies of the eastern satrapies to rely on, and Alexander was confident—too confident, as it turned out—that he would not be greatly troubled by them. The Achaemenid Empire had come to an end, after two hundred years; the Greek war of revenge was over. And so Alexander dismissed his Greek troops, many of whom immediately re-enlisted as mercenaries.

Naturally, Alexander had been giving some thought to administration. He continued to retain the Achaemenid satrapal system, as he had in Anatolia, but in the Near Eastern and eastern satrapies he sometimes appointed or reappointed Iranians or other easterners. They were experienced men, so it made sense to make use of those he could trust, and they came with networks of subordinate loyalties, but Alexander circumscribed their power by simultaneously appointing Macedonians as garrison commanders and financial controllers. Local administrative systems were left in place; he tweaked only the top layers.

Appointing easterners to high office was a way of ensuring a smooth transition of power, but it was also a necessity. There simply were not enough Macedonians to run the empire, and few Greeks were highly placed in Alexander's court. The new empire would have to include both European and Asian institutions and personnel, and Alexander symbolized this in his own person by starting—first in Babylon—to dress in a way that was distinctively royal, but not exclusively either eastern or western. Nevertheless, it proved too eastern for some of those close to him.

The End of the Achaemenids

The focus of the Alexander historians is so squarely on his forward motion that we have little information about what was happening behind him. One thing we do know, however, is that in the autumn of 331, around the time of the battle of Gaugamela, Agis III, the Eurypontid king of Sparta, called on his fellow Greeks to rise up against Macedon. Earlier in the fourth century, Persian money had forced Agesilaus out of Persian territory and back to Greece for the Corinthian War, and, after Issus, Darius had sent envoys to the Greeks, hoping to do the same again. His encouragement had found receptive ears in Sparta. Agis, acting as the Persian agent in Greece, had even won over to the cause the Cretan cities, which were usually tied up with their own affairs.

Something went wrong with Agis' timing, however, or he was unlucky. It turned out that the Persian fleet in the Aegean was hard pressed at the time of his uprising and could not make good on the king's promise of help. By the spring of 330, after defeating the Macedonian garrison from Corinth, Agis had gained support—but only from other Peloponnesian states. None of the central or northern Greek states chose to get involved, not even Athens, perhaps because they had men serving with Alexander who would have faced his wrath. As a reward for Athenian quietism, Alexander would send them three thousand talents and the statues of Harmodius and Aristogeiton that Xerxes had stolen when he sacked the city in 480.

It can hardly have been a coincidence that the Macedonian governor of Thrace simultaneously initiated an attempt at independence. But Antipater was up to the task. After quelling the rebellion in Thrace by diplomacy or bribery, he marched south, collecting Greek allies from the League of Corinth on the way, to supplement his Macedonians. Battle was joined at Megalopolis, a Macedonian ally that the Spartans had attacked, and the Spartans were defeated. There was significant loss of life on both sides, with Agis himself one of the casualties. Again, as after Leuctra, the Spartans had to "let tradition sleep" to avoid the implosion of their society (p. 298). The Spartans played little part in broader events for a long while. Some of them—even kings—appear in the historical record only when they hired themselves out as mercenary commanders.

Alexander was unexpectedly merciful: the Spartans were required only to pay a token indemnity to Megalopolis, and give hostages. The battle had been hard fought, and if Agis had won, Macedonian rule in Greece would have been precarious, and this would have affected the eastern expedition. Nevertheless, when Alexander at Persepolis heard news of the victory, he is said to have sneered at it: "Apparently, gentlemen, while we've been defeating Darius here, a battle of mice has taken place back home in Arcadia."[5]

Meanwhile, in the East, Alexander set out from Hecatompylus after Bessus, who was heading for his home satrapy of Bactria (northern Afghanistan,

5 Plutarch, *Agesilaus* 15.4.

roughly) and had declared himself king, as Artaxerxes V. This was a setback for Alexander, who was trying to present himself as the legitimate king, a king by conquest and by the acceptance of the Iranian noblemen he had already won over. Further setbacks followed, of a military nature, as Alexander subdued the southeastern satrapies in order to confine Artaxerxes to the northeastern satrapies of Bactria and Sogdiana, and then hunted him in the mountains and valleys there.

Artaxerxes was betrayed to Alexander in the middle of 329 and was duly put to death, but it still took another two years of costly warfare in these provinces before Alexander felt he could move on to further conquests. He never really pacified Sogdiana, and had to resort to massacres and terror tactics to make any kind of impression at all. The best he could do was leave garrisons there, in the towns (some of them new foundations) or in fortresses established for this purpose. He also took his first wife, Rhoxane. She was the daughter of a Sogdianan nobleman called Oxyartes, formerly a fierce foe, but now one of the men on whom Alexander was chiefly relying to keep the eastern satrapies quiet. The Alexander historians present the marriage as a love match, but its purpose was strategic. She was the oriental queen to suit Alexander. Their children would have both Asian and European blood, and Alexander's style of kingship was the same mixture.

Internal Troubles and Intimations of Immortality

These were difficult years for Alexander. Casualties were heavy, the men's morale was often low, and there was much talk in the ranks about returning home now that the job was done. But the most serious disaffection was in the upper echelons of the army, where it manifested, in the way typical of royal courts, as a contest for power and Alexander's favor.

Philotas had served with distinction throughout the campaign, but he was an arrogant man and it was known that he thought his father, Parmenion, should receive more credit for the part he was playing in Alexander's successes. Late in 330, in the province of Drangiana, he made a fatal mistake: for some reason, when he heard about a plot to kill Alexander, he failed to pass on the information. When news of the conspiracy leaked out and it was also discovered that Philotas already knew about it, he was inevitably impli-cated, and was put to death along with the conspirators. Was he guilty? We shall never know. It may be that what brought him down was that he was disliked by courtiers close to Alexander who felt that he was obstructing their promotion.

Alexander could not stop there, however: he had to kill Parmenion as well, who was too powerful to be left alive and angry, and many of those who formed Parmenion's primary networks. It is not impossible that Alexander had intended all along to do something like this, because it removed the last of the old guard, the men who had been loyal to Philip, and Alexander now promoted his own men: Macedonians, a few Greeks, and a few Iranians. Alexander's conflicts with members of the Macedonian nobility were not over, but they now became less significant.

Then, in Samarkand in 328, things got out of hand at a drunken sym-posium, and Alexander and Cleitus, the man who had saved his life at the Granicus, got into a ferocious row that ended with Alexander running his friend through with a spear. The issue—or what Cleitus focused on in his drunken rage—was Alexander's adoption of eastern habits. Many were as concerned as Cleitus (and the late Philotas) that Alexander was apparently increasing his reliance on eastern troops and eastern governors, when these were the men they had come to conquer. They were concerned also that he had chosen an eastern rather than a Macedonian wife, and they hated seeing their king becoming so Persianized that he now behaved like an oriental king, with practices such as limiting access to his presence, seating himself on a golden throne for official meetings, and accepting obeisance from his eastern subjects (Europeans were spared this ritual). And whereas in Macedon those closest to the king had been free to speak their minds, that was now becoming a rare and sometimes dangerous privilege.

Back home in Macedon, where the king and his advisers met more in symposia than in a formal manner, no one was required to call the king "your majesty" or anything like that; they addressed him by his first name. Alexander was the first Macedonian king to call himself "King Alexander," rather than just "Alexander, son of Philip." Macedonians were not used to being treated with oriental disdain. But Alexander had to find ways to make his rule acceptable to members of the local elites; in order to present himself as the legitimate successor of the Achaemenid kings, he had to adopt some of their customs.

Alexander may already have begun to think of himself as more than human. Things had moved on since he had been named a son of Ammon by the oracle. Many of his new subjects in Egypt and the East were ready to acknowledge his godhood, not just because it was traditional for them to regard kings as gods or the gods' instruments, but because Alexander's achievements were incredible, and incredible achievements were a sign of divinity. His godhood was discussed in his court, and a contemporary historian tells us that Alexander used to dress up as various gods and was honored on such occasions with incense and reverential silence.[6] Some places in Anatolia began to worship him before his death, and in 324 and 323 the question was debated in the cities of the Greek mainland too, where many states, including Sparta, Megalopolis, and Athens, instituted his cult. Alexander was a new phenomenon, wielding massive power, and regarding him as a god helped the Greeks accommodate him within their worldview. Hence most cults of Alexander (and then of his Successors too) were initiated by the Greek cities, not by the kings themselves.

It was perfectly possible within Greek religion for a man to be a god. Of course, there were uncrossable gulfs between humanity and divinity—not least the one that Homer stressed: the gods do not die. But it was always possible for a person to be taken over temporarily by a god; as long as Alexander was performing miraculous deeds, he could be regarded as an incarnate god.

Lysander of Sparta was the first we know of to receive cult while he was alive: the oligarchs he restored in Samos and elsewhere instituted his cult as a savior god. After Alexander, it was common for the great kings to receive cult when alive (and certainly when dead) and to have festivals instituted in their names by grateful states; that was an intrinsic part of their style of kingship. Their womenfolk soon began to receive cults as well, especially as Aphrodite, the goddess of femininity and, increasingly, of marriage. Only the Antigonid rulers of Macedon stood apart from this trend; they had no use for it because the people they ruled had no tradition of divine or semidivine kingship. When addressed as a god, Antigonus Gonatas of Macedon scorned the title, saying: "The slave who collects my chamber pot knows better."[7]

---

6 Arrian, *Anabasis* 4.10–11 (Austin no. 12); Ephippus, *FGrH* 126 F 5.
7 Plutarch, *Moralia* 360c–d (*On Isis and Osiris*).

But when great events were afoot, as they were in the time of Alexander and his immediate Successors, gods walked the earth.

To the Ends of the Earth

In the late spring of 327, having suppressed a conspiracy against his life from some of the Royal Pages (who had personal, not ideological reasons for wanting him dead), Alexander left Afghanistan, hopefully in the safe hands of his new father-in-law, and set out for India. Only the Punjab ("Five Rivers"), in today's Pakistan, had paid tribute to the Achaemenid Empire, and Alexander's intention was first to impress his rule upon this very wealthy province, and then to see what lay beyond it.

The Indian states were disunited, so his task was far easier than it might have been. A number of rajahs were happy to ally themselves with him as a way of getting the better of their neighbors; others surrendered without a fight once they had seen how terrible were the consequences of resistance. Alexander certainly had a cruel side to his nature, but his terrible savagery in Pakistan was partly strategic: he wanted to deter others, because, having finally discovered how enormous the country was, he was in a hurry to get on. He had to fight only two major battles, one against Porus, the king of the fertile land between the Jhelum and Chenab rivers, which is still Pakistan's major breadbasket. Porus lost, but Alexander reinstated him, as he did other kings in the region.

In the end, it was not the Indians who defeated Alexander, but his own men and the weather. By the time they reached the Beas River late in 326, just inside modern India, they had been marching for weeks in the monsoon rains. There is nothing worse for foot soldiers on the march: clothes and shoes rot, weapons rust, marching is uncomfortable, disease rampant. Up until then, serious dissension seems to have been more or less confined to Alexander's court, but now the ordinary soldiers simply refused to go on. Alexander wanted new conquests, and he wanted to see if India was the end of the world, with nothing beyond it except the legendary river Ocean, which encircled the continents in the Greek imagination. No mortal man had ever seen the Ocean, and that alone aroused Alexander's longing to do so. But his men could not be moved. Alexander sulked and raged, but the omens from the gods were unfavorable as well. With both gods and men against him, he turned back.

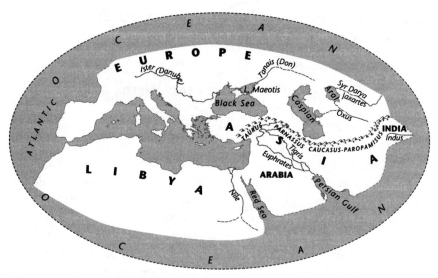

Map 19.1. Alexander's world-view.

Instead of retracing his route, he chose to sail the 1,200 kilometers (750 miles) down the Indus to the Arabian Sea. Since his men now numbered nearly 100,000, this required the construction of hundreds of ships. Garrisons were left along the way to discourage future rebellion. When Alexander heard that the Malava and another tribe were going to attack in large numbers, outnumbering even his enormous army, he ordered a preemptive strike. As usual, he was the first to scale the wall of the Malavan citadel—but this time he found himself isolated, with only two or three men beside him. It was not in his nature to retreat or wait to be shot down, and his men were approaching, so they leaped off the wall and into the citadel. They resisted with furious desperation, but before long Alexander took an arrow in the chest, and blood bubbled up from a pierced lung. Miraculously, the others kept the enemy at bay until the rest of the army arrived. The slaughter was immense. This was not the first time Alexander had been wounded, but it was by far the worst. Fortunately, though there were further tests, there were no more major battles to be won.

The army finally reached the Arabian Sea in the summer of 325. No Europeans had ever set eyes on it before, and previously Alexander had thought that the Indus was an extension of the Nile, and that they would find a vast desert between India and Egypt.[8] But it was always going

8 Arrian, *Anabasis* 6.1.2–6.

to be impossible to govern such remote lands, and soon all his efforts in Pakistan were undone. Within two years, after the assassination of one of his satraps, he had removed the other two from the region and given much of the territory he had conquered into the hands of two native kings, Porus and Taxiles. By 317, a young man called Chandragupta Maurya, driven by imperialist ambitions of his own, had taken over the Indian satrapies. He controlled all of northern India from the Khyber Pass to the Ganges Delta in Bengal, and was turning his attention not only southwards but also northwards, toward the Greco-Macedonian satrapies that ringed his new empire from the Himalayas to the Arabian Sea. Chandragupta has every right to be considered as great a conqueror as his Macedonian contemporary, and his empire lasted much longer, from 322 until 185.

A Purge and Some Celebrations

Alexander explored the Indus Delta for some months, until the weather was suitable and everything was ready for the next leg of the great journey west. The army would be divided into three, and would reunite at the Persian (or Arabian) Gulf. Craterus would take one division of the army by an inland route; Nearchus of Crete, Alexander's admiral, would take the fleet along the desolate Gedrosian coast, to map and describe this unexplored region; and Alexander would take an inland route close to the coast, so that he could leave food and dig wells for the fleet as it sailed along the inhospitable coastline. Exploration was always part of Alexander's mission, and many contingents of men had been sent here and there along his route to reconnoiter and observe. There were scientists in his retinue, and his patronage of them paved the way for later kings as well. Greek learning was hugely stimulated by his conquests and by the accounts of men like Nearchus (now lost to us) of the lands, peoples, flora, and fauna they encountered. This was the time when the study of geography as we understand it began.

Alexander's desert march turned out to be disastrous. On some stretches, there was not enough food and water for his men, let alone the fleet, which was therefore left largely to fend for itself and suffered appalling hardship. Alexander's division suffered worse than Craterus'. Once they had eaten all the baggage animals, people began to die of hunger and thirst, with the slaves, women, and children of the baggage train suffering worst. Hundreds of Alexander's men died during the sixty days of the march of about eight hundred kilometers (five hundred miles). It is not clear how much of this Alexander could have foreseen and avoided, or indeed whether he deliberately chose a difficult route to keep proving his superhuman nature. In Carmania the two land columns were reunited and the troops celebrated with days of drunken indulgence, an extravagant Dionysian revel, with the encouragement and participation of Alexander, who dressed as the god himself. Nearchus' fleet arrived some time later.

Many of the powerful men of the new empire, Asians and Europeans alike, had not expected Alexander to reappear from his far-eastern adventures, and had begun to behave with independent arrogance. Misrule and maladministration were rife, and Alexander had to put a stop to it. As the historian Arrian put it:[9]

> The demonstration that in Alexander's kingdom the ruled were not to be wronged by their rulers was more responsible than anything else for keeping both the conquered peoples and those who had joined him of their own accord in an orderly state, for all their vast numbers and the vast distances that separated them.

In Carmania, therefore, over the winter of 325/4, Alexander instituted a massive purge. Many of the arrangements he had made on the way east had been ad hoc, while he was single-mindedly focused on conquest. Now that the main Asian conquests were over, it was time to make things more permanent. In a few weeks, six of the twenty or so satraps of the empire were executed, four were replaced, and four others conveniently died.

At the same time, Alexander ordered all the satraps to disband their mercenary forces, which several had been using to prop up oppressive regimes; native troops would be used for the defense of the satrapies. Many of the mercenaries joined Alexander's army (an anticipated benefit), while others in their thousands turned to brigandage or returned to Greece, perhaps to resume a domestic life of peace, or perhaps to wait for further recruitment at Cape Taenarum, the southernmost tip of Greece, which had become a huge mercenary camp. Many of the returning mercenaries were brought safely home and left at Taenarum by an Athenian, Leosthenes, and later events suggest that he may already have had in mind some use for these men.

By March of 324, Alexander's army had reached Susa, and the following month he and dozens of the Macedonian elite took eastern wives in a

---

9 Arrian, *Anabasis* 6.27.5 (Austin no. 14).

simultaneous mass wedding. Alexander himself took two more wives, daughters of two previous Achaemenid kings. The purpose of this strange experiment may have been to create future generations of mixed-blood leaders who would be acceptable to the native populations, to match Alexander's mixed-blood heirs by his wives. But it could also be read as a supremacist statement, along the lines of "We've taken your land and now we'll take your women." At the same time as this elite affair, thousands of ordinary soldiers had the liaisons they had struck up with local women officially recognized, perhaps as a way of encouraging at least some of them to stay in the East.

Death in Babylon

Alexander's final destination was Babylon. There he would rest and take thought for the future. Since the future was sure to involve further conquests—Arabia for certain, but possibly also North Africa—even while on the march he sent orders around the empire for more troops to be sent to him, and he ordered the construction of warships in all the eastern Mediterranean ports. He would see out the summer heat in Ecbatana, in the mountains, and then a vast army would assemble in Babylonia and Cilicia. As Arrian remarked: "None of Alexander's plans was small or mean, nor would he have rested content with any of his possessions even if he had added Europe to Asia and the British islands to Europe."[10]

At Opis, on the way to Ecbatana, Alexander announced the demobilization of thousands of his Macedonian veterans, who were to be repatriated with Craterus, while Antipater came out with fresh troops. The veterans had fought long and hard; many of them were in their fifties or even sixties. But resentment had been building up for a long time about Alexander's use of eastern troops. Only a few weeks earlier in Carmania there had been a massive military display by thirty thousand eastern youngsters who had spent the past three years being trained as Macedonian phalangites. The veterans did not enjoy the prospect of being replaced by easterners, and they spoke their minds to Alexander—until he had the ringleaders executed. Harmony was restored by a legendary banquet for nine thousand men, hosted by their king, but the rank and file had once again found their voice.

Throughout the eastern campaigns—ever since childhood, in fact—Alexander's closest friend had been Hephaestion, and he had been promoted

10 Arrian, *Anabasis* 7.1.4 (Austin no. 20).

(once Philotas was out of the way) until he was Alexander's second-in-command. It is very likely that they were lovers. In Ecbatana, in the autumn of 324, Hephaestion died of an illness, exacerbated by heavy drinking. Alexander was inconsolable. He ordered mourning throughout the army and the empire, organized lavish funeral games, gained permission from Siwah to institute the worship of Hephaestion as a hero, and planned an extravagantly expensive tomb for his friend in Babylon.

Alexander's expenses were enormous. In addition to paying the tens of thousands of men serving in the army and navy, there were costly public works such as Hephaestion's tomb and rebuilding the huge temple of Baal in Babylon, not to mention the building of cities, fortresses, temples, and victory monuments, the funding of festivals and athletic competitions, the maintenance of warships, and the upkeep of a glittering court. Alexander was also obliged to be extraordinarily generous with everyone, both friends and potential enemies. But he had the money. From the treasuries and cities of the Achaemenid Empire, he looted at least 180,000 talents of precious metals, coined and uncoined, as well as other valuables. When the empire was at its fullest extent and functioning properly, it brought in a regular income of perhaps thirty thousand talents a year. Many of the more backward districts of the eastern empire had hardly been monetized earlier, but Alexander took over or established mints from Amphipolis to Susa, and spread coined money throughout his empire.

Early in 323, Alexander returned to Babylon. On June 11, around 3:30 in the afternoon, he died, just short of his thirty-third birthday. He was taken ill during a symposium at which, in the Macedonian manner, much wine was consumed, and died after days of gradual weakening and deterioration. Naturally, there are countless theories about his death. Ten years earlier, he had probably contracted malaria in Cilicia; perhaps that was his killer now. We have two descriptions of his symptoms, but they scarcely help in identifying the cause of death.[11]

The most dramatic possibility is raised by the fact that his symptoms are not incompatible with the effects of a slow-acting poison such as white hellebore, which is native to Anatolia. Many found Alexander's death hard to comprehend, while others found it a useful propaganda tool, and for both reasons rumors very quickly sprung up that he had been murdered. And, as in an Agatha Christie novel, there were plenty of people close at hand

11 Plutarch, *Alexander* 73–77; Arrian, *Anabasis* 7.25–26.

who might have liked to see him dead. It was not just that some of them entertained world-spanning ambitions, soon to be revealed. It was more that Alexander's recent purge, his megalomaniacal desire for further conquests, and his ongoing assumption of divinity could have turned even some of those closest to him.

Now or later, Olympias stirred the pot from Epirus, where for some years she had been living in exile, having fallen out irredeemably with Antipater. She knew, then, where to point the finger over her son's death. And she had a plausible case: Antipater's replacement by Craterus might well have made the viceroy resentful, and there are many small signs that relations between Antipater and Alexander were strained. We have already seen, for instance, the contempt with which Alexander treated Antipater's victory at Megalopolis in 331.

Antipater had good reason to think that, as another member of the old guard, on arriving in Babylon he would be executed, as Parmenion had been, on some charge or other, even though he was seventy-five years old. Then again, two of Antipater's sons were in Babylon—and one of them, Iolaus, was well placed to act as a poisoner, since he was Alexander's cupbearer, and Alexander had fallen ill while drinking. Indeed, when news of Alexander's death reached Athens, the anti-Macedonian politician Hyperides proposed honors for Iolaus, precisely for having done away with the king. The second of Antipater's sons, Cassander, had arrived only a few weeks earlier to plead for his father's retention in Macedon. All in all, it seems impossible to discount the idea that Alexander the Great was murdered. The main fact that tells against it is that his death was followed by chaos, as we shall shortly see. If it had been murder, presumably the conspirators would have arranged a smoother transfer of power to their hands or to those of their chosen successor.

ACT III

The Hellenistic Period (323–30)

Greeks, Macedonians, and Romans

PART III

20

The Successor Kingdoms

The Hellenistic period, and independent Greek or Greco-Macedonian history, ended in the year 30 with the fall to Rome of the final Successor kingdom, that of the Ptolemies in Egypt. It is said that when Octavian, the future Roman emperor Augustus, entered the Egyptian capital, Alexandria, he honored the tomb of Alexander the Great with offerings of a golden crown and flowers. When he was asked if he would like to see the tombs of the Ptolemies as well, he refused, saying that "he wanted to see a king, not corpses."[1] The new ruler of the world was extravagantly honoring the first ruler of the world, but he did have a point. There was a sense in which Alexander had stayed alive, while others died. The Greeks of the Hellenistic period continued to live in Alexander's shadow. It was his ambitions that had laid the foundations of the new world, and his spirit lingered in its constant and frequently brilliant search for new horizons.

Augustus' contempt had a long history, however. Until recently, it was not uncommon for accounts of ancient history to skip from Alexander's death to the rise of Rome, ignoring the decades in between as though nothing important happened: men turned into mere corpses, but did not bestride the world the way a true king does. This attitude is misplaced. As a result of Alexander's conquests, Greeks and Macedonians came to rule and inhabit huge new territories. They were living, in effect, in a new world, and this made the Hellenistic period one of the most thrilling periods of history, as everyone at every level of society, from potentates to peasants, adjusted to their new situations. The period pulsates with fresh energy and with a sense—reminiscent of the excitement of the Archaic period—that anything was possible, that there were further boundaries, cultural as well as geographical, to discover and overcome.

1 Suetonius, *Augustus* 18 (early second century CE).

After the end of the Classical period, the sources become even more difficult than usual. This is largely because literary critics later in antiquity thought Hellenistic writers inferior to those of the Classical period, and hardly bothered to preserve them. The only continuous narrative account, that of Diodorus of Sicily, written in the first century, breaks off into fragments after the year 302. But the lack of macrohistorical narrative is compensated by the microhistorical insights afforded by tens of thousands of inscriptions and papyri, coins and cuneiform documents from Babylon. One way and another, enough survives for us to see that the Hellenistic period was a time of vibrant energy and creativity. It held a certain nostalgia for the past, but this did not make it a time of decadence after the glorious Classical period. Nowadays, it is seen as a time when many of the foundations of the modern European world were being laid, including

Figure 20.1. Papyrus fragment. This papyrus fragment, dating from the third century CE and found at Oxyrhynchus in Egypt (Oxyrhynchus Papyrus 2547), contains some of the Hippocratic Oath—the oath of good practice sworn by doctors—which was composed in the fourth century BCE. Photo: Wikimedia.

the ways in which political power was conceived and constructed, how intellectual studies should be approached, what counts as aesthetic beauty, and the relations between individuals and their societies. Things unthinkable in the Classical period—in realpolitik as in artwork—became possible in the Hellenistic period. Alexander's extraordinary conquests propelled the Greek world in many new directions.

The Threat of Chaos

Succession to the Macedonian throne was often an untidy business, littered with coups and corpses, but this one was especially difficult, because there was no obvious heir, and Alexander had not made his will known. There were only three realistic possibilities for the next king, given that he had to be a male Argead. Of his close family, Alexander had left alive only his half-brother Arrhidaeus, saved by the fact that he was less than fully mentally competent. Then there was Heracles, the five-year-old son of Alexander's former mistress Barsine, but the fact that he was not the product of a legitimate marriage made him an unlikely candidate. Then, of Alexander's three wives, Rhoxane was pregnant and due to deliver in a couple of months' time. If she came to term—she had already miscarried once—and if the child was male, he would become a serious claimant to the throne, although he would of course need a regent.

Trouble was also looming in Greece. Just a year before his death, Alexander had ordered the Greek cities to take back their exiles. There were sound reasons for the edict, because there were thousands of rootless Greeks, political exiles or demobilized professional soldiers, in both Asia and Europe, threatening disorder. Besides, Alexander wanted to sow the Greek cities with men who would be grateful to him. But he had unilaterally issued this order without involving the League of Corinth, as he should for matters relating to the Greek states. It might have been a charade to have got them involved, but protocol and the maintenance of good relations still demanded it.

The most severe disruption caused by the Exiles Decree would be not political, stemming from the return of opponents of current regimes, but economic, arising from the need to accommodate thousands of shiftless men and to settle legal claims for long-lost property. To make matters worse, these were years of drought and grain shortages: an inscription from Cyrene lists over forty Greek cities that received cheap grain from them.[2] The worst affected by the Exiles Decree were the Thessalians, Aetolians, and Athenians, whose possession of Samos was at stake. The returning Samian exiles would evict Athenian families who in some cases had been there for forty years.

A long decree from Tegea shows the kind of complex steps that were required to reincorporate the returning exiles in an orderly manner:[3] a time limit of sixty days was set for claims to be registered with the courts; the status of the property claimed had to be assessed, and whether or not it had a plot of land attached; the status (married or unmarried, male or female) of the returning exiles who were claiming the property had to be taken into consideration; and, most delicate of all, some fair means had to be found to deprive current landowners of property that was claimed by returning exiles. Basically, the Tegeans' solution was to offer only a portion of their property to the returning exiles, so that current owners could retain some, and both parties were to be compensated by the state itself for their shortfalls.

At the time of Alexander's death, many of the Greek states were up in diplomatic arms over the decree, trying to negotiate better solutions for themselves. But political exiles were massing on borders, anticipating their imminent return, and local conflicts were already breaking out as some refugees tried to sneak home before the decree had come into force. Greece was a powder keg.

The Succession

Immediately after Alexander's death, those of his senior officers who were present in Babylon met in Nebuchadnezzar's great palace and began to make arrangements for the future. The power play began. All seven of Alexander's Royal Bodyguards were there, the men who had been closest to him; the most important were Perdiccas (who had become Alexander's second-in-command after Hephaestion's death), Leonnatus (head of a powerful baronial house in Macedon), Thessalian Lysimachus (a brilliant general), and Ptolemy (a childhood friend of Alexander's).

---

2 Rhodes/Osborne no. 96 = (translated) Bagnall/Derow no. 3; Harding no. 116.
3 Rhodes/Osborne no. 101 = (translated) Bagnall/Derow no. 4; Harding no. 122.

Some very important people were not in Babylon. Apart from Olympias, the queen mother, two leading men were absent—Antipater and Craterus. By virtue of his viceregal position, Antipater was the most powerful man in the empire after Alexander—or he had been until Alexander had ordered him replaced by Craterus. At the time of Alexander's death, Craterus was no closer to Macedon than Cilicia, where he had been supervising the buildup of armaments with the help of another Macedonian returnee called Polyperchon. Then there was Antigonus Monophthalmus, who by now was not just the satrap of Phrygia, but had also taken on responsibility for the southern provinces of Anatolia as well. He had a huge army under his command. No doubt the only reason such a powerful and experienced man was not in Babylon was because he had not heard in time about Alexander's death.

It was the job of the senior officers in Babylon to choose a successor and present their choice to the Macedonian troops for acclamation. Their preference was to wait to see if Rhoxane's baby was male, and make him king, and the elite cavalry agreed with them, but the infantry wanted no interregnum, and promoted Arrhidaeus, Alexander's half-brother, calling him King Philip after his father. He may have been not fully competent, but he was at least fully Macedonian, and he was there in Babylon. With senior officers championing this position or that in their personal bids for power, turbulent days followed, both at the conference table and outside.

In the end, Perdiccas violently suppressed the opposition and pushed through a kind of compromise: Rhoxane's unborn baby, if male, and Arrhidaeus would both be kings, with Perdiccas as their regent and Seleucus, previously the commander of a crack infantry regiment, as his second-in-command. Antipater and Craterus were made joint "Generals in Europe," but since Antipater was elderly, it was expected that Craterus would soon hold the position on his own, which would hopefully be enough to satisfy his ambitions. So, in the name of the new king Philip III, Perdiccas replaced Alexander's satraps or confirmed them in their posts. Few easterners were retained in any senior posts, and certainly not as satraps; that particular measure of Alexander's seems to have been set aside. It would of necessity be resurrected within two or three generations, by which time prejudice had died down and talented and hellenized natives played prominent roles in the various administrations.

A few weeks later, in September 323, Rhoxane gave birth to a boy, who was proclaimed Alexander IV—and, to be on the safe side, she eliminated

Alexander's other two wives. But a dual kingship was a recipe for disaster, especially since neither of the kings was fully competent. For the foreseeable future, both would be pawns in the hands of those who, by fair means or foul, gained or assumed the position of "protector of the kings" and attempted to rule the empire by speaking in their names. The Macedonian infantry swore oaths of personal allegiance to new kings on their accession, and tended to be loyal to the throne, so the names of the kings carried a great deal of weight.

Three Rebellions

Alexander's death seduced many parts of the empire into restiveness, but the most formidable rebellions were Greek. The Rhodians were the most successful: they threw out their Macedonian garrison and remained free for decades to come, albeit with strong links to Egypt. Less successful were thousands of homesick Greek mercenaries, who set out home from Bactria and Sogdiana, "longing for Greek customs and the Greek way of life";[4] they were massacred on Perdiccas' orders as a deterrent.

Meanwhile, the mainland Greeks were also preparing for rebellion, with Delphi adding its blessing to the enterprise. The Spartans, still reduced by their defeat in 331, stayed away, and the Boeotians, profiting from the removal of Thebes in 335, fought for Macedon, but nearly all the other central and southern Greek states flocked to the banner raised by the Athenians and Aetolians. Aristotle's residence in Athens became untenable—he had, after all, been Alexander's tutor—and he fled into exile, saying, with a reference to Socrates' trial, that he was doing so "lest Athens sin twice against philosophy."[5] The elderly philosopher died the following year.

Ironically, the war was funded by some of Alexander's own money, confiscated from the former Imperial Treasurer, Harpalus, who had fled before Alexander's wrath at his corruption and had tried to secure his refuge in Athens by bribery. He was an honorary citizen of Athens, for an earlier gift of grain. Even supposedly incorruptible Demosthenes succumbed to the glitter of eastern gold and was sent into exile, while, on being rejected by the Athenians, Harpalus fled to Crete, where he was assassinated.

4 Diodorus of Sicily, *Library of History* 18.7.1; Austin no. 27.
5 *Vita Aristotelis Marciana* 41; *Vita vulgata* 19; *Vita Latina* 43.

With the help of Harpalus' money, Leosthenes, now officially an Athenian General, recruited his mercenaries from Cape Taenarum and marched north at the head of twenty-five thousand men. The number would have been greater had the Macedonian garrison at Corinth not prevented most of the Peloponnesian contingents from linking up with the central Greek forces. When Antipater marched south to meet the Greeks, Leosthenes defeated him in battle and put him under siege in Lamia, the main town of the district of Malis; hence the war is known as the Lamian War. Even after Leosthenes fell, Greek hopes were high, but then Leonnatus arrived, in the spring of 322, with reinforcements. He had his eye on the Macedonian throne, and Olympias had offered him the most prestigious wife of all—Alexander's sister, her daughter Cleopatra. But Leonnatus lost his life outside Lamia. His forces managed to break the siege, though, and the Macedonians pulled back north.

At sea, however, Antipater's fleet, reinforced by a large number of ships from Cilicia, defeated the mainly Athenian navy of the Greeks three times in succession in the summer of 322. Macedonian control of the sea was so complete that their admiral took to styling himself Poseidon. That was the end of the war; the opening of the sea made it possible for Craterus to sail over, and in August the outnumbered Greeks were defeated at Crannon in Thessaly. Only the Aetolians never surrendered, and late in 321 Antipater and Craterus launched a massive invasion of the rugged land—but they were called away by more urgent business, as we shall see.

Many in Athens expected their city to be razed, as Alexander had razed rebel Thebes in 335. Intense negotiations by Phocion again secured less harsh terms, as after Chaeronea, but they were still devastating. After 180 years, the democracy was replaced by a limited franchise, with the threshold of citizenship set at a property level of two thousand drachmas, so that twelve thousand poorer citizens were suddenly disenfranchised; power was transferred from the people to the men of property, and the Assembly was required to do no more than rubber-stamp their decisions.

A garrison was installed in Piraeus, cutting Athens off from its fleet (which was, in any case, greatly reduced) and making commerce with the port city a matter of checkpoints and delays, and a massive indemnity was imposed. Thousands of the newly disenfranchised Athenians were relocated to Thrace, perhaps to make room for the Samian cleruchs when they returned. Naturally, the most prominent anti-Macedonians were killed. Demosthenes, who had been brought back from exile for the war, took poison rather than fall into Antipater's ungentle hands.

Nor was it just Athens that was reduced. Antipater dissolved the League of Corinth in favor of more direct, less benign means of control. He made sure that all the major states in Greece were governed by tyrants or pro-Macedonian oligarchies, supported where necessary by garrisons of mercenaries. Tyrants returned to mainland Greece for the first time since the sixth century, deserving the title because it would take rebellion to remove them; their regimes were not usually oppressive, but they were living symbols of Macedonian dominance. Mainland Greece was effectively occupied territory, and resentment of Macedonian rule seethed below the surface.

The Murder of Perdiccas

After Alexander's death, the Greek world descended into about fifty years of unrelenting warfare on a vast scale. At last, from the blood-soaked dust of dozens of battlefields there arose a small number of kingdoms. Not a few of the men who played a part in these wars were trying to emulate Alexander and take over the entirety of the empire for themselves, and they were thwarted only because they came up against the equal ambitions of others. As Plutarch wrote about them:[6]

> When men whose greed recognizes no limits set by sea or mountain or desert, and whose desires overleap even the boundaries that define Europe and Asia—when such men are neighbors, with adjacent territories, it would be foolish to think that they could remain content with what they have, without doing one another wrong.

Perdiccas, the regent of the kings, was supported by those who wanted to see Macedon remain a legitimate monarchy. One of the most important of these loyalists was Eumenes of Cardia, Alexander's Greek secretary and a not incompetent general, as events would show. Lined up against them were chiefly those who had their own personal ambitions. Perdiccas' hand was greatly strengthened when, after the death of Leonnatus, Olympias offered him Cleopatra in marriage. If Perdiccas was married to Alexander's sister, favored by Alexander's mother, the protector of Alexander's brother

---

6 Plutarch, *Pyrrhus* 12.2.

Figure 20.2. Successor coins. Here we see (from left to right) likenesses of Ptolemy I, Seleucus, and Demetrius Poliorcetes. Notice the adoption of the diadem as a sign of royalty, and, in imitation of Alexander, the new habit of shaving. BM 1863,0728.1; ANS WSM.1366; ANS N.108. © Trustees of the British Museum; © American Numismatic Society.

and son, and the commander of the army with which Alexander had conquered the East, his position would be virtually unassailable. This was Olympias' bid to forge an alliance of such strength that it would be able to keep her and her grandson alive until he was old enough to succeed to the throne.

Alexander's name remained a powerful talisman, and all the Successors did their best to ally themselves as closely as possible with the Argead house, by marriage and by protecting the two kings; Ptolemy even hijacked Alexander's corpse, claiming the right to bury it in Egypt rather than Macedon, and making himself Alexander's successor. All the Successors, if they could, made sure that everyone knew how vital a role they had played in Alexander's eastern campaigns, and more generally in his life. Ptolemy claimed to be Alexander's secret half-brother, Seleucus to have been born on the same day. Many of them dressed and wore their hair like Alexander, and went beardless in his manner. All those who established kingdoms founded cities bearing Alexander's name and minted coins with Alexander's head in the place of divinity; even when they portrayed themselves on their coins, there were still echoes of Alexander.

Valuable as Olympias' friendship was, it was not enough. While Perdiccas invaded Egypt—provoked not only by the hijacking of Alexander's corpse, but by Ptolemy's general stance of independence—her enemies Craterus and Antipater made a truce with the Aetolians, and Lysimachus allowed their army to pass through Thrace, his satrapy, and into Anatolia. There they joined forces with their new ally Antigonus Monophthalmus and prepared to face Eumenes. Things were going badly for Perdiccas in Egypt, but his life might have been saved if news had arrived on time of Eumenes' early successes in Anatolia (including the killing of Craterus), but in the summer of 320 Perdiccas was murdered in Egypt by his senior officers, and by the spring of 318, with Antipater safely back in Macedon with the kings, Antigonus had defeated the loyalist forces in Anatolia as well.

Cassander's Bid for Power

Shortly after his return to Macedon, however, aged Antipater died and bequeathed his regency to Polyperchon. But his son Cassander had been expecting the position himself, and he joined forces with Antigonus. While Cassander saw to Greece, Antigonus was to check Eumenes and Polyperchon's other friends in Asia. Fighting broke out in 318, the second war of the Successors. In need of allies, Polyperchon offered to support Greek attempts to overthrow their current regimes in favor of democracy. The offer, sweetened with the promise to return Samos, was enough to gain him Athens, where the democrats seized power amid great jubilation. The democratic heart of Athens was still beating. Phocion and others who had held power under Antipater were executed or sent into exile. But as the weeks passed and Polyperchon proved incapable of taking Piraeus from Cassander's forces, popular support ebbed away from the democrats, and in 317 the Athenians came to terms with Cassander, who was now personally resident in Piraeus.

The newly restored democracy was dissolved, and Cassander installed as his puppet ruler the Aristotelian philosopher Demetrius of Phalerum. Demetrius oversaw a less restricted oligarchy than the one imposed by Antipater, since he halved the property qualification for citizenship to a thousand drachmas; but he gave sweeping powers to a single Secretary, and to a board of seven elected Guardians of the Law, whose job, like that of the Areopagus Council of old, was to keep officers on the straight and narrow and to make sure that the people did not generate any inappropriate proposals. The charge of introducing an illegal or undemocratic proposal, which had served for a century as a vital democratic instrument, was removed from the statute books. The city's needs were now so few that the liturgy system could safely be brought to an end also, in favor of voluntary or solicited donations from the rich. Direct taxation of individuals ceased and was never resurrected in Athens. If Demetrius was a dictator, he seems to have been a fairly benign one.

Polyperchon had considerable success in the Peloponnese, where he seems to have wanted to form the cities into some kind of league, but it was in the north that the critical action took place. Philip III, the perhaps autistic king, had been married since 321 to his niece Eurydice, who was as ambitious as her rival Olympias, each championing one of the kings. In 317 Eurydice decided to risk all, and she prevailed upon her husband to declare his support for Cassander over Polyperchon. Her gamble did not pay off: when Polyperchon and Olympias marched on Macedon from Epirus—for the first war between women, proposed a melodramatically inclined historian[7]—Eurydice's forces deserted her. They had to choose between two Argead kings, and the talismanic presence of Alexander's mother tipped the scales toward the five-year-old boy. Now restored to Macedon at last, Olympias ruthlessly slaughtered her enemies—including, finally, both Philip and Eurydice.

But within a few weeks Cassander had marched north from Greece and unleashed a blitzkrieg. Polyperchon joined his son in a mini-kingdom in the Peloponnese, sprawling from Messene to Corinth. Olympias fled to Pydna, but Cassander took the city early in 316 and put her to death after a show trial. Her grandson, Alexander IV, he kept along with Rhoxane under house arrest in Amphipolis. Meanwhile, Eumenes fled east from Anatolia, pursued by Antigonus, and found allies among some of the eastern satraps. Twice he almost defeated Antigonus in battle, but he was eventually betrayed by his allies in Iran and executed in January 316.

The war was over. Cassander was supreme in Greece and Macedon, while in the space of a few years Antigonus, well over sixty years old now, had made himself the master of almost all the former Achaemenid Empire, excluding Egypt. His resources and power were vast, and he began to behave accordingly, disposing satraps and satrapies as he wished. In 316, on his way west after defeating Eumenes and settling the eastern satrapies, he expelled Seleucus from Babylonia, his legitimate satrapy. Seleucus was taken in by Ptolemy, and before long the other major Successors—not just Lysimachus, but even Cassander, recently Antigonus' ally—agreed to try to curb Antigonus, who clearly wanted the entirety of Alexander's empire for

---

7 Duris of Samos, *FGrH* 76 F 52.

himself, and to reinstate Seleucus. The third war of the Successors broke out in 315, pitting Antigonus and his son Demetrius against the rest.

The Peace of the Dynasts

Antigonus secured Anatolia, appointed Polyperchon his General in Europe, and then turned his attention to Ptolemy. He marched south in the summer of 315 through Phoenicia, expelling Ptolemaic garrisons from cities and accepting their surrender. By 314, following a fifteen-month siege of Tyre, he had all the coastal cities of Cilicia and Phoenicia under his control, and he started building a fleet with which to invade Egypt. Leaving Demetrius in charge in Syria, he went to Anatolia to see to Cassander. By the late summer of 312, he was preparing to invade Europe across the Hellespont. He had won many of the cities to his side with the promise of freedom. Assuming he could overcome Lysimachus, he would come at Macedon from the east, while the Aetolians came from the south and the Illyrians from the west. It was going to take a miracle to save Cassander—and the miracle happened.

Ptolemy launched an attempt to recover Palestine, and inflicted a severe defeat on Demetrius outside Gaza. The heartland of the Antigonid Empire was under threat, and the new city, Antigonea, that was being built in northern Syria as the imperial capital. Antigonus canceled the invasion of Europe and hurried east. By the time he reached Syria, however, early in 311, Ptolemy had launched another attack, hoping to extend farther up the coast—and this time Demetrius had defeated him so convincingly that Ptolemy had abandoned his gains and withdrawn to Egypt.

While the Antigonids plundered northern Arabia, Seleucus seized the opportunity to return to Babylon. Even though Ptolemy loaned him only a small force, it was easier than it might have been, because he was popular with the local elites—not least because he was the only senior follower of Alexander, who did not repudiate the Iranian wife he had been assigned at Susa in the mass marriage of 324. But since the restoration of Seleucus had been one of the main objectives of the anti-Antigonid cause, the war lost impetus. After four years of fighting no one had made significant gains. The Peace of the Dynasts, as it is known, came into force in 311 and more or less recognized the status quo. But recognizing Antigonus' right to all Asia left Seleucus as a conspicuous loose end. Over the next couple of years, the Antigonids more than once came very close to driving him out of Babylonia, but he displayed true brilliance and, growing ever stronger by incorporating the soldiers of the armies he defeated, forced the Antigonids to come to terms with him in 308.

Antigonus abandoned the eastern satrapies, and over the next few years Seleucus spread east and took them over one by one, establishing his authority far more successfully than Alexander had, again by using his ability to get on with the local elites. Trouble from India was averted in 304 by ceding much of the frontier satrapies of southern Afghanistan, Pakistan, and southern Iran to the emperor Chandragupta Maurya, in exchange for several hundred war elephants. Seleucus ended up with a huge but manageable kingdom, and had made himself a force to be reckoned with alongside the other major players. The Seleucid Empire became so important to the East that the year of Seleucus' return, 312, became Year One for the entire region, even in places that owed the Seleucids no allegiance (the dating system is still in use among Yemenite Jews). Once Seleucus' son, Antiochus, as a way of suggesting that the Seleucid dynasty would go on and on, had decided to perpetuate the system (rather than marking his accession as the first year of a new regime), it became the first continuous dating system, the precursor of all others, including our own.

By implicitly acknowledging that the empire had been divided up, the Peace of the Dynasts made the life of Alexander IV forfeit. None of the Successors was going to return to being a subordinate when Alexander came of age and claimed the entire empire as his inheritance. And the first throne he claimed would have been that of Macedon—so, perhaps in 308, Cassander quietly had the teenaged king poisoned, along with Rhoxane. There was a telling lack of protest from any of the others. Cassander had now killed the mother, wife, and son of Alexander the Great. At much the same time, Alexander's illegitimate son Heracles was eliminated as well, the last act of a now aged Polyperchon. After over three hundred years of rulership, it was the end of the main branch of the Argead line. Only one of Alexander's half-sisters remained alive (Thessalonice, who was married to Cassander and had three sons), and his full sister, Cleopatra, was soon to be killed by Antigonus because she was poised to marry Ptolemy and legitimate his claim to the Macedonian throne. She was past the age of childbearing anyway.

Alexander IV's death removed the last obstacle to kingship. Antigonus had been recognized as the king of Asia for some time, and in 307 the Athenians had hailed both him and his son as kings, but now they all assumed the title—the Antigonids first in 306, as joint kings, with the others (including Agathocles of Syracuse) following suit within a few years. As kings, they proceeded to ensure the perpetuation of their line, mint coins in their own names, found cities to anchor their territories, and undertake all the duties of kingship, if they had not already been doing so. But this did not mean that they felt their territories were settled. Macedonian kings were warlords. Military success brought wealth and increased territory, which gave a king both more revenue and more men at his service, so that he could gain more military success. The Successors legitimized their rule by military victory— they had no choice, because they could boast of no royal ancestry—and their descendants, the Hellenistic kings, inherited this militaristic ethos from them.

The Battle of Ipsus

In 307 Antigonus triggered the fourth war of the Successors by sending Demetrius with a fleet of 250 ships and a purse of five thousand talents to establish an Antigonid bridgehead in Athens. The Phalerean Demetrius fled and ended up ultimately in Egypt, where he became Ptolemy's adviser for the famous Library of Alexandria, modeling it on Aristotle's library, which he knew well. The Athenians regained their pride as the Antigonid Demetrius restored democracy, removed the garrison from Piraeus that had been there for fifteen years, returned Lemnos and Imbros (which his father had taken some years earlier), and promised them grain, timber, and money to rebuild their fleet and their fortifications. Just as after the downfall of the Thirty in 403, a board of Legislators was appointed to revise the laws. The democrats set to work with a will, and a torrent of decrees was issued over the next few years.

The Athenians heaped honors on Demetrius and his father, worshipping them as savior gods. They made them the eponymous heroes of two new civic tribes (made up of demes removed from other tribes), added to the ten that had done service since the time of Cleisthenes, and made the appropriate institutional adjustments, so that membership of the Council, for instance, was raised from five to six hundred. But if anyone in Athens hoped for a new period of democratic freedom, they were mistaken; Demetrius' yes-men did not have everything their own way, but opposition was muted. As far as the Antigonids were concerned, Athens was to be the western capital of their empire, and their subjects were expected to do their bidding.

Demetrius made considerable progress against Cassander in Greece. But by 306 the Antigonid fleet was ready in the shipyards of Cilicia and Phoenicia, and Antigonus, too old and overweight now to do the job himself, recalled Demetrius for the invasion of Egypt. The first task was to gain Cyprus—an important island for its harbors and its resources (chiefly minerals, salt, and ship-quality timber). Demetrius' army swept across the island, finally pinning Ptolemy's brother Menelaus in Salamis. Ptolemy sent a huge force to relieve his brother, but Demetrius crushed the Egyptian fleet before it could make land, and gained thousands of mercenaries for himself. This was the star campaign of Demetrius' career, and he was only thirty years old.

The invasion of Egypt, however, late in 306, was stymied by Ptolemy's defenses and the onset of winter. Antigonus decided to try again the next year, and to start by taking Rhodes, which commanded the eastern entrance to the Aegean and had close commercial ties with Egypt: it was the clearing house and banking center for Egyptian grain, and exported wine there in large quantities. After Rhodes, he would move on to Egypt. In the event, however, the resourceful Rhodians withstood a siege for over a year, until early in 304, when Antigonus called it off because Demetrius was urgently needed in Greece. The Rhodians had bought Ptolemy time to regroup.

If Ptolemy had reason to be grateful to the Rhodians, they too were grateful to him, for the many blockade runners he had sent during the siege with vital troops and supplies; they instituted a cult of Ptolemy Soter ("Savior"), and he adopted the title as his official designation. Henceforth, all the Ptolemies had epithets, usually indicating their divinity or military prowess, and in Asia the Seleucids did the same.

Demetrius too gained an appellation. The siege became famous not just for the intensity of the fighting, but also for the innovatory towers and engines that were built under his supervision. These were so huge and elaborate—it took over three thousand men to trundle one of them into place—that, despite the siege's ultimate failure, Demetrius became known from then on as Demetrius Poliorcetes, Besieger of Cities. In thanks for their survival, the Rhodians erected a huge bronze statue of Helios—the Sun god, their patron deity—at the entrance to their harbor. With a height of thirty meters (a hundred feet), the Colossus of Rhodes, as it is known, was considered one of the wonders of the world—this was an age that admired gigantism—but it snapped at the knees and fell during an earthquake in 227.

Once the siege had been called off, Demetrius returned to Athens, just in time to prevent it from falling to Cassander, and made it his base for the next couple of years. Building on his earlier successes, he had soon brought so many of the Greek states under his control—they were governed by his chosen men—that he was able to form them into a new Hellenic League, a revival of Philip II's League of Corinth, with him and his father as life presidents. Only Sparta, Messene, and Thessaly refused to join. The League duly appointed Demetrius its commander-in-chief for the war against Cassander, and he marched north. It looked as though the final showdown for possession of Macedon was about to take place.

Cassander, however, had already formed all the other major players into a fresh anti-Antigonid alliance. Early in the summer of 302, while he kept Demetrius pinned in Thessaly, Lysimachus invaded Anatolia from Thrace. Antigonus heaved himself out of retirement and marched north from Syria. Little happened for the rest of the year, as Lysimachus withdrew before Antigonus while waiting for Seleucus to arrive from Babylonia, with thousands of men and hundreds of war elephants. Demetrius abandoned Greece to Cassander and took his army to Anatolia to support his father. Once Seleucus arrived, battle was joined at Ipsus in Phrygia. Each side was commanded by two kings and fielded about eighty thousand men; all the peoples of the empire were represented. It was the greatest battle of the Successors, and the most significant. If the Antigonids won, they would or would soon have the entirety of Alexander's empire.

But it was an outright victory for the anti-Antigonid alliance. Octogenarian Antigonus died appropriately on the battlefield in a shower of javelins, while Demetrius escaped by the skin of his teeth. After the battle, "the victorious kings proceeded to slice up the whole of Antigonus' and Demetrius' domain like an enormous carcass, each taking his portion."[8] Lysimachus, already the king of Thrace, took all of Anatolia up to the Halys River. Cassander, who had not fought in the battle, gained nothing directly, but he could expect to recover control of Greece and his brother Pleistarchus, who had fought in the battle, was given Cilicia. Seleucus added Mesopotamia and Syria to his enormous kingdom, knowing that this would bring him into conflict

8 Plutarch, *Demetrius* 30.1.

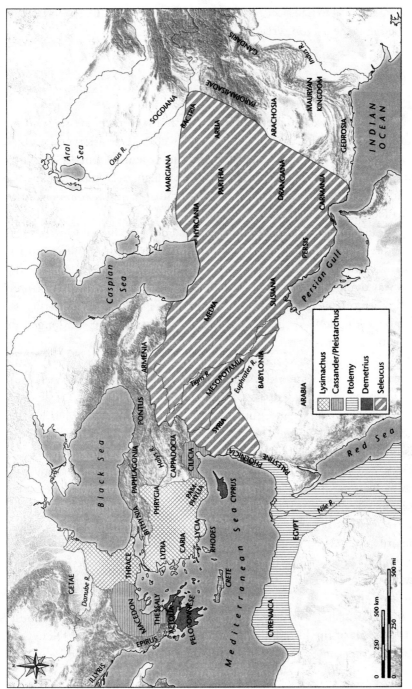

Map 20.1. The division of the spoils after Ipsus.

with Ptolemy, who had occupied Phoenicia up to the Eleutherus River and claimed it as spear-won territory.

The Tragedy of Demetrius

Demetrius fled the battlefield with several thousand men. He still had the strongest fleet, great wealth, Cyprus, and scattered possessions here and there. He thought he had Athens too, but the Athenians refused him entry and expelled his family. His Hellenic League fell apart. Demetrius expected to survive by moving between his havens and making raids as opportunities presented themselves, like a pirate king.

He could also expect the coalition that had defeated him at Ipsus to break up before long, and so it did. By 298 two potentially hostile factions had arisen: Lysimachus and Ptolemy versus Seleucus and Demetrius. Cassander, who was dying of tuberculosis, stayed aloof even when Demetrius threw his brother out of Cilicia and took it for himself. By 296 Demetrius had built up a kingdom in the eastern Mediterranean, but he still longed for Macedon.

In 297 Cassander died and his eldest son, Philip IV, followed his father to the grave within a few months; he too was probably consumptive. Cassander's two younger sons divided the country between them, with Alexander V west of the river Axius and Antipater I to the east, and with their mother, Thessalonice, favoring the younger brother, Alexander. Demetrius felt that this unsettled situation boded well for him. In 296 he returned in force to Greece, and by the summer of 295, once he had deterred blockade runners by hanging the captain of a grain ship that was trying to get through, he had starved Athens into submission. Anecdotes tell of a father fighting his son for the right to eat the corpse of a mouse, and of the philosopher Epicurus counting out the daily ration of beans for the members of his commune.[9] This time, Demetrius made no promises about democracy and leaving the city ungarrisoned; the city was uneasily ruled by a junta of those loyal to him.

When Antipater murdered his mother and drove his younger brother from his half of the kingdom, Alexander appealed for help to Demetrius. This was the opportunity Demetrius had been waiting for. When the

9 Plutarch, *Demetrius* 34.2.

appeal arrived, he was poised to take Sparta, for the first time in its history, but he gave up even that claim to fame. Leaving his son, Antigonus Gonatas, in charge of southern Greece, Demetrius marched north. Alexander, however, had also turned to Pyrrhus of Epirus, a cousin of Alexander the Great. At the age of eighteen Pyrrhus had fought for the Antigonids at Ipsus, but he subsequently transferred his allegiance to Ptolemy, and it was with his support that he made himself king of Epirus in 297. Pyrrhus' assistance to Alexander came with a heavy price tag—the cantons of Macedon that bordered Epirus, and some of his Greek neighbors too—but Alexander agreed, and Pyrrhus very quickly chastised Antipater and then, with the help of Lysimachus, the neighboring power, reconciled the two brothers.

But when Demetrius arrived, he killed Alexander and terrified Antipater into flight. Lysimachus was disinclined to take action, preferring to trade his recognition of Demetrius' right to Macedon for Demetrius' abandonment of the remaining Greek cities of Anatolia that still owed him allegiance but were now within Lysimachus' territory. Over the next few years, Demetrius also lost all his other territories to his rivals: Ptolemy gained the Cycladic islands (the Confederacy of Islanders) and Cyprus, Seleucus took Cilicia. Demetrius seems not to have cared; if he had Macedon, he had all he wanted, and he secured his control of Greece with garrisons.

For much of the late 290s and early 280s, Demetrius defended Thessaly and Macedon against Pyrrhus' threatening but ultimately futile attempts to expand at his expense. By 288, Macedon was reasonably secure. This was good for Macedon, but bad for Demetrius, because he immediately began to dream of recovering all the former Antigonid territories in Asia. To this end, he was planning to amass an army of 100,000 men, and a fleet of five hundred warships was being prepared in the shipyards of Greece.

Triremes, too unstable (unless two of them were yoked together) to hold the siege equipment and artillery that modern warfare required, were in the process of being superseded (but never entirely replaced) all over the Greek world by quadriremes and quinqueremes, but Demetrius, whose hobby was engineering, was building some monsters as well. A quadrireme, with four files of oarsmen per side, had roughly the same size of crew as a trireme (though the oarsmen were in a different configuration), but was considered an upgrade because it was heavier and carried a larger ram; a quinquereme, with five files of oarsmen on each side, was larger both in terms of crew size and overall bulk. But Demetrius was building ships with fifteen and sixteen files of oarsmen, which, we are assured, were seaworthy despite their enormous bulk.[10]

Once again, Antigonid schemes united all the other kings, including Pyrrhus. In 287, while Ptolemy's admiral sailed for southern Greece to stir the Greek states into rebellion, Lysimachus and Pyrrhus invaded Macedon from the east and west respectively. Demetrius took steps to meet the threats—but resentment had been building up in Macedon over his autocratic style of kingship and his assumption that Macedon was no more than a springboard for eastern conquest. His men abandoned him.

Lysimachus and Pyrrhus gained their halves of Macedon almost without a blow. Once again, the Macedonian army (probably led by their commanders) had assumed the right to make policy. Antipater, in exile in Thrace, pointed out that he was the rightful king of Macedon, so Lysimachus, his father-in-law, had him killed. Demetrius fled south to what remained of his Greek possessions, and he and Antigonus Gonatas used their wealth to rebuild a substantial army. And then, driven by insane dreams of conquest, in 285 Demetrius invaded Anatolia, leaving his son in Greece. A year later, he was trapped in the Taurus Mountains, with Lysimachus' son Agathocles blocking his way north into Anatolia and Seleucus blocking his other routes. Seeing the hopelessness of the situation, his men were deserting in droves, and Demetrius soon fell into Seleucus' hands. He died in captivity two years later, having drunk himself to death. His body was returned with pomp to Gonatas and buried in Demetrias, the fortress city he had founded in Thessaly.

The Last Successors

Lysimachus now had half of Macedon, all of Thrace, and much of Anatolia. But, true to the ethos of Macedonian kingship, he wanted more, and, aged in his seventies, he was in a hurry. In 284 he drove Pyrrhus out of western Macedon, and reunited the kingdom under his rule. Seleucus and the Ptolemies—the future Ptolemy II had been made joint king with his father in 285—became alarmed. It was common practice among the Successors (and an intermittent practice subsequently) to make their sons joint kings

10 Plutarch, *Demetrius* 43.7.

before their deaths: how else could they guarantee the succession when they themselves had no lineage and had conquered their territories by force?

But, as it turned out, Lysimachus was his own worst enemy. In 300, he had married Arsinoe, a daughter of Ptolemy, and by the mid-280s he was making clear his preference for his sons by this marriage over those of his other marriages, including his very competent adult son, Agathocles. We do not know the details, but Lysimachus had Agathocles killed at Arsinoe's instigation, and his sons' supporters fled in fear of their lives, many to the court of Seleucus, who was quite willing to be stirred into action against his former ally. He too was of a similar age and in a similar hurry, and late in 282 he set out for Anatolia. The decisive battle of the final war of the Successors was fought in February 281 at Corupedium, west of Sardis. It was a complete victory for Seleucus; Lysimachus died on the field. Arsinoe fled to Cassandreia (the former Potidaea, refounded by Cassander in 316), perhaps to try to claim Macedon for her sons, one of whom was in his teens.

Seleucus now held all Asia from the Aegean to the Tigris, and in 293 he had made his son Antiochus joint king, responsible for the satrapies east of the Tigris. Ptolemy must have felt threatened, especially since Seleucus had accepted his elder half-brother into his court, Ptolemy Ceraunus (the Thunderbolt), who had an excellent claim to the Egyptian throne, being the son of an earlier marriage than the one that had produced Ptolemy II. Seleucus spent a few months organizing his new territories, before taking the next step and invading Europe to take Lysimachus' former possessions there as well. We can only imagine what had been happening in Macedon and Greece during those few months. Seleucus was close to ruling the entirety of Alexander's empire, apart from Egypt. But Ceraunus wanted Macedon for himself, and he treacherously killed Seleucus with his own hand. The last of the true Successors—those who had known and ridden with Alexander the Great—both died in blood within a few months of each other.

Macedon on the Rack

Ceraunus' murder of Seleucus, the most powerful king in the world, was bound to lead to chaos. Antiochus urgently needed to prevent Anatolia from falling apart, but he had to deal first with uprisings in the Middle East that were supported by Ptolemaic troops, and it was not until 279 that he was able to send an army to Anatolia. By then, Ptolemy II (his father had died in 283) had made such huge gains that his court poet, Theocritus of Syracuse, could truthfully claim:[11]

> A portion he possesses of Phoenicia and Arabia,
> Of Syria, Libya, and the land of the black Ethiopians.
> All Pamphylians obey his commands, as do the fierce Cilicians,
> The Lycians, the war-loving Carians, and the islands of the Cyclades.

Taking into account the fact that he also had the friendship of Rhodes, Ptolemy effectively held the entire eastern Mediterranean and Aegean coastline, and before long he had further naval bases in Thrace and Crete, and even one at Methana in the Peloponnese (which was renamed Arsinoe). After the downfall of Poliorcetes, he had the strongest fleet in the eastern Mediterranean, and he made good use of it.

In Europe, Ceraunus, who must have laid his plans carefully and made suitable friends in advance, was acclaimed king of Macedon by the fickle army. Antigonus Gonatas sailed north to claim Macedon as his by inheritance, but was repulsed in a major sea battle. Arsinoe's children could have had a good claim for the throne as well, but, to avoid warfare, Ceraunus agreed to marry his half-sister and adopt her children as his heirs. But within a few months he had butchered her younger sons, the eldest having sensibly fled, it seems; he reappears years later as the lord of the city of Telmessus, on the borders of Caria and Lycia. Arsinoe too fled, and ended up in Egypt, where she became a queen for the third time.

Ceraunus made himself the master of Macedon, and recovered all Thessaly except for Demetrias, which remained in Antigonid hands. But in 279 a huge war party of Celts approached from the northern Balkans, where they had settled after being displaced from central Europe a hundred or so years earlier. They destroyed the Odrysian kingdom of Thrace, and continued on toward Macedon. When it came to battle, the Macedonian army was cut to pieces and Ceraunus' head was paraded on a spear.

The Celts went on the rampage, but lacked siegecraft, so that people huddled in towns and fortresses while their land was plundered. A Macedonian general called Sosthenes drove them off, but a second wave arrived, even larger than the first, and made for central Greece. Delphi itself was threatened, but the Celts were repulsed by bad weather and the guerrilla tactics of

---

11 Theocritus, *Idyll* 17.86–90; Austin no. 255.

a combined Greek army, led by the Aetolians and Phocians. This was a great victory for the Greeks, and the hordes dispersed, mostly to Serbia or Thrace.

Ceraunus left no heir, and over the next few years five pretenders vied for the throne—a prize that was rarely held for more than a few weeks. Gonatas was fighting in Anatolia, but when Macedon was threatened by the Celts as they returned from central Greece, he came to terms with Antiochus: they would not interfere in each other's territory, with the border between them set at Abdera. So ended the impossible Antigonid dream of recovering an Asian empire. Back in Thrace, Gonatas managed to lure a large force of Celts into an ambush and wiped them out. Declaring himself the savior of Macedon, and legitimizing his rule by reference to his father's brief reign, he drove out the last pretenders and in 276 had himself acclaimed king.

Gonatas reigned for long enough to establish the Antigonid dynasty in Macedon. By the 270s, then, the fundamental blocs of Alexander's former empire were clear: the Antigonids had Macedon and hegemony in Greece, the Seleucids held Asia, and the Ptolemies Egypt, with extensive overseas possessions. But the kings remained warlords, eager to expand their territories, and there was little relief from warfare over the subsequent decades.

21

A Time of Adjustment

The larger world that the Greeks now inhabited demanded that they look beyond the structures and institutions of single cities. Huge kingdoms, in which Greeks were both subjects and partners, formed the topmost layer of political life, and many Greek states responded by forming themselves into great confederacies and forging new kinds of diplomatic links. The polis had to adjust and give up its particularist ways; even ultra-traditionalist Sparta succumbed to new pressures. Only the Western Greeks of Sicily and southern Italy remained more or less unaffected by the new currents farther east. Meanwhile, the Successor kingdoms were establishing themselves and sorting out their relationships with their subjects and their neighbors. Both inevitably required the spilling of blood.

The three main Greco-Macedonian kingdoms—Macedon itself, Egypt, and Syria—have their own separate histories which, despite plenty of intertwining, demand separate narrative sections in this chapter, but there is a common theme: the ways in which all the kings sought to dominate and control their subjects. They came as conquerors, but now they needed to stabilize their kingdoms. Their central intention was to maximize their revenue from taxes and plunder, in order to retain and if possible expand their kingdoms. They all practiced a rolling economy, using money raised in one campaign to fund another, and using the extra territory gained by a successful campaign to raise more troops for further campaigns. For this they needed as much internal stability as they could provide, and stability required means of control that varied from the stringent (such as Macedonian repression of the Greek cities) to the diplomatic (such as Seleucid and Ptolemaic appeasement of the power-possessors in their lands). They could even be quite extraordinary: the Ptolemies' attempts to secure their dynasty, for instance, included the practice of sibling marriage.

The Greeks under Macedon

By 272 Antigonus Gonatas had secured his rule over Macedon. He had fought off challenges from pretenders and Pyrrhus and restored Macedonian control over Thessaly and Paeonia, and he had in place a nonaggression pact with Antiochus. He was happy to leave the cantons that Pyrrhus had been awarded by Alexander V in Epirote hands, because they acted as a buffer against the Illyrians. Pyrrhus had left Greece in 280 for adventures in Italy and Sicily, but in 275 he returned, so short of money that he invaded Macedon for plunder. Soon he had control of much of the country, and he resurrected his claim to the throne, but he lost his life in 272 in the Peloponnese, and Gonatas recovered his losses.

His job was reconstruction. For that, he needed stability in Greece, where hopes of independence flared into life from time to time. Following in his father's (and Cassander's) footsteps, he adopted a policy of repression: the major Greek cities were ruled by tyrants or friendly politicians, with his overt or implicit support, and backed up by mercenary garrisons. This was a risky policy, and indeed resentment built up. In 268 Areus of Sparta, bidding for international recognition as the equal of other Hellenistic kings (he had just minted Sparta's first silver coins, and they looked exactly like the "Alexanders" of all the other kings), arranged a coalition between the Spartan alliance, Ptolemy of Egypt, and the Athenians. Ptolemy was concerned that his naval bases in the Aegean might be threatened by the current buildup of the Macedonian fleet; the Athenians wanted to get rid of their garrisons (they had evicted those in the city itself twenty years earlier, but the rest remained); Areus wanted to see Sparta regain hegemony in the Peloponnese.

The war is known as the Chremonidean War, after the Athenian politician who proposed the alliance with Areus and Ptolemy; in doing so, he glossed over the long enmity between Athens and Sparta and dwelled instead on the "noble struggles" undertaken by the two states in alliance in the past.[1] It was the last attempt by the old city-states of Greece to

---

1   Austin no. 61; Burstein no. 56; Bagnall/Derow no. 19.

win independence from Macedon, and it showed that they were no longer up to the task. Areus consistently failed to get past the Macedonian garrison in Corinth to link up with his allies, and died in the attempt in 265, at which point Sparta more or less dropped out. Gonatas held Piraeus and had Athens under siege, but Ptolemaic forces patrolled both the Attic countryside and the Aegean, and the Athenians were able to hold out for a few years, until giving up in 261. Chremonides fled, and Gonatas forced Ptolemy to make peace after beating him so severely, in a naval battle off the island of Cos, that he lost control of the Cycladic Islands.

In punishment, Athens itself was again garrisoned and Gonatas intervened for a few years to make sure that his friends were in high office. But when he saw that the Athenians accepted that they would never again play a lead role in Greek affairs, he removed the garrison. The Athenians had no fleet to speak of, and rather than initiating aggression abroad, defense of the countryside became the main military goal, for them as for others. Even Salamis, for so long no more than an extension of Athenian hinterland, was out of their control for much of the third century. Honored by all the kings out of respect for its past, Athens began its drift toward becoming a university town and a tourist destination. Financial support continued to come mainly from Egypt, and in 224/3 the grateful Athenians added a thirteenth tribe, Ptolemais, to the existing twelve.

But Gonatas' mastery of Greece was short-lived. In the Peloponnese, he had to quell a rebellion in the early 240s by his nephew, and then in 243 he lost Corinth to a surprise attack by the Achaean General, Aratus of Sicyon. The Achaeans made no secret of the fact that their fundamental aim was to absorb all the Peloponnesian states into their confederacy, as an end in itself, but also as a way to resist their powerful neighbors in Aetolia. For this program to succeed, they needed Corinth, the key to the Peloponnese and one of the three "fetters of Greece," as a later Macedonian king was to describe it, along with Chalcis and Demetrias.[2]

The apparently unstoppable energy of the Achaeans under Aratus immediately attracted further states into the confederacy, until the only friends remaining to Gonatas in the Peloponnese were Argos and Megalopolis. Instead of responding directly to the seizure of Corinth, Gonatas persuaded the Aetolians to act on his behalf, but the Achaeans repulsed their invasion

2 Polybius, *Histories* 18.11.5, Livy 32.37.3.

in 241. This was a lackadaisical response from Gonatas; he was an old man now, and he died early in 239, aged eighty.

The Demetrian War

For a long time, the Aetolians and the Epirotes had been on good terms, but at some point, possibly in the 250s, they had divided Acarnania between them, with the Epirotes taking the northern half and the Aetolians the south. Acarnania simply ceased to exist as a political entity. But half of Acarnania was not enough for the Aetolians, and in 239 they were poised to take the Epirote half as well. The Epirotes asked for help from Demetrius II, Gonatas' son and heir, whose wife was an Epirote princess. The ensuing war occupied the entire ten years of his reign.

Now it was the Aetolians' turn to look for help—and in a complete reversal of the trend of the past thirty or forty years, they formed an alliance with the Achaeans. This was an extremely powerful union, with great potential for the future of the Greeks, and a real threat to the hegemony of Macedon; almost all of central and southern Greece was united in military action for the first time ever. Just as importantly, they had chosen to unite; it was not imposed on them by an outside power, as all the various leagues of earlier times had been. It is tempting to think that, had circumstances been different (had the Romans not arrived, perhaps), the Greeks might have moved closer toward the creation of a single federal state—toward becoming one instead of many.

We know little about the war that began in 238. By the end of it, Megalopolis had joined the Achaean Confederacy, Boeotia had been detached from the Aetolian Confederacy, and Epirus had become a republic, albeit a deeply troubled one, on the assassination of the last member of the royal house. The Aetolians naturally seized the opportunity created by Epirote turmoil to renew their attempt on northern Acarnania. Unable to respond himself, Demetrius paid the Illyrians to help the Epirotes. Then the Athenians, awakening from years of slumber, paid off their garrisons and regained their freedom. Since Athens, as a Macedonian enclave, had been the constant target of Achaean attacks, the war lost energy—and then in the spring of 229 the death of Demetrius, fighting the Dardanians (a powerful Illyrian tribe), brought it to a close. Aratus had even given the Athenians

---

some of the money with which they bought off their garrisons, and he was displeased when they ignored the hint and remained outside the Achaean Confederacy. The Laurium mines were once again in full operation, and Athens entered a phase of renewed prosperity until its sack early in the first century, based on the ready acceptance around the Mediterranean of a new Athenian silver coinage, the so-called New Style tetradrachms, which became almost as popular as the owl coinage had been in the fifth century.

The Spartan Reformation

In 244 or thereabouts Agis IV ascended to the Eurypontid throne of Sparta. Over the past 125 years, Sparta had been repeatedly humbled; recent attempts on Aetolia, Megalopolis, and Mantinea had been signal failures; the *agōgē* had fallen into disuse; the messes were being used for ostentatious displays of wealth; and much wealth and political power were in the hands of women. Agis decided to do something about all this, under the banner of restoring what he claimed to be the original Lycurgan constitution of Sparta.

The loss of Messenia a hundred years earlier had accelerated the decline in the number of Spartiates, full citizens. By the time of Agis' accession,[3]

> of the fewer than seven hundred Spartiates who remained, only perhaps a hundred possessed land or even their allotted farm, while the general mass of Spartans sat idly in the city without resources or rights, defending themselves sluggishly and irresolutely against external threats, and constantly on the look-out for opportunities for revolutionary change.

At the same time, the number of Inferiors, degraded citizens, had reached perhaps two thousand. Following the lead of other reforms or attempted reforms elsewhere in the Greek world, Agis decided to cancel debts, confiscate all farmland, and then divide it into equal lots to be distributed afresh to Spartiates, Inferiors, and deserving Perioeci, who would all thereby become Spartiates and form the backbone of the new state and its army.

But Agis failed. He had the support of the younger generation of Spartiates, but it would take a stronger hand than his to push through such radical reforms. He was condemned to death in 241 by a kangaroo court. Ironically, since he had worked so hard to make himself the only

---

3 Plutarch, *Agis* 5.7; Austin no. 69a.

sovereign power in Sparta, his death left Leonidas II, his Agiad counterpart, in full control, since Agis' Eurypontid heir was underage. In fact,
as it turned out, the dual kingship of Sparta had come to an end: the
trend begun by Areus and Agis came to fruition. After Cleomenes III,
burning to restore Sparta to greatness, came to the Agiad throne on the
death of Leonidas in 235, the Eurypontid boy conveniently died, and the
next in line was murdered within days of returning from exile to claim
his throne. Charismatic Cleomenes remained the sole king, and in 227,
on the back of a string of military successes, he was ready to revive Agis'
program of reforms and possessed the ruthlessness to make it happen. He
was married to Agis' former wife, and had the backing of her powerful
family and others.

Anticipating resistance from the Ephors, he killed them (though one
escaped, wounded) and abolished the institution, resurrecting the old claim
that it was not part of the original Lycurgan constitution. The Council
of Elders was made toothless, and the five Ephors were replaced by six
Patronomoi, Custodians of Ancestral Law and Custom, whose job was
essentially to maintain this latest version of Sparta's "ancestral" constitution. Cleomenes placed his Agiad brother on the Eurypontid throne, exiled
about eighty of his opponents, and confiscated their land. Then he activated
Agis' reforms: debts were cancelled, and all land in Laconia was pooled
and divided into four thousand lots for the new citizens. Cleomenes led
the way by giving his own estates to the pool. The revival of the *agōgē*
was entrusted to a Stoic philosopher, Sphaerus of Borysthenes. Finally,
the Spartan hoplites—now a citizen army loyal to Cleomenes—were re-
equipped in the Macedonian style.

This was not class warfare; the changes were generated by the privileged
class and designed only to reform the privileged class. Nor was Cleomenes
much of an ideologue; he was concerned only with Sparta. Nevertheless, as
a result of his reforms, throughout the Peloponnese "the common people
hoped for a redistribution of the land and a remission of debts."[4] Nothing
came of this. There had been earlier cases of land-redistribution or debt-
cancellation here and there in the Greek world (as by Solon of Athens early
in the sixth century), and there would be others, but this time the Achaeans,
governed by the landed gentry, made sure that unrest did not trigger revolution or any kind of class consciousness. But one beneficial outcome of the

4 Plutarch, *Cleomenes* 17.3.

unrest was that many communities created debt-relief programs to keep their impoverished masses quiet.

Antigonus Doson

On Demetrius' death in 229, his son Philip was only eight years old. The boy inherited nothing but trouble. The Dardanians (from modern Kosovo, roughly) who had just killed Demetrius were on the rampage in Paeonia, and the Aetolians had annexed much of Thessaly during the Demetrian War. The Achaeans had continued to expand as well, and had gained Argos. Macedonian authority in Greece was more or less extinct. Hegemony urgently needed to be reimposed. As regent for Philip, the Macedonian elite chose a nephew of Gonatas called Antigonus, known as Antigonus Doson (like Gonatas, a Macedonian word whose meaning we do not know). By dint of marrying Philip's mother, Doson had himself acclaimed king, and to secure the succession he adopted Philip as his son. Then he bought off the Dardanians, and by 228 he had also recovered much of Thessaly from the Aetolians.

While Doson was dealing with the Aetolians, skirmishing between the Spartans and Achaeans in the Peloponnese developed into full-blown war. This was Cleomenes' bid to restore Spartan hegemony in the Peloponnese—to resuscitate the Peloponnesian League—and by 225 his powerful new army had occupied most of central and north-eastern Peloponnese, includ-ing much of Arcadia, Corinth, and Argos—the first time the Spartans had subjected their old enemy. Sparta controlled the entire eastern half of the Peloponnese. The Achaeans were on the ropes; the confederacy was facing extinction. Ptolemy III transferred his financial support to Cleomenes, who now seemed the more effective counterweight to Macedon. The Achaeans asked for help from their allies, the Aetolians, but the Aetolians were still suffering from the aftereffects of the resounding defeat Doson had inflicted on them in Thessaly.

This refusal by the Aetolians was ill-judged, and it caused the unravel-ing of their alliance with the Achaeans—if the refusal was not a sign that it had already unraveled. The consequences were momentous. In despera-tion, at Aratus' urging, the Achaeans performed a sensational about-face and approached the Macedonian king for an alliance. Doson agreed to help—he must have been delighted—but the price he demanded was high: the

Achaeans were to cede Corinth, which would once again be garrisoned by Macedonian troops and governed by friends of Macedon, recognize Doson as the leader of the Greeks, cede Megara to the Boeotians, and pay the costs of the war. In 224 Doson marched south and faced Cleomenes. He was unable to break through Cleomenes' well-prepared defenses at the isthmus, near Corinth, but the Spartan king was forced to fall back to Argos by a threat to his garrison there, and Doson was able to drive him back from there to Sparta.

Doson was anxious to secure his revived authority in Greece. Where his predecessor, Antigonus Gonatas, had employed a policy of repression, Doson preferred gentler treatment of his subjects. In order to secure his position in Greece and give it a permanent structure, in the autumn of 224 he formed his Greek allies into a Common Alliance. As a sop to the Greeks, Doson allowed it to be a rather loose arrangement, since all decisions reached by the main council had to be ratified by the assemblies of the member states. This meant, for instance, that (if they dared to displease Doson) they were not obliged to supply troops for any given campaign. Members were also free to make war and peace on their own, as long as they did not fight other members. It was a sign of the times that not one of the original members was a city-state; the era of the polis had passed. All the major confederacies were members, all as committed to oligarchy as Doson himself, but the independent city-states at first stayed aloof, or neutral. Relations with the Aetolians being poor, they were excluded; even if in the short term the target of the alliance was Cleomenes, it looked as though it would soon be the Aetolians. This was another hegemonial alliance, like the Peloponnesian League, the Delian League of Athens, Philip and Alexander's League of Corinth, Polyperchon's abortive Peloponnesian League of 318, and the Hellenic League of Demetrius Poliorcetes. Macedonian influence in Greece was back at the level of the 250s. When the Achaeans bloodily reincorporated Mantinea into their confederacy in 223, they obsequiously renamed the city Antigonea.

Cleomenes continued to fight well, though with his back increasingly against the wall, and in 223 succeeded in destroying Megalopolis "with such malignant savagery," says Polybius, a citizen of Megalopolis himself, "that it was impossible to imagine that a community might ever again be formed there."[5] (Actually, as Polybius knew, it was refounded a few years later.) But

5 Polybius, *Histories* 2.55.8.

the next year Doson convincingly defeated Cleomenes near the village of Sellasia, not far north of Sparta. Cleomenes fled to Egypt, where he died three years later, vainly trying to get an indifferent Alexandrian population to rise up against Ptolemy IV, who had placed the former Spartan king under house arrest.

For the first time in its history, Sparta fell to an invading army. Doson installed a governor and at least some of Cleomenes' reforms were canceled. Under the protection of Macedon, the landed rich of Sparta resumed their former practices, starting with taking over the property of those who had fallen at Sellasia, so that a few years later the leader of a failed attempt on the throne was again offering the program of debt-cancellation and land-redistribution. Cleomenes' reforms had failed, but Spartan society had still undergone a permanent change.

In gratitude for their recovery, the Achaeans showered Doson with honors. But he had to hurry back north to deal with an Illyrian raid into Macedon. He succeeded in repelling them, but he was consumptive and the strain of battle brought on his death in the autumn of 221. The accession to the throne of sixteen-year-old Philip V was uncontested; he would prove to be one of the greatest of Macedonian kings, in extremely difficult times.

Hellenistic Syracuse

The changed circumstances of the new world created by Alexander's eastern conquests created few ripples among the Western Greeks; they were, or were soon to be, more concerned by the growing power of Rome. In Syracuse, the reign of Dionysius I's successor, his son Dionysius II, is known chiefly for his rivalry with Dion, who was married to Dionysius I's daughter. But it is impossible to mention Dionysius II without also mentioning that, very early in his first reign (367–357), Dion persuaded him to bring Plato to his court. Dion had met Plato while the Athenian philosopher was traveling in Sicily. The idea was to turn Dionysius II into a Platonic philosopher–king. In his *Republic*, Plato had argued that the only hope for the Greek states was if philosophically trained men—and, remarkably, women—held the reins of government, because they were the only ones who could institute the kind of regime in which everyone would prosper to the best of his or her ability.

The attempt to turn worldly Dionysius II into such a ruler was doomed from the start, and only exacerbated the tension between him and Dion.

Plato left in frustration, and Dion was sent into exile. In 357 he returned, however, at the head of an army and deposed Dionysius, to the delight of the Syracusans, who were finding his reign burdensome. But Dion was assassinated in 354, and the chaos that followed was scarcely relieved at all by the return of Dionysius in 346. Eventually, the desperate Syracusans appealed for help to their old mother city, Corinth.

In 344 the Corinthians dispatched a general called Timoleon, a man apparently of no more than ordinary distinction, but he successfully—miraculously, one might say—reconciled the warring factions in Syracuse (Dionysius left Syracuse for comfortable retirement in Corinth), pinned the Carthaginians in the west of the island (especially as a result of his victory in the bloody battle of the Crimisus River in 339), expelled the tyrants from several Greek cities, instituted a moderate oligarchy at Syracuse and elsewhere, and arranged a number of the Greek cities in an alliance with Syracuse at its head. The prospect of peace on the island, and an active advertising campaign, enticed tens of thousands of new Greek settlers to come and revive the cities, which had become depopulated by the constant warfare. Timoleon may have behaved very like his predecessors, the Syracusan tyrants, but he was working for the good of all, not just of himself.

But not long after Timoleon's retirement in 337 (he died the following year), another of the island's great lurches took place when this fragile alliance broke apart. Tyrannies returned to the cities and oligarchy to Syracuse. Those who felt excluded by this oligarchy found a champion in a successful general called Agathocles and, once he had removed his opponents in their thousands, he became tyrant of Syracuse in 316. In 304, on the strength of his defeat of the Carthaginians, he changed his title to "king," as a way of legitimizing his position and aligning Sicily with the monarchies of the eastern Mediterranean, newly declared by Alexander's Successors. The towns and cities of Sicily were organized into something like a nation-state under a Syracusan monarchy. This was as close as the Sicilian Greeks came to unification.

On Agathocles' death in 289, Syracuse once more descended into chaos, with internal struggles and a renewed threat from Carthage. In 279 the Syracusan aristocrats summoned the warlord and adventurer, Pyrrhus of Epirus, who was then in southern Italy with an army, helping the great Greek city of Tarentum resist the Romans. Pyrrhus achieved some success against the Carthaginians—but he then installed himself as king of Sicily (with his sons dubbed the kings of Italy and Epirus). This did not go down well with his allies, and he returned to Epirus, leaving one of his generals, a man called Hieron, to seize power in Syracuse in 275 with the help of the common people, and declare himself king as Hieron II. During Hieron's long reign, Syracuse regained its position as one of the leaders of the Mediterranean, with the help of an alliance with Rome, which was just then beginning to extend its power outside Italy.

Syria

It makes sense to follow Polybius and speak of the Seleucids as kings of Syria. For a while, they ruled much of Asia, but they were eventually reduced to northern Syria, and Seleucus I himself made it the heart of his empire with an intensive program of city-building in the late 300s and 290s. Apart from anything else, these cities were a bulwark against Ptolemy, who occupied territories in Phoenicia, Palestine, and timber-rich Coele Syria (the Bekaa valley, inland from the Phoenician coast) that were technically Seleucus'. The conflict and rivalry between the two kingdoms was a sink-hole of energy for much of the Hellenistic period, and in due course even the Romans got sucked in and manipulated matters from the sidelines.

Achaemenid kings (like many medieval European rulers) had maintained a mobile court, moving between several royal cities, depending on the season and their need to be seen somewhere. The Seleucids followed suit—in this, as in many other aspects of their administration—and indeed built palaces in cities the length and breadth of their empire (doubtless the governors' residences, between royal visits), but they were more usually to be found in northern Syria. Seleucus was not the first to see the advantages and potential of this region, which came to be called Seleucis: Antioch, the greatest of the four new cities there—Antiocheia-on-the-Orontes, to give it its full name—was built in part from stones salvaged from Antigonea, the nearby city Antigonus Monophthalmus left half-built on his death.

The Seleucids were the major city-builders of the era, with over a hundred new foundations and refoundations to their names, from fortresses to cities. Seleucus alone was astonishingly prolific: "He built cities throughout his empire. Sixteen of them were named after his father, five after his mother, nine after himself, and four after his wives."[6] There is an implied

---

6 Appian, *The Syrian Wars* 57; Austin no. 57.

contrast with Alexander, all of whose city foundations were named after himself. Another of Seleucus' great foundations was Seleucia-on-the-Tigris, not far north of Babylon (and not far south of modern Baghdad). There are substantial remains, and archaeology is ongoing when geopolitical conditions allow it. Seleucia remained an important city for centuries, under various empires. In Seleucid times, it was the second greatest Greek city in the world after Alexandria, with a population of about 200,000 to compare with Alexandria's 300,000, and it became the most important commercial center in the East. But as the Seleucid gaze came to be drawn west rather than east, so Seleucia came to be rivaled by Antioch.

The fertility of Anatolia and other parts of their empire made it easy to attract settlers from Greece, in competition with other kings. Just as the citizens of Old Greece had created foundation myths for their cities, so the Seleucids stressed the blessing of Greek gods on their building work and assimilated local deities to their Greek equivalents, to make it clear that immigrants would not be coming to an alien land. Since the greatest of the new cities bore the names of members of the Seleucid household, they were symbolically planting themselves in the land as its rulers and marking their regime as a new start.

The new towns, with mixed populations of immigrants and natives, had both military and commercial functions as ports, on roads or river crossings, or near borders, and served as hubs for the collection of agricultural taxes. The Seleucids populated the land also with their mercenaries, who could be paid, if they chose, with plots of land, to be farmed by themselves or as absentee landlords. In the Macedonian and Achaemenid fashion, these men, and then their male descendants, owed military service to the crown, and always formed the core of Seleucid armies. This was an economical policy: it was cheaper than maintaining a standing army, it reduced the number of mercenaries to be hired, and it brought more royal land into taxable production. One of the primary Seleucid means of control of their subjects was the presence throughout their empire of a great many soldiers.

The Fault Lines of the Seleucid Empire

Antiochus I inherited a fragmented empire. Its most salient features were its size and the variety of climates and cultures within it—from the ancient civilization of Babylonia to hill tribes led by warrior chieftains. At its peak, the empire occupied over 3,750,000 square kilometers (about 1,500,000 square miles) and had a population of perhaps thirty million. The immigrant population was never more than 5 percent, but it was not native resentment that proved to be the undoing of the Seleucids. Like the Achaemenids before them, the Seleucids had to depend on the loyalty of subordinates to hold it all together, and were careful to maintain good relations with important cities, temples, and estate-owners—by, for instance, performing in Babylon all the rituals that had been expected of Babylonian kings for centuries, and by maintaining and improving economic infrastructures such as irrigation systems, roads, and harbors. Powerful men were kept happy with grants of estates. This was the velvet hand of Seleucid control of their subjects and their perennial search for stability.

Nevertheless, at times when the center was weak or under threat, subordinates tended to feel that they should be loyal first to themselves. Ultimately, its sheer size was the undoing of the Seleucid Empire: it proved impossible for the center to retain control of the peripheries against aggressive external enemies and the internal desire for independence of the cities, barons, vassal kings (who came to replace satraps in several parts of the eastern empire), mountain tribes, and so on that made up the empire. Its military resources, though great, were always stretched thin, and it lacked the great wealth of Egypt. The Seleucid Empire endured for a long time, but neither it nor Egypt were nation-states with fixed borders; the series of Syrian wars alone shows how flexible their borders were—constantly shifting beyond their core territories, expanding or contracting. The eastern Seleucid Empire is a case in point. We know little of its history, but we can say that, for much of the third century, several of the northern satrapies east of Media and Persis—a huge chunk of the empire—were more or less out of Seleucid control, and the kings were generally too preoccupied to do much about it. It was not until the eastern campaign of Antiochus III between 212 and 205 that some degree of order was restored.

Antiochus I's western empire had also broken up. The passage through the Taurus mountains between Syria and Anatolia was always difficult, and virtually impossible in winter, so that Anatolian rebellions had been common in the Achaemenid period too. By the middle of 279, when he was able to send an army there after his father's murder, Anatolia had been without a strong Seleucid presence for more than two years, and a great deal had changed. Cappadocia was poised to become an independent kingdom, and Thracian Bithynia already was; the powerful Greek cities of Heraclea Pontica and Byzantium had joined with others in the region to form a Northern Confederacy, whose Lysimachean coinage showed that they rejected the legitimacy of Seleucid authority; rugged Paphlagonia was ruled by one or more kings (or, sometimes, divided between its neighbors); and the rest of the southern Black Sea coastline was part of the new kingdom of Pontus. Most of the southern cities around the coastline up to Caria, and some way inland, were part of Greater Egypt, and there were also many barons with greater or smaller estates; Persian, Greek, and Macedonian, they had been favored by some king or other. And then there was Pergamum: in return for financial

Figure 21.1. The Ludovisi Gaul. A Roman copy of a bronze original, which was sculpted in Pergamum late in the third century. The suicidal pair were originally the centerpiece of a huge monument commemorating a battle won by Attalus I, and showing other Celts (or Gauls) in pathetic poses. Museo Nazionale Romano (Palazzo Altemps) no. 8608. Photo © Vanni Archive / Art Resource, NY.

help in his war against Lysimachus, a man called Philetaerus had been allowed by Seleucus to rule this wealthy and impregnable city in north-western Anatolia (the word "Pergamum" means "citadel") as a kind of semi-independent governor.

The most pressing problem in Anatolia, however, was the Celts. During a succession wrangle in Bithynia, a large force of Celts had been hired as mercenaries from Thrace, where they had settled since invading Macedon and Greece. These Celts had been followed by others, until there were three huge tribes on the move, sowing death and destruction wherever they went. Antiochus had to prove himself to his Greek subjects and potential subjects by eliminating this barbarian menace, and once the First Syrian War with Egypt was over in 271—a futile business, in which neither side made significant gains—he turned to the Celts.

It would have been easy for the Celts simply to replace the Persians as the "barbarian" Other in the Greek mind, but over the long years during which Antiochus, and after him many another Greco-Macedonian leader, fought the Celts, a reluctant strain of admiration crept into Greek discourses about them—and into their artwork. By the end of the 260s, there were Celtic pockets here and there in Anatolia, but most of them had taken over part of Phrygia, which came to be called Galatia, the "land of the warriors." A form of Celtic was spoken there until the sixth century CE, but it is not clear to what degree the several tribes ever united. They remained loose cannons, ever ready to sell themselves as mercenaries to the highest bidder, and given to demanding protection money from their neighbors. But Seleucid suppression of the Celts appeased their Anatolian subjects and gave them greater control of their western empire.

Pergamum

In 261 Antiochus I died, after a few years of peace in his kingdom, and his son Antiochus II came to the throne. Conflict with Egypt—the Second Syrian War—occupied the early years of his reign, but he emerged the winner, with gains in Anatolia. But when he died in 246, each of his two wives championed their sons for the throne, and both had wide support within the kingdom. One of the wives also had support outside the kingdom, since she was the sister of the new Egyptian king, Ptolemy III, and Ptolemy invaded Syria, initiating the Third Syrian War.

By the time he got there, his sister and her son had been done away with, and Seleucus II was on the throne, but Ptolemy still made great inroads, partly because of local support, but partly just because Seleucus was far away in western Anatolia. Ptolemy even got as far as Babylon, and a document that appears or pretends to be his own campaign record talks of how he was made welcome in Antioch.[7] By 241, however, Seleucus had undone many of Ptolemy's gains in the eastern Mediterranean, at the cost of losing some of what he had gained in Anatolia in the previous war, and Antigonus Gonatas had followed up his earlier defeat of the Ptolemaic navy at Cos with another off Andros, warning Ptolemy not to think about regaining the Aegean.

In 241, Seleucus appointed his brother Antiochus Hierax (the Hawk) his joint king in Anatolia. Hierax was a young teenager, but, spurred on by his mother, he declared himself sole king. Hierax gained the support of Ptolemy, allied himself with some of the Galatians, and the brothers fell to fighting. But Seleucus had troubles to attend to farther east—in Parthia, above all, where he compelled the ruler of the Parni, who had recently invaded, to become a vassal king—and after being badly mauled by his brother's troops in 239 at Ancyra (modern Ankara), he gave up, leaving Hierax to dispute Anatolia with the Pergamenes.

These decades of turmoil in Anatolia were the making of Pergamum. In 263 Philetaerus' successor, his nephew Eumenes, declared Pergamum independent, and then confirmed it by defeating the army Antiochus sent to put him down. By the time of his death in 241, Eumenes had consolidated the position of Pergamum in Mysia and Aeolis, largely by peaceful means, and had gained a crucial naval base at Elaea. He was succeeded by his cousin and adopted son, Attalus. There were never any disputed successions in the Attalid household.

Eumenes had already made it clear to the wider world by his patronage of the arts and support for the Athenian philosophical schools that, in this time of chaos, he saw Pergamum as being the preserver and perpetuator of Greek culture, so it suited Attalus to present himself, in his turn, as the champion of Greeks against barbarians. When the Celts attacked over his refusal to pay them protection money, he responded with a stunning victory, on the strength of which he declared himself king, changing his status from Seleucid vassal to rival. Pergamene coins from now on showed the head

---

7 *FGrH* 160 = (translated) Austin no. 266; Bagnall/Derow no. 27; Burstein no. 98.

of Philetaerus, no longer of Seleucid kings. Over subsequent decades, the idea that Pergamum was the protector of the freedom of the Greek cities of Anatolia against the forces of barbarism was perpetuated by monuments not just in Pergamum, but in all the major centers in Greece. By 227, in a series of stunning victories, Attalus had also driven Hierax out of Anatolia. Almost all of Seleucid Anatolia was in Pergamene hands. Attalus saw that Pergamum had the opportunity of becoming one of the great Hellenistic kingdoms.

In 226 Seleucus fell from his horse and died, and his eldest son came to the throne as Seleucus III. Almost all we know of his brief reign is that he launched successive attempts to recover Anatolia, and was rewarded for his failure to do so by being assassinated in 223 by his generals. Achaeus, one of the great barons of Anatolia and a relative of the royal house, was acclaimed king by the army—the Macedonian troops turning kingmakers once again—but he refused, and Seleucus' younger brother came to the throne, aged twenty, as Antiochus III.

But Attalus had overstretched himself. By 221 Achaeus, clearly a man of great talent, had undone all of his recent gains and reduced Pergamum to its original frontiers, as a large city-state but not a hegemonial power. Ptolemy IV transferred his support from Attalus, and the following year Achaeus felt ready to face his destiny. He negotiated a ceasefire with Attalus and marched on Syria, declaring himself king as he did so. But his troops mutinied, not so much because they doubted Achaeus' kingship as because they felt he was leading them into a fight they could only lose; after all, Antiochus had just put down a far more serious rebellion by Molon, the Median satrap and self-declared king, who had had wide support in the eastern satrapies.

Antiochus could ignore Achaeus for a while, so he launched the Fourth Syrian War to drive the occupying Egyptian forces out of his territories, while Achaeus consolidated his position in the south of Anatolia and Attalus recovered some of the territory in the northwest that he had lost over the previous years. But in 216 Antiochus was ready to face Achaeus. He made an alliance with Attalus on the understanding that the Pergamene king could keep his recent gains—so the Seleucids now acknowledged the independent existence of Pergamum as a hegemonial power in Anatolia—and by 213 Achaeus had been defeated and put to death. This was a savage war; in the course of it, Sardis was sacked by Antiochus' troops so thoroughly that he had to rebuild it afterwards.

Antiochus recovered all the former Seleucid territory in Anatolia, except for what he had conceded to Attalus. Could he keep it this time? It helped enormously that relations with Pergamum remained good for the next twenty years, but it would also depend in part on his choice of viceroy. Sensibly, he appointed Zeuxis, the general who had been responsible for the defeat of Molon, rather than a family member, and Zeuxis proved loyal. Having done all he could to stabilize things in Anatolia, the ever-restless Antiochus turned to the lost eastern satrapies. He succeeded in getting the independent kings of Armenia and Bactria to acknowledge his suzerainty and pay him tribute, and to reaffirm the vassal status of the king of the Parthians, and on the strength of these successes he took the title "the Great," as though he had conquered the East like Alexander. The Greek kingdom of Bactria was wiped out around the middle of the second century by a massive invasion of nomads, part of a large-scale population movement, but the Parthian kingdom would in due course become the Parthian Empire and challenge Rome for dominance in the East.

Egypt

Egypt was a relatively self-contained unit, geographically speaking; it consisted of the Nile Delta on the Mediterranean and a thin strip of fertile flood plains a thousand kilometers (620 miles) south up the river valley to the First Cataract (the first stretch of shallows), never wider than thirty kilometers (twenty miles) at any point and bounded by desert to east and west. The kingdom comprised about 23,000 square kilometers (about 8,880 square miles) and had a population of four or five million.

Settlements along the river were perched on high ground, to avoid the annual mud-depositing floods, the source of the country's great fertility and wealth; at the time of the floods, they were turned into islands. There were three main areas of settlement. Lower Egypt, the Delta region in the north, was densely settled; it was on the far west of the Delta that Alexander chose to site Alexandria. To the southwest of the Delta lay a large, fertile depression called the Fayyum, where the arable land was hugely increased by a massive drainage and canalization project initiated by the Ptolemies. Then Middle and Upper Egypt sprawled up the Nile, and included two great cities: Memphis in the north, the religious center of Egypt, and Thebes in the south, famous for the temples of Karnak and Luxor. The many-streamed and marshy Delta was hard to cross, so Memphis (near modern

Cairo) was the usual gateway to Egypt from the east—though there was the Sinai Desert to cross first.

Egypt had been a major center of culture for hundreds of years before the Macedonians arrived to form its thirty-first and final dynasty, and Ptolemy I had less city-building to do than the Seleucids. Many Egyptian Greeks therefore lived in non-Greek environments, in close relationships with the native populations. Ptolemy's only large foundation (or refoundation: it replaced a smaller Greek settlement) was Ptolemais in the southern Thebaid, which, with its different dialect and ethnic makeup, had a perennial tendency to regard itself as a separate state, and so needed a regional administrative center.

The Ptolemies, like all Hellenistic kings, also founded many smaller settlements (for instance, by settling mercenaries on the land, like the Seleucids), but there were only ever the three Greek cities in Egypt itself (not counting Egypt's overseas possessions)—Alexandria, Ptolemais, and Naucratis. But Alexandria by itself was an enormous project. Founded in 331, it was still largely a building site when Ptolemy designated it his capital, perhaps in 313, and marked the occasion by moving Alexander's body there from Memphis, where he had first laid it to rest after the hijacking. The city was divided into three sections: one for Greeks and Macedonians (who were the only full citizens and were privileged with tax exemptions), one for Egyptians, and one for everyone else, who were mainly Jews—the second largest Jewish population after Jerusalem. Until the growth of Rome, Alexandria was the greatest city in the Mediterranean. Even in the first century, one visitor could say: "It leaves all other cities a long way behind in terms of its beauty, size, financial liquidity, and everything that contributes to graceful living."[8] But it was also beset with all the usual urban problems, from corruption to ethnic tension.

The Ptolemies

Ptolemy II's chief concern early in his reign was to secure his rule against the possibility of any interdynastic disputation of the throne. When his sister Arsinoe arrived in 280 or thereabouts from the northern Aegean, in flight

---

8 Diodorus of Sicily, *Library of History* 17.52.5.

from her disastrous marriage to Ptolemy Ceraunus, he made her marry him and adopt his children, so that there were no loose ends. Marrying his full sister was an extraordinary step for Ptolemy to take. There were only faint traces of such a practice in Egyptian and Persian pasts (though Mausolus and other fourth-century dynasts of Caria had married siblings), but Ptolemy gloried in it: around 272 he inaugurated a joint cult of Alexander and the Sibling Deities—himself and Arsinoe, though both were still alive (she died in 270). Nor were these minor cults: in both the Seleucid and Ptolemaic kingdoms, the priests of dynastic cults were always important men, and royal appointees. There came to be several such cults in each kingdom, often conjoined with those of Alexander, and the Greek cities followed the kings' lead.

Brother–sister marriage was supposed to guarantee the purity of the bloodline, to advertise the solidity of the royal family, and to secure stability by eliminating the possibility of rival claimants to the throne; the king was effectively cloning himself, and so every generation of Egyptian kings took the same name. Perhaps surprisingly, there is no real evidence of genetic deterioration over the more than two hundred years that the Ptolemies, or some of them, practiced sibling marriage. Strife within the

Figure 21.2. **Ptolemy II and Arsinoe II.** Brother and sister, husband and wife, the original power couple. They seem almost to be two heads of a single body. The bulging eyes are a sign of potency. This is a gold octadrachm (eight drachmas). BM 1964,1303.3. © The Trustees of the British Museum.

royal family became increasingly savage, but savagery has characterized many courts throughout the ages. Sibling marriage was a symbol of power, a way for the Ptolemies to claim that conventional morality did not apply to them. If the satirical poet Sotades' reaction is typical, the Greeks were appalled: "Unholy the hole into which you push your prick."[9] Sotades paid for the quip with his life.

The mainspring of Ptolemaic foreign policy was the need to keep intact the extensive buffer zones that the first two Ptolemies had put in place around Egypt by the middle of the third century. Apart from their defensive function, these overseas possessions made up for Egypt's deficiencies in minerals and ship-quality timber, and enabled them to control the trade routes of the eastern Mediterranean, the Aegean, and the Black Sea approaches. They were the major suppliers to the Greek world of grain and other commodities, and they needed to make sure that their cargoes were safe.

In Greece and Anatolia, as we have seen, the Ptolemies supported whichever state or states seemed best able to check Antigonid and Seleucid ambitions. In the Aegean, they did their best to retain their possessions against a strengthening Macedonian navy. In Palestine, Coele Syria, and Phoenicia, they fought a series of wars against the Syrian kings. In Cyrenaica, the earliest Ptolemaic external possession and one of the most important, they used diplomacy to keep the peace and allowed the rulers to think of themselves for a while as royalty. In Africa, they extended south into Nubia, especially to safeguard the provision of war elephants and gold.

From the moment he ascended to the Syrian throne in 223, Antiochus III intended to recover the entirety of the kingdom when it had been at its greatest extent, under Seleucus I, as though he still had rights to it. He was delayed by Molon's rebellion, but once it had been put down, Antiochus drove the Ptolemaic forces out of Coele Syria and coastal Phoenicia. This task occupied the first two years of the Fourth Syrian War. But Ptolemy IV, who had come to the Egyptian throne in 221, belied his reputation for being more interested in poetry than politics, or took the advice of his powerful chief ministers. Having restructured his army and greatly increased the number of native Egyptians serving in it, he inflicted a massive defeat on Antiochus at the battle of Raphia in 217. With over 140,000 men (and 175

9 Plutarch, *Moralia* 11a (*On the Education of Children*).

elephants) between the two sides, which were fairly evenly matched, this was the greatest battle since Ipsus. After acknowledging defeat, Antiochus withdrew to northern Syria, and over the next few weeks almost every single place that he had gained or regained returned to Ptolemaic control.

This was a great victory for the Egyptians, but it proved to be a peak from which they could only fall. Trouble had been brewing for a long time, with occasional outbursts, since a good number of Egyptians, especially in the south, resented being a subject race and the exploitation of their land by foreigners. Before the battle of Raphia, the Ptolemaic governor of Coele Syria had gone over to Antiochus, and Ptolemy's queen is said to have offered every soldier in the Egyptian army two gold minas.[10] Even with the exaggeration, it seems that the Ptolemies were finding it hard to retain the loyalty of their men.

To judge by the concessions that were made when the troubles were over (reductions in tax, for instance, and concessions to the priesthood), social discontent was the major factor. Very probably, Egyptian priests were behind the disturbances; during the decades of Persian rule, the temples had grown hugely powerful, forming a kind of nationalist underground, much as the Greek Orthodox Church did during the Turkish rule of Greece, and the Catholic Church did in Ireland under British occupation. When the Ptolemies arrived, they did their best to appease the powerful priesthoods, by performing all the rituals appropriate to their position as pharaohs, by allowing the temples to prosper, and by personally funding the building and rebuilding of temples. Many of the monumental Egyptian remains that survive today date from the Ptolemaic era.

Nevertheless, it was clear that this velvet glove concealed an iron fist. There were garrisons everywhere; soldiers were a common sight on any town or city street, especially since the country was so often on a war footing; the kings presented themselves as warriors. Polybius described the inhabitants of Alexandria as Egyptians, Greeks, and mercenaries, "heavily armed, numerous, and coarse."[11] Ptolemy II's far-famed parade, held in Alexandria perhaps in 278, included eighty thousand soldiers; even Adolf Hitler's fiftieth birthday in 1939 was celebrated by only fifty thousand.

Disturbances began not long after Raphia, both in the Delta and in Upper Egypt, and the Egyptian soldiers who had fought in the battle were right at

10   3 Maccabees 1.4.
11   Polybius, *Histories* 34.14; Austin no. 323.

Figure 21.3. The Rosetta Stone. This trilingual stele, whose discovery enabled the decipherment of hieroglyphics, records a decree issued in 196 by the Egyptian priesthood in honor of Ptolemy V. It refers, among many other things, to the execution by Ptolemy of some of the southern rebels who had troubled his father. BM EA24. © The Trustees of the British Museum.

the center of them. Although the kings were never seriously threatened, and probably retained control of the Nile valley, there were occasions between 205 and 186 when men in Thebes were calling themselves pharaohs, or perhaps were being allowed to call themselves pharaohs. The country was seriously weakened by two decades of internal strife, and, as we shall see, only Roman intervention stopped it falling to the Seleucids.

22

The Greek Cities in
the New World

The rise of the Successor kingdoms changed the status of the Greek polis. Although the Eastern Greek cities had long been subject to kingdoms, they had always aspired to the recovery of their full autonomy. It was now clear that this was out of the question not just for them, but for the mainland Greek communities as well. The cities, being nominally free, were not strictly parts of the kingdoms, but the monarchies were a noticeable presence. Some cities had permanent garrisons; many had governors appointed by the king and answerable only to him; all prioritized the king's business in their assembly meetings. The gradual loss of Athenian energy and autonomy that I have traced over the decades following the Macedonian conquest was, we may assume, typical and paralleled elsewhere. A degree of freedom had been lost forever.

While most cities were formally exempt from paying regular tribute, they were in no position to refuse a request from above for a contribution, and they had regular taxes to pay. Most of the new cities that were founded owed their very existence to kings, which immediately put them in a position of subservience, since city-founders always had religious authority. In return for a king's benefactions, a city might hail him as its Savior and Benefactor and grant him rewards and honors, up to and including status as a god. State consultation of the Delphic and other oracles declined, because now it was the kings who had the answers.

The kings' demands for money and men were insistent. They had enormous expenses—warfare on a massive scale, cities to build, fortunes to give away to deserving men, brilliant courts to maintain—and a lot of the burden fell on the cities. There was a simple reason for this. The generation of revenue was always the kings' primary concern; old cities already had long-established taxation systems, and new cities could quickly be equipped with one, so it was easier to extract money from cities than from elsewhere. Hence kings gave a lot of land to cities, in order to bring it more readily into the taxation system. The cities of Egypt and Asia acted as hubs for the collection of taxes in cash and kind, which were then passed on to the central government.

Generalizations about how the kings treated cities need to be tempered by the reminder that factors such as location and prestige determined how bluntly or diplomatically a king intervened in a city's affairs. It also depended on the king; although in other respects the Attalids of Pergamum were typical Hellenistic kings, they shared power to such an extent with the cities in their realm that it was almost as though they were kings of a confederacy—but then they owed less to the colonial style of monarchy adopted by the others, and even their palaces were modest compared to those of the other kings. But one consequence of the new situation was almost universal: nearly all cities of any size or importance found themselves worse off financially than before—or, rather, their usual rather meager revenues proved to be no longer sufficient. This was due above all to the unrelenting warfare.

Farming, trade, mining—all the usual sources of income—were likely to be interrupted, and the seas were rife with pirate fleets, so that merchantmen often needed to be convoyed by warships. The greatest problem was the sheer cost of warfare. Even if a city was not directly involved in the fighting, whether supporting friends or defending itself against enemies, the expenses were horrendous. There were mercenaries to hire, and in an era of siege warfare, the first things a city needed were stout defensive walls and towers, preferably made out of well-worked stone, and a secure water supply. Ephesus' fortifications had sixty towers—but the entire city was first moved to a new, more defensible location. The expenses were so great that kings and other benefactors had to step in, if it suited them to do so. When Rhodes, vital to Mediterranean commerce, was devastated by an earthquake in 227, kings from as far west as Syracuse rushed to help.

Benefaction was a distinct mode of power-wielding in the Hellenistic period. This was the time when, thanks to rich citizens and kings, the centers of the greatest cities became truly magnificent, adorned with beautifully wrought structures. Cities needed kings, but kings needed cities too, because doing cities favors enhanced their prestige and gained them goodwill, an investment in the future, and because, as I have just said, revenue-extraction was made easier by cities. It was a form of reciprocal gift-exchange, favors in return for honors. But every time a king paid for fortifications—or built a stoa in the agora, or donated grain or money, or awarded certain privileges—the city fell further into debt. Petitions created a kind of dialogue between city and court, and were invariably couched in terms that helped the citizens feel better about themselves, but this was a pantomime of mastery and subservience, and the dialogue resulted only in the increased dependency of cities on kings. The hand that gives is above the hand that receives, as Napoleon is supposed to have said.

The Freedom of the Greek Cities

The slogan of freedom had been cynically bandied about ever since, in the run-up to the Peloponnesian War, the Spartans had promised to free the Greeks from the Athenians. The Greek cities were good sources of men and expertise, and, just as importantly, if they were content there was no need to go to all the expense of garrisoning them. But in the mouths of men as powerful as the Successors and Hellenistic kings, every promise of freedom could realistically be read as a veiled threat, a reminder that freedom was in their hands and that the cities simply lacked the resources to mount a serious challenge. Observing this trend, the clear-sighted historian Polybius wrote: "All kings mouth platitudes about freedom at the beginning of their reigns . . . but once they have gained their ends they soon treat those who believed them as slaves, not as allies."[1]

But there was still plenty for citizens to do; a man still identified himself first by his community and was likely to want to play his part in making it a better place to live. The city-state was still regarded as the ideal setting for civilized life. Dozens of vigorous new cities were created in the Hellenistic period, such as Alexandria and Antioch, in the newly conquered territories; and even if some cities declined, others grew or regrew in size and influence—Messene, Patrae, Sicyon, and Miletus are examples. Two of the islands, Rhodes and Delos, enjoyed or embarked upon the most prosperous phases of their histories.

For much of the Hellenistic period (until the arrival of the Romans), since the kings had learned how unpopular oligarchies were, most cities

1 Polybius, *Histories* 15.24.4.

were constitutionally tempered democracies, with all the Athenian-style apparatus of tribes, demes, popular courts, a combination of sortition and election, council, boards of officers, and assembly. In such a set-up, citizens still had a lot to do. They met and determined their relations with both their neighbors (up to and including going to war with them) and the local kings, defended themselves against pirates, organized the *ephēbeia*, elected officers, hired public doctors, ratified treaties, worried about their food supply, employed citizens of neutral states to arbitrate their disputes (a common Hellenistic practice), decided who were and were not citizens, passed laws and decrees, organized festivals, tried to increase revenues and spend them wisely, minted coins (if they had a mint), and administered justice. Large-scale foreign policy was out of their hands, but they were, in theory, self-governing as regards domestic policy. Their incomes and expenditures were qualitatively much the same as before, though often less in quantity. But an exclusive focus on domestic policy could give a city a bourgeois, provincial character.

Cities continued to act as though they were independent, and the pace of local political life scarcely slackened in the Hellenistic period. Kings too pretended that cities were independent, and generally disguised their commands as polite requests, or praised certain behaviors as a way of showing how they should behave in the future. When democracy returned briefly to Athens in 319, the Macedonian viceroy Polyperchon wanted the Athenians to condemn to death the leaders of the previous oligarchy; he got the king, Philip III, to write a letter to the Athenians the gist of which was "that while he had no doubt of the men's treachery, he left it up to them, as free and autonomous agents, to reach a verdict."[2] The "free and autonomous agents" duly put the men to death. The pretense in public documents was that relations between kings and cities were cordial, even if at the time they were strained; the pretense was that the kings were not being manipulative.

But, while it is true that any of a city's decisions could be undone at a stroke if it displeased the local king or dynast, this was rare. One of the reasons the practice of arbitrating disputes between cities increased in the Hellenistic period is that such disputes, if they escalated into fighting, were likely to irritate a king, so it was best to dissolve the dispute before it came to his attention. As long as the kings were receiving their tributes and taxes from the cities, they were content. For a Hellenistic city, negotiating a safe

2 Plutarch, *Phocion* 34.3.

path among kings, and then Romans too, was not much different from the earlier necessity of doing the same among rival Greek states. The polis continued to function much as it ever had, but citizens were aware that the presence of the kings gave everything they said and did the potential for insignificance.

The Rule of the Landowners

On a day-to-day basis, there were more immediate restrictions than the usually distant kings; these stemmed above all from the increasing power of the rich in their cities. We often find the same families holding office, or otherwise prominent, generation after generation. They had to be rich, because they were expected to pay for some of the city's functions themselves, by voluntary donation or in response to a request from the assembly; even generals often had to supply arms and armor for their men. A long inscription that survives from third-century Samos shows the range of services a rich man might be expected to provide: a prominent citizen is thanked for pestering Antiochus II on behalf of some people who had lost their land, for acting as public prosecutor and as superintendent of the gymnasium, for having paid out of his own pocket for a delegation to a festival in Alexandria, and for contributing toward or paying in full for three shipments of grain to the city.[3]

We have seen the beginning of this trend toward dependency on the rich in the fourth century, but it accelerated rapidly in the third. Typically, these men would be called on to relieve poverty and hunger among their fellow citizens, embellish the city in some way, or just make a contribution to the public treasury. By making such contributions in the first place, the rich—just like the kings, whose benefactions they mirrored in miniature—laid themselves open to moral pressure to do so again in the future. Some cities even came to stipulate the minimum level at which contributions were to be made. Many cities implicitly encouraged competition among the rich—and some did so explicitly: ". . . so that more people may compete to provide benefits for the city when they see worthy men being honored."[4] The institution allowed the rich to make a display of their wealth

---

3 Austin no. 132; Bagnall/Derow no. 76.
4 *Syll.*[3] 493.

and to compete with one another for the good of the city, as they always had done.

The gap between rich and poor widened considerably in the Hellenistic period, as we can tell by, for instance, measuring house sizes; there was a rapid increase from the late fourth century onward, when ostentation came back in fashion. At some point, the limitation in Athens on the amount of land anyone could own had been lifted, or was no longer enforced, because we hear of larger estates, there and elsewhere in Greece; in spacious Anatolia, they could be huge. There was also a prosperous middle-income group, but taxation was heavy in the Hellenistic period, and the poor suffered. Many small farmers went under, and their land began to be absorbed by their more prosperous neighbors. Kings and rich citizens frequently had to distribute grain to prevent famine. Mercenary service and emigration were attractive options for many.

The rich were also vital to cities because they were the only ones with access to the kings. The best-case scenario was if a fellow citizen was a Friend of a king, one of his inner circle, but at least he had to be rich enough to know how to move in that world. The petitions these men brought to the ears of kings could mean the difference between starvation and plenty, war and peace, decay or modernization, and they were effusively thanked and honored. The cost to independence was high: the people (in so far as they were still attending assemblies) sacrificed political rights for charity.

A cycle was created whereby a man earned gratitude and distinction for benefiting his state (whether in or out of office at the time), and then translated this into further offices, priesthoods, and opportunities for distinction for himself or other members of his family. Thus a new hereditary aristocracy emerged in the Greek world, and though cities were institutionally democracies, in practice they were oligarchies. Astonishingly, from the third quarter of the fourth century men began once again to worship at Mycenaean tombs, legitimizing their power just as their elite forebears had four hundred years previously (p. 47). The gap between rich and poor was underlined symbolically: whereas in the Classical period, after a major sacrifice the meat was distributed in equal portions to all, regardless of status, in the Hellenistic period the rich expected to be honored with the larger portions.

This aristocratization of Greek cities accelerated under Roman rule; in fact, Roman legislation made it the official constitutional norm. By the time of the Roman Empire, no popular assembly anywhere had any function

apart from rubber-stamping elite decisions. The old idea of citizen equality evaporated in the chasm between rich and poor, and hereditary elites
then remained in power for much of European history, until democracy re-
emerged—at any rate, as an ideal—during the American and French revo-
lutions of the late eighteenth century. From a broad historical perspective,
democracy in ancient Greece begins to seem an unusual and short-term
experiment.

The Achaean and Aetolian Confederacies

Another restriction on the Greek communities was that in the course of the
third century many of them became members of confederacies, sacrificing
full independence for greater security. The formation or further development of federal states was a major phenomenon of the times. In part, it was
a response to the failure of the hegemonial alliances set up by Athens and
Sparta to guarantee peace, but mainly it was a form of military and economic protectionism: in the new world of superpowers, strength lay in the
reduction of local competition in favor of cooperation. The two major confederacies of the Hellenistic period, the Aetolian and the Achaean, evolved
in mountainous regions that had been considered backward, and would
have remained so had they not united.

The Achaeans of the rugged south coast of the Corinthian Gulf had long
had a sense of ethnic identity, and this led, in the first half of the fourth century, to federation. This early confederacy broke up, but it began to reform
in the late 280s. At first, members came just from Achaea itself, but a significant moment came in 251, by which time the confederacy already had nine
members. Aratus, aged only twenty, seized control in his native Sicyon and
took it into the confederacy, despite the fact that it was not an Achaean city.
The Aetolian Confederacy was already ahead of them on this, but now the
Achaean state burst its ethnic bounds. The next turning-point was Aratus'
seizure of Corinth in 243. The Achaeans now had real international power,
and by the middle of the 230s they were well on the way to achieving
their goal of unifying the Peloponnese; in city after city, the Macedonian-
imposed tyrant either voluntarily stepped down or was forcibly ejected.
Lacking Corinth, the Macedonians were helpless to retaliate.

The Aetolian Confederacy had a parallel history. There had long been
people identified as "the Aetolians," as though they were ethnically

distinct, but we cannot be sure that they had created federal structures until the second quarter of the fourth century, and even then nothing significant came of it for a while. The turning point was their leadership in repelling the Celtic invasion of 279. This brought them much-deserved international recognition—they themselves were quick to compare it to the defeat of the Persians two hundred years earlier—which over subsequent years they translated into dominance over Delphi and the incorporation of its neighbors (and their votes on the Amphictyonic Council). Then, as a result of warfare in 245, they gained the Boeotians as well.

The confederacy now controlled the entirety of central Greece, from coast to coast, and even had influence among the Aegean islands. Up to this point, the Aetolians had been regarded as bandits, who preyed on their neighbors and everyone else in ways that had not been seen in civilized Greece since the Archaic period, but now they entered the economic and military mainstream of Greek history. To address the problem of their poor

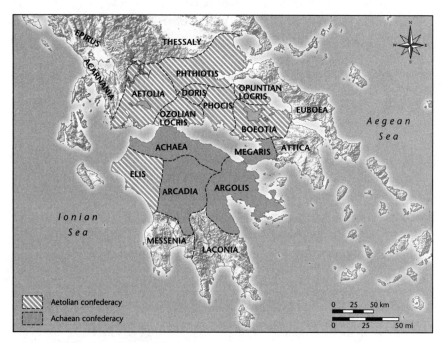

Map 22.1. The Aetolian and Achaean confederacies.

reputation, they were generous with grants of *asylia* (p. 167), guaranteeing to punish any of their citizens who treated their friends abroad with violence.

Both confederacies had similar institutional structures. Each year a General was appointed as the head of state, and he was supported by a small group of other elected officers, responsible for, say, organizing military levies or for the state finances. The General had to leave an interval of one year (in the Achaean Confederacy), or perhaps three years (in the Aetolian Confederacy), before being re-elected, but within this constraint re-election was common. Aratus was first elected General of the Achaeans in 245, and then every other year for the rest of his life. The legislative branch of each confederacy was the assembly of all male citizens of military age, but this met only a few times a year (four for the Achaeans, two for the Aetolians), so there were smaller councils of representatives to meet more frequently for day-to-day business and to prepare the agenda for the assembly. The council wielded a lot of power, then, since it had to take care of much business by itself, without consulting the assembly, and the councils of both confederacies were generally populated by the better-off members of society, since no one else could afford to give up the time. Polybius, himself an Achaean (though a native Arcadian), loyally claimed that the Achaean Confederacy was a model democracy,[5] but in reality it and the Aetolian Confederacy were oligarchies of landowners, just like pretty much everywhere else at the time.

The Greek Diaspora

Despite the long hostility between Greeks and Persians, Greeks had played peaceful roles in the Achaemenid Empire. As mercenaries, traders, artists, artisans, doctors, secretaries, engineers, envoys, entertainers, explorers, and translators, they had passed through or been resident in the domains of satraps, and even occasionally in the court of the Great King himself. But the numbers involved were nothing compared to the influx of Greek settlers in the wake of Alexander's conquests. We are told that in 323 at least twenty thousand Greek soldiers rebelled and began the long trek home from the eastern satrapies before being massacred (p. 356)[6]—and that was just the

5 Polybius, *Histories* 2.38.6.
6 Diodorus of Sicily, *Library of History* 18.7.2.

fighting men from two satrapies, not counting their dependents. This gives some idea of the numbers involved in this wave of emigration; hundreds of thousands of Greeks moved from cities around the Mediterranean to Egypt or Asia, and tens of thousands to Sicily too.

Now the Greeks were a presence not just in the termini of the eastern trade routes but on the routes themselves, and finds of Greek coins as far east as India show that businessmen took advantage. The greater interconnectedness of the Hellenistic world stimulated trade and craft, enlarging the prosperous middle-income group. Cities increasingly entered into favorable trade agreements with one another. Trading associations sprang up to share knowledge and infrastructures, and some of them became rich and powerful enough to negotiate with kings.

Frontiers were being pushed back, and intrepid explorers pushed them further. In the last quarter of the fourth century, Pytheas of Massalia sailed from the western Mediterranean, circumnavigated the British Isles, and explored the amber coasts of the Baltic; at much the same time, Patrocles, a Friend of Seleucus I, was sailing around the Caspian Sea. A little later, Eudoxus of Cyzicus opened up trade in the Arabian Sea, building on Nearchus of Crete's preliminary exploration (p. 343). Long-distance travel and navigation became more scientific, as astronomers developed more precise models to account for the apparent movement of the heavenly bodies, and, late in the fourth century, the first map of the known world was drawn that showed a few orientation lines, the precursors of longitude and latitude.

Literal mobility across geographical borders found metaphorical echoes in society. Certain conventions did not survive the transposition to the East, and social mobility increased. Fortunes were made by men from outside the highest social classes, and even by slaves. The manumission of slaves became much more common, and there was a huge increase in the awarding of divine honors to human beings, as though even the barrier between humanity and divinity had become permeable.

Mobility led to the erosion of old family-based structures, not just in the sense that families themselves were physically broken up as one or more members emigrated, but also because these emigrants were uprooted from their ancestors and their kinship groups, with all that this implied in terms of family pride and cult. Formerly, people had been reluctant to leave the place of their birth. Their roots were there, and they felt that without them, like a plant, they would perish, or at least not thrive. But the old beliefs now had less of a hold on people and they were less reluctant to emigrate. Hence, in part, the importance of gymnasia and social clubs in these far-flung foundations: they were substitutes for extended families and havens of tradition for expatriate Greeks.

Greek became by far the most common supra-regional language throughout the known world. A new dialect evolved to act as the common tongue of the new world—and that was its name, koine (Greek *koinē*), "the common tongue." Inscriptions and literature show that local dialects persisted, but koine was now the dominant version of Greek. It was essentially the Attic dialect of Classical Athens, shorn of a few peculiarities. The plays that were put on in the theaters were invariably Athenian or Athenian-style dramas; Isocratean rhetoric was an important element in education; cities, as I have already mentioned, were moderate democracies in the Athenian mold; most coinage was on the Attic standard. As Isocrates said in the middle of the fourth century, people had come to be called Greek more because of their absorption of Athenian culture than because of their birth.[7] The emigrants' sense of Greekness could no longer depend on local ethnicities (such as being Athenian or Corinthian) or on existence in an ancestral homeland; they were Greeks because they shared the common culture of the Greek cities, old and new.

The main wave of west-to-east emigration lasted no more than two or three generations after Alexander's conquests. There were two phases. In the first, land needed to be secured in the short term, and so the first settlers were usually men who had been hired as mercenaries and were now detailed to garrison an existing town or a fortress. In the second, these mercenaries were given a grant of land, some fortresses grew in size, and new cities were founded as well, attracting further immigrants. The pace of city-foundation or refoundation peaked in the second generation of kings, when immigrants with peacetime skills were in as much demand as soldiers.

Archaeologists have discovered in Afghanistan a major Greek city, of whose existence we would otherwise have been entirely unaware; founded late in the fourth century on the site of a former Achaemenid settlement, it is called Ai Khanoum, after a nearby village. It grew to be very large, with a main street a kilometer in length, and wealthy from the trade in lapis lazuli—eastern Bactria was the only known source at the time. One of the most astonishing discoveries was an inscription showing that a philosopher transcribed the famous moral maxims from the sanctuary of Apollo

7 Isocrates, 4.50 (*Panegyricus*).

at Delphi, and brought the copy thousands of kilometers east as a kind of foundation document for the new city.[8] The story underscores the astonishing mobility of the period, and also shows, since the Delphic maxims (such as "Know yourself," "Nothing in excess," and "Die without regrets") formed the heart of Greek popular morality, that Ai Khanoum was to be a Greek city, even if it lay on the banks of the Oxus (the Amu Darya, today). The presence there of a few eastern structures and designs would hardly have dented a visitor's impression that this was essentially a Greek city; after all, there had always been eastern artwork in Greek cities—sphinxes and Egyptian-style *kouros* statues, for instance.

The new cities were created as oases of Greek culture. Every city was bound to have a theater, for instance, and so the Guild of Dionysus came into existence as an organization that supplied actors and the expertise needed to stage plays all over the world. Each new foundation also had to have a gymnasium, a stadium, and Greek-style temples, administrative buildings, and stoas in an agora. All over the world, people were in agreement about what a Greek city should be like. Their public and private buildings looked alike, the new cities were laid out with barracks-like uniformity as rough rectangles crisscrossed by streets, and they shared a common culture; an Athenian or a Syracusan would not have felt out of place in Ai Khanoum or Alexandria. They were not living in Greece, but that did not mean that they could not live in an idea of Greece.

The Spread of Hellenism

This uniformity is remarkable. One might have expected literature and art in Afghanistan to have developed in different directions from those they took in Egypt, but this was not so to any great extent. To the degree that native styles infiltrated, obviously it was different styles doing the infiltration in Egypt than in Afghanistan, but there was not that much infiltration. There is much archaeological work to do in Asia especially, but at Ai Khanoum, the only Hellenistic city to have been excavated east of the Tigris, there is minimal hybridity of artistic and architectural styles. Most structures are purely Greek, with little more than the palace (in Greek-style

8   Austin no. 186; Burstein no. 49.

architecture, but scarcely a traditional Greek institution) and a temple built in the squat Mesopotamian style to relieve this impression. Much the same could be said of Seleucia-on-the-Tigris, where eastern and European styles of buildings rubbed shoulders, but rarely blended their architectural styles. Of course, hybrid artifacts can be found, and in gradually increasing numbers over the years, but their overall scarcity is telling. Greeks had a long history of considering their culture superior to that of anyone else, and seem to have regarded local styles as devoid of cultural interest, or at least as not for them.

There are hints that the Greeks considered themselves superior to the native populations they ruled and lived beside. In one of Theocritus' poems a Greek woman expresses contempt for Egyptians, calling them "ants, numberless and uncounted." Presumably not everyone shared such views, but we may guess that many did. In one papyrus document, for instance, a camel-driver complains to his Greek superior that he is being badly treated because he is a barbarian and cannot speak Greek. In another, we see the other side of the coin: a Macedonian complains of being treated badly by Egyptians "because I'm Greek."[9] There were occasional outbreaks of ethnic tension, especially in Alexandria.

Greco-Macedonian rulership turned the kingdoms into two-faced societies, in cultural terms, since both Greek and native artistic and architectural traditions continued side by side. Alexandria sported obelisks and sphinxes as adornments; as in London today, these were purely decorative elements, not integrated into a hybrid architectural order. The Ptolemies acted and had themselves portrayed as Egyptian pharaohs as well as Greek kings. In both countries two sets of laws ran in parallel for the two populations; both kingdoms used two official languages (Greek and Aramaic or Akkadian, depending on location; Greek and demotic Egyptian) and even had double calendrical systems, which were not quite in sync.

The town of Uruk in Babylonia has been well excavated, but, outside of official documents and the limited adoption by individuals of Greek names, not a trace of the use of Greek has been found there, and very little even in the way of Greek pottery (though Greek pottery styles were popular). There was of course plenty of intermarriage and other forms of

9 Theocritus, *Idyll* 15.45. Austin no. 307; Bagnall/Derow no. 137. Austin no. 320; Bagnall/Derow no. 138.

Figure 22.1. Ptolemy VIII as pharaoh. Ptolemy, depicted entirely in the Egyptian artistic style, is being crowned as pharaoh by the goddesses Nechbet (right) and Wachjet (left). This is a relief sculpture from the temple of Horus at Edfu. Photo © Olaf Tausch.

social intercourse, but culturally it seems clear that the Greeks liked to keep themselves separate. The official name of Alexandria was not "Alexandria-in-Egypt," but "Alexandria-by-Egypt." It is an often-repeated but still telling fact that Cleopatra VII, the last Macedonian ruler of Egypt, was also, according to Plutarch, the first to know the Egyptian language.[10]

10 Plutarch, *Antony* 27.4.

But if Greeks generally found it easy to resist the lure of orientalism, it was not so the other way around. Throughout the fourth century, cities and peoples on the margins of the Greek world had become increasingly hellenized (the cities of Cyprus and Phoenicia, for example, where kingship died out in tandem with hellenization); now the phenomenon continued on a much larger scale. The functioning of the bureaucracies required that a number of natives learn Greek. Since Greeks were the dominant elite and Greek was the lingua franca, a certain proportion of the native population came to assume at least some of the trappings of Greek culture as a way of gaining a share of the power. This is the familiar colonial phenomenon whereby the closer one gets to the ruling class, the more cultural differences are eliminated.

It became a sign of prestige for a native to be a member of the local gymnasium or to worship at a Greek temple, and so over time Greek culture began to filter out of the Greek compounds. Moreover, by gaining the right to be classified as a Greek, a native came in for tax exemptions. From early on, there were a few educated natives who knew Greek—the Egyptian historian Manetho wrote a history of Egypt in Greek around 285, for instance, and a couple of decades later Berossus of Babylon did the same for his city—but the numbers increased as the years passed.

The two-faced nature of Seleucid Asia and Ptolemaic Egypt—the choice not to impose institutional uniformity but to allow native traditions to continue—meant that, for many, the coming of the conquerors made little difference. The Macedonian newcomers had to react to the realities of the lands they now controlled, and in both kingdoms the administrative systems remained essentially the same as before the conquest, with some Greek institutions (such as tax-farming and banking) grafted on. The trickle-down from hellenized natives was limited, in the sense that it was largely restricted to the cities, and to elites within the cities. The majority of the population, the peasant farmers, found their daily lives more or less untouched by regime changes and international markets. They were still selling or exchanging their products locally; their ignorance of Greek was an uncrossable barrier. If their lives changed at all, it was as a result of different taxes, increased monetization, and the introduction of Greek agricultural stock and methods; viticulture took off in Egypt, for instance, and different varieties of wheat and breeds of sheep were introduced here and there.

The Greeks were there to make prosperous new lives for themselves. They did not see themselves as bearing any ancient equivalent of the White Man's Burden to civilize barbarian races, nor did they pretend they were bringing freedom and fair trade. The ideal of cosmopolitanism—of a world in which different cultures mingled and met as equals—was a philosophers' fancy, and had little bearing on Greek and Macedonian attitudes or policies. Nevertheless, an unintended result of the mass emigration was the diffusion of a layer of Greek culture all over the known world.

23

Social Life and Intellectual Culture

The Hellenistic period was a time of relentless, bloody warfare, the scale of which dwarfed earlier wars, but it was also a time of great originality in cultural and intellectual fields. This might seem surprising, but one common denominator was the kings, who enhanced their prestige not only by conquest, but also by promoting Greek culture. Alexander led the way, in this as in so much else: he was said to sleep with both a dagger and a copy of Homer's *Iliad* under his pillow.[1] Cosseted by the wealth of kings, writers and scientists had the leisure to open up new horizons. Another aspect, which also helps to explain the conjunction of violence and cultural creativity, was the escapist desire to avert one's gaze from the brutality of the real world.

Women in the Hellenistic World

Some of the power of kings was shared with their womenfolk. There were several ways in which royal women could gain power. First, they were useful to kings; their marriages were an essential part of the kings' dynastic maneuvering. Second, it was their job to produce and protect the heir to the throne. Third, the royal bloodline could pass through women; that was why Alexander the Great, for instance, married the daughters of two previous Achaemenid kings, why the Ptolemies practiced sibling marriage (so that the bloodline remained single), and why Antigonus Monophthalmus felt he had to do away with Alexander's sister Cleopatra before she married Ptolemy. It was also why family factions could form up behind royal

---

1 E.g. Plutarch, *Alexander* 8.

women, so that they could make or break a court. And, fourth, they functioned as priestesses for cults of female deities. Less constrained by southern Greek practices, Macedonian women—and royal Macedonian women
above all—had more freedom than most of their Greek cousins.

Even so, most royal women of the Hellenistic period were prominent—
by the side of their husbands, so to speak—rather than powerful, and their
public roles and goals were mostly set by men rather than themselves. But
the opportunity was there for power if a royal woman had the character
to seize it. We have seen Olympias and Arsinoe achieve things that were
unthinkable for others. Arsinoe's name could even be attached to policy
decisions; shortly after her death, her brother–husband Ptolemy II said that,
in joining the Greek alliance for the Chremonidean War, he was following
her desire to foster Greek freedom.[2] Cleopatra I ruled as regent for her son
after her husband Ptolemy V had died, the first to do so, but not the last.
Berenice II (273–221) exercised real power in Cyrenaica, and owned a fleet
of grain-transport boats on the Nile. Laodice, the wife of Antiochus III,
represented him for certain functions while he was away at war. The most
famous female sole ruler of Egypt was, of course, Cleopatra VII, the con-
sort of both Julius Caesar and Mark Antony, who kept her throne through
twenty-one turbulent years.

This tradition of prominent or powerful queens (or, on occasion in
Egypt, concubines) was more a feature of the Ptolemaic and Seleucid
dynasties, where queens had cities named after them and received worship
as goddesses, than it was of Macedon itself, where royal women were far less
prominent. We hear little about Pergamene queens either. But Ptolemaic
and Seleucid royal women had their own wealth and the right to dispose of
it as they wished, and they had staffs to help them with their public duties;
the wife of Antiochus II even had her own bodyguard.

Some of the freedoms of royal women were faintly echoed in the lives
of Greek women lower down the social scale. Poems by Theocritus and his
Alexandrian colleague Herodas have women setting up a commemorative
plaque in a temple, pushing their way through crowded streets, shopping,
visiting friends—in short, living ordinary lives that were less restricted to
the home. Greater freedom for women was one result of mass emigration
from mainland Greece with its traditions. Not that patronizing attitudes

2   Austin no. 61; Burstein no. 56; Bagnall/Derow no. 19.

ceased; many Hellenistic cities, for instance, had an officer, called a *gynaiko-nomos*, whose job it was to regulate the public behavior of women.

Nor were women's public roles restricted to the sphere of religion, as they had been earlier. All over the Greek world, women, just like their male counterparts (though in far smaller numbers), made public benefactions in their own names (such as repairing city walls or the Council House) and were even on occasion appointed to official positions that required financial outlay. Late in the Hellenistic period, for instance, a woman called Phile was appointed to the senior magistracy of Priene, and she used her position to improve the city's water supply.[3] The goods that accompanied women in their graves begin to be more nearly equal in value and kind to those found in male graves, suggesting greater equality. We even find women signing their own marriage contracts, which would have been the job of a male guardian in the Classical era.[4] Women did not gain official power—they never got the vote, for instance—but wealth could give them influence, as the wealthy women of Hellenistic Sparta found (p. 229).

Education

The most important way in which women's lives changed in the Hellenistic period was that it became more acceptable for them to receive an education. The most striking evidence for this is the number of women authors we hear about—poets, doctors, philosophers, grammarians, a musicologist—though we usually hear only their names, not the content of their work (but that is the case for many male writers too). The change of attitude that made it possible for girls to be educated was part of the general acceptance of greater social mobility in the new world. The majority of girls were still receiving no more than a basic grounding in reading, writing, and arithmetic, which was enough to enable them to run a household, but more of them were receiving it than before, and some were able to take their education much farther.

Education remained essentially the same as in earlier times, but became more programmatic in the Hellenistic period. The evidence is uncertain, but some teachers may even have instituted the practice of formally testing

3 Burstein no. 45.
4 P. *Tebtunis* 104.

proficiency by examination. It was widely accepted that children would first learn to read and write, and then study literature (by means of a rather narrow selection of works, as likely to be chosen for moral edification as for any other qualities), music, arithmetic, and geometry. This curriculum would give children some basics and steep them in Greek literature and popular morality. Poorer children would perhaps omit some of the more refined and complex subjects, such as music. That was as far it went for most children, but a few would go on in their teens to study the subjects that later formed the medieval trivium: grammar, rhetoric, and philosophy. Riding and weapons training were optional extras for rich children, as in the Classical era. Education in the trivium was expensive, but the lower levels of schooling were cheap, and were paid for by the child's parents or by a fund set up by the community.

The value of education as giving a child a good start in life was recognized in the Hellenistic period. Literacy spread wider (though it is still impossible to guess at precise levels), and it began to be more normal, for instance, for written contracts to be drawn up for business deals. The sprawling Ptolemaic bureaucracy relied heavily on the written word. Works of literature began to be read to oneself rather than aloud, as had been the universal practice in earlier times, when a slave, most likely, would have read a book to his master and friends. More books were written, and collections of papyrus rolls—libraries—were established.

Children were either taught at home by private tutors or went out to schools, but a great deal of education, whether physical or intellectual, was also based on the gymnasium. Gymnasia had always been frequented by educators: both Plato and Aristotle, for instance, two of the giants of fourth-century philosophy, held their discussions in gymnasia. In the Hellenistic period, the gymnasium became an essential element of Greek life, and indeed a mark of Hellenism and a symbol of civilization. When in the second century a small town in Phrygia wanted to be recognized as a polis, it asked the Pergamene king for permission not just to develop its own laws and to administer itself, but also for permission to build a gymnasium.[5] Greek settlers in Asia and Egypt built gymnasia even in villages, let alone towns, which might boast several gymnasia, perhaps specifically for different age-groups. The gymnasium complex in Pergamum was one of the most striking of its architectural wonders. A long inscription survives

5 Austin no. 236; Bagnall/Derow no. 43.

Figure 23.1. The Apoxyomenos. The title means "Athlete cleaning himself with a strigil." This was a conventional subject for Greek sculpture, said to have been perfected by Lysippus of Sicyon in the mid-fourth century. This unique bronze version, slightly over lifesize, was discovered in the Adriatic Sea in 1996. Photo © Alinari / Art Resource, NY.

from Beroea in Macedon, detailing the complex regulations for use of the gymnasium—who was allowed in, who was allowed to exercise naked, the duties of the gymnasium staff, the levels of fines for misbehavior, and so on. Shopkeepers, prostitutes, slaves, and freed slaves were categories excluded by the snobbish elite.[6]

6 Austin no. 137; Bagnall/Derow no. 78; Arnaoutoglou no. 98.

A gymnasium was a multi-use facility. Typically, it had a large square central court, for wrestling and other sports, which was surrounded on all sides by a colonnade, off which there were rooms for all the various functions of a gymnasium—bathing, training, changing, meeting friends, or attending lectures. A running-track, covered or open, might be attached. A gymnasium was the responsibility of a gymnasiarch, and he was often a very important person in the community. He also had to be rich, or persuasive, since the upkeep of a gymnasium was expensive; apart from anything else, olive oil was used in large quantities, for lighting and for oiling the body before exercise (the oil was taken off afterwards by a kind of cleansing scraper called a strigil). Non-Greeks could join a gymnasium, but they would need proficiency in Greek (if that was not already a prerequisite for joining) to get the most out of it. Along with the staging of Greek dramas in the theaters, gymnasia were the primary movers of hellenization all over the Hellenistic world.

Hellenistic Culture

The recognition of the value of education went hand in hand with new developments in all the arts. In the past, most statues had been for public display, and the subjects were therefore portrayed as bearers of civic virtues—modest women, sternly serious warriors, beautiful youths, august deities. Of course, such portraits continued, given the desire of kings and great men to commemorate themselves—kings especially liked their statues to show them young, virile, and heroically nude, or as cuirassed cavalry generals—and given also a fashion for the emulation of classical artistic ideals. But increasing wealth also opened up the private market, and with it the demand for something more suitable for the domestic courtyard. A much greater degree of realism became the fashion in all artistic fields, and works were commissioned on a less monumental, more human scale. It is tempting to think that the Hellenistic period was when art as we understand it was born.

Hellenistic comedy is represented for us chiefly by the surviving plays of Menander of Athens, dating from the last quarter of the fourth century and the beginning of the third. They are delightful, soap-operatic light comedies. The protagonists are recognizable types, but they are not political types; they are, for instance, clever slaves, young women with illegitimate children, grumpy old men, braggart soldiers, and worthless young men-about-town, all depicted with great skill. The plots often center on a thwarted love affair, which comes out well for the young lovers in the end. Where earlier comedy engaged directly with contemporary events, for Menander they form no more than the background: women might be abducted by pirates, or have children by foreign soldiers; men contemplate enlisting as mercenaries, or are assumed to have died on service abroad, or return with a spear-won concubine. Menander's work was considered so realistic that one critic exclaimed: "O Menander! O Life! Which of you imitated the other?"[7]

Menander was writing at a time when thousands of lives were being lost on the battlefields of Asia and Europe, and he seems to have felt that it was his job to distract his audience's attention from such harsh realities. Escapism is apparent in other fields as well. Rich town-dwellers commissioned pastoral paintings to adorn their domestic quarters—the first manifestation of the long European tradition of landscape painting. None of these paintings has survived, but they are known through later imitations, such as those preserved in the ruins of Pompeii and Herculaneum in southern Italy by the eruption of Vesuvius in 79 CE. Vitruvius of Rome, author of an encyclopedic work on architecture, described typical scenes as "harbors, headlands, woods, hills, and the wanderings of Odysseus."[8] Such scenes were considered relaxing—which is to say that they took one's mind off current affairs. But then it had always been the job of the Muses to bring, along with the arts, "forgetfulness of ills and relief from cares."[9]

The evidence for Hellenistic tragedy is slight, but bears out these generalizations. Tragedy had to compete on the stage not just with comedy but with forms of entertainment such as mimes, dance shows, and virtuoso monologues. As in comedy and sculpture, more precise characterization replaced the portrayal of people as larger-than-life types; sentiment replaced emotion. Plots became less straightforward, so that the audience's attention focused on the twists and turns of the story line rather than on any big questions that might underlie it. The goal now was entertainment rather than education. Composers experimented with a wider range of meters and musical modes, authors with lighter plots. These are only generalizations: Exekiel

7 Aristophanes of Byzantium (third century) in Syrianus, *Commentary on Hermogenes* 4.101.
8 Vitruvius, *On Architecture* 7.5.2–3 (first century CE).
9 Hesiod, *Theogony* 55.

the Tragedian, for instance, wrote a play about the flight of Moses and the Jews from Egypt. Epic poetry continued to be written and sometimes celebrated real events, as when Simonides of Magnesia, an otherwise unknown third-century poet, wrote about the wars of Antiochus III.

Pastoral paintings quite often occupied panels that were displayed in a room in such a way that they could be read as a continuous narrative. Around the middle of the third century, poets such as Theocritus began to echo this trend by creating in some of his *Idylls* ("vignettes") a fictional bucolic world. Theocritus displays the typical Hellenistic focus on ordinary men and women rather than heroes—or, rather, he creates fictionalized versions of ordinary people. Sculptors were doing the same. The new canon for the human body introduced by Lysippus of Sicyon and his school in the mid-fourth century allowed sculptors to experiment with more sensuous poses. The full range of emotions could now be expressed on face and body together—a satyr turning to look at his tail, a dancer dancing free. Realism was the name of the game. An anecdote tells how Alexander the Great's horse, Bucephalas, whinnied at the portrait Apelles of Colophon had painted of him.[10]

Every such portrait is a mini-biography, and it is not surprising that the literary genre of biography also gained momentum in the Hellenistic period, developing from mere eulogy—the written equivalent of a heroic sculpture—to serious attempts to uncover character. Realistic coin portraits preserved a person's character forever. The epigram, previously used almost entirely for commemorative purposes (on tombstones and votive offerings, especially—the word *epigramma* originally meant just "inscription") became a very popular verse form, with its often poignant focus on ordinary folk and their feelings:[11]

> All Nicomache's favorite things, her trinkets and her Sapphic
>   conversations with other girls beside the shuttle at dawn,
> Fate took away prematurely. The city of the Argives
>   cried aloud in lament for that poor maiden,
> a young shoot reared in Hera's arms. Cold, alas, remain
>   the beds of the youths who courted her.

The Hellenistic emphasis on ordinary people and ordinary emotions stands in striking contrast with earlier eras. It is unimaginable that the

10 Aelian, *Miscellany* 2.3; Pliny, *Natural History* 35.95.
11 Posidippus of Pella 55; Austin/Bastianini (third century); translation by Kathryn Gutzwiller.

clients of Classical artists would have asked them to dedicate their skills to portraying social inferiors such as laborers and slaves, women and children, but these are the typical subjects of much Hellenistic work. It is equally hard to imagine that Jason, the heroic gatherer of the Golden Fleece, could have been portrayed as he was in the often tongue-in-cheek epic *Argonautica* of Apollonius of Rhodes (born c. 295, and the

Figure 23.2. The Boxer at Rest. With his cauliflower ears, scarred face, battered body, and thonged hands, this famous statue, made c. 200, displays the Hellenistic love of realism. One of the most powerful statues to survive from the Hellenistic period, it was probably made for a rich Roman patron. Museo Nazionale Romano no. 1055. Photo © Scala / Art Resource, NY.

second librarian of the Alexandrian Museum)—not as a mighty warrior, but as a team-builder. Both heroes and gods tend to become reduced in Hellenistic poetry to a human level; treating Heracles this way was almost a subgenre of literature.

The miniaturization—the focus on the norms of daily life—that gave epigrams their poignancy is evident also in other fields, such as the engraving of coins and seal rings, and especially in jewelry, the most significant of the luxury arts of the Hellenistic period. A new aesthetic emerged. Poetry and the visual arts focused on technique and subtle displays of learning, and reflected each other. What was assonance in poetry and repeated motif in music became the periodic placing of color and form in painting; poetry in particular was full of such devices, designed to enhance its musicality, playfulness, and suggestiveness. Techniques such as filigree, chiaroscuro, and gilding were the visual counterparts of the wit and refinement of Hellenistic poetry. Poets returned the favor by valuing vividness, the ability to bring a matter directly before the mind's eye. The subjects of all media were similar: not just heroes and kings, but pets, plants, children, ordinary people, domestic scenes, comic characters, tragic characters—portrayed with vigor, a love of detail, and psychological insight. In some cases, artists chose grotesquery and caricature (here we find hunchbacks, dwarfs, and cripples, for instance); in others, pathos or a gentle eroticism. It was all a far cry from the incessant warfare of the Hellenistic era.

The Museum and Library of Alexandria

Kings in all times and places have displayed their power by patronizing the arts, and the Hellenistic courts were no exception. Apart from anything else, it was important for these warlike kings to demonstrate that they were men of peace as well. There were philosophers, scientists, artists, and writers at the court of every king, but the main driver of innovation was the Museum of Alexandria—a *Mouseion*, a shrine to the Muses, the goddesses of culture—which occupied a prestigious site within the palace compound. The Museum functioned both as a temple of learning (literally, since its director was also its high priest) and as a residential college for scholars, focusing particularly on science and literature. It flourished until 144, when in a fit of paranoia Ptolemy VIII expelled many Jews and intellectuals from Alexandria.

All expenses in this "birdcage of the Muses," as an Antigonid protégé, the satirist Timon of Phleious, called it,[12] were covered by the king, including generous salaries and the development of the scholars' major resource, a library, established in an annex to the Museum. Ptolemy I's intention in creating the library—apart from enhancing his status—was typically ambitious: to collect a copy of every book ever written in Greek. But translation of non-Greek works took place too, most famously the translation, over many decades, of the Old Testament into Greek by Alexandrian Jewish scholars.

It is impossible to know how many papyrus rolls the library contained at any given time, and many books occupied more than one roll. If each roll held about thirty thousand words, this book, for instance, would make six rolls. But the rolls certainly numbered in the tens of thousands—few enough by today's lights, but an incredible achievement in the ancient world. By the 230s, the catalog alone, drawn up by Callimachus of Cyrene (who was also a famous writer of prose and verse), ran to 120 volumes; each entry contained the title of the work, the name and a thumbnail biography of the author listing all his other works, the opening line of each work, and the number of verses if it was poetry. The catalog was an inventory of Greek literature and thought. The library came to be so unwieldy that a second one was opened in the nearby sanctuary of Serapis, which was perhaps open to the public rather than being the exclusive (and walled-off) domain of the live-in scholars. After the Museum was badly damaged by fire in 48 (when Julius Caesar burned the Ptolemaic fleet in the harbor and the fire spread), the Serapeum library became the main one, and there were further subsidiaries as well. Then the library died of neglect over the next few centuries before being finally destroyed in the seventh century CE.

As soon as the books began to arrive and to be studied, it was clear that there were many different versions even of well-known texts, and that forgeries and interpolations abounded. So the necessity of classifying every work for the catalog had to be supplemented by the attempt to establish authentic texts, and that involved in part the drawing up of rules for the Greek language. Thus were philology and literary scholarship born. Standard texts were established, especially of Homer's poems; dictionaries and grammars were written; canons were created, such as the ten orators who were taken to write the purest Attic Greek, or the nine great lyric poets, to the

12 Timon, F 60 Wachsmuth.

detriment and often the ultimate loss of authors who fell outside these canons. Hellenistic oratory is consequently as closed a book to us as Hellenistic tragedy, and hardly any Greek poetry survives from the entire second and first centuries.

All over the Hellenistic world, royal patronage was the main engine of cultural development in science, mathematics, medicine, technology, art, and literature. Some philosophers stayed away, expressing horror at the decadence of court life and preferring the lively philosophical scene in Athens, but others became tutors to princes and Royal Pages, and most scholars took patronage as an honor, a sign that they had won or deserved international renown. Hence artists and writers paid for their privileged lifestyles with fulsome praise of the king—like Theocritus' sixteenth *Idyll*, in which Ptolemy II is the perfection of military prowess, piety, munificence, and so on. Callimachus' quasi-historical poem *Aetia* made Ptolemaic Alexandria the culmination of Greek cultural evolution. By means of such poems, the residents of the Museum vied with one another, and with other courtiers, for the king's attention and generosity.

The erudition that the Museum fostered had a powerful impact on the kind of literature that was written. It is not just that didactic poetry in the manner of Hesiod was resurrected as a genre, but that a great deal of lighter verse was colored by allusions of such obscurity that only the author could be expected to get all of them. In addition to learned references, obscure words and neologisms abounded. Whereas in the past poems had been written for performance and accompanied by music, they were written now also for private readers, who had time to linger over the texts and pick up at least some of the allusions and nuances. This was an artificial, escapist universe, and it was one from which the uneducated masses were largely excluded. Literature, as in most periods of history, was largely for the elite. To a certain extent, Alexandrian literature was a kind of refined game between author and reader. The poems were read out at court symposia, where guests would compete to see how many of the allusions they could get. It is not surprising that clever tricks such as acrostics and pattern poetry (in which a poem about wings, say, has the shape of wings when written down) first appear from Alexandrian pens.

Excessively clever verse can of course be frigid and indigestible, and this would certainly be a fair description of some Hellenistic literature. The best of it preserves the spirit of the Museum in which it was written, in its attempt to honor the past and engage with it creatively by echoing, imitating, and parodying the old masters, while at the same time branching out in new directions. A writer's display of erudition mirrored in miniature the ostentation of the whole Museum. Wit, learning, experimentation, and technical mastery were the hallmarks of Alexandria.

The library was not entirely without precedent. Egyptian temples had collections of texts and treatises. In seventh-century Nineveh, Ashurbanipal, king of Assyria, collected a library of thirty thousand cuneiform tablets, ranging from legal texts to magical spells, via epic poetry. Scientific research seems to have become institutionalized in Babylonian temples in the fourth century. Private collectors had begun to accumulate libraries—Aristotle's was particularly famous. What was unprecedented was the sheer scale of the project. As the Hellenistic period progressed, other cities established great libraries—Antioch, Pella, and Pergamum, especially—but none compared with the library of Alexandria.

Science and Technology

Literature was not the only specialty of the Museum of Alexandria. Scientists too were encouraged to draw on the resources of the library. So, for instance, the school of medicine based on the island of Cos (the birth-place of the fifth-century founder of scientific medicine, Hippocrates) moved its headquarters to the Museum. Many scientists worked outside Alexandria as well, either attached to the court of some other king or in the medical schools of Cnidus and Rhodes. The main drivers of progress in science and technology were warfare, trade, the quest for improve-ments in food and water supply, and the kings' constant hunger for inno-vations that would enhance their prestige. Sheer competitiveness was another factor, as many theories were explicitly developed to improve on a colleague's ideas.

The practical applications of science were always uppermost in every-one's minds, not least because of the possibility of generous rewards from a king if, say, one learned enough about poisons to save his life; or invented a more powerful catapult; or entertained him with a novel gadget, such as the mechanical snail that Demetrius of Phalerum had lead a procession in Athens in 308, excreting slime, or the water-organ, driven by compressed air (a stupendous advance), invented by one of the mechanical geniuses of the era, Ctesibius of Alexandria, the son of a barber.

This is the time when science as we understand it came into being, based on Aristotle's clarification of scientific method. As we have seen, earlier thinkers were bound to rely on imagination as much as logic or experimentation to reach conclusions. How else could they investigate distant objects, events in the remote past, or things that were invisible to them, such as embryos? Scientists in the Hellenistic period were scarcely better off, but were more prepared to approach empirical data with uncluttered minds.

The third and second centuries were a golden age of science and mathematics, when scientists wrote ingenious and learned monographs on particular topics—optics, mechanics, conic sections, the liver, the pulse, botany, and so on. In the Classical era, the search had been for perfection—to capture the perfect human body in a statue, to come up with a theory that explained everything all at once—but Hellenistic scientists were happy to work in a more piecemeal fashion. Polymathy was therefore normal: in the early first century, for instance, Posidonius of Syria wrote not only on all branches of philosophy, but also on astronomy, meteorology, mathematics, geography, seismology, zoology, military tactics, geography, anthropology, botany, and history. Not a single one of his books has survived intact.

Euclid wrote his *Elements*, a compendium of geometry and number theory that is still used today as a textbook. Archimedes of Syracuse, who was killed during the Roman sack of Syracuse in 212, wrote on a number of mathematical subjects, but is best known for his inventions (such as a screw for raising water) and for his exclaiming "*Eureka!*"—"Got it!"— when he cracked one particularly tricky problem. Nothing testifies better to the importance of Greek mathematical work than the fact that Euclid and Archimedes (along with sixth-century Pythagoras) are still household names today.

Aristarchus of Samos used geometry to work out the distances of the sun and the moon from the earth, and, seventeen centuries before Copernicus, boldly proposed that the sun was the center of the universe rather than the earth. The theory did not catch on, and astronomers developed increasingly complex models to explain the apparent motion of the heavenly bodies in a geocentric universe. The famous Antikythera Mechanism, a few fragments of which were pulled up from a shipwreck off the island of Antikythera in 1900 and which dates to between 100 and 50, was a kind of planetarium, consisting of an ingenious system of geared wheels that meshed to show the relative positions of the sun and moon and the five known planets at any given point of time and from any location on earth, and could be used to predict eclipses or plot horoscopes. The major coup of Eratosthenes of Cyrene, another polymath and the head librarian of the Museum under Ptolemy III, was coming up with the first good measurement of the circumference of the earth; he was off by only about 16 percent.

But the greatest advances were made in medicine. Anatomy—how the bodily organs work—received the most attention in the third century. Researchers were hugely helped by the temporary lifting of the taboo against using corpses for medical research. Some even practiced vivisection on criminals, and criminals were also used as guinea pigs for the effects of poisons. This was another advantage of working for kings, who had the power of life and death over their subjects. We may condemn such practices, but they reveal how intense was the desire to learn that motivated Hellenistic scientists.

Hellenistic Philosophy

Not only did Plato's and Aristotle's schools flourish, and continue to teach and argue about (and alter) their founders' thought, but four major new schools arose in the Hellenistic period: Cynicism, Stoicism, Epicureanism, and Skepticism. These new philosophies argued among themselves, often with considerable rancor. Nevertheless, there was common ground. Philosophy climbed down from the abstract realms of Platonic metaphysics or Aristotelian polymathy and learned to appeal to a wider audience with promises of self-improvement. That is why we can still apply the names of the Hellenistic schools to ordinary people; even though the meanings of the words have altered over the centuries, we still say that people are stoical or epicurean (or skeptical, or cynical), but not usually that they are Platonist or Aristotelian.

The word "Cynic" means "dog-like"; it was applied to these practical philosophers as an insult, because true Cynics lived like beggars or tramps. They adopted the term as a compliment, however, saying that they were the watchdogs of people's morals. The most famous Cynic was the founder, Diogenes of Sinope (c. 405–c. 325), who notoriously lived out on the street in a large ceramic jar. Two of the very many apocryphal stories about him will serve to introduce Cynicism.[13]

---

13 The first is from Plutarch, *Alexander* 14, the second from Diogenes Laertius, *Lives of Eminent Philosophers* 16.37.

> Alexander the Great paid Diogenes a visit [in Corinth] and found him relax-
> ing in the sun. Diogenes raised himself up a bit when the huge crowd of
> people appeared and looked at Alexander, who greeted him and asked if there
> was anything he wanted. "Yes," replied Diogenes. "Would you move aside a
> little, out of my sunlight?"

In the second story, Diogenes had reduced his needs so that all he carried or
wore was a thin tunic, a plate, and a cup for drinking water. One day he saw a
boy cupping his hands to drink from a stream—so he threw away his cup: it
was another thing he could do without. The Cynics did not have an organized philosophy so much as a distinct way of life, in which happiness was
attained by reducing one's needs and living apart from the distractions of life.

The Skeptics believed that the purpose of life was continual investigation.
They withheld their assent from all answers, believing that it was impossible
for us to attain certainty about anything. The common charge against them
was that without beliefs it is impossible to act, but they were prepared to
give temporary assent to sense data and to what *appeared* right and wrong,
while ultimately reserving judgment. They came up with arguments by
which they could challenge any dogma and force anyone to suspend judgment on any matter whatsoever.

But the two most famous and influential schools—influential throughout the Roman Empire, not just in the Greek world—were Stoicism and
Epicureanism. The Stoics were named after the Painted Stoa in Athens,
where they originally met under the guidance of their teacher, Zeno of
Citium (335–263). The common meaning of the word in English to denote
not being affected by emotion is only half a truth. They believed that the
goal of life was to align oneself with nature. Since nature is governed by
rational principles, the supreme part of a human being was the rational
mind. The emotions were a hindrance to the working of the rational mind,
but a Stoic's objective was not to feel no emotions, so much as not to let
them influence him. For if everything is rationally predetermined, as they
believed, then even if my child dies in horrible pain, there is no point in my
getting distressed, because it must have been for the best. Besides, the only
truly good thing there is is moral virtue and the only bad thing is moral evil,
so my child's death is neither good nor bad; it is one of the host of things
the Stoics called "indifferent." They also developed sophisticated systems of
logic and physics, but everything was subordinated to the goal of trying to
become a sage, someone truly aligned with the cosmos. Their model sage
was Socrates.

The Epicureans were not, as the modern use of the word would have one think, gluttons and hedonists. It is true that they took pleasure to be the goal of life, but the idea was not to maximize pleasure but to enjoy what they called tranquility, peace of mind. They achieved tranquility originally by living apart, in communes—Epicurus' school in Athens was simply called "the Garden"—avoiding all the agitation of daily life, and obeying and learning by heart the precepts of the master, which were designed to appeal to reason. He was a materialist, believing that everything is made up of atoms (atomic theory had been invented in the late fifth century by Leucippus and Democritus of Abdera), and that absolutely everything can be explained by the behavior of atoms and their movements. Even the gods are just relatively long-lived agglomerations of atoms; dreams are atoms left over from prior perceptions. Understanding that the world is like this is a giant step toward tranquility, because in such a world there is nothing to fear. "Death is nothing to us, because nothing is 'good' or 'bad' unless sense-experience is involved, and death is the absence of sense-experience"—death is simply annihilation, the dissolution of one's atomic structure.[14] The good life is achieved by the avoidance of irrational fears, by moderating one's appetites, and by kindness to others. The reason Epicureanism attracted a hostile press, such that they were accused of indecency and so on, is that they tried to live self-sufficiently, apart from society, and that the school was open to all comers, even women and slaves.

All the schools, then, set out to demonstrate how individual human beings should live and provided methods and theoretical contexts for achieving this goal. They all saw philosophy as the remedy for human ills, but differed in what they saw as the fundamental problems and in how to go about attaining peace of mind. The three main branches into which philosophy was divided by the schools were logic (understood as the way or ways of discovering the truth of any matter), physics (the nature of the world and the laws that govern it), and ethics (how to achieve happiness). Already in the last quarter of the fourth century, Xenocrates of Chalcedon, the third head of Plato's Academy, had declared that there was no point to philosophy unless it relieved people of the stresses of life.[15]

14 Epicurus, *Letter to Menoeceus* (in Diogenes Laertius, *Lives of Eminent Philosophers* 10.124).
15 Xenocrates, F 4 Heinze.

So philosophy in the Hellenistic period went in two incompatible directions. High philosophy, as we may call it, was the impersonal presentation of often very subtle ideas and arguments; some of the work of the Stoics, for instance, on logic and epistemology is as challenging as philosophical work of any era. Low philosophy, on the other hand, was the attempt to make philosophy practical and accessible to the common man and woman. Hence philosophers presented a public image that stressed poverty, or at least frugality, as a way of advertising the success of their teaching: they themselves had moved beyond the superficial values of the world, and could teach others to do so as well. The pupils they wanted were those who already felt somewhat at odds with the world. We meet again the escapist aspect of Hellenistic culture.

Hellenistic Religions

The hazards and mobility of the early Hellenistic period made it a time of anxiety, as old structures were abandoned or found wanting. Fundamental concepts, such as the importance of ritual purity and the avoidance of pollution, remained the same, but anxiety left its marks on religious practice. For instance, a dominant Hellenistic desire was just for safety, for self and kin, and so people's attitudes toward the gods shifted slightly: rather than bargaining with the deity—"I've done such-and-such for you and I expect something in return"—deities were approached much more as superior beings, the divine equivalent, perhaps, of the absolute rulers who possessed the earth. People wanted to put themselves into the gods' hands.

Anxious people are also inclined to look elsewhere. When Demetrius Poliorcetes was in Athens in 290, a hymn was composed in his honor that included the words: "While other gods are far away, or lack ears, or do not exist, or pay no attention to us, we see you present here, not in wood or stone, but in reality."[16] The Greeks had prayed for safety in a time of turmoil to their usual gods, and they had not responded. Perhaps Demetrius could do better.

The Olympian gods continued to be worshipped, naturally, and not just in the old cities. The Seleucids traced their lineage back to Apollo, the Ptolemies to Zeus and Heracles, and the Attalids to Athena and Dionysus,

16 Austin no. 43; Burstein no. 7.

so these cults thrived in their regimes. Callimachus wrote a series of beautiful hymns to Olympian deities, for performance at their festivals. The god of healing, Asclepius, received magnificent new temples in Messene, Cos, Pergamum, and elsewhere, and his famous sanctuary at Epidaurus was refurbished. If in other sanctuaries building work decreased, that was largely because they already had sufficient and sufficiently grand buildings.

But in the new cities there was greater variety, partly as a result of syncretism. In Bactria, for instance, Artemis was identified with the great Iranian goddess Anahita. Syncretism came naturally in the sphere of religion, because polytheists find it easy to identify their gods with those of other peoples, and because their religion is not the product of some exclusive revelation by a prophet. We have already seen that there was little blending of East and West in art and architecture, but the same cannot be said for people's personal lives, including forms of worship. Easterners made Greek-style dedications to their local deities. Some of the first portraits of the Buddha, from the Kushana dynasty of first-century Afghanistan, bear a striking resemblance to Greek portraits of Apollo. International centers such as Delos had temples for Egyptian, Syrian, Palestinian, Jewish, and Babylonian deities, as well as for the Olympians, and they all used Greek as their language. Whereas a fifth-century Greek would instinctively have gone to a temple of Asclepius for healing, a second-century Greek could choose between Asclepius and Serapis.

This element of choice made religion more personal, and many of the gods that were popular in the Hellenistic period were those, like Asclepius, who offered security to people and their families. Deities with mystery cults consequently flourished, as did those with ecstatic cults (such as Dionysus and Cybele, the Great Mother of Anatolia), but one of the most remarkable phenomena was the very rapid spread of the worship of the Egyptian deities Serapis and Isis. Their popularity was due to the fact that they were imagined as being more responsive to human needs than the Olympians.

The development of the cult of Serapis was attributed to Ptolemy I,[17] and the temple of Serapis (in the Greek style, but with Egyptian as well as Greek statuary) became one of the most magnificent buildings in Alexandria. Serapis already existed as an Egyptian deity (an amalgam of Osiris and Apis), but Ptolemy developed his cult in a European form. The combination of near monotheism with salvationism was irresistible, and a cult that Ptolemy originally intended

17 Plutarch, *Moralia* 361f–362a (*On Isis and Osiris*).

Figure 23.3. Serapis and Isis. In this Roman-period statue group, we see Isis as Persephone and Serapis as Hades, the god of the underworld. Hence he is accompanied by Cerberus, the three-headed hound that guarded the entrance to Hades' realm. Archaeological Museum of Heraklion, Crete. Photo © Jebelon.

to suit cosmopolitan Alexandria spread throughout the Greek world. The philosophers had long been arguing for monotheism; the success of Serapis shows that the tendency had spread far beyond the schoolroom.

The cult of Serapis was joined, in the form of a new, Greek-style mystery religion, with that of his sister–wife Isis. Devotees came to regard Serapis and Isis as the primordial masculine and feminine principles of the universe; when the Ptolemies practiced sibling marriage, they became avatars of the divine pair. Isis became "the Goddess of Countless Names," and absorbed the functions of almost every other female deity in the Egyptian and Greek pantheons. She became the source of all human wisdom and grace, beloved especially by her female worshippers:[18]

18 SEG 8 548.

The Syrians call you Astarte-Artemis-Anaia, and the peoples of Lycia Queen Leto; the Thracians too call you Mother of the Gods, and the Greeks high-throned Hera, Aphrodite, kind Hestia, Rhea, and Demeter, but the Egyptians call you the Only One, because you are all the other goddesses named by other peoples.

Another important phenomenon was an increase in the number of abstractions that received cult, such as Peace, Rumor, Fame, Shame, and Victory. On the darker side, we are told that, before carrying out a mission, a pirate chieftain employed by Philip V of Macedon used to set up altars to Impiety and Lawlessness.[19] Abstractions had been worshipped before, especially in Sparta, but their increased attractiveness in the Hellenistic period was perhaps due to the fact that they were easily movable, rather than being tied to a particular location, as many Olympian cults were.

By far the most important of these abstractions was Fortune. Reflecting on the Macedonian conquest of the Persians, Demetrius of Phalerum explained why:[20]

Suppose that, fifty years ago, some god had foretold the future to the Persians or their kings, or to the Macedonians or their kings. Would they, do you think, have believed that the very name of the Persians would now be altogether lost, who at one time were the masters of almost the whole inhabited world, while the Macedonians, whose name was formerly unknown, would now be masters of it all?

In a world of rapidly changing circumstances, the only certainty was uncertainty, so you wanted to appease Lady Fortune and gain her support. Astrology was supposed to be one way of gaining knowledge of the future, and so making oneself master of one's fate and no longer subject to Fortune.

Fortune was a great, irrational, female principle, and the spread of the worship of Isis was helped by her early identification with Good Fortune. Fortune was worshipped by private individuals, but also as a civic deity, as the Fortune of entire cities or peoples. Seleucus I gave Antioch a magnificent temple to Fortune, which contained a famous cult statue; another grand temple was a neighbor of the Museum in Alexandria. Under the pen of historians such as Polybius of Megalopolis and Diodorus of Sicily, Fortune became a major force in history, as a kind of divine impresario,

19 Polybius, *Histories* 18.54.10.
20 Demetrius of Phalerum, F 82A Stork/van Ophuijsen/Dorandi; Austin no. 25.

Figure 23.4. The Fortune of Antioch. This is a small Roman copy of a famous monumental original, commissioned by Seleucus I when he founded his new capital city in northern Syria. The Orontes River (which flowed through the city) swims at the goddess's feet; she is crowned with the fortifications of the city, and she brings prosperity in the form of sheaves of wheat. Vatican Museums. Photo © Jastrow.

producing tragedies and comedies out of human lives. Wherever there were Greeks or hellenized peoples, the cult of Fortune was to be found.

Individualism

A noticeable feature of Hellenistic culture, in all its forms, is its focus on the human individual. Quite why this should have happened is unclear, but

I would pick on two possible factors. First, many people were uprooted from their traditional collectives and social groups, and forced to face life's challenges on their own. Second, there may have been a trickle-down from the cult of personality that grew up around Alexander and then the kings who followed him.

Strange though it may seem, a citizen of a Greek community of the Classical period would have struggled to understand the value of individualism. We use the term to describe part of a spectrum of possibility, ranging from absolute individualism (or anarchy) at one end, to absolute collectivism (communism, perhaps) at the other. We think of ourselves as individuals by contrast with the soulless, faceless apparatus of state control—and there lay the difference, because the Classical Greek state was not soulless and faceless, but was animated by and wore the faces of each generation of its citizens. Collectivism was a very pronounced characteristic of all Greek states. A citizen had a far more restricted sense of privacy than we do. Almost everything he did, from fathering sons to worshipping gods, was done for the good of the state—that is, for the good of his fellow citizens. But now, under the Hellenistic kings, a pancake model, in which all citizens of a state were theoretically equal, had been replaced by a pyramidal model, with powerful individuals occupying the top layers.

The relative disempowerment of citizens as political agents made it possible for them to see themselves, to a greater extent, as individuals, rather than just as contributors to the greater good. Of course, people had chosen not to play a part in the public life of their cities before—they were called *idiōtai*, the remote origin of our "idiots"—but as the Hellenistic period progressed, fewer citizens played significant roles in politics and larger numbers gained more of a private life, and hence the context within which the value of the individual might be recognized.

The most popular philosophers were precisely those who appealed to the new sense of individual worth. The same went in religion; that was why there was a surge of interest in cults that offered individual salvation. By the same token, small-scale, more personal forms of worship thrived in increasing numbers alongside the great civic cults of gods and rulers. And we have seen how sculptors, comedians, and workers in all the arts focused on portraying individuals. The Hellenistic period is when Western men and women discovered their worth as individuals for the first time.

24

The Roman Conquest

In 229 the Romans' military attention was first drawn east. Of course, there had been contacts between Greeks and Romans for centuries. The coastline of northwestern Greece is separated by only seventy-two kilometers (forty-five miles) of water from the heel of Italy, so that the various peoples had always had trade contacts, and the Romans had conquered the Greeks of southern Italy and Sicily by the second half of the third century. But this was the first time they had landed on the soil of Old Greece with an army. In 146, eighty-three years later, the city of Corinth was infamously destroyed by them and their control of Greece was complete. This was a big year for the Romans, because it was also in 146 that they finally settled their long and hideously bloody series of conflicts with the North African city of Carthage—the Punic Wars—by destroying it as well. The Mediterranean, from east to west, was more or less securely in Roman hands.

We are fortunate that the speed of the Roman conquest attracted the attention of one of the great Greek historians, Polybius of Megalopolis. He was fascinated by the fact that, as Rome grew more powerful, all the events of the known world became interconnected under the Roman umbrella. He was contemporaneous with at least some of the events he narrated, and in fact played a not inconsiderable part in some of them. He was originally a politician of the Achaean Confederacy, but he fell foul of the Romans and was exiled to Italy. There he became friends with powerful Romans and discovered an alternative life's work as a historian (and in part an executant) of the Roman takeover of the Mediterranean. For Polybius, the mere chronicling of events was not enough; events demand an explanation and he attributed Roman success to their political and military institutions—and to the Greeks' inability to unite against what could have been a common enemy. Far from all his work has survived, but some of the gaps are filled by the Roman historian Livy (Titus Livius), who drew heavily for this period on his Greek predecessor.

The Illyrian Wars

The Illyrians had taken advantage of the chaos afflicting the west coast of Greece (p. 378) to expand at the expense of the Epirotes. Since the Illyrians were notorious pirates, the Romans were concerned about the threat to their shipping, especially because they were busy at the time, and for the next thirty or forty years, in subduing the Celtic tribes that occupied the fertile Po valley in what is now northern Italy. Access to the Adriatic Sea would be important for that venture. One of the envoys they sent in 230 to the court of the Illyrian queen, Teuta, was murdered, and the Romans declared war. They quickly defeated Teuta in 229 and put an end to Illyrian expansion, but they had to come back and do it again in 219, because the man they had left in charge—Demetrius, the Greek lord of the island of Pharos (modern Hvar)—began to threaten the Romans' new friends in Illyris, chiefly the Greek cities on the west coast of Illyris (in modern Albania). Again, the Romans evacuated their entire army after doing what they had come for. They had no military presence, but they had made their mark and made some new Greek friends.

As foreigners on Greek soil, the Romans had an obligation to explain themselves. After the first war, they sent envoys to the two most powerful Greek states, the Aetolian and Achaean confederacies; they even sent envoys to Athens and Corinth, which had not been involved at all, and were presumably chosen as representative Greek cities. But they signally failed to send envoys to Macedon. We have seen that Macedon's influence in Greece was weak by the early 220s, but even so the Macedonian king should have been the very first person to whom the Romans explained their actions. The Macedonians had been the protectors of Greece for over a century. The Romans came and started to take over that function themselves, and then they did not send a diplomatic mission to Macedon. Nor did they after the second war.

This was not a blunder; the Romans were not stupid. It was a deliberate insult. The Common Alliance into which Antigonus Doson formed the Greek states in the 220s was a response, a reminder that the Greeks fell into his sphere. But by the end of the Second Illyrian War the Romans were looking to the longer term. They chose not to make diplomatic contact with the Macedonian king because, as I believe, they could already foresee at least the possibility that they might take over his role in Greece, and so that he might become the enemy. And, indeed, after the Second Illyrian War, a trickle, later a flood of Greek states began to send envoys to Rome for one reason or another. They began to defer to Rome rather than Macedon.

Two Macedonian Wars

No one can have been surprised when, after the defeat of the Spartans at Sellasia in 222, the Common Alliance was next turned against the Aetolians. By the end of the three-year Social War in 217, the Aetolians had been considerably reduced, though not as much as the allies had intended. They were still dominant in the Amphictyonic Council, for instance. But Philip V ended the war prematurely, and Polybius assures us that this was because he had decided to save his strength for tackling the Romans.[1]

The Romans were indeed vulnerable. In 218 the Carthaginian general Hannibal had crossed the Alps and invaded Italy from the north, launching the Second Punic (Carthaginian) War. By 215, after a series of devastating victories, he had the Romans on the ropes, and at this point Philip entered into a treaty with him. The treaty (whose terms the Romans knew from an intercepted document) explicitly committed Philip and his Common Alliance to help Hannibal defeat the Romans in Italy. In return, Hannibal promised that the Romans, once he had defeated them, would never make war on Macedon and would renounce their authority over their Greek friends in Illyris.[2]

As things turned out, the treaty came to little in practical terms, but the Romans could not know that, and they were bound to react. The Greeks of southern Italy were flocking to Hannibal's banner, and even the new (and last) king of Syracuse, Hieronymus, broke with Rome in favor of Hannibal, when Syracuse had been Rome's most important ally in the region for decades. Everywhere, Greeks were inclining to treat the Romans as enemies. But Hieronymus was assassinated in 214, and Syracuse endured a long siege before falling to the Romans in 212. The Roman general Marcus Claudius Marcellus allowed his troops to rape and plunder to their hearts' content, though he left the buildings essentially intact. So much booty was taken to Rome that it was said to mark the moment when the Romans

---

1 Polybius, *Histories* 5.103–105; Austin no. 73.
2 Polybius, *Histories* 7.9; Austin no. 76.

came to appreciate Greek artwork.[3] Syracuse never fully recovered, and it joined the other cities of Sicily as part of Rome's first overseas province.

In Greece, the first two Macedonian Wars were really part of a single process, because the Romans, overstretched by fighting on two fronts, withdrew from the first after only a couple of years, leaving their allies, the Aetolians, to do their fighting in Greece for them, while they concentrated on Hannibal in Italy. The Romans and Aetolians agreed to divide the spoils between them:[4]

> And if the Romans capture by force any cities of these peoples, let it be permitted, as far as the Roman people is concerned, for the Aetolian people to have these cities and their territories; and whatever the Romans take apart from the city and its territory, let the Romans have it. And if any of these cities is captured jointly by the Romans and the Aetolians, let it be permitted, as far as the Roman people is concerned, for the Aetolians to have these cities; and whatever they capture apart from the city, let it belong jointly to both parties.

But Philip defeated the Aetolians and made a separate peace with them, leaving enough unfinished business for a second war to be inevitable. Still, the Romans had remained in Greece long enough to acquire a reputation for brutality that they were never able to shake off. They may even have cultivated it on purpose: it enabled them to withdraw their troops as usual, but still maintain a degree of remote control by the threat of returning once more with overwhelming force. Terror is an economical tool of control.

The Romans were furious with the Aetolians for letting them down, and as soon as they were free—that is, once they had finally defeated Hannibal in 202—they returned to Greece. In the meantime, Philip had continued to provoke and alarm the Romans, not least by entering into an agreement with Antiochus III of Syria to take advantage of current Egyptian weakness. On the back of this agreement Philip helped himself to Egyptian (and Rhodian) possessions in the Aegean and coastal Caria, while Antiochus did the same in inland Caria and elsewhere in Anatolia. Antiochus then launched the Fifth Syrian War (202–195), in which he gained Coele Syria for the first time, and regained Phoenicia and Palestine once and for all after a hundred years of intermittent attempts. By the end of the war, Greater Egypt had been permanently reduced to Cyprus, Cyrenaica, and a handful of bases in the Aegean.

---

3 Plutarch, *Marcellus* 21.5.
4 Austin no. 77b; Bagnall/Derow no. 33; Sherk no. 2.

The Romans, meanwhile, concentrated their efforts on dividing the Greeks against themselves. In the First Macedonian War, they had created an alliance to rival Philip's Common Alliance out of their Illyrian Greek friends, the Aetolians, Eleans, Spartans, and Attalus I of Pergamum. Then, in the run-up to the second war, they gained the Rhodians, Byzantines, and Athenians as well. The Athenians were too insignificant to do more than make war with words: they abolished the two tribes Antigonis and Demetrias, obsequiously created a hundred years earlier, and brought the number of tribes up to twelve again (having created Ptolemais in 223) by decreeing a new one, Attalis, in honor of the Pergamene king. Finally, the Romans sent envoys around the mainland Greek states, offering them protection—in other words, threatening them with retaliation if they chose the wrong side.

The major coup was that they detached the Achaean Confederacy from Macedon, when it had been the backbone of the Common Alliance for twenty years. The dominant personality in the confederacy since Aratus' death in 213 was Philopoemen of Megalopolis; he had re-equipped the Achaean army in the Macedonian style, and he had for some time been an advocate of independence from Macedon. The Romans persuaded them to make the break, under their protection. Every state in Greece now had to consider carefully whereabouts, on a spectrum from subservience to hostility to Rome, it was safe to stand. Many a state was riven by factional fighting over this vital issue, on which its future existence might depend.

In 200, once Philip had firmly rejected an ultimatum from the Romans—to desist from aggression against Greek states and Egyptian possessions, or suffer the consequences—another Roman army landed in Illyris. The Romans made little progress in the first two years of the war, consistently failing to break through to threaten Macedon itself. But in 198 a dynamic new general arrived, Titus Quinctius Flamininus. He was a canny diplomat as well, and he wielded against Philip the old Greek slogan of freedom, demanding in effect that he give up the long-standing Macedonian hegemony in Greece.

The war was decided, as ancient wars often were, by a single battle, at Cynoscephalae in Thessaly in 197. It was closely fought, but ultimately a decisive defeat for Philip. But even had he won, the Romans would simply have waited a year or two and returned in greater force. In the post-war settlement, Macedonian territory and influence were reduced to what they had been 150 years earlier, before Philip II's great work. The Romans had added the mainland Greeks to the southern Italian and Sicilian Greeks whose destinies they already controlled.

The Isthmian Declaration

Despite its success, however, the Roman alliance was in trouble. Flamininus had insisted that Philip was to allow the Greeks to be free. But his allies, the Aetolians—who had allied themselves with Rome only because they saw the war as an opportunity for them to attain their long-desired goal of hegemony in Greece—forcefully pointed out to Flamininus that, logically, the freedom of the Greek states meant freedom not just from Macedon, but from Rome as well. To be consistent, the Romans should simply leave.

A short while later, therefore, at the Isthmian Games of 196, Flamininus made a dramatic announcement, to the effect that everywhere that had formerly been under Macedonian hegemony or had been members of the Common Alliance was, thanks to "the Roman Senate and Titus Quinctius, general and consul" to be "free, ungarrisoned, untaxed, and autonomous."[5] The Romans were imitating the kingly habit of disposing the world with a few words. The Greeks were ecstatic; their long subservience to Macedon was over.

In fact, it was not until a couple of years after the Isthmian Declaration that Flamininus could realistically lead his men home, and he had to suffer increasingly rancorous harassment from the Aetolians. He received permission from the Senate to extend his stay in order to deal with Nabis of Sparta. The years since the battle of Sellasia had been troubled for Sparta; an attempt by the Ephors to revive the dual kingship had failed, and a series of sole kings had not restored Sparta's fortunes; they had managed to resist constant pressure from the Achaeans to join their confederacy, but they had led the Spartans on military ventures which had resulted only in further humiliation (first by Philip V, and then by Philopoemen) and loss of manpower.

Nabis—intriguingly, though he was a Spartiate, his name is not Greek—had come to the Spartan throne in 207, as sole king in the Hellenistic style, with a grand palace (the first to be built in Greece since the Mycenaean era), a mercenary bodyguard, a tendency to patronize the arts, and a silver

---

5 Polybius, *Histories* 18.46.5; Livy, *History of Rome* 33.32.5; Plutarch, *Flamininus* 10.4.

coinage proclaiming him "king." He revived Cleomenes' reforms, and gained a loyal army by banishing the rich among his opponents and giving their land to mercenaries and helots. He completed Sparta's defensive walls, so that for the first time it resembled a normal Greek city, introduced regular taxation (apparently for the first time), built up Sparta's navy, and ruled as a sole king, with institutions such as the Council of Elders and the ephorate abolished or reduced to powerlessness.

Flamininus' excuse for attacking Sparta was that it was treating Argos as a subject state and interfering with its constitution (that is, banishing the rich, who were Roman supporters, and giving their land to the poor). Argos had seceded from the Achaean Confederacy in 198, disgusted by the decision to join the Roman alliance, and had ended up under Spartan control. The Romans and their allies put together a massive invading force of fifty thousand, the largest army ever seen in Laconia. Once Gytheum, Sparta's port, had fallen, supplies could no longer reach the city, and it did not take Flamininus much of the summer of 195 to defeat Nabis and recover Argos for the Achaean Confederacy. His Greek allies had wanted Sparta destroyed, but Flamininus, who did not want to see the entire Peloponnese fall into Achaean hands, prevailed, and Sparta was punished by having its territory partitioned, with the coastal towns (which soon formed themselves into a

Figure 24.1. Nabis of Sparta. Here we see Nabis as the virile reviver of Sparta's fortunes. The legend on the reverse reads: "King Nabis." The seated figure is Heracles, who had been a fixture on Spartan coins for decades, a symbol of Spartan endurance in these difficult times. British Museum 1896,0601.49. Photo © Olga Palagia.

confederacy of their own, the Confederacy of Free Laconians) placed under the protection of the Achaeans. Nabis was left in place as king.

Finally, in 194 the Romans left, after having been a presence on Greek soil for six years. But the withdrawal of the troops was little more than an exercise in public relations, since the Romans had forcefully demonstrated their ability to return if they felt it necessary. They did not leave the Greeks free, as promised, in any meaningful sense. Rome now had the authority to broker every important piece of business in the Mediterranean. From now on, the Greek states could do nothing major without incurring the approval or disapproval of the Senate, and the Romans kept them on their toes by occasionally intervening even in relatively minor matters. Before long, kings, let alone less dignified emissaries, supported their more delicate petitions by literally prostrating themselves on the floor of the Senate.

If at this period of their history the Romans chose a stripped-down, indirect form of imperialism in Greece, dependent only on securing deference from their subjects, that was not because they were unaware of the more direct form, which they were practicing themselves elsewhere in the Mediterranean. As early as 227, the Senate officially recognized both Sicily and Sardinia-cum-Corsica as the first provinces of an overseas empire. But the Romans hoped to be able to leave the Greeks to administer themselves within a suitably oligarchic version of their existing structures, while they themselves remained a more remote presence. As the British discovered in India, bribing local elites with political power works well as a tool of remote control.

The Reduction of Nabis and Antiochus

Despite the Roman departure in 194, everyone recognized that they might soon be back. The Aetolians were openly hostile, and no one knew how Philip would react to the reduction of Macedon to a rump state. In 193 the Aetolians made the first move: they raised with Philip, Antiochus III of Syria, and Nabis of Sparta the possibility of their forming an anti-Roman alliance.

Nabis leaped at the chance, and immediately began trying to recover from the Achaeans some of the Perioecic towns he had lost a few years earlier, as though he already had Aetolian protection. This premature action irritated the Aetolians—neither of their other prospective allies had yet committed himself—and, judging Nabis too loose a cannon, they decided to kill him and incorporate Sparta into their confederacy. They succeeded in the first task, but not the second, and in fact it was Philopoemen who rushed in and brought Sparta into the Achaean Confederacy instead. A few years later, after having brutally crushed a Spartan rebellion, Philopoemen changed Sparta into an Achaean-style city, sweeping away the last traces of the "Lycurgan" constitution. It would not be overly romantic to describe Nabis as "the last of the Spartans."

The incorporation of Sparta was the fulfillment of a long Achaean dream, but a major source of trouble for them over the ensuing decades, as many Spartans had no desire to remain in the confederacy and wanted a return to some version of their old constitution. It also made trouble with the Romans, who took on the role of protectors of Sparta. They eventually expressed their disapproval in such strongly worded terms that the council of the Achaean Confederacy was split, with Philopoemen's faction, insisting on their right to self-government, matched by one led by Callicrates, for whom Achaean survival, even at the cost of deference to Rome, was more important than Achaean pride. Philopoemen's death in 182 left Callicrates' group in control.

But how would Antiochus respond to the Aetolians' suggestion? The Romans had been wary of Antiochus ever since his anti-Egyptian pact with Philip, and there were more recent factors too: there were many Greek cities in Antiochus' Anatolia, some of whom had appealed to Rome to keep them "free"; and Attalus of Pergamum—and then, after 197, his successor, Eumenes II—had been complaining to them of the threat Antiochus posed to their territory. Pergamum and the Seleucids had been on good terms for twenty years, but Eumenes was prepared to betray that trust, because he saw the possibility of guiding Pergamum to greatness with Roman help.

The Seleucid Empire was larger than it had been since the time of Seleucus I, and Antiochus was a true Hellenistic king, not as effete as many of those who came after, especially in Egypt. The Romans knew he would expand his empire if he could. They first warned him to stay away from Greece and then, when Antiochus told them off for meddling in his business, they upped the ante by insisting that he should free the Greek cities of Anatolia as well. This extension gave them a pretext for taking the war to Anatolia, should the need arise. Both sides began preparing for war, and Antiochus provoked the Romans further by accepting into his court

Hannibal, in exile from Carthage thanks to Roman intrigues. Philip, however, prudentially sided with the Romans.

At the spring 192 assembly of the confederacy, the Aetolians drafted a formal invitation to Antiochus "to free Greece and arbitrate the dispute between the Aetolians and the Romans."[6] In October Antiochus sailed for Greece. He arrived with a surprisingly small force, expecting reinforcements from the Aetolians and others, and achieved considerable success in gaining new allies along the east coast of Greece. But the following year Thermopylae once again proved the graveyard of Greek freedom. Aetolian power was permanently curtailed, and the Romans followed up victory in Greece by defeating Antiochus more decisively the year after that in Anatolia, at Magnesia-by-Sipylus, and slaughtering the Galatian tribes that had sided with him. Hannibal fled to the Bithynian court, but Flamininus saw to his death there a few years later. In a very short space of time, the tentacles of Roman authority had spread throughout the Greek world.

The Peace of Apamea

The terms imposed on Antiochus by the Romans in the Peace of Apamea were harsh. He was to pay, over time, a crippling indemnity of fifteen thousand talents (the largest ever imposed up to then, and a major boost to the Roman economy) and withdraw from Thrace and Anatolia altogether, back to Syria, beyond the Taurus Mountains. Given how difficult it had been for Seleucid kings to retain control of Anatolia, the humiliation of losing it perhaps hurt more than the loss. After all, what remained to Antiochus was very substantial. But he died in 188 in the East, where he was trying to recover both territory and dignity. He was succeeded by his eldest son, Seleucus IV.

The Romans' settlement was radical. Seleucid Anatolia was divided between their friends at the river Maeander, with the northern half going to Pergamum and the southern half to Rhodes. These two would be Roman proxies in Anatolia. Rhodes, a Greek city-state, was elevated to hegemonial status. Pergamum's long-held ambitions were richly fulfilled, and this was the time of the city's greatest prosperity, testified to by glorious building projects such as the Great Altar of Zeus, one of the most outstanding pieces of work from the ancient world (which has been well preserved and

6 Livy, *History of Rome* 35.33.8.

restored, and is housed in a special museum in Berlin). Those cities that had supported the Roman effort were left free, subject to neither Pergamum nor Rhodes. It was very noticeable that there was no discussion of the possibility of returning Ptolemaic possessions in Anatolia. Egypt was to remain weak, as far as the Romans were concerned. They were looking for a balance of powers in the eastern Mediterranean, with no state outweighing any other.

The system the Romans had put in place for the Greeks worked satisfactorily for a while in Greece itself, where Macedon and the Achaeans were the powers chosen to balance each other, but it was a disaster from the outset in Anatolia. The Romans had hoped that they would be able to exercise remote control as in Greece, but Anatolia was just that much more distant, and both their friends and their enemies were constantly infringing what the Romans saw as the boundaries of proper behavior.

Gradually the Romans withdrew their favor from both Rhodes and Pergamum. They courted Eumenes' brother Attalus for a while, declared the Galatians autonomous after Eumenes had defeated them in battle, and allowed the Bithynians to go to war against Pergamum. They listened to the complaints of Eumenes' neighbors and even once refused him entry to Rome. Chastened, Eumenes learned his lesson and was left in place,

Figure 24.2. The Great Altar of Pergamum. This huge monumental altar was commissioned by Eumenes II. The frieze at its base, every sculpture a masterpiece, focuses on Zeus' victory over the Giants as parallel to the Attalids' ongoing victories over the barbarian Galatians. Berlin, Staatliche Museen. Photo © Vanni Archive / Art Resource, NY.

and future Pergamene kings also accepted their constraints. When Attalus III died childless in 133, he declared the city free, but asked the Romans to see that his will was done. Pergamum descended into civil war, with many of the other dynasts of Anatolia supporting one side or the other. The Romans stepped in. They finally quelled the fighting in 130, and the following year began the process of turning Pergamene territory into the province the Romans grandiosely named "Asia." In 123 Roman tax-farmers gained the right to collect the taxes of Anatolia, or as much of it as was then in Roman hands, initiating the Roman exploitation of the East. For a while, no province contributed more to the Roman treasury than Asia. Bithynia was annexed in 74, Pontus in 63, and before long the entirety of Anatolia was made up of Roman provinces.

As for the Rhodians, they had much of the territory they had gained after the war taken away from them, and they were further undermined when the Romans made the island of Delos a free port under the supervision of Athens. From now on, a certain amount of Mediterranean trade avoided Rhodes and its expensive duties in favor of Delos, which became the center of the eastern Mediterranean trade in, among other things, slaves. Piraeus remained prosperous, and Alexandria continued to grow as a commercial hub, but Rhodes settled into a slow political and economic decline, and became, like Athens, a center of culture and education.

The End of the Macedonian Monarchy

While fighting the Aetolians during the war, Philip had regained quite a bit of territory, and he hoped, given his good behavior, that he would be allowed to keep it. But, from the Roman point of view, that would make Greece imbalanced, and Macedon was once more reduced to its "ancient borders."[7] Over the next few years, however, Philip rebuilt his military strength, chiefly by annexing bits of Thrace and then recruiting his new subjects for the army. His enemies—Eumenes above all—told the Romans that he was gearing up for war, and the Romans agreed.

But Philip died in 179 before coming to blows again with the Romans. He bequeathed that task to his son, Perseus, the last king of Macedon—but not before the Romans had tried to install his brother Demetrius on

---

7 Livy, *History of Rome* 39.26.14.

the throne in his place. One of Philip's last actions had been the killing of Demetrius, accused by Perseus (with the help of probably forged documents) of treachery and conspiracy. It was the only such murderous incident in the history of the Antigonid household.

Perseus walked a fine line between keeping the peace and behaving as the ruler of a great kingdom, but the Romans had plainly decided to eliminate the Macedonian monarchy once and for all, and they bullied Perseus into war. The outcome was perhaps a foregone conclusion, but for the first couple of years the Macedonian king performed better than expected, given the lack of support he received from the southern Greeks. The long Greek resentment of Macedonian hegemony was a telling factor. Again, it was a single battle, the battle of Pydna in 168, that decided the war in Rome's favor, and finally proved the superiority of the Roman legion over the Macedonian phalanx. Following the battle, Perseus was imprisoned in Italy, and the monarchy was dissolved. Within a couple of years, Perseus had starved himself to death in prison. The first of the three greatest Hellenistic kingdoms had fallen to Rome.

From Macedon to Macedonia

Lucius Aemilius Paullus, the conqueror of Macedon, announced its future at a conference in Amphipolis, his equivalent of Flamininus' Isthmian Declaration. Macedon was to be divided into four separate statelets or "sections," and half of their revenue was to go to Rome. Senior Macedonians who had survived the slaughter at Pydna were interned in Italy. The gold and silver mines, which, along with timber, were central to the Macedonian economy, were closed—to hinder short-term economic recovery, but also just because Rome had no particular need for precious metals at that time. None of the four statelets was allowed more ships or troops than it might need to defend its borders, and they were not allowed to enter into economic or social relations with one another. Illyris, whose king, Genthius, had come in on Perseus' side, suffered the same fate and was divided into three statelets. Genthius too died in prison in Italy.

Once again, when the fighting was over and the new dispensation for Greece and Macedon was in place, the Romans withdrew their forces. As they marched back through Epirus toward Illyris and Italy, they sacked Molossis, which had sided with Perseus. Whole towns were plundered and destroyed, and no fewer than 150,000 men, women, and children were seized as slaves. At a stroke, the population of Epirus was more or less halved, and the region was reduced to poverty. Warfare in Macedon, Greece, and Anatolia was so profitable for the Romans that they were able to cancel direct taxation of their citizens for a hundred years.

Macedon remained troubled, however, and eventually the Romans realized that they had to find a more direct solution. Starting perhaps in 146, a Roman general and troops (probably no more than a single legion of 4,500 men) were sent out every year. It was the beginning of the process of turning Macedon into a permanent province of the Roman Empire. Little was done immediately beyond the installation of the army and governor, but a new calendar was introduced, indicating a new era. Although the governor's primary responsibilities were military (especially checking raids from the northern tribes), he also oversaw the collection of tribute and responded to local petitions that came now to his door, not to that of the Senate in Rome; and so, over the years, he became as much an administrator as a military man. Gradually, the Romans came to see Macedon as a whole, overarching the four sections into which it had been divided, and administrative structures evolved that enabled Macedon (as I have called it for the sake of convenience—the Greeks spoke of either "Macedon" or "Macedonia") to become, with the inclusion of Thesssaly, Macedonia, a formal province of the Roman Empire, perhaps by the end of the second century.

The Achaean War

The major event in Achaean political life of the 160s and 150s was the transportation to Italy of a thousand of their leading men, including Polybius, as part of the Roman settlement of Greece following Pydna. The Romans felt, rightly, that the Achaeans had not been truly committed to seeing Rome take power in Greece. In 151, seventeen years and very many petitions later, three hundred survivors were allowed to return. If this was a Roman attempt to appease the confederacy and keep it quiet, it was a signal failure.

The returnees must have harbored a great deal of resentment. And then, as so often in history, the passage of time had allowed a new generation to grow up, to whom prudential policies (such as those, in this case, of Callicrates) were anathema. As Pindar was the first to say, "War is sweet to those who have no experience of it."[8] In 149 Sparta once again seceded from the confederacy, and the Achaeans used force to try to bring it back in. The Roman response, still in the name of Greek freedom, was to attempt to break up the confederacy—to reduce it to its original ethnically Achaean members. At this critical juncture, Callicrates died of old age, and Critolaus was elected General on a wave of anti-Roman feeling. When he declared war on Sparta, everyone knew that this meant war with Rome. That this was no more than a magnificent gesture in the face of certain doom was confirmed when they were joined by too few Greeks.

So in 146 the Achaeans were crushed and Corinth was sacked: its inhabitants murdered or sold into slavery, its antiquities looted by the victorious Roman and Pergamene troops, its fortifications and major public buildings destroyed, and its territory made the public property of Rome and rented out to Sicyon. No atrocity on this scale had been seen in Greece since Alexander the Great had razed Thebes almost two hundred years earlier. In the past, Roman wars had ended with treaties; that time was truly over.

Greece after 146

The Achaean War would prove to be the last flicker of Greek independence for almost sixty years. Not just Achaea but Megaris and much of central Greece were put under the direct authority of the Macedonian governor, and from now on paid taxes to Rome. Any remaining democracies were replaced by oligarchies; all confederacies were broken up; all public land became the property of Rome. Polybius was the Romans' agent for overseeing these changes in the Achaean cities.

The Greeks were part of the growing Roman Empire, and their history was now Roman history. A people creates its own history if it makes its own political decisions, but few important decisions remained in Greek hands. By the middle of the first century, almost all the honorific statues being erected in Greece were of Romans. As Plutarch noted, Philopoemen was called "the last of the Greeks," because he was the last to try to exclude Rome from Greek political life.[9] There was a final flurry of Greek sentiment in the early 80s, when the Athenians joined the uprising of Mithridates

8 Pindar, F 110 Snell/Maehler.
9 Plutarch, *Aratus* 24.2.

VI of Pontus against Rome, but this was insanity, and the Athenians were savagely punished, with thousands slaughtered and massive looting. Athens consistently supported the losing side in the Roman civil wars of the 40s and 30s, some of the campaigns of which took place in Greece, but this was bad luck rather than defiance. Along with the rest of Greece, the once-great city gradually fell asleep.

By the last quarter of the first century, Greece had been turned into a province of the empire, which the Romans called Achaea, in part as an insult to the Achaean Confederacy. By the fourth century CE, and perhaps earlier, Greeks were not even calling themselves Greeks, but identified themselves as Christians and as Romans, *Rōmaioi*. After 146 BCE, Greece embarked on two thousand years of unfreedom, as part of successive empires—Roman, Byzantine, Ottoman. Freedom was finally gained in 1832 CE, when the independent nation-state of Greece came into being.

Apart from temporary woes, such as the disruption of trade, large parts of mainland Greece were permanently damaged by the years of the Roman conquest. Literary sources, whether Roman or Greek, in the second and first centuries, give an unrelievedly bleak picture, one of depopulation, barren fields, and ruined cities. Even though this evidence is contaminated by the sentimental, tourist-friendly theme of "Greece's Glorious Past," archaeology confirms that many areas saw a dramatic drop in rural occupation. Others—Athens, Thessaly (which became a major supplier of wheat to Rome), Messenia, and Delphi—gained in prosperity, but in many places subsistence farming became unattractive or unviable, farmers sold out to the owners (Greeks or Italians) of increasingly large estates, who were also their political masters, and people clustered more in towns and cities, if they did not emigrate. The gap between rich and poor, ever-widening throughout the Hellenistic period, continued to widen under Roman support for the landowning class.

Another cause of Greek impoverishment was simply the amount of plunder that was taken back to Rome and Italy during the decades of the initial Roman conquest. A victorious Roman general often gained a "triumph" on his return to Rome—a magnificent military–religious parade in celebration of his victories. Descriptions of the loot displayed in these triumphs are astonishing: tons of bullion, tons of coined money, thousands of statues and vases in bronze, marble, and precious metals, paintings by Greek masters, tens of thousands of slaves. Rome took the best from Greece. So much artwork was shipped to Italy—and, later, manufactured specifically for the

Italian market—that the Romans rather than the Greeks became the preservers of Greek culture. But even this ill wind was good for some: Greek thinkers, artists, and artisans abandoned impoverished Greece, which could hardly now support their work, and flocked to Italy to exploit this new passion for Greek cultural artifacts.

Other forms of economic exploitation were slower to develop. Even before provincialization and the creation of the empire, Italian businessmen had profited from Roman expansion, above all because it was they who supplied the armies. In peacetime, once provinces had been created, Italians became the managers and farmers of Roman public land and resources (previously the possessions of kings), and were responsible, above all, for the collection of some taxes, for the rights to which they bid in the traditional way. These *publicani*, to use the Latin word, were essential to the Roman economy, and they used that power to get away with various forms of extortion, which were likely to be overlooked as long as they were not too outrageous.

The abuses of the *publicani* and the occasional corrupt governor were largely responsible for the uprising of Mithridates VI of Pontus, whose defeat required three wars between 89 and 63. One of his first acts was the massacre of all the Romans and Italians he could find in Anatolia—men, women, and children. The smallest figure preserved by our sources for the victims is eighty thousand, which gives some idea of the numbers of Italian businessmen in the East.[10] But, by and large, the tax system worked smoothly, so that we hear about it only when things went wrong and some corruption hit the headlines. Eventually, the Greek cities were able to settle into bourgeois contentment under the *pax Romana*. Writing at the end of the first century CE, Plutarch put it well: "All war, whether against Greeks or foreigners, has been banished from our lives until it is nowhere to be seen, and we have as much freedom as our masters allow us."[11]

The End of the Hellenistic Kingdoms

Away from the Balkan peninsula, the rest of the story can be quickly told—the unhappy tale of the terminal decline of Egypt and Syria as a result of their own suicidal dynastic squabbling, meddling in each other's affairs,

10 Valerius Maximus, *Memorable Deeds and Sayings* 9.2.3 ext (first century CE).
11 Plutarch, *Moralia* 824c (*Precepts of Statecraft*).

and interference from Rome. When Seleucus IV died in 175, the obvious successor to the Syrian throne was his son Demetrius. But Demetrius was a hostage in Rome for Seleucid good behavior, and the Romans refused to release him, so Eumenes II of Pergamum, the Roman puppet, placed Antiochus IV on the throne instead, a son of Antiochus III, saying that he was restoring him to his ancestral kingdom.[12] For much of the rest of its history, the Syrian kingdom was weakened by the factional rivalry of these two branches of the royal household, or by further rivalries stemming from this first one. Palace intrigues and civil wars sapped the state.

In 168, when Antiochus IV had Alexandria under siege in the course of the Sixth Syrian War and was poised to take all of Lower Egypt, a Roman troubleshooter called Gaius Popillius Laenas, emboldened by the freshly arrived news of the Roman victory over Perseus of Macedon, demanded that Antiochus call off the invasion and come to terms. When Antiochus prevaricated, Popillius, in an astounding display of arrogance, drew a circle around him in the sand and told him not to step outside it until he had given his answer. Antiochus caved in.

It was an extraordinary moment. Rome had come a long way if it could threaten the most powerful king in the known world and deny him the right to pursue a foreign policy of his own choosing. In fact, it turned out to be a cardinal moment, marking the start of the tortuous decline of Seleucid power in the Near East. A couple of years later, Antiochus provocatively held an enormous military parade in the course of a festival of Apollo, involving fifty thousand soldiers; since this was proof that he was building up his armaments beyond the level stipulated by the Peace of Apamea, the Romans had to respond: they burned his fleet and hamstrung his elephants.

After Demetrius escaped from Rome in 162 and reclaimed his kingdom, the Romans did all they could to destabilize his reign. They supported a pretender to the throne and helped the enemies of Syria—above all, the Jewish rebellion of Judas Maccabeus, which led, by the 120s, to independence for Judaea and possession of a substantial territory, a huge extension of the hinterland of Jerusalem. The Jews were not alone; many other statelets and cities within the Seleucid Empire gained their independence by war or diplomacy, and the Parthians continued to whittle away at the eastern

12 Austin no. 208; Burstein no. 38.

satrapies, until in about 140 they even took Babylonia, and the Seleucids controlled only northern Syria and eastern Cilicia. Antiochus VII, who came to the throne in 139, made a huge effort to recover the lost territories, and did indeed briefly recover Mesopotamia, Babylonia, and Media, but his success made him careless, and he lost his life in 129. No subsequent king dared to take on the Parthians.

In 95 Lucius Cornelius Sulla, the future dictator of Rome, came east to make a treaty with the Parthians, stipulating the Euphrates as the frontier between them, even though neither of them was currently exercising direct rule there. This was very ominous: the Near East was being disposed with no reference to the Seleucids. Meanwhile, the Seleucids were spiraling out of control, with simultaneous rulers claiming legitimacy from their thrones in Antioch, Cilicia, or Damascus, and endless civil wars to support their claims, while further cities within the kingdom seized the opportunity for independence.

It was not to be the Romans or the Parthians, however, who brought the Seleucid kingdom to an end, but a new power, Tigranes II of Armenia. After taking over the western provinces of the Parthians, in 83 he occupied Syria as well. A final Seleucid, Antiochus XIII, based in Cilicia, lacked the strength to dislodge him. When Tigranes was brought to heel by the Romans, almost all former Seleucid territory was in either Roman or Parthian hands. In 64, the Roman general Gnaeus Pompeius (Pompey the Great) simply ordered Antiochus into retirement, and Syria was turned into a province of the Roman Empire, along with Cilicia.

Egypt remained troubled even after the recovery of the Thebaid in 186. The deadly factional fighting of the court led to widespread corruption, several serious rebellions, riots in Alexandria, lynchings, uprisings in the countryside, the breakdown of orderly government, and periods of civil war. Internal affairs occupied so much energy that there was little in the way of foreign policy, and Egypt's last overseas possessions were gradually lost. A series of general amnesties did little to heal the rifts, no reforms really worked, and the country's finances suffered badly. Sometimes Egypt, Cyprus, and Cyrenaica were ruled by different members of the royal family.

Increasingly, kings and queens turned to Rome for help in their vicious squabbles, and rulers were recognized in Egypt only if they had disbursed enough money among the senators to be recognized in Rome. For a long time, the Romans refused to help them militarily, but senators made frequent visits, to observe and advise. The turn to Rome was so determined that in 154 Ptolemy VIII legally bequeathed the kingdom to Rome if he died without heirs—warning his brother that he would gain nothing by murdering him. In fact, he lived on and had many children—but he was a forerunner, and only twenty years later, as already mentioned, Attalus III left Pergamum to Rome.

In 96 the ruler of Cyrenaica, Ptolemy Apion, left his kingdom to Rome (perhaps to make sure a rival did not get it, or perhaps because he knew the Romans would take it sooner or later anyway), and in the mid-70s it was turned into a province of the empire. In 87 the Romans finally received Egypt as a bequest from Ptolemy X, but they did nothing for a while,

Figure 24.3. Cleopatra. A Roman bust of Cleopatra VII, wearing a diadem to signify her royalty. This likeness suggests she was as beautiful and alluring as legend claims, but she was known also for her intellectual accomplishments, which included the writing of a medical treatise. Berlin, Staatliche Museen. Photo © Sailko.

because a governor of Egypt would have kingly resources at his disposal, and might pose a threat to the Republic back home. Subsequent Egyptian rulers fostered this concern, in a final attempt to cling on to some degree of independence. But the Romans became much more of a presence in Egypt, and the possibility of annexing the country was hotly debated in the Senate. One result was that Cyprus was annexed in 58; Ptolemy XII was too frightened to protest.

The beginning of the end came when Cleopatra VII turned to Julius Caesar in the early 40s for help against her brother, Ptolemy XIII. A hard-fought civil war made Cleopatra sole ruler, under the protection of Caesar, who had also become her lover. But Caesar was murdered in 44 (at a time when Cleopatra was in Rome with him), and in 42, after defeating Caesar's assassins, Mark Antony (Marcus Antonius) was given the job of organizing the East. Canny Cleopatra soon won him over to her side and her bed, and nurtured his ambitions in order to protect and expand her kingdom. By the end of the 30s, Antony had made Alexandria the capital of his prospective eastern empire, with Cleopatra as his queen, and their children (and Caesarion, Cleopatra's son by Julius Caesar) as their dynastic heirs.

After their defeat in 31 at the battle of Actium (on the west coast of Greece), in the final civil war of the Roman Republic, Antony and Cleopatra returned to Egypt and prepared their defenses. Gaius Julius Caesar Octavianus—soon to be Rome's first emperor, Augustus—entered Alexandria on August 3, 30, after Antony's troops had defected. Antony had already killed himself, and Cleopatra followed him as soon as she could. Three centuries of Greco-Macedonian monarchy came to an end as the last of the Hellenistic kingdoms fell to Rome. One of the stories of the last days of Alexander the Great had him promising that, after his death, his empire would fall "to the strongest."[13] It turned out that only Rome had sufficient strength.

13 Arrian, *Anabasis* 7.26.3; Diodorus of Sicily, *Library of History* 17.117.4.

25

A Feat of Imagination

Greek political culture has been the main subject of this book, and the quality for which the Greeks have most commonly been admired is freedom. This is due partly to the emphasis they themselves placed on political freedom, and partly to the fact that the time of the rediscovery of Greece—the late eighteenth and early nineteenth centuries, when the country first began to receive regular visits from northern Europeans—was also the time when the Greeks were beginning their struggle for independence from the Ottoman Empire. Inevitably, the alleged freedom of the ancient Greeks was contrasted with the submission and submissiveness of contemporary Greeks. This led, in the Victorian era and the early twentieth century, to quite a bit of silly idealization of the ancient Greeks as the originators of all that is good and noble, but there was a kernel of truth: the Greeks clearly did value their freedom.

But freedom, for states just as much as for individuals, is bound to bring them into conflict with others, who seek equally to protect and perpetuate their own integrities. Despite the fact that Greek states were not just individual entities, but were parts of systems (ethnic, religious, commercial), exclusivity and particularism were hardwired into every Greek state. Plato agreed: "Every polis," he said, "is inevitably engaged in undeclared warfare with every other polis."[1] Here is the root of the one–many problem: Greeks were always in competition against other Greeks. This is why they never achieved political unification on their own, and rarely even sought it or conceived of it as a goal. The Achaeans actively wanted and pursued the unification of the Peloponnese, but it is not clear that they ever wanted to unify all Greeks into a federal state, or conceived of that as a possibility.

1 Plato, *Laws* 626a.

I spoke earlier in the book of different tiers of identity, such that a man was at the same time Greek, Dorian, and from Argos, let's say. At any given moment, external events, moral persuasion (by a speech, or a tract, or a politically engaged theatrical production), or his own internal motivations might prompt him to accept one tier over the others. Every moment had the potential for a switch from one tier to another. The events of history happen when enough people share the same framework in a sufficiently coherent form, and choose the same set of loyalties. Then they act as Greeks, or as Dorians, or as Argives, or as a political faction. Coherent and long-term identification was needed with the top tier, with Greekness, before full unification was possible or even conceivable.

The Greeks acknowledged their cultural unity, but there were many impediments to political unity. A number of states might unite in a military alliance, as in the face of the Persian or Macedonian threat, but they soon fell to fighting one another again. Aristophanes, in his *Lysistrata* (produced in 411) spoke bitterly of men who frequented the pan-Hellenic sites "as though they were kinsmen," and yet fought wars against other Greeks.[2] Plutarch claims that, at Pericles' instigation, the Athenians wanted to try to turn the Delian League into a pan-Hellenic alliance, but this was a fantasy, a backward projection from Plutarch's own time to the Classical period.[3] There were always switch-points, but for much of their history the Greeks invariably chose the smaller rather than the larger tier of identity—the particular state rather than the Greek nation.

The competitive values of the heroes in the Homeric poems—their ethos being "to strive always to be the best, superior to others"[4]—outlasted their Archaic origins by centuries. Elite individuals were driven by the same motivation throughout Greek history, making it unsurprising that the ethos resurfaced at the time of the Hellenistic kings. States too saw themselves as occupying rungs in an international hierarchy in relation to other states; the Peloponnesian War was all about whether Sparta or Athens would be "the best, superior to others." Competition was the default position for both individuals and states. Cooperation was far harder to attain, and usually needed divine sanction: "The gods love those who restrain themselves," says Athena in Sophocles' *Ajax*.[5]

---

2 Aristophanes, *Lysistrata* 1128–1134, translated in the Preface.
3 Plutarch, *Pericles* 17.
4 Homer, *Iliad* 6.208, 11.783.
5 Sophocles, *Ajax* 132–133.

By the fourth and third centuries, the position had changed, as an increasing number of men saw the advantages of cooperation. Gorgias and Lysias, two of the most famous speakers of their day, called for Greek unity in speeches delivered at the Olympic festival (respectively in 408 and 388), where they found pan-Hellenic audiences. In the words of Gorgias: "Trophies erected over fallen barbarians call for hymns of praise, while those erected over fallen fellow Greeks call for lamentation."[6] Demosthenes and Isocrates noted the mutual hostility that prevented the Greeks from uniting; Isocrates wanted the Greeks to recognize their cultural unity as a springboard to united political action; Aristotle thought the Greeks could have ruled the world if they united as a single state.[7]

As a result, the Greeks found ways of forming more stable and longer-lasting unions. The precedents were the less limited leagues of the fifth century—the Peloponnesian League, the Hellenic League against Persia, and the Delian League—none of which was limited in time, and each of which had the potential to incorporate ever more members. The main manifestation of this tendency toward political unification in the Hellenistic period was the phenomenon of confederation, but there were also lesser political gestures such as sharing citizenship with other states and finding peaceful means to resolve conflicts. Otherwise, unity was generally thrust on the mainland Greeks, always in more or less incomplete forms, by outsiders—by those who wanted to rule or control them and found it hard to do so as long as the bickering and fighting endemic to their usual political institutions continued. It was above all the Macedonians who began to bundle the people together in leagues and treat them as "the Greeks," and this tendency was inherited by the Romans, who, by establishing Greece as a province of the empire, finally recognized the Greeks as a distinct people, bringing to its conclusion the long trend toward increasing political unification.

From Cultural to Political Unity

To the Persians, Macedonians, and Romans, the Greeks had a recognizable, distinct ethnic identity, and in the treaties they made and leagues they

---

6 Gorgias F 5b Diels/Kranz; Lysias 33 (*Olympic Speech*).
7 Demosthenes 14.3 (*On the Symmories*); Isocrates 4.15 and 50 (*Panegyricus*); Aristotle, *Politics* 1327b32–33. See also Herodotus, *Histories* 8.3, written in the 420s.

formed, they imposed this view on the Greeks. Even so, Greek political unification would never have happened if the potential had not been there. As we have seen, as soon as the Greeks emerged in the Mediterranean, they became aware of themselves as cultural cousins. In the words of Herodotus, written in the 420s (a passage we have already glanced at), Greekness (*to Hellēnikon*, "the Greek thing") consisted of shared culture, language, and lineage.[8] The Greeks were always aware of a shared substrate underlying their regional and other differences, and the idea of a pan-Hellenic community was supported by cult at sites such as Delphi and Olympia, by shared values, by warfare against barbarians, and by the pan-Greek past constructed by poems such as Homer's *Iliad* and the genealogies of *The Catalog of Women*. This sense of cultural unity, of an imagined community, only increased in the Hellenistic period as a result of the Greek diaspora and expatriate clinging to tradition, and there was a genuine sense that Greeks all around the world shared values, ideas, and institutions, and formed a worldwide community. "The Greek world" was an abstract cultural construct, much like Christendom in the Middle Ages.

The Greeks, then, had long imagined themselves as forming a pan-Hellenic community by virtue of their shared culture, and, like any powerful act of imagination, the idea exerted pressure and edged closer to realization. It was not a smooth progression: pan-Hellenism was a salient issue in some places (such as Athens) more than in others, and at some times (the fifth and fourth centuries) more than others. One of the triggers, or reminders, was the flourishing of federal states and leagues, because their constitutions always allowed for the political independence of their members, giving the Greeks a blueprint for the idea of a federal state of a nonhegemonial kind, voluntarily entered into. Another was sustained contact with quasi-Greeks such as Macedonians, which entailed the adoption of a larger idea of what it was to be Greek. But responsibility lay chiefly with Alexander the Great, who gave an enormous boost to the idea of Greek unity by undertaking an expressly pan-Hellenic war against the barbarian, a continuation of the Trojan War, and whose vast empire opened up new horizons that made it possible for Greeks to transcend the parochialism of the city-state culture of Old Greece.

After Alexander, then, the Greeks came to give their kinship political weight. We can measure the trend by means of kinship diplomacy, the practice of appealing to another state for help on the basis of kinship. There had been cases of this kind of diplomacy in the Classical period. When, for

8   Herodotus, *Histories* 8.144.2.

instance, the Greeks of the Balkan peninsula appealed for help before the Persian Wars to the Greeks in the Ionian Islands, Sicily, and southern Italy, they did so on the grounds of kinship, but generally speaking awareness of kinship was limited to one's own immediate neighbors, to fellow Ionians (or Dorians, or Aeolians), or to colonies in relation to their mother cities. In the Hellenistic period, however, kinship diplomacy was a very common tactic; dozens of inscriptions survive in which cities base a claim of kinship on a shared genealogy in the mythical past.

The frequency of the practice was matched by its scale. Late in the third century, the city of Magnesia-on-the-Maeander sent ambassadors inviting states all over the Greek world to participate in a festival and to recognize (among other things) their mutual kinship. A great many cities responded; although we can read now the names of only sixty, there was room on the original inscription for two hundred.[9] Or again, when the little town of Cytenium in Doris, the homeland of the Dorians, needed financial assistance to repair earthquake damage, it did not just turn to Dorian states, which would have been easy, but constructed complex genealogies and journeyings of both gods and heroes to demonstrate its kinship not just with the city of Xanthus in Lycia (where the surviving inscription comes from), but even with the Seleucids and Ptolemies, whose courts the Cytenian envoys were headed for when they stopped in Xanthus. The mythology they came up with could have linked them to almost any other state in the Greek world.[10] So the external pressure for unification exerted by the Macedonians and Romans met a growing internal recognition of the political implications of Greek cultural unity.

The Greek Nation

Over time, then, more people than just a few intellectuals began to take seriously the idea that the Greeks were one in blood as well as in culture, and to take steps to consolidate the Greek world on that basis. The Roman creation of the provinces of Achaea and Macedonia, and the Greek provinces of Anatolia, was the culmination of that trend. In the first and second centuries CE, super-confederacies were formed out of the confederacies of both Greece and Anatolia. These could not be political unions, since politically the Greek confederacies were members of the Roman provinces,

9 Burstein no. 30; Rigsby no. 66.
10 *SEG* 38 1476.

so they were given a religious purpose: they were founded on the worship of the emperor—Caligula for the first-century league, and Hadrian for the second-century one. The delegates called themselves "Panhellenes" and met, in the second century, in a temple called the Panhellenion, built in Hadrianopolis, the new suburb of Athens built by Hadrian. Neither of these leagues lasted more than a few decades, but they show that the Greeks' awareness of themselves as a potential nation survived the imposition of the Roman provinces. In our own day, we know all too well how borders imposed by superpowers can cut across groupings that natives find more salient.

But there was always one thing missing. The Greeks could stress their shared language, their kinship, their similar forms of worship, of dress, of warfare. Despite the fact that so much of their history involved Greeks fighting against one another, they could even create a sense of a shared history, by stressing pan-Hellenic moments such as the Trojan War, the Persian Wars, and the long resistance to Macedon. But they could never point to a common territory, a Greek homeland, and in most definitions of ethnicity a shared territory, or at least a claimed territory, is a central aspect. The French would not be the French if they did not occupy France or at least claim some ancestral connection to France. The Greeks shared the sea, impossible to encompass and possess, but they had no land.

In the fourth century, however, some politicians began to speak of Greece as "the common fatherland" of the Greeks. Isocrates, for instance, projected back onto earlier Greeks the idea that "while they regarded their native cities as their several places of abode, yet they considered Greece to be their common fatherland." In other words, he supposed that earlier Greeks were capable of transcending the particularist tier of identification with one's birthplace and of recognizing a higher level of shared Greekness. This confirms what I have been saying—that in the fourth and third centuries there was a far stronger sense than before of political unification and the necessity of it—but the idea of a shared Greek homeland was a fantasy, no more than a rhetorical appeal for unity.[11] Nevertheless, it was true that the road to political unification would never reach an end until there was a Greek homeland; until then, it would always be partial, and cultural more

---

11 Isocrates 4.81 (*Panegyricus*); Diodorus of Sicily, *Library of History* 18.10.3, paraphrasing a fourth-century decree.

than political. For long centuries, as members of the eastern Roman Empire and then of the Ottoman Empire, the Greeks remembered that they were one and held in their imaginations a sense of community. Finally, in 1832, as a result of the War of Independence, Greece became a proper nation-state, with its own territory, government, history, religion, language, and culture.

Glossary

Academy the school established in Athens in the fourth century by Plato, which met originally in the gymnasium attached to the shrine of the Attic hero Academus, just outside the city walls to the northwest.

Achaemenid words ending in "-id" (Antigonid, Seleucid, Eupatrid, Alcmaeonid, etc.) mean "descendants of" or "from the family of." The rulers of the Persian Empire claimed to be descended from Achaemenes (Haxamaniš), the perhaps legendary founder of their house.

Acropolis the high point of a city, used especially for refuge, as a religious center, and as a commanding place to house a garrison and control the city.

Agiad, Eurypontid the two royal houses of Sparta.

Agōgē the "raising," the name for the Spartan educational system; see pp. 108–10.

Agora the civic center, marketplace, and administrative heart of an ancient Greek town.

Amphictyony a council formed of *amphiktuones*, "neighboring states," with the job of administering an important international shrine, such as that of Apollo on the island of Delos, or that of Apollo at Delphi.

Anatolia the same as Asia Minor, i.e. most of modern Turkey.

Archon literally "ruler" or "leader." The title was used for senior officials of many states. In Archaic and Classical Athens, nine Archons were chosen each year, and after their year of office they joined the Areopagus Council. The "Eponymous Archon" gave his name to the year for dating purposes.

Areopagus a hill in Athens (the "rock of Ares") a little to the northwest of the Acropolis, where meetings were held of the council of former Archons, known therefore as the Areopagus Council. The council's powers were curtailed in the 460s, and it was reduced to little more than an intentional homicide court.

Assembly the assembly of citizens constituted the chief legislative organ of democratic Athens and other democracies, but had lesser powers under oligarchies and monarchies.

Asylia the word, meaning "inviolability," designated a place where seizure of goods or persons was forbidden (hence our "asylum"). Originally applied to individuals or temples, in the Hellenistic period whole cities were granted *asylia*, as a form of general protection or in order to protect visitors to particular festivals with a truce that would allow them to travel in safety.

Attica the territory and farmland of the ancient city of Athens.

Autonomy self-government and independence.

Barbarian the word used by Greeks for non-Greeks (in Greek, *barbaros*). It was probably onomatopoeic, in the sense that they thought that foreign languages sounded like "*bar-bar-bar.*"

Chorus a group of men, women, or children singing hymns and dancing in a religious festival or show.

Cleruchy an overseas settlement on land confiscated by the Athenians, where the emigrant cleruchs ("allotment-owners") lost neither the privileges nor the obligations of Athenian citizenship. Cleruchies often served as garrisons for restive states in the Athenian alliance.

Confederacy *see Koinon.*

Consul two consuls were elected in Republican Rome every year as its leaders, with both military and domestic political responsibilities and powers, which were constrained only by the Senate (q.v.) and tribunes of the plebs.

Delian League the grand naval alliance formed after the Persian Wars by the Athenians out of Aegean, eastern Mediterranean, and Black Sea states, in order to continue the fight against the Persians and keep the newly liberated Greek states free.

Deme a parish or ward in Attica (and elsewhere). After Cleisthenes' reforms in Athens, on attaining his majority at age 18, man had to be registered with his ancestral deme to count as a citizen.

*Eph**ē**beia* a formal program of acculturation and military training, instituted in Athens in the fourth century and widely imitated by other states.

Ephor in Sparta, five Ephors ("overseers") were chosen each year, with a range of powers; see pp. 114–15.

Ethnos, **plural** *ethn**ē*** a "people," or a group of villages and towns that have agreed to self-identify as kin. *See also Koinon.*

Eupatridae "the descendants of good fathers," literally—the group of aristocratic families of Athens who formed the administration in the early Archaic period.

Eurypontid *see Agiad*

Faction a group of people with common political views, a pressure group. There were no political parties in ancient Greece. Political factions formed around particular issues and leaders, and were generally referred to as "So-and-so and his friends." They lasted as long as the shared interests endured, whereas a political party can last for generations and is concerned with the widest possible range of political issues. Groups might on occasion become as large as parties by forming alliances, but these were temporary.

Frieze the central section of the entablature of a building (above the columns), often decorated with relief sculptures on grand temples and other buildings.

Hegemony literally "leadership," but used especially where one state subordinates its allies to itself, by political and economic means, and by the real or implied threat of military intervention, while allowing them formally to retain their autonomy (q.v.). Hence, for instance, the Delian League was a "hegemonial alliance."

Heliaea the Athenian people meeting in a judicial capacity. The Heliaea was refashioned in the 460s as a number of separate jury courts, known as the *Dikastēria*, the People's Courts.

Helots agricultural serfs in Laconia and Messenia, owned by the Spartan state, but used to farm individual Spartiates' allotments; see pp. 106–8.

Heraion a sanctuary with a temple dedicated to the goddess Hera.

Hero more than human, but less than gods, heroes were people who during their lifetime had displayed such power that after their deaths they received worship, in order to harness or turn aside that power.

Hoplite a heavy-armed Greek foot soldier, typically armed with a thrusting spear and a short sword, and protected by various pieces of armor and, above all, a large shield; see pp. 61–4, 157–60. Hoplites fought typically in phalanxes (q.v.).

Koinon*, plural *koina a federal state, or confederacy. An *ethnos* (q.v.) as a political entity; see pp. 39–41.

Kouros/Korē a *kouros* is a young male, a *korē* an unmarried girl, a "maiden." The names are commonly used for a kind of monumental statue that was made in the Archaic period, but Korē, the Maiden, is also a common way of referring to Persephone, Demeter's daughter and the wife of Hades.

League in this book I have reserved "league" for alliances such as the Athenian Delian League and the Peloponnesian League, and "confederacy" for *koina* (q.v.).

Liturgies public services undertaken by the rich in Athens and elsewhere; see pp. 212–13.

Medimnos a *medimnos* was a dry measure equivalent (in Athens) to about 50 liters (11 gallons); 20 *medimnoi* of barley was enough to feed a family of four for a year.

Medize to "medize" was to collaborate with the Persians, who were not distinguished by the Greeks from Medes.

Meltemi violent northerly winds that scour the Aegean intermittently from late May to September; called the "etesian" or "periodic" winds by the Greeks because of their regularity.

Metic in Athens and elsewhere, a resident alien of free status. From the Greek *metoikos*, "immigrant."

Near East roughly the same as what we usually call the Middle East today, from Iran to Turkey to Egypt.

Obol, drachma, mina, talent the basic units of Greek money; 1 silver talent = 60 minas = 6,000 drachmas = 36,000 obols.

Oligarchy "government by the few," who were necessarily rich; opposed to "democracy," the term used for government by all the people (all male citizens), or at least a good proportion of them.

Ostracism The voting process in fifth-century Athens by which prominent men could be sent into exile for purely political reasons; see pp. 97–8. There was a similar process in democratic Syracuse, called *petalismos*.

Ostrakon a shard or fragment of pottery, used for many purposes (as we today use scraps of paper), including the casting of votes for an ostracism.

Pan-Hellenism the idea that all Greeks everywhere were related, and shared certain features that distinguished them from (and made them better than) non-Greeks. Politically, it was the idea that Greeks should put aside their squabbles and unite against a common foreign enemy.

Panoply a full suit of armor.

Papyrus a kind of wetland sedge grown especially in Egypt, the pith of which was used to make paper (hence the term).

Pediment a kind of gable, usually triangular in shape, that was situated above the columns at either end of a Greek temple, and was often adorned with relief sculptures.

Peisistratid descended from Peisistratus, i.e. the regime of his two sons, Hippias and Hipparchus. The term is also used more loosely to refer to the combined tyranny of both Peisistratus and his sons.

Penteconter a ship used for war or commerce and rowed by fifty men, often in two banks of oars on either side. Penteconters were superseded for military purposes by triremes toward the end of the sixth century.

Perioeci literally "those who dwell around us," the free inhabitants of Laconia and Messenia under Spartan rule, who formed the commercial class of traders, craftsmen, artisans, etc.

Phalanx a rectangular formation, usually with a much greater front than depth, of closely packed infantry troops. The word originally meant "log," as though a phalanx rolled inexorably along.

Pharaoh the title used for the kings of ancient Egypt.

Polemarch literally, "war leader." A senior position in many Greek states; in Athens, one of the nine Archons. Soon after the establishment of the Board of Generals in Classical Athens, the Polemarch was reduced to purely judiciary functions.

Polis a Greek city or city-state, comprising an urban center and its surrounding farmland; see especially pp. 37–8.

Presocratics the name used for the philosophers and proto-scientists whose work preceded Socrates in spirit, even if not always in time, since the last of the Presocratics were his contemporaries.

Province in Roman terms, a task or theater of military operations assigned by the Senate to a consul or praetor; later, an administrative unit of the empire.

Prytany a 35- or 36-day stretch of the year when, in Athens, the fifty councilors from one of the ten Athenian tribes were in charge of daily administrative functions; hence they were called the *prytaneis*, "the presidents."

Republic a nonmonarchical or nontheocratic state.

Satrap a governor of a province (a satrapy) of the Achaemenid Empire, and afterwards of the Seleucid Empire. The word is derived from the Old Persian *khsha-thrapavan*, "Protector of the Kingdom."

Senate despite being a deliberative body, the Senate was effectively the ruling council of Republican Rome. A debate in the Senate led to a resolution, a *senatus consultum*, which was then presented to the appropriate popular assembly (of which there were several in Rome) for ratification or passage into law.

Sophist an educator or intellectual. The word is no more than a noun formed from the Greek word for "clever," and just as educators and intellectuals come in all guises, so the sophists taught different subjects and used different methods. Except in the reaction they met from conservatives and rivals, they were far from being a unified school or movement.

Sortition the use of a random lottery to select people for official positions, in Athens and other democracies, for jobs where it was felt that no particular expertise was required, just general goodwill toward the democracy.

Spartiate a full Spartan citizen, a member of the Spartan landowning elite.

Stoa a long, covered, and often splendid portico or colonnade for shade, shelter, and shopping, typical of Greek cities. The philosophical school Stoicism was so called because the first Stoics met in the Painted Stoa in Athens.

Symposium a highly ritualized private drinking party for the elite; see pp. 48–52.

Tax-farming the practice of auctioning off the right to collect this or that tax; the farmer paid up front the total the state expected from the tax, and it was then his job to collect it from those who owed it. He expected to make a profit. The system released the administration from the bother of collecting taxes itself.

Thesmothete nine Archons were appointed annually in Classical Athens, with the six *thesmothetai* ("regulators") being the most junior. Their earliest functions are unknown, but later it was their job to receive the charges for a wide range of suits and make arrangements for the cases to come to court. After the revision of the laws at the end of the fifth century, they were also given the job of regularly reviewing the laws and reporting problems to the Assembly.

Thete a wage laborer. The word was taken over by Solon for the members of the lowest of the census classes he established in Athens (p. 80). Thetes made up the majority of the Athenian population and supplied most of the oarsmen for the fleet.

Tribe for the purposes of civic and military administration, citizens were divided into tribes—ten at first in democratic Athens, but different numbers at other times and in other places.

Trierarch nominally, the "captain of a trireme," but actually the man who supplied the money to maintain the ship, not the expertise to sail it.

Trireme from the end of the sixth century, the most common type of Greek warship. Light and maneuverable, and propelled by three banks of oarsmen on either side, it was used largely as a guided missile to ram and disable enemy ships.

Specifications varied somewhat from state to state; in this book, the Athenian trireme, about which we know most, has been taken as standard.

Tyrant an unconstitutional monarch, common in the Greek cities in the Archaic period, in the Sicilian cities throughout their history, and all over the Greek world as imposed especially by Persian and Macedonian rulers. A tyrant was not necessarily a despot.

Urbanization movement of people from the countryside into cities, an essential component of the formation of cities. Ruralization is the opposite, but at times of considerable population increase, both processes occur in tandem.

Xenia "the condition of being a host or a guest." The word is chiefly used of a kind of international friendship between members of the wealth and political elite—a ritualized friendship initiated and maintained by the exchange of valuable gifts.

Recommended Reading

The bibliography for the hundreds of years of history covered in this book is vast; the history and culture of ancient Greece have been extensively and intensively worked on for over two hundred years. Since the primary readership of this book will not consist of hard-core scholars (who, in any case, know where to go for reading material), I have limited this bibliography to what I consider to be the next level of accessible books to read after this one. There are, of course, further levels beyond that, and many of the books I have listed contain good bibliographies to guide the curious reader into the byways of scholarship.

TRANSLATIONS

To understand ancient Greek history, it is essential to read ancient Greek literature—not just the historians, but other genres as well. There is no substitute for immersing oneself in Greek ways of thinking. Many translations are now available of Greek works, far too many to list. A lot of the good ones are published in one of two famous series: Oxford World's Classics and Penguin Classics.

REFERENCE WORKS

The Oxford Classical Dictionary, now in its fourth edition (2012), and its fifth edition online (http://classics.oxfordre.com/), is a treasury of information on all aspects of the ancient world; it is rivaled by *The Cambridge Dictionary of Classical Civilization* (2008). Either of these is as indispensable as the best atlas, *The Barrington Atlas of the Greek and Roman World*, edited by R. Talbert (Princeton University Press, 2000). There are also a great many useful maps, battle plans, and town plans in R. Talbert (ed.), *Atlas of Classical History* (Croom Helm, 1985).

WEBSITES

There is an increasing number of excellent open-access websites relevant to the study of ancient history. I would single out the Athenian Agora Excavations, Attic Inscriptions Online, the Beazley Archive, Bryn Mawr Classical Review, the Centre for the Study of Ancient Documents, the Packard Humanities Institute, the Perseus Project, and the Stoa Consortium.

GENERAL BOOKS

A very attractive thematic/cultural rather than chronological/historical book on ancient Greece, and therefore a good complement to the one you hold in your hands, is P. Cartledge (ed.), *The Cambridge Illustrated History of Ancient Greece* (rev. ed., Cambridge University Press, 2002). The relevant volumes of the *Cambridge Ancient History* series (2nd ed., volumes III.3 to VIII) add up to a very substantial and authoritative account of Greek history. Sixty-eight short but informative essays on all aspects of ancient Greece are crammed into G. Boys-Stones, B. Graziosi, and P. Vasunia (eds.), *The Oxford Handbook of Hellenic Studies* (Oxford University Press, 2009). A. Erskine (ed.), *A Companion to Ancient History* (Wiley-Blackwell, 2009), is another very valuable collection, containing hardly fewer essays.

There is a thorough and excellent general history of Anatolia: C. Marek (with P. Frei), *In the Land of a Thousand Gods: A History of Asia Minor in the Ancient World* (Princeton University Press, 2016; trans. by S. Rendall; 2nd ed., first German pub. 2010).

INTRODUCTION I

Environmental Background

The essential book on ancient Greek geology, topography, climate, demography, diet, etc., is R. Sallares, *The Ecology of the Ancient Greek World* (Cornell University Press, 1991), but L. Thommen, *An Environmental History of Ancient Greece and Rome* (2nd ed., Cambridge University Press, 2012), is shorter. All aspects of ancient Greek life relevant to the economy are covered, with unexpected readability, in W. Scheidel, I. Morris, and R. Saller (eds.), *The Cambridge Economic History of the Greco-Roman World* (Cambridge University Press, 2007). The Mediterranean environment is enthusiastically and exhaustively examined by P. Horden and N. Purcell, *The Corrupting Sea: A Study of Mediterranean History* (Blackwell, 2000). P. Garnsey, *Food and Society in Classical Antiquity* (Cambridge University Press, 1999), is fascinating on food and food supply.

The nature of ancient Greek farming is controversial. Books mentioned in the previous paragraph will be relevant, but also dedicated studies such as P. Halstead, *Two Oxen Ahead: Pre-Mechanized Farming in the Mediterranean* (Wiley-Blackwell, 2014); V. Hanson, *The Other Greeks: The Family Farm and the Agrarian Roots of Western Civilization* (2nd ed., University of California Press, 1999); and S. Isager and J. Skydsgaard, *Ancient Greek Agriculture: An Introduction* (Routledge, 1992). A brilliant book on the inseparability of Greek cities and their farmland is R. Osborne, *Classical Landscape with Figures: The Ancient Greek City and Its Countryside* (George Philip, 1987).

INTRODUCTION II

Historical Background

The best starting-point for the prehistorical period is C. Thomas and C. Conant, *Citadel to City-State: The Transformation of Greece, 1200–700 BC* (Indiana University

Press, 1999). Also very useful is O. Dickinson, *The Aegean from Bronze Age to Iron Age: Continuity and Change between the Twelfth and Eighth Centuries BC* (Routledge, 2006). C. Shelmerdine (ed.), *The Cambridge Companion to the Aegean Bronze Age* (Cambridge University Press, 2008), gives a bit more detail. An outstanding introduction to the so-called Dark Age in particular is C. Thomas, *Myth Becomes History: Pre-Classical Greece* (Regina Books, 1993).

The Archaic Period

The most accessible introduction is O. Murray, *Early Greece* (2nd ed., Harvard University Press, 1993). There are two good, thorough narrative histories, very different from each other: J. Hall, *A History of the Archaic Greek World, ca. 1200–479 BCE* (2nd ed., Wiley-Blackwell, 2013), and R. Osborne, *Greece in the Making, 1200–479 BC* (2nd ed., Routledge, 2009). These should be supplemented by H. Shapiro (ed.), *The Cambridge Companion to Archaic Greece* (Cambridge University Press, 2007), and especially by K. Raaflaub and H. van Wees (eds.), *A Companion to Archaic Greece* (Wiley-Blackwell, 2009). The material culture of Archaic Greece is well covered by J. Whitley, *The Archaeology of Ancient Greece* (Cambridge University Press, 2001). All of these books contain material relevant to Chapters 1 to 9, if not farther.

CHAPTER I

The Emergence of the Greeks

The best introduction to the dynamic Early Archaic period remains A. Snodgrass, *Archaic Greece: The Age of Experiment* (University of California Press, 1980). The emigrations of the period are clearly written up by J. Boardman, *The Greeks Overseas: Their Early Colonies and Trade* (4th ed., Thames and Hudson, 1999), and R. Garland, *Wandering Greeks: The Ancient Greek Diaspora from the Age of Homer to the Death of Alexander the Great* (Princeton University Press, 2014). How did the local populations react to the arrival of the Greeks? T. Hodos, *Local Responses to Colonization in the Iron Age Mediterranean* (Routledge, 2006), has some answers. The effects on Greek ethnicity are discussed by J. Hall, *Hellenicity: Between Ethnicity and Culture* (University of Chicago Press, 2002), and by K. Vlassopoulos, *Greeks and Barbarians* (Cambridge University Press, 2013).

The main topic of this chapter is state formation. N. Yoffee, *Myths of the Archaic State: Evolution of the Earliest Cities, States, and Civilizations* (Cambridge University Press, 2005), is superb on the subject in general, and for ancient Greece I recommend P. Manville, *The Origins of Citizenship in Ancient Athens* (Princeton University Press, 1990), and L. Mitchell and P. Rhodes (eds.), *The Development of the Polis in Archaic Greece* (Routledge, 1997). D. Tandy, *Warriors into Traders: The Power of the Market in Early Greece* (University of California Press, 1997) is a well-argued study of early Archaic trade and its impact on state formation. On the architecture of Greek temples and all other edifices: M. Miles (ed.), *A Companion to Greek Architecture* (Wiley-Blackwell, 2016).

The outstanding introduction to the polis is M. Hansen, *Polis: An Introduction to the Ancient Greek City-State* (Oxford University Press, 2006), and A. Zuiderhoek, *The Ancient City* (Cambridge University Press, 2017), is excellent on the distinctive qualities of urbanism in the ancient Mediterranean. For *koina* see H. Beck and P. Funke (eds.), *Federalism in Greek Antiquity* (Cambridge University Press, 2015). For the varieties of administration: H. Beck (ed.), *A Companion to Ancient Greek Government* (Wiley-Blackwell, 2013).

CHAPTER 2

Aristocracy and the Archaic State

For Greek aristocracy in general, C. Starr, *The Aristocratic Temper of Greek Civilization* (Oxford University Press, 1992), is an excellent introduction, to be supported by W. Donlan, *The Aristocratic Ideal and Selected Papers* (Bolchazy-Carducci, 1999). The symposium in this period is discussed by M. Wecowski, *The Rise of the Greek Aristocratic Banquet* (Oxford University Press, 2014), and the essays in F. Budelmann (ed.), *The Cambridge Companion to Greek Lyric* (Cambridge University Press, 2009), afford a good introduction to the kinds of poetry that was sung there. The artwork of the period is enthusiastically displayed and discussed by J. Hurwit, *The Art and Culture of Early Greece, 1100–480 BC* (Cornell University Press, 1985), and its eastern origins are engagingly illuminated by two books by W. Burkert: *The Orientalizing Revolution: Near Eastern Influence on Greek Culture in the Early Archaic Age* (Harvard University Press, 1992; trans. by M. Pinder and W. Burkert; first German pub. 1984), and *Babylon, Memphis, Persepolis: Eastern Contexts of Greek Culture* (Harvard University Press, 2004).

On *xenia*, G. Herman, *Ritualised Friendship and the Greek City* (Cambridge University Press, 1987), is essential. On Olympia: T. Nielsen, *Olympia and the Classical Hellenic State City-Culture* (Royal Danish Academy of Sciences and Letters, 2007). On Delphi: M. Scott, *Delphi: A History of the Center of the Ancient World* (Princeton University Press, 2014).

CHAPTER 3

The Archaic Greek World

The standout books on lawmaking in this period are both by M. Gagarin: *Early Greek Law* (University of California Press, 1986) and *Writing Greek Law* (Cambridge University Press, 2008).

The controversy about when hoplite weaponry and tactics were adopted, and what the sociopolitical implications were, is best approached via essays in D. Kagan and G. Viggiano (eds.), *Men of Bronze: Hoplite Warfare in Ancient Greece* (Princeton University Press, 2013). The starting-point for the study of ancient Greek tyranny is S. Lewis, *Greek Tyranny* (Bristol Phoenix Press, 2009), followed closely by L. Mitchell, *The Heroic Rulers of Archaic and Classical Greece* (Bloomsbury, 2013).

S. von Reden, *Money in Classical Antiquity* (Cambridge University Press, 2010), and M. Peacock, *Introducing Money: Economics as Social Theory* (Routledge, 2013), are superb introductions to the invention and use of coined money in ancient Greece.

Good introductions to the work of the Presocratic philosopher–scientists are R. Waterfield, *The First Philosophers: The Presocratics and Sophists* (Oxford University Press, 2000), and J. Warren, *The Presocratics* (Acumen, 2007). On early prose, S. Goldhill, *The Invention of Prose* (Oxford University Press, 2002), is short but very satisfying.

There are countless studies of black-figure and red-figure ceramics. R. Osborne, *Archaic and Classical Greek Art* (Oxford University Press, 1998), constitutes a good introduction, but see also J. Barringer, *The Art and Archaeology of Ancient Greece* (Cambridge University Press, 2014). A. Stewart, *Classical Greece and the Birth of Western Art* (Cambridge University Press, 2008), sets the art of the fifth and fourth centuries in its social and political contexts.

CHAPTER 4

Early Athens

General histories already listed will afford the best approach to Archaic Athens. There is an extended discussion of Dracon in D. Leão and P. Rhodes, *The Laws of Solon: A New Edition with Introduction, Translation and Commentary* (I. B. Tauris, 2015), an outstanding edition of and commentary on Solon's verse. Solon's political intentions are somewhat obscure; good starting points are chapters in Manville 1990, in Mitchell/Rhodes (eds.) 1997—both of these are listed above under Chapter 1—and in P. Cartledge, *Ancient Greek Political Thought in Practice* (Cambridge University Press, 2009). The Peisistratid tyranny is best approached through general books on tyranny (listed under Chapter 3) or general books on Athens, but there is also a good collection of essays: H. Sancisi-Weerdenburg (ed.), *Peisistratos and the Tyranny: A Reappraisal of the Evidence* (Gieben, 2000).

CHAPTER 5

The Democratic Revolution

For the political history of Archaic Athens, we are blessed with G. Anderson, *The Athenian Experiment: Building an Imagined Political Community in Ancient Attica, 508– 490 BC* (University of Michigan Press, 2003); for its financial history, with H. van Wees, *Ships and Silver, Taxes and Tribute: A Fiscal History of Archaic Athens* (I. B. Tauris, 2013); and for its material culture, with J. Camp, *The Archaeology of Athens* (Yale University Press, 2001).

The best introductions to Cleisthenes' work are books that survey Athenian democracy in general. Here I would recommend P. Cartledge, *Democracy: A Life* (Oxford University Press, 2016), P. Rhodes (ed.), *Athenian Democracy* (Edinburgh University Press, 2004), and D. Stockton, *The Classical Athenian Democracy* (Oxford

University Press, 1990). On the way politics worked in Classical Athens: W. Connor, *The New Politicians of Fifth-century Athens* (Princeton University Press, 1971; repr. Hackett, 1992). On metics, see D. Kamen, *Status in Classical Athens* (Princeton University Press, 2013).

The development of the Agora under the democracy is covered by J. Camp, *The Athenian Agora: Excavations in the Heart of Classical Athens* (Thames and Hudson, 1986), and that of the Acropolis by J. Hurwit, *The Athenian Acropolis: History, Mythology, and Archaeology from the Neolithic Era to the Present* (Cambridge University Press, 1999).

J. O'Neil, *The Origins and Development of Ancient Greek Democracy* (Rowman & Littlefield, 1995), and E. Robinson, *Democracy beyond Athens: Popular Government in the Greek Classical Age* (Cambridge University Press, 2011), are very interesting studies of non-Athenian democracies.

CHAPTER 6

Sparta

The best short introductions to Sparta are P. Cartledge, *The Spartans: An Epic History* (Macmillan, 2002), and N. Kennell, *Spartans: A New History* (Wiley-Blackwell, 2010). The best general history for the Classical city is P. Cartledge, *Sparta and Lakonia: A Regional History, 1300 to 362 BC* (2nd ed., Routledge, 2002). A. Powell, *Athens and Sparta: Constructing Greek Political and Social History from 478 BC* (3rd ed., Routledge, 2016), contains a very readable account of Spartan history and culture in the fifth century. The best place to start thinking about helots is the relevant chapter in K. Bradley and P. Cartledge (eds.), *The Cambridge History of Slavery*, vol. 1: *The Ancient Mediterranean World* (Cambridge University Press, 2011). A revolutionary and important book on the Spartan economy, but a demanding read, is S. Hodkinson, *Property and Wealth in Classical Sparta* (Classical Press of Wales, 2000).

CHAPTER 7

Greek Religion

The best way to approach ancient Greek religion is through the essays in D. Ogden (ed.), *A Companion to Ancient Greek Religion* (Wiley-Blackwell, 2010). E. Kearns, *Ancient Greek Religion: A Sourcebook* (Wiley-Blackwell, 2010), is a very useful collection of passages in translation.

There are a number of accessible books on divination: K. Beerden, *Worlds Full of Signs: Ancient Greek Divination in Context* (Brill, 2013); M. Flower, *The Seer in Ancient Greece* (University of California Press, 2008); and S. Johnston, *Ancient Greek Divination* (Wiley-Blackwell, 2008).

The gods and their worship are the focus of J. Bremmer and A. Erskine (eds.), *The Gods of Ancient Greece: Identities and Transformations* (Edinburgh University Press, 2010), and J. Larson, *Ancient Greek Cults: A Guide* (Routledge, 2008). For women's roles in religion: J. Connelly, *Portrait of a Priestess: Women and Ritual in Ancient Greece* (2nd ed., Princeton University Press, 2010), and M. Dillon, *Girls and Women in Classical Greek Religion* (Routledge, 2002). J. Pedley, *Sanctuaries and the Sacred in the Ancient Greek World* (Cambridge University Press, 2005), is outstanding. As usual, much of our evidence comes from Athens: R. Parker, *Athenian Religion: A History* (Oxford University Press, 1996).

Increasingly, scholars are working on the margins of Greek religion, away from the central, civic aspects. Orphism is brilliantly illuminated by F. Graf and S. Johnston, *Ritual Texts for the Afterlife: Orpheus and the Bacchic Gold Tablets* (2nd ed., Routledge, 2007). What little we know about the main mystery cults is displayed by H. Bowden, *Mystery Cults of the Ancient World* (Princeton University Press, 2010).

The best introduction to Athenian tragedy is J. Gregory (ed.), *A Companion to Greek Tragedy* (Wiley-Blackwell, 2005). A. Pickard-Cambridge, *The Dramatic Festivals of Athens*, revised by J. Gould and D. Lewis (Oxford University Press, 1988), is authoritative on the City Dionysia. A good introduction to how the concerns of the polis are reflected in the dramas is D. Carter, *The Politics of Greek Tragedy* (Bristol Phoenix Press, 2007). J. Robson, *Aristophanes: An Introduction* (Duckworth, 2009), is a very good introduction to Old Comedy.

CHAPTER 8

The Persian Wars

M. Waters, *Ancient Persia: A Concise History of the Achaemenid Empire, 550–330 BCE* (Cambridge University Press, 2014), is an excellent, shortish introduction to the Achaemenid Empire. J. Lazenby, *The Defence of Greece* (Aris & Phillips, 1993), is a good account of the Persian Wars in general. For more contextualization: A. Burn, *The Persian Wars: The Greeks and the Defence of the West, c. 546–478 BC* (2nd ed., Duckworth, 1984). G. Cawkwell, *The Greek Wars: The Failure of Persia* (Oxford University Press, 2005), is an account of all the Greeks' military engagements with the Persians down to Alexander the Great. An unusual perspective on the conflict is taken by R. Garland, *Athens Burning: The Persian Invasion of Greece and the Evacuation of Attica* (Johns Hopkins University Press, 2017)—a very readable book.

CHAPTER 9

The Greeks at War

The best introductions to ancient Greek warfare are J. Lendon, *Soldiers and Ghosts: A History of Battle in Classical Antiquity* (Yale University Press, 2005); L.

Rawlings, *The Ancient Greeks at War* (Manchester University Press, 2007); and H. van Wees, *Greek Warfare: Myths and Realities* (Duckworth, 2004). For more detail, go to B. Campbell and L. Tritle (eds.), *The Oxford Handbook of Warfare in the Classical World* (Oxford University Press, 2013). V. Hanson, *Warfare and Agriculture in Classical Greece* (2nd ed., University of California Press, 1998), changed the way we think about the effects of ancient Greek warfare on farming.

The experience of hoplite warfare is well illuminated by V. Hanson, *The Western Way of War: Infantry Battle in Classical Greece* (2nd ed., University of California Press, 2000), and by J. Crowley, *The Psychology of the Athenian Hoplite: The Culture of Combat in Classical Athens* (Cambridge University Press, 2012). The outstanding book on hoplite equipment is A. Schwartz, *Reinstating the Hoplite: Arms, Armour and Phalanx Fighting in Archaic and Classical Greece* (Steiner, 2009), and, for ancient Greek armor in general, A. Snodgrass, *Arms and Armour of the Greeks* (2nd ed., Johns Hopkins University Press, 1999). Use of mercenaries is surveyed by M. Trundle, *Greek Mercenaries from the Late Archaic Period to Alexander* (Routledge, 2004). L. Worley, *Hippeis: The Cavalry of Ancient Greece* (Westview, 1994), and R. Gaebel, *Cavalry Operations in the Ancient Greek World* (University of Oklahoma Press, 2002), are surveys of the use of cavalry in Greek warfare. P. de Souza, *Piracy in the Graeco-Roman World* (Cambridge University Press, 1999), is the standard work on piracy.

The topics of diplomacy and interstate relations are best approached with the help of L. Mitchell, *Greeks Bearing Gifts: The Public Use of Private Relationships in the Greek World, 435–323 BC* (Cambridge University Press, 1997), D. Bederman, *International Law in Antiquity* (Cambridge University Press, 2001), and P. Low, *Interstate Relations in Classical Greece: Morality and Power* (Cambridge University Press, 2007), but there are important chapters in Beck/Funke (eds.) 2015 (listed under Chapter 1), in P. Hunt, *War, Peace, and Alliance in Demosthenes' Athens* (Cambridge University Press, 2010), and in M. Christ, *The Limits of Altruism in Democratic Athens* (Cambridge University Press, 2012). A. Eckstein, *Mediterranean Anarchy, Interstate War, and the Rise of Rome* (University of California Press, 2006), argues that, in reality, a state of anarchy characterized interstate relations in the Mediterranean.

The Classical Period

The best general histories of the Classical period of ancient Greek history are P. Rhodes, *A History of the Classical Greek World, 478–323 BC* (2nd ed., Wiley-Blackwell, 2010), and S. Hornblower, *The Greek World, 479–323 BC* (4th ed., Routledge, 2011). J. Davies, *Democracy and Classical Greece* (2nd ed., Harvard University Press, 1993), is shorter, and very good indeed. R. Osborne (ed.), *Classical Greece* (Oxford University Press, 2000) has a thematic approach, with chapters written by different hands. K. Kinzl (ed.), *A Companion to the Classical Greek World* (Wiley-Blackwell, 2006), is a collection of introductory essays. The material culture of Classical Greece is well covered by J. Whitley, *The Archaeology of Ancient Greece* (Cambridge University Press, 2001). All of these books contain material that is relevant to Chapters 10 to 18, if not beyond.

CHAPTER 10

The Delian League

A good short introduction to the league is contained in Powell 2016 (listed under Chapter 6); essays in P. Low (ed.), *The Athenian Empire* (Edinburgh University Press, 2008), will add more depth. The finances of the empire are clearly explained by L. Samons, *Empire of the Owl: Athenian Imperial Finance* (Steiner, 2000).

CHAPTER 11

The Economy of Greece

The essential book is Scheidel/Morris/Saller (eds.) 2007 (listed under Introduction I), and the best short introduction is L. Migeotte, *The Economy of the Greek Cities from the Archaic Period to the Early Roman Empire* (University of California Press, 2009; trans. by J. Lloyd; first French pub. 2002). A. Bresson, *The Making of the Ancient Greek Economy: Institutions, Markets, and Growth in the City-States* (Princeton University Press, 2016; trans. by S. Rendall; first French pub. in two vols., 2007/2008), is much longer and more comprehensive, and argues that the Greeks were not as poor as they have commonly been made out to be. A similar argument can be found in J. Ober, *The Rise and Fall of Classical Greece* (Princeton University Press, 2015).

P. Acton, *Poiesis: Manufacturing in Classical Athens* (Oxford University Press, 2014), proves that manufacturing was an important sector of the economy. Trade is the subject of N. Morley, *Trade in Classical Antiquity* (Cambridge University Press, 2007), and C. Reed, *Maritime Traders in the Ancient Greek World* (Cambridge University Press, 2003). For labor in the ancient world, see A. Burford, *Land and Labor in the Greek World* (Johns Hopkins University Press, 1993); for wages, W. Loomis, *Wages, Welfare Costs, and Inflation in Classical Athens* (University of Michigan Press, 1998). Technological advances of course contribute greatly to the economy; the best single book on ancient technology is J. Oleson (ed.), *The Oxford Handbook of Engineering and Technology in the Classical World* (Oxford University Press, 2008). For Piraeus, Athens' port-of-trade: R. Garland, *The Piraeus* (2nd ed., Bristol Classical Press, 2001).

For slavery and serfdom, N. Fisher, *Slavery in Classical Greece* (2nd ed., Bristol Classical Press, 2001), is introductory, and the up-to-date longer treatment is Bradley/Cartledge (eds.) 2011 (listed under Chapter 6).

CHAPTER 12

Athens in the Age of Pericles

Books on the Classical Athenian democracy have already been mentioned under Chapter 5. Here I will add books on the democracy's strengths and weaknesses, starting by repeating Cartledge 2016. In addition, three books by J. Ober on Athenian political culture: *Mass and Elite in Democratic Athens* (Princeton University

Press, 1989), *Political Dissent in Democratic Athens: Intellectual Critics of Popular Rule* (Princeton University Press, 1998), and *Democracy and Knowledge: Innovation and Learning in Classical Athens* (Princeton University Press, 2008). M. Ostwald, *From Popular Sovereignty to the Sovereignty of Law: Law, Society, and Politics in Fifth-century Athens* (University of California Press, 1986), is a tour de force, a massive account of the development of the Athenian democracy in the fifth century toward (he says) the sovereignty of law.

D. Pritchard, *Public Spending and Democracy in Classical Athens* (University of Texas Press, 2015), is a clear account of how much it cost to run the democracy. J. Davies, *Wealth and the Power of Wealth in Classical Athens* (Ayer, 1984), reveals the lives of the super-rich. M. Christ, *The Bad Citizen in Classical Athens* (Cambridge University Press, 2006), reveals another aspect of their lives.

Pericles has two excellent recent biographies: V. Azoulay, *Pericles of Athens* (Princeton University Press, 2014; trans. by J. Lloyd; first French pub. 2010), and T. Martin, *Pericles: A Biography in Context* (Cambridge University Press, 2016). L. Samons (ed.), *The Cambridge Companion to the Age of Pericles* (Cambridge University Press, 2007), is a collection of accessible essays about Athenian life and culture during Pericles' time. T. Shear, *Trophies of Victory: Public Building in Periklean Athens* (Princeton University Press, 2016), is a thorough account and analysis of the Periclean building program as a whole. For the Parthenon, there is a wonderful narrative account by M. Beard, *The Parthenon* (Profile, 2002).

CHAPTER 13

Women, Sexuality, and Family Life

Ancient Greek attitudes toward women are contextualized by P. Cartledge, *The Greeks: A Portrait of Self and Others* (2nd ed., Oxford University Press, 2002). The best book is E. Fantham, H. Foley, N. Kampen, S. Pomeroy, and H. Shapiro, *Women in the Classical World* (Oxford University Press, 1994). This is a text-based account, almost a sourcebook of passages in translation, very thorough and clear. R. Just, *Women in Athenian Law and Life* (Routledge, 1989), makes impressive use of the Athenian evidence, while Dillon 2002 (listed under Chapter 7) is authoritative on women's religious roles. S. Pomeroy, *Spartan Women* (Oxford University Press, 2002), has that topic covered, but Hodkinson 2000 (listed under Chapter 6) is far better on their economic roles.

The study of ancient Greek housing, largely based on archaeology, is quite technical, but two books by L. Nevett are as introductory as they come: *House and Society in the Ancient Greek World* (Cambridge University Press, 1999), and *Domestic Space in Classical Antiquity* (Cambridge University Press, 2010). From adultery to inheritance, the stand-out book on family life is C. Patterson, *The Family in Greek History* (Harvard University Press, 1998). B. Rawson (ed.), *A Companion to Families in the Greek and Roman Worlds* (Wiley-Blackwell, 2011), is full of fascinating material, and C. Cox, *Household Interests: Family, Property, Marriage Strategies, and Family Dynamics in Ancient Athens* (Princeton University Press, 1998), is brilliant on what counted as "the household."

J. Robson, *Sex and Sexuality in Classical Athens* (Edinburgh University Press, 2013), and J. Davidson, *Courtesans and Fishcakes: The Consuming Passions of Classical Athens* (Fontana, 1997), are the places to start for attitudes toward sex. The topic of homosexuality was opened up by K. Dover, *Greek Homosexuality* (Duckworth, 1978), and this important book has been reissued with new introductions by Bloomsbury (2016). D. Hamel, *Trying Neaira: The True Story of a Courtesan's Scandalous Life in Ancient Greece* (Yale University Press, 2003), is an entertaining account of one prostitute's business in fourth-century Athens.

CHAPTER 14

The Peloponnesian War

J. Lendon, *Song of Wrath: The Peloponnesian War Begins* (Basic Books, 2010), is brilliant on the early years of the war. Of the many books on the war as a whole, I would recommend L. Tritle, *A New History of the Peloponnesian War* (Wiley-Blackwell, 2010), V. Hanson, *A War Like No Other: How the Athenians and Spartans Fought the Peloponnesian War* (Random House, 2005), and J. Roberts, *The Plague of War: Athens, Sparta, and the Struggle for Ancient Greece* (Oxford University Press, 2017).

There is a dedicated book, a very good one, on the Sicilian expedition: P. Green, *Armada from Athens* (Hodder & Stoughton, 1970). The demagogues who rose in influence during the war are the subject of Connor 1971 (listed under Chapter 5). The dynamics of democratic and oligarchic factionalism are explored in A. Lintott, *Violence, Civil Strife and Revolution in the Classical City, 750–330 BC* (Croom Helm, 1982), and the best account of the oligarchic coup of 411 can be found in Ostwald 1986 (listed under Chapter 12). Some of the consequences of the oligarchic coups are discussed by J. Shear, *Polis and Revolution: Responding to Oligarchy in Classical Athens* (Cambridge University Press, 2011).

CHAPTER 15

The Instability of Syracuse

P. Cartledge, *Ancient Greece: A History in Eleven Cities* (Oxford University Press, 2009; repr. 2011 as *Ancient Greece: A Very Short Introduction*), has a good introductory chapter on Syracuse, and M. Finley, *Ancient Sicily* (2nd ed., Chatto & Windus, 1979), is an accessible history of the island as a whole up to the Byzantine period. The settlement of Sicily is covered by Boardman 1999 (listed under Chapter 1), and its consequences explained by F. De Angelis, *Archaic and Classical Greek Sicily: A Social and Economic History* (Oxford University Press, 2016). B. Caven, *Dionysius I: Warlord of Sicily* (Yale University Press, 1990), is a revisionist study of Dionysius. The nature of the democracy at Syracuse is taken up by Robinson 2011 (listed under Chapter 5). S. Berger, *Revolution and Society in Greek Sicily and Southern Italy* (Steiner, 1992), sheds light on the violence of Syracusan society.

On rich and poor in Athens, and the reasons for the stability of the Athenian democracy, Ober 1989 (listed under Chapter 12) is utterly convincing.

CHAPTER 16

Socrates and the Thirty Tyrants

The essential book on the regime of the Thirty Tyrants in Athens is P. Krentz, *The Thirty at Athens* (Cornell University Press, 1982). The crisis as a whole is reviewed by A. Rubel, *Fear and Loathing in Ancient Athens: Religion and Politics during the Peloponnesian War* (Acumen, 2014; trans. by M. Vickers and A. Piftor; first German pub. 2000). How the Athenians coped afterwards is the focus of B. Strauss, *Athens after the Peloponnesian War: Class, Faction and Policy 403–386 BC* (Croom Helm, 1986), and A. Wolpert, *Remembering Defeat: Civil War and Civic Memory in Ancient Athens* (Johns Hopkins University Press, 2002).

The best place to start on ancient education is W. Bloomer (ed.), *A Companion to Ancient Education* (Wiley-Blackwell, 2015). M. Joyal, J. Yardley, and I. McDougall, *Greek and Roman Education: A Sourcebook* (Routledge, 2008), usefully pulls together a lot of scattered material. Literacy levels in ancient Greece are impossible to measure, but it is important to try: W. Harris, *Ancient Literacy* (Harvard University Press, 1989), and R. Thomas, *Literacy and Orality in Ancient Greece* (Cambridge University Press, 1992).

The sophistic movement is best approached via P. O'Grady (ed.), *The Sophists: An Introduction* (Duckworth, 2008), which has a chapter on each of the major sophists, and H. Tell, *Plato's Counterfeit Sophists* (Center for Hellenic Studies, 2011), which sets the movement in context. There is a good survey of Greek philosophy of the Classical period in T. Irwin, *Classical Thought* (Oxford University Press, 1989). For rhetoric and rhetorical teaching, G. Kennedy, *The Art of Persuasion in Greece* (Princeton University Press, 1963), remains unsurpassed as an introduction.

By far the best short book on Socrates as a philosopher is C. Taylor, *Socrates: A Very Short Introduction* (Oxford University Press, 1998). There is much more to Socrates' work than what might have got him into trouble with the authorities, but those particular aspects are discussed by R. Waterfield, *Why Socrates Died: Dispelling the Myths* (Faber, 2009), and in the relevant chapter in Cartledge 2009 (listed under Chapter 4). For more on Socrates' trial, see T. Brickhouse and N. Smith, *Plato and the Trial of Socrates* (Routledge, 2004).

The Athenian legal system has been the subject of a lot of good recent work. The two fundamental books are D. MacDowell, *The Law in Classical Athens* (Cornell University Press, 1978), and S. Todd, *The Shape of Athenian Law* (Oxford University Press, 1993). M. Gagarin and D. Cohen (eds.), *The Cambridge Companion to Ancient*

Greek Law (Cambridge University Press, 2005), is a superb collection of essays, on law outside Athens as well.

CHAPTER 17

The Futility of War

M. Scott, *From Democrats to Kings: The Downfall of Athens to the Rise of Alexander the Great* (Icon Books, 2009), is a brave attempt to write a popular account of the confusing events of the fourth century. More details can be found in the usual general history books, and in J. Buckler, *Aegean Greece in the Fourth Century BC* (Brill, 2003), R. Sealey, *Demosthenes and His Time: A Study in Defeat* (Oxford University Press, 1993), and L. Tritle (ed.), *The Greek World in the Fourth Century* (Routledge, 1997).

There is a readable account of Cyrus the Younger's attempt on the Persian throne by R. Waterfield, *Xenophon's Retreat: Greece, Persia, and the End of the Golden Age* (Faber, 2006). The Corinthian War is the subject of C. Hamilton, *Sparta's Bitter Victories: Politics and Diplomacy in the Corinthian War* (Cornell University Press, 1979). The Boeotian War is well discussed by M. Munn, *The Defense of Attica: The Dema Wall and the Boiotian War of 378–375 BC* (University of California Press, 1993). Thebes' brief ascendancy is covered by J. Buckler, *The Theban Hegemony 371–362* (Harvard University Press, 1980).

The one and only book on common peaces is T. Ryder, *Koine Eirene: General Peace and Local Independence in Ancient Greece* (Oxford University Press/University of Hull, 1965), though there are some excellent relevant essays toward the end of Beck/Funke (eds.) 2015 (listed under Chapter 1).

A good introduction to fourth-century Athens, written for a broad audience, is P. Harding, *Athens Transformed, 404–262 BC: From Popular Sovereignty to the Dominion of Wealth* (Routledge, 2015). The first book to read on the Second Athenian League is J. Cargill, *The Second Athenian League: Empire or Free Alliance?* (University of California Press, 1981). M. Hansen, *The Athenian Democracy in the Age of Demosthenes: Structure, Principles, Ideology* (2nd ed., Bristol Classical Press, 1999), is brilliant, but perhaps a bit overstated, on the ways in which the democracy changed. The best biography of Demosthenes is I. Worthington, *Demosthenes of Athens and the Fall of Classical Athens* (Oxford University Press, 2013).

CHAPTER 18

The Macedonian Conquest

For Macedonian history: N. Hammond, *The Macedonian State: The Origins, Institutions, and History* (Oxford University Press, 1989), and R. Errington, *A History of Macedonia* (University of California Press, 1990; trans. by C. Errington; first German pub. 1986). E. Carney, *Women and Monarchy in Macedonia* (University of Oklahoma Press, 2000), investigates the lives of royal Macedonian women.

Z. Archibald, *Ancient Economies of the Northern Aegean, Fifth to First Centuries BC* (Oxford University Press, 2013), illuminates the Macedonian economy.

I. Worthington, *Philip II of Macedonia* (Yale University Press, 2008), is an excellent biography. On the Vergina tombs, the book written by the archaeologist himself is breathtaking: M. Andronicos, *Vergina: The Royal Tombs* (Athenon, 1992). On the League of Corinth, see Beck/Funke (eds.) 2015 (listed under Chapter 1).

All aspects of Athenian history in the Hellenistic period are superbly covered by the award-winning C. Habicht, *Athens from Alexander to Antony* (Harvard University Press, 1997; trans. by D. Schneider; first German pub. 1995).

CHAPTER 19

Alexander the Great
Good short introductions: H. Bowden, *Alexander the Great: A Very Short Introduction* (Oxford University Press, 2014), and W. Adams, *Alexander the Great: Legacy of a Conqueror* (Longman, 2004). Good longer accounts: A. Bosworth, *Conquest and Empire: The Reign of Alexander the Great* (Cambridge University Press, 1988), and W. Heckel and L. Tritle (eds.), *Alexander the Great: A New History* (Wiley-Blackwell, 2009). P. Briant, *Alexander the Great and His Empire: A Short Introduction* (Princeton University Press, 2010; trans. by A. Kuhrt; first French pub. 2002), usefully sets the conquests in the context of the history of the East. I. Worthington, *By the Spear: Philip II, Alexander the Great, and the Rise and Fall of the Macedonian Empire* (Oxford University Press, 2014), allows one to compare father and son. F. Holt, *The Treasures of Alexander the Great: How One Man's Wealth Shaped the World* (Oxford University Press, 2016), is outstanding on Alexander's finances.

The Hellenistic Period
There are two very good, short, and very different introductions to the Hellenistic period: P. Green, *The Hellenistic Age: A Short History* (The Modern Library, 2007), and P. Thonemann, *The Hellenistic Age* (Oxford University Press, 2016). The most useful of the general histories is G. Shipley, *The Greek World after Alexander, 323–30 BC* (Routledge, 2000), though for all its heft P. Green, *Alexander to Actium: The Historical Evolution of the Hellenistic Age* (University of California Press, 1990), is very readable. R. Errington, *A History of the Hellenistic World, 323–30 BC* (Wiley-Blackwell, 2008), is outstandingly good, but limited to politics and warfare. G. Bugh (ed.), *The Cambridge Companion to the Hellenistic World* (Cambridge University Press, 2006), and A. Erskine (ed.), *A Companion to the Hellenistic World* (Oxford: Blackwell, 2003), are indispensable collections of essays. D. Ogden, *Polygamy, Prostitutes, and Death: The Hellenistic Dynasties* (Classical Press of Wales, 1999), is a brilliant account of the family dynamics of the Hellenistic courts. All of these books contain material relevant from Chapter 20 through to the end of the book.

CHAPTER 20

The Successor Kingdoms

R. Waterfield, *Dividing the Spoils: The War for Alexander the Great's Empire* (Oxford University Press, 2011), is an accessible narrative history of the forty years following Alexander's death. The first decade or so is brilliantly described by J. Romm, *Ghost on the Throne: The War for the Corpse, Crown, and Empire of Alexander the Great* (Simon & Schuster, 2011). E. Anson, *Alexander's Heirs: The Age of the Successors, 323–281 BC* (Wiley-Blackwell, 2014), is a scholarly general history, and J. Roisman, *Alexander's Veterans and the Early Wars of the Successors* (University of Texas Press, 2012), considers the period from the viewpoint of the Macedonian soldiery.

Many of the Successors have received dedicated biographies: E. Anson, *Eumenes of Cardia: A Greek among Macedonians* (2nd ed., Brill, 2015); R. Billows, *Antigonos the One-Eyed and the Creation of the Hellenistic State* (University of California Press, 1990); I. Worthington, *Ptolemy I: King and Pharaoh of Egypt* (Oxford University Press, 2016); J. Grainger, *Seleukos Nikator* (Routledge, 1990); H. Lund, *Lysimachus: A Study in Early Hellenistic Kingship* (Routledge, 1992). Two prominent women are the subjects of good biographies as well, both by E. Carney: *Olympias: Mother of Alexander the Great* (Routledge, 2006), and *Arsinoë of Egypt and Macedon: A Royal Life* (Oxford University Press, 2013). Many of the uses of Alexander's image by his successors are revealed by A. Stewart, *Faces of Power: Alexander's Image and Hellenistic Politics* (University of California Press, 1993).

CHAPTER 21

A Time of Adjustment

This period of Athenian history is illuminated by Habicht 1997 (listed under Chapter 18) and Harding 2015 (listed under Chapter 17). Cartledge 2009 (listed under Chapter 4) has a short introductory chapter on the reforms of Agis and Cleomenes in Sparta, and more detail can be found in M. Michalopoulos, *In the Name of Lykourgos: The Rise and Fall of the Spartan Revolutionary Movement, 243–146 BC* (Pen & Sword, 2016; trans. by M. Kavallieros and M.-A. Niforos; first Greek pub. 2009), and in P. Cartledge and A. Spawforth, *Hellenistic and Roman Sparta: A Tale of Two Cities* (2nd ed., Routledge, 2001).

R. Talbert, *Timoleon and the Revival of Greek Sicily, 344–317 BC* (Cambridge University Press, 1974), is the essential book on Timoleon's work. Pergamene affairs are covered by R. Allen, *The Attalid Kingdom: A Constitutional History* (Oxford University Press, 1983), and R. Evans, *A History of Pergamum: Beyond Hellenistic Kingship* (Bloomsbury, 2012).

There is an accessible general history of the Seleucids, in three shortish volumes, written by J. Grainger and published by Pen & Sword: *The Rise of the Seleukid Empire, 323–223 BC* (2014), *The Seleukid Empire of Antiochus III, 223–187 BC* (2015), and *The Fall of the Seleukid Empire, 187–75 BC* (2015). The dynamics of center and peripheries, and of kings and usurpers, are illuminated by B. Chrubasik, *Kings and Usurpers in the Seleukid Empire: The Men Who Would Be King* (Oxford University Press, 2016). G. Aperghis, *The Seleukid Royal Economy: The Finances and Financial Administration of the Seleukid Empire* (Cambridge University Press, 2004), speculates convincingly about the economy. There is no better description of the Seleucid empire than P. Kosmin, *The Land of the Elephant Kings: Space, Territory, and Ideology in the Seleucid Empire* (Harvard University Press, 2014). R. Strootman, *Courts and Elites in the Hellenistic Empires: The Near East after the Achaemenids, c. 330–30 BCE* (Edinburgh University Press, 2014), is outstanding on the Seleucid court. The eastern satrapies are the topic of R. Mairs, *The Hellenistic Far East: Archaeology, Language, and Identity in Greek Central Asia* (University of California Press, 2014).

A. Samuel, *The Shifting Sands of History: Interpretations of Ptolemaic Egypt* (University Press of America, 1989), is an excellent short introduction to the modern study of the Ptolemaic kingdom, and G. Hölbl, *A History of the Ptolemaic Empire* (Routledge, 2000; trans. by T. Saavedra; first German pub. 1994), is a really good general history. The first hundred years of Ptolemaic rule of Egypt is illuminated by S. Caneva, *From Alexander to the Theoi Adelphoi: Foundation and Legitimation of a Dynasty* (Peeters, 2016). J. Manning, *Land and Power in Ptolemaic Egypt: The Structure of Land Tenure* (Cambridge University Press, 2003), is the place to start for the economy, and his *The Last Pharaohs: Egypt under the Ptolemies, 305–30 BC* (Princeton University Press, 2010), is an account of how they made their kingdom work. J. Bingen, *Hellenistic Egypt: Monarchy, Society, Economy, Culture*, ed. R. Bagnall (University of California Press, 2007), is also important reading on this.

CHAPTER 22

The Greek Cities in the New World

There is a three-volume gazetteer of all the Greek settlements of the Hellenistic period by G. Cohen, published by the University of California Press: *The Hellenistic Settlements in Europe, the Islands, and Asia Minor* (1995); *The Hellenistic Settlements in Syria, the Red Sea Basin, and North Africa* (2006); *The Hellenistic Settlements in the East from Armenia and Mesopotamia to Bactria and India* (2013). City fortifications are nicely illustrated in A. McNicoll and N. Milner, *Hellenistic Fortifications from the Aegean to the Euphrates* (Oxford University Press, 1997).

For confederacies, I can only repeat Beck/Funke (eds.) 2015 (listed under Chapter 1). There is also a very long and brilliant study: E. Mackil, *Creating a Common Polity: Religion, Economy, and Politics in the Making of the Greek Koinon* (University of California Press, 2013). There are two very good books on the Aetolian Confederacy—J. Grainger, *The League of the Aitolians* (Brill, 1999), and J. Scholten, *The Politics of Plunder: Aitolians and Their Koinon in the Early Hellenistic Era, 279–217 BC* (University of California Press, 2000)—but the best way to approach the Achaean Confederacy is through two biographies: F. Walbank, *Aratos of Sicyon* (Cambridge University Press, 1933), and R. Errington, *Philopoemen* (Oxford University Press, 1969).

Books on reciprocal gift-giving between cities and kings or other patrons, being based largely on inscriptional evidence, tend to be quite complex. The place to start is M. Domingo Gygax, *Benefaction and Rewards in the Ancient Greek City: The Origins of Euergetism* (Cambridge University Press, 2016). Two quite challenging books by J. Ma explore the phenomenon in the Hellenistic period: *Antiochos III and the Cities of Western Asia Minor* (Oxford University Press, 2000) and *Statues and Cities: Honorific Portraits and Civic Identity in the Hellenistic World* (Oxford University Press, 2013).

CHAPTER 23

Social Life and Intellectual Culture

The best book on the Hellenistic world in general is F. Chamoux, *Hellenistic Civilization* (Blackwell, 2003; trans. by M. Roussel; first French pub. 1983), a mid-length account of all aspects of Hellenistic culture. A. Chaniotis, *War in the Hellenistic World* (Blackwell, 2005), cleverly and convincingly reads Hellenistic culture as a product of the constant warfare.

The foundational study of royal women, still worth reading, is G. Macurdy, *Hellenistic Queens: A Study of Woman-Power in Macedonia, Seleucid Syria, and Ptolemaic Egypt* (Johns Hopkins University Press, 1929; repr. Ares, 1985). J. Whitehorne, *Cleopatras* (Routledge, 1994), nicely focuses on all those named Cleopatra. R. Smith, *Hellenistic Royal Portraits* (Oxford University Press, 1988), is outstanding on the ways queens and kings liked to be portrayed. The bibliography for women and families is the same as for Chapter 13, with the important addition of S. James and S. Dillon (eds.), *A Companion to Women in the Ancient World* (Wiley-Blackwell, 2012). The bibliography for education is the same as for Chapter 15.

B. Fowler, *The Hellenistic Aesthetic* (University of Wisconsin Press, 1989), is a very nice book on the subject. On Hellenistic art in general: J. Pollitt, *Art in the Hellenistic Age* (Cambridge University Press, 1986), and A. Stewart, *Art in the Hellenistic World: An Introduction* (Cambridge University Press, 2014). On Hellenistic literature: K. Gutzwiller, *A Guide to Hellenistic Literature* (Wiley-Blackwell, 2007), and J. Clauss and M. Cuypers (eds.), *A Companion to Hellenistic Literature* (Wiley-Blackwell, 2010).

L. Casson, *Libraries in the Ancient World* (Yale University Press, 2001), is a general account of ancient libraries, and there is an outstanding collection of accessible essays on the Alexandrian library in R. MacLeod (ed.), *The Library of Alexandria: Centre of Learning in the Ancient World* (I. B. Tauris, 2000). On patronage, R. Strootman, *The Birdcage of the Muses: Patronage of the Arts and Sciences at the Ptolemaic Imperial Court, 305–222 BCE* (Peeters, 2017), is indispensable.

T. Rihll, *Greek Science* (Cambridge University Press, 1999), is an unrivaled short introduction to Greek science, as her *Technology and Society in the Ancient Greek and Roman Worlds* (American Historical Association, 2013) is for technology. T. Dantzig, *Mathematics in Ancient Greece* (Charles Scribner's Sons, 1955; repr. Dover Books, 2006), is the most accessible work. A. Jones, *A Portable Cosmos: Revealing the Antikythera Mechanism, a Scientific Wonder of the Ancient World* (Oxford University Press, 2017), is brilliant not just on the mechanism itself, but on Hellenistic astronomy in general. Medicine made great progress in the Hellenistic period: V. Nutton, *Ancient Medicine* (2nd ed., Routledge, 2013), is the best imaginable introduction to the subject.

A good introduction to the therapeutic side of Hellenistic philosophy is P. Hadot, *What Is Ancient Philosophy?* (Harvard University Press, 2002; trans. by M. Chase; first French pub. 1995). A. Long, *Hellenistic Philosophy: Stoics, Epicureans, Sceptics* (2nd ed., University of California Press, 1986), is a well-established classic. Hellenistic religion has not yet been very well served, but L. Martin, *Hellenistic Religions: An Introduction* (Oxford University Press, 1987), complemented by F. Grant (ed.), *Hellenistic Religions* (Bobbs-Merrill, 1953), which is a sourcebook of passages in translation, will do. We are better off for Athenian religion: J. Mikalson, *Religion in Hellenistic Athens* (University of California Press, 1998).

CHAPTER 24

The Roman Conquest

The most accessible account of the Roman conquest of Greece is R. Waterfield, *Taken at the Flood: The Roman Conquest of Greece* (Oxford University Press, 2014), but see also A. Eckstein, *Rome Enters the Greek East: From Anarchy to Hierarchy in the Hellenistic Mediterranean* (Blackwell, 2008). N. Rosenstein, *Rome and the Mediterranean, 290–146 BC: The Imperial Republic* (Edinburgh University Press, 2012), is an excellent introduction to the Roman takeover of the entire Mediterranean. For the archaeology of post-conquest Greece: S. Alcock, *Graecia Capta: The Landscape of Roman Greece* (Cambridge University Press, 1993).

The bibliography for the Ptolemies and Seleucids is the same as for Chapter 21. On Cleopatra: D. Roller, *Cleopatra: A Biography* (Oxford University Press, 2010). On Rhodes: R. Berthold, *Rhodes in the Hellenistic Age* (Cornell University Press, 1984). On Philip V: F. Walbank, *Philip V of Macedon* (Cambridge University Press, 1940).

CHAPTER 25

A Feat of Imagination

The development of the concept of freedom in ancient Greece is ably discussed by K. Raaflaub, *The Discovery of Freedom in Ancient Greece* (University of Chicago Press, 2004; rev. ed. trans. by R. Franciscono and K. Raaflaub; first German pub. 1985). What I call the imagined community of the Greeks is the subject especially of L. Mitchell, *Panhellenism and the Barbarian in Archaic and Classical Greece* (Classical Press of Wales, 2007), a very important book. The basic book now on Greek ethnicity is J. McInerney (ed.), *A Companion to Ethnicity in the Ancient Mediterranean* (Wiley-Blackwell, 2014). Another essential book is E. Gruen, *Rethinking the Other in Antiquity* (Princeton University Press, 2011). On kinship diplomacy: L. Patterson, *Kinship Myth in Ancient Greece* (University of Texas Press, 2010).

Index

Note: **bold letters** refer to the maps on pp. xxiii–xxix

Megalopolis, **A**, 299, 337, 340, 347, 377-8, 379, 382
Megara, -ians, Megaris, **A**, 28-9, 46, 75, 82, 116, 181-2, 184, 237, 240, 241, 242, 382, 453
Melkart (Phoenician god), 123
Melos (island), **A**, 13, 139, 241, 245
Memnon of Rhodes, 330-2
Memphis, **E**, 392-3
Menander of Athens (playwright), 420-1
Menelaus (hero), 116
Menelaus (Macedonian), 365
mercenaries, 35, 62, 82, 116, 163-4, 186, 230, 248, 263-4, 268, 269, 276-8, 289, 293, 294, 302, 312-13, 315, 322, 330, 332, 336, 337, 344, 356-7, 358, 365, 376, 386, 389, 393, 396, 400, 404, 409, 444, 445
Mesopotamia, **F**, 17, 143, 366, 411, 457
Messapians, **D**, 186
Messene, **A**, 299, 361, 366, 401, 433
Messenia, -ians, **A**, 3, 16, 26, 38, 105-8, 115, 180-2, 205, 241-2, 248, 299, 301-2, 379, 454
Methana, **A**, 372
Methone, **B**, 57, 180-1, 314
Methymna, 76
metics, 99-100, 135, 166, 192-3, 201, 204, 207, 211, 212, 214-15, 225, 227, 233, 273, 275-7, 305, 319
Miletus, Milesians, **C**, 28, 36, 69-71, 128, 141, 143, 186, 204, 331, 401
Miltiades of Athens, 83, 143-4, 146
Minoan civilization, 13-15
Mithridates VI of Pontus, 453-5
Molon, 391-2, 395
Molossis, -ians, **B**, 40, 451
monarchy, *see* kingship; tyranny
Muses (goddesses), 123, 421, 424-5
music, song, 45, 47, 49-50, 52, 53, 54, 86, 109, 122, 125, 135, 136, 218, 229, 233, 279, 307, 418, 421, 424, 426
Mycale, Mt., 154
Mycenae, **A**, 14
Mycenaean civilization, 14-18, 21, 25, 39, 47, 122, 178, 404, 444
Myronides of Athens, 182
Mysia, **C**, 390
Mysteries, Eleusinian, 131-2, 188, 247, 253-4

Samothracian, 131-3
Mytilene, **C**, 45, 241, 244, 255

Nabis of Sparta, 444-7
Naucratis, **E**, 28, 30, 393
Naupactus, **A**, 182, 241-2
Naxos (island), **A**, 13, 36, 75, 179, 186
Nearchus of Crete, 343-4, 408
Near East, 15, 17, 25, 31, 48, 58, 66, 104, 141, 335, 336, 456, 457
Nebuchadnezzar II of Babylon, 35, 354
Nemea River, battle of, 291
Newgrange (Ireland), 47
Nicias of Athens, 202, 244-5, 248
Nile (river), **E**, 28, 329, 342, 392, 398, 416
Nineveh, 427
Nisaea, **A**, 242, 244, 254
Notium, 254
Nubia, 395

Ocean (legendary river), 341
Odeon (Athens), 219
Odrysians, **C**, 300, 314, 372
Odysseus (hero), 8, 19, 421
Odyssey (Homer), 15, 19, 35, 127
"Old Oligarch," the, 198
oligarchy, 41, 43, 46, 75-6, 115, 116, 186, 241, 245, 249-50, 254, 256, 260, 290, 319, 325, 331, 340, 358, 382, 384, 401, 404, 407, 446, 453; *see also* Athens, oligarchy
olive oil, 6, 9, 55, 79, 420
Olympia, **A**, **D**, 53-6, 104, 123, 125, 128, 132, 176, 219, 263, 267, 464; *see also* games, Olympic
Olympias, 314, 323, 334, 347, 355, 357-9, 361, 416
Olympus, Mt., **B**, 1, 50, 122-3
Olynthus, **B**, 40, 295, 300, 315-16
Opis, **F**, 345
oracles, *see* divination
Orchomenus, **A**, 291
Orestes (hero), 116
Orestis, **B**, 313
Oreus, **B**, 185
orientalizing fashion, 47-8, 72
Orontes (river), **E**, 28, 385, 436
Oropus, **A**, 319
Orpheus (hero), Orphism, 131